Practice Problems for FINANCIAL ALGEBRA
Advanced Algebra with Financial Applications
Tax Code Update

Practice Problems for FINANCIAL ALGEBRA
Advanced Algebra with Financial Applications
Tax Code Update

Second Edition

Robert Gerver

Richard Sgroi

Australia • Brazil • Mexico • Singapore • United Kingdom • United States

Illustrator Credits
Cover app icons created by Michael Gerver

National Geographic Learning | Cengage
1 N. State Street, Suite 900
Chicago, IL 60602

National Geographic Learning, a Cengage company, is a provider of quality core and supplemental educational materials for the PreK-12, adult education, and ELT markets. Cengage is a leading provider of customized learning solutions with employees residing in nearly 40 different countries and sales in more than 125 countries around the world. Find your local representative at **NGL.Cengage.com/RepFinder.**

Visit National Geographic Learning online at **NGL.Cengage.com/school**

ISBN: 978-0-357-42357-8

Printed in Mexico
Print Number: 02   Print Year: 2022

Table of Contents

1-1 Discretionary and Essential Expenses

Exercises

1. For most people, the cost of a subscription to streaming music services is definitely a discretionary expense. Marshal researched subscription costs and found the following rates for streaming services:

   $10/mo., $6/mo., $33/year, $3/mo., $5/mo., $10/mo., $10/mo., $4/mo., $12/mo., $60/year

   a. In order to analyze the data, the subscription rates must cover the same time period. Change the yearly rates to monthly rates.

   b. What is the mean monthly subscription fee? Round your answer to the nearest cent.

   c. What is the median monthly subscription fee?

   d. What is the mode monthly membership fee?

2. Carla is a carpenter. She wants to purchase new high-quality tools for her business. She found the following prices for the exact same set of tools from various sellers:

   $6,700 $7,450 $8,000 $7,600 $7,450 $8,200 $7,210

   a. What is the mean price? Round your answer to the nearest cent.

   b. What is the median price?

   c. What is the mode price?

3. According to the Bureau of Economic Analysis, the monthly percentage change of disposable income in the United States over the course of a year from February to February was reported as follows:

   0.3%   0%   0.6%   0.5%   0.5%   0.4%   0.3%   0.2%   0.3%   0.2%   0.3%   0.4%   0.2%

   a. What was the mean percent change over this period? Round your answer to the nearest hundredth of a percent.

   b. What was the median percent change over this period.

   c. From January to February of the second year, a 0.2% change in disposable income was reported. If the January amount was 12.43 billion dollars, what would the February amount be? Round your answer to two decimal places.

4. In their brochure, AutoNation Career School estimated the average discretionary personal expenses for a student attending to be $2,850. Martin is a student and feels that the amount is too high. He polled his co-students and made a list of their actual school year expenses:

   $2,500 $2,600 $3,000 $3,200 $2,700 $2,900 $2,850

   a. What is the mean of these students' personal expenses? Round your answer to the nearest cent.

   b. How does that average compare with the estimate?

   c. What would Martin's actual personal expenses for that school year have to be so that his amount and his co-students' amounts together would have an average of $2,850?

Use the following table to answer questions 5–8.

Monthly Cell Phone Bills

Jan	Feb	Mar	Apr	May	June	July	Aug	Sept	Oct	Nov	Dec
x_1	x_2	x_3	x_4	x_5	x_6	x_7	x_8	x_9	x_{10}	x_{11}	x_{12}
$83	$86	$78	$82	$95	$87	$90	$76	$88	$82	$83	$71

5. Write the formula for the mean cell phone bill for the entire year using sigma notation and determine that mean. Round your answer to the nearest cent.

6. Write the formula for the mean cell phone bill for the last six months of the year using sigma notation and determine that mean. Round your answer to the nearest cent.

7. Write the formula for the mean cell phone bill from March to September using sigma notation and determine that mean. Round your answer to the nearest cent.

8. Write the sigma notation mean formula for the 3 consecutive month period that would have the highest mean of the year.

Use the following table to answer questions 9–11.

⬤Janet attends State University and lives in an on-campus dorm suite with 5 friends. They share the cost of the monthly upgraded cable bill for their suite. Below is a listing of the bills for their freshman year.

Monthly Cable Bill

Sept	Oct	Nov	Dec	Jan	Feb	Mar	Apr	May
x_1	x_2	x_3	x_4	x_5	x_6	x_7	x_8	x_9
$65	$70	$84	$76	$50	$80	$78	$78	$67

9. Round the following value $\dfrac{1}{9}\sum\limits_{i=1}^{9} x_i$ to the nearest dollar.

    Interpret the answer in the context of the problem.

10. Round the following value $\dfrac{1}{4}\sum\limits_{i=1}^{4} x_i$ to the nearest dollar.

    Interpret the answer in the context of the problem.

11. Write the sigma notation mean formula for the second semester beginning in February and determine that semester average rounded to the nearest dollar.

12. The New York Premier Theater is hosting a concert at which all proceeds will go to the charity. The seating chart is shown here:

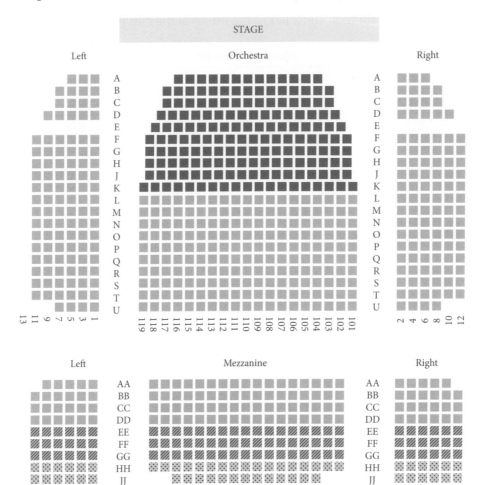

The seating options for the color-coded seats are priced as follows:

▨ Rear Mezzanine 54 seats, each at $150

▨ Middle Mezzanine 87 seats, each at $200

▨ Front Mezzanine and Orchestra 512 seats, each at $300

■ Front and Center Orchestra 167 seats, each at $500

a. Construct a frequency distribution with column headings "Seat Type", "Price", and "Number of Seats".

b. If all of the seats were sold for this concert, what would be the total amount to be donated to charity?

c. Determine the mean, median, and mode seat prices. Round to the nearest cent.

13. Although companies would like consumers to believe that identity theft protection is an essential expense, in reality it is discretionary. A consumer organization compared the monthly costs of similar identity theft protection plans on the market and published the following list:

$14.99 $12.75 $14.99 $14.99 $9.99 $25 $25 $10 $14.99 $10 $20 $10 $20

$14.99 $10 $25 $20 $12 $14.99 $25 $25 $20 $12.75 $10 $9.99

a. Write the formula for the mean in sigma notation and use it to calculate the mean monthly plan price. Round your answer to the nearest cent,

b. Construct a frequency distribution for the data.

c. Use the frequency distribution to determine the mean. Round to the nearest cent.

d. Use the frequency distribution to determine the median and the mode.

1-2   Travel Expenses

Exercises

1. A certain rail company uses a method called demand pricing for setting the prices of their seats. The price per seat starts at a fixed amount. As the train starts to fill up, the prices gradually increase. A consumer watchdog agency selected a random coach car on a train traveling between New York and Philadelphia. They asked each traveler for the price paid for the seat. The following is the result of their survey.

   a. Extend the graph by adding a cumulative frequency column. Calculate the 6 entries for that column and answer the questions below.

   b. How many passengers paid a fare at or below $45?

   c. How many passengers paid a fare at or above $70?

Price	Frequency	Cumulative Frequency
$39	12	
$45	17	
$55	14	
$70	7	
$88	5	
$107	4	

   d. How many passengers paid a fare that was at least $45 and at most $88?

2. Use the table in problem 1 to answer these questions.

   a. Add a relative frequency column. Calculate the relative frequencies. Round each to the nearest thousandth.

   b. Which ticket prices have a relative frequency greater than 0.2 and less than 0.3?

   c. Interpret the relative frequency for the $88 ticket price in terms of a percent.

3. Many people travel to Florida to visit the popular theme parks there. The table below lists yearly attendance at one of those parks for 6 consecutive years.

Year	Attendance in millions
2009	17.3
2010	16.97
2011	17.14
2012	17.54
2013	18.59
2014	19.33

Use the table to answer the questions below.

a. Add a "Relative Frequency" column to the table and determine all of the entries in that column. Round your entries to three decimal places.

b. Add a "Cumulative Frequency" column to the table and determine all of the entries in that column. Express your answer in millions to two decimal places.

c. Add a "Relative Cumulative Frequency" column to the table and determine all of the entries in that column. Round your entries to three decimal places.

d. What was the average monthly number of visitors in millions attending this theme park over this 6-year period? Round to the nearest tenth of a million.

e. What was the median number of park visitors?

f. Use your completed chart. What percent of the total number of visitors attended in 2014?

g. Use your chart. Approximately what percent of all people entering the park did so in 2009, 2010, and 2011 combined? Where would you find this information in your chart?

4. Jim lives in San Francisco and attends school at a university in New York City. He wants to travel home for his sister's wedding next month and has researched round trip airfares. The table lists all available itineraries with fares below $400.

RT Fares	Frequency	Rel. Freq.	Cum. Freq.	Re. Cum. Freq.
$326	2	0.024	2	0.024
$336	10	0.119	12	0.143
$340	2	0.024	14	0.167
$344	4	b.	18	0.214
$350	5	0.060	23	f.
$357	9	0.107	d.	0.381
$366	15	0.179	47	0.560
$371	3	0.036	50	0.595
$376	2	c.	52	0.619
$379	6	0.071	58	g.
$384	17	0.202	e.	0.893
$392	9	0.107	84	1.000
Total	a.			

Use the table to determine the missing values a–g.

5. Four car rental prices were quoted for a 1-day rental. The frequencies are listed. Let Y represent the frequency of the $83 price quote. Use the information shown in the chart to write algebraic expressions for the entries labeled a–e.

1-day Car Rental	Frequency	Relative Frequency	Cumulative Frequency	Relative Cumulative Frequency
$65	4			
$72	2	b.		
$83	Y	c.		
$100	3		d.	e.
Total	a.			

6. Tesa lives in a major city. Her employer pays for her round trip taxicab fare from home to work each day. She must keep receipts for each trip and turn them in at the end of each month for reimbursement. The fares are based on distance and time so they change each day due to traffic, construction, weather, and other factors. Below is an ordered list of her round-trip fares for the 23 workdays in August.

23.00   23.00   24.25   24.25   24.25   24.25   24.25   24.75

25.50   25.50   25.50   25.50   25.50   25.50   25.60   25.75

25.80   25.80   25.80   25.90   25.90   25.95   25.95

a. Find the percentile rank for a fare of $25.50. Interpret your results.

b. Find the percentile rank for a fare of $25.90. Interpret your results.

c. Based on your answers to parts a and b of this problem, which fare would have a percentile rank of about 70%?

7. The table below lists all train fares quoted from Washington, DC, to Philadelphia, PA, on a given day.

a. Write an algebraic expression for the percentile rank of $42.

Cost to Airport	Frequency
$42	a
$48	b
$55	c
$68	d
$90	e
$109	f

b. Write an algebraic expression for the percentile rank of $48.

c. Write an algebraic expression for the percentile rank of $55.

d. Write an algebraic expression for the percentile rank of $68.

e. Write an algebraic expression for the percentile rank of $90.

f. Write an algebraic expression for the percentile rank of $109.

1-3 Entertainment Expenses

Exercises

1. Following are the prices of 12 tickets listed on the *Ticket Racket* ticket broker site for a Bruce Springsteen concert.

   $75, 120, 120, 145, 150, 150, 150, 175, 175, 200, 225, 275

   Round your answers to the nearest hundredth.

   a. What is the mean ticket price?

   b. What is the median ticket price?

   c. What is the mode ticket price?

   d. What is the range?

   e. What is the variance?

   f. What is the standard deviation?

2. The variance of a distribution is 50. What is the standard deviation, rounded to the nearest thousandth?

3. The following is a list of Relay for Life donations given by several community businesses in the Maple Glen High School vicinity.

   $10, $50, $100, $100, $100, $120, $120, $125, $150, $150, $250.

   Round your answers to the nearest hundredth.

   a. What is the mean donation amount?

   b. What is the range?

   c. What is the variance?

   d. What is the standard deviation?

4. Airline fares can vary greatly, even from the same carrier within the same day. The following are fares from New York to Burbank, CA, over the past week.

   $430, $567, $334, $701, $424, $555, $890, $455, $450, $1,122

   What is the standard deviation for this distribution? Round your answers to the nearest dollar.

5. The distribution of cell phone bills for families in Smithtown North High School has mean $183 and standard deviation 11. At Smithtown South High School, the mean is $181 and the standard deviation is 21. Which distribution is more spread out?

6. The following is a distribution of the number of individual song downloads made by students in Arlington High School's Acoustic Café Club last year.

    12, 11, 21, 43, 23, 51, 19, 22, 88, 60

    a. Find the mean number of downloads per club member.

    b. If each club member increased their downloads by 6, what happens to the mean?

    c. If each club member multiplies their downloads by 3, what happens to the mean?

    d. Find the median number of downloads per club member.

    e. If each club member increased their downloads by 6, what happens to the median?

    f. If each club member multiplies their downloads by 3, what happens to the median?

    g. Find the range of the distribution.

    h. If each club member increased their downloads by 6, what happens to the range?

    i. If each club member multiplies their downloads by 3, what happens to the range?

    j. Find the standard deviation of the original distribution to the nearest thousandth.

    k. If each club member increased their downloads by 6, what happens to the standard deviation?

    l. If each club member multiplies their downloads by 3, what happens to the standard deviation?

7. Look at the original data in problem 6. Suppose the number 60 was changed to 600 and the rest of the numbers remained the same.

    a. Would the mean be affected?   **b.** Would the median be affected?

    c. Would the range be affected?   **d.** Would the standard deviation be affected?

Name _____   Date _____

8. A high school theater production had an admission price of $10. During the show, 876 people paid to enter.

   a. What is the range of the distribution of admission fees?

   b. What is the standard deviation of the distribution of admission fees?

   c. If the standard deviation of a distribution is 0, must all of the data be the same number? Explain.

9. A class of 31 students averaged 82 on a recent exam. Two students were absent and took the exam the next day. The two students averaged 88 on their exam. What was the average for the entire class, including the two students who took the test one day later?

10. The number of cars owned by households in the Lakebridge Condominium Complex is shown in the table.

Number of Cars Owned	Frequency, f	$x_i f$	$x_i - \bar{x}$	$(x_i - \bar{x})^2$	$(x_i - \bar{x})^2 f$
0	22	c.	h.	l.	p.
1	43	d.	i.	m.	q.
2	52	e.	j.	n.	r.
3	3	f.	k.	o.	s.
TOTAL	$n = 120$	g.			t.

   a. Find the mean number of cars owned per household.

   b. Fill in the missing entries in the table to the nearest hundredth.

   c. Find the standard deviation of the distribution to the nearest hundredth.

12. A distribution consists of 30 scores of 10 and 30 scores of 20. Find the ratio of the range to the standard deviation.

13. Create a distribution of five numbers that has range 10, maximum score 20, and mean 12.

1-4 | Vacation Expenses

Exercises

1. A travel agency did a survey and found that the average local family spends $1,900 on a summer vacation. The distribution is normally distributed with standard deviation $390.

   a. What percent of the families took vacations that cost under $1,500? Round to the nearest percent.

   b. What percent of the families took vacations that cost over $2,800? Round to the nearest percent.

   c. Find the amount a family would have spent to be the 60th percentile. Round to the nearest dollar.

2. A distribution is normal with mean 60 and standard deviation 8. Find the area of each of the following shaded regions to four decimal places.

   a.
   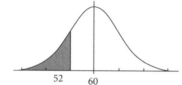

   b.
   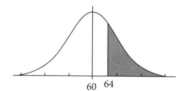

   c.
   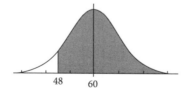

   d.
   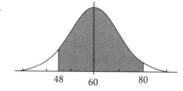

3. A family of two adults and two children on vacation in the United States will pay an average of $247 per day for food and lodging with a standard deviation of $60 per day, according to a recent survey by a national travel association.

    a. Find, to the nearest hundredth, the z-score for $150 for vacation food and lodging expenses.

    b. If a vacationer had a z-score of 2.1, what were their daily expenses for food and lodging?

    c. If the data is normally distributed, find the percent of these vacationers who spent less than $307 per day.

    d. What is the variance?

    e. What is the mean expense for food and lodging for a 7-day vacation?

4. The Vacation Times website rates recreational vehicle campgrounds using integers from 0 to 15. Last year they rated over 1,000 campsites. The ratings were normally distributed with mean 7.6 and standard deviation 1.7.

    a. How high would a campsite's rating have to be for it to be considered in the top 10% of rated campsites? Round to the nearest hundredth.

    b. Find the z-score for a rating of 5. Round to the nearest hundredth.

    c. Find the percentile for a rating of 7.5. Round to the nearest percent.

    d. A campsite had a z-score of 2. What was its rating?

5. A certain amusement park ride requires riders to be at least 48 inches tall. If the heights of children in a summer camp are normally distributed with mean 52 and standard deviation 2.5, how many of the 140 campers will be allowed on the ride? Round to the nearest integer.

6. What z-score on the Normal Curve table has an area of 0.8849 to its left?

7. What z-score on the Normal Curve table has an area of 0.6808 to its right?

8. *Travel Times Journal* found that the average per person cost of a 10-day trip along the Pacific coast, per person, is $1,015. This includes transportation, food, lodging, and entertainment.

   a. If the data is normally distributed with standard deviation $198, find the percent of vacationers who spent less than $1,200 per day. Round to the nearest hundredth of a percent.

   b. Find the per-day expense for one of these travelers who had a *z*-score of −1.6.

   c. A *Bargain Times Vacation Blog* writer claimed to have done this vacation for a cost of $710 per person. What percentile is represented by $710? Round to the nearest hundredth of a percentile.

9. The school nurse at West Side Elementary School weighs all of the 230 children by the end of September. She finds that the students' weights are normally distributed with mean 98 and standard deviation 16. After compiling all the data, she realizes that the scale was incorrect—it was reading two pounds over the actual weight. She adjusts the records for all 230 children.

   a. What is the effect of the correction on the mean?

   b. What is the correct mean?

   c. What is the effect of the correction on the standard deviation?

10. During a recent summer month, airfares from Miami, FL, to Seattle, WA, were normally distributed with mean $760 and standard deviation $136.

   a. Sketch a normal curve and shade in the interval below $500.

   b. Find the *z*-score for a fare of $500.

   c. What percent of the airfares were below $500?

   d. The lowest 5% of airfares represents a real bargain. What airfare represents the 5th percentile?

   e. What percent of the airfares were below the median?

Financial Algebra Workbook 1-4

1-5 Personal Expenses

Exercises

1. Each month you have $200 automatically deposited from your checking account into a discretionary savings account. Your plan is to leave the money in this account for the next 10 years in order to use the total at that time at your discretion. A scatter plot shows the number of months that have passed and the amount in your discretionary spending account each month. The explanatory *x*-variable is the number of months that have passed. The response *y*-variable is the amount in your savings account. Is there a positive or negative correlation? Explain.

2. Determine if the scatter plot below depicts a positive correlation or a negative correlation.

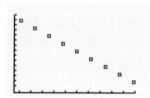

3. Describe each of the following correlation coefficients using the terms strong, moderate, or weak and negative or positive.

   a. $r = -0.19$ **b.** $r = -0.93$ **c.** $r = 0.57$

   d. $r = 0.0999$ **e.** $r = -0.97$ **f.** $r = -0.45$

4. Lori created a scatter plot where the explanatory variable was the side of a square, and the response variable was the perimeter of the square. Is the data positively or negatively correlated? Explain.

5. In each situation of bivariate data there is causation, so the variables can be named explanatory and response variables. Identify each explanatory variable and response variable.

   a. number of days worked, amount earned

   b. amount earned in the year, income taxes paid

   c. temperature, number of swimmers at the beach

   d. price of a dress, number of dresses sold

6. MoviePlay is an online movie rental service. They have a sliding price list based upon the popularity of the movies. The table below shows the rentals by price category for the month of September. Let x represent the price and y represent the number of movies rented at that price.

Price	# of rentals
5.99	800
4.99	1,000
3.99	1,200
2.99	1,380
1.99	1,672
0.99	1,903

a. Examine the data without drawing a scatter plot. Describe any trends you see.

b. Draw a scatter plot. Describe the correlation.

c. Based on this information, how many rentals might be anticipated if the company instituted a new price category of $6.99. Explain your reasoning.

7. The table below lists the percentage of households with an income of $100,000 or more that spent money on fitness-related activities over the course of one year as reported by statista.com.

Fitness Spending in dollars (d)	Percent of households with an income of $100,00 or more
0	53.7%
$0 < d < 250$	17.8%
$250 \le d < 500$	12.5%
$500 \le d < 1000$	8.4%
$1000 \le d < 2000$	5%
$2000 \le d < 3000$	1.5%
$3000 \le d < 5000$	0.7%
$5000 \le d < 10,000$	0.2%

a. Without making a scatter plot, what trend do you see in the data.

b. Draw a scatter plot. Let x represent the spending interval number ($x = 1$ when d = 0, $x = 2$ when $0 < d < 250$, $x = 3$ when $250 \le d < 500$ etc.) Describe the correlation.

c. Based on the trend, scatter plot, and correlation, what might you predict the percentage to be for households that had $10,000 to $15,000 fitness-related expenses?

Name _____   Date _____

8. In Application 6 for section 1-5 in the textbook, you were given the following table about discretionary personal back-to-school personal expenses.

   a. Determine the linear regression equation that best fits the data presented in the table. Let x represent the year and y represent the back-to-school spending amount per family. Round numbers to the nearest hundredth.

   b. Determine the correlation coefficient for the bivariate data. Round to the nearest hundredth. Interpret that correlation coefficient.

   c. Use the linear regression equation to predict the spending amount in 2016. Round your answer to the nearest cent.

Year	Back to School Spending in Dollars per Family
2004	$483.28
2005	$443.77
2006	$527.08
2007	$563.49
2008	$594.24
2009	$548.72
2010	$606.40
2011	$603.63
2012	$688.82
2013	$634.79
2014	$669.28
2015	$630.36

   d. Rather than using the actual year values, x could have represented the year number where $x = 1$ represents 2004, $x = 2$ represents 2005, and so on. Replace the year numbers for x in your list. Determine the regression line using this bivariate data set. Do you get the same regression equation as in part a?

   e. What similarities and differences do you see in the two regression equations? Explain.

   f. Use the second linear regression equation to predict the spending for 2016. What x-value will you use in this case to represent 2016?

9. The Super Bowl is a big money-making and money-spending event. The discretionary spending amounts on Super Bowl weekends are in the billions of dollars. Examine the chart below that lists TV viewer numbers and Super Bowl weekend-related expenses by year.

Year	TV Viewers in millions	Money Spent in billions
2007	93.18	8.71
2008	92.45	9.47
2009	98.73	9.56
2010	106.48	8.87
2011	111	10.15
2012	111.3	11.02
2013	108.4	12.28
2014	111.5	12.37
2015	114.4	14.31
2016	111.9	15.53

a. Determine the linear regression equation where x represents the year number ($x = 1$ represents 2007, $x = 2$ represents 2008, etc.) and y represents the money spent. Round all numbers to the nearest thousandth. What is the correlation coefficient? What can you infer from the coefficient?

b. Determine the linear regression equation where x represents the number of TV viewers and y represents the money spent. Round all numbers to the nearest thousandth. What is the correlation coefficient? What can you infer from the differences between this coefficient and the one found in part a?

2-1 Checking Accounts

Exercises

1. Mitchell has a balance of $1,200 in his First State Bank checking account. He deposits a $387.89 paycheck, a $437.12 dividend check, and a personal check for $250 into his account. He wants to receive $400 in cash. How much will he have in his account after the transaction?

2. Meg has a total of d dollars in her checking account. She makes a cash deposit of c dollars and a deposit of three checks each worth s dollars. She would like e dollars in cash from this transaction. She has enough money in her account to cover the cash received. Express her new checking account balance after the transaction as an algebraic expression.

3. Neal deposited a $489.50 paycheck, an x dollar stock dividend check, a y dollar rebate check, and $85 cash into his checking account. His original account balance was w dollars. Assume each check clears. Write an expression for the balance in his account after the deposits?

4. Elaine has m dollars in her checking account. On December 8, she deposited $1,200, r dollars, and $568.90. She also cashed a check for t dollars and one for $73.70. Write an algebraic expression that represents the amount of money in her account after the transactions.

5. Del and Jen have a joint checking account. Their balance at the beginning of October was $6,238.67. During the month they made deposits totaling d dollars, wrote checks totaling $1,459.98, paid a maintenance fee of z dollars, and earned b dollars in interest on the account. Write an algebraic expression that represents the balance at the end of the month?

6. New Merrick Bank charges a $21-per-check overdraft protection fee. On June 5, Lewis had $989.00 in his account. Over the next few days, the following checks were submitted for payment at his bank: June 6, $875.15, $340.50, and $450.63; June 7, $330; and June 8, $560.00.

   a. How much will he pay in overdraft protection fees?

   b. How much will he owe the bank after June 8?

7. Dean has a checking account at City Center Bank. During the month of April, he made deposits totaling $2,458.52 and wrote checks totaling $789.23. He paid a maintenance fee of $25 and earned $3.24 in interest. His balance at the end of the month was $4,492.76. What was the balance at the beginning of April?

8. Bellrose Bank charges a monthly maintenance fee of $17 and a check-writing fee of $0.05 per check. Last year, Patricia wrote 445 checks from her account at Bellrose. What was the total of all fees she paid on that account last year?

9. Create a check register for the transactions listed.

   a. Your balance on 1/5 is $822.67.

   b. You write check 1076 on 1/6 for $600.00 to Excel Health Club.

   c. You deposit a paycheck for $227.45 on 1/11.

   d. You deposit a $50 rebate check on 1/15.

   e. On 1/16, you begin writing a donation check to Clothes for Kids but make an error and have to void the check. You write the very next check for $100 to this organization.

   f. On 1/20, you withdraw $200 from the ATM at the mall. The company owning the ATM charges you $3.50 and your bank charges you $2.50 for the ATM transaction.

   g. On 1/21, you made a debit card purchase at Stacy's Store for $134.87.

   h. Your friend gave you the $1,300 he owed you and you deposit it on 1/22.

   i. You write the next check on 1/23 to iBiz for $744.24 for a new computer.

   j. You deposit your paycheck for $227.45 on 1/23.

   k. On 1/24, you withdraw $50 from the ATM affiliated with your bank. There are no fees.

   l. On 1/24, you write the next check for $75.00 to iTel Wireless.

   m. On 1/25, you write a check for $120 concert tickets to Ticket King.

NUMBER OR CODE	DATE	TRANSACTION DESCRIPTION	PAYMENT AMOUNT	✓	FEE	DEPOSIT AMOUNT	$ BALANCE
			$				

10. Create a check register for the transactions listed.

   a. Your balance on 2/25 is $769.22.

   b. On 2/25, you write check 747 for $18 to Steve Smith.

   c. On 2/27, you deposit your paycheck in the amount of $450.80.

   d. Your grandparents send you a check for $50, which you deposit into your account on 2/28.

   e. On 3/2 you write a check to North State College for $300.00 and another check to Middle Island Auto Parts for $120.65.

   f. Later in the day on 3/2 you write two more checks: Metro Transit for $85.00 and Bling's Department Store for $58.76.

   g. On 3/3, at Border Barns Books, as you write the next check for $105.85, you make a mistake and void that check. You pay with the next available check in your checkbook.

   h. On 3/5, you deposit a rebate check for $425 into your checking account.

   i. On 3/8, you pay your car insurance with an e-check to AllFarm Insurance for $521.30.

   j. On 3/10, you withdraw $300 from the ATM. There is a $4.50 charge for using the ATM.

   k. On 3/11, you deposit your paycheck in the amount of $450.00.

   l. On 3/12, you use your debit card to make three purchases at Sports Master: $88.91, $23.50, and $100.70.

   m. On 3/13, you transfer $1,000 from your savings account into your checking account.

   n. On 3/13, you write a check to Empire Properties for your first month's rent in your new apartment in the amount of $820.00.

   o. On 3/15, you use your debit card to purchase a $150.00 microwave at Kitchen Supply.

Name _____   Date _____

(Transactions are listed on the previous page.)

NUMBER OR CODE	DATE	TRANSACTION DESCRIPTION	PAYMENT AMOUNT	✓	FEE	DEPOSIT AMOUNT	$ BALANCE
			$				

Name _____ Date _____

2-2 Reconcile a Bank Statement

Exercises

1. On the back of Elise's monthly statement, she listed the following outstanding withdrawals: #123, $76.09; #117, $400; #130, $560.25; debit card, $340.50; and #138, $83.71. She also determined that a deposit for $500 and another for $328.90 are outstanding. Using these outstanding transactions, what adjustment will have to be made to her statement balance?

2. Pina filled out the following information on the back of her monthly statement:

   Ending balance from statement $1,139.78
   Deposits outstanding   + $280.67
   Total of checks outstanding   – $656.91
   Revised statement balance $_____
   Balance from checkbook $763.54

   Find Pina's revised statement balance. Does her account reconcile?

3. Tasha filled out the following information on the back of her bank statement:

   Ending balance from statement $764.22
   Deposits outstanding   + $387.11
   Total of checks outstanding   – $455.32
   Revised statement balance $_____
   Balance from checkbook $669.01

   Find Tasha's revised statement balance. Does her account reconcile?

4. Lenny opened a checking account last month. Today he received his first statement. The statement listed five deposits and 24 checks that cleared. Lenny's check register shows nine outstanding checks. How many checks has Lenny written since the account was opened?

5. Arden's checking account charges a $21 monthly maintenance fee with no per-check fee. He wants to switch to a different account with a fee of 18 cents per check and a $15 monthly maintenance fee. The following information is about his last five monthly statements.

Month	Number of Checks on Statement	Month	Number of Checks on Statement	Month	Number of Checks on Statement
Feb	24	Mar	37	Apr	35
May	33	June	41		

   a. What is the mean number of checks Arden wrote per month during the last five months?

   b. About how much should Arden expect to pay per month for the new checking account?

   c. What advice would you give Arden?

6. Below you will find Mitch West's monthly statement and his check register. Use them to complete parts a–e in his checking account summary. Does his account reconcile?

Mitch West
23 Sycamore Lane
Benridge, NY 10506

ACCOUNT NUMBER: 456213-A232
STATEMENT PERIOD: 5/15 - 6/15

STARTING BALANCE ⟶ **$ 2,312.70**

DATE	DESCRIPTION	CHECK NUMBER	TRANSACTION AMOUNT	BALANCE
8/16	W/D	1056	$ 256.00	
8/20	DEPOSIT		$ 1,200.80	
8/22	W/D	Debit card	$ 234.81	
8/22	W/D	1058	$ 334.90	
8/23	W/D	Debit Card	$ 34.72	
8/25	W/D	1060	$ 145.78	
8/26	W/D	1059	$ 56.00	
8/27	DEPOSIT		$ 150.00	
9/1	W/D	1061	$ 230.00	

ENDING BALANCE ⟶ **$2,368.29**

NUMBER OR CODE	DATE	TRANSACTION DESCRIPTION	PAYMENT AMOUNT	✓	FEE	DEPOSIT AMOUNT	$ BALANCE
							2,309.70
1056	8/15	Best Offer Inc.	256 00				− 256.00
							2,053.70
1057	8/16	Dept. of Motor Vehicles	86 50				− 86.50
							1,967.20
1058	8/16	AutoWorld	334 90				− 334.90
							1,632.30
	8/18	Car Nation	234 81				− 234.81
							1,397.49
	8/20	Deposit				1,200 80	+ 1,200.80
							2,598.29
1059	8/21	Print Makers	56 00				− 56.00
							2,542.29
1060	8/22	Book Bonanza	145 78				− 145.78
							2,396.51
	8/23	Fast Freddy's Fast Food	34 72				− 34.72
							2,361.79
	8/27	Deposit				150 00	+ 150.00
							2,511.79
1061	8/30	Lincoln Savings Bank	230 00				− 230.00
							2,281.79
1062	9/1	VOID					
1063	9/1	Pasta Pete's	32 50				− 32.50
							2,249.29
	9/2	Deposit				300 00	+ 300.00
							2,549.29

Checking Account Summary

Ending Balance from Statement	a.
Deposits Outstanding	+ b.
Total of Checks Outstanding	− c.
Revised statement balance	d.
Balance from Checkbook	e.

2-3 | Savings Accounts

Exercises

1. Gary deposits $3,700 in an account that pays 2.15% simple interest. He keeps the money in the account for three years, but doesn't make any deposits or withdrawals. How much interest will he receive after the three years?

2. How much simple interest is earned on $6,000 at an interest rate of 2.25% in $4\frac{1}{2}$ years?

3. How much principal would you have to deposit to earn $700 simple interest in $1\frac{1}{2}$ years at a rate of 2%.?

4. Jesse estimates that it will cost $300,000 to send his newborn son to a private college in 18 years. He currently has $65,000 to deposit in an account. What simple interest rate would he need so that $65,000 grows into $300,000 in 18 years? Round to the nearest percent.

5. Dillon has a bank account that pays 3.2% simple interest. His balance is $1,766. How long will it take for the amount in the account to grow to $2,000? Round to the nearest year.

6. How long will it take $5,000 to double in an account that pays 1.6% simple interest? Round to the nearest year.

7. How much simple interest would $1,500 earn in 11 months at an interest rate of 3.75%?

8. How much simple interest would $1,000 earn in 275 days at an interest rate of 4.21%? (There are 365 days in a year.)

9. Colin deposited $1,230 in an account that pays 2.19% simple interest for three years.

    a. What will the interest be for the three years?

    b. What will be the new balance after three years?

    c. How much interest did the account earn the first year, to the nearest cent?

    d. How much interest did the account earn the second year, to the nearest cent?

    e. How much interest did the account earn the third year, to the nearest cent?

10. Gerry deposited $1,230 in an account that pays 2.19% simple interest for one year.

    a. How much interest will he earn in one year?

    b. What will his balance be after one year?

    c. Gerry withdraws all of the principal and interest after the first year and deposits it into another one-year account at the same rate. What will his interest be for the second year?

    d. What will his balance be after two years?

    e. Compare the accounts of Gerry and Colin from Exercise 9. Who earned more interest the second year, Gerry or Colin? Explain.

11. Use the simple interest formula to find the missing entries in the following table. Round monetary amounts to the nearest cent, percents to the nearest hundredth of a percent, and time to the nearest month. Use 365 days = 1 year.

	Interest	Principal	Rate	Time
a.		$980	2.6%	1 yr
b.		$2,900	3.05%	15 mo
	$400	$3,500	4.5%	**c.**
	$400	**d.**	0.66%	4 years
	$400	$3,000	**e.**	3 yr
f.		$750,000	1.2%	100 days
	y dollars	p	2.11%	**g.**

12. How much simple interest would x dollars earn in 13 months at a rate of r percent?

13. How long would $100,000 take to double at a simple interest rate of 8%?

14. How long would $450 take to double at a simple interest rate of 100%?

15. What simple interest rate, to the nearest tenth, is needed for $15,000 to double in 8 years?

16. Arrange these fractions of a year in ascending order: 190 days, 5 months, 160 days, 7 months, 200 days.

17. Max has $17 in a fund he is creating to save for a bike. He adds $6 per week of his babysitting earnings to the fund. If his weekly fund balance is represented by an arithmetic sequence, find the 27th term.

2-4 Explore Compound Interest

Exercises

Round to the nearest cent where necessary.

1. How much interest would $2,000 earn in one year at the rate of 1.2%?

2. How much interest would $2,000 earn, compounded annually, in two years at the rate of 1.2%?

3. How much interest would $2,000 earn, with simple interest, in two years at the rate of 1.2%?

4. Compare your answers to Exercises 2 and 3. Explain why they differ.

5. How much would d dollars earn in one year at the rate of p percent compounded annually?

6. Margaret deposits $1,000 in a savings account that pays 1.4% interest compounded semiannually. What is her balance after one year?

7. How much interest does $5,300 earn at a rate of 2.8% interest compounded quarterly, in three months?

8. Mr. Guny deposits $4,900 in a savings account that pays 1.5% interest compounded quarterly.

    a. Find the first quarter's interest.   b. Find the first quarter's balance.

    c. Find the second quarter's interest.   d. Find the second quarter's balance.

    e. Find the third quarter's interest.   f. Find the third quarter's balance.

    g. Find the fourth quarter's interest.   h. Find the fourth quarter's balance.

    i. How much interest does the account earn in the first year?

9. Jonathan deposits $6,000 in a savings account that pays 2.1% interest compounded quarterly. What is his balance after one year?

10. How much interest would $1,000,000 earn at 2% compounded daily, in one day?

11. How much interest would y dollars earn in one day at a rate of 1.75% compounded daily?

12. Mrs. Huber opened a savings account on June 26 with a $1,300 deposit. The account pays 1.6% interest compounded daily. On June 27, she deposited $450 and on June 28 she withdrew $110. Complete the table based on Mrs. Huber's banking activity.

	June 26	June 27	June 28
Opening balance	a.	f.	k.
Deposit	b.	g.	—
Withdrawal	—	—	l.
Principal used to Compute Interest	c.	h.	m.
Interest	d.	i.	n.
Ending Balance	e.	j.	o.

13. Mr. Nolan has a bank account that compounds interest daily at a rate of 1.7%. On the morning of December 7, the principal is $2,644.08. That day he withdraws $550 to pay for a snow blower. Later that day he receives a $934 paycheck from his employer, and he deposits that in the bank. On December 8, he withdraws $300 to go holiday shopping. What is his balance at the end of the day on December 8?

14. Mrs. Platt has an account that pays p percent interest compounded daily. On April 27, she had an opening balance of b dollars. Also on April 27, she made a w dollars withdrawal and a d dollars deposit. Express her interest for April 27 algebraically.

15. This morning, Mrs. Rullan had a balance of 1,000 dollars in an account that pays 2.05% interest compounded weekly. Express her interest for the following week if she makes no deposits or withdrawals.

16. Kristin deposited $9,000 in an account that has an annual interest rate of 2.1% compounded monthly. How much interest will she earn at the end of one month?

17. How much would $25,000 earn in one hour at the rate of 5%, compounded hourly?

18. The Jules Server Scholarship Fund gives a graduation award of $250 to a graduating senior at North End High School. Currently the fund has a balance of $8,300 in an account that pays 2.2% interest compounded annually. Will the amount earned in annual interest be enough to pay for the award?

19. Kelly has d dollars in an account that pays 1.4% interest compounded weekly. Express her balance after one week algebraically.

2-5 Compound Interest Formula

Exercises

Round to the nearest cent wherever necessary.

1. Mr. Mady opens a savings account with principal *P* dollars that pays 2.11% interest compounded quarterly. Express his ending balance after one year algebraically.

2. Jeff deposits $2,300 at 1.13% interest compounded weekly. What will be his ending balance after one year?

3. Nancy has $4,111 in an account that pays 1.07% interest compounded monthly. What is her ending balance after two years?

4. Mr. Weinstein has a savings account with a balance of $19,211.34. It pays 1.1% interest compounded daily. What is his ending balance after three years, if no other deposits or withdrawals are made? How much interest does he earn over the three years?

5. If you invested $10,000 at 3.8% compounded hourly for five years, what would be your ending balance?

6. Danielle has a CD at Crossland Bank. She invests $22,350 for four years at 1.55% interest, compounded monthly. What is her ending balance? How much interest did she make?

7. Ms. Santoro is opening a one-year CD for $16,000. The interest is compounded daily. She is told by the bank representative that the annual percentage rate (APR) is 1.8%. What is the annual percentage yield (APY) for this account?

8. Knob Hill Savings Bank offers a one-year CD at 1.88% interest compounded daily. What is the APY for this account? Round to the nearest hundredth of a percent.

9. Kings Park Bank is advertising a special 1.66% APR for CDs. Kevin takes out a one-year CD for $24,000. The interest is compounded daily. Find the APY for Kevin's account.

10. Imagine that you invest $100,000 in an account that pays 5.9% annual interest compounded monthly. What will your balance be at the end of 18 years?

11. Yurik invests $88,000 in a CD that is locked into a 1.75% interest rate compounded monthly, for seven years. How much will Yurik have in the account when the CD matures?

12. Stephanie has created a study tool to help her study compound interest. She writes the compound interest formula with letters different than the traditional representations.

$$X = M\left(1 + \frac{Q}{K}\right)^{KB}$$

  a. If Q is increased, does the new balance increase or decrease? Explain your answer.

  b. If K is decreased, does the new balance increase or decrease? Explain.

  c. If B is increased, does the new balance increase or decrease? Explain.

  d. Is it possible that $M > X$? Explain.

  e. Using Stephanie's variable representation, express the amount of interest earned on the account.

13. Compare the simple interest for one year on a principal of 1 million dollars at an interest rate of 6.3% to compounding every second for the same principal and interest rate.

  a. How many seconds are in an hour?

  b. How many seconds are in a day?

  c. How many seconds are in a year?

  d. How much interest does $1,000,000 earn in one year at 6.3% interest, compounded every second?

  e. How much does the same $1,000,000 earn at 6.3% in one year, under simple interest?

  f. How much more interest did the compounded every second account earn when compared to the simple-interest account?

14. Britney invested $4,000 in a CD at TTYL Bank that pays 1.4% interest compounded monthly.

  a. How much will Britney have in her account at the end of one year?

  b. What is the APY for this account? Round to the nearest hundredth of a percent.

15. How much more would $5,000 earn in 10 years, compounded daily at 2%, when compared to the interest on $5,000 over 10 years, at 2% compounded semiannually?

2-6 Continuous Compounding

Exercises

Round to the nearest cent wherever necessary.

1. Given the function $f(x) = \frac{1,234,999}{x}$, as the values of x increase toward infinity, what happens to the values of $f(x)$?

2. As the values of x increase toward infinity, what happens to the values of $g(x) = 3x - 19$?

3. Given the function, $h(x) = \frac{8x - 3}{4x + 5}$, as the values of x increase towards infinity, use a table to find out what happens to the values of $h(x)$.

4. If $f(x) = \frac{10}{x^2}$ use a table and your calculator to find $\lim\limits_{x \to \infty} f(x)$.

5. Given the function $f(x) = 2^x$, find $\lim\limits_{x \to \infty} f(x)$.

6. Given the function $f(x) = \left(\frac{1}{2}\right)^x$, use a table to compute $\lim\limits_{x \to \infty} f(x)$.

7. If you deposit $1,000 at 100% simple interest, what will your ending balance be after one year?

In 8–12, you compare simple interest with daily compounding and continuous compounding.

8. If you deposit $10,000 at 1.85% simple interest, what would your ending balance be after three years?

9. If you deposit $10,000 at 1.85% interest, compounded daily, what would your ending balance be after three years?

10. If you deposit $10,000 at 1.85% interest, compounded continuously, what would your ending balance be after three years?

11. How much more did the account that was compounded continuously earn compared to the account compounded daily?

12. How much more did the account that was compounded daily earn compared to the simple-interest account?

13. Eric deposits $4,700 at 1.03% interest, compounded continuously for five years.

    a. What is his ending balance?

    b. How much interest did the account earn?

14. Write the verbal sentence that is the translation of $\lim\limits_{x \to \infty} f(x) = 3.66$.

15. Write the verbal sentence given below symbolically using limit notation.

    The limit of g(x), as x approaches zero, is fifteen.

16. Given the function $f(x) = \dfrac{2x - 17}{x}$, use a table to find $\lim\limits_{x \to \infty} f(x)$.

17. Find the balance for each compounding period on $50,000 for $2\frac{1}{2}$ years at a rate of 1.3%.

    a. Annually   **b.** Semiannually

    c. Quarterly   **d.** Monthly

    e. Daily   **f.** Hourly

    g. Continuously

18. A private university has an endowment fund that currently has 49 million dollars in it. If it is invested in a one-year CD that pays 2% interest compounded continuously, how much interest will it earn?

19. Use a table of increasing values of x to find each of the following limits.

    a. $\lim\limits_{x \to \infty} f(x)$ if $f(x) = \dfrac{5x - 2}{x + 3}$ **b.** $\lim\limits_{x \to \infty} g(x)$ if $g(x) = \dfrac{12x + 5}{4x + 3}$

    c. $\lim\limits_{x \to \infty} f(x)$ if $f(x) = \dfrac{5x^3 - 100}{x^2}$ **d.** $\lim\limits_{x \to \infty} f(x)$ if $f(x) = \dfrac{7x^2 - 1}{x^3 + 2}$

20. Find the interest earned on a $14,000 balance for nine months at 1.1% interest compounded continuously.

21. Assume you had P dollars to invest in an account that paid 5% interest compounded continuously. How long would it take your money to double? (Hint: Try substituting different numbers of years into the continuous compounding formula). Round to the nearest year.

2-7 | Future Value of Investments

Exercises

1. Vincent made a $2,000 deposit into an account on August 1 that yields 2% interest compounded annually. How much money will be in that account at the end of 5 years?

2. On December 31, Juan Carlos made a $7,000 deposit in an account that pays 0.9% interest compounded semi annually. How much will be in that account at the end of two years?

3. Liam was born on October 1, 2009. His grandparents put $20,000 into an account that yielded 3% interest compounded quarterly. When Liam turns 18, his grandparents will give him the money for a college education. How much will Liam get on his 18th birthday?

4. Colleen is 15 years from retiring. She opens an account at the Savings Bank. She plans to deposit $10,000 each year into the account, which pays 1.7% interest, compounded annually.

    a. How much will be in the account in 15 years?

    b. How much interest would be earned?

5. Anton opened an account at Bradley Bank by depositing $1,250. The account pays 2.325% interest compounded monthly. He deposits $1,250 every month for the next two years.

    a. How much will he have in the account at the end of the two-year period?

    b. Write the future value function. Let x represent each of the monthly interest periods.

    c. Graph the future value function.

    d. Using your graph, what will the approximate balance be after one year?

6. Sylvia wants to go on a cruise around the world in 5 years. If she puts $50 into an account each week that pays 2.25% interest compounded weekly, how much will she have at the end of the five-year period?

7. Fatima opened a savings account with $7,500. She decided to deposit that same amount semiannually. This account earns 1.975% interest compounded semiannually.

   a. What is the future value of the account after 10 years?

   b. Write the future value function. Let x represent the number of semiannual interest periods.

   c. Graph the future value function.

   d. Using your graph, what is the approximate amount in her account after 18 months?

8. Marina invests $200 every quarter into an account that pays 1.5% annual interest rate compounded quarterly. Adriana invests $180 in an account that pays 3% annual interest rate compounded quarterly.

   a. Determine the amount in Marina's account after 10 years.

   b. Determine the amount in Adriana's account after 10 years.

   c. Who had more money in the account after 10 years?

   d. Write the future value function for Marina's account.

   e. Write the future value function for Adriana's account.

   f. Graph Marina and Adriana's future value function on the same axes.

   g. Interpret the graph in the context of the two future value functions.

2-8 Present Value of Investments

Exercises

1. Complete the table to find the single deposit investment amounts.

Future Value	Rate	Time	Deposit (to nearest cent)
$200	2% compounded annually	2 yr	a.
$400	1.5% compounded semiannually	4 yr	b.
$5,000	1.1% compounded quarterly	8 yr	c.
$25,000	2.1% compounded monthly	64 mo	d.

2. Complete the table to find the periodic deposit investment amounts.

Future Value	Rate	Time	Deposit (to nearest cent)
$7,000	1.25% compounded annually	5 yr	a.
$9,500	2.6% compounded semiannually	8 yr	b.
$500,000	1.625% compounded quarterly	15 yr	c.
$1,000,000	2% compounded monthly	246 mo	d.

3. When his daughter Alisa was born, Mike began saving for her wedding. He wanted to have saved about $30,000 by the end of 20 years. How much should Mike deposit into an account that yields 3% interest compounded annually in order to have that amount? Round your answer to the nearest thousand dollars.

4. How long will it take for $5,000 to grow to $10,000 in an account that yields 1.2% interest compounded annually. Experiment with the formula in your calculator using different years or use logarithms.

5. Martina will be attending 4 years of undergraduate school and four more years of graduate school. She wants to have $200,000 in her savings account when she graduates in 8 years. How much must she deposit in an account now at a 2.6% interest rate that compounds monthly to meet her goal? Round your answer to the nearest dollar.

6. Kate wants to install an in ground pool in five years. She estimates the cost will be $50,000. How much should she deposit monthly into an account that pays 1.6% interest compounded monthly in order to have enough money to pay for the pool in 5 years? Round your answer to the nearest dollar.

7. Amber wants to have saved $300,000 by some point in the future. She set up a direct deposit account with a 1.75% APR compounded monthly, but she is unsure of how much to periodically deposit for varying lengths of time. Set up a present value function and graph that function to depict the present values for this situation from 12 months to 240 months.

8. Geri wants $30,000 at the end of five years in order to pay for new siding on her house. If her bank pays 2.2% interest compounded annually, how much does she have to deposit each year in order to have that amount?

9. Uncle Al wants to open an account for his nieces and nephews that he hopes will have $100,000 in it after 25 years. How much should he deposit now into an account that yields 1.75% interest compounded monthly so he can be assured of meeting that goal amount?

10. Althea will need $30,000 for her nursing school tuition in 18 months. She has a bank account that pays 2.45% interest compounded monthly. How much does she have to put in each month to have enough money for the tuition?

11. Art opened an account online that pays 1.8% interest compounded monthly. He has a goal of saving $20,000 by the end of four years. How much will he need to deposit each month?

12. Anthony wants to repay the loan his parents gave him in three years. How much does he need to deposit into an account semiannually that pays 1.25% interest twice a year in order to have $35,000 to repay the loan?

13. Lorna needs $40,000 for a down payment when she buys her boat in 4 years. How much does she need to deposit into an account that pays 1.15% interest compounded quarterly in order to meet her goal?

Graph the present value function for this situation.

14. How much should Sandy deposit each month into a 2.85% account, which compounds interest monthly, if she wants to save $85,000? Use a span from year 0 to year 10 in months.

2-9   The Term of a Single Deposit Account

Exercises

1. In each of the following compound interest equations with t representing the account term, determine the number of times the account is compounded per year and the interest rate percent.

   a. $314{,}961.92 = 280{,}000(1.04)^t$

   b. $4{,}050 = 1{,}800(1.0125)^{4t}$

   c. $2{,}142 = 350(1.006)^{2t}$

   d. $10{,}008 = 1{,}200(1.0036)^{12t}$

   e. $578.88 = 500(1.007)^{3t}$

2. Rewrite each of the compound interest equations in #2 as an exponential equation in the standard form $a = b^c$.

3. Solve for t in each of the following compound interest equations. Leave your answer in terms of a logarithm.

   a. $12{,}800 = 640(1.008)^{2t}$

   b. $32{,}500 = 5{,}000(1.04)^t$

   c. $9{,}800 = 1{,}000(1.0025)^{12t}$

   d. $18{,}500 = 500(1.00375)^{4t}$

   e. $39{,}000 = 30{,}000(1.006)^{3t}$

4. In each of the equations below, t represents the term of a savings account. Find the value of t to the nearest tenth of a year.

   a. $t = \dfrac{\log_{1.02}(2.875)}{12}$

   b. $t = \dfrac{\log_{1.12}(3.4)}{3}$

   c. $t = \dfrac{\log_{1.011}(100.15)}{2}$

   d. $t = \dfrac{\log_{1.025}(20.7)}{6}$

   e. $t = \dfrac{\log_{1.009}(8.125)}{12}$

5. In each of the following compound interest equations, the variable n represents the number of times per year that the interest is compounded. Use logarithms to write an expression for n. Evaluate the expression to the nearest integer.

a. $6{,}720 = 6{,}400(1.00125)^{6n}$

b. $12{,}150 = 9{,}000(1.005)^{10n}$

c. $762.5 = 625(1.008)^{4n}$

d. $232{,}200 = 180(1.051)^{12n}$

e. $1{,}860 = 150(1.0625)^{3n}$

6. Shannon wants to start saving for her retirement. Her goal is to save $350,000. If she deposits $250,000 into an account that pays 2.04% interest compounded monthly, approximately how long will it take for her money to grow to the desired amount? Round your answer to the nearest tenth of a year.

7. Steve has $125,000 to invest in a savings account that pays 3.25% interest compounded quarterly. How many years will it take for the account to earn $15,000 in interest? Round your answer to the nearest tenth of a year.

8. Daisy deposited $600 into an account that compounds interest daily at a rate of 1.46%. At the end of a certain period of time, he had a balance in the account of $645.

a. Write an expression for the account term t but do not evaluate it.

b. Using the expression you determined in part **a** and the change-of-base formula with common logarithms, determine a value of the account term t.

c. Using the expression you determined in part **a** and the change-of-base formula with natural logarithms, determine a value of the account term t. Round the term to the nearest year.

d. What do you notice about the values of t found in parts **c** and **d**? Explain your reasoning for the results.

9. Jasper deposits $20,000 into an account that compounds interest continuously at a rate of 3.4%. To the nearest tenth of a year, how long will it take his money to grow to $30,500?

10. The time it takes for money to quadruple in an account where r is the interest rate expressed as a decimal compounded annually is given by the formula $t = \dfrac{\log 4}{\log(1+r)}$. Use the compound interest formula to derive this result.

11. Andy deposited $15,000 in an account that yields 2.8% interest compounded quarterly. How long will it take for his balance to increase by 25%?

2-10 The Term of a Systematic Account

Exercises

1. Use the Power Property of logarithms to determine the value. In some cases, there will be a numerical answer. In others the answer will be an algebraic expression.

   a. $\log(10^5)$

   b. $\log(a^2)$

   c. $\log_y 3^x$

   d. $\ln e^m$

   e. $\ln(a + b)^c$

2. Use the change of base property to write the given logarithm as a quotient of common logs. Do not evaluate.

   a. $\log_6 144$

   b. $\log_a(b - c)$

   c. $\log_7 t$

   d. $\log_{ab} 5$

   e. $\ln k$

3. Use the One-To-One Property and the Power Property to find the value of t to the nearest tenth in each of the following.

   a. $15.625 = (2.5)^t$

   b. $8^t = 26{,}2144$

   c. $5^{2t} = 9{,}765{,}625$

   d. $(3.5)^{2t+1} = 525.21875$

   e. $3^{\frac{t}{2}} + 10 = 6{,}571$

4. Use the compound interest formula $B = P\left(1 + \frac{r}{n}\right)^{nt}$ in each of the following to express t in terms of a logarithm by rewriting the exponential equation in logarithmic form. Simplify where possible but do not evaluate.

   a. $B = 800$, $P = 500$, $r = .02$, $n = 2$

   b. $B = 13{,}520$, $P = 5{,}200$, $r = .03$, $n = 6$

   c. $B = 750{,}000$, $P = 500{,}000$, $r = .036$, $n = 4$

Use the following situation for questions 5 and 6. Barbara has deposited money into a savings account at Center City Bank. The account pays 3% interest compounded monthly. How long will it take for $5,000 to grow to $5,600.

5. Use the steps below to find the value of t to the nearest year.

   a. Substitute the values in the compound interest formula.

   b. Simplify the value inside the parentheses.

   c. Divide both sides by the value of P. You should now have an exponential equation in standard form.

   d. Rewrite the exponential equation in an equivalent logarithmic form.

   e. Apply the change of base formula to change the logarithm into a quotient of two common logs.

   f. Find the value of the quotient to the nearest thousandth.

   g. Divide both sides by the coefficient of t. Round to the nearest tenth of a year.

6. Use the steps below to find the value of t to the nearest year.

   a. Substitute the values in the compound interest formula.

   b. Simplify the value inside the parentheses.

   c. Divide both sides by the value of P. You should now have an exponential equation in standard form.

   d. Apply the One-To-One Property using common logs.

   e. Simplify the side of the equation with the exponent by applying the Power Property.

   f. Solve for t. This will be a three-step process. Divide both sides by the logarithmic coefficient; divide both sides by the value of n; simplify and round to the nearest tenth of a year.

Name _____   Date _____

Questions 5 and 6 offered the steps for finding the term of a savings account using two different methods. Select either method to solve questions 7 and 8.

7. iPartner is an online bank that offers a locked-in interest rate of 3.6% compounded monthly. Rich makes an initial deposit of $10,000. How long does he have to keep the money in this account in order to have a balance of $12,000? Round to the nearest year.

8. Danka opened a savings account that pays 1.8% interest compounded continuously. Her initial deposit was $160. How long would she have to leave the money in the account for it to reach $250?

9. Bill want to make monthly deposits of $75 into a savings account that offers 2.7% interest compounded monthly. Use the future balance of a periodic investment formula to determine how long will it take for the account balance to reach $2000. Round to the nearest tenth of a year.

10. If Graziela makes quarterly deposits of $800 into an account that pays 1.8% interest quarterly, how long will it take for her principal to grow to $20,000? Use the future balance of a periodic investment formula to answer the question. Round to the nearest tenth of a year.

11. An alternative method for solution to problems similar to Exercises 9 and 10 would have been to use the present value formula from section 2-8 as shown here:

$$P = \frac{B \times \dfrac{r}{n}}{\left(1 + \dfrac{r}{n}\right)^{nt} - 1}$$

In a–h below, write the equations that result when you follow the steps to use this formula to solve exercise 10.

a. Let $B = 20{,}000$, $P = 800$, $r = 0.018$, and $n = 4$. Substitute these values into the present value formula.

b. Simplify wherever possible.

c. Eliminate the denominator. Multiply both sides of the equation by the expression in the denominator.

d. You will now try to isolate the variable t on one side of the equation. Divide both sides by 800.

e. Add 1 to both sides of the equation.

f. You now should have an exponential equation in standard form. Apply the One-To-One Property by taking the common log of both sides of the equation.

g. Apply the Power Property to remove the exponent.

h. Solve for t. Round your answer to the nearest tenth. Your result should match the answer in exercise 11.

12. In **a–h** below, write the equations that result when you follow the steps to use the systematic

withdrawal formula, $P = W \dfrac{1-(1+\frac{r}{n})^{-nt}}{\frac{r}{n}}$ to determine how long it will take for a savings account

to reach $0. The account was set up with an initial deposit of $8000. Interest is compounded monthly at 1.2% with a monthly withdrawal of $400.

a. Substitute $P = 8{,}000$, $W = 400$, $r = .012$, and $n = 12$ in the systematic withdrawal formula.

b. Simplify wherever possible.

c. Divide both sides by 400.

d. Multiply both sides by .001.

e. Subtract 1 from both sides.

f. Divide both sides by –1.

g. Take the log of both sides (One-To-One Property).

h. Apply the Power Property.

i. Divide both sides by log(1.001).

j. Divide both sides by –12.

k. Simplify.

13. Burt deposited $100,000 into an account that compounds interest semiannually at a rate of 2.66%. At the end of each 6-month period, a withdrawal of $8000 is made from the account. How long will it take until the account has a balance of $0? Round your answer to the nearest tenth of a year.

3-1 Introduction to Consumer Credit

Exercises

1. Monique purchases a $5,100 dining room set. She can't afford to pay cash, so she uses the installment plan, which requires an 18% down payment. How much is the down payment?

2. Joe wants to purchase an electric keyboard. The price of the keyboard at Macelli's, with tax, is $2,344. He can save $150 per month. How long will it take him to save for the keyboard?

3. Lisa purchases a professional racing bicycle that sells for $3,000, including tax. It requires a $200 down payment. The remainder, plus a finance charge, is paid back monthly over the next $2\frac{1}{2}$ years. The monthly payment is $111.75. What is the finance charge?

4. The price of a stove is *s* dollars. Pedro makes a 10% down payment for a two-year installment purchase. The monthly payment is *m* dollars. Express the finance charge algebraically.

5. Depot Headquarters has a new promotional payment plan. All purchases can be paid off on the installment plan with no interest, as long as the total is paid in full within 12 months. There is a $25 minimum monthly payment required. If the Koslow family buys a hot tub for $4,355, and they make only the minimum payment for 11 months, how much will they have to pay in the 12th month?

6. The White family purchases a new pool table on a no-interest-for-one-year plan. The cost is $2,665. There is a *d* dollars down payment. If they make a minimum monthly payment of *m* dollars until the last month, express their last month's payment algebraically.

7. Snow-House sells a $1,980 snow thrower on the installment plan. The installment agreement includes a 20% down payment and 12 monthly payments of $161 each.

   a. How much is the down payment?

   b. What is the total amount of the monthly payments?

   c. What is the total cost of the snow thrower on the installment plan?

   d. What is the finance charge?

8. Carey bought a $2,100 computer system on the installment plan. He made a $400 down payment, and he has to make monthly payments of $79.50 for the next two years. How much interest will he pay?

9. Mike bought a set of golf clubs that cost k dollars. He signed an installment agreement requiring a 5% down payment and monthly payments of g dollars for $1\frac{1}{2}$ years.

    a. Express his down payment algebraically.

    b. How many monthly payments must Mike make?

    c. Write expressions for the total amount of the monthly payments and the finance charge.

10. Mrs. Grudman bought a dishwasher at a special sale. The dishwasher regularly sold for $912. No down payment was required. Mrs. Grudman has to pay $160 for the next six months. What is the average amount she pays in interest each month?

11. The Hut sells a $2,445 entertainment system credenza on a six-month layaway plan.

    a. If the monthly payment is $440, what is the sum of the monthly payments?

    b. What is the fee charged for the layaway plan?

    c. Where is the credenza kept during the six months of the layaway plan?

12. Jessica has $70,000 in the bank and is earning 1.7% compounded monthly. She plans to purchase a used car, for which the down payment is $500 and the monthly payments are $280.

    a. Will her monthly interest cover the cost of the down payment? Explain.

    b. Will her monthly interest cover the cost of the monthly payment?

13. Joseph purchased a laptop that regularly sold for w dollars but was on sale at 10% off. He had to pay t dollars for sales tax. He bought it on the installment plan and had to pay 15% of the total cost with tax as a down payment. His monthly payments were m dollars per month for three years.

    a. Write expressions for the amount of the discount and the sale price.

    b. Write expressions for the total cost of the laptop, with tax, and the down payment.

    c. What was the total of all of the monthly payments? What was the total he paid for the laptop on the installment plan?

    d. What was the finance charge?

3-2 Loans

Exercises

Round to the nearest cent wherever necessary.

1. Refer to the table to find the monthly payments necessary to complete parts a–e.

   a. What is the monthly payment for a $3,200 five-year loan with an APR of 3%?

   b. Mia borrows $66,000 for four years at an APR of 4%. What is the monthly payment?

   c. What is the total amount of the monthly payments for a $6,100, two-year loan with an APR of 5%? Round to the nearest dollar.

   Monthly Payment Per $1,000 of Loan

Interest Rate (APR)	2-Year Loan	3-Year Loan	4-Year Loan	5-Year Loan
1%	$42.10	$28.21	$21.26	$17.09
2%	$42.54	$28.64	$21.70	$17.53
3%	$42.98	$29.08	$22.13	$17.97
4%	$43.42	$29.52	$22.58	$18.42
5%	$43.87	$29.97	$23.03	$18.87
6%	$44.32	$30.42	$23.49	$19.33
7%	$44.77	$30.88	$23.95	$19.80

   d. The total of monthly payments for a three-year loan is $22,317.12. The APR is 4%. How much money was originally borrowed?

   e. What is the finance charge for a $7,000, two-year loan with a 6% APR?

2. Ray borrows b dollars over a $2\frac{1}{2}$-year period. The monthly payment is m dollars. Express his finance charge algebraically.

3. Cecilia bought a new car. The total amount she needs to borrow is $29,541. She plans to take out a four-year loan at an APR of 6.3%. What is the monthly payment?

4. Claire needs to borrow $12,000 from a local bank. She compares the monthly payments for a 5.1% loan for three different periods of time. What is the monthly payment for a one-year loan? A two-year loan? A five-year loan?

5. The Star Pawnshop will lend up to 45% of the value of a borrower's collateral. Ryan wants to use $4,000 worth of jewelry as collateral for a loan. What is the maximum amount that he could borrow from Star?

6. Solomon is taking out a loan of x dollars for y years, which has a monthly payment of m dollars. Express the finance charge for this loan algebraically.

7. Jeanne has a $14,800, $3\frac{1}{2}$-year loan with a high APR of 8.56% due to her less-than-average credit rating.

    a. What is the monthly payment for this loan?

    b. If she changes the loan to a three-year loan, what is the monthly payment?

    c. What is the difference in the monthly payments for the two loans?

    d. Which loan has the higher finance charge? What is the difference in the finance charge for these two loans?

    e. Do you feel that it is worth paying the higher monthly payment to have the loan finish six months earlier?

8. Liz found an error in the monthly payment her bank charged her for a four-year, $19,500 loan. She took the loan out at an APR of 5%. Her bank was charging her $459.07 per month.

    a. What is the correct monthly payment?

    b. Liz noticed the error just before making the last payment. The bank told her that they would credit all of the overpayments and adjust her last month's payment accordingly. What should her last month's payment be after the adjustment? Explain.

9. The Bartolotti family took out a loan to have a garage built next to their house. The 10-year, 10.4% loan was for $56,188. The monthly payment was $475, but the promissory note stated that there was a balloon payment at the end.

    a. How many monthly payments do the Bartolotti's have to make?

    b. What is the sum of all but the last monthly payment?

    c. If the finance charge is $34,415.60, what must the total of all of the monthly payments be?

    d. What is the amount of the balloon payment for the final month of this loan?

10. Christina is a police officer, so she can use the Police and Fire Credit Union. The credit union will lend her $11,000 for three years at 4.05% APR. The same loan at her savings bank has an APR of 6.82%.

    a. How much would Christina save on the monthly payment if she takes the loan from the credit union?

    b. How much would she save in finance charges by taking the loan from the credit union?

3-3 Student Loans

Use the following situation to answer questions 1–5.

Marlie will be starting college next month. She was approved for a 10-year, Federal Unsubsidized student loan in the amount of $18,800 at 4.29%. She knows she has the option of beginning repayment of the loan in 4.5 years. She also knows that during this non-payment time, interest will accrue at 4.29%.

1. How much interest will Marlie accrue during the 4.5-year non-payment period?

2. Marlie has to decide whether she can afford to make interest-only payments for the first 4.5 years or defer all payments for that period of time. If she decides to make no payments during the 4.5 years, the interest will be capitalized at the end of that period. Suppose Marlie decides to defer the payments.

    a. What will be the new principal when she begins making loan payments?

    b. How much interest will she pay over the life of the loan?

3. Suppose Marlie only paid the interest during her 4 years in school and the six-month grace period. What will she now pay in interest over the term of the loan?

4. Marlie made her last monthly interest-only payment on December 1. Her next payment is due on January 1. What will be the amount of that interest-only payment?

5. Suppose that Marlie had decided to apply for a private loan rather than a federal loan. She has been offered a private loan for 10 years with an APR of 7.8%.

    a. Determine her monthly payment.

    b. What is the total amount she will pay back?

    c. What is the total interest amount?

6. Jim's parents paid for the first three years of his college costs. When he was a college senior, he was approved for an unsubsidized loan in the amount of $15,200 at a 4.29% interest rate for 10 years.

   a. If he chooses to make interest-only payments until the monthly loan payments are due, for how long will he be making interest only payments?

   b. What is the total amount of his interest-only payments?

   c. If he begins the loan repayment with no interest capitalization because he already paid the interest when he was in school and during the six-month grace period, how much will he have paid in interest for this loan by the end of the 10-year loan period?

7. Barb is a freshman attending a 4-year college. She has been approved for a $12000 subsidized federal loan at 4.29% for 10 years. How much will the U.S. Department of Education pick up in interest costs during her 4.5-year non-payment period?

Use the following situation to answer questions 8–12.

Phil has been accepted into a 2-year Radiology Technician Program at a career school. He has been awarded a $9000 unsubsidized 10-year federal loan at 4.29%. He knows he has the option of beginning repayment of the loan in 2.5 years. He also knows that during this non-payment time, interest will accrue at 4.29%.

8. How much interest will Phil accrue during the 2.5-year non-payment period?

9. If Phil decides to make no payments during the 2.5 years, the interest will be capitalized at the end of that period. What will be the new principal when he begins making loan payments?

10. Suppose Phil only paid the interest during his 2 years in school and the six-month grace period. What will he pay in interest over the term of his loan?

11. Phil made his last monthly interest-only payment on April 12. His next payment is due on May. What will be the amount of that interest-only payment?

12. Suppose that Phil had decided to take out a private loan for $9,000 where loan payments start as soon as the loan amount is deposited in his student account and continue for 10 years. The interest rate is 8.1%.

   a. Determine his monthly payment.   b. What is the total amount he will pay back?

   c. What is the total interest amount?

3-4 Loan Calculations and Regression

Exercises

1. What is the monthly payment for a 10-year, $20,000 loan at 4.625% APR? What is the total interest paid on this loan?

2. Max is taking out a 5.1% loan in order to purchase a $17,000 car. The length of the loan is five years. How much will he pay in interest?

3. Merissa wants to borrow $12,000 to purchase a used boat. After looking at her monthly budget, she realizes that all she can afford to pay per month is $250. The bank is offering a 6.1% loan. What should the length of her loan be so that she can keep within her budget? Round to the nearest year.

4. What is the total interest on a 15-year, 4.98% loan with a principal of $40,000?

5. Ansel wants to borrow $10,000 from the Hampton County Bank. They offered him a 6-year loan with an APR of 6.35%. How much will he pay in interest over the life of the loan?

6. Tom and Kathy want to borrow $35,000 in order to build an addition to their home. Their bank will lend them the money for 12 years at an interest rate of $5\frac{3}{8}$%. How much will they pay in interest to the bank over the life of the loan?

Use the Yearly Payment Schedule to answer Exercises 7–10.

Year	Principal Paid	Interest Paid	Loan Balance	Year	Principal Paid	Interest Paid	Loan Balance
							$76,000.00
2016	$3,702.31	$3,158.45	$72,297.69	2024	$5,198.46	$1,662.30	$36,279.09
2017	$3,862.78	$2,997.98	$68,434.91	2025	$5,423.74	$1,437.02	$30,855.35
2018	$4,030.18	$2,830.58	$64,404.73	2026	$5,658.80	$1,201.96	$25,196.55
2019	$4,204.85	$2,655.91	$60,199.88	2027	$5,904.04	$956.72	$19,292.51
2020	$4,387.07	$2,473.69	$55,812.81	2028	$6,159.90	$700.86	$13,132.61
2021	$4,577.18	$2,283.58	$51,235.63	2029	$6,426.88	$433.88	$6,705.73
2022	$4,775.56	$2,085.20	$46,460.07	2030	$6,705.73	$157.40	$0.00
2023	$4,982.52	$1,878.24	$41,477.55				

7. What is the loan amount?

8. What is the length of the loan?

9. What is the monthly payment?

10. What is the total interest over the loan's life?

11. Neville is considering taking out a $9,000 loan. He went to two lending institutions. Sunset Park Company offered him a 10-year loan with an interest rate of 5.2%. Carroll Gardens Bank offered him an 8-year loan with an interest rate of 6.6%. Which loan will have the lowest interest over its lifetime?

12. JFK Federal Bank offers a $50,000 loan at an interest rate of 4.875% that can be paid back over 3 to 15 years.

   a. Write the monthly payment formula for this loan situation. Let t represent the number of years from 3 to 15 inclusive.

   b. Write the total interest formula for this loan situation. Let t represent the number of years from 3 to 15 inclusive.

Use the table of decreasing loan balances for a $230,000 loan at 5.5% for 20 years to answer questions 13–15.

	Loan Balance
0	$230,000.00
1	$223,502.14
2	$216,637.75
3	$209,386.16
4	$201,725.52
5	$193,632.76
6	$185,083.51
7	$176,052.02
8	$166,511.07
9	$156,431.94
10	$145,784.26
11	$134,535.97
12	$122,653.20
13	$110,100.15
14	$96,839.02
15	$82,829.83
16	$68,030.43
17	$52,396.21
18	$35,880.12
19	$18,432.38
20	$0.00

13. Write a linear regression equation that models the data with numbers rounded to the nearest tenth.

14. Write a quadratic regression equation that models the data with numbers rounded to the nearest tenth.

15. Write a cubic regression equation that models the data with numbers rounded to the nearest tenth.

3-5 Credit Cards

Exercises

Round to the nearest cent wherever necessary.

1. If the APR on a credit card is 22.2%, what is the monthly interest rate?

2. If the monthly interest rate on a credit card is p percent, express the APR algebraically.

3. The average daily balance for Dave's last credit card statement was $1,213.44, and he had to pay a finance charge. The APR is 20.4%. What is the monthly interest rate? What is the finance charge for the month?

4. Mr. Reis had these daily balances on his credit card for his last billing period. He did not pay the card in full the previous month, so he will have to pay a finance charge. The APR is 19.8%.

   six days @ $341.22   ten days @ $987.45
   three days @ $2,122.33   eleven days @ $2,310.10

   a. What is the average daily balance?

   b. What is the finance charge?

5. Mrs. Fagin's daily balances for the past billing period are given below.
   For five days she owed $233.49.   For three days she owed $651.11.
   For nine days she owed $991.08.   For seven days she owed $770.00.
   For seven days she owed $778.25.

   Find Mrs. Fagin's average daily balance.

6. Mike Bauer had a daily balance of x dollars for d days, y dollars for 9 days, r dollars for 4 days, and m dollars for 5 days. Express his average daily balance algebraically.

7. Mrs. Cykman's credit card was stolen, and she did not realize it for several days. The thief charged a $440 watch while using it. According to the Truth-in-Lending Act, at most how much of this is Mrs. Cykman responsible for paying?

8. Mr. Kramden's credit card was lost on a vacation. He immediately reported it missing. The person who found it days later used it and charged c dollars worth of merchandise on the card, where $c > \$50$. How much of the c dollars is Mr. Kramden responsible for paying?

9. The average daily balance for Pete's credit card last month was a dollars. The finance charge was f dollars. Express the APR algebraically.

10. Brett and Andy applied for the same credit card from the same bank. The bank checked both of their FICO scores. Brett had an excellent credit rating, and Andy had a poor credit rating.

    a. Brett was given a card with an APR of 12.6%. What was his monthly percentage rate?

    b. Andy was given a card with an APR of 16.2%. What was his monthly percentage rate?

    c. If each of them had an average daily balance of $7,980, and had to pay a finance charge for that month, how much more would Andy pay than Brett?

11. A set of daily balances for one billing cycle are expressed algebraically below.

    w days @ r dollars   5 days @ x dollars n days @ q dollars p days @ $765

    If the APR is 21.6%, express the billing cycle's finance charge algebraically.

12. Mrs. Imperiale's credit card has an APR of 13.2%. She does not ever pay her balance off in full, so she always pays a finance charge. Her next billing cycle starts today. The billing period is 31 days long. She is planning to purchase $7,400 worth of new kitchen cabinets this billing cycle. She will use her tax refund to pay off her entire bill next month. If she purchases the kitchen cabinets on the last day of the billing cycle instead of the first day, how much would she save in finance charges? Round to the nearest ten dollars.

13. Pat's ending balance on his debit card last month was $233.55. This month he had $542 worth of purchases and $710 worth of deposits. What is his ending balance for this month?

14. Tomika's credit rating was lowered, and the credit card company raised her APR from 18% to 25.2%.

    a. If her average daily balance this month is $8,237, what is the increase in this month's finance charge due to the higher APR?

    b. If this amount is typical of Tomika's average daily balance all year, how much would the rise in interest rate cost her in a typical year? Round to the nearest ten dollars.

15. Linda and Rob charged a $67.44 restaurant bill on their credit card. They gave the card to the waitress, who accidentally transposed two digits and charged them $76.44. They did not notice this until they received their statement later that month. Their card has an 18% APR.

    a. How much were Linda and Rob overcharged?

    b. They plan to pay their monthly statement amount in full, but they need to deduct the amount they were overcharged, plus the finance charge that was based on the incorrect amount. If the overcharged amount was on their statement for 18 of the 31-day billing cycle, how much should they deduct from this monthly statement, including the amount they were overcharged?

3-6 Credit Card Statement

Exercises

1. The summary portion of Manny Ramira's credit card statement is shown. Determine the new balance amount.

SUMMARY	Previous Balance	Payments / Credits	Transactions	Late Charge	Finance Charge	New Balance	Minimum Payment
	1,237.56	$1,200.00	$2,560.67	$0.00	$9.56		

2. Lizzy has a credit line of $9,000 on her credit card. Her summary is shown. What is her available credit balance?

SUMMARY	Previous Balance	Payments / Credits	Transactions	Late Charge	Finance Charge	New Balance	Minimum Payment
	$6,500.56	$5,200.00	$978.45	$20.00	$12.88		

3. Rich had a previous balance of x dollars and made an on-time credit card payment of y dollars where y < x. He has a credit line of 10,000 dollars and will have to pay $15.50 in finance charges. Rich made purchases totaling $1,300.30. Write an algebraic expression that represents his current available credit.

4. Determine the error that was made using the following summary statement.

SUMMARY	Previous Balance	Payments / Credits	Transactions	Late Charge	Finance Charge	New Balance	Minimum Payment
	$350.90	$200.00	$200.00	$0.00	$8.68	$759.58	

5. Marianne has a credit card with a line of credit at $15,000. She made the following purchases: $1,374.90, $266.21, 39.46, and $903.01. What is Marianne's available credit?

6. Luke has a credit line of $8,500 on his credit card. He had a previous balance of $4,236.87 and made a $3,200.00 payment. The total of his purchases is $989.42. What is Luke's available credit?

7. The APR on Ramona's credit card is currently 24.6%. What is the monthly periodic rate?

8. Sheila's monthly periodic rate is 2.41%. What is her APR?

9. Examine the summary section of a monthly credit card statement. Calculate the new balance.

SUMMARY	Previous Balance	Payments / Credits	Transactions	Late Charge	Finance Charge	New Balance	Minimum Payment
	$876.34	$800.00	$1,009.56	$30.00	$29.67		$18.00

10. Jack set up a spreadsheet to model his credit card statement. The summary statement portion of the spreadsheet is shown. Write the formula for available credit that would be entered in cell J32.

	D	E	F	G	H	I	J
	Previous Balance	**Payments**	**New Purchases**	**Late Charge**	**Finance Charges**	**Credit Line**	**Available Credit**
31							
32							

11. Use the credit card statement to answer the questions below.

Liam DeWitt						6915 Maple Creek Dr. West Chester, OH

ACCOUNT INFORMATION						
Account Number	4-10700000		Billing Date	13 Sept	**Payment Due**	30 Sept

TRANSACTIONS					DEBITS / CREDITS (–)
22 Aug	Propane Home Heat				$250.50
23 Aug	TJ Marsha's Department Store				$87.60
25 Aug	Brighton University				$1,300.00
1 Sept	Middle Island Auto Parts				$470.63
2 Sept	Payment				– $2,000.00
3 Sept	Al's Mobal Gas Station				$34.76
5 Sept	Stop, Shop and Go				$102.71
10 Sept	Federal Express				$45.90
12 Sept	Computer Depot				$848.60

SUMMARY	Previous Balance	Payments / Credits	Transactions	Late Charge	Finance Charge	New Balance	Minimum Payment
	$3,240.50			$0.00			$50.00

		Average Daily Balance	# Days in Billing Cycle	APR	Monthly Periodic Rate
Total Credit Line	$ 5,000.00				
Total Available Credit	$ 5,000.00				
Credit Line for Cash	$ 4,000.00				
Available Credit for Cash	$ 4,000.00		30	19.8%	

a. How many purchases (debits) were made during the billing cycle?

b. What is the sum of all purchases (debits) made during the billing cycle?

c. When is the payment for this statement due?

d. What is the minimum amount that can be paid?

e. How many days are in the billing cycle?

f. What is the previous balance?

3-7 Average Daily Balance

Exercises

Use Liam DeWitt's Flash Card statement and the blank credit calendar for Exercises 1–4.

Liam DeWitt					6915 Maple Creek Dr. West Chester, OH

ACCOUNT INFORMATION					
Account Number	4-10700000		Billing Date	13 Sept	**Payment Due** 30 Sept

TRANSACTIONS					DEBITS / CREDITS (−)
22 Aug	Propane Home Heat				$250.50
23 Aug	TJ Marsha's Department Store				$87.60
25 Aug	Brighton University				$1,300.00
1 Sept	Middle Island Auto Parts				$470.63
2 Sept	Payment				− $2,000.00
3 Sept	Al's Mobal Gas Station				$34.76
5 Sept	Stop, Shop and Go				$102.71
10 Sept	Federal Express				$45.90
12 Sept	Computer Depot				$848.60

SUMMARY	Previous Balance	Payments / Credits	Transactions	Late Charge	Finance Charge	New Balance	**Minimum Payment**
	$3,240.50			$0.00			$30.00

		Average Daily Balance	# Days in Billing Cycle	APR	Monthly Periodic Rate
Total Credit Line	$ 5.000.00				
Total Available Credit	$ 5.000.00		30	19.8%	
Credit Line for Cash	$ 4,000.00				
Available Credit for Cash	$ 4,000.00				

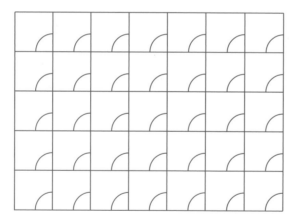

1. What is Liam's average daily balance?

2. What is Liam's monthly periodic rate?

3. What is Liam's finance charge?

4. What is Liam's new balance?

5. What is Liam's available credit?

Name _____   Date _____

Use Shannon Houston's credit card statement and the blank calendar for Exercises 6–11.

Shannon Houston						720 Timber Trail Dr Indianapolis, IN

ACCOUNT INFORMATION						
Account Number	16677289-02		Billing Date	6 Apr	**Payment Due**	30 Apr

TRANSACTIONS		DEBITS / CREDITS ()
9 Mar	Gingham Pastry Shop	$27.68
11 Mar	Corner Clothes	$127.35
16 Mar	Le Petite Menu	$87.40
22 Mar	Payment	– $190.60
26 Mar	Dutchess Pharmacy	57.30
28 Mar	Sparrow Jewelers	$325.90
4 Apr	Elder's Antiques	$870.21

SUMMARY	Previous Balance	Payments / Credits	Transactions	Late Charge	Finance Charge	New Balance	Minimum Payment
	$560.30			$0.00			$25.00

		Average Daily Balance	# Days in Billing Cycle	APR	Monthly Periodic Rate
Total Credit Line	$ 5.000.00				
Total Available Credit			30	15.6%	
Credit Line for Cash	$ 4,000.00				
Available Credit for Cash	$ 4,000.00				

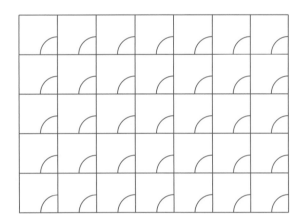

6. What amount should be in the box for "Payment/Credits"?

7. What amount should be in the box for "Transactions"?

8. What is Shannon's average daily balance?

9. What is Shannon's finance charge?

10. What is Shannon's new balance?

11. What is Shannon's available credit?

4-1   Classified Ads

Exercises

1. Enrique plans to sell his car and places a 6-line ad. His paper charges $42 for the first two lines and $6.75 per extra line, to run the ad for one week. What will Enrique's ad cost to run for three weeks?

2. The following piecewise function gives the cost, $c(x)$, of a classified ad in a car magazine.

$$c(x) = \begin{cases} 35.50 & \text{when } x \leq 4 \\ 35.50 + 5.25(x-4) & \text{when } x > 4 \end{cases}$$

   a. Graph the function.

   b. If x is the number of lines in the ad, what is the cost of each extra line?

   c. Is the cost of one line the same as the cost of four lines?

3. Griffith purchased a used car for $9,400. He paid 6.5% sales tax. How much tax did he pay?

4. Ms. Boyrer is writing a program to compute ad costs. She needs to enter an algebraic representation of the costs of a local paper's ad. The charge is $32.25 for up to three lines for a classified ad. Each additional line costs $6. Express the cost of an ad $f(x)$ with x lines as a function of x algebraically.

5. *The Fort Salonga News* charges $29.50 for a classified ad that is four or fewer lines long. Each line above four lines costs an additional $5.25. Express the cost of an ad algebraically as a piecewise function.

6. Roxanne set up the following split function, which represents the cost of an auto classified ad from her hometown newspaper.

$$f(x) = \begin{cases} 31.50 & \text{when } x \le 5 \\ 31.50 + 5.50(x-5) & \text{when } x > 5 \end{cases}$$

If x is the number of lines in the ad, express the price $c(x)$ of a classified ad from this paper in words.

7. Dr. Mandel purchased a used car for $11,325. Her state charges 8% tax for the car, $53 for license plates, and $40 for a state safety and emissions inspection. How much does she need to pay for these extra charges, not including the price of the car?

8. Leeanne plans to sell her car and places an x-line ad. The newspaper charges p dollars for the first k lines and e dollars per extra line, to run the ad for a week.

a. When $x > k$, write an algebraic expression for the cost of running the ad for a week.

b. When $x < k$, write an algebraic expression for the cost of running the ad for two weeks.

9. A local *Pennysaver* paper charges f dollars weekly for a five-line classified ad. Each additional line costs a dollars. Express algebraically the cost of a four-line ad that runs for a year.

10. a. Graph the piecewise function: $f(x) = \begin{cases} 22.50 & \text{when } x \le 6 \\ 22.50 + 5.75(x-6) & \text{when } x > 6 \end{cases}$

b. What are the coordinates of the cusp?

c. What is the slope of the graph where $x > 6$?

d. What is the slope of the graph where $x < 6$?

11. Mr. Ciangiola placed this ad in the *Collector Car Digest:*

> 2014 Chevrolet HHR SUV. Orange, 4 cyl.
> automatic, leather, chrome wheels, wood
> trim, running boards, PS, PB, AM/FM/CD.
> Mint! $18,500. 555-7331.

a. If the newspaper charges $45 for the first four lines and $7 for each extra line, how much will this ad cost?

b. Sue buys the car for 5% less than the advertised price. How much does she pay?

c. Sue must pay her state 4% sales tax on the sale. How much must she pay in sales tax?

12. Express the classified ad rate, $36 for the first four lines and $4.25 for each additional line, as a piecewise function. Use a "Let" statement to identify what x and y represent.

13. The following piecewise function represents the cost of an x-line classified ad from the *Rhinebeck Register.*

$$f(x) = \begin{cases} D & \text{when } x \leq w \\ D + K(x-w) & \text{when } x > w \end{cases}$$

a. What is the cost of a p-line ad, if $p < w$?

b. What is the cost of a b-line ad, if $b > w$?

c. Express algebraically the total cost, with 6% sales tax, of a w-line ad.

4-2 | Automobile Transactions

Exercises

1. The following automobile prices are listed in descending order: *a, b, c, d, x, y,* and *w.* Express the difference between the median and the mean of these prices algebraically.

2. A local charity wants to purchase a classic 1956 Thunderbird for use as a prize in a fundraiser. They find the following eight prices in the paper.

$48,000	$57,000	$31,000	$58,999
$61,200	$59,000	$97,500	$42,500

   a. What is the best measure of central tendency to use to get a reasonable estimate for the cost of the car? Explain.

   b. What is the range?

3. Given is the list of prices for a set of used original hubcaps for a 1957 Chevrolet. They vary depending on the condition. Find the following statistics for the hubcap prices.

$120	$50	$320	$220	$310	$100	$260	$300	$155	$125
$600	$250	$200	$200	$125					

   a. mean, to the nearest dollar

   b. median

   c. mode

   d. four quartiles

   e. range

   f. interquartile range

   g. boundary for the lower outliers; any lower outliers

   h. boundary for the upper outliers; any upper outliers

4. The data below gives the MPG ratings for cars owned by 15 Placid High School seniors. Find the following statistics about the MPG ratings.

15.9, 17.8, 21.6, 25.2, 31.1, 29, 28.6, 32, 34, 14, 19.8, 19.5, 20.1, 27.7, 25.5

a. Mean

b. Median

c. median of the lowest seven scores

d. lower quartile, Q_1

e. median of the highest seven scores

f. upper quartile, Q_3

g. interquartile range

h. range

i. boundary for the upper outliers

j. boundary for the lower outliers

k. How many outliers are in this data set?

5. The following scores are written in ascending order: $a, b, c, d, e, f, g, h,$ and i.

a. What measure of central tendency does score e represent?

b. What measure of central tendency is represented by $\frac{a+b+c+d+e+f+g+h+i}{9}$?

c. Which quartile is represented by $\frac{b+c}{2}$?

6. The boxplot summarizes information about the numbers of hours worked in December for 220 seniors at Tomah High School.

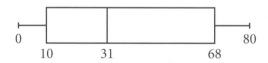

a. What is the range? What is the interquartile range?

b. What percent of the students worked 68 or more hours?

c. How many students worked 31 hours or less?

d. Does the boxplot give the median of the distribution? What is the median?

Name _____   Date _____

7. Jerry is looking to purchase a set of used chrome wheels for his SUV. He found 23 ads for the wheels he wants online and in the classified ads of his local newspaper and arranged the prices in ascending order, which is given below.

$350	$350	$350	$420	$450	$450	$500	$500	$500	$500
$600	$700	$725	$725	$725	$725	$725	$775	$775	$800
$825	$825	$850							

a. Make a frequency table to display the data.

b. Find the mean.

c. Draw a box-and-whisker plot for the data.

8. *Collector Car Magazine* has a listing for many Chevrolet Nomads.

Price	Frequency
$29,000	2
$34,000	1
$35,000	1
$42,900	1
$48,000	5
$51,000	3
$56,000	1
$59,000	4

a. Find the total frequency.

b. Find the range.

c. Find the mean to the nearest cent.

d. Draw a box-and-whisker plot for the data.

9. Use the modified boxplot to determine if Statements a – g are True or False. When the statement is false, explain.

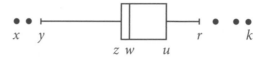

a. The range is $r - y$.

b. 25% of the scores are at or below y.

c. The interquartile range is $u - z$.

d. The median is w.

e. The boundary for lower outliers is r.

f. The boundary for upper outliers is y.

10. The side-by-side boxplots for distributions A and B were drawn on the same axes.

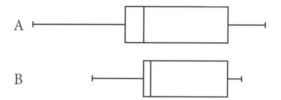

a. Which distribution has the greater range?

b. Which distribution has the lower first quartile?

c. Which distribution has the smallest interquartile range?

d. What percent of the scores in distribution A is above distribution B's maximum score?

e. Which distribution has scores that are the most varied?

f. What percent of scores in distribution A are less than distribution B's first quartile?

4-3 Automobile Insurance

Exercises

1. Mr. Cousins has 100/300 bodily injury insurance. He was in an auto accident caused by his negligence. Five people were injured in the accident. They sued in court and were awarded money. One person was awarded $150,000, and each of the other two was awarded $95,000. How much will the insurance company pay for these lawsuits?

2. Ronaldo has 50/250 BI liability insurance. He loses control of his car and injures 18 children in a Little League game, and each child is awarded $20,000 as a result of a lawsuit. How much will the insurance company pay in total for this lawsuit? How much will Ronaldo be personally responsible for?

3. Cai's annual premium is p dollars. If she pays her premium semiannually, there is a 1% surcharge on each payment. Write an expression for the amount of her semiannual payment.

4. Jake has $25,000 worth of property damage insurance and $1,000-deductible collision insurance. He caused an accident that damaged a $2,000 sign, and he also did $2,400 worth of damage to another car. His car had $2,980 worth of damage done.

   a. How much will the insurance company pay under Jake's property damage insurance?

   b. How much will the insurance company pay under Jake's collision insurance?

   c. How much of the damage must Jake pay for?

5. Allen Siegell has a personal injury protection policy that covers each person in, on, around, or under his car for medical expenses up to $50,000. He is involved in an accident and five people in his car are hurt. One person has $3,000 of medical expenses, three people each have $500 worth of medical expenses, and Allen himself has medical expenses totaling $62,000. How much money must the insurance company pay out for these five people?

6. The Chow family just bought a second car. The annual premium would have been a dollars to insure the car, but they are entitled to a 12% discount since they have another car insured by the company.

   a. Express their annual premium after the discount algebraically.

   b. If they pay their premium quarterly, and have to pay a quarterly b dollars surcharge for this arrangement, express their quarterly payment algebraically.

7. Mrs. Lennon has 100/275/50 liability insurance and $50,000 PIP insurance. During an ice storm, she hits a fence and bounces into a storefront with 11 people inside. Some are hurt and sue her. A passenger in Mrs. Lennon's car is also hurt.

   a. The storefront will cost $24,000 to replace. There was $1,450 worth of damage to the fence. What insurance will cover this, and how much will the company pay?

   b. A professional soccer player was in the store, and due to the injuries, he can never play soccer again. He sues for $3,000,000 and is awarded that money in court. What type of insurance covers this, and how much will the insurance company pay?

   c. The passenger in the car had medical bills totaling $20,000. What type of insurance covers this, and how much will the insurance company pay?

   d. The 11 people in the store are hurt and each requires $12,000 or less for medical attention. Will the company pay for all of these injuries?

8. In 2007, Roslyn High School instituted a safe driver course for all students who have licenses. They want to statistically analyze if the course is working. The side-by-side box-and-whisker plots give the annual number of car accidents involving Roslyn students for those two 10-year periods.

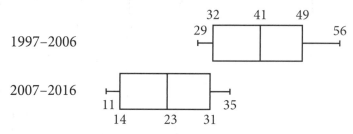

   a. What is the median number of annual accidents for the years 1997–2006? The years 2007–2016?

   b. What is the range of the annual accident figures for the years 1997–2006? The years 2007–2016?

   c. What do the side-by-side boxplots tell about the safe driver program that Roslyn High School instituted? Explain.

   d. John claims that 75% of the data for the years 2007–2016 are less than the first quartile for the years 1997–2006. Is he correct? Explain.

9. Manuel has x dollar-deductible collision insurance. His car is involved in an accident, and has w dollars worth of damage to it, where $x > w$. How much must the insurance company pay him for the damages?

4-4 Probability—The Basis of Insurance

Exercises

1. The distribution of ages of drivers at the Darcy Insurance Agency is normally distributed with mean 48 and standard deviation 10. As part of an advertising campaign, a driver is going to be selected at random to receive free car insurance for a year. What is the probability that the randomly selected person will be less than 30 years old?

2. The ratio of male drivers to female drivers with parking passes at Plandome High School is 5:3. If there are 64 students with parking passes, how many are female?

3. The following two-way table shows student lunch preferences for underclassmen at Minisink High School. Express your answers in fraction form.

	Freshman (F)	Sophomore (S)	Junior (J)	Total
Buy Lunch In School (B)	46	25	49	120
Bring Own Lunch (L)	36	65	44	145
Total	82	90	93	265

   a. Find the probability that a randomly selected person from this group brings their own lunch.

   b. What is the probability that a randomly selected person from this group is a freshman who brings their own lunch?

   c. Find the probability that a randomly selected person from this group is a junior given that they buy lunch at school.

   d. Find the probability that a randomly selected person from this group buys lunch at school given that they are a junior.

   e. Find P(F) in decimal form. Round to two decimal places.

   f. Find P(B) in decimal form. Round to two decimal places.

   g. Which is greater, P(J) or P(J|L)?

   h. Which is greater, P(S|L) or P(L|S)?

   i. Find P(F|B) and explain if events F and B are independent or associated events.

4. The yearbook committee of Huntington High School is randomly selecting a student's car for the "Senior Life" section of the yearbook. If 42 of the seniors own cars, and twins Robert and Leslie each own their own cars, what is the probability that neither of their cars will be selected for the yearbook page?

5. The following Venn diagram describes cars sold during last winter at Gervy's Garage. The letter A represents air conditioning, C represents it has a CD player, and T represents automatic transmission.

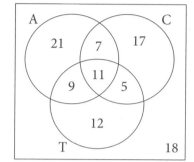

   a. How many people bought cars with air conditioning?

   b. How many people bought cars with automatic transmission and CD player?

   c. How many people purchased cars with all three options?

   d. How many people purchased cars with exactly one of these options?

   e. How many people purchased cars at Gervy's Garage last summer?

   f. A buyer from this group is selected at random to receive free satellite radio. What is the probability that they purchased the CD player?

   g. One person from this group is going to be selected at random. Find P(T).

   h. Determine if A and C are independent events and explain your answer.

   i. Examine the three shaded regions below. Describe what characteristic makes these three regions alike.

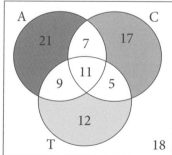

6. The distribution of weekly gasoline expenses for parents of teenagers in the Glennon Soccer Club is normally distributed with mean $46 and standard deviation 8. A parent will be selected at random. Round your answers to the nearest hundredth.

a. What is the probability that the person spends more than $54 on gas weekly?

b. What is the probability that the person spends less than $54 for gas weekly?

c. What is the probability that the person spends between $22 and $70?

d. What is the probability that the person selected spends less than $50 for gas weekly?

7. A fair, six-sided numbered cube has one of these digits on each face:

   2, 4, 6, 7, 8, 9

a. If the cube is rolled, what is the probability of rolling an even number?

b. What is the probability of rolling a prime number?

c. What is the probability of rolling a number not divisible by 3?

d. Mike rolls the die and gets a 3. He plans to roll it a second time. What is the probability of Mike rolling a 3 on the second roll?

8. The Student Council at Merrick High School is having a meeting on student parking issues for their 210 seniors. The event "goes out for lunch with their cars" is represented by L. The event "has a first period class" is represented by F. From a survey, they find out that there are 90 students who go out for lunch with their cars, 60 of which do not have a first period class. They also find out that 80 students do not go out for lunch with their cars and these 80 students also do not have a first period class. How many students have a first period class but do not take their cars out for lunch? (Hint: Draw a Venn diagram.)

4-5 Linear Automobile Depreciation

Exercises

1. Jason purchased a car for $22,995. According to his research, this make and model of car loses all of its marketable value after 9 years. If this car depreciates in a straight line form, what are the coordinates of the intercepts of the depreciation equation?

2. Suppose Phyllis knows that her car straight line depreciates at a rate of $1,997 per year over an 11-year period. What was the original price of her car?

3. Ina's car straight line depreciates at a rate of D dollars per year. Her car originally cost C dollars. What are the coordinates of the intercepts of the straight line depreciation equation?

4. A new car sells for $29,250. It straight line depreciates in 13 years. What is the slope of the straight line depreciation equation?

5. A new car straight line depreciates according to the equation $y = -1,875x + 20,625$.

   a. What is the original price of the car?

   b. How many years will it take for this car to fully straight line depreciate?

6. Write and graph a straight line depreciation equation for a car that was purchased at $27,450 and completely depreciates after 10 years.

7. Caroline purchased a car 4 years ago at a price of $28,400. According to research on this make and model, similar cars have straight line depreciated to zero value after 8 years. How much will this car be worth after 51 months?

8. The straight line depreciation equation for a luxury car is $y = -4{,}150x + 49{,}800$. In approximately how many years will the car's value drop by 30%?

9. Katie purchased a new car for $27,599. This make and model straight line depreciates for 13 years.

    a. Identify the coordinates of the x- and y-intercepts for the depreciation equation.

    b. Determine the slope of the depreciation equation.

    c. Write the straight line depreciation equation that models this situation.

    d. Draw the graph of the straight line depreciation equation.

10. Geoff purchased a used car for $16,208. This make and model used car straight line depreciates after 8 years.

    a. Identify the coordinates of the x- and y-intercepts for the depreciation equation.

    b. Determine the slope of the depreciation equation.

    c. Write the straight line depreciation equation that models this situation.

    d. Draw the graph of the straight line depreciation equation.

11. The straight line depreciation equation for a truck is $y = -4{,}265x + 59{,}710$.

    a. What is the original price of the truck?

    b. How much value does the truck lose per year?

    c. How many years will it take for the truck to totally depreciate?

12. Examine the straight line depreciation graph for a car.

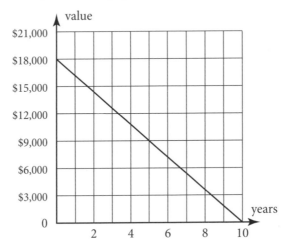

    a. At what price was the car purchased?

    b. After how many years does the car totally depreciate?

    c. Write the equation of the straight line depreciation graph shown.

13. The straight line depreciation equation for a car is $y = -2{,}682x + 32{,}184$.

    a. What is the car worth after 6 years?

    b. What is the car worth after 12 years?

    c. Suppose that *T* represents a length of time in years when the car still has value. Write an algebraic expression to represent the value of the car after *T* years.

    d. Suppose that after *a* years, the car depreciates to *b* dollars. Write an algebraic expression for *a*.

14. The graph of a straight line depreciation equation is shown.

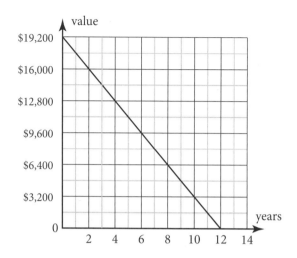

a. Use the graph to approximate the value of the car after 4 years.

b. Use the graph to approximate the value of the car after 5 years.

c. Use the graph to approximate when the car will be worth half its original value.

15. Tom purchased a new car for $36,000. He has determined that it straight line depreciates over 12 years. When he purchased the car, he made a $6,000 down payment and financed the rest with a 5-year loan where he pays $610 per month.

a. Create an expense and depreciation function where x represents the number of months.

b. After how many months will the amount invested in the car be equal to the value of the car? Round your answer to the nearest month.

16. Suppose that your car straight line depreciates monthly over time. You know that after 7 months your car was worth $13,200. According to an online car value calculator, after 11 months, you car is now worth $4,400. Set up an arithmetic sequence to determine how much the car depreciates each month?

4-6 Historical and Exponential Depreciation

Exercises

1. Tanya's new car sold for $23,856. Her online research indicates that the car will depreciate exponentially at a rate of $6\frac{3}{8}\%$ per year. Write the exponential depreciation formula for Tanya's car.

2. The screen to the right is from a graphing calculator after running an exponential regression analysis of a set of automobile data. The variable x represents years and y represents car value. Using the numbers on the screen, write the exponential regression equation.

   ```
   ExpReg
    y=a*b^x
    a=43754.00259
    b=.8223288103
    r²=.8405850061
    r=-.9168342304
   ```

3. The screen to the right is from a graphing calculator after running an exponential regression analysis of a set of automobile data. The variable x represents years and y represents car value. What is the annual depreciation percentage for this car? Round your answer to the nearest tenth of a percent.

   ```
   ExpReg
    y=a*b^x
    a=26092.73333
    b=.8865688485
    r².9616674348
    r=-.9806464372
   ```

4. Sharon purchased a used car for $24,600. The car depreciates exponentially by 8% per year. How much will the car be worth after 5 years? Round your answer to the nearest penny.

5. Brad purchased a 5-year old car for $14,200. When the car was new, it sold for $24,000. Find the depreciation rate to the nearest hundredth of a percent.

6. Lyle's new car cost him $28,000. He was told that this make and model depreciates exponentially at a rate of 11.5% per year. How much will his car be worth after 57 months?

7. Gina bought a used car for A dollars. B years ago, when the car was new, it sold for C dollars. Express the depreciation rate in terms of A, B, and C.

8. A car exponentially depreciates at a rate of 8.5% per year. Mia purchased a 4-year-old car for $17,500. What was the original price of the car when it was new? Round your answer to the nearest thousand dollars.

9. Nancy and Bob bought a used car for $22,800. When this car was new, it sold for $30,000. If the car depreciates exponentially at a rate of 9.2% per year, approximately how old is the car? Round your answer to the nearest hundredth of a year.

10. A car originally sold for $21,000. It depreciates exponentially at a rate of 6.2% per year. When purchasing the car, Jon put $5,000 down and pays $3,000 per year to pay off the balance.

    a. Write the exponential depreciation equation. Write the expense equation.

    b. Graph these two equations on the same axes.

    c. After how many years will his car value equal the amount he paid to date for the car? Round your answer to the nearest year.

    d. What is the approximate value of the car at this point? Round to the nearest hundred dollars.

11. The historical prices of a car are recorded for 14 years as shown.

Age	Value	Age	Value	Age	Value
0	21,000	5	13,105	10	8,178
1	19,110	6	11,925	11	7,448
2	17,390	7	10,852	12	6,772
3	15,825	8	9,875	13	6,163
4	14,401	9	8,987	14	5,608

    a. Use exponential regression to determine the exponential depreciation equation that models this data. Round to the nearest hundredth. Note: Due to rounding, some values might not calculate to the exact amount as shown in the table.

    b. Determine the depreciation rate.

12. Use the table of values in Exercise 11. Consider the values to represent a geometric sequence.

    a. What is the common ratio?   **b.** What is the general term for this geometric sequence?

13. The car that Dana bought is 5 years old. She paid $11,100. This make and model depreciates exponentially at a rate of 10.25% per year. What was the original price of the car when it was new? Round your answer to the nearest dollar.

14. Arnold bought a 3-year old car. He paid A dollars for it. This make and model depreciates at a rate of D percent per year. Write an expression for the original selling price of the car when it was new.

15. A new car sells for $31,400. It exponentially depreciates at a rate of 4.95% to $26,500. How long did it take for the car to depreciate to this amount? Round your answer to the nearest tenth of a year.

4-7   Driving Data

Exercises

1. A car travels at an average rate of speed of 60 miles per hour for $7\frac{1}{2}$ hours. How many miles does this car travel?

2. A car travels m miles in t hours. Express its average speed algebraically.

3. Juanita has a hybrid car that averages 44 miles per gallon. Her car has a 12-gallon tank. How far can she travel on one full tank of gas?

4. Ruth is planning a 1,543-mile trip to a math teachers' conference in San Diego. She plans to average 50 miles per hour on the trip. At that speed, for how many hours will she be driving? Express your answer to the nearest hour.

5. Lisa is a trucker and needs to keep track of her mileage for business purposes. She begins a trip with an odometer reading of x miles and ends the trip with an odometer reading of y miles.

   a. Express the total number of miles covered algebraically.

   b. If the trip takes h hours of driving, express the average speed algebraically.

   c. If the truck used g gallons of gas during the trip, express the mpg the truck averaged during the trip algebraically.

   d. If gas costs c dollars per gallon, write an algebraic expression that represents the fuel expense for the trip.

6. Abby's car gets approximately 24 miles per gallon. She is planning a 1,200-mile trip.

   a. About how many gallons of gas should she plan to buy?

   b. At an average price of $2.40 per gallon, how much should she expect to spend for gas?

7. Sarah drives at an average speed of s miles per hour for h hours. Express algebraically the number of miles she covers.

8. Raquel is driving from New York City to Daytona, Florida, a distance of 1,034 miles. How much time is saved by doing the trip at an average speed of 60 mph as compared with 55 mph? Round to the nearest half-hour.

9. Complete the table. Round entries to the nearest hundredth.

Distance (mi)	Rate (mph)	Time (hours)	MPG	Gallons Used	Price per gallon ($)	Cost for Fuel ($)
200	40	a.	b.	12	$2.33	c.
d.	55	6	20	e.	G	f.
1,000	60	g.	h.	45.4	i.	T
1,000	r	j.	x	k.	G	l.

10. Monique is away at college, and realized she left her laptop at home, 625 miles away. She arranges to meet her father at a location somewhere between home and college, so he can bring her the laptop.

   a. Monique averages 55 mph, and her part of the trip takes h hours. Represent the miles she covered algebraically.

   b. Her father takes 2 more hours than Monique to make his part of the trip, and his average speed is 50 mph. Represent the distance he covered algebraically.

   c. What is the sum of the distances they covered, expressed algebraically, using your answers from parts a and b?

   d. What is the numerical sum of the distances they covered?

   e. Write an equation that can be used to find the number of hours they traveled.

   f. How many hours did it take Monique to do her part of the trip?

   g. How many miles did Monique drive?

   h. How many hours did it take her father to do his part of the trip? How many miles did her father drive?

11. Francois' car gets about 12.5 kilometers per liter. He is planning a 1,600-kilometer trip.

   a. About how many liters of gas should Francois plan to buy? Round your answer to the nearest liter.

   b. At an average price of $0.90 US per liter, how much should Francois expect to spend for gas?

12. Ace Car Rental charges customers $0.18 per mile driven. You picked up a car and the odometer read x miles and brought it back with the odometer reading y miles. Write an algebraic expression for the total cost Ace would charge you for mileage use on a rented car.

4-8 Driving Safety Data

Exercises

Answer each hour and minute question to the nearest unit. Answer each second question to the nearest tenth.

5,280 feet = 1 mile; 1,000 meters = 1 kilometer

1. How many miles does a car traveling at 57 mph cover in one hour?

2. How many feet does a car traveling at 57 mph cover in one hour? In one minute? In one second?

3. How many miles does a car traveling at 70 mph cover in one hour?

4. How many feet does a car traveling at 70 mph cover in one hour? In one minute? In one second?

5. How many miles does a car traveling at *a* mph cover in one hour?

6. How many feet does a car traveling at *a* mph cover in one hour? In one minute? In one second?

7. How many kilometers does a car traveling at 50 kph cover in one hour?

8. How many meters does a car traveling at 50 kph cover in one hour? In one minute? In one second?

9. How many kilometers does a car traveling at *a* kph cover in one hour?

10. How many meters does a car traveling at *a* kph cover in one hour? In one minute? In one second?

11. Complete the chart:

Speed	Reaction Distance	Braking Distance
75 mph		
65 mph		
55 mph		
45 mph		
5 mph		

12. Jerry is driving 35 miles per hour as he approaches a park. A dog darts out into the street between two parked cars, and Jerry reacts in about three-quarters of a second. What is his approximate reaction distance (do not use the estimate)?

13. Manuel is driving 60 miles per hour on a state road with a 65 mph speed limit. He sees a fallen tree up ahead and must come to a quick, complete stop.

  a. What is his estimated reaction distance?

  b. What is his approximate braking distance?

  c. About how many feet does the car travel from the time he switches pedals until the car has completely stopped?

14. Anita is driving on the highway at the legal speed limit of 63 mph. She sees a police road block about 300 feet ahead and must come to a complete stop. Her reaction time is approximately $\frac{3}{4}$ of a second. Is she far enough away to safely bring the car to a complete stop? Explain your answer.

15. Rob is driving on a Canadian highway near Montreal at 63 kph. He sees an accident about 30 meters ahead and needs to bring the car to a complete stop. His reaction time is approximately $\frac{3}{4}$ of a second. Is he far enough away from the accident to safely bring the car to a complete stop?

16. Model the total stopping distance by the equation $y = \frac{x^2}{20} + x$ where x represents the speed in mph, and y represents the total stopping distance in feet.

  a. Graph this equation for the values of x where $x \geq 10$ and $x \leq 65$.

  b. Use the graph to approximate the stopping distance for a car traveling at 30 mph.

  c. Use the graph to approximate the speed for a car that completely stops after 240 feet.

17. A spreadsheet user inputs a speed in kph into cell A1.

  a. Write a formula that would enter the approximate equivalent of that speed in mph in cell A2.

  b. Write a spreadsheet formula that would enter the approximate total stopping distance in meters in cell A3.

4-9 Accident Investigation Data

Exercises

1. A car is traveling on a cement road with a drag factor of 1.1. The speed limit on this portion of the road is 45 mph. It was determined that the brakes were operating at 85% efficiency. The driver notices that the drawbridge is up ahead and that traffic is stopped. The driver immediately applies the brakes and the tires leave four distinct skid marks each 50 feet in length.

    a. What is the minimum speed the car was traveling when it entered the skid? Round your answer to the nearest tenth.

    b. Did the driver exceed the speed limit when entering the skid?

2. Highway 21 has a surface drag factor of 0.72. A car with a b percent braking efficiency is approaching an accident causing the driver to apply the brakes for an immediate stop. The tires leave four distinct skid marks of c feet each. Write an expression for determining the minimum speed of the car when entering into the skid.

3. Mark was traveling at 40 mph on a road with a drag factor of 0.85. His brakes were working at 80% efficiency. To the nearest tenth of a foot, what would you expect the average length of the skid marks to be if he applied his brakes in order to come to an immediate stop?

4. Davia is traveling on an asphalt road at 50 miles per hour when she immediately applies the brakes in order to avoid hitting a deer. The road has a drag factor of A, and her brakes are operating at 90% efficiency. Her car leaves three skid marks each of length r. Write an algebraic expression that represents the skid distance.

5. Determine the radius of the yaw mark made when brakes are immediately applied to avoid a collision based upon a yaw mark chord measuring 59.5 feet and a middle ordinate measuring 6 feet. Round your answer to the nearest tenth.

6. Arami's car left three skid marks on the road after she slammed her foot on the brake pedal to make an emergency stop. The police measured them to be 45 feet, 40 feet, and 44 feet. What skid distance will be used when calculating the skid speed formula?

7. Grace's car left four skid marks on the road surface during a highway accident. Two of the skid marks were each 52 feet, and two of the skid marks were each 56 feet. What skid distance will be used when calculating the skid speed formula?

8. Sam's car left three skid marks. Two of the marks were each *A* feet long, and one skid mark was *B* feet long. Write the algebraic expression that represents the skid distance that will be used in the skid speed formula.

9. Russell was driving on a gravel road that had a 20 mph speed limit posted. A car ahead of him pulled out from a parking lot causing Russell to immediately apply the brakes. His tires left two skid marks of lengths 60 feet and 62 feet. The road had a drag factor of 0.47. His brakes were operating at 95% efficiency. The police gave Russell a ticket for speeding. Russell insisted that he was driving under the limit. Who is correct (the police or Russell)? Explain.

10. Delia was driving on an asphalt road with a drag factor of 0.80. Her brakes were working at 78% efficiency. She hit the brakes in order to avoid a cat that ran out in front of her car. Three of her tires made skid marks of 38 feet, 42 feet, and 45 feet respectively. What was the minimum speed Delia was going at the time she went into the skid?

11. A car is traveling at 52 mph before it enters into a skid. The drag factor of the road surface is 0.86, and the braking efficiency is 88%. How long might the average skid mark be to the nearest tenth of a foot?

12. Bill is driving his car at 41 mph when he makes an emergency stop. His wheels lock and leave four skid marks of equal length. The drag factor for the road surface was 0.94, and his brakes were operating at 95% efficiency. How long might the skid marks be to the nearest foot?

13. Andrea was traveling down a road at 45 mph when she was forced to immediately apply her brakes in order to come to a complete stop. Her car left two skid marks that averaged 60 feet in length with a difference of 6 feet between them. Her brakes were operating at 90% efficiency at the time of the incident. What was the possible drag factor of this road surface? What were integer lengths of each skid mark?

14. An accident reconstructionist takes measurements of the yaw marks at the scene of an accident. What is the radius of the curve if the middle ordinate measures 5.3 feet when using a chord with a length of 39 feet? Round your answer to the nearest tenth of a foot.

15. The measure of the middle ordinate of a yaw mark is 7 feet. The radius of the arc is determined to be 64 feet. What was the length of the chord used in this situation? Round your answer to the nearest tenth of a foot.

16. The following measurements from yaw marks left at the scene of an accident were taken by police. Using a 40-foot length chord, the middle ordinate measured approximately 4 feet. The drag factor for the road surface was determined to be 0.95.

   a. Determine the radius of the curved yaw mark to the nearest tenth of a foot.

   b. Determine the minimum speed that the car was going when the skid occurred to the nearest tenth.

17. A consumer safety organization wants to test the strength of auto roof straps in crash conditions. Cargo was secured to the roof of a car at a height of 5.1 feet above the ground. The car was remotely operated and traveled at 60 mph before hitting a concrete block head-on. The researchers noticed that as soon as the front of the car hit the concrete block, the straps snapped and the cargo projected off the top of the roof in a downward half-parabolic path. Let y represent height in feet, x represent horizontal distance in feet, and t represent time in seconds in the following projectile motion equations: $y = -16.1t^2 + 5.1$ and $y = -0.0021x^2 + 5.1$.

   a. How long does it take for the cargo to hit the ground? Round your answer to the nearest hundredth of a second.

   b. What is the horizontal distance that the cargo travels? Round your answer to the nearest tenth of a foot.

5-1 | Looking for Employment

Exercises

1. Mitchell found a job listed in the classified ads that pays a yearly salary of $57.3K. What is the weekly salary based on this annual salary?

2. Clarissa is considering two job offers. One has an annual salary of $61.1K and the other has an annual salary of $63.4K. What is the difference in the weekly pay for these two jobs, rounded to the nearest dollar?

3. Mr. Leonard took a job through an employment agency. The job pays $88K per year. He must pay a fee to the employment agency. The fee is 22% of his first 4 weeks' pay. How much money must Mr. Leonard pay the agency, to the nearest cent?

4. The Ludwig Employment Agency posted a job in the advertising field. The fee is 18% of 3 weeks' pay. The job pays d dollars annually. Express the agency fee algebraically.

5. Arielle owns Levitt Construction Corporation. She needs a welder and is placing a seven-line classified ad. The cost of an ad that is x lines long is given by the following piecewise function. Find the cost of a seven-line ad.

$$c(x) = \begin{cases} 33 & \text{when } x \le 4 \\ 33 + 5(x - 4) & \text{when } x > 4 \end{cases}$$

6. The *Carpenter's Chronicle* charges $12 for each of the first three lines of a classified ad and $7.25 for each additional line. Express the cost of an x-line ad, $c(x)$, algebraically as a piecewise function.

7. Job-Finder charges employers d dollars to post a job on their website. They offer a 12% discount if 10 or more jobs are posted. If 24 jobs are posted by a specific employer, write an algebraic expression for the cost of the 24 ads with the discount.

8. Art's Printing Service charges $27.50 to print 100 high-quality copies of a one-page resume. Each additional set of 100 copies costs $14.99. Express the cost, $c(r)$, of printing r sets of 100 resumes, as a piecewise function.

9. Yoko needs 300 copies of her resume printed. Dakota Printing charges $19.50 for the first 200 copies and $9 for every 100 additional copies.

   a. How much will 300 copies cost, including a sales tax of $4\frac{1}{2}$%? Round to the nearest cent.

   b. If the number of sets of 100 resumes is represented by r, express the cost of the resumes, $c(r)$, algebraically as a piecewise function.

Name _____   Date _____

10. Kim answered a help-wanted ad. The ad states that the job pays d dollars semiannually. Express Kim's monthly salary algebraically.

11. Rudy's job pays him $1,550 per week. Express his annual salary using the 'K' notation.

12. Teach-Tech is an online job-listing site for prospective teachers. The charge to teachers looking for jobs is $19 per week, for the first 4 weeks, to post their resumes. After four weeks, the cost is $7 per week.

   a. If w represents the number of weeks, represent the cost $c(w)$ as a piecewise function.

   b. Find the cost of listing a resume for 8 weeks.

13. Charleen earns m dollars per month as a police officer. Express algebraically her annual salary using the K abbreviation found in classified ads.

14. Marty is a dentist. He is placing an eight-line classified ad for a hygienist. The following piecewise function gives the price of an x-line ad.
$$c(x) = \begin{cases} 31 & \text{when } x \leq 5 \\ 20 + 6(x - 5) & \text{when } x > 5 \end{cases}$$

   a. What is the cost of the first five lines if Marty purchases five lines?

   b. What is the cost of the first five lines if Marty purchases more than five lines?

   c. How much less is a six-line ad compared to a five-line ad?

15. Kevin is looking for a job as a piano technician. One classified ad lists a job that pays 64.6K. Another job he found has a weekly salary of $1,120. What is the difference in the weekly salaries of these two jobs? Round to the nearest dollar.

16. Michelle got a new job through the McCartney Employment Agency. The job pays $49,400 per year, and the agency fee is equal to 35% of one month's pay. How much must Michelle pay the agency? Round to the nearest cent.

17. Todd is looking for a job as a chemistry teacher. He plans to send resumes to 145 schools in his city. His local printer charges $34 per 100 copies and sells them only in sets of 100.

   a. How many copies must Todd purchase if he is to have enough resumes?

   b. How much will the copies cost Todd, including 5% sales tax?

5-2 Pay Periods and Hourly Rates

Exercises

1. Mr. Varello is paid semimonthly. His annual salary is $64,333. What is his semimonthly salary, rounded to the nearest cent?

2. Mr. Whittaker earns b dollars biweekly. His employer is changing the pay procedure to monthly, but no annual salaries are changing. Express his monthly salary algebraically.

3. Mrs. Frederick is paid semimonthly. Her semimonthly salary is $1,641.55. What is her annual salary?

4. Ms. Saevitz is paid semimonthly. Her annual salary is a dollars. Her office is considering going to a biweekly pay schedule. Express the difference between her biweekly salary and her semimonthly salary algebraically.

5. Julianne works as a waitress at a local Emerald Monday restaurant. Her regular hourly wage is $15.50

    a. She regularly works 40 hours per week. What is her regular weekly pay?

    b. If she works 50 weeks each year at this rate, what is her annual salary?

6. Mr. Lewis regularly works h hours per week at a rate of y dollars per hour. Express his annual salary algebraically.

7. Mrs. Roper works 40 hours per week regularly, at a rate of $16.20 per hour. When she works overtime, her rate is time and a half of her regular hourly rate. What is Mrs. Roper's hourly overtime rate?

8. If you earned d dollars per hour regularly, express your hourly overtime rate algebraically if you are paid time-and-a-half for overtime.

9. Mr. Ed earns $15.50 per hour. His regular hours are 40 hours per week, and he receives time-and-a-half overtime. Find his total pay for a week in which he works 45 hours.

10. Mrs. Trobiano regularly works 40 hours per week, at a rate of d dollars per hour. Last week she worked h overtime hours at double time. Express her total weekly salary algebraically.

11. Krissy worked her 40 regular hours last week, plus 8 overtime hours at the time-and-a-half rate. Her gross pay was $785.20. What was her hourly rate?

12. Mrs. Frasier worked her 40 regular hours last week, plus 4 overtime hours at the double-time rate. Her gross pay was $734.40. What was her hourly rate?

13. Last year Andrea's annual salary was a dollars, and she was paid biweekly. This year she received a raise of r dollars per year. She is now paid semimonthly.

   a. Express her biweekly salary last year algebraically.

   b. Express her semimonthly salary this year algebraically.

   c. How many more checks did Andrea receive each year when she was paid biweekly, as compared to the new semimonthly arrangement?

14. This week, Sean worked h regular hours and t overtime hours at the time-and-a-half rate. He earned $950. If r represents his hourly rate, express r algebraically in terms of h and t.

15. Mr. Harrison earns $32 per hour. He regularly works 40 hours per week. If he works 26 overtime hours (at time-and-a-half), would his overtime pay exceed his regular gross pay? Explain.

16. In 2003, Carlos Zambrano earned $340,000 pitching for the Chicago Cubs. In 2009, his salary was $18,750,000.

   a. Zambrano pitched in 32 games in 2003. What was his salary per game in 2003?

   b. He pitched in 28 games in 2009. What was his salary per game in 2009? Round to the nearest cent.

   c. Did he earn more per game in 2009 than he did for the entire 2003 season?

17. Last year, Mrs. Sclair's annual salary was $88,441. This year she received a raise and now earns $96,402 annually. She is paid weekly.

   a. What was her weekly salary last year? Round to the nearest cent.

   b. What is Mrs. Sclair's weekly salary this year? Round to the nearest cent.

   c. On a weekly basis, how much more does Mrs. Sclair earn as a result of her raise?

18. Leah is paid semimonthly. How many fewer paychecks does she receive in 2 years compared to someone who is paid weekly?

5-3 Commissions, Royalties, and Piecework Pay

Exercises

1. Enid wrote a textbook for high school students. She receives a 5% royalty based on the total sales of the book. The book sells for $51.95, and 12,341 copies were sold last year. How much did Enid receive in royalty payments for last year, to the nearest cent?

2. Rich wrote a novel that sells for n dollars each. He received a bonus of $50,000 to sign the contract to write the book, and he receives 9% commission on each book sale. Express the total amount of income he earns from selling b books algebraically.

3. Dafna makes sport jackets. She is paid d dollars per hour, plus a piece rate of p dollars for each jacket. Last week she made j jackets in h hours. Write an expression for her total earnings.

4. Rock singer and writer Beep Blair is paid 11.5% on her CD sales and music downloads. Last year, she sold 1.22 million CDs and 2.1 million music downloads. The CDs were sold to music stores for $5 each, and the music downloads were $1 each.

   a. What was the total amount of income from CD sales?

   b. What was the total amount of download sales?

   c. How much did Beep Blair receive in royalties last year?

5. Mr. Corona sells magazines part-time. He is paid a monthly commission. He receives 21% of his first $1,500 in sales and 14% of the balance of his sales. Last month he sold $2,233 worth of magazine subscriptions. How much commission did he earn last month?

6. Carter Cadillac pays commission to its car sales staff. They are paid a percent of the profit the dealership makes on the car, not on the selling price of the car. If the profit is less than or equal to $500, the commission rate is 18%. If the profit is greater than $500 and less than or equal to $2,000, the commission rate is 24% of the profit. If the profit is above $2,000, the rate is 27% of the profit.
   If p represents the profit, express the commission $c(p)$ algebraically as a split function.

7. Mrs. Lohrius sells electronics on commission. She receives 10% of her first x dollars in sales and 12% of the balance of her sales. Last month, she sold y dollars worth of electronics, where $y > x$. Express the commission she earned last month algebraically.

8. Abbey Road Motors pays a percent commission to its sales people. They are paid a percent of the profit the dealership makes on a car. If the profit is less than or equal to $1,000, the commission rate is 20%. If the profit is greater than $1,000 and less than or equal to $2,000, the commission rate is 20% of the first $1,000 and 24% of the remainder of the profit. If the profit is above $2,000, the rate is 20% of the first $1,000 of profit, 24% of the next $1,000 of profit, and 29% of the amount of profit over $2,000. If p represents the profit, express the commission $c(p)$ algebraically as a split function.

9. Casey is a real estate agent. She earns 8.15% commission on each sale she makes. After working with a potential buyer for $3\frac{1}{2}$ months, she finally sold a house for $877,000.

   a. What did Casey earn in commissions for this sale?

   b. This was her only sale for the entire $3\frac{1}{2}$-month period. What was her average salary per month for this period, to the nearest cent?

   c. For the next 4 months, Casey is not able to sell a house due to a faltering economy. What is her average monthly salary for the past $7\frac{1}{2}$ months, to the nearest cent?

10. Barry works at Larry's Computer Outlet. He receives a weekly salary of $310 plus 3.05% commission based on his sales. Last year, he sold $1,015,092 worth of computer equipment. How much money did Barry earn last year, to the nearest cent?

11. Jill picks corn and gets paid at a piecework rate of 55 cents per container for the first 300 containers picked. She receives 60 cents per container for every container over 300 that she picks. Last week, Jill picked 370 containers. How much did she earn?

12. Vicki works at Apple Appliances. She earns d dollars per hour, but is also paid p% commission on all sales. Last week she sold w dollars worth of appliances in the h hours she worked. Write an expression that represents her salary for the week.

13. Ms. Halloran works in a factory. She receives a salary of $15 per hour and piecework pay of 15 cents per unit produced. Last week she worked 40 hours and produced 988 units.

   a. What was her piecework pay? What was her total hourly pay for the week? What was her total pay for the week?

   b. If her boss offered to pay her a straight $18 per hour and no piecework pay for the week, would she earn more or less than under the piecework pay system?

   c. Under her current pay plan, what would her total weekly salary have been if she produced 0 units?

5-4   Employee Benefits

Exercises

1. Ali has worked at a fashion magazine for the last 5 years. Her current annual salary is $64,000. When she was hired, she was told that she had four days of paid vacation time. For each year that she worked at the magazine, she would gain another three days of paid vacation time to a maximum of 26 days. How many paid vacation days does she now get at the end of 5 years of employment?

2. Ina's employer offers a sliding paid vacation. When she started work, she was given two paid days of vacation. For each 4-month period she stays at the job, her vacation is increased by one day.

    a. Let x represent the number of 4-month periods worked and y represent the total number of vacation days. Write an equation that models the relationship between these variables.

    b. How much vacation time will she have after working for this employer for 6.5 years?

3. When Tyler started at his current job, his employer gave him five days of paid vacation time with a promise of five additional paid vacation days for each 2-year period he remains with the company to a maximum of 5 work weeks of paid vacation time.

    a. Let x represent the number of years he has worked for this employer and y represent the number of paid vacation days he has earned. Write an equation that models the relationship of these variables.

    b. It has been 8 years since Tyler began working for this employer. How many paid vacation days has he earned?

    c. When will Tyler reach the maximum number of paid vacation days allowable?

4. When Alton started his current job, his employer told him that he had one day of paid vacation until he reaches his first year with the company. Then, at the end of the first year, he would have three vacation days. After each year, his number of vacation days would triple up to 27 days of paid vacation.

    a. Let x represent the number of years worked and y represent the number of paid vacation days. Write an equation that models the relationship between these variables.

    b. How many vacation days will he have earned after 2 years?

    c. In what year will he have maxed out his vacation days?

5. Martha's employee benefits include family health-care coverage. She contributes 18% of the cost. Martha gets paid biweekly and $108.00 is taken out of each paycheck for family health-care coverage. How much does her employer contribute annually for the family coverage?

6. Rachel contributes 20% of the cost of her individual health care. This is a $38 deduction from each of her weekly paychecks. What is the total value of her individual coverage for the year?

7. At Chocolatier Incorporated, there are two factors that determine the cost of health care. If an employee makes less than $65,000 per year, he pays $52 per month for individual coverage and $98 per month for family coverage. If an employee makes at least $65,000 per year, individual coverage is $67 per month and family coverage is $122 per month.

   a. Graham makes $62,800 per year. He has individual health care. His yearly contribution is 10% of the total cost. How much does his employer contribute?

   b. Claudia 's annual salary is $75,400. She has family health care. Her employer contributes $1,052 per month toward her total coverage cost. What percent does Claudia contribute toward the total coverage? Round to the nearest tenth of a percent.

8. Dan's employee benefits include health-care coverage. His employer covers 78% of the cost, which is a contribution of $1,599.78 toward the total coverage amount. How much does Dan pay for his coverage?

9. Liz works at *Food For Thought* magazine. Her employer offers her a pension. Liz's employer uses a formula to calculate the pension. Retiring employees receive 2.1% of their average salary over the last 4 years of employment for every year worked. Liz is planning on retiring at the end of this year after, 20 years of employment. Her salaries for the last 4 years are $66,000; $66,000; $73,000; and $75,000. Calculate Liz's annual pension.

10. As part of their employee benefits, all workers at Light and Power Electric Company receive a pension that is calculated by multiplying the number of years worked times 1.875% of the average of their three highest years' salaries. Mia has worked for LPEC for 30 years and is retiring. Her highest salaries were $92,000, $94,800, and $96,250. Calculate Mia's pension.

11. In Ben's state, the weekly unemployment compensation is 55% of the 26-week average for the two highest-salaried quarters. A quarter is three consecutive months. For July, August, and September, Ben earned a total of $22,400. In October, November, and December, he earned a total of $22,800. Determine Ben's weekly unemployment compensation.

12. Carol's weekly unemployment compensation is *W* percent of the 26-week average for the two highest salaried quarters. For January, February, and March, Carol earned *X* dollars. In April, May, and June, she earned *Y* dollars. Write an algebraic expression that represents Carol's weekly unemployment compensation.

5-5   Social Security and Medicare

Exercises

1. Dr. Grumman got his first job in 2020. In that year, the government took out 6.2% of a person's income for Social Security, until a person made $137,700. If Dr. Grumman earned $141,340 in 2020, how much did he pay to Social Security?

2. Lauren earned a total of d dollars last year, where $d < $99,000$. The government took out 6.2% for Social Security and 1.45% for Medicare. Write an algebraic expression that represents what she paid to Social Security and Medicare combined.

3. In 1978, the Social Security and Medicare rate combined was 6.05%, and this was deducted from all earnings up to a maximum taxable income of $17,700.

   a. Express the combined Social Security and Medicare tax $s(x)$ for 1978 as a piecewise function.

   b. Ten years later, the combined percent had increased to 7.51% and the maximum taxable income had increased to $45,000. Express the Social Security tax $s(x)$ for 1988 as a piecewise function.

   c. If a person earned $50,000 in 1978, and $50,000 in 1988, what was the difference in the Social Security and Medicare taxes paid?

4. In 2016, the government took out 6.2% of earnings for Social Security to a maximum taxable income of $118,500. For Medicare, 1.45% of all earnings was paid. How much money should someone have earned in 2016 so that their payments into Medicare were equal to their payments into Social Security? Round to the nearest dollar.

5. In 1998, Lisa earned $149,461.20. The Social Security maximum taxable income was $68,400, and the Social Security percent was 6.2%.

   a. What was her monthly gross pay?

   b. In what month did Lisa hit the maximum taxable Social Security income?

   c. How much Social Security tax did Lisa pay in May, to the nearest cent?

   d. How much Social Security tax did Lisa pay in July, to the nearest cent?

   e. How much Social Security tax did Lisa pay in June, to the nearest cent?

Name _____ Date _____

The following table gives a historical look at Social Security and Medicare taxes for the years 2000–2020. Use the table for Exercises 6–10.

Year	Social Security Percent	Social Security Maximum Taxable Income	Medicare Percent	Income Subject to Medicare Tax
2000	6.2%	76,200	1.45%	All income
2001	6.2%	80,400	1.45%	All income
2002	6.2%	84,900	1.45%	All income
2003	6.2%	87,900	1.45%	All income
2004	6.2%	87,900	1.45%	All income
2005	6.2%	90,000	1.45%	All income
2006	6.2%	94,200	1.45%	All income
2007	6.2%	97,500	1.45%	All income
2008	6.2%	102,000	1.45%	All income
2009	6.2%	106,800	1.45%	All income
2010	6.2%	106,800	1.45%	All income
2011	4.2%	106,800	1.45%	All income
2012	4.2%	110,100	1.45%	All income
2013	6.2%	113,700	1.45%	All income
2014	6.2%	117,000	1.45%	All income
2015	6.2%	118,500	1.45%	All income
2016	6.2%	118,500	1.45%	All income
2017	6.2%	127,200	1.45%	All income
2018	6.2%	128,400	1.45%	All income
2019	6.2%	132,900	1.45%	All income
2020	6.2%	137,700	1.45%	All income

6. In 2010, for the first time since 2004 the maximum taxable income was not raised. Find the maximum a person could pay into Social Security for 2010.

7. In 2011, the percent deducted for Social Security was lowered to 4.2% to help stimulate the economy. How much did a taxpayer earning more than the maximum taxable income save in 2011 due to the lower rate?

8. Let $t(x)$ represent the total combined Social Security and Medicare taxes for the year 2007. If x represents the income, express this total as a piecewise function.

9. Mr. Jackson had two jobs in 2005. The first job, in which he earned $74,007, was from January to August, and the second job, in which he earned $35,311, was from August to the end of the year. The employer for the second job took out Social Security taxes on all of Mr. Jackson's income. As a result, he paid too much Social Security tax. How much should he be refunded?

10. In 2015, Dr. Kirmser's gross pay was $381,318.60.

   a. What was her monthly gross pay?

   b. In what month did she hit the maximum taxable Social Security income?

   c. How much Social Security tax did she pay in February? Round to the nearest cent.

   d. How much Social Security tax did she pay in September? Round to the nearest cent.

   e. How much Social Security tax did Dr. Kirmser pay in April? Round to the nearest dollar.

11. Use the information from the table to examine Social Security and Medicare taxes for 2005.

   a. If x represents income, express the Social Security function $s(x)$ for 2005 as a piecewise function.

   b. Graph the Social Security function for 2005.

   c. Find the coordinates of the cusp.

   d. If x represents income, what is the Medicare function $m(x)$ for 2005?

   e. Graph the Medicare function for 2005 on the same axes as the Social Security function in part b.

   f. Elena worked three jobs in 2005. The total of her three incomes was less than $90,000. At Hamburger Coach, she made h dollars. At the Binghamton Book Exchange, she made b dollars. At Ruby's Restaurant, she made r dollars. Express the combined total of her social security and Medicare taxes as an algebraic expression.

   g. In 2005, how much money would someone have to have earned so that their payments into Medicare were equal to their payments into Social Security? Round to the nearest dollar.

6-1 Tax Tables, Worksheets, and Schedules

Exercises

Use the portion of the tax table shown here to answer Exercises 1–7.

If line 10 (taxable income) is—		And you are—				If line 10 (taxable income) is—		And you are—				If line 10 (taxable income) is—		And you are—			
At least	But less than	Single	Married filing jointly *	Married filing separately	Head of a household	At least	But less than	Single	Married filing jointly *	Married filing separately	Head of a household	At least	But less than	Single	Married filing jointly *	Married filing separately	Head of a household
		Your tax is—						Your tax is—						Your tax is—			
77,000						**80,000**						**83,000**					
77,000	77,050	12,885	8,862	12,885	11,494	80,000	80,050	13,545	9,485	13,545	12,154	83,000	83,050	14,216	10,145	14,216	12,824
77,050	77,100	12,896	8,868	12,896	11,505	80,050	80,100	13,556	9,496	13,556	12,165	83,050	83,100	14,228	10,156	14,228	12,836
77,100	77,150	12,907	8,874	12,907	11,516	80,100	80,150	13,567	9,507	13,567	12,176	83,100	83,150	14,240	10,167	14,240	12,848
77,150	77,200	12,918	8,880	12,918	11,527	80,150	80,200	13,578	9,518	13,578	12,187	83,150	83,200	14,252	10,178	14,252	12,860
77,200	77,250	12,929	8,886	12,929	11,538	80,200	80,250	13,589	9,529	13,589	12,198	83,200	83,250	14,264	10,189	14,264	12,872
77,250	77,300	12,940	8,892	12,940	11,549	80,250	80,300	13,600	9,540	13,600	12,209	83,250	83,300	14,276	10,200	14,276	12,884
77,300	77,350	12,951	8,898	12,951	11,560	80,300	80,350	13,611	9,551	13,611	12,220	83,300	83,350	14,288	10,211	14,288	12,896
77,350	77,400	12,962	8,904	12,962	11,571	80,350	80,400	13,622	9,562	13,622	12,231	83,350	83,400	14,300	10,222	14,300	12,908
77,400	77,450	12,973	8,913	12,973	11,582	80,400	80,450	13,633	9,573	13,633	12,242	83,400	83,450	14,312	10,233	14,312	12,920
77,450	77,500	12,984	8,924	12,984	11,593	80,450	80,500	13,644	9,584	13,644	12,253	83,450	83,500	14,324	10,244	14,324	12,932
77,500	77,550	12,995	8,935	12,995	11,604	80,500	80,550	13,655	9,595	13,655	12,264	83,500	83,550	14,336	10,255	14,336	12,944
77,550	77,600	13,006	8,946	13,006	11,615	80,550	80,600	13,666	9,606	13,666	12,275	83,550	83,600	14,348	10,266	14,348	12,956
77,600	77,650	13,017	8,957	13,017	11,626	80,600	80,650	13,677	9,617	13,677	12,286	83,600	83,650	14,360	10,277	14,360	12,968
77,650	77,700	13,028	8,968	13,028	11,637	80,650	80,700	13,688	9,628	13,688	12,297	83,650	83,700	14,372	10,288	14,372	12,980
77,700	77,750	13,039	8,979	13,039	11,648	80,700	80,750	13,699	9,639	13,699	12,308	83,700	83,750	14,384	10,299	14,384	12,992
77,750	77,800	13,050	8,990	13,050	11,659	80,750	80,800	13,710	9,650	13,710	12,319	83,750	83,800	14,396	10,310	14,396	13,004
77,800	77,850	13,061	9,001	13,061	11,670	80,800	80,850	13,721	9,661	13,721	12,330	83,800	83,850	14,408	10,321	14,408	13,016
77,850	77,900	13,072	9,012	13,072	11,681	80,850	80,900	13,732	9,672	13,732	12,341	83,850	83,900	14,420	10,332	14,420	13,028
77,900	77,950	13,083	9,023	13,083	11,692	80,900	80,950	13,743	9,683	13,743	12,352	83,900	83,950	14,432	10,343	14,432	13,040
77,950	78,000	13,094	9,034	13,094	11,703	80,950	81,000	13,754	9,694	13,754	12,363	83,950	84,000	14,444	10,354	14,444	13,052

1. Abe is single. His taxable income is $83,492. How much does Abe owe in taxes?

2. Roberta is married and filing a joint return with her husband Steve. Their combined taxable income is $80,997. How much do they owe in taxes?

3. Quinn files as Head of Household. His tax is $12,220. What is his range of income according to the tax table?

4. Determine the tax for each filing status and taxable income amount listed.

   a. single $80,602

   b. head of household $83,572

   c. married filing jointly $77,777

   d. married filing separately $83,050

5. Given a taxable income amount, express the tax table line that would be used in compound inequality notation.

   a. $i = \$80,154$

   b. $i = \$83,221$

6. Given the taxable income amount, express the tax table line that would be used in interval notation.

    a. $i = \$80,101$ **b.** $i = 77,686$

7. Given the filing status and the tax, identify the taxable income interval that was used to determine that tax. Express your answer in interval notation.

    a. head of household $12,352   **b.** single $13,545

    c. married filing jointly $10,321   **d.** married filing separately $13,589

Use the Tax Schedule for Head of Household to answer Exercises 8–12.

Schedule Z—If your filing status is **Head of household**

If your taxable income is:		The tax is:	of the amount
Over—	But not over—		over—
$0	$13,600	---------- 10%	$0
13,600	51,800	$1,360.00 + 12%	13,600
51,800	82,500	5,944.00 + 22%	51,800
82,500	157,500	12,698.00 + 24%	82,500
157,500	200,000	30,698.00 + 32%	157,500
200,000	500,000	44,298.00 + 35%	200,000
500,000	----------	149,298.00 + 37%	500,000

8. Calculate the tax for each of the taxable incomes of a head of household taxpayer.

    a. $200,000   **b.** $23,872

    c. $121,890   **d.** $82,251

9. For what taxable income would a taxpayer have to pay $30,698.00 in taxes?

10. According to the tax schedule, Ann has to pay about $40,000 in taxes. What is Ann's taxable income interval?

11. Sam's taxable income is $92,300. What percent of his taxable income is his tax? Round to the nearest percent.

12. Manny's taxable income, t, is between $200,000 and $500,000. Write an algebraic expression that represents the amount of his tax.

Use the tax computation worksheet for a single taxpayer to answer Exercises 13–15.

Section A—Use if your filing status is **Single.** Complete the row below that applies to you.

Taxable income If line 10 is—	(a) Enter the amount from line 10	(b) Multiplication amount	(c) Multiply (a) by (b)	(d) Subtraction amount	Tax Subtract (d) from (c). Enter the result here and on the entry space on line 11a.
At least $100,000 but not over $157,500	$	× 24% (0.24)	$	$ 5,710.50	$
Over $157,500 but not over $200,000	$	× 32% (0.32)	$	$18,310.50	$
Over $200,000 but not over $500,000	$	× 35% (0.35)	$	$24,310.50	$
Over $500,000	$	× 37% (0.37)	$	$34,310.50	$

13. Calculate the tax for each of the taxable incomes using the tax computation worksheet above.

    a. $189,000

    b. $415,221

    c. $572,951

14. Let x represent a single taxpayer's taxable income that is over $157,500 but not over $200,000. Write an expression for this taxpayer's tax in terms of x.

15. Let w represent the tax for any taxable income t on the interval $t > 500,000$.

    a. Calculate the lowest tax on this interval.

    b. Calculate the highest tax on this interval.

    c. Express the tax for this row of the worksheet in interval notation in terms of w.

6-2 | Modeling Tax Schedules

Exercises

Use the past year's schedule below for a married filing jointly taxpayer to answer Exercise 1.

Schedule Y-1— If your filing status is **Married filing jointly** or **Qualifying widow(er)**

If your taxable income is:		The tax is:	of the amount over—
Over—	But not over—		
$0	$18,450	--------- 10%	$0
18,450	74,900	$1,845.00 + 15%	18,450
74,900	151,200	10,312.50 + 25%	74,900
151,200	230,450	29,387.50 + 28%	151,200
230,450	411,500	51,577.50 + 33%	230,450
411,500	464,850	111,324.00 + 35%	411,850
464,850	---------	129,996.50 + 39.6%	464,850

1. There are six taxable income intervals in this chart. Let x represent any taxable income. Express those intervals in tax schedule notation, interval notation, and compound inequality.

Tax Schedule Notation	Interval Notation	Compound Inequality Notation

2. Let y represent the tax and x represent the taxable income of a head of household taxpayer. Use a past year's worksheet below to write four equations in $y = mx + b$ form for values of x that are greater than or equal to $100,000.

Section D— Use if your filing status is **Head of household**. Complete the row below that applies to you.

Taxable income If line 43 is—	(a) Enter the amount from line 43	(b) Multiplication amount	(c) Multiply (a) by (b)	(d) Subtraction amount	Tax Subtract (d) from (c). Enter the result here and on Form 1040, line 44
At least $100,000 but not over $129,600	$	× 25% (0.25)	$	$ 5,677.50	$
Over $129,600 but not over $209,850	$	× 28% (0.28)	$	$ 9,565.50	$
Over $209,850 but not over $411,500	$	× 33% (0.33)	$	$ 20,058.00	$
Over $411,500 but not over $439,000	$	× 35% (0.35)	$	$ 28,288.00	$
Over $413,200	$	× 39.6% (0.396)	$	$ 48,482.00	$

3. Write a piecewise function to represent the tax $f(x)$ for the first three taxable income intervals in a past year's schedule below for a single taxpayer.

Schedule X— If your filing status is **Single**

If your taxable income is:		The tax is:	of the amount over—
Over—	But not over—		
$0	$9,225	‑‑‑‑‑‑‑‑ 10%	$0
9,225	37,450	$922.50 + 15%	9,225
37,450	90,750	5,156.25 + 25%	37,450
90,750	189,300	18,481.25 + 28%	90,750
189,300	411,500	46,075.25 + 33%	189,300
411,500	413,200	119,401.25 + 35%	411,500
413,200	‑‑‑‑‑‑‑‑	119,996.25 + 39.6%	413,200

4. Examine the tax schedule for the years 1914 and 2018 after a new tax law went into effect. The schedule in 1914 applied to all taxpayers. The schedule for 2018 is for a single taxpayer. **Marginal Tax Rate** is the rate of tax a taxpayer pays at his/her income level.

1914			2018		
Marginal Tax Rate	Tax Brackets		Marginal Tax Rate	Tax Brackets	
	Over	But not over		Over	But not over
1.0%	$0	$20,000	10.0%	$0	$9,525
2.0%	$20,000	$50,000	12.0%	$9,525	$38,700
3.0%	$50,000	$75,000	22.0%	$38,700	$82,500
4.0%	$75,000	$100,000	24.0%	$82,500	$157,500
5.0%	$100,000	$250,000	32.0%	$157,500	$200,000
6.0%	$250,000	$500,000	35.0%	$200,000	$500,000
7.0%	$500,000		37.0%	$500,000	

a. What was the marginal tax rate for a taxpayer with a taxable income of $40,000 in 1914?

b. What was the marginal tax rate for a taxpayer with a taxable income of $40,000 in 2018?

c. Based on the marginal tax rate, find the difference in tax between a single taxpayer in 1914 making $90,000 and a single taxpayer in 2018 making the same amount.

5. Examine the following piecewise function that models the tax computation worksheet for a single taxpayer in a past year. Write the tax equations in $y = mx + b$ form.

$$c(x) = \begin{cases} 14,652.50 + 0.28(x - 71,950) & 100,000 < x \le 150,150 \\ 36,548.50 + 0.33(x - 150,150) & 150,150 < x \le 326,450 \\ 94,727.50 + 0.35(x - 326,450) & x > 326,450 \end{cases}$$

6-3 | Income Statements

Exercises

1. Jack's employer just switched to a new payroll system. He wants to make sure that his net pay has been computed correctly. His gross pay per pay period is $587.34. He has the following deductions: Social Security tax (6.2%), Medicare tax (1.45%), federal withholding tax $164.45, state withholding tax $76.34, retirement insurance contribution $50.00, disability insurance fee $8.00, medical insurance fee $23.00, and dental insurance fee $8.00. What should his net pay be for this pay period?

2. Tony makes an hourly salary of $15.40 for 40 regular hours of work. For any time worked beyond 40 hours, he is paid at a rate of time-and-a-half per hour. Last week, Tony worked 46 hours. Find each of the following for this period.

   a. Tony's gross pay

   b. Social Security tax

   c. Medicare tax

3. Elizabeth works for Picasso Paint Supplies. Her annual salary is $72,580.

   a. What is Elizabeth's annual Social Security deduction?

   b. What is Elizabeth's annual Medicare deduction?

   c. Elizabeth is paid every other week. What is her biweekly gross pay?

   d. Each pay period, Elizabeth's employer deducts 21% for federal withholding tax. What is the total amount withheld for federal tax from Elizabeth's annual salary?

   e. If Elizabeth is taxed at an annual rate of 2.875% for city tax, how much is deducted from her salary per paycheck to withhold that tax?

   f. As of January 1, Elizabeth will receive a 9.1% raise. What will Elizabeth's annual salary be?

4. A taxpayer's annual Social Security tax is $6,107. What is the taxpayer's gross annual salary?

5. A taxpayer's annual Medicare tax is $841. What is the taxpayer's gross annual salary?

Name _____ Date _____

6. Let x represent the gross paycheck amount for a weekly pay period. Let y represent the number of the week in the year (1 = first week, 2 = second week, etc.)

    a. Write an expression to represent the calendar year-to-date amount.

    b. Write an expression for the Social Security tax for each pay period.

    c. Write an expression for the year-to-date Social Security tax.

    d. Write an expression for the Medicare tax for each pay period.

    e. Write an expression for the year-to-date Medicare tax.

    f. If C percent of the gross pay is withheld for federal taxes, write an expression for the weekly amount withheld for those taxes.

    g. Write an expression for the total annual federal tax withheld.

7. Use the partial information given in this electronic W-2 form to calculate the amount in Box 3.

8. Melanie is taxed at a 19% tax rate for her federal taxes. Last year, she reduced her taxable income by contributing X dollars per biweekly paycheck to her tax deferred retirement account and Y dollars per biweekly paycheck to her FSA. Write an expression for the amount she reduced her taxes by if her gross biweekly pay is Z dollars.

1 Wages, tips, other compensation	2 Federal income tax withheld
3 Social security wages	4 Social security tax withheld **$6,361.20**
5 Medicare wages and tips	6 Medicare tax withheld
7 Social security tips	8 Allocated tips
9 Verification code	10 Dependent care benefits
11 Nonqualified plans	12a **E** $2,400.00
13 Statutory employee ☐ Retirement plan ☒ Third-party sick pay ☐	12b
14 Other **caf125 $5,600.00**	12c

9. Examine Alfredo Plata's incomplete W-2 form. Based on the information determine the amounts in each of the following boxes.

    a. Box 1

    b. Box 3

    c. Box 4

    d. Box 5

a Employee's social security number **000-00-0000**	OMB No. 1545-0008	Safe, accurate, FAST! Use	Visit the IRS website at www.irs.gov/efile.
b Employer identification number (EIN) **00-0000000**		1 Wages, tips, other compensation	2 Federal income tax withheld **$14,662.50**
c Employer's name, address, and ZIP code **Blake Industries 234 Washington Blvd Seven Bridges, NY 10515**		3 Social security wages	4 Social security tax withheld
		5 Medicare wages and tips	6 Medicare tax withheld **$1,346.04**
		7 Social security tips	8 Allocated tips
d Control number		9 Advance EIC payment	10 Dependent care benefits
e Employee's first name and initial **Alfredo** Last name **Plata** Suff.		11 Nonqualified plans	12a See instructions for box 12 **E** $2,300.00
		13 Statutory employee ☐ Retirement plan ☒ Third-party sick pay ☐	12b
137 Michigan Rd. Seven Bridges, NY 10515		14 Other **caf125 $4,280.00**	12c
			12d
f Employee's address and ZIP code			
15 State Employer's state ID number **00-0000000**	16 State wages, tips, etc.	17 State income tax	18 Local wages, tips, etc.	19 Local income tax	20 Locality name

6-4 Form 1040—Reporting Taxable Income

Exercises

1. Arthur's employer withheld $15,987.76 in federal income tax. After completing his return, Arthur has determined that his tax is $18,945.22. Will Art get a refund, or does he owe the IRS and how much?

2. Latoya is an accountant who also works as a part-time museum tour guide. Information from her tax worksheet includes wages from the accounting job, $85,290.45; wages from the museum job, $12,670.34; interest, $563.99; and dividends, $234.67. What is Latoya's total income?

3. Drew is single with a taxable income for last year of $83,472. His employer withheld $16,998 in federal taxes.

   a. Use the tax tables from Section 6-1 in this workbook to determine Drew's tax.

   b. Does Drew get a refund?

   c. Find the difference between Drew's tax and the amount withheld by his employer.

4. Davia and Bill are married and file their taxes jointly. Davia's taxable income was $50,675 and Bill's was $32,802. Davia's employer withheld $11,654 in federal taxes. Bill's employer withheld $7,345 in federal taxes.

   a. What is their combined taxable income?

   b. Use the tax tables from section 6-1 in this workbook to determine their tax.

   c. Do they get a refund?

   d. Find the difference between their tax and the amount withheld by their employers.

5. Parker is single and paying off his graduate student loan. The monthly payment is $679.34. He is hoping to receive an income tax refund that is large enough to make at least one monthly payment. His taxable income is $77,911 and his employer withheld $19,458 in federal taxes.

   a. Use the tax tables from section 6-1 of this workbook. How much of a refund will Parker receive?

   b. How many loan payments will Parker be able to make with this refund?

6. Eileen is a married taxpayer who files jointly with her husband. Their combined taxable income is X dollars and their tax is Y dollars. Eileen's employer withheld A dollars from her salary and her husband's employer withheld B dollars from his salary during the year.

   a. Write an algebraic expression for the amount they would receive should they get a refund.

   b. Write an algebraic expression for the amount they would owe in taxes if the combined amount withheld was not enough to cover the tax they owe.

In problem 7, complete Form 1040 and appropriate schedules for the Boyd family. Use 000-00-0000 for all Social Security numbers. Current tax forms, tables, and instructions are available at www.irs.gov.

7. George and Patty Boyd are married filing jointly with two children, John and Paul. George is a mechanic and Patty is a plumber. She was unemployed for part of the year. She also won $500 in the state lottery. George has a side business fixing guitars and used Schedule C to find his taxable business income. Here are their W-2 Forms:

W-2 (George Boyd)

a Employee's social security number	000-00-0000
b Employer identification number (EIN)	00-2222222
1 Wages, tips, other compensation	$77,566
2 Federal income tax withheld	$9,262.21
3 Social security wages	$77,566
4 Social security tax withheld	$4,809.09
5 Medicare wages and tips	$77,566
6 Medicare tax withheld	$1,124.71

c Employer's name, address, and ZIP code
Mizzi Ace Auto Repair
20 Maple Avenue
Livingston, MT 59047

e Employee's first name and initial   Last name
George Boyd
3 Abbey Road
Livingston, MT 59047

15 State	Employer's state ID number	16 State wages, tips, etc.	17 State income tax
		$77,566	$2,232

Form **W-2** Wage and Tax Statement
Department of the Treasury—Internal Revenue Service

W-2 (Patty Boyd)

a Employee's social security number	000-00-0000
b Employer identification number (EIN)	00-7777777
1 Wages, tips, other compensation	$61,222
2 Federal income tax withheld	$9,262.21
3 Social security wages	$61,222
4 Social security tax withheld	$3,795.76
5 Medicare wages and tips	$61,222
6 Medicare tax withheld	$887.72

c Employer's name, address, and ZIP code
Rosenberg Plumbing
8 Mattituck Street
Livingston, MT 59047

e Employee's first name and initial   Last name
Patty Boyd
3 Abbey Road
Livingston, MT 59047

15 State	Employer's state ID number	16 State wages, tips, etc.	17 State income tax
		$61,222	$2,191

Form **W-2** Wage and Tax Statement
Department of the Treasury—Internal Revenue Service

Here is their important financial information for the past tax year:

Interest: Regal Savings Bank $876

Dividends: Exxon Mobil $315

Unemployment compensation: $2,600

Schedule C Business Income: $3,661

Rodeo Bank: $891

Chrysler: $1,139

Prize: $500

6-5 Reducing Your Form 1040 Tax Liability

Exercises

1. Mike and Lisa Lerner had combined wages of $91,301 last year. They also had a bank interest of $792 and $667. They received stock dividends of $287 and $530. During the year, Lisa won a $1,000 prize. Find the total income from wages, bank interest, dividends, and the prize.

2. Paul and Mary had $78,111.19 in income from their jobs and their bank interest. They also had $2,139 worth of student loan interest, and Paul paid $6,000 in alimony. These two expenses are deductions from income. Find their adjusted gross income.

3. The Starkey family had a total income of i dollars. They also had a dollars in adjustments to income. Express their adjusted gross income algebraically.

4. The Kivetsky family had an adjusted gross income of $119,245.61. They included medical deductions on Schedule A. They had $14,191 in medical expenses. Medical insurance covered 80% of these expenses. The IRS allows medical and dental expenses deductions for the amount that exceeds 7.5% of a taxpayer's adjusted gross income. How much can they claim as a medical deduction?

5. Anita's adjusted gross income was a dollars last year. If she had m dollars of medical expenses last year, and 80% of these expenses were covered by her insurance, express her medical expense deduction algebraically.

6. The Mazzeo family donated c dollars in cash to charity last tax year. They also donated b bags of used clothing valued at $50 each. They donated two used computers valued at x dollars each to the local food pantry. Express their total charitable contributions algebraically.

7. The Holfester family took $5\frac{1}{2}$ hours to gather information for their Schedule A. The itemized deductions saved them $4,095 in taxes. What was the mean savings per hour to fill out Schedule A? Round to the nearest dollar.

8. The Lowatsky family had $9,441 worth of hurricane damage that was not covered by insurance. They need to follow IRS procedures to take a casualty deduction on Schedule A.

   a. The IRS requires that $100 be deducted from each casualty. What is the total casualty loss after the $100 is deducted?

   b. Their adjusted gross income is $67,481. Find 10% of their adjusted gross income.

   c. Their Schedule A casualty deduction can be found by subtracting 10% of the adjusted gross income from the answer to part a. What is their casualty loss deduction?

9. Maria's adjusted gross income was *a* dollars. She had three different casualties last year that were not covered by insurance. A laptop computer valued at *x* dollars was taken from her gym locker, and her car was stolen, and she did not have comprehensive insurance, so she lost *y* dollars. An ice storm caused *z* dollars worth of damage that was not covered by insurance. Express her casualty loss algebraically.

10. Jessica Filipowitz filed as a Single taxpayer and had a taxable income of $77,989. Then she learned that $876 of her student loan interest was tax deductible, so revised her Form 1040. Using the tax tables from Lesson 6-1 of this book, find out how much the student loan deduction saved her on her tax liability.

11. Raoul and Alice Cramden are married and have three children, Norton, Fred, and Cardi. Raoul is a security guard and Alice is yoga instructor. They file as Married Filing Jointly. Raoul has a car detailing business, so he also filed Schedule C. He also is paying off his student loan and will deduct the interest. Raoul was unemployed for several weeks during the year. Their W-2 forms are shown below.

a Employee's social security number		
000-00-0000		

b Employer identification number (EIN)	1 Wages, tips, other compensation	2 Federal income tax withheld
00-3333333	**$71,981**	**$8,765.43**

c Employer's name, address, and ZIP code	3 Social security wages	4 Social security tax withheld
	$71,981	**$4,462.82**
Guardian Security	5 Medicare wages and tips	6 Medicare tax withheld
88 Dorset Ridge	**$71,981**	**$1,043.72**
Dyersville, IA 52040	7 Social security tips	8 Allocated tips

d Control number	9 Verification code	10 Dependent care benefits

e Employee's first name and initial Last name	Suff.	11 Nonqualified plans	12a
		13 Statutory employee / Retirement plan / Third-party sick pay	12b
Raoul Cramden		14 Other	12c
112 Elk Drive			12d
New Vienna, IA 52040			

f Employee's address and ZIP code						
15 State Employer's state ID number	16 State wages, tips, etc.	17 State income tax	18 Local wages, tips, etc.	19 Local income tax	20 Locality name
	$71,981	**$3,007**			

Form W-2 Wage and Tax Statement   Department of the Treasury—Internal Revenue Service

	a Employee's social security number **000-00-0000**		
b Employer identification number (EIN) **00-9999999**		**1** Wages, tips, other compensation **$63,009**	**2** Federal income tax withheld **$8,212.21**
c Employer's name, address, and ZIP code		**3** Social security wages **$63,009**	**4** Social security tax withheld
Field of Yoga **19 Shoeless Street** **Dyersville, IA 52040**		**5** Medicare wages and tips **$63,009**	**6** Medicare tax withheld
		7 Social security tips	**8** Allocated tips
d Control number		**9** Verification code	**10** Dependent care benefits
e Employee's first name and initial Last name Suff.		**11** Nonqualified plans	**12a**
Alice Cramden **112 Elk Drive** **New Vienna, IA 52040**		**13** Statutory employee ☐ Retirement plan ☐ Third-party sick pay ☐	**12b**
		14 Other	**12c**
			12d
f Employee's address and ZIP code			

15 State Employer's state ID number	**16** State wages, tips, etc. **$63,009**	**17** State income tax **$2,011**	**18** Local wages, tips, etc.	**19** Local income tax	**20** Locality name

Form **W-2** Wage and Tax Statement

Department of the Treasury—Internal Revenue Service

a. Fill in Box 4, FICA tax withheld, with the correct entry, for Alice's W-2.
b. Fill in Box 6, Medicare tax withheld, with the correct entry, for Alice's W-2.
c. Complete their Form 1040, with Schedule 1 and Schedules A and B, using Social Security numbers 000-00-0000 and their financial information below.

Taxable interest: Troy Savings $762   Hendrix County Bank $441
Dividends: Boeing $340   Amazon $1,115

Refund from last year's state income tax: $657
Taxable business income from Schedule C: $2,442 from Raoul's business
Unemployment compensation: $1,977
Prize from state lottery: $1,000
Penalty for early withdrawal of interest: $28
Student loan interest that is deductible: $1,871 for the year
Medical Expenses: Insurance $11,098; Prescriptions $310; Doctors $5,111; Dentists $2,816; Eyeglasses $390. Their insurance covered 80% of the medical expenses.
Taxes: State income tax is from W-2; real estate taxes $6,213
Home mortgage interest paid: $8,177
Contributions: cash $907, used clothing and furniture $850
Casualty and theft losses: They had flood damage, not covered by insurance, of $15,098, and a designer wallet (worth $250) with $600 cash was stolen while on vacation.
Child care credits: $1,215 (They had to pay for day care when both parents were working).

7-1   Finding a Place to Live

Exercises

1. Use the interval 25%–30% to find the monetary range that is recommended for the monthly housing budget in each situation. Round to the nearest dollar.

    a. Enrique makes $109,992 per year.   **b.** Barbara makes $5,000 per month.

2. Hannah's financial advisor believes that she should spend no more than 26% of her gross monthly income for housing. She has determined that amount is $1,794 per month. Based on this amount and her advisor's recommendation, what is Hannah's annual salary?

3. Adina makes $53,112 per year and is looking to find a new apartment rental in her city. She searched online and found an apartment for $1,500 per month. The recommendation is to budget between 25% and 30% of your monthly income for rent. Can Adina afford this apartment based upon the recommended interval? Explain.

4. Rex makes $12.50 per hour. He works 35 hours a week. He pays 24% of his gross earnings in federal and state taxes and saves 10% of his monthly gross income. He is considering renting an apartment that will cost $1,600 per month.

    a. Is this monthly rental fee within the recommended 25%–30% housing expense range?

    b. Based upon his expenses, can he make the monthly payments?

5. Brian's monthly gross income is $2,950. He pays 22% of his monthly gross earnings in federal and state taxes and spends 10% of that monthly income to pay off his credit card debt. Brian is also paying off a loan his parents gave him for a new car by sending them 8% of his income per month. Brian found an apartment near his work that rents for $1,300 per month. Will he be able to make the payments without changing the amounts he pays toward his loan and credit card debt?

6. Larry is renting an apartment that will cost r dollars per month. He must pay a D dollars application fee and C dollars for a credit application. His security deposit is two month's rent and he must also pay the last month's rent upon signing the lease. His broker charges 7% of the total year's rent as the fee for finding the apartment. Write an algebraic expression that represents the total cost of signing the lease.

7. The square footage and monthly rental of 10 similar one-bedroom apartments yield the linear regression $y = 0.775x + 950.25$ where x represents the square footage of the apartment and y represents the monthly rental price. Grace can afford $1,500 per month rent. Using the equation, what size apartment should she expect to be able to rent for that price?

8. Carla wants to rent a new apartment. She made a table listing the square footage of the apartments and their rents as shown. Use linear regression analysis to determine if there is a correlation between the square footage (*x*) and the amount charged for the monthly rent (*y*).

Square feet (*x*)	600	790	800	850	925	980	1,050	1,400
Monthly Rent (*y*)	$795	$1,523	$1,600	$1,800	$2,000	$2,100	$2,300	$3,000

   a. What is the linear regression equation? Round the numbers to the nearest hundredth.

   b. Interpret the correlation coefficient.

9. The square footage and monthly rental of 15 similar one-bedroom apartments yield the linear regression formula $y = 1.3485x + 840.51$, where *x* represents the square footage and *y* represents the monthly rental price. Round answers to the nearest whole number.

   a. Determine the monthly rent for an apartment with 1,200 square feet.

   b. Determine the square footage of an apartment with a monthly rent of $1,900.

10. Conan is moving into a two-bedroom apartment in Valley Oaks. The monthly rent is $2,000. His up-front fees are shown. How much can he expect to pay up front for this apartment?

   | **Application fee:** 3% of one month's rent |
   | **Credit application fee:** $20 |
   | **Security deposit:** 1 month's rent and last month's rent |
   | **Broker's fee:** 14% of year's rent |

11. Debbie wants to rent a one-bedroom apartment in April Acres. The apartment has a monthly rent of *D* dollars. The fees are shown below. Write an algebraic expression that represents the amount she is expected to pay before renting the apartment.

   Application fee: 2% of one month's rent   Security deposit: $\frac{1}{2}$ month's rent
   Last month's rent paid up front   Broker's fee: 4% of one year's rent

12. NuHome Movers charges $95 per hour for loading/unloading services and $80 per hour for packing/unpacking services. Their charge is $2.50 per mile for truck rental. Jay is moving a distance of 200 miles and needs 9 hours of loading/unloading and 7 hours of packing/unpacking. What will his moving cost be if the service also charges 7.25% tax on the total?

13. iVan charges an hourly rate for a moving team to load and unload a truck. The charge is a different hourly rate for a team to pack and unpack boxes. Use the quotes to determine the iVan hourly rates.

Weekday Move	**Weekend Move**
8 hours of loading/unloading	5 hours of loading/unloading
6 hours of packing/unpacking	3 hours of packing/unpacking
$890 total cost	$515 total cost

Name _____   Date _____

Exercises

1. The length of a room is $19\frac{1}{2}$ feet. When using $\frac{1}{4}$ inch = 1 foot scale, what would be the length of the wall on a floor plan?

2. Kim is building a large gazebo for her backyard. It is in the shape of a regular hexagon. Each side of the gazebo is 12 feet long. The apothem is 10.4 feet. She needs to purchase stones for the floor. It costs $9.50 per square foot for a special type of interlocking stone. Find the cost of the gazebo's floor. Round to the nearest ten dollars.

3. Find the volume of a rectangular room that measures 13 feet by 15.5 feet, with an 8-foot ceiling.

4. A rectangular room has length L and width W. Its volume is 2,455 cubic feet. Express the height of the ceiling algebraically in terms of x.

5. A regular heptagon (7 sides) has perimeter 126 and area A. Express the apothem a of the heptagon algebraically in terms of the area A.

6. An irregular plane figure drawn on graph paper is framed inside of a 15 by 40 rectangle. To find its area, 10,000 random points are generated, and 5,710 of them land inside the irregular region. What is the area of the irregular region, to the nearest integer?

7. The main meeting room of the Glen Oaks Community Center measures 46 feet by 34 feet and has a 12-foot ceiling. It is well insulated and faces the east side of his house. The manager wants to purchase an air conditioner. How large an air conditioner should he purchase? Round up to the next thousand BTUs.

8. Circle O is situated in rectangle $ACDE$ as shown.

   a. Find the area of the rectangle.

   b. Find the radius of the circle.

   c. Find the area of the circle to the nearest integer.

   d. Find the area of the shaded region.

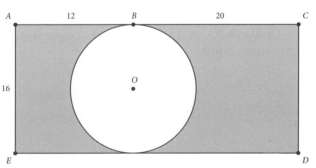

9. Kyoko plans to put a new wood floor in her den, which is shown in the floor plan.

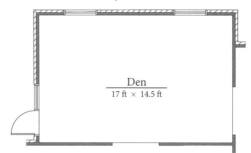

Den
17 ft × 14.5 ft

a. What is the area of the floor?

b. At a cost of $11 per square foot, how much will it cost to put down the new floor?

c. Kyoko plans to put a rectangular area rug in the room. The rug will be large enough so that only a 2-foot wide section of the wood floor will be exposed on each side. Find the dimensions of the area rug.

d. What is the area of the area rug?

e. Find the area of the wood floor that will be exposed once the area rug is laid down.

10. A rectangular room has length L, width W, and height H, where L, W, and H are measured in feet.

a. Express the volume in cubic feet algebraically.

b. If carpeting costs $72 per square yard, write an expression for the cost of carpeting the floor of this room.

11. A rectangular room measures 16 feet by 18 feet. The ceiling is 9 feet high.

a. Find the total area of the four walls in the room.

b. If a gallon of paint costs $37.99 and it covers 400 square feet on average, what is the cost of painting the room, including the ceiling, with two coats of paint? Explain your answer.

c. This room is well insulated and is on the north side of the house. How large of an air conditioner would this room require? Round to the next highest thousand BTUs.

d. A scale drawing is made of this room using the scale 1 sq ft = $\frac{1}{4}$ sq in. What are the dimensions of this room on the drawing?

12. A rectangular room measures L feet by W feet. The ceiling is 8 feet high. The walls and the ceiling will be painted the same color. Express the total area of the walls and ceiling algebraically.

7-3 Mortgage Application Process

Exercises

1. The Jacobs family is planning to buy a home. They have some money for a down payment already. They see a home they like and compute that they would need to borrow $213,000 from a bank over a 30-year period. The APR is 3.75%.

   a. What is the monthly payment, to the nearest cent?

   b. What is the total of all of the monthly payments over the 30 years?

   c. What is her total interest for the 30 years?

2. Pam and Chris found a home for which they would have to borrow H dollars. If they take out a 25-year loan with monthly payment M, express the interest I in terms of H and M.

3. A bank requires that the Dotkoms pay their homeowner's insurance, property taxes, and mortgage in one monthly payment to the bank. If their monthly mortgage payment is $1,711.22, their semi-annual property tax bill is $3,239, and their annual homeowner's insurance bill is $980, how much do they pay the bank each month?

4. If you borrow $200,000 at an APR of 4% for 25 years, you will pay more per month than if you borrow the money for 30 years at 4%.

   a. What is the monthly payment on the 25-year mortgage, to the nearest cent?

   b. What is the total interest paid on the 25-year mortgage?

   c. What is the monthly payment on the 30-year mortgage?

   d. What is the total interest paid on the 30-year mortgage?

   e. How much more interest is paid on the 30-year loan? Round to the nearest dollar.

   f. What is the difference between the monthly payments of the two different loans? Round to the nearest dollar.

5. The assessed value of the Kreiner family's house is $457,000. The annual property tax rate is 2.66% of assessed value. What is the annual property tax on the Kreiner's home?

6. Tom and Gwen have an adjusted gross income of $144,112. Their monthly mortgage payment for the house they want would be $1,483. Their annual property taxes would be $9,330, and the homeowner's insurance premium would cost them $1,099 per year. They have a monthly $444 car payment, and their credit card monthly payment averages $4,021.

   a. Based on the front-end ratio, would the bank lend them $220,000 to purchase the house they want? Explain your answer.

   b. Based on the back-end ratio, would the bank lend them $220,000 to purchase the house they want? Explain your answer.

7. The market value of Jennifer and Neil's home is $319,000. The assessed value is $280,000. The annual property tax rate is $19.70 per $1,000 of assessed value.

   a. What is the property tax on their home?

   b. How much do they pay monthly toward property taxes? Round to the nearest cent.

8. Rowena has an adjusted gross income of k dollars. She is looking at a new house. Her monthly mortgage payment would be m. The annual property taxes would be p, and the annual homeowner's premium would be h. Express her front-end ratio algebraically.

9. Britney and Jakob have an annual adjusted gross income of x dollars. Their monthly mortgage payment is m. Their annual property taxes are p, and their annual homeowner's premium is h. They have a monthly credit card bill of c and a monthly car loan of l. They also have an annual college tuition bill represented by t. Write an expression for each ratio.

   a. front-end ratio   b. back-end ratio

10. Find the monthly payment (before the balloon payment) for a 25-year, interest-only balloon mortgage for $300,000 at an APR of 3.1%. Round to the nearest ten dollars.

11. An interest-only balloon mortgage of a principal p for 20 years has total interest of i dollars. Write an expression for the amount of each monthly payment before the balloon payment.

12. Ted has an adjusted gross income of $120,006. He wants a house with a monthly mortgage payment of $1,921 and annual property taxes of $7,112. His semiannual homeowner's premium would be $897. Ted has a credit card bill that averages $300 per month.

   a. What is the back-end ratio to the nearest percent? The front-end ratio?

   b. Assume that his credit rating is good. Based on the back-end ratio, would the bank offer him a loan? Explain.

   c. Based on the front-end ratio, would the bank offer him a loan? Explain.

7-4 Purchasing a Home

Exercises

1. Let L represent a loan amount, P represent the percent of the APR on that loan, D represent the daily interest that would be charged on the loan at that rate, M represent the number of days in a month, and C represent the closing date on a loan.

    a. If I represents the interest on the loan for one year, write an algebraic expression for the interest I.

    b. Write an algebraic expression for the daily interest in terms of I.

    c. Let Z represent the interest due on a loan from the closing date to the end of the month. Write an algebraic expression for Z.

2. Liz and Nick are buying a $725,000 home. They have been approved for a 3.25% APR, 30-year mortgage. They made a 20% down payment and will be closing on March 11.

    a. What is their interest on the loan for one year?

    b. What is the daily interest?

    c. How much should they expect to pay in prepaid interest at the closing?

3. How much will be charged in prepaid interest on a $500,000 loan with an APR of 3.725% that was closed on August 26?

4. Lars has been approved for a $420,000, 20-year mortgage with an APR of 5.125%.

    a. What is his monthly payment?

    b. How much interest would he expect to pay on the loan in the first month?

    c. How much of that monthly payment will go toward the principal?

5. The bank approved Sylvie for a $250,000, 15-year mortgage with an APR of 3.95%.

    a. What is her monthly payment?

    b. How much interest would she expect to pay on the loan in the first month?

    c. How much of that monthly payment will go toward the principal?

6. Hillary was told that based on the price of her home, her approximated closing costs would range from $11,600 to $40,600. How much was the price of her home?

7. Laura and Rich have been approved for a $325,000, 15-year mortgage with an APR of 5.3%. Using the mortgage and interest formulas, complete the two-month amortization table.

Payment Number	Beginning Balance	Monthly Payment	Toward Interest	Toward Principal	Ending Balance
1					
2					

8. Examine the following loan amortization table for the first 5 months of a $475,000, 25-year mortgage with an APR of 5.45%. Complete the table.

Payment Number	Beginning Balance	Monthly Payment	Toward Interest	Toward Principal	Ending Balance
1	475,000.00		2,157.29	745.46	474,254.54
2			2,153.91	748.84	473,505.70
3	473,505.70			752.24	472,753.46
4	472,753.46		2,147.09		471,997.80
5	471,997.80	2,902.75	2,143.66	759.09	
6	471,238.71	2,902.75	2,140.21		470,476.17

9. Examine the loan amortization table for months 92–95 of a $200,000, 8-year mortgage with an APR of 5.025%. Determine the amounts missing in the table.

Payment Number	Beginning Balance	Monthly Payment	Toward Interest	Toward Principal	Ending Balance
92	12,514.18		52.40	2,481.97	
93	10,032.21		42.01	2,492.36	7,539.85
94			31.57	2,502.80	5,037.05
95	5,037.05			2,513.28	2,523.77

10. Shay took out a $560,000, 10-year mortgage with an APR of 3.5%. The first month she made an extra payment of $1,200. What was the ending balance at the end of her first month?

11. Randy took out an adjustable rate mortgage for $375,000 over 20 years. It had an introductory rate of 3.25% for the first year, and then it rose to 4.5%. Complete the chart for the 13th payment.

Payment Number	Beginning Balance	Monthly Payment	Toward Interest	Toward Principal	Ending Balance
12	362,608.15	2,126.98	982.06	1,144.92	361,463.23
13					

7-5 Mortgage Points

Exercises

1. Determine the cost of the points and the new interest rate for each loan amount and interest rate. Assume each point costs 1% of the loan amount.

   a. $280,000, original APR 4.18%, 1 point with a 0.2% discount

   b. $350,000, original APR 2.95%, 2 points with a 0.275% discount per point.

   c. $600,000, original APR 4.6%, 3 points with a 0.225% discount per point.

   d. $450,000, original APR 3.75%, 1 point with a 0.3% discount

   e. $2,000,000, original APR 3.55%, 2 points with a 0.235% discount per point.

2. Juanita wants to take out a 15-year, $350,000 loan with a 3.4% APR. She is not sure as to whether or not she should purchase points to reduce the loan APR. If she purchases two points, it will decrease her APR by 0.125% per point. Each point will cost 1% of her loan. Compare her monthly payments with and without the purchase of the points.

3. Ansel was approved for an 18-year, $450,000 loan with a 3.9% APR. If he purchases 1 point, his APR will reduce to 3.7%. How much will his monthly payment savings be?

4. Akiko purchased 4 points, each of which reduced her APR by 0.165%. Each point cost 1% of her loan value. Her new APR is 2.8% and the points cost her $19,200.

   a. What was the original APR?

   b. What is her principal?

5. Hamed purchased x points. Each point lowered his APR by y%. The cost per point was z% of the loan amount. His new APR is A% and his points cost him B dollars. Write an algebraic expression for

   a. the original APR

   b. the principal

6. The Bedford Shore Credit Union offered Patti a $220,000 30-year mortgage at 3.17%. The credit union offers up to 4 points that will reduce her APR by 0.25% per point. Each point will cost 1% of the loan value. Patti is considering buying 3 points.

   a. Calculate her monthly payments with the points.

   b. Calculate her monthly payments without the points.

   c. Determine the breakeven month.

7. National Savings Bank approved Caroline for a $300,000 12-year loan at a 3.875% APR. Should Caroline purchase 1 point or no points? Each point lowers the APR by 0.125% and costs 1% of the loan amount. Justify your reasoning.

8. Alena wants to take out a $600,000 loan to purchase a new waterfront home. The bank offers a 30-year loan with an APR of 4.15%. If she purchases one point for 1% of the value of the loan, she will reduce her APR by 0.3%.

   a. What is her monthly savings with the point purchase?

   b. When will she break even?

9. Technical Savings Bank offers borrowers a zero closing cost loan. Each negative point reduces the closing costs by 1% of the principal and increases the APR by 0.125%. Jared wants to borrow $540,000 from Technical Savings at 3.48% for 25 years. The estimated closing costs are $10,000.

   a. How many negative points does he need to have a zero closing cost loan?

   b. What will his new APR be on the loan?

   c. There is a chance that in 15 years, his company may be moving to a different state. Are these negative points worth the investment?

10. Teachers' Federal Credit Union offers a 3.25%, 10-year mortgage. Moira wants to borrow $380,000 and "purchase" enough negative points to eliminate her $14,000 closing costs. Each negative point reduces the closing costs by 1% of the principal and increases the APR by 0.135%.

   a. How many points will she need?

   b. What will her new APR be?

   c. What is the breakeven time for Moira's loan?

7-6 Rentals, Condominiums, and Cooperatives

Exercises

1. On March 1, Antonio purchased a new condominium. He pays a monthly maintenance fee of $1,030. His monthly property taxes equal 13.5% of the monthly fee. How much will Anton pay in property taxes for this calendar year?

2. Sarah purchased a condominium at Tulip Meadows. She pays $3,196.80 in property taxes each year. These taxes are taken out of her monthly maintenance fee of $1,480. What percentage of this monthly fee goes to property taxes?

3. Last year, one-fifth of the Fitzgerald's $800 dollar monthly co-op maintenance fee went toward property taxes. How much property tax did the Fitzgerald's pay last year?

4. Luella's monthly maintenance fee is $720, of which p percent is tax deductible for property tax purposes. Express the annual property tax deduction algebraically.

5. The Sea Cottage Cooperative is owned by the shareholders. The co-op has a total of 32,000 shares. Linda has an apartment at Sea Cottage and owns 480 shares of the cooperative. What percentage of Sea Cottage does Linda own?

6. Last year, p percent of Shannon's x-dollar co-op monthly maintenance fee went toward property taxes. Write an algebraic expression for Shannon's annual property taxes.

7. Petra has a co-op in Sunset Village. The cooperative consists of a total of 28,000 shares. If Petra owns s shares, what percentage of the cooperative corporation does she own?

8. The South Hills Apartment Complex has just announced rate increases. All rents will increase by 3.2%, and the security deposit, which was formerly 50% of one month's rent, must now equal 60% of the new rent. Eddie rented an apartment for $1,600. In what amount should he write a check to cover the new rent and the extra security deposit?

9. Joey rented an apartment from a landlord in his hometown. His rent was R dollars per month until he moved out last week. The new tenants pay N dollars per month. Write an algebraic expression to represent the percent increase.

10. In 1998, Ben bought a co-op for $120,000. He borrowed $90,000 from the bank to make the purchase. Now he wants to sell the co-op, but the market value has decreased to $80,000. His equity in the co-op is $46,800. If he sells the co-op, he will have to pay off the mortgage. How much will he make after he pays off the mortgage?

Name _____ Date _____

11. Nick moved into an apartment in the city. He pays $3,200 rent per month. The landlord told him the rent has increased 3% per year on average.

    a. Express the rent y as an exponential function of the number of years x.

    b. Suppose the rent had increased $100 each year. Express the rent y as a function of the number of years x.

    c. Determine the predicted rent after 5 years using each of the two equations.

12. The monthly rents for Jillian's one-bedroom apartment, at the North Haven Towers, for a 10-year period, are given in the table.

    a. Write the exponential regression equation that models these rents. Round the numbers to the nearest hundredth.

    b. According to your equation, what is the approximate yearly rent increase percentage?

    c. Using your equation, what will the rent be in 15 years?

Year	Monthly Rent ($)
1	1,680
2	1,700
3	1,750
4	1,790
5	1,825
6	1,855
7	1,885
8	1,920
9	1,965
10	2,000

13. Beth moved into an apartment close to her new job. She will be paying $2,000 per month in rent and expects a 2.5% rent increase each year.

    a. Express the rent y as an exponential function of the number of years rented, x.

    b. What can she expect the rent to be in the 10th year?

14. Monthly rent at The Breakers Co-ops has increased annually, modeled by the exponential equation $y = 2,700(1.045)^x$. What was the percent increase per year?

15. Margot bought a condominium at a time when prices were at their highest. She paid $185,000. Since then, she has watched the market value decrease by 5% per year.

    a. Write an exponential depreciation equation to model this situation.

    b. Based on your equation, approximately when will her condominium be worth less than $145,000?

7-7   Home Maintenance and Improvement

Exercises

1. Ruth is setting up the locations of the corners of a 10' by 24' rectangular deck she is going to build in her backyard. To make sure she has a perfect rectangle, she checks to make sure the diagonals are the same.

   a. What should the length of each diagonal be?

   b. What angle does the diagonal make with the longer side of the deck? Round to the nearest degree.

   c. What angle does the diagonal make with the shorter side of the deck? Round to the nearest degree.

2. Jake is installing a staircase so his children can have access to a tree house he built. The rise of the stairs is 7 inches and the run of each stair is 10 inches. What is the slope of the staircase, expressed as a fraction?

3. The Golf King Driving Range is installing a huge net to catch long golf drives. The poles to hold the net up are 50 feet high. The contractor needs to run a wire from the top of the pole to the ground to keep the poles and the net secure. This wire is called a *guy wire*.

   a. If the guy wire runs from the top of the pole to a point on the ground 22 feet from the base of the pole, how long must the guy wire be? Round up to the next highest foot.

   b. What is the slope of the guy wire, expressed as a fraction?

4. Bill bought a set of car ramps so he can work under his car. He drives the car up the ramp and then the wheel sits on top of the shaded rectangle, as shown in the picture.

   a. If side MA has length 9 inches, what is the slope of the ramp, expressed as a fraction?

   b. If side MA has length 9 inches, what is the angle of elevation, <R, of the ramp? Round to the nearest degree.

5. A side view of Rajan's roof is shown in the diagram below.

   a. What is the length of the run of the roof?

   b. What is the pitch of the roof?

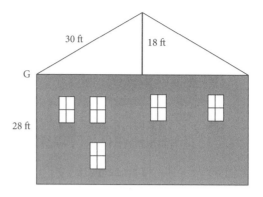

   c. Rajan plans to clean out his gutters, located at G, and he needs to purchase a ladder long enough. If the recommended angle of elevation for the ladder is 66 degrees, how far must he place the foot of the ladder from the house to clean his gutters? Round to the nearest tenth.

   d. How long a ladder must Rajan purchase? Round to the next highest foot.

6. Mark has a tree in his backyard that he wants to make sure cannot fall on his neighbor's house if there is a bad storm. The tree is 49 feet from his neighbor's house. From a point on the ground 35 feet from the tree, the angle of elevation of the top of the tree is 50 degrees. How tall is the tree? Round to the nearest foot.

7. The Glen Head Girl Scout troop is planning to build a ramp for a local park. The Americans with Disabilities Act (ADA) states that handicap ramps for wheelchairs should have a slope of 1/12 or less. A diagram of the ramp is shown below,

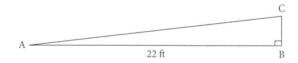

   a. Convert the 22-foot horizontal length into inches.

   b. What, in inches, is the maximum height, BC, the ramp can be to adhere to ADA guidelines? Round to the nearest tenth of an inch.

   c. If BC has length 9 inches, what is the slope of the ramp?

   d. If BC has length 10 inches, what is the angle of elevation of the ramp? Round to the nearest tenth.

8. The Fickman Construction Company is building a rectangular deck that measures 40′ by 20′. They need to run an electric line across the diagonal, underneath the deck. How long is the diagonal of the deck, to the nearest foot?

9. The Wright family purchased a portable movie screen for their backyard. It is held up with poles and guy wires on each side of the screen, as shown in the diagram.

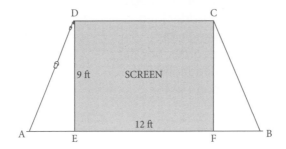

a. If AE = 6 feet, what is the angle of elevation of the guy wire AD? Round to the nearest degree.

b. What is the length of the guy wire? Round to the nearest tenth.

c. How much wire is needed for the two guy wires?

d. How long is AB?

10. From a point 30 feet from the base of a tree, the angle of elevation is 65 degrees, as shown in the diagram. The eye level height is 6 feet.

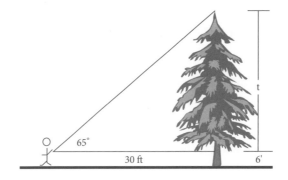

a. Find the value of t to the nearest foot.

b. Find the height of the tree, to the nearest foot.

8-1 Business Organizations

Exercises

1. Avril invested $60,000 in a partnership with Lane, Jules, Ray, Ravi, and Petra. The total investment of all partners was $320,000. What percent of the business does Avril own?

2. The Metropolitan Corporation has issued a total of 2,400,000 shares. The North Side Investment Group owns 7.5% of those shares. How many shares does North Side own?

3. Enid, Eve, and Tammy have formed a partnership. The total investment was $400,000. Enid owns 35.4% and Eve owns 28.8% of the partnership. How much did Tammy invest?

4. Three partners are investing a total of $1,200,000 in a new restaurant. Their investments are in the ratio of 6:8:11. How much did each invest?

5. Alli, Beth, Catie, Dave, Eddie, Franny, and George invested $4,914,000 in a business venture in the ratio of 1:2:3:4:5:6:7 respectively. How much did Alli and George each invest?

6. Dennis owns 24% of a partnership. Bob owns 48% of the partnership. If Rich is the third partner, what percent of the partnership does he own? Write a simplified ratio to represent their investments in the partnership.

7. Angel owns five-eighths of a partnership in a bakery.
    a. What percent of the bakery does Angel own?

    b. Angel's partner, Lisa, owns the remaining portion of the bakery. Write a simplified ratio to represent Angel's ownership to Lisa's ownership in the bakery.

8. Austen owns seven-sixteenths of a jewelry store. The total investment for the store was $832,000. What is the value of Austen's share of the business?

9. Penny owns five-ninths of a movie theater. Penny's investment is worth $450,000. What is the total investment that was made for the movie theater?

10. The Barnaby Corporation issued 2,700,000 shares of stock at its beginning to shareholders. How many shares must a shareowner own to have a majority of the shares?

11. Ella owns 15% of Fitz Incorporated. The rest of the shares are owned equally by the remaining 5 shareholders. What percent of the corporation does each of the other shareholders own?

12. Clinton and Barbara are the partners in a local music shop. They needed $448,500 to start the business. They invested in the ratio of 11:12.

    a. How much money did each invest?

    b. What percent of the business is owned by Clinton? Round to the nearest tenth of a percent.

13. Andrea, Dina, and Lindsay invested in a partnership in the ratio of 7:9:14, respectively. Ten years later, their partnership was worth $1,800,000. Dina decided to move to Europe and sold her part of the partnership to Andrea.

    a. How much did Andrea pay Dina for her share of the partnership? Round to the nearest dollar.

    b. What percent of the business did Andrea own after she bought out Dina? Round to the nearest tenth of a percent.

    c. What was the new ratio of ownership once the business was owned by only Andrea and Lindsay?

14. Mike, Rob, Jon, and Kristy own shares in the Arlington Partnership in the ratio of $a:b:c:d$ respectively. Arlington is now worth E dollars.

    a. Write an algebraic expression for the percent of the partnership that represents Mike's investment.

    b. Jon decides to sell his portion of the partnership to Kristy. Write the new ratio of ownership for Mike, Rob, and Kristy.

    c. Write an algebraic expression for the new percent representing Kristy's ownership.

15. Fifty-five and one-half percent of the shareholders in a fast food chain are under the age of 40. If the corporation is owned by 86,000 investors, how many of the shareholders are 40 and over?

16. The North Salem Stock Club owns x percent of the shares of a certain corporation. Each of the 10 club members owns y shares of that stock. The corporation's ownership is represented by a total of S shares of stock. Express the number of shares of the corporation owned by each club member algebraically.

17. A partnership owned by 25 partners is worth 5.4 million dollars. The partnership loses a lawsuit worth 6.2 million dollars. How much of the settlement is each partner liable for after the partnership is sold? Explain.

8-2 | Stock Market Data

Exercises

1. Use the trading data for Friday, October 20 and Friday, October 27 to answer the questions.

Discovery Group	
October 20	
Last	$38.50
Trade Time	4:00 P.M. ET
Chg	$1.56
Open	$37.22
52-week High	$76.19
52-week Low	$22.78
Sales in 100s	19,700
High	$40.10
Low	$36.77

Discovery Group	
October 27	
Last	$42.00
Trade Time	4:00 P.M. ET
Chg	$1.50
Open	$42.50
52-week High	$76.19
52-week Low	$22.78
Sales in 100s	23,600
High	$42.50
Low	$42.00

a. What was the difference between the high and the low prices on October 20?

b. On October 27, what was the actual volume of Discovery Group shares posted? Write the volume in numerals.

c. At what price did Discovery Group close on October 19?

d. Use the October 19 closing price from above and the October 20 opening price to find the difference in prices as a percent increase. Round to the nearest hundredth percent.

e. On October 21, Discovery Group announced that they would close one of their manufacturing plants. This resulted in a drop in their stock price. It closed at $32. Express the net change from October 20 to October 21 as a percent, rounded to the nearest tenth of a percent.

f. On October 28, Discovery Group announced that they would not be closing the plant. This news caused the price of their stock to rise. It closed at $48.20. Express the net change from October 27 to October 28 as a percent, rounded to the nearest tenth of a percent.

g. Explain why the 52-week high and 52-week low numbers are the same in both charts.

h. Examine the closing price of Discovery Group on October 27. One year earlier, one share closed at 30% higher than that amount. What was the closing price one year earlier?

2. Write each of the following volumes using complete numerals.

    a. Sales in 100s: 82,567

    b. Sales in 100s: 321.78

    c. Sales in 1000s: 12,856

    d. Sales in 10,000s: 6,478.98

    e. Sales in 100,000s: 35,495.235

    f. Sales in 100,000: 3.2

Use the spreadsheet to answer the Exercises 3–7. Use the left side of the equation to indicate in which cell to store the formula.

	A	B	C	D	E	F	G	H
1	Symbol	Stock	Aug. 21 Last	Change	% Change from Aug. 20	Aug. 20 Close	Volume in 100s	Volume in 1000s
2	ABC	American Bicycle Corp.	34.89	3.02		31.87	12345	
3	DEF	Detroit Energy Fund	8.56	0.35	4.3		121	
4	GHI	General Hospital Incorporated	14.7	−0.28		14.98	8123	
5	JKL	Juniper Kansas Luxuries	121.45	−2.95			763542	
6	MNO	Middle Network Offices	75		−0.6	75.45	2637	
7	PQR	Prince Queen Resalers	11.29	0.88				239.478
8	STU	Southern Texas Underwriters	54.92	−3.37				23754.2
9	VWX	Valley Windmill Xperience, Inc.			−1.83	64.88		493004

3. Write a formula that will convert the volume given in 100s into a volume given in 1000s.

    a. Juniper Kansas

    b. Detroit Energy

4. Write a formula that will store the exact volume for each stock in column I.

    a. Valley Windmill

    b. Middle Network

5. Write a formula to determine the close on August 20 for each of the following.

    a. Southern Texas

    b. Prince Queen Resalers

6. Write a formula to determine the percent change for each of the following.

    a. ABC

    b. GHI

7. Calculate each net change.

    a. MNO

    b. VWX

8-3 Stock Market Data Charts

Exercises

Use the stock chart to answer the exercises below for December 14–18.

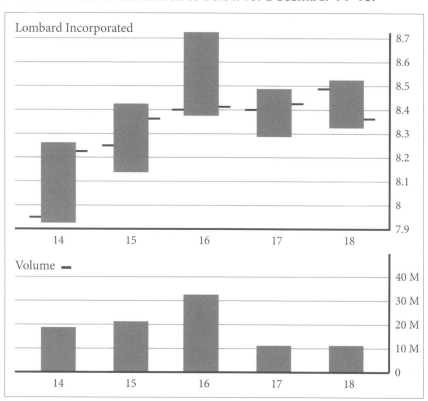

1. Which day had the highest price? Which day had the least low price?

2. Approximately how many shares of Lombard Incorporated were traded over the five days?

3. On what date did the stock close at a price lower than it opened?

4. Find each price.

   a. opening on December 16

   b. high on December 18

   c. low on December 14

   d. closing on December 15

5. Express each net change as a monetary amount and as a percent to the nearest tenth.

   a. from December 14 to December 15

   b. from December 17 to December 18

6. Approximately how many fewer shares were traded on December 18 than on December 16?

Name _____ Date _____

Use the candlestick chart to answer the exercises below for December 14–18.

7. On which days were opening prices higher than the closing prices?

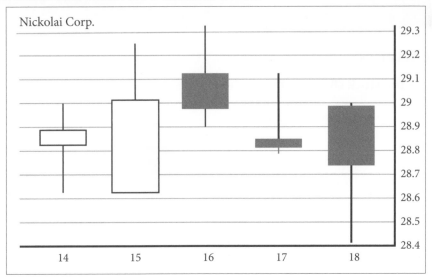

Nickolai Corp.

8. On which days were the closing prices higher than the opening prices?

9. On 12/16, what was the approximate closing price? approximate lowest price?

10. What was the difference between the lowest and highest prices recorded for this period?

11. What does the absence of a line at the bottom of the December 15 bar indicate?

12. Construct a bar chart for the following 5-day period, December 14–December 18.

Day	Open	Close	High	Low	Volume
14	15.98	15.95	16.07	15.93	41,000,000
15	15.83	15.75	16.01	15.65	80,000,000
16	15.80	15.69	15.85	15.67	75,000,000
17	15.59	15.80	15.95	15.56	70,000,000
18	15.91	15.59	15.91	15.59	80,000,000

8-4 Trends In Stock Closing Prices

Exercises

1. Determine the 3-day simple moving averages for the 10 consecutive day closing prices.

   7.78, 7.90, 8.00, 7.97, 7.86, 7.67, 7.60, 7.65, 7.65, 7.70

2. Determine the 5-day simple moving averages for the 10 consecutive day closing prices.

   121.56, 121.60, 121.65, 121.65, 121.60, 121.52, 120, 120.67, 121.50, 121.45

3. Determine the 6-day simple moving averages for the 10 consecutive day closing prices.

   97.70, 97.70, 98, 98.45, 99, 99.68, 101, 101.50, 100, 100.56

4. Determine the 7-day simple moving averages for the 14 consecutive day closing prices for Exxon Mobil listed.

   43.23, 43.23, 43.21, 43, 43.50, 43.55, 43.45, 43.56, 43.76, 44, 44.03, 44.09, 44, 44.02

Determine the simple moving averages (SMA) by subtraction and addition for each set of 10 consecutive day closing prices.

5. 3-day SMA

   $11.97, $11.85, $11.52, $13.17, $14.24
   $15.02, $15.26, $14.96, $13.56, $13.38

6. 4-day SMA

   $26.31, $25.94, $27.65, $27.13, $26.81
   $26.65, $26.55, $25.89, $25.82, $25.87

7. 5-day SMA

   $221.49, $222.15, $221.70, $223.81, $223.00
   $223.03, $222.99, $224.04, $224.12, $224.16

8. 6-day SMA

   $0.65, $0.53, $0.60, $0.63, $0.50,
   $0.55, $0.56, $0.58, $0.59, $0.67

9. Use a spreadsheet to determine the 10-day simple moving averages for General Electric.

17-Sep	16.97	24-Sep	17.06	1-Oct	16.31	8-Oct	16.46	15-Oct	16.79
18-Sep	16.88	25-Sep	16.35	2-Oct	15.45	9-Oct	16.20	16-Oct	16.35
21-Sep	16.43	28-Sep	16.47	5-Oct	15.59	12-Oct	16.36	19-Oct	16.05
22-Sep	17.06	29-Sep	16.91	6-Oct	16.14	13-Oct	16.32	20-Oct	15.80
23-Sep	17.17	30-Sep	16.83	7-Oct	16.03	14-Oct	16.77	21-Oct	15.51

10. Use a spreadsheet to determine the 12-day simple moving averages for Motorola.

4-Aug	7.24	10-Aug	7.17	14-Aug	7.26	20-Aug	7.37	26-Aug	7.48
5-Aug	7.13	11-Aug	7.03	17-Aug	7.06	21-Aug	7.58	27-Aug	7.34
6-Aug	7.11	12-Aug	7.07	18-Aug	7.21	24-Aug	7.48	28-Aug	7.21
7-Aug	7.13	13-Aug	7.28	19-Aug	7.29	25-Aug	7.53	31-Aug	7.18

11. The closing prices for 10 consecutive trading days for a particular stock are given here. Calculate the 5-day simple moving averages and plot both the closing prices and the averages on a graph.

15.19, 15.21, 15.32, 15.40, 15.40, 15.38, 15.41, 15.50, 15.55, 15.47

12. Discuss the implication of the crossover on the 4th day in the graph.

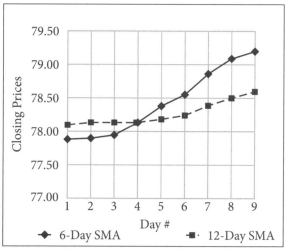

13. Examine the following SMA graph to determine an implication for each crossover.

a. on Day 3

b. on Day 5

c. on Day 9

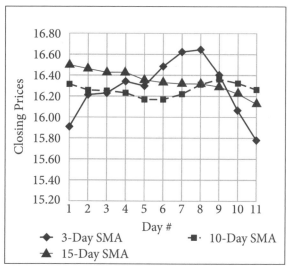

14. Examine the closing prices for 15 consecutive trading days of PDGN.

Trading Day	CLOSE
1	89.67
2	89.5
3	90.12
4	90.69
5	91
6	91.1
7	91.05
8	92.75
9	93
10	94.2
11	94
12	94.9
13	94.95
14	95
15	95.1

a. Determine a linear regression equation that fits the data. Round numbers to the nearest hundredth.

b. Determine a quadratic regression equation that fits this data. Round numbers to the nearest thousandth.

c. Use the equations you found in parts a and b to determine the predicted closing price on the 16th trading day. The actual closing price was $95.99. Which regression equation was a better predictor?

8-5 | Stock Market Ticker

Exercises

Use the following ticker to answer Exercises 1–6. The stock symbols represent the corporations: C, CitiGroup Inc; BAC, Bank of America; F, Ford Motor Corp; and MSI, Motorola Solutions.

> MSI 4.2K @ 72.59 ▼ 0.16   BAC .65K @ 15.28 ▲ 1.11
>
> F 61.8K @ 13.67 ▼ 2.07 C 76K @ 43.54 ▲ 0.09

1. Millie is following the trades of Motorola Solutions. The result of the latest trade is posted on the ticker.

   a. How many shares of MSI were traded and at what price per share?

   b. What was the value of the MSI trade?

   c. Suppose the next MSI trade represents a sale of 1,200 shares at a price that is $0.23 lower than the last transaction. What will Millie see scrolling on the ticker for this transaction?

2. Susan sold her Bank of America shares as indicated on the ticker above.

   a. How many shares did she sell?

   b. For how much did each share sell?

   c. What was the total value of all the shares Susan sold?

   d. Suppose that the next BAC trade that comes across the ticker represents a sale of 34,000 shares at a price that is $2.31 higher than the last transaction. What will Susan see scrolling across her screen for this transaction of BAC?

3. How many shares of Ford are indicated on the ticker?

4. What is the total value of all of the CitiGroup shares traded?

5. Interpret each of the following.

   a. @43.54   b. MSI 4.2K   c. ▲1.11

6. What was the previous day's closing price for each stock?

7. Ron knows that JP Morgan Chase & Co has the ticker symbol JPM. What can Ron learn from the following line of symbols: JPM 0.26K @ 43.43 ▼ 0.98?

8. For their 16th birthday, Liz gave her twin daughters, Adriana and Marina, 3,500 shares of IBM to be split evenly between them. Ten years later, on September 13, the twins sold all of the shares at a price of $127.91. The closing price of IBM on September 12 was $126.13. How did this trade appear on the stock ticker?

9. Jenna contacted her broker and asked him to sell all 4,000 of her Pepsico (PEP) shares on Friday as soon as the trading price hit $59.48 per share. Jenna knew that PEP closed at $58 on Thursday. How will her trade appear on the ticker?

Use the following ticker information to answer Exercises 10–14. The stock symbols represent the corporations: BMY, Bristol-Myers Squibb; AA, Alcoa; INTC, Intel Corp; and MSFT, Microsoft.

> BMY 0.88K @ 62.87 ▼ 0.93   AA 78K @ 10.73 ▲ 1.12
>
> INTC 17.9K @ 32.09 ▼ 1.06   MSFT 0.81K @ 53.52 ▲ 2.23

10. Lucinda put in an order for some shares of Bristol-Myers Squibb.

   a. As shown on the ticker, how many shares did Lucinda buy and for what price per share?

   b. What was the value of Lucinda's trade?

11. Jared has sold his shares of Intel, as indicated on the above ticker.

   a. How many shares did he sell and for what price per share?

   b. What was the total value of all the shares Jared sold?

12. How many shares of Alcoa are indicated on the ticker?

13. What is the total value of all of the Microsoft shares traded?

14. Interpret each of the following.

   a. AA 1.1K   **b.** ▼1.06   **c.** @10.73

15. Write the ticker symbols for each situation.

   a. 1,500 shares of RJS at a price of $13.19, which is $0.92, lower than the previous day's close.

   b. 38,700 shares of EPZ at $39.22, which is $1.83 higher than the previous day's close.

8-6 | Stock Transactions

Exercises

1. Five years ago, Julianne purchased stock for $9,433. Yesterday, she sold the stock for $10,219. What was her gross capital gain?

2. A few years ago, Melky bought 100 shares of a cologne company's stock for $16.77 per share. Last month she sold all of the shares for $11.88 per share. What was her loss?

3. In March of 2009, Jennifer bought shares of stock in the Pepsi-Cola Company for $47 per share. In March 2016, she sold them for $101 per share. Express the increase in price as a percent of the purchase price. Round to the nearest tenth of a percent.

4. Mike bought shares of a brand new corporation that manufactures dish antennas. He bought the stock years ago for $4,100. He recently sold this stock for $7,100. Express his capital gain as a percent of the original purchase price. Round to the nearest tenth of a percent.

5. Fran bought shares in a supermarket chain in early 2016 for $21.11 per share. She sold them later in that same year for $20 per share. Express her loss as a percent of the purchase price. Round to the nearest percent.

6. Andy bought 300 shares of a corporation that manufactures kitchen cabinets. He bought the stock years ago for x dollars. He recently sold this stock for y dollars. Express his capital gain as a percent of the original purchase price algebraically.

7. Ashley bought $1,200 worth of stock in a home improvement store. She does not know what she will sell it for, so let x represent the selling price of all the shares. Express the percent value of Ashley's capital gain algebraically.

8. Jake bought 540 shares of Sound Foundations stock years ago for $44.50 per share. He sold them yesterday for $49.54 per share.

    a. What was the percent increase in the price per share, rounded to the nearest percent?

    b. What was the percent capital gain for the 540 shares, rounded to the nearest percent?

9. Lisa bought h shares of Home Depot stock for x dollars per share. She sold all of the shares years later for y dollars per share. Express her capital gain algebraically.

10. Jack bought w shares of Xerox stock for a total of t dollars. Write an expression for the price he paid per share.

11. Bill purchased shares of Apple for *a* dollars per share. He plans to sell them as soon as the price rises 20%. Express the price he will sell his shares at algebraically.

12. Maria purchased 1,000 shares of stock for $65.50 per share in 2009. She sold them in 2016 for $55.10 per share. Express her loss as a percent of the purchase price, rounded to the nearest tenth of a percent.

13. Allen purchased shares of stock for *x* dollars in 2016. He sold them weeks later for *y* dollars per share. Express his capital gain as a percent of the purchase price.

14. Anna bought 350 shares of stock for *p* dollars per share. She sold them last week for *s* dollars per share. Express her capital gain algebraically in terms of *p* and s.

15. Max bought *x* shares of stock for *y* dollars per share. His broker told him to sell them when they earn a *p* percent capital gain. Express the total selling price of the shares algebraically.

16. Donnie bought *x* shares of stock for *y* dollars per share years ago. His stock rose in price, and eventually hit a price that would earn him a 137% capital gain. He decided to sell 75% of his *x* shares.

   a. Represent 75% of the *x* shares algebraically.

   b. Represent the capital gain earned on each of the shares that were sold algebraically.

   c. Represent the capital gain earned on all of the shares that were sold algebraically.

   d. Represent the total value of the shares that were sold algebraically.

   e. Years later, the company stock falls to its lowest price of $3 per share. Donnie sells the rest of his shares. Write an expression for the total selling price of all the shares sold at $3.

17. Fill in the missing purchase prices and selling prices for stock trades in the table.

Number of Shares	Purchase Price per Share	Selling Price per Share	Capital Gain or Loss	Percent Gain or Loss (nearest tenth of a percent)
500	$54	$62	a.	b.
100	c.	$12	$700	d.
650	$31	e.	f.	15% (gain)
1,300	g.	$23	–$7,800	h.

8-7 Stock Transaction Fees

Exercises

1. Juaquin made three trades through his online discount broker, Electro-Trade. Electro-Trade charges a fee of x dollars per trade. Juaquin's first purchase was for $2,456 without the fee, his second purchase was for $3,000 without the fee, and his third purchase was for $2,119 without the fee. If the total of the purchases was $7,623 including broker fees, what does Electro-Trade charge per trade?

2. Ted made x transactions last month using Trades-Are-Us online brokers, which charges y dollars per trade. Each transaction was a sale of stock. The total value of all the shares Ted sold was t dollars. The brokers sold the stock, took out their fees, and sent Ted a check for the rest of the money he was owed. Express the value of the check Ted received from the broker algebraically.

3. The fee schedule for the Glen Head Brokerage Firm is shown in the table below.

Fee Schedule for Glen Head Brokerage Firm	Online Trades	Telephone Trades (automated)	Trades Using a Broker
Portfolio Value less than $100,000	x dollars per trade	online fee plus r dollars	c percent commission plus online fee
Portfolio Value greater than $100,000	y dollars per trade	online fee plus q dollars	p percent of commission plus online fee

   a. Joy purchased s dollars worth of stock using a broker from Glen Head Brokerage Firm. The current value of her portfolio is $21,771. Express algebraically the broker fee she must pay for this transaction.

   b. Jonathan has a portfolio worth 1.1 million dollars. He made w automated telephone trades during the past year, buying and selling $90,000 worth of stock. Express his total broker fee algebraically.

4. Meghan purchases $41,655 worth of stock on her broker's advice and pays her broker a 1.5% broker fee. She sells it when it increases to $47,300, months later, and uses a discount broker who charges $19 per trade. Compute her net proceeds after the broker fees are taken out. Round to the nearest dollar.

5. Fred is a broker who charges 1% per stock transaction. A competing online broker charges $26 per trade. If someone is planning to purchase stock, at what purchase price would Fred's commission be the same as the online broker fee?

6. Barbara purchased stock last year for $8,500 and paid a 1.25% broker fee. She sold it for $7,324 and had to pay a 0.5% broker fee. Compute her net proceeds.

7. Adam purchased stock several years ago for *x* dollars and had to pay a 1.5% broker fee. He sold that stock last month for *y* dollars and paid a discount broker $15 for the sale. Express his net proceeds algebraically.

8. Steven purchases *x* dollars worth of stock on his broker's advice and pays his broker a flat $12 broker fee. The value of the shares falls to *f* dollars months later, and Steven uses a broker who charges 1% commission to make the sale. Express his net proceeds algebraically.

9. Rich bought 20,000 dollars worth of stock and paid a *y* percent commission. Dan purchased 17,000 dollars worth of stock and paid a *q* percent commission. Find a value of *y* and a value of *q*, where *y* and *q* are each less than 3, such that Rich's commission is less than Dan's.

10. If you bought 600 shares of stock for $41 per share, paid a 1% commission, and then sold them 6 months later for $41.75 per share, with a $30 flat fee, are your net proceeds positive or negative? Explain.

11. Mr. Wankel bought *x* shares of stock for *y* dollars per share last month. He paid his broker a flat fee of $14. He sold the stock this month for *p* dollars per share, and paid his broker a 2% commission. Express his net proceeds algebraically.

12. Michelle Miranda Investing charges their customers a 1% commission. The Halloran Group, a discount broker, charges $13.75 per trade. For what dollar amount of stock would Miranda charge double the commission of Halloran?

13. CoronaCorp, a discount broker, charges their customers *x* dollars per trade. The Sclair Bear & Bull House charges a 1.5% commission. For what value of stock would both brokers charge the same commission? Express your answer algebraically.

14. Mrs. Cowley purchases $32,000 worth of stock on her broker's advice and pays her broker a 0.75% broker fee. She is forced to sell it when it falls to $25,100 two years later, and uses a discount broker who charges $17 per trade. Compute her net loss after the broker fees are taken out.

15. Sal bought *x* shares of a stock that sold for $31.50 per share. He paid a 1% commission on the sale. The total cost of his investment, including the broker fee, was $5,726.70. How many shares did he purchase?

16. Mrs. Didamo purchased stock years ago for *d* dollars and had to pay a flat $20 broker fee. The price dropped but she needed money for college so she sold it at a loss, for *x* dollars, plus a 1% broker fee. Express her net loss algebraically.

8-8   Stock Splits

Exercises

1. Yesterday the Rockville Corporation instituted a 2-for-1 stock split. Before the split, the market share price was $63.44 per share and the corporation had 2.3 billion shares outstanding.

    a. What was the pre-split market cap for Rockville?

    b. What was the post-split number of shares outstanding for Rockville?

    c. What was the post-split market price per share for Rockville?

2. Suppose that a corporation has a market capitalization of $97,000,000,000 with 450M outstanding shares. Calculate the price per share to the nearest cent.

3. Tele-Mart instituted a 5-for-1 split in April. After the split, Roberta owned 1,860 shares. How many shares had she owned before the split?

4. In May, the Black Oyster Corporation instituted a 3-for-1 split. After the split, the price of one share was x dollars. What was the pre-split price per share, expressed algebraically?

5. Patterson's Appliances was considering a 2-for-3 reverse split. If the pre-split market cap was $634,000,000, what would the post split market cap be?

6. Faye owned 1,300 shares of Wonderband Corp. Last week, a 2-for-1 split was executed. The pre-split price per share was w dollars.

    a. Determine the number of shares Faye owned after the split.

    b. Write an algebraic expression for the price per share after the split.

    c. Express the total value of the Wonderband stock Faye owned algebraically after the split.

7. Suppose that before a stock split, a share was selling for x dollars. After the stock split, the price was $\frac{2x}{3}$ dollars per share. What was the stock split ratio?

8. On December 14, XTO Energy Inc. executed a 5-for-4 split. At that time, Ed owned 553 shares of that stock. The price per share was $55.60 before the split. After the split, he received a check for a fractional part of a share. What was the amount of that check?

9. Yesterday, Tenser Inc. executed a 2-for-1 split. Jamie was holding 500 shares of the stock before the split and each was worth $34.12.

    a. What was the total value of her shares before the split?

    b. How many shares did she hold after the split?

    c. What was the post-split price per share?

    d. What was the total value of Jamie's shares after the split?

10. On May 30, Universe Inc. announced a 5-for-2 stock split. Before the split, the corporation had 340 million shares outstanding with a market value of $73.25 per share.

    a. How many shares were outstanding after the split?

    b. What was the post-split price per share?

    c. Show that this split was a "monetary non-event" for the corporation.

11. Two days ago, Lisa owned y shares of Postaero. Yesterday, the corporation instituted a 3-for-2 stock split. Before the split, each share was worth x dollars.

    a. How many shares did she hold after the split? Express your answer algebraically.

    b. What was the price per share after the split? Express your answer algebraically.

    c. Show that the split was a "monetary non-event" for Lisa.

12. Last week, Donna owned x shares of Spoonaire stock. Yesterday, the company instituted a 2-for-5 reverse split. The pre-split price per share was $3.40. The number of shares outstanding before the split was y.

    a. How many shares did Donna hold after the split? What was the post-split price per share?

    b. What was the post-split number of outstanding shares? What was the post-split market cap?

13. After a 5-for-2 stock split, Laura owned x shares of Skroyco stock. Each share was worth $16 after the split. What was the value of one share before the split?

8-9 Dividend Income

Exercises

1. Jared is purchasing a stock that pays an annual dividend of $3.42 per share.

   a. If he purchases 400 shares for $53.18 per share, what would his annual income be from dividends?

   b. What is the yield, to the nearest tenth of a percent?

2. Marianne purchased s shares of a corporation that pays a d dollars quarterly dividend per share. What is her annual dividend income, expressed algebraically?

3. Adrianna owns 1,000 shares of a corporation that pays an annual dividend of $2.17 per share. How much should she expect to receive on a quarterly dividend check?

4. Mr. Fierro owns x shares of stock. The annual dividend per share is q dollars. Express Mr. Fierro's quarterly dividend amount algebraically.

5. The annual dividend per share of a certain stock is d dollars. The current price of the stock is x dollars per share. What is the percent yield of the stock, expressed algebraically?

6. You bought x shares of a stock for y dollars per share. The annual dividend per share is d. Express the percent yield algebraically.

7. Stock in the Sister Golden Hair Shampoo Company was selling for $44.64 per share, and it was paying a $2.08 annual dividend. It underwent a 2-for-1 split.

   a. What was the new price of one share after the split?

   b. If you owned 300 shares before the split, how many shares did you own after the split?

   c. What was the annual dividend per share after the split?

   d. What was the yield, to the nearest tenth of a percent, before the split?

   e. What was the yield, to the nearest tenth of a percent, after the split?

8. One share of West World stock pays an annual dividend of $1.50. Today West World closed at $26.50 with a net change of −3.50. What was the stock's yield at yesterday's closing price?

9. The stock in a real estate corporation was selling for $6 per share, with an annual dividend of $0.12. It underwent a 2-for-5 reverse split.

   a. What was the value of a share after the reverse split?

   b. What was the annual dividend after the reverse split?

   c. What was the yield after the reverse split?

10. One share of Liam Corp. stock pays an annual dividend of d dollars. Today Liam closed at c dollars with a net change of $+h$. Write an expression for the stock's yield at yesterday's close.

11. In the summer of 2016, Apple was paying a $0.57 annual dividend. What would you receive on a quarterly dividend check if you had x shares of Apple at that time? Express your answer algebraically.

12. A corporation was paying a $4.20 annual dividend. The stock underwent a 3-for-2 split. What is the new annual dividend per share?

13. If you received a dividend check for d dollars and your stock had a quarterly dividend of p dollars, express the number of shares you owned algebraically.

14. Complete the missing entries in the table below. Round all dollar amounts to the nearest cent, and round all percents to the nearest tenth of a percent.

Price per Share at Wednesday's Close	Dividend	Wednesday's Net Change	Tuesday's Closing Price	Tuesday's Yield	Wednesday's Yield
$23	$0.96	+1	a.	b.	c.
$54.10	$2	d.	$54.88	e.	f.
W	D	C	g.	h.	i.

15. Pat owned 2,500 shares of Speed King Corporation, and received a quarterly dividend check for $925. What was the annual dividend for one share of Speed King?

16. Janet owned 114 shares of a corporation, and received a quarterly dividend check for y dollars. Express the annual dividend for one share algebraically.

17. A stock's dividend is not changing, yet its yield has fallen over the past five consecutive days. What had happened to the price of the stock over those last five days?

18. A stock's dividend was decreased on Tuesday. Does that mean its yield is lower on Tuesday than it was on Monday? Explain.

9-1 | Inventions

Exercises

1. Decide whether each of the following questions or statements are biased or not. (The random number table appears on page 145 and the normal curve table appears on page 146.)

   a. Do you think a person who doesn't vote is irresponsible?

   b. Do you agree or disagree with the fact that eating in class is not permitted?

   c. Don't you think Mr. Menchel should let us use calculators more often?

   d. How would you describe Mr. Rogala's car?

   e. Do you feel that hockey is more exciting than tennis?

   f. Do you avoid fast-food restaurants as part of a healthy diet?

2. A cosmetics company is deciding whether or not to modify a lipstick product they manufacture. They need to do some research. They want to test if women react differently to medicated lipsticks. They randomly select 500 women and randomly assign them to two different groups. One uses the medicated lipstick and the other uses non-medicated lipstick. Is this an example of an observational study or an experimental study?

3. A music school needs to test some new music stand designs, and they need to select 100 students randomly from an enrollment of 719 students.

   a. If they use the random number table, how many digits will they need to use to represent the students?

   b. If they use the random number table and start on line 10, what are the numbers of the first five students who will be selected?

4. A random group of 90 gas stations, from the 121,000 gas stations in the United States, is to be taken using the random number table.

   a. How many digits will be needed to be assigned to each gas station?

   b. Would it be possible for the random sample of 90 gas stations to contain only California gas stations?

   c. Would it be probable for the random sample of 90 gas stations to be all from California?

   d. Would it be possible for the random sample of 90 gas stations to be all the same brand?

   e. Would it be probable for the random sample of 90 gas stations to be the same brand?

5. A pharmaceutical company is testing a new drug to see if its effectiveness on lowering blood pressure is superior to the old drug. They randomly select 2,000 people and split them into two groups. One group takes the old drug and the other group takes the new medication. Is this an example of an observational study or an experiment?

6. The Plastico Plastics Company wants to test if its new cell phone screen protector is more resistant to scratches for a longer period of time than the current type of screen protector they manufacture. They will test 100 old covers and 100 new covers.

   a. Draw a diagram for a completely randomized design that describes the experiment.

   b. The life of the old protector is normally distributed with mean 42 months and standard deviation 3 months. The average life of the new protector was 52 months with a standard deviation of 2 months. Explain if you think the new protector is superior.

   c. If the new protector from part b had an average life of 43 months, would you believe the new protector is superior? Explain.

7. The Forever Tread Tire Company manufactures bicycle tires. They have developed a new type of tire that they plan to test on 200 customers' bicycles, randomly selected from their list of 8,476 customers.

   a. If they start on line 18 of the random number table, what will be the numbers of the first three customers selected?

   b. Why will a matched-pairs design be better than a completely randomized design for this study?

8. A holiday tree farm has developed a soil additive they think will make their trees grow faster, and taller. They need to conduct an experiment. They need to plant trees randomly into different containers—some with the soil additive and some without.

   a. Does a random assignment of trees guarantee that all the naturally heartier trees will not all be tested with the soil additive?

   b. Is it probable that all the heartier seeds will be placed with only the soil additive?

   c. If the test is conducted and the trees treated with the new fertilizer do in fact grow taller, and faster, would the company believe the soil additive worked as intended or that all the better, heartier trees happened to be, by chance, assigned to the new fertilizer containers?

9. The Power-Sure Battery Company designed a new type of long-lasting battery and they are testing it so they can set up an advertising campaign. They are going to pick 80 batteries from the first lot of 900 batteries to see if the batteries will last as many hours as they claim.

a. If they number the batteries 001–900 and start at line 3 on the random number table, what are the numbers of the first five batteries that will be tested for defects?

b. If the lifetime of the new batteries in a flashlight is normally distributed with mean 110 hours and standard deviation 10 hours, and they guarantee that their batteries will last at least 100 hours, what percent of the batteries will not meet that standard?

TABLE 1   Random Numbers

Row																				
1	4	5	1	8	5	0	3	3	7	1	2	8	4	5	1	1	0	9	5	7
2	4	2	2	5	8	0	4	5	7	0	7	0	3	6	6	1	3	1	3	1
3	8	9	9	3	4	3	5	0	6	3	9	1	1	8	2	6	9	2	0	9
4	8	9	0	7	2	9	9	0	4	7	6	7	4	7	1	3	4	3	5	3
5	5	7	3	1	0	3	7	4	7	8	5	2	0	1	3	7	7	6	3	6
6	0	9	3	8	7	6	7	9	9	5	6	2	5	6	5	8	4	2	6	4
7	4	1	0	1	0	2	2	0	4	7	5	1	1	9	4	7	9	7	5	1
8	6	4	7	3	6	3	4	5	1	2	3	1	1	8	0	0	4	8	2	0
9	8	0	2	8	7	9	3	8	4	0	4	2	0	8	9	1	2	3	3	2
10	9	4	6	0	6	9	7	8	8	2	5	2	9	6	0	1	4	6	0	5
11	6	6	9	5	7	4	4	6	3	2	0	6	0	8	9	1	3	6	1	8
12	0	7	1	7	7	7	2	9	7	8	7	5	8	8	6	9	8	4	1	0
13	6	1	3	0	9	7	3	3	6	6	0	4	1	8	3	2	6	7	6	8
14	2	2	3	6	2	1	3	0	2	2	6	6	9	7	0	2	1	2	5	8
15	0	7	1	7	4	2	0	0	0	1	3	1	2	0	4	7	8	4	1	0
16	6	6	5	1	6	1	8	1	5	5	2	6	2	0	1	1	5	2	3	6
17	9	9	6	2	5	3	5	9	8	3	7	5	0	1	3	9	3	8	0	8
18	9	9	9	6	1	2	9	3	4	6	5	6	4	6	5	8	2	7	4	0
19	2	5	6	3	1	9	8	1	1	0	3	5	6	7	9	1	4	5	2	0
20	5	1	1	9	8	1	2	1	1	6	9	8	1	8	1	9	9	1	2	0
21	1	9	8	0	7	4	6	8	4	0	3	0	8	1	1	0	6	2	3	2
22	9	7	0	9	6	3	8	9	9	7	0	6	5	4	3	6	5	0	3	2
23	1	7	6	4	8	2	0	3	9	6	3	6	2	1	0	7	7	3	1	7
24	6	2	5	8	2	0	7	8	6	4	6	6	8	9	2	0	6	9	0	4
25	1	5	7	1	1	1	9	5	1	4	5	2	8	3	4	3	0	7	3	5
26	1	4	6	6	5	6	0	1	9	4	0	5	2	7	6	4	3	6	8	8
27	1	8	5	0	2	1	6	8	0	7	7	2	6	2	6	7	5	4	8	7
28	7	8	7	4	6	5	4	3	7	9	3	9	2	7	9	5	4	2	3	1
29	1	6	3	2	8	3	7	3	0	7	2	4	8	0	9	9	9	4	7	0
30	2	8	9	0	8	1	6	8	1	7	3	1	3	0	9	7	2	5	7	9
31	0	7	8	8	6	5	7	5	5	4	0	0	3	4	1	2	7	3	7	9
32	8	4	0	1	4	5	1	9	1	1	2	1	5	3	2	8	5	5	7	5
33	7	3	5	9	7	0	4	9	1	2	1	3	2	5	1	9	3	3	8	3
34	4	7	2	6	7	6	9	9	2	7	8	7	5	5	5	2	4	4	3	4
35	9	3	3	7	0	7	0	5	7	5	6	9	5	4	3	1	4	6	6	8
36	0	2	4	9	7	8	1	6	3	8	7	8	0	5	6	7	2	7	5	0
37	7	1	0	1	8	4	7	1	2	9	3	8	0	0	8	7	9	2	8	6
38	9	7	9	4	4	5	3	1	9	3	4	5	0	6	3	5	9	6	9	8
39	0	4	2	5	0	0	9	9	6	4	0	6	9	0	3	8	3	5	7	2
40	0	7	1	2	3	6	1	7	9	3	9	5	4	6	8	4	8	8	0	6
41	3	5	6	6	2	4	4	5	6	3	7	8	7	6	5	2	0	4	3	2
42	6	6	8	5	5	2	9	7	9	3	3	1	6	9	5	9	7	1	1	2
43	9	5	0	4	3	1	1	7	3	9	2	7	7	4	7	0	3	1	2	8
44	5	1	7	8	9	4	2	2	9	2	8	9	9	8	0	6	3	7	2	1
45	1	6	3	9	4	1	3	2	1	1	8	5	6	3	4	1	9	3	1	7
46	4	4	8	6	4	0	3	8	3	8	3	5	9	5	9	4	8	3	9	4
47	7	7	6	6	4	5	4	4	8	4	4	0	3	9	8	5	2	0	2	3
48	2	5	6	6	3	7	0	6	5	6	9	0	1	9	5	2	6	9	1	2

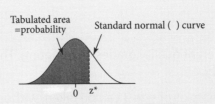

Standard normal
probabilities (continued)

Tabulated area
=probability

Standard normal ( ) curve

0   z*

z*	.00	.01	.02	.03	.04	.05	.06	.07	.08	.09
0.0	.5000	.5040	.5080	.5120	.5160	.5199	.5239	.5279	.5319	.5359
0.1	.5398	.5438	.5478	.5517	.5557	.5596	.5636	.5675	.5714	.5753
0.2	.5793	.5832	.5871	.5910	.5948	.5987	.6026	.6064	.6103	.6141
0.3	.6179	.6217	.6255	.6293	.6331	.6368	.6406	.6443	.6480	.6517
0.4	.6554	.6591	.6628	.6664	.6700	.6736	.6772	.6808	.6844	.6879
0.5	.6915	.6950	.6985	.7019	.7054	.7088	.7123	.7157	.7190	.7224
0.6	.7257	.7291	.7324	.7357	.7389	.7422	.7454	.7486	.7517	.7549
0.7	.7580	.7611	.7642	.7673	.7704	.7734	.7764	.7794	.7823	.7852
0.8	.7881	.7910	.7939	.7967	.7995	.8023	.8051	.8078	.8106	.8133
0.9	.8159	.8186	.8212	.8238	.8264	.8289	.8315	.8340	.8365	.8389
1.0	.8413	.8438	.8461	.8485	.8508	.8531	.8554	.8577	.8599	.8621
1.1	.8643	.8665	.8686	.8708	.8729	.8749	.8770	.8790	.8810	.8830
1.2	.8849	.8869	.8888	.8907	.8925	.8944	.8962	.8980	.8997	.9015
1.3	.9032	.9049	.9066	.9082	.9099	.9115	.9131	.9147	.9162	.9177
1.4	.9192	.9207	.9222	.9236	.9251	.9265	.9279	.9292	.9306	.9319
1.5	.9332	.9345	.9357	.9370	.9382	.9394	.9406	.9418	.9429	.9441
1.6	.9452	.9463	.9474	.9484	.9495	.9505	.9515	.9525	.9535	.9545
1.7	.9554	.9564	.9573	.9582	.9591	.9599	.9608	.9616	.9625	.9633
1.8	.9641	.9649	.9656	.9664	.9671	.9678	.9686	.9693	.9699	.9706
1.9	.9713	.9719	.9726	.9732	.9738	.9744	.9750	.9756	.9761	.9767
2.0	.9772	.9778	.9783	.9788	.9793	.9798	.9803	.9808	.9812	.9817
2.1	.9821	.9826	.9830	.9834	.9838	.9842	.9846	.9850	.9854	.9857
2.2	.9861	.9864	.9868	.9871	.9875	.9878	.9881	.9884	.9887	.9890
2.3	.9893	.9896	.9898	.9901	.9904	.9906	.9909	.9911	.9913	.9916
2.4	.9918	.9920	.9922	.9925	.9927	.9929	.9931	.9932	.9934	.9936
2.5	.9938	.9940	.9941	.9943	.9945	.9946	.9948	.9949	.9951	.9952
2.6	.9953	.9955	.9956	.9957	.9959	.9960	.9961	.9962	.9963	.9964
2.7	.9965	.9966	.9967	.9968	.9969	.9970	.9971	.9972	.9973	.9974
2.8	.9974	.9975	.9976	.9977	.9977	.9978	.9979	.9979	.9980	.9981
2.9	.9981	.9982	.9982	.9983	.9984	.9984	.9985	.9985	.9986	.9986
3.0	.9987	.9987	.9987	.9988	.9988	.9989	.9989	.9989	.9990	.9990
3.1	.9990	.9991	.9991	.9991	.9992	.9992	.9992	.9992	.9993	.9993
3.2	.9993	.9993	.9994	.9994	.9994	.9994	.9994	.9995	.9995	.9995
3.3	.9995	.9995	.9995	.9996	.9996	.9996	.9996	.9996	.9996	.9997
3.4	.9997	.9997	.9997	.9997	.9997	.9997	.9997	.9997	.9997	.9998
3.5	.9998	.9998	.9998	.9998	.9998	.9998	.9998	.9998	.9998	.9998
3.6	.9998	.9998	.9999	.9999	.9999	.9999	.9999	.9999	.9999	.9999
3.7	.9999	.9999	.9999	.9999	.9999	.9999	.9999	.9999	.9999	.9999
3.8	.9999	.9999	.9999	.9999	.9999	.9999	.9999	.9999	.9999	1.0000

9-2 Market Research

Exercises

1. Just Carpets has eight different quality grades of carpeting. Three types are being selected for a corporate test on durability.

   a. How many different samples of size 3 can be taken, without replacement?

   b. How many different samples of size 5 can be taken without replacement?

2. The Smithtown Highway Department is doing a survey on potholes and road conditions. They send a survey to all registered voters in their locale. Explain why this surveying technique is poor due to undercoverage.

3. As part of a quality control test on tennis racquets, Xander has to use a new racquet for 60 minutes each day for a month. Xander skips days, sometimes doesn't do the entire 60 minutes, and sometimes he plays for more than 60 minutes. Is this an example of undercoverage or nonresponse? Explain.

4. A sporting goods store sells 10 brands of golf clubs. Four will be randomly chosen to be put on sale this week. If one of the four must be the Golf King brand, how many different combinations of four can be put on sale?

5. A local YMCA is looking to get feedback on its swim program from the 200 people who are enrolled in swimming lessons. They are taking a stratified random sample of 50 swimming students because they want the sample to have the same percentage breakdown as the entire group of swimmers. The following table gives the percent breakdown of swim students at this YMCA:

   a. How many elementary aged students should be randomly selected for this survey?

Age Group	Percent
Elementary School	20%
Teenagers	32%
Adults	48%

   b. How many adults should be randomly selected for this survey?

   c. If the YMCA had taken a simple random sample, would have it been possible to have the sample be comprised solely of elementary school students? Explain.

6. The Bel Air Vintage Car Company manufactures replacement parts for old cars. A new machine that manufactures steering wheels produced the following number of defective wheels during the last five-day work week:

Monday (M) 7
Tuesday (U) 18
Wednesday (W) 21
Thursday (H) 31
Friday (F) 33

a. Find the range of the distribution of defects.

b. There are five different samples of size 4 possible. List the five possible samples using the letters M, U, W, H, F.

c. Find the range of each of the five samples found in part b.

d. Find the mean of the five sample ranges from part c.

e. Does the mean of the five sample ranges equal the original range you found in part a?

f. Is the range an unbiased estimator?

g. Find the mean of the original distribution of defects.

h. Is the mean an unbiased estimator?

i. Find the standard deviation σ of the original distribution. Round to the nearest hundredth.

7. The economics department of a local college is looking to determine the banking knowledge of their graduating seniors. Professor Klopfer has a class of seniors in his macroeconomics class and agrees to give the survey there. Explain why this survey is biased.

8. The Ticket to Read bookstore is planning to analyze the spending habits of college students. A professor of freshman physics volunteers to have his class take the survey.

a. What type of sample is this?

b. Can you give a disadvantage of surveying this way?

c. Is limiting the survey to freshman is an example of undercoverage or nonresponse?

9. A local Honda dealer is looking to determine the public's opinion on foreign versus domestic automobiles. They send a survey to all of their customers. Explain why this survey is biased.

10. The Fit It Fast tool company is planning to address a recent problem with theft of tools. The management is doing a survey of random employees. They randomly select 100 employees and have them fill out an anonymous questionnaire. Which do you think is a greater problem in this scenario, nonresponse or undercoverage? Explain.

11. Lawnmasters Landscaping is planning a marketing strategy for the upcoming year. They plan on doing on survey to see how many residents in their neighborhoods mow their own lawns. They have their secretaries randomly call home weekdays during their 9am–5pm work shift, and find out that only 17% of the homeowners mow their own lawns. Do you think this is an overestimate, underestimate, or good approximation of the actual population percent of people who mow their own lawns? Explain.

12. The local tax assessor of Peconic County is seeking information on requiring taxpayers to pay their taxes electronically instead of with checks in the mail. They send a survey to all residents who served jury duty within the past two years in their locale. Explain why this surveying technique is poor.

9-3 Supply and Demand

Exercises

1. Wayne's Widget World sells widgets to stores for $9.20 each. A local store marks them up $8.79. What is the retail price at this store?

2. The wholesale price of an item is w dollars. The retail price is p percent higher. Express the retail price algebraically.

3. The Knockey Corporation sells hockey sticks at a wholesale price of $103. If a store marks this up 106%, what is the retail price?

4. A tire company sells bicycle tires to retailers for t dollars. The Mineola Bike Shop marks them up 80%. Express the retail price at the Mineola Bike Shop algebraically.

5. The following graph shows the supply and demand curves for a widget.

   a. Explain what will happen if the price is set at $9.

   b. Use the graph above to explain what will happen if the price is set at $2.75.

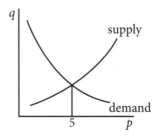

6. An automobile DVD/navigation system sells to stores at a wholesale price of $497. A popular national chain store sells them for $879.99. What is the markup?

7. A guitar sells for a retail price of g dollars. The wholesale price of the guitar is w. Write an expression for the markup and an expression for the percent of the markup.

8. An automobile ski rack is sold to stores at a wholesale price of $38. If a store has a $23 markup, what is the retail price of the ski rack? Find the percent of the markup, to the nearest percent.

9. A manufacturer takes a poll of several retailers to determine how many widgets they would buy at different wholesale prices. The results are shown. What is the equation of the demand function? Round values to the nearest hundredth. Use the demand function to determine how many widgets, to the nearest hundred, retailers would buy at a price of $20.

Wholesale Price	23	26	28	30	33	35	37	40
Quantities Retailers Will Purchase (1,000s)	4,000	3,450	3,100	2,550	2,000	1,900	1,750	1,400

10. The graph shows supply and demand curves for the AquaPod, a digital music player for scuba divers.

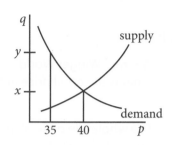

  a. What is the equilibrium price?

  b. What will happen if the price is set at $35?

  c. How many AquaPods are demanded at a price of $35?

  d. How many AquaPods are supplied at a price of $40?

  e. What will happen if the price is set at $45?

11. The Greencup Company produces paper cups. They have developed a new type of insulated cup that is biodegradable and doesn't allow the cup to get too hot to hold. They want to use the demand function to help them set a price. They survey dozens of retailers to get an approximation of how many cups would be demanded at each price.

Wholesale Price p (pack of 50)	$5	$5.50	$6	$6.50	$7	$7.50	$8	$8.50	$9	$9.50
Quantity, q (1,000s)	5,100	4,900	4,600	4,200	3,700	2,400	2,100	1,600	700	200

  a. Find the equation of the linear regression line. Round to the nearest thousandth.

  b. Give the slope of the regression line and give an interpretation of its units.

  c. Find the correlation coefficient and interpret the value. Round to the nearest thousandth.

  d. Based on the regression line, how many packages of cups would be demanded at a wholesale price of $4? Round to the nearest hundred.

  e. Was your answer to part d an example of extrapolation or interpolation? Explain.

  f. If the company sold 5,100,000 packages of cups at a price of $5 each, how much money would they take in?

  g. If the company sold 200,000 packages of cups at a price of $9.50 each, how much money would they take in?

  h. Compare your answers to parts f and g. Why is it not correct to conclude that more profit is made by selling for $5 than for $9.50?

9-4 Fixed and Variable Expenses

Exercises

1. The fixed expenses for producing widgets are $947,900. The labor and materials required for each widget produced costs $16.44. Represent the total expenses as a function of the quantity q produced.

2. A widget manufacturer's expense equation is $E = 14q + 29,000$. What are the variable costs to produce one widget?

3. The Catania Cat Corporation manufactures litter boxes for cats. Their expense function is $E = 4.18q + 82,000$. Find the average cost of producing 10,000 litter boxes.

4. The expense function for a certain item is $E = 2.95q + 712,000$. Express the average cost of producing q items algebraically.

5. The Mizzi Corporation has created a demand function for one of its wrench sets. It expresses the quantity demanded in terms of the wholesale price p, and it was created by surveying retailers and using linear regression. The demand function is $q = -98p + 5,788$. Their expense function is $E = 23q + 68,000$. Express the expense function as a function in terms of p.

6. A corporation's expense function is $E = 7.50q + 34,000$. The demand function was determined to be $q = -5.5p + 6,000$. Express the expense function in terms of the price.

7. Wexler's manufactures widgets. They create a monthly expense equation of all expenses in one month of manufacturing. The expense equation is $E = 2.10q + 7,600$. They plan to sell the widgets to retailers at a wholesale price of $3.50 each.

   a. How many widgets must be sold so that the income from the widgets is equal to the expense of producing them? Round to the nearest widget.

   b. If the company sells 2,900 widgets, how much money will they lose?

8. Find the breakeven point for the expense equation $E = 6.25q + 259,325$ and the revenue function $R = 12q$.

9. The NFW Corporation produces a product with fixed expenses of f dollars and variable expenses of v dollars per item. If q represents quantity produced, write the expense function.

10. The Burden Corporation manufactures racquets. The racquets have the expense equation $E = rq + f$. What is the average cost of producing x racquets?

11. The DiMonte Corporation invented a new type of sunglass lens. Their variable expenses are $12.66 per unit, and their fixed expenses are $111,200.

    a. How much does it cost them to produce one lens? 15,000 lenses?

    b. Express the expense function algebraically. What is the slope of the expense function?

    c. If the slope is interpreted as a rate, give the units to use.

    d. What is the average cost, to the nearest cent, of producing 15,000 lenses?

    e. What is the average cost, to the nearest cent, of producing 17,000 lenses?

    f. As the number of lenses increased from 15,000 to 17,000, did the average expense per lens increase or decrease?

12. The expense equation for a new business venture is $E = 4.55q + 28,500$. If the owners have $100,000 to start up this operation, what quantity can they produce initially if they spend all of this money on production? Round to the nearest hundred units.

13. The graph shows Expense (*E*) and Revenue (*R*) functions and several different levels of quantity produced.

    a. What are the coordinates of the breakeven point?

    b. If *U* units are produced, will there be a profit or a loss?

    c. Compare the profit made if *W* units are produced to the profit made if *T* units are produced. Which level of production yields a greater profit? How can you tell?

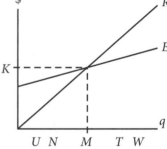

14. The fixed costs of producing a Winner Widget are *f* dollars. The variable costs are *v* dollars per widget. If the average cost of producing *q* Winner Widgets is *a*, express the fixed cost *f* in terms of *a*, *v*, and *q*.

15. Explain why the *y*-intercept of the expense function is never 0, while the *y*-intercept of the revenue function is always 0.

9-5 | Graphs of Expense and Revenue Functions

Exercises

1. Examine the graphs of an expense function and a revenue function.

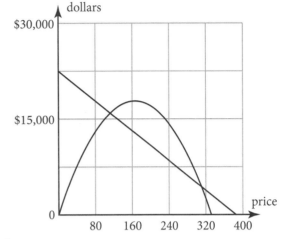

   a. What is the price at which the maximum revenue is attained?

   b. Estimate the maximum revenue.

   c. Estimate the leftmost breakeven point.

   d. Estimate the rightmost breakeven point.

2. Identify the maximum point by using the axis of symmetry.

   a. $R = -2,000p^2 + 44,000p$

   b. $R = -125p^2 + 3,200p$

3. Geoff's company manufactures customized T-shirts. Each shirt costs $2.00 to manufacture and print. The fixed costs for this product line are $2,000. The demand function is $q = -1,200p + 7,800$, where p is the price for each shirt.

   a. Write the expense equation in terms of the demand q.

   b. Express the expense equation from part a in terms of the price p.

   c. Write the revenue function in terms of the price.

   d. Graph the functions in an appropriate viewing window. What price yields the maximum revenue? What is the revenue at that price? Identify the price at the breakeven points. Round answers to the nearest cent.

   e. Use any of the methods you learned in this section to determine the roots of the revenue equation. Interpret those roots in the context of this problem.

4. Mobile Tech manufactures cell phone accessories. A particular item in their product line costs $40 each to manufacture. The fixed costs are $120,000. The demand function is $q = -120p + 8,000$, where q is the quantity the public will buy given the price p.

a. Write the expense function in terms of p.

b. Identity an appropriate viewing window for the domain of the expense function.

c. Construct the graph of the expense function from part a.

d. What is the revenue equation for this Mobile Tech product? Write the revenue equation in terms of the price.

e. Use the revenue equation from part d. What would the revenue be if the price of the item was set at $60?

f. Use any of the methods you learned in this section to determine the roots of the revenue equation. Interpret those roots in the context of this problem.

g. Graph the revenue function found in part d.

h. Which price would yield the higher revenue, $20 or $40?

i. Graph the expense and revenue functions found above. Interpret the graph.

9-6 | Breakeven Analysis

Exercises

1. AVS Industries has determined that the combined fixed and variable expenses for the production and sale of 800,000 items are $24,000,000. What is the price at the breakeven point for this item?

2. The expense equation for the production of a certain audio player is $E = 1{,}250q + 700{,}000$, where q is the quantity demanded. At a particular price, the breakeven revenue is $3,800,000. What is the quantity demanded at the breakeven point?

3. A manufacturer determines that a product will reach the breakeven point if sold at either $30 or $120. At $30, the expense and revenue values are both $120,000. At $120, the expense and revenue values are both $400,000. Graph possible revenue and expense functions that would depict this situation. Label the maximum and minimum values for each of the axes. Circle the breakeven points.

4. Estimate the breakeven points of the expense and revenue functions in each graph.

a.
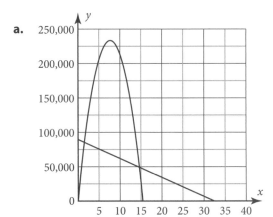

b.
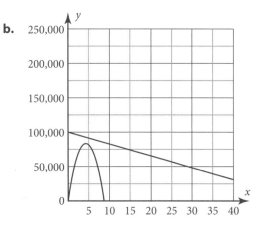

5. Sound Foundations Inc. is a firm that manufactures concrete building supplies. Their research department has invented a new product that they want to sell to builders. After extensive analysis, they have found that their breakeven point will occur only once when the price of the item is $1,200. At this price, the expense and revenue will be $3,500,000. Graph possible revenue and expense functions that would depict this situation. Label the maximum and minimum values for each of the axes. Circle the breakeven point and interpret the graph.

6. Sunset Park Equipment produces camping gear. They are considering manufacturing a new energy-efficient lantern. The expense function is $E = -54{,}000p + 7{,}000{,}000$ and the revenue function is $R = -1{,}800p^2 + 200{,}000p$.

    a. Sketch the graphs of the expense and revenue functions.

    b. Determine the prices at the breakeven points. Round to the nearest cent.

    c. Use your answers from part b to determine the revenue and expense amounts for each of the breakeven points. Round to the nearest cent.

7. Baby-B-Good manufactures affordable plastic baby rattles. The expense equation is $E = -3{,}400p + 50{,}000$, and the revenue equation is $R = -1{,}800p^2 + 20{,}000p$.

    a. Sketch the graph of the expense and revenue functions.

    b. Determine the prices at the breakeven points. Round to the nearest cent.

    c. Use your answers from part b to determine the revenue and expense amounts for each of the breakeven points. Round to the nearest cent.

8. Approximate both the expense and revenue functions shown in the graph in terms of price x.

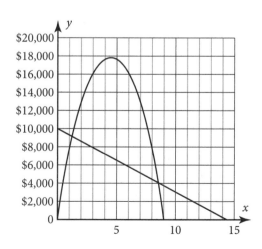

9-7 | The Profit Equation

Exercises

1. Maximum profit can be found on the graph where the difference between the revenue and expense functions is the greatest. Examine each of the following graphs and estimate the maximum profit price and the maximum profit at that price.

a.
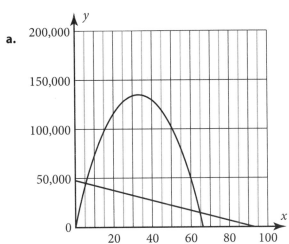

b.
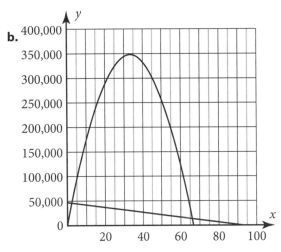

c.
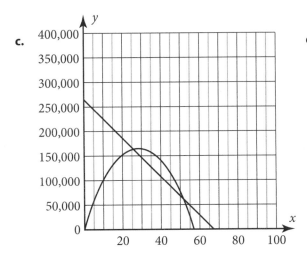

d.
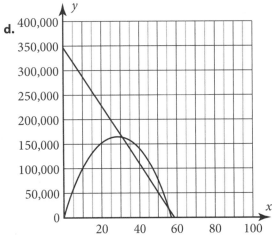

Determine the profit equation.

2. $E = -14,000p + 80,000$ $R = -32,200p^2 + 106,000p$

3. $E = -2,100p + 100,000$ $R = -900p^2 + 20,000p$

4. $E = -1,100p + 40,000$ $R = -150p^2 + 3,800p$

5. The expense and revenue function can yield a profit function. That equation can represent no profit made for any price.

    a. Use your graphing calculator and the revenue equation from Exercise 2 to determine an expense equation that would yield a situation where no profit can be made.

    b. Use your graphing calculator and the expense equation from Exercise 3 to determine a revenue equation that would yield a situation where no profit can be made.

6. Determine the maximum profit and the price that would yield the maximum profit for each equation.

    a. $P = -500p^2 + 67{,}600p - 20{,}000$ **b.** $P = -370p^2 + 8{,}800p - 25{,}000$

    c. $P = -31p^2 + 4{,}540p - 9{,}251$

7. Listen Up sells external computer speakers. Their new product has the following expense and revenue functions: $E = -828p + 400{,}000$ and $R = -38p^2 + 8{,}000p$.

    a. Determine the profit function.

    b. Determine the price, to the nearest cent, which yields the maximum profit.

    c. Determine the maximum profit to the nearest cent.

8. FunFleece Incorporated manufactures fleece hats. It is considering making a new type of weatherproof fleece hat. The expense and revenue functions are $E = -300p + 150{,}000$ and $R = -300p^2 + 29{,}000p$.

    a. Determine the profit function.

    b. Determine the price, to the nearest cent, which yields the maximum profit.

    c. Determine the maximum profit to the nearest cent.

9. Determine the expense equation given the profit and revenue equations.

    $P = -468p^2 + 45{,}599p - 299{,}000$ $R = -468p^2 + 45{,}000p$

10. Determine the revenue equation given the profit and expense equations.

    $P = -525p^2 + 65{,}326p - 185{,}000$ $E = -326p + 185{,}000$

11. Hi-Res Industries is a new company with a single product in production. They calculate their profit equation to be $P = -150p^2 + 30,000p - 2,343,750$.

Determine the price values where the profit is equal to zero and the price at which the profit is a maximum.

9-8 Mathematically Modeling a Business

Exercises

Use the graph of the expense function (Y₁), the revenue function (Y₂), and the profit function (Y₃) to answer Exercises 1–3.

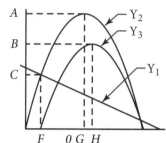

1. Name the coordinates of the maximum revenue point.

2. Name the coordinates of the maximum profit point.

3. What is the significance of the point (F, C)?

You are the CEO of Widget World Corporation. Researchers have developed a new electronic widget. The fixed costs to make the widget will be $30,000, and the variable cost will be $150 per widget. Exercises 4–13 are about the Widget World Corporation.

4. Write the expense function for the electronic widget in terms of q where q is the quantity that will be produced.

5. The market research department conducted consumer surveys and reported the following results. In these ordered pairs, the first number represents the **possible price** and the second number represents the **quantity demanded.** The points are listed as (p, q).

   (75, 6500), (100, 5900), (125, 4500), (150, 3900), (175, 2800), (200, 1500), (225, 900)

   You now need to set up a demand function using the ordered pairs from the market research department. Enter these ordered pairs into graphing calculator lists. Write the linear regression equation that models this set of ordered pairs. Round each coefficient to the nearest integer.

6. The equations used are in terms of q and p. Replace y with q and replace x with p. Write the new equation for q in terms of p.

7. Recall that the revenue equation is $R = pq$. Substitute the quantity (demand) equation from Exercise 6 into the revenue equation and simplify.

8. Use the equation for the demand from Exercise 6. Substitute this into your expense equation from Exercise 4 to write an expense equation in terms of p rather than q.

9. Enter the equation for R as Y_1 and the equation for E as Y_2 in your graphing calculator. What viewing window will you use to graph Y_1 and Y_2 in the same window?

10. Make a sketch of the graphs.

11. Find the coordinates of the breakeven points in your graph in Exercise 10. Round the coordinates to the nearest whole number.

12. Write the profit equation in terms of x (the price variable) by subtracting the expense equation from the revenue equation. Let Y_3 represent the profit. What will you enter in your calculator?

13. Enter the profit equation into your graphing calculator and determine the maximum profit price and amount to the nearest integer.

   a. The x-value represents the price at which each widget should be set in order to get maximum profit. What is that price?

   b. The y-value represents the maximum profit. What is that profit?

9-9 Optimal Outcomes

Exercises

1. Determine whether each of the following points falls within the profit feasible region defined by $x \geq 0, y \geq 0, 7x + 3y \leq 45$.

   a. $(2, 2)$ **b.** $(5, 1)$ **c.** $(6, 4)$

   d. $(4, 8)$ **e.** $(0, 15)$

2. The vertices of a feasible region are listed below. What is the maximum profit for the objective equation $P = 120x + 170y$

   a. $(0,300), (0,0), (1200,0)$

   b. $(20,70), (60,80), (80,90), (40,10)$

3. The vertices of a feasible region are listed below. What is the minimum cost for the objective equation $C = 57x + 88y$

   a. $(2,9), (10,20), (15,13), (8,2)$

   b. $(50,80), (70,120), (90,180), (120,90)$

4. In each of the following, you are given an objective function and the vertices of a feasible region. Determine both the maximum and minimum values of the objective function as well as the point at which they occur.

   a. $P = 81x + 57y$ $(6, 3), (10, 10), (15, 7)$

   b. $C = 98.15x + 63.5y$ $(0, 800), (40, 1000), (100, 900), (60, 200), (50, 50)$

5. Circuitry Inc. produces two types of circuit boards. Their profits are $400 for Circuit 1 and $300 for Circuit 2. The process involves both types of circuits to be manufactured on both machine A and machine B. It takes 2 hours on machine A and 1.5 hours on machine B to manufacture Circuit 1. It takes 1 hour on machine A and 1.5 hours on machine B to manufacture Circuit 2. Because the company produces other electronics, they can allocate no more than 100 hours per day for circuit production on machine A and no more than 90 hours a day for circuit production on machine B. Let x represent the number of Circuit 1s produced and y represent the number of Circuit 2s produced.

a. Write the profit objective function.

b. Write the machine A constraint inequality.

c. Write the machine B constraint inequality.

d. Graph the constraint inequalities. Identify the coordinates of the feasible region.

e. How many of each type of circuits must they sell to maximize their profits?

6. A financial manager wants to invest up to $600,000 of his client's money in two investment plans. The Focused Plan pays an annual interest rate of 4% and the Strategic Plan pays an annual interest rate of 7%. The manager feels that in order to get the best return, the client should invest no less than $150,000 in the Focused Plan and no less than $250,000 in the Strategic Plan. How much should be invested in each plan to maximize the return?

a. Let x represent the amount invested in the Focused Plan. Write an expression for the interest received from this investment.

b. Let y represent the amount invested in the Strategic Plan. Write an expression for the interest received from this investment.

c. Use parts a and b to write the return (R) objective function.

d. Write the constraint that represents the limit on the total amount that can be invested. This will be one of the constraints that form the feasible region.

e. Write an inequality that represents the suggested amount to be invested in the Focused Plan.

f. Write an inequality that represents the suggested amount to be invested in the Strategic Plan.

g. Graph the feasible region.

h. Determine the vertices of the feasible region.

i. Which vertex of the feasible region will maximize the return on the investment? What is that maximum return?

Name _____   Date _____

7. Liam Anthony is a financial advisor. He wants to invest up to $250,000 of his client's money in two investment plans. The Apex Plan pays an annual interest rate of 5% and the Multi- Plan pays an annual interest rate of 6%. Although the Multi-Plan pays a higher interest rate, there is some risk involved. Liam and the client have agreed to invest at most 50% of the total in the Multi-Plan. Liam feels that in order to get the best return, the client should invest no less than $100,000. How much should be invested in each plan to maximize the return?

a. Let x represent the amount invested in the Apex Plan. Write an expression for the interest received from this investment.

b. Let y represent the amount invested in the Multi-Plan. Write an expression for the interest received from this investment.

c. Use parts a and b to write the return objective function.

d. Write the constraint that represents the limit on the total amount that can be invested. This will be one of the constraints that form the feasible region.

e. Write an expression that represents the total amount that can be invested.

f. Write an expression that represents 50% of the total amount found in part e.

g. Liam is recommending that the amount invested in the Multi-Plan be no more than the amount found in part f. Write this inequality.

h. Use the distributive property to simplify the inequality found in g.

i. Combine like terms. Simplify the inequality. This will be one of the constraints that form the feasible region.

j. Write the inequality representing the manager's recommendation for the total amount that should be invested. This will be one of the constraints that form the feasible region.

k. Graph the feasible region.

l. Determine the vertices of the feasible region.

m. Which vertex of the feasible region will maximize the return on the investment? What is that maximum return?

Financial Algebra **Workbook 9-9**

8. Extreme Climb makes camping fabric that is a mixture of polyester and nylon. Their warehouse has 6000 lots of polyester and 3000 lots of nylon available during the week of June 1 for production of their Peak Performance and Rugged Performance fabrics. A roll of Peak Performance fabric uses 80 lots of polyester and 30 lots of nylon. A roll of Rugged Performance uses 40 lots of polyester and 30 lots of nylon. They make a profit of $90 per roll on the Peak Performance and $150 per roll on the Rugged Performance. How many rolls of each type should they manufacture during this week to maximize profit?

9. Industry City is a start-up company that produces picnic table sets made from recycled metal. Right now, Industry City has two big clients—River Cottages and Oceanside Resorts. River Cottages needs at least 60 tables, and Oceanside Resorts needs at most 150 tables. Industry City is able to produce and send at most 400 tables to these two clients. It cost $80 per table to ship to River Cottages, and $60 per table to ship to Oceanside Resorts. In return for the purchases, River Cottages has agreed to give Industry City $20 in rebates for each table purchased. Oceanside gives $30 in rebates toward for each table purchased. The owner of Industry City has determined that the company needs at least $2400 in credits to keep shipping costs down. How many tables should be shipped to American and Oceanside to minimize shipping costs? What is the minimum cost?

   a. Let x represent the number of tables shipped to River Cottages and y represent the number of tables shipped to Oceanside Resorts. Set up the cost objective function.

   b. Write the River Cottages constraint inequality for the number of tables needed.

   c. Write the Oceanside Resorts constraint inequality for the number of tables needed.

   d. Write the constraint inequality for the total number of tables Industry City is able to ship to these two locations.

   e. Write the constraint inequality for the credits.

   f. Graph the feasible region.

   g. Identify the vertices.

   h. What values will minimize cost in the objective function?

10. Raul and Carla own The Cakery Bakery. They make specialty cakes for all occasions. They have just been hired to provide the desserts for a large convention that will be held in one week. They will need to hire bakers and cake decorators. Bakers make $600 per week and cake decorators $900 per week. The company knows that they will need at least 3 bakers and at least 5 cake decorators. A baker spends 4 hours designing and 15 hours creating the cakes. A cake decorator spends 8 hours designing and 15 hours creating the cakes. Raul and Carla know that they will need at least 80 hours of design and 180 hours of creation. How many bakers and decorators will be needed for this job in order to keep costs at a minimum?

a. Let x represent the number of bakers needed and y represent the number of decorators needed. Write the cost objective function.

b. Write the constraint inequality for the number of bakers needed for this job.

c. Write the constraint inequality for the number of decorators needed for this job.

d. Complete the following table.

	Design	Creation
Baker	____ hours	____ hours
Decorator	____ hours	____ hours

e. Use your table to write the constraint inequality for the design hours needed to complete this job.

f. Use your table to write the constraint inequality for the creation hours needed to complete this job.

g. Graph the feasible region. You will notice that it is not a closed polygon. Rather, this is a boundless region because there is no upper constraint to form the polygon. Because you will be looking to minimize the cost objective function, this will not be a problem.

h. Identify the vertices of the feasible region.

i. Use the vertices and the cost objective function to determine the number of bakers and the number of decorators who must be hired for the job to minimize cost.

10-1   Retirement Income from Savings

Exercises

1. Ethan is 48 years old. He is planning on retiring when he turns 62. He has opened an IRA with an APR of 2.95% compounded monthly. If he makes monthly deposits of $850 to the account, how much will he have in the account when he is ready to retire?

2. Conor is 21 years old and just started working after college. He has opened a retirement account that pays 2.5% interest compounded monthly. He plans on making monthly deposits of $200. How much will he have in the account when he reaches $59\frac{1}{2}$ years of age?

3. Carla opened a retirement account that pays P percent interest compounded monthly. If she has direct deposits of X dollars per month taken out of her paycheck, write an expression that represents her balance after Y years.

4. Gillian started a retirement account with $10,000 when she turned 35. The account compounds interest quarterly at a rate of 3.625%. She made no further deposits into the account. After 20 years, she decided to withdraw 40% of what had accumulated in the account so that she could make her home handicap accessible. She had to pay a 10% penalty on the early withdrawal. What was her penalty?

5. Tanya is 42 years old. She would like to open a retirement account so that she will have one-half million dollars in the account when she retires at the age of 65. How much must she deposit each month into an account with an APR of 2.75% compounded monthly in order to reach her goal?

6. John is $59\frac{1}{2}$ years old. He plans to retire in 3 years. He now has $600,000 in a savings account that yields 3.4% interest compounded continuously. He has calculated that his final working year's salary will be $115,000. He has been told by his financial advisor that he should have 60% to 70% of his final year annual income available for use each year when he is retired.

   a. What is the range of income that his financial advisor feels he must have per year after he retires?

   b. Use the continuous compounding formula to determine how much he will have in his account at the beginning of retirement.

   c. If he uses 60% of his final annual salary, not accounting for any interest accrued in the account, how many years will he be able to tap into this account in his retirement?

7. Melanie has been contributing to a retirement account that pays 3.875% interest with pretax dollars. This account compounds interest monthly. She has put $300 per month into the account. At the end of 8 years, she needed money for a down payment on a new home. She withdrew 25% of the money that was in the account.

   a. Rounded to the nearest dollar, how much did she withdraw?

   b. Because she is in the 21% tax bracket, what was her tax liability on the amount of the withdrawal (rounded to the nearest dollar)?

   c. She had to pay a 10% early withdrawal penalty. How much was she required to pay (rounded to the nearest dollar)?

   d. How much did this withdrawal "cost" her?

8. Van is an office supervisor who has been contributing to his retirement account for the last Y years with pre-tax dollars. The account compounds interest quarterly at a rate of P percent. He contributes D dollars into the account after each 3-month period and this has not changed over the life of the account.

   a. Write an expression to represent the balance in the account after Y years of saving.

   b. After M years of contributions (where M is greater than Y), he needed to withdraw W percent of the money in his account. Write an expression for the withdrawal amount.

   c. Van pays T percent of his income in taxes. Write an algebraic expression for the combined total of his tax liability and the 10% early withdrawal penalty.

9. Meryl contributed 500 pre-tax dollars per month into her retirement account last tax year. Her taxable income for the year was $77,480. She files taxes as a married filing separately taxpayer.

   a. What would her taxable income have been had she contributed to the account in after-tax dollars?

   b. Use the tax table below to calculate her tax liability in both the pre-tax and after-tax contribution situation

   c. How much did Meryl save in taxes during that year?

77,000

If line 10 (taxable income) is—		And you are—			
At least	But less than	Single	Married filing jointly *	Married filing separately	Head of a household
			Your tax is—		
77,000	77,050	12,885	8,862	12,885	11,494
77,050	77,100	12,896	8,868	12,896	11,505
77,100	77,150	12,907	8,874	12,907	11,516
77,150	77,200	12,918	8,880	12,918	11,527
77,200	77,250	12,929	8,886	12,929	11,538
77,250	77,300	12,940	8,892	12,940	11,549
77,300	77,350	12,951	8,898	12,951	11,560
77,350	77,400	12,962	8,904	12,962	11,571
77,400	77,450	12,973	8,913	12,973	11,582
77,450	77,500	12,984	8,924	12,984	11,593
77,500	77,550	12,995	8,935	12,995	11,604
77,550	77,600	13,006	8,946	13,006	11,615
77,600	77,650	13,017	8,957	13,017	11,626
77,650	77,700	13,028	8,968	13,028	11,637
77,700	77,750	13,039	8,979	13,039	11,648
77,750	77,800	13,050	8,990	13,050	11,659
77,800	77,850	13,061	9,001	13,061	11,670
77,850	77,900	13,072	9,012	13,072	11,681
77,900	77,950	13,083	9,023	13,083	11,692
77,950	78,000	13,094	9,034	13,094	11,703

80,000

If line 10 (taxable income) is—		And you are—			
At least	But less than	Single	Married filing jointly *	Married filing separately	Head of a household
			Your tax is—		
80,000	80,050	13,545	9,485	13,545	12,154
80,050	80,100	13,556	9,496	13,556	12,165
80,100	80,150	13,567	9,507	13,567	12,176
80,150	80,200	13,578	9,518	13,578	12,187
80,200	80,250	13,589	9,529	13,589	12,198
80,250	80,300	13,600	9,540	13,600	12,209
80,300	80,350	13,611	9,551	13,611	12,220
80,350	80,400	13,622	9,562	13,622	12,231
80,400	80,450	13,633	9,573	13,633	12,242
80,450	80,500	13,644	9,584	13,644	12,253
80,500	80,550	13,655	9,595	13,655	12,264
80,550	80,600	13,666	9,606	13,666	12,275
80,600	80,650	13,677	9,617	13,677	12,286
80,650	80,700	13,688	9,628	13,688	12,297
80,700	80,750	13,699	9,639	13,699	12,308
80,750	80,800	13,710	9,650	13,710	12,319
80,800	80,850	13,721	9,661	13,721	12,330
80,850	80,900	13,732	9,672	13,732	12,341
80,900	80,950	13,743	9,683	13,743	12,352
80,950	81,000	13,754	9,694	13,754	12,363

83,000

If line 10 (taxable income) is—		And you are—			
At least	But less than	Single	Married filing jointly *	Married filing separately	Head of a household
			Your tax is—		
83,000	83,050	14,216	10,145	14,216	12,824
83,050	83,100	14,228	10,156	14,228	12,836
83,100	83,150	14,240	10,167	14,240	12,848
83,150	83,200	14,252	10,178	14,252	12,860
83,200	83,250	14,264	10,189	14,264	12,872
83,250	83,300	14,276	10,200	14,276	12,884
83,300	83,350	14,288	10,211	14,288	12,896
83,350	83,400	14,300	10,222	14,300	12,908
83,400	83,450	14,312	10,233	14,312	12,920
83,450	83,500	14,324	10,244	14,324	12,932
83,500	83,550	14,336	10,255	14,336	12,944
83,550	83,600	14,348	10,266	14,348	12,956
83,600	83,650	14,360	10,277	14,360	12,968
83,650	83,700	14,372	10,288	14,372	12,980
83,700	83,750	14,384	10,299	14,384	12,992
83,750	83,800	14,396	10,310	14,396	13,004
83,800	83,850	14,408	10,321	14,408	13,016
83,850	83,900	14,420	10,332	14,420	13,028
83,900	83,950	14,432	10,343	14,432	13,040
83,950	84,000	14,444	10,354	14,444	13,052

10. Pei is a 26-year-old television executive. She files taxes as a single taxpayer. She needed to withdraw $30,000 from her tax-deferred retirement account to assist her parents with some financial problems. Pei's gross taxable income for the year in question was $162,983.

Schedule X—If your filing status is **Single**

If your taxable income is:		The tax is:	of the amount over—
Over—	But not over—		
$0	$9,525	---------- 10%	$0
9,525	38,700	$952.50 + 12%	9,525
38,700	82,500	4,453.50 + 22%	38,700
82,500	157,500	14,089.50 + 24%	82,500
157,500	200,000	32,089.50 + 32%	157,500
200,000	500,000	45,689.50 + 35%	200,000
500,000	---------	150,689.50 + 37%	500,000

a. Use the tax schedule to calculate Pei's tax liability had she not made the early withdrawal.

b. Use the same worksheet to calculate her liability with an increase in her taxable income of $30,000.

c. How much more in taxes did she pay because of the early withdrawal?

d. What was her early withdrawal penalty?

11. Annette makes $96,000 per year working for an online e-magazine. Her company offers a 401K retirement plan in which they will match 45% of her contributions to the 401K up to 9% of her salary. The company will only allow employees to make contributions to the 401K to a maximum of 25% of their salary. For the year in question, the maximum allowable contribution to any 401K is $22,000 because she is over the age of 55.

a. What is the maximum Annette's employer will allow for her contribution?

b. What is the maximum contribution she could make?

c. What is her employer's maximum contribution amount?

10-2 Social Security Benefits

Exercises

1. In 2020, the maximum taxable income for Social Security was $137,700 with a 6.2% tax rate.

    a. What is the maximum anyone could have paid into Social Security tax in the year 2020?

    b. Ravi had two jobs in 2020. One employer paid him $89,222 and the other paid him $61,200. Each employer took out 6.2% for Social Security. How much did Ravi overpay in Social Security for 2020?

2. In 2019, Giselle had two jobs. She earned $93,440 working the first 8 months of the year at a nursing home. She switched jobs in September and began to work in a hospital, where she earned $62,211. In 2019, the maximum taxable income for Social Security was $132,900. The Social Security tax rate was 6.2%. How much OASDI tax did Giselle overpay? Round to the nearest cent.

3. Alexandra had two employers last year. Both of her employers took out OASDI tax. The OASDI percent was p and the maximum taxable OASDI income was m dollars. She earned x dollars at one job and y dollars at her second job, and $x + y > m$. Express her OASDI refund algebraically.

For Exercises 4 and 5 use the Social Security worksheet below.

Social Security Benefits Worksheet—Lines 5a and 5b   *Keep for Your Records*

Before you begin:	✓ Figure any write-in adjustments to be entered on the dotted line next to Schedule 1, line 22 (see the instructions for Schedule 1, line 22).
	✓ If you are married filing separately and you lived apart from your spouse for all of 2019, enter "D" to the right of the word "benefits" on line 5a. If you don't, you may get a math error notice from the IRS.
	✓ Be sure you have read the *Exception* in the line 5a and 5b instructions to see if you can use this worksheet instead of a publication to find out if any of your benefits are taxable.

1. Enter the total amount from **box 5** of all your **Forms SSA-1099** and **RRB-1099**. Also, enter this amount on Form 1040 or 1040-SR, line 5a .... **1.** _____
2. Multiply line 1 by 50% (0.50) .... **2.** _____
3. Combine the amounts from Form 1040 or 1040-SR, lines 1, 2b, 3b, 4b, 4d, 6, and Schedule 1, line 9 .... **3.** _____
4. Enter the amount, if any, from Form 1040 or 1040-SR, line 2a .... **4.** _____
5. Combine lines 2, 3, and 4 .... **5.** _____
6. Enter the total of the amounts from Schedule 1, lines 10 through 19, plus any write-in adjustments you entered on the dotted line next to Schedule 1, line 22 .... **6.** _____
7. Is the amount on line 6 less than the amount on line 5?
    ☐ **No.** (STOP) None of your social security benefits are taxable. Enter -0- on Form 1040 or 1040-SR, line 5b.
    ☐ **Yes.** Subtract line 6 from line 5 .... **7.** _____
8. If you are:
    • Married filing jointly, enter $32,000
    • Single, head of household, qualifying widow(er), or married filing separately and you **lived apart** from your spouse for all of 2019, enter $25,000
    • Married filing separately and you lived with your spouse at any time in 2019, skip lines 8 through 15; multiply line 7 by 85% (0.85) and enter the result on line 16. Then, go to line 17 .... **8.** _____
9. Is the amount on line 8 less than the amount on line 7?
    ☐ **No.** (STOP) None of your social security benefits are taxable. Enter -0- on Form 1040 or 1040-SR, line 5b. If you are married filing separately and you **lived apart** from your spouse for all of 2019, be sure you entered "D" to the right of the word "benefits" on line 5a.
    ☐ **Yes.** Subtract line 8 from line 7 .... **9.** _____
10. Enter: $12,000 if married filing jointly; $9,000 if single, head of household, qualifying widow(er), or married filing separately and you **lived apart** from your spouse for all of 2019 .... **10.** _____
11. Subtract line 10 from line 9. If zero or less, enter -0- .... **11.** _____
12. Enter the **smaller** of line 9 or line 10 .... **12.** _____
13. Enter one-half of line 12 .... **13.** _____
14. Enter the **smaller** of line 2 or line 13 .... **14.** _____
15. Multiply line 11 by 85% (0.85). If line 11 is zero, enter -0- .... **15.** _____
16. Add lines 14 and 15 .... **16.** _____
17. Multiply line 1 by 85% (0.85) .... **17.** _____
18. **Taxable social security benefits.** Enter the **smaller** of line 16 or line 17. Also enter this amount on Form 1040 or 1040-SR, line 5b .... **18.** _____

(TIP) *If any of your benefits are taxable for 2019 **and** they include a lump-sum benefit payment that was for an earlier year, you may be able to reduce the taxable amount. See Lump-Sum Election in Pub. 915 for details.*

Need more information or forms? Visit IRS.gov.   -28-

4. Andrew and Julianne Coletti are married and filing a joint Form 1040. Andrew is collecting Social Security, but Julianne is not. They are filling out the Social Security worksheet on page 173 so they can determine the amount of Andrew's Social Security benefits that they will pay Federal income tax on. Number a blank sheet of paper 1–18. Fill in the following lines which were taken from their tax information:

- Line 1—Andrew received $31,555 in Social Security benefits.

- Line 3—the total of their other income from lines 1, 2b, 3b, 4b, 4d, and Schedule 1, line 9, is $143,677.

- Line 4—the amount from line 2a is $502.

- Line 6—the total to enter is $6,075.

a. Fill in the correct entries for the rest of the lines on their Social Security worksheet.

b. How much of Andrew's Social Security benefit must they pay Federal income tax on?

c. How much of Andrew's Social Security benefit is not taxed?

5. Sabrina is single. She is filling out the Social Security worksheet on page 173 so she can determine the amount of her Social Security benefits that she will pay Federal income tax on. Number a blank sheet of paper 1–18.

a. Fill in the following lines, which were taken from Sabrina's tax information:

- Line 1 —she received $29,612 in Social Security benefits.

- Line 3—the total of her other income from lines 1, 2b, 3b, 4b, 4d, and Schedule 1, line 9, is $67,891.

- Line 4—the amount from line 2a is $440.

- Line 6—the total to enter is $3,921.

b. How much of Sabrina's Social Security benefits does she have to pay tax on?

6. Mr. Stevens filled out a Social Security benefits worksheet. He received x dollars in Social Security benefits but had to pay taxes on t dollars of it.

a. Express the fraction of his Social Security income that he had to pay tax on as a percent.

b. Express algebraically the percent of his Social Security benefits that was not taxed.

7. Emanuel earned $87,098 last year and then retired. He now receives $31,234 in annual Social Security benefits. What is the difference between his monthly salary during his last year of work and his monthly Social Security benefit? Round to the nearest ten dollars.

8. This year Phil pays m dollars for Medicare Part B coverage. He reads that this cost will go up 11.5% next year. Express the difference between this year's and next year's cost algebraically.

10-3 Pensions

Exercises

1. Dyana worked at Litton Light Manufacturing for 25 years. Her employer offers a pension benefit package with a flat benefit formula using the flat amount of $60 for each year of service to calculate her monthly pension. How much will Dyana's monthly pension benefit be?

2. Frank worked for Morton Industries for 18 years. His company offered him a flat amount of $48 for each year of service as his monthly pension package. After one year, he was notified of a 1.625% cost of living adjustment to his monthly pension benefit. Determine Frank's current monthly pension benefit.

3. Aileen worked for Penultimate Inc. for Y years. Her company offered her a flat monthly pension benefit of D dollars for each year of service. After one year in retirement, she was notified of a P percent cost of living adjustment. Write an algebraic expression that represents her current monthly pension benefit.

4. George is retiring after 30 years at Peabody Motors. The company offers him a flat yearly retirement benefit of $870 for each year of service. What will be his monthly pension?

5. Mary is retiring after working for Fashonista Limited for 21 years. The company offered her a flat retirement benefit of $50 per month for each year of the first 15 years of service and $65 per month for each year of service thereafter.

   a. What was her monthly income in the first year after retirement?

   b. What was her annual income for the first year of retirement?

   c. After one year of retirement, she received a 0.9% cost of living adjustment to her monthly pension benefit. What was her new monthly benefit?

6. Statton Realty offers their employees a flat pension plan in which a predetermined dollar amount (multiplier) is multiplied by the number of years of service to determine the monthly pension benefit using the following schedule.

YEARS EMPLOYED	MULTIPLIER
15–19	$62.50
20–25	$75.80
26+	$83.25

   After working at Statton for 25 years, Gina has decided to open her own business. What would be the difference in her monthly pension benefit if she stays for an extra year?

7. Risa's employer offers an annual pension benefit calculated by multiplying 1.875% of the career average salary times the number of years employed. Here are Risa's annual salaries over the last 15 years of employment.

56,000	56,000	57,100	57,100	58,900	58,900	58,900	62,000
65,000	65,000	66,400	66,800	66,800	68,000	68,600	

a. What is Risa's career average salary?

b. What is Risa's annual pension under this plan?

c. What percentage of her final annual salary will her annual retirement salary be? Round your answer to the nearest percent.

d. What is Risa's monthly pension benefit? Round your answer to the nearest cent.

8. Kevin is planning on retiring after 25 years of employment. For the last 3 years he has made $132,000; $135,000; and $138,000. His employer offers a defined benefit plan in which the annual pension is calculated as the product of the final 3-year average salary, the number of years of service, and a 2.25% multiplier. What will Kevin's annual pension be?

9. Depot City uses a final average formula to calculate an employee's pension benefits. The amount used in the calculations is the salary average of the final 5 years of employment. The retiree will receive an annual benefit that is equivalent to 1.2% of the final average for each year of employment. Vilma is retiring at the end of this year, after 23 years of employment at Depot City. Calculate her annual retirement pension given that her final 5 years of salaries are $63,000; $63,700; $64,000; $64,000; and $64,800.

10. Singh's employer offers a defined contribution pension plan that uses a graded 6-year vesting formula as shown here.

Years Employed	Vesting Percentage
1–2	0%
3–10	25%
10–15	45%
15–20	70%
20–35	85%
30+	100%

His employer matches $0.75 on the dollar for all of his contributions. After 16 years, Singh decides to move to a different state. His personal contributions (adjusted for losses or gains in the investment) amount to $25,000. How much of his pension will he be able to take with him?

11. Alternate Universe Inc. offers their employees P percent of the average of their last 3 years of annual salaries for each year of service to the company. Helen began working at Alternate Universe Y years ago and is now planning to retire. Her final 3 years of salaries are A, B, and C dollars. Write an algebraic expression that will represent her annual retirement benefit.

12. Richie has contributed Y dollars per month to his pension plan for each of the last R years. His employer has matched P percent of each contribution. His employer uses a graded vesting formula according to the schedule below.

Years Employed	Vesting Percentage
0	0%
1	0%
2–8	B%
9–15	C%
16–30	D%
30+	100%

Richie has decided to change jobs after R years of service where $16 \le R \le 30$.

a. Write an algebraic expression that represents how much he has contributed to his retirement account.

b. How much of his contributions can he take with him?

c. Write an algebraic expression that represents how much his employer has contributed to his retirement account.

d. Write an algebraic expression that represents how much of the employer contributions Richie can take with him.

13. Logan has worked at Pendleton University for the last 20 years. The university calculates their employee's pension according to the following formula.

Determine the average of the highest 5 years of annual earnings.

Determine the monthly average using the above amount.

Subtract $1,000 from that amount.

Multiply the result by 45%.

Add $500 to that result.

For each year of employment over 15 years, add 0.5% of the average monthly salary.

The final result is the monthly pension benefit.

Logan's five highest annual salaries are $73,000; $73,900; $73,900; $74,000; and $75,000. Calculate Logan's monthly pension benefit if he retires after 20 years of employment. Round any calculations to the nearest cent.

10-4   Life Insurance

Exercises

1. Mr. Kurris is 50 years old. In 4 years, his house will be paid off and his daughter will be finished with college. He wants to take out a 5-year level-term life insurance policy with a face value $750,000. The monthly premium is $61.

   a. What will be his total cost for this policy over the 5-year period?

   b. If he dies after paying for the policy for 16 months, how much will the insurance company pay his beneficiaries?

   c. If he does not die during the 5 years, how much does the insurance company make on this policy?

   d. If he dies after paying for the policy for 13 months, how much will the insurance company lose on this policy?

2. The Apple Insurance Company offers 5-year term $100,000 policies to a 46-year-old female for $516 per year. The mortality rates are shown below. Fill in the missing entries a–g in the table.

Age at Death	46	47	48	49	50	Age ≥ 51
Mortality Rate	0.0016	0.0019	0.0022	0.0027	0.0032	a.
Insurance Company Profit at End of Each Year if Purchaser Dies in That Year	b.	c.	d.	e.	f.	g.

   h. What is the expected profit for one of these policies? Round to the nearest cent.

   i. If the company sold 5,000 of the same policies to 46-year-old females, what would their expected profit be for the 5,000 policies? Round to the nearest thousand dollars.

3. Julio has a universal life insurance policy with a face value of $200,000. The current cash value of the policy is $11,560. If the premium is $102 per month, for how many months can the cash value be used to pay the premium?

4. An insurance company sells a $500,000 5-year term policy to a female. The monthly policy is m dollars. If the person dies 20 months after taking out the policy, express the insurance company's profit algebraically.

5. Mr. DiPasquale's whole life premium increased from $115 to $149 per month when he increased his face value. Find the percent increase to the nearest percent.

6. Use the mortality table below to answer parts a–f.

	Mortality Table for Males			Mortality Table for Females	
Exact Age	Death Probability	Life Expectancy		Death Probability	Life Expectancy
56	0.008467	23.52		0.005148	26.94
57	0.009121	22.71		0.005627	26.07
58	0.009912	21.92		0.006166	25.22
59	0.010827	21.13		0.006765	24.37
60	0.011858	20.36		0.007445	23.53
65	0.017976	16.67		0.011511	19.50
66	0.019564	15.96		0.012572	18.72
67	0.021291	15.27		0.013772	17.95
68	0.023162	14.59		0.015130	17.19
69	0.025217	13.93		0.016651	16.45

a. What is the life expectancy for a 69-year-old female? Round to the nearest year.

b. Until what age is a 65-year-old male expected to live? Round to the nearest year.

c. If the company insures 10,000 males who are 58 years old, how many are expected to die before their 59th birthday? Round to the nearest integer.

d. Based on the table, what is the probability that a 68-year-old male will live to his 69th birthday?

7. The mortality rate for a certain female elderly age category is 0.0059. A company insures 10,000 people in this category. About how many of them will die before their next birthday?

8. Express the expected profit algebraically for the following expected value table.

Profit	a	b	c	d
Probability	0.01	0.02	0.9	0.01

9. Mr. Norton has a universal life insurance policy, and the current cash value of the policy is c. The premium is m dollars per month. He is going to use the cash value to pay for premiums as long as it can. In those months, the cash value will earn i dollars interest. Write an algebraic expression for the number of months the cash value can be used to pay the premium.

10. Use the definition of the greatest integer function to evaluate the following.

a. [109.999]

b. [87.007]

c. [−50.95]

d. $[34\frac{12}{13}]$

e. $[\sqrt{39}]$

f. $[\sqrt{35}]$

11. The Wonderland Miracle Carnival Company manages a game at a state fair. They charge $3 per game. Winners receive a $10 prize. The probability of winning the game is 0.15.

a. What is the probability of losing the game?

b. What profit does the company earn if a person wins the game?

c. What profit does the company earn if the person loses the game?

d. Set up a table indicating the profit and the probability of winning and losing.

e. What is the expected profit per game?

f. If 800 people play this game during the week-long state fair, what is the company's profit for the week?

12. Mr. Kite took out a 10-year term policy with a face-value of f dollars. Over the lifetime of the policy, he pays monthly payments of m dollars. He dies after 12 years.

a. Express the total he paid for the policy algebraically.

b. How much will his family receive from the insurance company?

13. Mr. Henderson takes out a term life insurance policy with a renewable annual premium. The first year premium is $350. Premiums increase by 7% each year.

a. What will the premiums be in the second year?

b. What will the premiums be in the third year? Round to the nearest cent.

c. What will the premiums be in the nth year?

d. Does the expression in your answer to part c model an arithmetic sequence or a geometric sequence?

10-5 Investment Diversification

Exercises

1. Rob is retiring from his teaching job. His annual pension will be $84,500, which he will receive every year until he dies. However, he has a choice to make. If he agrees to take a 10% reduction in his pension, his wife can continue to receive that annual payment even after his death, until she dies.

   a. What is the amount of the reduced annual pension?

   b. If Rob lives 10 years after retirement and receives the full $84,500 per year, how much will he have received in total?

   c. If Rob lives 20 years, and takes the reduced pension amount, and his wife lives 11 years past his death, how much will the pension have paid in total?

   d. If Rob lives 6 years after retirement and then dies, and he took the reduced pension, how much less did he receive than if he took the full $84,500 amount each year?

   e. For how many years would Rob's wife have to live to collect pension money that was more than the amount Rob sacrificed from part d?

2. The following circle graphs give the proportional breakdowns of two investors' diversified portfolios.

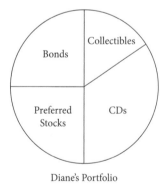

Diane's Portfolio

Jack's Portfolio

   a. Which investment in Diane's portfolio do you think is the most risky?

   b. Which is Jack's riskiest investment?

   c. Which portfolio do you consider to be the most risky?

   d. Out of the eight different types of investments, which one is the safest?

3. Kim is planning to set up a $90,000 investment portfolio. She plans on investing 30% into stock, 30% into bonds, 30% into collectibles, and the remainder into a 10-year certificate of deposit.

    a. How much is invested in the CD?

    b. If the CD earns 2.25% interest compounded continuously, how much will it grow to in 10 years? Round to the nearest cent.

    c. The same amount is invested in stocks as in collectibles. If the stock goes down 10%, and the collectibles gain 10% in value, what is the net gain from these two investments?

4. The Castellano family is planning to send their 1-year old twin daughters to college in 17 years. They plan on investing $4,000 each year per child to help meet their college costs.

    a. If the interest rate was 3% compounded annually, what will the value of each child's account be in 17 years? Assume the periodic, annual $4,000 deposit continues for each child.

    b. Would investing the money in a stock that had a yield of 5% earn more money than the CD? Explain.

    c. What are the advantages and disadvantages in investing the money in stock?

5. Charlotte invested $120,000 into stocks, bonds, and real estate several years ago. She diversified the investment according to the following percentages:

    Stocks: 33%

    Bonds: 42%

    Real estate: 25%

    If the stocks increase 9% in value, the bonds gain 8%, and the real estate loses 5%, what is the total monetary gain or loss from this diversified portfolio?

6. In 1985, Leslie bought a classic 1956 Chevrolet Nomad for $22,000. Over the next 31 years, he invested approximately $750 per year into restoring the car to its original condition. In 2016 he sold it for $61,000.

a. Imagine he chose not to invest in the car. Assume he invested the initial $22,000 in an account that paid an average of 9.11% interest compounded daily for the next 10 years. How much would that grow to in the 10 years? Round to the nearest hundred dollars.

b. Interest rates started to fall in the 1990s. Imagine he took the money the account had earned in part a (after rounding) and invested it in a CD that paid an average of 4% compounded daily for the remaining 21 years. How much would that grow to by 2016? Round to the nearest hundred dollars.

c. If he deposited $750 each year into an account that paid 4.09% compounded annually, how much would be in that account after the 31 years? Round to the nearest hundred dollars.

d. How much of a gain would the three accounts from parts a, b, and c make in the 31 years, to the nearest hundred dollars?

e. How much did he invest in the Nomad?

f. How much did he gain on the Nomad investment?

g. Which investment was more conservative?

11-1 | Utility Expenses

Exercises

1. LED light bulbs are replacing incandescent light bulbs because over 90% of the energy consumed by an incandescent bulb goes in to producing heat, not light. The 14-watt LightKing LED costs $1.32 in electricity per year. The 60-watt LightKing incandescent bulb gives the same amount of light but costs $6.09 in electricity per year. How much could be saved per year by using 25 of the LED bulbs in a house?

2. The Ricardo household used *w* cubic feet of water during a summer month. Express the number of ccf of water they used algebraically.

3. Mrs. Zorn works for a utility company and is reading the electric meter for a local pizza place, which is shown below.

    How many kWh of electricity are indicated by the dials?

4. A certain guitar amplifier requires 200 watts when it is being used. How much would it cost to run for 55 minutes, at a cost of $0.11 per kWh? Round to the nearest cent.

5. The dials shown below are from a natural gas meter and display the number of ccf used. How many ccf are indicated by the dials?

6. The Simpsons' previous water bill showed a meter reading of 433 ccf. Below is their meter's current reading. At a cost of $0.91 per ccf, what should their next water bill be?

7. The Robinsons' old dryer cost them $455 per year to run. The new one they purchased for $940 will save them 18% annually in energy costs to run it. In how many years will it pay for itself?

Financial Algebra **Workbook** 11-1

8. An appliance uses w watts to run. If you run it for h hours, and the cost per kilowatt-hour is c, express the cost of running the appliance per kwh algebraically.

9. The Nesmiths' old clothes washer costs c dollars to run for a year. They replace it with a new energy-efficient washer that costs w dollars, but saves p percent per year in energy usage. How many years will it take for the washer to pay for itself? Express your answer algebraically using the greatest integer function.

10. Two years ago the Lange family used $3,250 worth of electricity. Last year they switched to balanced billing.

    a. What was their monthly payment last year under balanced billing? Round to the nearest cent.

    b. During last year, they actually used $3,766 of electricity and their balanced billing payments were not enough to pay for their electrical usage. They had to pay the difference at the end of the year. How much did they owe the utility company?

11. Last winter, the Kranepool family used 431 gallons of heating oil at a price of $4.12 per gallon. If the price increases 8.25% next year, what will their approximate heating expense be for the year? Round to the nearest ten dollars.

12. A typical light bulb requires 60 watts to run when it is turned on. If a light fixture requires three of these bulbs, and the light is left on unnecessarily for four hours per day, how many kWh of electricity are wasted each year?

13. Mr. Denton's last water bill was for $109.56. The previous reading was 1,209 ccf and the present reading was 1,417 ccf. What does his water company charge for 100 cubic feet of water? Round to the nearest cent.

14. The Manilow family paid their electric bill using balanced billing all last year. The monthly payment was m dollars. At the end of the year, the electric company told them they used more electricity than they were billed for, and they owed d dollars. Express the value of the electricity used by the Manilows last year algebraically.

15. A water bill listed a previous reading of 4,501 ccf and a present reading of 4,971 ccf. The water company charges $0.86 per ccf of water. What should have been charged on this water bill?

16. One watt hour is equivalent to 3.413 BTUs per hour.

   a. If an air conditioner is rated at 10,000 BTU, how many watts does it require per hour? Round to the nearest hundred watts.

   b. Express your answer to part a in kWh.

   c. If you run an air conditioner for 15 hours per day, and electricity costs $0.12 per kWh, estimate the cost of running the air conditioner for 15 hours on 60 summer days. Round to the nearest dollar.

17. The following box-and-whisker plot gives the monthly costs of electricity for the Sharkey household for the year.

$112 $166 $202 $325 $398

   a. How many months was the bill $202 or less?

   b. How many months had bills greater than or equal to $166?

   c. If they have gas heat, and they live in Virginia, which month do you think had the $398 bill? Explain your reasoning.

   d. If they have electric heat, and they live in Minnesota, which month do you think had the $398 bill? Explain.

18. The Lennon family used x dollars worth of electricity two years ago and then switched to balanced billing.

   a. Express the amount of their monthly balanced billing payment algebraically.

   b. Last year, they underpaid their bill and were charged c dollars at the end of the year to make up for the underpaid charges. Express the amount of this year's balanced billing monthly payment algebraically, if it was based on last year's usage.

19. How many cubic feet are represented by the following water meter?

Financial Algebra Workbook 11-1

20. It has been reported that an electric clothes dryer can account for about 12% of the electricity used in an average household. With that much electrical consumption in mind, it is important to choose wisely when making a dryer purchase. WestEnd Electric manufactures two different types of clothes dryers. The Energy Dry model costs $700 and is expected to use $140 per year in electricity. The Vista model costs $400 and is expected to use $180 per year in electricity.

a. Set up a cost function, $E(x)$, to represent the cost of owning and operating the Energy Dry model over a period of x years.

b. Set up a cost function, $V(x)$, to represent the cost of owning and operating the Vista model over a period of x years.

c. Set up an average yearly cost rational function, $A(x)$, for the Energy Dry model.

d. Set up an average yearly cost rational function, $B(x)$, for the Vista model.

e. Graph both average yearly cost functions $A(x)$ and $B(x)$ on the same axes. Interpret the graphs in terms of the average yearly cost for owning and operating each dryer.

11-2 Electronic Utilities

Exercises

1. Micaela's cell phone plan has a monthly fee of $87, which includes unlimited free text messages and phone calls, and 4GB of data. Each extra GB of data costs $15. Find the cost of a month in which Micaela uses 5.2GB of data.

2. A wireless phone company's *Call-All* phone plan has a basic charge per month, which includes a certain amount of gigabytes. There is a charge for each additional gigabyte. The split function below gives the price $c(g)$ of using gigabytes for data. Fractions of a gigabyte are charged as if they were a full GB.

$$c(g) = \begin{cases} 59 & \text{when } g \leq 6 \\ 59 + 16.50(g - 6) & \text{when } g > 6 \text{ and } g \text{ is an integer} \\ 59 + 16.50\lceil g - 6\rceil + 1 & \text{when } g > 6 \text{ and } g \text{ is not an integer} \end{cases}$$

   a. Describe the cost of the *Call-All* phone plan by interpreting the split function.

   b. Find the monthly cost of the *Call-All* phone plan for someone that used 7.7GB.

3. The Tech-N-Text phone company charges $48 for unlimited texting per month, or $0.16 per text message sent or received. For what amount of text messages would the unlimited plan cost the same as the per-text plan?

4. Next-Text charges $19 for a pre-paid phone card with 250 text messages included. If the customer goes over the 250 messages, the cost is $0.12 per text message. They have an unlimited plan, which costs $45 per month.

   a. If t represents the number of text messages, and $c(t)$ represents the cost of the messages, express $c(t)$ as a split function in terms of t.

   b. Graph the function from part a. What are the coordinates of the cusp?

   c. On the same axes, graph the function $c(t) = 45$, which represents the cost under the unlimited plan.

   d. Find the coordinates of the point of intersection of the two graphs. Round to the nearest hundredth.

   e. For what number of text messages are the costs of the two different plans the same? Round to the nearest integer.

5. A cable TV provider charges Nina $99 per month for three services—Internet, land-line phone, and cable television. In addition, Nina's monthly bill for cell phone calls and text messages averages $59.70 per month. What is her average cost per day for these four services? Round to the nearest dollar.

6. Randi, a college student, is taking a semester abroad. She purchases a one-time use, 90-day international cell phone plan. There is a one-time fee of $85 and it includes 400MB of data usage. Each extra MB, or part thereof, of data costs $0.21. Express the cost of this plan as a piecewise function.

7. Examine the following split function which gives the cost $c(t)$ of t text messages per month.

$$c(t) = \begin{cases} w & \text{when } t \le r \\ w + k(t - r) & \text{when } t > r \end{cases}$$

a. If Sophie had r text messages, what is the cost for the month?

b. Is the cost of $2r$ text messages double the cost of r text messages? Explain.

8. Eleni uses 6.8 GB of data per month and plan, which costs $70 per month and includes 4GB of data. Each extra GB is x. Express algebraically the average cost per GB of using this plan when 6.8GB of data are used.

9. The Super Vision cable TV/Internet/phone provider advertises a flat $100 monthly fee for all three services for a new customer. The rate is guaranteed for 5 years. Cable Zone normally charges $46 for monthly home phone service, $36 for monthly Internet service, and $56 for monthly cable television.

a. How much could a customer save during the first year by switching from Cable Zone to Super Vision?

b. Super Vision raises the rates 23% after a new customer's first year, how much will a customer who switched from Super Vision save in the second year?

c. If Super Vision raises the rates 18% for the third year compared to the second year, which company is cheaper for the third year?

10. A phone company set the following rate schedule for an *m*-minute call from any of its airport pay phones.

$$c(m) = \begin{cases} 0.95 & \text{when } m \le 6 \\ 0.95 + 0.24(m-6) & \text{when } m > 6 \text{ and } m \text{ is an integer} \\ 0.95 + 0.24([m-6]+1) & \text{when } m > 6 \text{ and } m \text{ is not an integer} \end{cases}$$

What is the difference in the costs of a $10\frac{1}{2}$ minute call compared to an 11-minute call?

11. Tay wants to purchase a new cell phone and change her service provider to WestCell. She can either buy the phone through WestCell or purchase the phone on her own at an electronics store or website. If she buys the phone through WestCell, they are offering her a reduced price in which they subsidize the difference between the discounted and regular price of the phone. She will also need to purchase the service plan through them. If she buys the phone on her own, she will then need to shop around for a service plan provider. Tay found the following information on both types of plans for the latest version of a smart phone she wishes to purchase:

Subsidized by WestCell: $250 for the phone plus $80 per month for unlimited talk and text and 3 GB of data.

Unsubsidized: $700 for the phone purchased at Great Buy plus a monthly $60 service plan through the provider RingZ for unlimited talk and text and 3 GB of data.

Create an average cost rational function for each possibility. Graph the functions and interpret the intersection point.

11-3   Charting a Budget

Exercises

1. Construct a pie chart to represent the percentages that Theo has determined as his monthly expenses.

   Household: 32%

   Education: 23%

   Transportation: 16%

   Health: 12%

   Savings: 9%

   Miscellaneous: 8%

2. Identify the approximate percentages allocated for each of the categories in the pie chart.

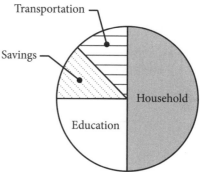

Budget Categories

3. The pie chart shows Winnie's monthly budget allocation of $4,000. Construct a bar graph using this information. Use the categories for the horizontal axis and the budgeted amounts for the vertical axis.

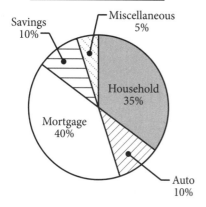

Winnie's Monthly Budget

Name _____   Date _____

4. Create a year-long budget matrix to chart the following medical related expenses: Healthcare premium: $120 twice a month; Prescriptions: $80 monthly; Physical exams: $225 semiannually; Dental insurance: $60 quarterly; Eyeglasses: $300 annually (June); Physical Therapy: $100 (bimonthly beginning in February).

5. Vinny's financial budget is as follows: The percentage budgeted for his retirement account is three times the percentage for his savings account. The percentage budgeted for his savings account is one-fourth the percentage budgeted for his checking account. The percentage budgeted for his stock investments is two-thirds the percentage budgeted for his retirement account. What is the percentage for checking? If $1,200 is budgeted for the entire category, how much goes to each account?

6. The bar graph shows budgeted monthly utility expenses for a 1-year period.

a. What is the total annual amount budgeted for utilities?

b. What percent of the total yearly amount was budgeted for the months of June–September?

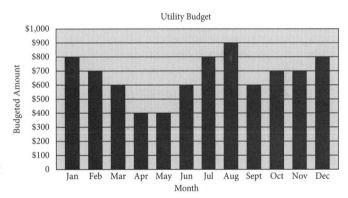

c. The homeowners replaced their furnace with a more energy efficient one. They were told that they could decrease their utility budget for the upcoming month of January by 20% from the previous January amount. How much will they budget for utilities in January?

7. Construct a bar graph for the September budget category "Personal Items" using the following amounts: Hair cut $20, Clothing purchases $60, Books $20, Newspapers/Magazines $65, Online Subscriptions $30, Gifts $80, Donations $40, and Other $50.

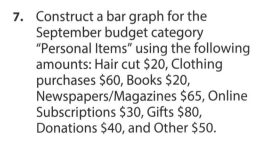

8. Tina's primary source of income pays a fixed amount and her secondary source of income varies monthly. In preparing her budget for the year, she has entered the amounts she has agreed to be paid when working her second job in the given months. She also has income from interest-bearing savings accounts and stock dividends. She used actual amounts from the previous year to set up this budget for the upcoming year.

	Jan	Feb	Mar	Apr	May	Jun	Jul	Aug	Sep	Oct	Nov	Dec
Primary Source	7,500	7,500	7,500	7,500	7,500	7,500	7,500	7,500	7,500	7,500	7,500	7,500
Secondary Source	1,300	1,800			1,500		2,500	1,500		2,200	2,000	4,000
Interest			250			280			310			350
Dividends			600			150			150			150
Other						3,000						3,000

a. What is her budgeted income for each month?

b. Construct a line graph of this budget.

c. Determine the average monthly income to the nearest dollar.

d. Draw a horizontal line on your graph representing that amount. What months fell below the average?

9. Aida created a double bar graph to illustrate the actual amounts spent this year for household expenses and the budgeted amounts for the following year. The following year's amounts reflect a 5% increase over the COLA. For June, the actual amount is $1,200 and the budgeted amount for Year 2 is $1,320.

a. What was the cost of living adjustment that Aida used to get the budgeted amounts?

b. Determine the budgeted amount for January of Year 2.

Household Expenses

Actual Amount Year 1
Budgeted Amount Year 2

c. The August actual amount was the exact amount Aida had budgeted for. This actual amount reflected an 8% increase over the previous year's actual amount for August. What was the previous year's actual amount for August rounded to the nearest dollar?

10. Under his "Garden Project" budget category, Steve has allocated $480 for two types of ground cover material. He can purchase "Premium Landscaping Rock" for $8 per bag or "Cedar Mulch Chips" for $4 per bag. Both bags cover the same square footage. He wants to buy a combination of both and stay within his budget.

   a. Determine a budget line equation for this situation.

   b. Graph the budget line depicting the different combinations of rock bags and cedar bags that Steve can purchase while still remaining within his budget.

   c. Name a combination of rock bags and cedar bags that will allow him to meet his budget exactly.

   d. Name a combination of rock bags and cedar bags that will keep him under budget.

   e. Name a combination of rock bags and cedar bags that will cause him to be over budget.

11. Jen's employer gives her a budget of $500 per month for transportation. She has determined that the cost of using a car-share vehicle is $20 per round trip and the cost of using a limousine service is $25 per round-trip. She wants to stay within the budget for these trips by using a combination of both.

   a. Write a budget line equation for this situation.

   b. Construct the budget line graph that models this situation.

   c. What do the points on the budget line represent?

   d. What do points below the budget line represent?

   e. Suppose that the budgeted amount increases to $600. Construct the new budget line and the old budget line on the same axes.

   f. What does the region in between the two lines represent?

11-4   Cash Flow and Budgeting

Exercises

1. Below is a budget table listing the actual amounts that were spent for each of the utilities categories during the first 6 months of the year. Freda wants to alter her current budget during the last 6 months and use the average of the actual amounts in each category. Complete the table with the average amount for each category.

	Jan	Feb	Mar	Apr	May	Jun	Average
Electric	110	140	135	135	130	140	a.
Water	90	85	76	80	85	85	b.
Cable	110	105	115	120	115	115	c.
Cell phone	80	90	120	140	110	110	d.
Land-line phone	40	35	35	35	40	45	e.
Sanitation	60	70	70	60	60	60	f.
Heating Fuel	450	520	500	300	100	50	g.

2. Quincy Gallois is single and owns a co-op. He has calculated the following assets and liabilities. Find Quincy's net worth.

ASSETS

Current value of the co-op: $180,000

Current value of car: $12,500

Checking account balance: $1,300

Combined savings: $18,000

Balance in retirement account: $30,000

Current value of owned electronics: $20,000

LIABILITIES

Remaining balance on mortgage: $120,000

Remaining balance on personal loan: $4,600

Combined credit card debt: $23,000

3. Celine's monthly liabilities and assets are given in the table. Determine Celine's debt-to-income ratio. Express that ratio as a percent.

Monthly Liabilities (Debt)		Monthly Pre-Tax Assets (Income)	
Mortgage Payment	$2,560	Gross Salary	$6,900
Student Loan Payment	$350	Income from Rental Property	$900
Minimum Credit Card Payment	$50		
Car Loan Payment	$120		

Use the following financial information for Bill Marshall to answer Exercises 4–8.

Financial Report			
Income			
Architect, monthly after-tax income: $8,000			
Consultant, monthly after-tax income: $2,000			
Monthly Expenses			
Rent	$2,800	Groceries	$220
Car loan	$200	Personal loan	$300
Electricity	$80	Land line phone	$40
Sanitation	$50	Auto insurance	$300
Cable/Internet	$100	Savings	$600
Dining out	$200	College loan	$260
Gasoline	$180	Cell phone	$90
Water	$40	Medical insurance	$60
Renter's insurance	$50	Entertainment	$200
Credit card debt	$500		

Non-Monthly Expenses
Medical: $300 in June, $160 in October
Auto-related: $1,200 in July
Home-related: $300 in March, $600 in September
Life insurance: $200 in February, June, October
Computer: $3,000 in January
Vacation: $1,200 in August
Gifts: $500 in May, $400 in December
Contributions: $20 each week of the year
Repairs: $1,500 in November

4. The Consumer Credit Counseling Service suggests that the monthly food budget be no greater than 30% of the income.

   a. What is Bill's total monthly food bill including dining out?

   b. What percent of his income is spent on food?

5. Examine Bill's non-monthly expenses. Find the total and the monthly average of these expenses.

Financial Algebra Workbook 11-4

6. Use the cash flow to construct a cash flow plan for Bill. What is his monthly cash flow?

INCOME				
Primary Employment				
Secondary Employment				
Other Employment				
TOTAL INCOME				
FIXED EXPENSES		NON-MONTHLY EXPENSES (per year)		
Rent/Mortgage		Medical/Dental		
Car Loan Payment		Auto-related		
Education Loan Payment		Home-related		
Personal Loan Payment		Life Insurance		
Health Insurance Premium		Computer		
Cable/Internet		Vacation		
Car Insurance Premium		Gifts		
Homeowner's/Renter's Insurance		Contributions		
TOTAL FIXED EXPENSES		Repairs		
		TOTAL NON-MONTHLY EXPENSES (per year)		
VARIABLE EXPENSES		TOTAL NON-MONTHLY EXPENSES (per month)		
Groceries (food)				
Dining Out				
Fuel (car)				
Cell Phone				
Land Line Phone				
Electricity				
Water				
Sanitation				
Entertainment				
Savings				
Debt Reduction				
Other				
TOTAL VARIABLE EXPENSES				
TOTAL EXPENSES				
MONTHLY CASH FLOW				

7. Create a frequency budget for Bill. Although his food, fuel, dining out, and entertainment expenses were listed as monthly for the cash flow, they should be considered as weekly expenses here. To find the weekly amount, multiply the monthly amount by 12 and then divide by 52 weeks. Round your answer up to the nearest dollar. Combine electricity, water, and sanitation under the "utilities" category. Any categories not mentioned in the template belong in the appropriate "other" section. What is Bill's surplus or deficit for the year?

AFTER TAX INCOME CATEGORIES	INCOME AMOUNTS	FREQUENCY	ANNUAL AMOUNT
Primary Employment			
Secondary Employment			
Interest			
Dividends			
Other Income			
TOTAL INCOME			
WEEKLY EXPENSES	**EXPENSE AMOUNTS**		
Food			
Personal Transportation			
Public Transportation			
Household			
Childcare			
Dining Out			
Entertainment			
Other (contributions)			
TOTAL WEEKLY EXPENSES			
MONTHLY EXPENSES			
Rent			
Utilities			
Land Line/Cellular Telephone			
Car Loan			
Education Loan			
Personal Loan			
Health Insurance			
Cable/Internet			
Car Insurance			
Renter's Insurance			
Savings			
Debt Reduction			
(continued on next page)			
(continued from previous page)			
Other			

TOTAL MONTHLY EXPENSES			
OTHER FREQUENCY EXPENSES			
Medical/Dental			
Auto-related			
Home-related			
Life insurance			
Computer purchase			
Vacation			
Gifts			
Contributions			
Repairs			
Taxes			
Other			
TOTAL OTHER FREQUENCY EXPENSES			
TOTAL EXPENSES			
ANNUAL SURPLUS or DEFICIT			

8. Use the year-long budget template on the next two pages to create a year-long budget for Bill.

	Jan	Feb	Mar	Apr	May	Jun	Jul	Aug	Sep	Oct	Nov	Dec
INCOME												
Primary Employment												
Secondary Employment												
Other Employment												
TOTAL INCOME												
FIXED EXPENSES												
Rent/Mortgage												
Car Loan Payment												
Education Loan Payment												
Personal Loan Payment												
Health Insurance Premium												
Cable/Internet												
Car Insurance Premium												
Homeowner's/Renter's Insurance												
Life Insurance												
VARIABLE EXPENSES												
Groceries (food)												
Dining Out												
Fuel (car)												
Cell Phone												

(continued on next page)

(continued from previous page)	Jan	Feb	Mar	Apr	May	Jun	Jul	Aug	Sep	Oct	Nov	Dec
Land Line Phone												
Electricity												
Water												
Sanitation												
Medical/Dental												
Auto-related												
Home-related												
Vacation												
Gifts												
Contributions												
Repairs												
Entertainment												
Savings												
Debt Reduction												
Computer												
Other												
TOTAL EXPENSES												

11-5 | Budget Matrices

Exercises

1. Examine these three matrices:

$$X = \begin{bmatrix} 2 & 5 & -1 \\ 3 & 0 & 4 \\ 6 & 1 & 1 \end{bmatrix}, \qquad Y = \begin{bmatrix} 4.5 & 10 \\ 8 & 9 \\ -7 & 3 \end{bmatrix}, \qquad Z = \begin{bmatrix} 7 & -2.5 & 6 \\ 3 & 4 & -5 \\ 5.2 & -1 & 0 \end{bmatrix}$$

a. What are the dimensions of Y?

b. List the elements of Z with their location symbols.

Determine each matrix in c–i.

c. $X + Z$

d. $Z + X$

e. $X - Z$

f. $Z - X$

g. $3Z$

h. $0.5X$

i. XY

2. Examine this portion of Chase's budget chart for April, May, and June:

Variable Expenses	April	May	June
Groceries	$800	$600	$750
Dining Out	250	100	50
Fuel (Car)	350	350	350
Cell Phone	90	70	85
Electricity	50	75	60
Water	40	40	40

Let matrix C be a 6 by 3 matrix whose elements are the entries in the budget chart above.

a. What is the value of the element $C_{2,3}$?

b. What is the value of the element $C_{5,1}$?

c. What is the value of the element $C_{6,2}$?

d. Which element has a value of 60?

e. Which element has a value of 90?

f. What would happen to each of the elements in the matrix $4C$?

3. What are the dimensions of each of the following matrices?

a. $\begin{bmatrix} 1 \\ 3 \end{bmatrix}$

b. $\begin{bmatrix} -0.5 \end{bmatrix}$

c. $\begin{bmatrix} 6 & 0 & 7 & 112 & 19 & 5 \end{bmatrix}$

d. $\begin{bmatrix} 2 & 1 & 0 & 0 \\ 0 & 1 & 0 & 1 \\ 0 & 0 & 1 & 2 \end{bmatrix}$

e. $\begin{bmatrix} 0.08 & 11 & 0 & 0.6 \\ 3 & 1 & 4 & 6 \\ \frac{1}{2} & \frac{1}{4} & \frac{3}{8} & \frac{4}{5} \\ 0.7 & 0.77 & 0.725 & 0.7 \\ 0 & 1 & 1 & 0 \end{bmatrix}$

4. Given $A = \begin{bmatrix} 1 & 2 & 3 & 4 \\ 4 & 3 & 2 & 1 \end{bmatrix}$, $B = \begin{bmatrix} 0 & 1 \\ 1 & 0 \\ 1 & 1 \end{bmatrix}$, $C = \begin{bmatrix} 8 & 8 & 2 \\ 2 & 8 & 8 \end{bmatrix}$, $D = \begin{bmatrix} -0.5 & 0.3 \end{bmatrix}$

$E = \begin{bmatrix} 1 & 2 & 3 \\ 4 & 5 & 6 \end{bmatrix}$, $F = \begin{bmatrix} 0 & 7 & 0 \\ 6 & 4 & 2 \\ 9 & 2 & 2 \end{bmatrix}$, $G = \begin{bmatrix} 1 & 0 \\ 7 & 8 \\ 2 & 5 \end{bmatrix}$, $H = \begin{bmatrix} 9 & 8 \\ -9 & -8 \end{bmatrix}$

Which of the following matrix operations are defined?

a. $A + B$ **b.** $E + H$ **c.** $4C - 3E$ **d.** $E + G$ **e.** BC **f.** AF **g.** A^2 **h.** F^2

5. Mason's Internet supplier is making a gradual increase in fees from January to June according to the following plan:

January $80

February 0.5% increase

March 0.65 % increase from January

April 0.8% increase from January

May 0.9% increase from January

June 1% increase from January.

Let matrix A be the matrix of 6 months of fees before the increase.

$A = \begin{bmatrix} 80 & 80 & 80 & 80 & 80 & 80 \end{bmatrix}$

Let matrix B be the percent increase matrix with entries written as equivalent decimals.

$B = \begin{bmatrix} 1 \\ 1.005 \\ 1.0065 \\ 1.008 \\ 1.009 \\ 1.01 \end{bmatrix}$

Calculate AB. What does that matrix represent?

6. Zeb and Avril are married computer specialists. Their job requires them to take graduate school computer science courses to keep their skills fresh. They keep individual budget charts of their education-related expenses for tax purposes. The charts below are for the spring semester.

Zeb's Expenses

Category	February	March	April	May
Tuition	$280	$280	$280	$280
Supplies	60	60	0	0
Transportation	90	90	90	90
Downloads	120	0	50	0
Fees	40	40	40	40

Avril's Expenses

Category	February	March	April	May
Tuition	$400	$400	$400	$400
Supplies	50	100	0	0
Transportation	150	200	150	150
Downloads	300	0	0	0
Fees	70	70	70	70

a. Let matrix Z be a 5 by 4 matrix consisting of Zeb's expenses. Write matrix Z.

b. Let matrix A be a 5 by 4 matrix consisting of Avril's expenses. Write matrix A.

c. What would $A + Z$ represent? Write matrix $A + Z$, their combined education-related expenses.

7. Use Avril's matrix *A* from exercise #6b above. Avril knows that in the next 4-month semester her tuition will decrease by 10%, her supplies will decrease by 5%, her transportation will remain the same, her download costs will remain the same, and her fees will increase by 10%. Write a 1 by 5 percent change matrix that could be multiplied times matrix *A* to yield a 1 by 4 matrix that will list the total education-related expenses for each month. Then determine that final matrix.

8. Determine the values of *a, b,* and *c* in the following matrix equation.

$$X = \begin{bmatrix} 3 & a & 2 \\ -1 & 4 & c \\ 5 & 6 & -7 \end{bmatrix} \quad Y = \begin{bmatrix} 1 & 6 \\ 5 & 0 \\ 8 & -2 \end{bmatrix}$$

$$XY = \begin{bmatrix} 24 & b \\ 51 & -14 \\ -21 & 44 \end{bmatrix}$$

9. The Verrazano High School Ski Club is having a fundraiser. They are selling school water bottles, ski caps, and stuffed mascots to make enough money to go to the ski competition in December. The following matrix gives the sales numbers for September, October, and November.

	September	October	November
Water Bottles	200	150	250
Ski Caps	180	100	150
Mascots	90	80	120

The profit that the club makes on each item sold is given here:

Water Bottles	Ski Caps	Mascots
$2.00	$4.00	$3.25

Find the product of the two matrices. Explain what the product represents.

For Practice

For Practice

For Practice

For Practice

For Practice

For Practice

For Practice

TABLE 4.1

Parametric and Nonparametric Statistical Tests to Assess Relationships and Differences for Two Groupings of Data and More Than (>) Two Groupings (all tests can be performed on SPSS)

Purpose and type of test	No. of data groupings	Paired groupings[a]	Name of test
Assessing relationships			
Parametric statistics (interval or ratio scales)	2	Yes	Pearson r
	> 2	Yes	Pearson r if testing each grouping against each other
	> 2	Yes	Multiple regression testing if two or more groupings predict another grouping
Nonparametric statistics (nominal or ordinal scales)	2	Yes	Spearman (rho) rank correlation (ordinal scale)[b]
Assessing differences			
Parametric statistics (interval or ratio scales)	2	Yes/no	Paired/independent t test
	> 2	Yes/no	Analysis of variance (ANOVA)
Nonparametric statistics (nominal or ordinal scales)	2	Yes	McNemar test (nominal scale) Wilcoxon matched-pairs signed-ranks test (ordinal scale)
	2	No	Chi-square (χ^2, nominal scale) Mann-Whitney U (ordinal scale)
	>2[c]	Yes	Cochran Q test (nominal scale) Friedman χ^2 (ordinal scale)
	> 2[c]	No	Chi-square (χ^2, nominal scale) Kruskal-Wallis H or k-sample median test (ordinal scale)

[a]Other names for paired data groupings are dependent groups, matched groups, related samples, repeated measures, and within-subjects testing. Yes/no means that versions of the test will accept either paired or independent data groupings.

[b]The table does not include nonparametric statistics for assessing relationships with *nominal* data (*phi coefficient* or *point biserial correlation* tests) because they are used mainly to assess effect size.

[c]If the design is a factorial—that is, it combines more than one independent variable (see Chapter 9), nonparametric statistics provide only an incomplete or fragmented analysis.

Sources: Siegel (1956) and Tabachnick & Fidell (2001)

Instructions: When using the table to identify the statistical test to use for an analysis, move from left to right, making four decisions:

1. Do you want to assess a relationship or a difference between your data groupings? If you're assessing a relationship, use only the upper half of the table; if difference, use only the lower half.

2. Are your data on an interval or ratio scale or on a nominal or ordinal scale? If interval or ratio, use only the shaded area (which covers only parametric statistics); if nominal or ordinal, use only the nonshaded area (nonparametric statistics).

3. How many data groupings will be included in the analysis?

4. Are the data in the groupings paired (such as, repeated measures or within subjects)?

Answering these questions in the listed order leads you to the correct statistic to use.

RESEARCH METHODS

USING PROCESSES
AND PROCEDURES
OF SCIENCE TO
UNDERSTAND BEHAVIOR

EDWARD P. SARAFINO
THE COLLEGE OF NEW JERSEY

PEARSON

Prentice
Hall

UPPER SADDLE RIVER, NEW JERSEY 07458

Library of Congress Cataloging-in-Publication Data

Sarafino, Edward P.
    Research methods : using processes and procedures of science to understand behavior / Edward P.
Sarafino.—1st ed.
        p. cm.
    Includes bibliographical references and indexes.
    ISBN 0-13-111161-2
    1. Psychology—Research—Methodology—Textbooks.   I. Title.

BF 76.5.S25 2005
150'.72—dc22

                                                                    2004012988

Editorial Director: Leah Jewell
Executive Editor: Jessica Mosher
Editorial Assistant: Kerri Scott
Assistant Managing Editor: Maureen Richardson
Production Liaison: Fran Russello
Manufacturing Buyer: Tricia Kenny
Cover Design: Bruce Kenselaar
Cover Illustration/Photo: JMG Design
Composition/Full-Service Project Management: Patty Donovan/Pine Tree Composition
Printer/Binder: RR Donnelley & Sons Company
Cover Printer: The Lehigh Press, Inc.

Pearson Education LTD., London
Pearson Education Singapore, Pte. Ltd
Pearson Education, Canada, Ltd
Pearson Education—Japan
Pearson Education Australia PTY, Limited
Pearson Education North Asia Ltd
Pearson Educación de Mexico, S.A. de C.V.
Pearson Education Malaysia, Pte. Ltd
Pearson Education, Upper Saddle River, New Jersey

10 9 8 7 6 5 4 3 2 1
ISBN 0-13-111161-2

TO PRECIOUS

AND TO MY STUDENTS
WHOSE QUESTIONS INSPIRED
MY CONTINUED LEARNING

Brief Contents

CONTENTS

PREFACE

Probably all instructors of research methods have had this experience: most students enter the course with feelings of trepidation, having heard it is "hard," and with questions about the relevance of the material to their lives because they don't expect to conduct research in their intended careers. The happy follow-up is that students generally finish the course having mastered the material pretty well and realized that they have acquired cognitive skills that will benefit them in subsequent courses, in nonresearch careers, and in daily judgments and thought processes. The course is challenging for students and instructors alike—and it's worth the effort. To promote student mastery, the textbook must present the material in an organized and clear way for students to understand its concepts and be able to integrate and apply them.

Early praise for Sarafino's Research Methods....

- " I very much admire Dr. Sarafino's clear, straightforward, and often humorous writing style. I enjoy the examples he gives and I think he is doing a nice job incorporating examples from many different areas of psychology."—Carrie Bulger, Quinnipiac College
- "The section on testing for main effects is EXCELLENT! Very clear description of how and why we test for main effects.... The entire section on interpreting interaction effects is great, well written with clear examples of interaction effects. The explanations of how to talk about interaction effects are excellent."—Paul Meritt, George Washington University

The book describes many dozens of basic and applied studies as examples of concepts in research methods. These studies include both classic and modern research on various topics published over the last few decades to show the substantial generality and uniformity of fundamental research concepts and strategies across time and fields in psychology.

PEDAGOGY AND ORGANIZATION

This book contains many pedagogical features. Each chapter begins with a *contents* list, giving students an overview of the progression of major topics and concepts. Then a *prologue* introduces the chapter with a lively and engaging vignette that describes a study with methods that are relevant to the chapter material and an overview of the basic ideas to be covered. The body of each chapter includes many *figures* and *tables* to clarify concepts or research findings. Important terms are **boldfaced,** and *italics* are used liberally for other terms and for emphasis. *Boxes* present additional interesting material to expand on and clarify concepts. Icons placed at appropriate points in the text indicate the availability of *Web tutorials* on a topic. Each chapter ends with a substantial *summary,* a list of *key terms,* essay-type *review questions,* lists of print and Internet *resources,* and a few *application activities.* All key terms are defined in a *glossary* at the back of the book.

The overall organizational framework follows the sequence of considerations and activities in the usual research process. As the contents shows, the book contains *12 chapters* and *two appendixes* in the following five parts.

- *Part I: Fundamentals of Research.* Chapter 1 gives an overview and brief history of science and then introduces students to the concepts of theories, hypotheses, and research strategies (experimental, quasi-experimental, correlational, and descriptive). Chapter 2 describes sources of research ideas, methods for searching the literature, and ways to form hypotheses. Chapter 3 focuses on ethics in research, giving the latest APA guidelines. Chapter 4 presents approaches to measurement, the types and features of data, and basic concepts in statistics and significance testing.

- *Part II: Essential Concepts of Research Strategies.* Chapter 5 discusses experimental strategies, focusing on the concepts of causal inference, systematic and nonsystematic variance, and methods for controlling unwanted variance, such as from extraneous variables. Chapter 6 describes nonexperimental strategies, particularly quasi-experimental and correlational strategies, indicating how they differ from experimental strategies and how correlational statistics are used, such as in assessing the reliability and validity of measurements.

- *Part III: Research Design, Analysis, and Preparation.* Chapter 7 discusses two-level and multilevel independent-groups designs with a single factor and procedures for statistical analysis of these designs. Chapter 8 covers two- and multilevel within-subjects and matched-groups designs with a single factor and methods for counterbalancing order effects and for statistical analysis of these designs. Chapter 9 describes factorial designs and statistical concepts and analyses of their data. Chapter 10 gives detailed instructions and checklists for designing and carrying out research.

- *Part IV: Applied, Descriptive, and Advanced Methods.* Chapter 11 discusses intra-subject (small-*N*) designs and methods of data analysis. Chapter 12 focuses on descriptive research strategies, program evaluation research, and advanced methods, such as meta-analysis. Like most research methods texts, I save the material in these chapters for the end of the book because students rarely conduct studies with these techniques in a research methods course.

- *Part V: Appendixes.* Appendix A focuses on writing research reports, giving general guidelines for effective writing and detailed information on preparing an APA-style research report. Appendix B covers statistical procedures, presenting step-by-step instructions for using SPSS to perform each of the parametric and nonparametric tests discussed in the book, directions for preparing tables and graphs, and statistical tables.

As this description indicates, this book's overall organization is similar to that used in most books on research methods. Some chapters were written to be relatively independent of others in content, providing a good deal of flexibility in the order with which they are covered. For example, Chapters 2 (on developing research ideas) and 3 (on ethics) can be placed later in the sequence, and Chapters 10 (on preparing to do research), 11 (on intrasubject designs), and 12 (on descriptive and program evaluation research) can be covered earlier.

UNIQUE FEATURES OF THE BOOK

This book has several unique features designed to address some of the challenges or problems the material on research methods presents for students. Most of the features I have included to solve these problems have been exceptionally well received from reviewers. Here are six noteworthy problems and the solutions I have incorporated.

1. *Problem:* The concepts are not psychological and are abstract and technical. *Solutions:* In addition to writing engagingly and presenting copious explanatory examples, figures, and tables, I have included two unique features. First, the prologue for each chapter consists of an interesting *vignette* that describes the rationale, method, and outcome of a relevant study that I then refer to later as an example of concepts, such as random assignment. Of this feature, one reviewer said, "I especially like the idea of beginning each chapter with a single vignette that is then used as a reference to illustrate key concepts." Second, the Companion Website has *tutorials,* each keyed with an icon in the chapter to specific material it addresses. Reviewers have commented that the integration of technology is timely and that the extensive tutorials are a plus.

2. *Problem:* Students have difficulty integrating and coordinating methods when designing and carrying out research. *Solutions:* Chapter 1 presents a brief *overview of the research strategies*—experimental, quasi-experimental, correlational, and descriptive—and a *diagram* comparing their ability meet the three criteria for cause–effect conclusions. Chapter 10 describes and gives *checklists for detailed activities to complete in designing and preparing to carry out a study* using any of the designs covered in the book. Regarding Chapter 10, a reviewer said, "I think this chapter is a very innovative one. It provides students with the 'nuts-and-bolts' of carrying out a study in the real world of research.... Many of the questions my students often raise with regard to [preparing a research proposal] are covered in this chapter. I like the way the author has cross-referenced the questions in Table 10.1 with relevant chapters in the book."

3. *Problem:* Students don't know which statistics to use. *Solution:* In addition to presenting descriptions of appropriate parametric and nonparametric tests for each type of research design, this book uses a unique procedure with *Table 4.1 by which students can identify the appropriate test* to use for their type of data and design. A reviewer said, "The diagrams and tables proposed to help students select appropriate statistical procedures are good (this point is one of the most difficult for my students to master)."

4. *Problem:* Students don't remember how to calculate statistics or know how to make tables and graphs. *Solutions:* Appendix B gives step-by-step *instructions for using SPSS* to calculate each of the inferential tests discussed in the book and presents detailed *directions for making tables and graphs* with computers. The student version of SPSS is available for purchase with this text (it will run all statistics covered in the book, except repeated measures ANOVA). A reviewer said, "I am particularly enchanted by the idea of step-by-step instructions for using SPSS."

5. *Problem:* Students have trouble integrating and following all the writing rules for APA-style reports. *Solution:* Appendix A not only describes general writing tips and the types of content in specific sections, but it also gives easy-to-follow *lists* of tips and of the ordering of content in sections.

6. *Problem:* Some students worry that they won't be able to design, conduct, and analyze data from a study. *Solution:* In addition to the features described earlier that will help students learn and coordinate the research methods material, I occasionally present brief descriptions of my own students' studies. One reviewer said, "I particularly like … examples of student research. This will be key in getting students to realize that research is not as daunting as they think it is."

LIST OF STUDENT RESEARCHERS

Over my decades of teaching research methods, I have been fortunate to have many fine students each semester who design and conduct impressive projects, some of which I've mentioned in this book as examples of methods and designs. I want to acknowledge these students at this time. They are, alphabetically: Danielle Benson, Jaime Bezek, Tracy Caldwell, Allison Carpenter, Marcia Deeny, Allison Durar, Rachel Engelson, Christine Gallagher, Jennifer Glass, Lauren Greenfield, Pavel Kloupar, Jonathan Lai, Tinera McNair, Karen Moore, Maria Pazos, Laura Petrick, Samantha Reece, Carolynn Ritter, Christen Rogers, April Stone, Tiffany Stone, Sara Termini, Jason Torchio, and Robert Werthwein.

SUPPLEMENTAL MATERIALS

An **Instructor's manual,** written by John E. Sparrow, University of New Hampshire at Manchester, is available to instructors and can be downloaded at www.prenhall .com/psychology. Please contact your local Prentice Hall representative for User

ID and Password information. It contains a test bank and information to help instructors (a) organize and present subject matter effectively and (b) enrich class experiences through activities and discussion, such as with laboratory and active learning exercises.

The **NEW Prentice Hall's TestGen (0-13-111223-6)** is available on one dual-platform CD-ROM. This test generator program provides instructors' "best in class" features in an easy-to-use program. Create tests using the TestGen Wizard and easily select questions with drag-and-drop or point-and-click functionality. Add or modify test questions using the built-in Question Editor and print tests in a variety of formats.

Research Navigator™ features three exclusive databases full of source material, including

- *EBSCO's ContentSelect Academic Journal Database,* organized by subject. Each subject contains 50 to100 of the leading academic journals for that discipline. Instructors and students can search the online journals by keyword, topic, or multiple topics. Articles include abstract and citation information and can be cut, pasted, e-mailed, or saved for later use.
- *The New York Times Search-by-Subject One Year Archive,* organized by subject and searchable by keyword or multiple keywords. Instructors and students can view the full text of the article.
- *Link Library,* organized by subject, offers editorially selected "best of the Web" sites. Link Libraries are continually scanned and kept up to date providing the most relevant and accurate links for research assignments.

To see how this resource works, take a tour at www.researchnavigator.com or contact your local Prentice Hall representative for more details.

INFORMATION FOR STUDENTS

How can learning about scientific methods be relevant and important for you? One way is in evaluating the claims and information you hear or read in the media about products to buy, lifestyle changes to make, or issues coming up for public vote. Is there scientific evidence for the claims, and is the evidence solid? Understanding the methods of research can help you to think through these issues more carefully and critically. Other ways by which learning about research methods is important relate to your future academic and career success. Knowledge of research methods will help you understand the material in other science-based courses in psychology and other disciplines and perform better in your career, even if it doesn't involve actually doing research. If your career is in mental health or in a public agency, for example, you will need to make decisions about the best course of action to take in treating clients or in hiring or training personnel. Often there is research evidence bearing on these decisions that you'll need to consider and assess.

THE BOOK

This book was designed for you, the student. First and foremost, it provides a thorough and up-to-date presentation of the concepts and procedures in conducting research. In doing this, the book often takes a "how-to" perspective, describing in paragraphs, lists, or diagrams how you would perform the activities in designing research, collecting and analyzing data, and preparing a report. Because the material the book discusses is often abstract and can be technical, I have made special efforts to write in a straightforward, clear, and engaging fashion and to prepare diagrams and tables to explain concepts and procedures.

THE COMPANION WEBSITE

The Companion Website for this text can be accessed at www.prenhall .com/sarafino and it contains several useful features to enhance your learning experience. These features include:

- A list of *learning objectives* for each chapter that will help you organize the concepts discussed.
- A student *study guide* contains quizzes with instant scoring and coaching on questions in multiple-choice, true–false, and fill-in-the-blank formats.
- Dynamic *weblinks* offer valuable sources of additional information about science and research techniques.

Go to the site and browse as you start the course so you'll know what is available there to help you master the material and make your research activities easier.

STUDY HINTS

You can enhance your learning by using the features of the Companion Website and by using this book effectively to learn and study well. I will describe one method for using the book that works well for many students.

Survey the chapter first. Read the contents list and browse through the chapter, examining the figures and tables. Some students also find it useful to read the summary first, even though it contains terms they may not yet understand. Then read the prologue. As you begin each new section of the chapter, look at its title and turn it into a *question*. Thus, the heading early in Chapter 1, "Ways of Acquiring Knowledge and Beliefs," might become "What are the ways by which people acquire knowledge and beliefs?" Doing this helps you focus on your reading. After reading the section, *reflect* on what you have just read. Can you answer the question you asked when you reworded the title?

When you have finished the body of the chapter, *review* what you have read by reading the summary and trying to define the items in the list of key terms. If there is something you don't understand, look it up in the chapter or glossary. You may find that this is a good time to use the *Web tutorials* for the chapter. Last, *reread* the chapter at least once, concentrating on the important concepts or ideas. You may find it helpful to underline or highlight selected material now that you have a good idea of what is important. If your exam will consist of "objective" questions, such as multiple choice, using this approach intensively and answering briefly the review questions at the end of the chapter should be effective. If your exam will have essay items, you will probably find it helpful to answer thoroughly the review questions and any other likely questions you may generate. For either type of exam, the online *study guide* will help clarify what you do and do not know well so you can focus on mastering these concepts.

I hope that you enjoy this book, that you learn a great deal from it, and that you will share my enthusiasm for the scientific enterprise by the time you finish the course.

ACKNOWLEDGEMENTS

Writing this book was a huge task. I am indebted first of all to the researchers whose important and creative work I have cited. Without such work, I'd have no examples to clarify the abstract and technical concepts of research methods. I also received a great deal of direct help and encouragement from a number of people whose contributions I gratefully acknowledge.

My heartfelt thanks go to Jayme Heffler, the acquisitions editor at Prentice Hall, who saw merit in my plan and signed the book. Other Prentice Hall staff helped establish my writing schedule, oversaw the review process, coordinated the production process, and generated the marketing plan. I also appreciate the fine work of, Karen Slaght, copyediting supervisor, and Patty Donovan, production supervisor.

The cover-to-cover review process generated many helpful suggestions that have made this a better book than it would have been otherwise. I thank the reviewers for reinforcing the work I did and prodding me to do still better. These reviewers are, alphabetically: *Carrie Bulger,* Quinnipiac University; *Kathleen Donovan,* Central OK; *Steven Isonio,* Golden West CC; *William Kelemen,* CSU at Long B.; *Paul Merrit,* George Washington University; *W. Daniel Phillips,* the College of New Jersey; *Kirsten Rewey,* University of Minnesota—Twin Cities Campus; *Kenneth Sacitsky,* Williams College; *Sherry L. Serdikoff,* JMU; *John E. Sparrow,* University of New Hampshire at Manchester; *Annette Taylor,* University of San Diego; *James Tittle,* Ohio State Univ.; *Robert West,* Notre Dame; and *Lynnette Zelezny,* California State University, Fresno.

Many other individuals were important, too. I thank Persis Sturges, the instructor in my very first research methods course, whose enthusiasm for research and interest in me as a student helped keep me on track, and my friend and colleague Jim Armstrong, who served as a sounding board for my ideas. I also thank the staff at The College of New Jersey library who acquired copies of journal articles and other needed materials and several students who read a draft of the book and provided feedback.

Very personal thanks go to the closest people in my life—family, friends, and colleagues—for encouraging and supporting my efforts to complete this book and tolerating my preoccupation.

TO CONTACT THE AUTHOR

I would be pleased to receive comments and suggestions about this book from students and instructors so that I may consider those ideas for future editions. You may contact me via an e-mail at: sarafino@tcnj.edu or use my postal address: Department of Psychology, The College of New Jersey, P. O. Box 7718, Ewing, NJ 08628.

Edward P. Sarafino

ABOUT THE AUTHOR

Edward P. Sarafino received his Ph.D. from the University of Colorado more than three decades ago when he began his affiliation with the Department of Psychology at The College of New Jersey. The departments research methods course has been a major part of his teaching schedule in most semesters. His scholarship has combined areas of health, developmental, and behavioral psychology and has applied most of the research methods he describes in this book. In addition to having published dozens of research articles and chapters, he has authored six books and many revised editions. He is a fellow of Division 38 (Health Psychology) of the American Psychological Association and has served as its Secretary and on several committees of that division and of the Society of Behavioral Medicine. When he is not working, he enjoys being with friends, traveling, hiking and other outdoor activities, and going to cultural events, especially music and visual arts.

CHAPTER 1
GOALS AND METHODS OF SCIENCE

What Is Science?
Ways of Acquiring Knowledge and Beliefs
Characteristics of Science
Science and Pseudoscience
Importance of Science for Psychology and You

How the Scientific Approach Emerged
Early Approaches
The Scientific Revolution
An Example: A Little "Experiment"

Research Goals and Strategies: The Basics
Theories, Models, and Hypotheses
Goals and Strategies of Scientific Research

PROLOGUE

Let's open with a true story about a scientific idea you've learned: how life begins—that is, the basic features of conception and fetal development. A sperm from the father joins with and fertilizes the egg of the mother, with each contributing half the offspring's genetic information. Then the fertilized egg attaches to the uterine wall and begins to form elements of the offspring's anatomy. In the 17th century, people didn't know this, and Western scholars generally believed that the offspring was a tiny, fully formed being before conception (Needham, 1975). The main debate focused on whether it was in the egg or the sperm. If the offspring was in the egg, the father's contribution was simply in providing sperm that stimulated fetal growth; if it was in the sperm, the mother's contribution was simply as an incubator. But poor testing methods initially led to errors. Although the compound microscope had been invented, the magnified images it produced were not very clear. As a result, when researchers tried to test these ideas in the mid- to late 1600s by examining sperm or eggs under microscopes, they reported incorrect conclusions. For example, some researchers who compared the sperm from donkeys and horses claimed they could see the tiny animals, and the ones in donkeys' sperm had longer ears! This seems amazing and somewhat amusing because we now know that there are no fully formed animals in sperm or eggs. We'll discuss in this chapter why those researchers thought they saw these things, and what we can do to prevent such errors today.

As we start on a journey to learn about methods in research, I welcome you to a course that will have many benefits that may not be immediately apparent. This chapter introduces you to the processes by which people acquire knowledge about their world, the role and characteristics of science in acquiring knowledge, the value of learning about science for making sound decisions in your life, and the goals and strategies of science endeavors. Let's start by considering what science is.

WHAT IS SCIENCE?

An important process for advancing each society is gaining knowledge. The most fruitful approaches to gain knowledge occur when people can choose questions and do careful, unbiased observations to seek answers. **Science** is a system of knowledge and procedures for gaining knowledge through careful and unbiased observation and analysis. We can describe this system best by first considering the various ways by which people acquire knowledge and develop beliefs.

WAYS OF ACQUIRING KNOWLEDGE AND BELIEFS

Think for a moment about something you believe is true. Maybe it could be that you think you are talented or bright, or that there is or is not a God. How do people develop strong beliefs? They start by acquiring an idea through experience, and then they "fix," or solidify, it into a belief. In the late 1800s, philosopher Charles Sanders Peirce (1877/1957) outlined several processes by which people fix beliefs, which have since been clarified (Helmstadter, 1970). These processes are called tenacity, authority, intuition, rationalism, and empiricism. The first three have shortcomings and apply more to everyday beliefs than to science.

Tenacity

By dictionary definition, *tenacity* means the state or quality of being persistent. An idea can be persistent in two ways: it can be present in people's experience repeatedly over a long time, and it can be durable in people who adopt it. As a process in fixing beliefs, **tenacity** refers to the tendency of people to accept an idea as valid because it has been repeated so often for a long time and to retain a belief because it reduces unpleasant feelings of uncertainty. Repetition in the absence of opposing information gives the idea an air of respectability and truth. This is part of the reason advertisers present a message over and over across many months or years. Because being uncertain is often unpleasant, people gain comfort from the beliefs they hold and resist changing them, even in the face of sound opposing evidence (Anderson, Lepper, & Ross, 1980). This resistance is clear in a person's prejudice against individuals whose ethnic background, race, religion, gender, sexuality, or age range differs from his or her own.

Authority

In fixing beliefs, the process of **authority** is the tendency for people to accept information as valid because it comes from a source they respect (which itself is a belief). The source can be a religious leader, a politician, a scholar, a news commentator, a movie star, one's parent or friend, or an organization, such as the World Health Organization. The actual correctness of the information will depend substantially on the source's biases and expertise. A politician or movie star may be less-expert sources on moral issues than religious leaders, and all these people may be biased in their views. Different religious leaders, even in the same religion, often differ in their views of morality and religious doctrine. Who's right?

Intuition

You've surely had a gut feeling or intuition that influenced your judgment, such as whether to date someone or take a certain college course. We all use hunches to make decisions when we lack evidence on an issue. In fixing beliefs, **intuition** is the tendency of people to accept an idea as valid, without applying logical thought or examining facts, because it seems self-evident. Before the journeys of Columbus and other explorers, it seemed intuitively obvious that the world was flat. Just look around you—doesn't it look flat? In today's world, we have other beliefs that seem self-evident and lack scientific evidence (Helmstadter, 1970; Slater, 2002). For instance, many people believe that college students get a better education at small institutions than at large ones. And many people believe that by raising self-esteem in adolescents, we can help them be happier, perform better in school, and avoid behavior problems, such as drug abuse. These beliefs may seem intuitively reasonable, but are they true?

   The processes of tenacity, authority, and intuition involve an uncritical acceptance of ideas, without careful thinking and observation, and are therefore more likely than other approaches to lead to false beliefs. All people, including scientists, use these processes to some extent in forming beliefs. For example, scientists often use intuition to develop ideas to test in research. But scientists make deliberate efforts to use two other processes, *rationalism* and *empiricism*, systematically to study and evaluate ideas and beliefs in their disciplines. These two processes give science a solid basis for developing valid knowledge.

Rationalism

In **rationalism,** individuals apply *reasoning*—that is, logical thinking—carefully to make plans, generate knowledge, and arrive at conclusions. Two types of reasoning are basic to science. In *deductive reasoning,* we begin with a set of general statements and arrive at a conclusion or prediction of a specific event, as in:

Stressful situations increase heart rate.

This person is in a stressful situation.

Therefore, this person has an elevated heart rate.

What if we swap the last two issues so that the statements become, "This person has an elevated heart rate" and "Therefore, this person is in a stressful situation." Logic would lead us to reject the conclusion. In contrast, *inductive reasoning* proceeds from specific facts or observations to arrive at a general conclusion. An example of inductive reasoning would be: "These 7-month-old babies got training in sign language and then used it to ask their fathers to read to them; therefore, babies can learn to communicate with adults."

Using logic to generate knowledge and reach conclusions has two limitations. First, the premise(s) must be true. If it were not true that stress increases heart rate, the prediction of the person's elevated heart rate would not be correct. Second, rationalism by itself can advance knowledge only so far and can fix belief prematurely through a process that Peirce called the *a priori method* ("a priori" translates from Latin as "from the former"). In a priori reasoning, the person uses propositions ("the former") that are self-evident, so a critical part of the process is intuitive. For example, in the reasoning of scholars in the opening story about whether the offspring was contained in the sperm or egg, they would have started with the self-evident proposition that a fully formed being exists before the act of intercourse.

Empiricism

"That's an empirical issue," you may have heard a scholar say, meaning that the issue's idea can be verified or disproved by observation or experiment. As a process in fixing belief, **empiricism** involves gaining knowledge by observations that can vary in the directness of the assessment. In methods using highly *direct assessment,* the observation occurs with our senses—for instance, we see or hear an event, such as one child hitting another. If highly *indirect assessment* is used, we don't actually observe the event, such as peoples' current or past feelings or attitudes, but rely on inferences from behavior or from self-reports in a questionnaire or an interview. Observations of internal physical states, such as blood pressure or brain activity, can be assessed fairly directly with mechanical or electrical devices.

Because not all observations are helpful in developing valid knowledge and beliefs, we will distinguish between two types, casual and systematic observation. In *casual observation,* people observe events incidentally or without very careful attention and structure. Our observations in everyday experience are of this type, as are intentional observations made in an inexact or uncontrolled manner. Casual observation can be risky, leading to incorrect conclusions. For example, people's perceptions can be influenced by cognitive biases based on what they want or expect to see (Bourne, Dominowski, Loftus, & Healy, 1986). In one such cognitive bias, called *illusory correlation,* people perceive an association between events or other things when none actually exists. Thus, people often rate children who do well in school as being better looking and more socially adept when, objectively, these characteristics are only weakly related. In another cognitive bias, called *confirmatory bias*, people tend to look for information that supports their beliefs and overlook or discount opposing information. Thus, someone who believes in astrology may notice and remember everyday instances that confirm astrological predictions and ignore or explain away instances that do not. In these examples, the beliefs may have begun through the processes of tenacity, authority, or intuition, and the "evidence" from casual empiricism methods makes them stronger.

In contrast, *systematic observation* is carefully planned, structured, and executed so that it is likely to reflect the actual situation and answer the questions it was designed to examine. This is the approach scientists use. They first identify the question they want to answer, then they determine where, when, and how they will observe the phenomenon under study. For instance, they decide whether to use direct or indirect assessment methods, exactly how observations will be carried out, and the type of training observers will need to assess events accurately. When the observations are conducted, the process is carefully structured so that no outside influences will affect them; for example, if we were observing children in social play in a small group, we would make sure no unexpected people entered the room.

A classic example contrasting casual and systematic observation can be found in the case of "Clever Hans," a horse in Germany at the turn of the 20th century that seemed to be able to do arithmetic calculations, such as addition and multiplication (Pfungst, 1911). When Hans' master, Mr. Von Osten, would state a problem, such as "Multiply 3 times 3," the horse would tap his hoof the correct number of times and stop. Von Osten denied using tricks, claimed that Hans could do the arithmetic, and gave performances in front of large audiences to prove it. The people in these audiences surely used casual observation, and they saw no tricks by Hans' master. Because of the notoriety that developed from newspaper accounts, a special commission was formed to examine the matter. Eventually systematic observation with different people giving Hans questions revealed several findings, particularly the following two. First, Hans could not answer correctly if he was fitted with blinders so he could not see the questioner. Second, Von Osten and other questioners typically gave subtle cues, such as bending forward slightly or glancing up, that Hans used to start and stop tapping. When the cue to stop tapping was given deliberately at the wrong time, the horse would stop at the wrong answer.

To summarize the ways by which people gain knowledge and fix beliefs, let's look back at the opening story about scientists trying to determine how conception and fetal development occured. Intuition, authority, and tenacity were almost certainly involved. What role did intuition play? The idea that the egg or sperm contained a fully formed, tiny animal probably seemed self-evident—after all, at birth or hatching, offspring are usually fully formed and small, and then they grow over time to adult size. Why wouldn't that happen before conception? The role of authority is very likely because most Western scholars believed the idea, differing mainly in whether the offspring was in the egg or the sperm. And tenacity was probably involved in two ways: the idea was present in most people's experience repeatedly over a long time, and it would have been durable in people who adopted it because there was no other satisfactory explanation before the 1700s. Although these processes affect scientific inquiry to some degree today, they are typically offset by rationalism and empiricism. Let's see how.

CHARACTERISTICS OF SCIENCE

Wouldn't someone have noticed that sometimes the children of two parents looked like the mother, sometimes they looked like the father, and often they had some features of each parent? Logically, wouldn't that suggest that both parents contribute some sort of partially formed material at conception that gets combined to form the fetus? These scholars were not using rationalism very effectively to explain conception. Maybe their high reliance on intuition, authority, and tenacity curbed the use of logic. And when the microscope made empiricism possible, there were two problems. First, their observations were probably influenced by confirmatory bias. Second, the poor quality of the images seen with microscopes of that time made observations less systematic than was needed to test the issue.

Today, the scientific approach, or *scientific method,* demands an integration of rational thinking and systematic observation. Scientists use rational thinking in developing ideas to test and in planning their research. Then they use systematic observation to collect data and use rational thinking again to analyze and interpret the outcome. The emphases on *rational thinking* and *systematic observation* are two features that distinguish science from other forms of inquiry and scholarship. We turn now to a description of other characteristics of science.

Assuming Lawfulness of Events

Do the events we experience happen randomly, or can they be predicted? If they were random, nature would be chaotic. But it isn't. Many events can be predicted quite well. You (and scientists) know that tomorrow will happen in the world, and the sun will rise in the east and set in the west. You can also predict many other things with nearly 100% accuracy. For one thing, if you call people in authority, such as your parent or boss, a nasty name to their face, your behavior will be disapproved and, maybe, punished. You may even be able to predict what the punishment will be. Also, when you are driving and see a car approaching in the opposite direction, it will almost certainly stay in its lane and not crash into you. For other events, such as the weather a week from now, the ability to predict may not be very good at this time, but scientists (and maybe you) believe it will improve with more knowledge and better instruments. A basic assumption of science is that events in our world are **lawful**—that is, their occurrence is orderly, is predictable, and follows certain rules of cause and effect. Thus, scientists believe that if we were to know the rules underlying an event fully and assess all factors that contribute to them precisely, we could predict the event with a high degree of accuracy.

For many decades in the 20th century, the issue of lawfulness of behavior was the center of a major debate—called *determinism versus free will*—among philosophers and psychologists. Each side took extreme positions. Determinists thought that behavior was entirely controlled by natural forces, such as genetics and past experience, and we could predict a person's every movement if we knew everything about him or her and the situation. Oppositely, scholars taking the free will position claimed that individuals have complete freedom of choice and decide whether to perform each conscious behavior. If this is so, we can never know all the information we would need to predict with much accuracy. Because it is now clear that many behaviors can be predicted accurately, but research has shown that the occurrence of natural events, such as some activity of atoms, is random and therefore unpredictable, most psychologists today hold a composite view (Sutton, 1987). They believe that each person's behavior is for the most part lawful but impossible to predict perfectly. This view leaves room for a process such as free will to influence behavior and sidesteps the issue of *how much* influence it has, which is probably the most reasonable position to take with the knowledge we currently have.

Asking Empirical Questions and Using Data

We have seen that an important approach by which scientists gain knowledge and fix beliefs is empiricism—that is, through direct or indirect observation. When they plan their research, they start by identifying the question(s) they want to answer. Some questions cannot be answered by way of observation, usually because we lack sufficient knowledge of or access to the events we want to study. We cannot determine through observation whether there is a God or what such a deity is like, and maybe we'll never be able to answer such questions empirically. Before necessary biochemical analyses were available, scientists could not examine how people's body systems reacted to psychological stress. Today we can answer many such questions, such as, "What happens to the killer T cells of the immune system during stressful events?" Thus, one can pose empirical and nonempirical questions. Scientists focus on asking **empirical questions,** those that can be answered through direct or indirect systematic observation in research.

By doing systematic observations in research, scientists can collect **data**— factual information, usually in numerical form, that can be used in two ways. First, analyses of research data enable scientists to find answers to the empirical questions they posed when designing the study. Suppose the empirical question was, "Do children who watch a lot of TV violence engage in aggressive play behavior more than children who watch little violence?" The data from systematic observations, say, on a playground, should answer the question—for instance, by showing higher amounts of fighting among children who do versus those who don't watch a lot of violence. Second, the data from prior research can be used in rational thought processes to lead to new ideas for research. After research finds a link between watching TV violence and engaging in aggressive behavior, researchers might ask a new empirical question: "Is the relationship between watching TV violence and aggressive behavior similar for children of different ages, such as 4, 7, and 10 years of age?"

Applying Control and Being Objective

Two other characteristics of science are that researchers apply control systematically and endeavor to be objective. The term **control** refers to procedures used in research to guide or manage events or conditions. Scientists apply control in two main ways. First, events or conditions in a study can be *manipulated*—that is, varied in a deliberate and systematic manner by the researcher—to see their influence on a phenomenon. For example, in the case of Clever Hans, testing his arithmetic performance with and without blinders to block his view of the questioner is an example of a manipulation. Or, if you conducted a study in which you introduced different noise levels to see the effects of noise on people's ability to remember what they read, you'd be manipulating noise levels. The second way scientists apply control is by isolating or eliminating unwanted or extraneous conditions that might unfairly influence the outcome of the study. For instance, in your study on noise levels, you'd want to control the types of noise and reading material, keeping them the same for all noise levels you introduce. If you don't apply control in this way, any differences in the people's memory of the material might be the result of the type of noise or material, and not the noise levels.

Scientists also endeavor to be **objective;** that is, they try to deal with facts or conditions relating to research or their disciplines impartially, without the influence of personal feelings or expectations. Being objective is an ideal that is difficult to achieve, but scientists try to do so by making conscious efforts to minimize their own subjectivity or by applying control procedures in their research. Let's consider how they do this in three components of their work. First, scientists endeavor to apply rational thought and logical statements when interpreting their own and others' findings or ideas. If the data from a well-designed and conducted study appear to support a view a scientist doesn't believe, colleagues would expect him or her to examine the situation logically and focus a rebuttal or follow-up study on rationally, rather than emotionally, derived ideas.

Second, doing systematic observations in research requires that data be collected impartially. In the research described in the opening story, scientists who examined the sperm of horses and donkeys through a microscope claimed they saw tiny animals and differences in ear size. These observations were subjective and not conducted in a fully systematic manner. Because the observers expected to see tiny horses and donkeys, their observations probably reflected confirmatory bias. Chances are that the observers really believed they saw the animals, and we do not need to assume that they were *lying.* How could the researchers have taken more objective observations? They could have made sure the observers did not know exactly what they would be viewing. Sometimes the sperm would be of horses, sometimes of donkeys, and sometimes of other animals, such as chickens, but the observer would not be told in advance which is which. By doing this, researchers can eliminate unwanted factors (expectations) that might unfairly influence the outcome of the study. This is a method of control called a **blind** procedure: the observer is unaware of, or "blind" to, what will be seen. As an example of the blind procedure in psychology research, suppose you were an observer in a study of the influence of watching TV violence on children's play behavior. When observing and assessing their play, you would not know which children watch a lot of TV violence and which do not.

Third, scientists should be objective in designing and carrying out their research to create a fair test of the conditions being studied. For example, if you were conducting a survey of the attitudes of males and females on controversial topics, such as abortion, the questions in the survey should not use biased or emotionally charged language ("Do you approve of killing poor defenseless embryos?"). Also, the questions should not lead the respondent to a particular answer ("Most people think abortion is acceptable in many circumstances. What do you think?"). And, if the survey is done as in-person interviews, the interviewer should not present the questions or react to answers in ways that might lead the respondent's answers. Sometimes these and other types of bias occur in research when the organization that funds it has a vested interest in the outcome. For instance, a biased study might be done if a manufacturer funds a test of one of its products against one of a competitor. For this reason, some journals that publish research reports, such as of pharmaceutical tests or comparisons, require that the authors state in the report that the study had funding from an organization with a vested interest.

Being a Self-Correcting Discipline

Another important feature of science is that it is **self-correcting:** the processes of science find errors in the knowledge it generates and revise that information. One way science finds errors is through the process of **replication**—that is, by performing a retest of the conditions in a study. Sometimes the subsequent study is an exact repeat of the original one, with no additional issues being examined, particularly if the original results are controversial and very important. More commonly, the subsequent study either replicates only part of the original one or repeats the original test within a larger study to examine other conditions or issues as well. Using either replication approach, a result that differs from that of the original study may be found, suggesting that the existing knowledge may be incorrect or limited in some way. Further studies may determine which finding is correct and the reason for the different outcomes.

An example of conflicting outcomes for a very important issue comes from the field of health psychology. Studies of medical patients with cancer had found originally that those who received psychotherapy, such as through group discussion and by learning methods to manage and cope with their stress, had better immune function months later and lived substantially longer than those who got only medical treatment (Fawzy et al., 1993; Spiegel, Bloom, Kraemer, & Gottheil, 1989). But similar treatments in subsequent studies were not successful, and we don't yet know why (Cunningham et al., 1998; Edelman, Lemon, Bell, & Kidman, 1999).

No single study resolves an issue. In trying to summarize the knowledge science has produced on a particular issue, we need to examine the research literature on that topic as a whole. Conflicting findings often lead to more research that enhances our understanding so that we can make refinements to our knowledge. This was the case in understanding the role of cholesterol on the development of heart disease. Initially, research indicated that the total level of cholesterol in people's blood was the problem, and we needed to lower that level to reduce their chances of getting heart disease. But scientists didn't know until more research was done that different types of cholesterol have different effects and that one type of cholesterol protects us from heart disease and another type of cholesterol, low-density lipoprotein, is the real culprit (Sarafino, 2002).

In summary, doing high-quality scientific investigations is a complicated and self-correcting process that requires rational thinking and systematic observation of events, the occurrence of which scientists assume is lawful. In doing research, scientists ask empirical questions, collect and analyze data, apply control procedures, and try to be objective. The activities in research typically occur in phases, as described in **Box 1.1**.

SCIENCE AND PSEUDOSCIENCE

Do you believe in *biorhythms,* the idea that astrological cycles of the sun and moon affect three spheres of your behavior: emotions and physical and mental abilities? According to this view, each of these spheres has a separate cycle—going from very positive to very negative and back again—taking 23 days for physical abilities, 28 days for emotions, and 33 days for mental abilities (Bio-Chart, 2002). Understanding your personal calendar of cycles supposedly helps you plan your life activities to maximize success and happiness. For instance, you can avoid having surgery when your physical cycle will be negative and try to schedule job interviews when your mental abilities will be positive. The field called biorhythms is an example of a pseudoscience (*pseudo* means "sham" or "false").

A **pseudoscience** is a system of knowledge and methods that many people erroneously view as scientific. Why do people believe in pseudosciences? They do partly because of the processes of intuition, tenacity, and authority. After all, wouldn't it be nifty to have a system like a biorhythms calendar that you could follow to maximize success and happiness? And most people don't think in scientific ways, such as knowing the value of using controls and systematic observation when testing predictions. As we are about to see, pseudosciences have three characteristics that may get people to believe that they contain knowledge as valid as that of sciences.

Pseudosciences Have the "Trappings" of Science

Listen to this: "When the curve of any cycle is above the midline, we experience a 'high' in the corresponding field (physical, emotional, or mental)." That's what a biorhythms Website says (Bio-Chart, 2002). Doesn't that sound scientific? Curves in a graph, even! It sounds like they actually have data to bear it out, but pseudosciences rarely do. Instead, they make efforts to seem like and associate themselves with sciences: notice the name BIOrhythms. Sometimes pseudoscientists advertise; when they do, they often try to look like scientists, perhaps wearing a lab coat. In some cases, pseudosciences may have elements that originate in science: surely many people see the real scientific concept of menstrual cycles as an analogy for the biorhythm concept. Many pseudosciences also make predictions, as the biorhythm view does for people's physical, emotional, and mental processes, thereby suggesting the events are lawful. And those predictions could be framed as empirical questions and tested in scientific research, but pseudoscience proponents rarely do that.

Box 1.1

Scientific research generally proceeds through a series of phases from start to finish. In our examination of the phases, you'll see examples of the features we just considered that characterize science.

Identifying Ideas to Test

To identify ideas to study in research, scientists start by examining their own and others' beliefs, which have developed through some combination of intuition, tenacity, authority, rationalism, and empiricism. Then they refine these ideas to arrive at a specific empirical question, such as "Do first graders spend more time working on academic tasks in class if the end-of-day activities, such as finger painting, that they get as rewards for working hard are chosen by the teacher or by themselves?" Using rational thinking and assumptions about lawful events, they make a prediction, such as "Students will work harder on academic tasks if they choose end-of-day rewards themselves." Sometimes more than one question and prediction are made.

Designing Test Procedures

The next phase involves determining how to structure the testing, especially deciding the conditions under which observations will be made and who will be tested. These decisions require objectivity and careful rational thinking, and they typically address control procedures. For instance, in the study of rewards with first graders, the researcher will need to decide how to make sure that the students who get to choose are equivalent to those who do not get to choose and that the academic tasks are the same for students in both conditions. In addition, what will the reward activities be? Exactly how will the students and teacher choose activities? How often will observations occur? Who will do them, and what specific data will he or she record? What statistical analyses are planned?

Observation and Data Collection

This is the main empirical phase. The researcher carries out the previously determined procedures exactly as designed. All observations need to be conducted systematically, with great care and objectivity.

Data Analysis and Interpretation

The statistical analyses must be appropriate for answering the empirical question(s) identified in the first phase. Given that the statistical procedures were for the most part identified in the design phase, data analysis begins with organizing the data, such as by tallying up scores and entering them into a statistics database. Once the calculations are performed, the researcher determines whether they confirm the prediction(s) he or she made and what conclusions they suggest. Thus, rational thinking and assumptions about lawful events play a role again.

continued

Communication

Because science generally operates as a public enterprise, researchers try to communicate to other people what they did and found. These communications typically take the form of research reports published in professional journals or presented at conventions. These reports describe the rationale for the study, the original prediction(s), the exact testing procedures (so that they can be replicated), the statistical analyses conducted, and the outcome and interpretation.

Pseudosciences Use Observation (But It's Casual)

Virtually all the evidence for the validity of pseudosciences comes from testimonials and anecdotes. There are two problems with this type of evidence. First, it is usually collected and retained in a selective way, keeping data that support the pseudoscience and discounting those that do not. Second, although some of the retained evidence may be reliable, most has been obtained through casual observation and is suspect with good reason: it's easy to get confirmatory testimonials. The magician James "The Amazing" Randi (1982) has shown this many times in his efforts to expose pseudosciences, such as those involved in graphology, psychic, and ESP phenomena. For instance, on a radio show, he asked listeners to send in handwriting samples and birth dates for graphology analysis. He then contacted three respondents so that he could "read" their personalities and have them rate his accuracy on a 0-to-10 scale, with 10 points being the highest. Their ratings were two 10s and a 9. How did he arrive at the personality descriptions? He simply read the exact words a pseudoscientist had given to three other people on another show!

Pseudosciences Evade Disproof

A common feature of pseudosciences is that their concepts usually enable them to explain away disconfirming research results. Suppose a well-designed scientific study was done to test biorhythm predictions about mental ability by testing people for solving crossword puzzles, and they performed better at negative than positive times in their mental cycles. This finding would disconfirm biorhythm predictions. Biorhythm advocates might argue that the emotional and physical cycles interfered with the people's mental performance, such as by making them anxious or tired. Or maybe they would say that the influences of the moon and sun on mental function cannot be measured in standard ways. The problem here is not so much whether their arguments are true, it's that their predictions cannot be tested definitively. One mark of science is that the empirical questions it generates can be tested.

Why do pseudosciences exist and thrive? As long as pseudosciences can evade disproof, they have tenacity, intuition, and, often, authority on their side to fix people's beliefs. Pseudoscience is big business, with proponents making large amounts of money from selling books, tapes, and other materials through media advertising and the Internet; writing newspaper and magazine columns; and appearing on radio and TV shows.

By now you surely know why science is important for psychology: Science enables the field to advance its development of valid knowledge. A major reason for needing this knowledge is for improving people's lives. This can be seen in the many ways knowledge from psychology research has been applied successfully, such as in:

- *Mental health* with improved methods for diagnosis and psychotherapy
- *Physical health* through programs to promote healthful behaviors and reduce stress and the transmission of HIV
- *Education* with techniques to enhance students' learning and to reduce classroom conduct problems
- *Law* by showing that eyewitness memory may easily be biased and can be enhanced with special cognitive procedures in police interviews

How can learning about science be important for you? We will consider three ways.

First, learning about science can improve your critical thinking in everyday life. We are exposed daily to claims and information based on science and pseudoscience that we may need or want to evaluate. Do schools using voucher systems provide better or worse education than other schools? Can we learn through or be influenced by visual or auditory messages presented subliminally, that is, below perceptual threshold? Are children with gay parents more likely than others to become gay? Does one kind of analgesic reduce headaches better than another? These are all empirical questions that research can answer. When we hear or read a claim indicating that an answer exists, we need to determine whether there is scientific evidence for it and how good the evidence is. Knowing the features of high-quality scientific research will help you think critically about a claim and figure out what to believe.

Second, learning about scientific methods will help you understand the content in your science-based courses, especially psychology, because you will know the processes by which that knowledge developed. This will be true regardless of the course topic—for instance, developmental, abnormal, cognitive, social, or health psychology. Suppose the course was on cognitive or developmental psychology, and your textbook was describing a study of age and time of testing on memory (May, Hasher, & Stoltzfus, 1993). The book said:

> The researchers compared the memory performance of young adults and elderly adults, testing half of each age group in the morning and half in the afternoon. Each adult read 10 short stories and was tested immediately for memory by having to recognize which of many sentences had actually been in the stories they had read. The results revealed that the younger adults performed much better than the elderly adults when tested in the afternoon, but the age groups did not differ when tested in the morning.

How many separate conditions or groups were there in this study? You could figure it out (there were four), but someone familiar with research methods would have processed or organized that information into the first reading. And when you're familiar with research methods, you'll probably process in your mind a picture of what a graph of the results would look like. Being able to do these things automatically is efficient, and it will help you remember the study and its findings better. You may also start to ask questions that might serve as ideas for future research, such as, "What would happen if they were tested in the evening or late at night?"

Third, learning about research methods will benefit your education and work performance if you pursue a career in psychology, even if you don't actually conduct research. For example, if you become a mental health professional, you will need to make decisions about the best treatment approach to use for particular clients or justify plans for treatment on the basis of past research. If you choose a career in government agencies or business, you may need to improve hiring or training procedures and justify your plans based on past research. Of course, if you become a research psychologist working in an academic department or in a governmental or business setting, the knowledge you gain in this course will be at the core of all your professional activities. And regardless of the specific field you choose, if you decide to pursue a graduate degree, you'll find that graduate schools prefer students who have taken and done well in undergraduate research courses and have actually performed research, such as in an independent study course. In many ways, the concepts in research methods will be among the most useful ones you'll learn in psychology. Students who continue in the field often find that they refer back to the materials they saved from the course for later courses and in their careers. (Go to **Box 1.2**)

Box 1.2   **PROFESSIONAL ORGANIZATIONS IN PSYCHOLOGY**

The largest professional organization for psychology is the American Psychological Association (APA). It was formed in 1892 and currently has over 84,000 members and over 50 divisions that focus on specific areas, including experimental, developmental, clinical, personality and social, and industrial and organizational psychology. (Many of these areas also have separate organizations outside APA.) The APA promotes scientific research in a variety of ways, such as by publishing journals and holding conventions to report research findings, developing guidelines for the structure of research reports, establishing ethical standards for conducting research, and giving awards for scientific contributions in psychology. The APA also offers membership for students and provides services especially for them, including information on careers and graduate programs in psychology. Another organization, the American Psychological Society (APS), was formed in 1988, focuses mainly on scientific issues, has about 15,000 members, and also offers student membership. You can get information about the APA and APS by using the Internet addresses given in the Resources section at the end of this chapter. Log on and see!

HOW THE SCIENTIFIC APPROACH EMERGED

When was the scientific approach created? Many people would say that it began in the 16th and 17th centuries with the works of the Polish astronomer Copernicus, the Italian astronomer–physicist Galileo, and the British physicist Newton. These works had a great impact and set the scientific approach in motion, but elements of the approach had been discovered and used 2,000 years earlier.

EARLY APPROACHES

Before the era of ancient Greece, people's understanding of the world and events was based mainly on mythical ideas, such as spirits, demons, and gods. Greek philosophers in the 6th to 4th centuries B.C. made the earliest known contributions to the development of the modern scientific method (Marx & Hillix, 1963). Although they used rationalism and tried to observe events, their observations were subjective and not very systematic. This situation endured in Western cultures, especially once they entered the Middle Ages after the fall of the Roman Empire in the 5th century A.D. From then until the 13th century, little progress was made toward developing scientific methods, and scholars' knowledge was based mainly on intuition, tenacity, authority, and logic. The authorities were mainly religious leaders, particularly the Pope, and scholars.

During that time, Arab scholars made major contributions to science, particularly in the concept of systematic observation (Powers, 1999). An 11th-century Arab scholar named Ibn al-Haytham, who is little known today, introduced systematic observation to resolve a continuing dispute that began in ancient Greece: Did vision occur by light traveling from an object to the eye or the other way around? One of his observations simply involved having people stare at the sun, which created discomfort in the eye, suggesting that light travels from the object. Because translations of his works weren't made until about 1300 A.D., his impact was delayed 300 years.

THE SCIENTIFIC REVOLUTION

During the Middle Ages, Christian theologians placed limitations on empirical testing in Europe. The most critical restriction was that knowledge obtained through empirical tests was not allowed to contradict theological dogma. The ultimate authority in disputes was the church, and empirical tests were permitted only if they served religious goals. These positions were the basis for the prohibition against dissecting human and animal bodies after death because these creatures had souls, making them sacrosanct and immune from being violated (Marx & Hillix, 1963).

The restrictions of the Middle Ages declined when the Renaissance emerged in the 14th and 15th centuries and fostered a rebirth of inquiry. The freer intellectual climate enabled many early scientists—Copernicus, Galileo, and Newton, for instance—to make major and lasting discoveries using the scientific method in the 16th and 17th centuries. But there were still two limitations in research. First, scientific discovery was not without political risk: Galileo was tried, convicted, and persecuted for supporting the Copernican view that the Earth revolves around the Sun. Second, methods of observation were not sufficiently systematic and objective, as we saw in the opening story about microscopic examinations of sperm. By the 18th and 19th centuries, the scientific method was widely accepted, and universities had established facilities for scientific study.

Before the late 1800s, psychology and philosophy were a joint discipline. But the advances in scientific development led to the belief that behavior is lawful, setting the stage for psychology to become a science and a separate discipline from philosophy (Marx & Hillix, 1963). Trained as a physiologist, Wundt established the first laboratory to study psychological processes in Leipzig, Germany, in 1879. In the research he and his students conducted, they used the procedure called **introspection,** or self-observation, in which people were trained to pay very close attention to their own immediate sensations and perceptions (Haynie, 2001). The main drawback to this procedure is its *subjectivity:* the participant is also the observer. For example, the person might be asked to form a mental image of something just seen and then describe not only its physical features, but also whether it seemed to appear "on the eyelids" or efforts made to move the eyeball to get or maintain the image (Marx & Hillix, 1963). Subjective reports of experiences are useful, but valid conclusions about them require verification with reports of the same events by other people and by observations taken in more objective ways. Let's look next at a more objective method to study memory.

AN EXAMPLE: A LITTLE "EXPERIMENT"

We'll try a little "experiment" on learning and memory to give you a glimpse into what it is like to be a participant in research, to get you thinking about issues involved in doing a study, and to provide an example of methods that we can refer back to later.

Instructions

Take out a blank sheet of paper and something to write with. You will be reading *a list of nouns slowly two times in different orders.* Then you'll be asked to write on your sheet of paper as many of the words as you can remember. When you go to the words, you'll find them listed in four columns. *For the first reading,* you should start with the left column and read the words from the top to the bottom of each column; read each word once and allow about 2 seconds between words. *For the second reading,* start at the bottom of the rightmost column and read the words in reverse order (bottom to top) of each column at the same 2-second pace. The amount of time to participate is much shorter than for most studies; you'll spend under 10 minutes in the exercise, including counting up the words recalled.

When I ask you to go to the page with the list, you'll use your sheet of paper to cover the page and then slide it down just past the titles, "Application Activities" and "Activity 1–1," until you start to see some more instructions. OK, turn to page 32 at the end of this chapter.

Outcome

How many of the listed related and unrelated words did you recall? When my students in many different semesters have done this task with a similar procedure, they have gotten an average of 14 or so related words and 9 or 10 unrelated words correct. And when we conducted statistical analyses on their combined data, we have always found that they recalled significantly more related than unrelated words. Why would this be? There are many possible reasons. For example, memory may be structured in such a way that each word has a direct path to all similar words, but not to dissimilar words. Or, knowing that several words in the list belong to the same category allows us to limit what we search for in our memory. In both cases, we would recall related words more easily. Researchers in psychology try to use systematic observation whenever possible to answer the empirical questions they test. (Go to **Box 1.3**)

RESEARCH GOALS AND STRATEGIES: THE BASICS

When researchers design studies, they apply particular strategies that are matched to the specific goals they have regarding what they want the data to demonstrate. For instance, the research strategies we would use to test the prediction that stress can *cause* headaches would be different from those we'd use to test the prediction that stress and headache are *related* or associated. Where do predictions come from?

THEORIES, MODELS, AND HYPOTHESES

"My theory is that the butler did it," you may have heard someone say about a murder mystery. The word *theory* has several meanings and often means *belief* in everyday conversation. In science, the word has a special meaning. A **theory** is a plausible, organized, and logical set of principles and facts presented to explain why and under what circumstances a phenomenon occurs. Theories should not be taken as entirely and actually "true," but as "working truths," or ideas to be tested and modified on the basis of additional evidence. They have three main functions: to *explain* phenomena, *organize* existing knowledge, and *make predictions* for researchers to pose as empirical questions and test. If a theory's predictions are upheld in research, it continues to be useful; but if its predictions are refuted, it is revised or discarded. Because theories present something like a "road map" of issues to test in future investigations, they provide one of many rich sources for research ideas and predictions.

Some theories apply to a very broad range of phenomena, as in Darwin's theory of evolution and Freud's psychodynamic theory of personality development. Freud's theory, for example, attempts to explain the overall processes of personality change as children grow toward adulthood and factors that affect specific personality attributes of individuals, such as whether they are stingy, sociable, or well adjusted. Other theories apply to a narrower range of phenomena, such as the structure of people's memory processes: Are they divided into

BOX 1.3 PORTRAITS OF PSYCHOLOGY RESEARCHERS

Each year, the APA presents *Awards for Distinguished Scientific Contributions* to a few psychologists whose work has been especially important. The following brief portraits are of award winners from the last several decades who were chosen for this box to represent a wide range of research interests. As you read each portrait, you'll learn about the exciting discoveries they made, and you can find references to some of their major writings in the Resources section at the end of this chapter.

B. F. Skinner (1904–1990), an experimental psychologist who received his award in 1958, is well known to students and one of the most famous psychologists ever. His seminal work on operant conditioning in animals examined phenomena relating to reinforcement, such as the effects of extinction (when reinforcement is stopped) on behavior. This and later work formed the basis for a subfield in psychology called the experimental analysis of behavior and for many techniques used today in psychotherapy, education, and industry.

John Garcia (1917–1986), an experimental psychologist, received his award in 1979. His research demonstrated two important phenomena. First, organisms may be genetically prepared to learn to associate certain events they experience, even when the events are separated by a long period of time. Second, exposure to a nausea-producing stimulus, such as radiation, can lead to a dislike of recently consumed food tastes; this finding has led to research on reducing learned food aversions of cancer patients who receive radiation therapy.

Mary D. Salter Ainsworth (1913–1999), a developmental psychologist who received her award in 1989 for her work on the infant–parent affectionate interpersonal bond called attachment. Her research with parents and children charted the course of attachment development and identified types of attachment behavior in children. Securely attached children seek interaction and proximity toward their mothers, and anxiously attached children either avoid their mothers or approach but resist contact and interaction.

Richard S. Lazarus (1922–2003), a personality psychologist, received his award in 1989 for his work on stress and coping processes. His research demonstrated the critical role of cognition and everyday hassles, such as being stuck in traffic or taking exams, in people's psychological stress and coping. This work enabled him to develop a new and widely accepted conceptualization of the nature and process of stress that involves continuous interactions, assessments, and adjustments between people and their environments.

Larry R. Squire, a physiological psychologist, received his award in 1993 for his research on brain structures and memory. Although his early work was on memory impairments in people with amnesia, his later work with humans and primates identified different types of learning and mem-

ory systems, relationships of these systems to each other, and areas of the brain involved in each system. For example, he found that people with damage to a part of the brain called the hippocampus have difficulty forming new memories.

Ellen S. Berscheid is a social psychologist who received her award in 1997 for her work on interpersonal attraction and relationships. Her research demonstrated the importance of physical attractiveness, liking, and dependence in dating and marriage choices and led to a conceptualization of different types of love. Passionate love involves strong emotions and sexual feelings; companionate love refers to the affectionate attachment that develops from long-term passionate love and among relatives and close friends.

separate systems? If so, are they separated on the basis of the types of information stored there or the length of time information remains there? The broader theories are not necessarily better or of higher quality than the narrower ones.

What characteristics distinguish good theories from others? Good theories have three main characteristics: They organize concepts well, are parsimonious, and make clear and testable predictions.

Well-Organized Theories

Good theories bring together and describe reasonable relationships among previously unconnected facts or ideas. For example, here are some facts about people's memory that were widely known before the 1960s but not yet pulled together or organized well. First, some information we take in stays in our memory for a long time, perhaps forever, even if we don't use it. Examples of this are easy to find—we remember a song, a word in a foreign language, or a person's name we haven't heard or used in many years. Second, new material that is prominent, learned with lots of repetition, and consistent with our existing knowledge tends to stay in memory a long time. Third, we quickly forget much of the information that comes in through our senses; the classic example is when we are driving on a freeway and are not able to recall having driven the last several miles. The fact that we hadn't crashed indicates that we had been taking in information. To pull together and organize these and other facts, Atkinson and Shiffrin (1971) proposed a theory with three memory systems:

- *Long-term storage,* where huge amounts of relatively permanent memories are held essentially forever and organized conceptually.
- *Short-term storage,* in which active memories are retained for a temporary period—10 to 30 seconds, for instance—so we can work on them. This information can be new material we need to use briefly or want to move to long-term storage, or it can be old material retrieved from long-term storage. In either event, the amount of information short-term storage can process at any given time is fairly small. To move information to long-term

storage, we may try to make it more prominent, repeat it over and over, or identify how it fits with other material we already know.

- ■ *Sensory storage,* which holds sensory impressions only briefly, generally less than a second.

Information comes into the memory system through sensory storage, moves to short-term storage if we pay attention to it, and moves to long-term storage if we make it prominent, repeat it, and identify how it fits with other material there. Notice how this theory uses the widely known facts outlined earlier, nicely organizes the flow of information in the system, and explains what happens to move material from one storage type to another.

Parsimonious Theories

Good theories are **parsimonious;** that is, the explanations they provide are *economical,* or as simple and straightforward as possible. This means that the explanations should rely as little as possible on assumptions, which are often intuitive, and constructs. **Constructs** are unobservable, hypothetical entities or processes that are inferred from specific events, such as behavior, and assumed to change or occur under certain circumstances. *Learning* and *anxiety* are examples: we don't actually observe these processes, but we infer them from behavior. Obviously, relying on some constructs is necessary. The preference for parsimonious theories does not mean that complex explanations that use constructs make for poor theories. It means that if two competing theories have equal validity but differ in parsimony, science prefers the one that gives a simpler explanation, covers a wider array of phenomena, and uses fewer constructs (Marx & Hillix, 1963). Keep in mind also that some constructs may eventually become observable with the invention of appropriate instruments, as happened with genetic materials: Before genes could be seen, Darwin proposed that the sperm and egg contain "gemmules" that guide development.

Let's look at two examples to clarify what parsimony and constructs mean. First, in the 19th century, theories of animal behavior tended to anthropomorphize, or attribute human qualities to animals, a great deal (Marx & Hillix, 1963). Theories explaining how animals learned to find food at the end of a maze would propose, for instance, that they could *plan* their route each time from their prior experiences. This was part of the reason for the great interest in Clever Hans' mathematical ability at the turn of the 20th century. What alternative would there be to attributing higher cognitive processes to animals? A more parsimonious explanation proposed that the improvements they show in their maze behavior with experience reflect habits they acquire through trial-and-error learning. The learning simply involves associations, not thinking, and tests of this view supported it.

As a second example, we'll compare the way two psychology theories explain how children become negativistic and aggressive (see Sarafino & Armstrong, 1986). Freud's theory is very complex and includes many constructs, such as *identification* and *fixation* processes and the *id, ego,* and *superego.* According to this theory, personality development advances through five stages, the second of which is the *anal stage,* in which 1- to 3-year-olds are preoccupied with toilet training and the pleasure experienced by elimination processes. Parents who are either very severe or overindulgent in their toilet training practices lead the child to *fixate* the personality at that stage, thereby retaining into adulthood characteristics that were successful in early childhood, such as stubbornness, negativism, and aggression. (The italicized words are some of the many constructs of the theory.) In comparison, learning theory, as described by Skinner and others, proposes a more parsimonious explanation. People develop a behavior pattern, such as being negativistic and aggressive, because they've been *reinforced,* or rewarded, repeatedly for those behaviors, such as by getting their way when they behave like that, and because they've seen others model those behaviors and not get punished.

Clearly Stated and Testable Theories

Good theories are stated clearly so that researchers can make specific predictions and test them. This way, it is possible to support or falsify them and advance our knowledge. This is a principle called **falsifiability;** that is, by making specific predictions, theories can be refuted or disproved. You may have noticed an important aspect of the wording in the last two sentences: I said we could disprove a theory or support (not "prove") a theory. When findings consistently disconfirm a theory's predictions, that theory, or at least part of it, is disproved. But findings that consistently confirm a theory's predictions *do not prove* it is correct. Why?

Let's refer to Freud's theory again: Parts of the theory have been criticized for not being testable, but the relationships it proposes of stages to later personality provide testable predictions. Many studies have found that children who experienced severe toilet training are more aggressive in adolescence than others who had moderate training (Sears, Whiting, Nowlis, & Sears, 1953). Does this finding mean that Freud's view is correct—there is an anal stage and the children's personalities had been fixated there? Not necessarily. Even if severe toilet training is associated with later aggressiveness, other factors can also account for the relationship (Beloff, 1962; Hetherington & Brackbill, 1963). For example, Beloff concluded that "anal" traits are associated more with the mother's personality characteristics than with the method of toilet training employed. It may be that mothers who use severe toilet training methods use harsh parenting methods in most aspects of child rearing, and perhaps they encourage the child's aggression by modeling that behavior and rewarding it inadvertently. Research has shown that children do learn to perform aggressive behaviors in these ways (Bandura, Ross, & Ross, 1963; Walters & Brown, 1963). Regardless of which theory is more valid, both theories provide falsifiable predictions on this issue that can be tested in research.

Models and Hypotheses

Sometimes explanations of phenomena in science are called models or hypotheses. How do they differ from theories? In this context, models and hypotheses are subclasses or types of theories and, as such, can yield predictions for research (Marx & Hillix, 1963). As we examine distinctions among these types of explanations, keep in mind that there are no clear cutoffs for classifying one as a theory, model, or hypothesis. The distinctions among and use of these terms are approximate.

The term **model** can have two meanings in science. As a type of theory, a *model* provides mainly a representation or description of the processes in a phenomenon and their relationships, rather than a full and organized explanation. Atkinson and Shiffrin's conceptualization of memory with three storage systems that we discussed earlier is more exactly a model, a subclass of theory. The second meaning of the term *model* refers to an analogy to or substitution for a related entity or process. For example, a physiological psychologist might use an *animal model* of brain function when studying how areas of the rat brain react to sounds to infer or estimate how similar areas of the human brain would react to the same sounds. Animal models are often used in early stages of medical and drug research.

The term **hypothesis** can also have two meanings. As a type of theory, *hypothesis* means a very tentative explanation or description that applies to a relatively narrow set of phenomena. For example, researchers have offered the *buffering hypothesis* to explain research findings that people who have high levels of social support in their lives have better health than those with little social support (see Sarafino, 2002). The buffering hypothesis proposes that social support protects people's health by curbing the negative health effects of potentially stressful situations, such as by enabling a person to interpret these situations as less stressful. The second meaning of the term *hypothesis* refers to a specific prediction for the outcome of a study. Theories (and the subclasses, models and hypotheses) often provide the source or basis for a specific hypothesis (prediction) of a study.

GOALS AND STRATEGIES OF SCIENTIFIC RESEARCH

When researchers design a study, they have in mind a specific *goal,* or idea of what they want it to accomplish, and a **research strategy,** or scientific approach for accomplishing the goal. The goals and strategies are coordinated, and a single study can have more than one goal and use more than one strategy. Using systematic observations of events or phenomena, scientists pursue goals of four broad types:

■ *Description*—that is, to detail or categorize events or phenomena or to chart their course. Let's look at three examples. First, researchers have monitored drug use by thousands of American adolescents annually to describe current levels for each drug and chart changes across years (Johnston, O'Malley, & Bachman, 2000). Second, researchers described many years ago the average course of motor development in infants: they sit without support by 6 months, stand while holding on furniture by 8 months, and walk well by 13 months (see Sarafino & Armstrong, 1986). Third, mental health researchers have developed the *Diagnostic and Statistical Manual of Mental Disorders* (DSM-IV; American Psychiatric Association, 1994) to classify and characterize many dozens of mental disorders, such as posttraumatic stress disorder and anorexia nervosa.

- *Prediction*—to forecast events or phenomena or to show associations between them. For example, studies have shown that adolescents are more likely to use marijuana if their parents and friends use mood-altering substances (Petraitis, Flay, Miller, Torpy, & Greiner, 1998). Other research with prediction as a goal have found that children who score high on intelligence tests tend to achieve higher school grades than those who score lower (Matarazzo, 1972). And studies have shown that the more stress people report experiencing, the more likely they are to develop infectious diseases (Jemmott & Locke, 1984).

- *Understanding*—to determine why and under what conditions events or phenomena occur. The main issue in this goal is determining what *causes* events or phenomena to occur. For example, once researchers knew that experience played a role in drug use, they were able to show that drug-related stimuli become conditioned to the drug's effects and elicit physiological reactions like those the drug itself produces (Childress, 1996). As another example, once researchers knew that stress is associated with contracting infections, they set out to determine why. One cause they found for the link is that stress produces chemical changes in the body that impair the functioning of the immune system (Jemmott & Locke, 1984; Rozlog, Kiecolt-Glaser, Marucha, Sheridan, & Glaser, 1999).

- *Application*—to employ an understanding of events and phenomena to influence their future occurrence. For example, once psychologists understood processes in classical conditioning whereby a person can learn to crave drugs when drug-related stimuli appear, they were able to apply conditioning principles in therapy to help individuals reduce their drug cravings (Childress, 1996). Like all scientific fields, psychology gains knowledge from research that can be applied to benefit (but sometimes harm) individual people and societies.

We saw earlier that researchers coordinate the strategies they employ with the goals they have for a study. Some strategies are better suited than others for specific research goals.

An Overview of Strategies

Suppose you were interested in testing Freud's psychodynamic theory, particularly with respect to the role of toilet training on later personality development. As you think about the processes involved, you'll realize that both the child's personality and the theoretical cause, toilet training severity, can vary from one time to another and from one individual to another. They are not constant. Because these things *vary*, they are called variables. A *variable* is any measurable characteristic of people, objects, or events that can change. In most research, there are two types of variables: an **independent variable** is tested for its potential or suspected influence, and a **dependent variable** is assessed to see if its value corresponds to, or "depends on," variations in the independent variable. For example, in testing Freud's theory, toilet training severity would be the independent variable and the child's later personality would be the dependent variable. In a study to examine the role of stress in illness, the amount of stress would be the independent variable, and there might be two dependent variables: the level of the participants' immune function and whether they developed an illness.

In the remaining sections of this chapter, we will discuss the four main strategies of research design that scientists employ (Campbell & Stanley, 1963; Cook & Campbell, 1979). These strategies are called *experimental, quasi-experimental, correlational,* and *descriptive* strategies. In later chapters we'll examine each of them in greater detail. As we discuss each strategy, we will use as our main examples research designs that might be used to study children's aggression with respect to the role of toilet training in its development.

The Experimental Strategy

We considered earlier how scientists apply *control* in their research: They can manipulate variables and isolate or eliminate unwanted or extraneous conditions. The **experimental strategy** uses a high degree of control to examine differences in the effects of specific conditions by manipulating the independent variable(s), looking for resulting changes in the dependent variable(s), and isolating or eliminating unwanted or extraneous factors. Let's see how we could use the experimental strategy to study the role of toilet training on the development of aggression.

Freud's psychodynamic theory predicts that children who experience harsh toilet training methods during the anal stage will show relatively high levels of aggressiveness later, having become fixated at that stage. Suppose we can recruit first-time parents (for each family, the one who has the larger child-rearing role) of 10-month-olds through a pediatrician's office. We use only those who have not yet begun toilet training and who indicate in answering hypothetical questions that they would use toileting methods psychologists consider harsh. How could we manipulate the parents' toilet training procedures? One way would be to form two groups: an *experimental group* in research receives a special treatment or condition, the *control group* does not. In our study, parents in the experimental group would receive instruction on using moderate toilet training procedures, but those in the control group would not. (The second parent could give independent assessments regarding the harshness of the procedures used.) In this way, we would manipulate the children's toilet training experiences.

How would we form the groups? We would need to control a critical unwanted or extraneous factor: groups that are unequal before the manipulation. If the groups are not equal at the start, whatever differences we observe in the dependent variable may be the result of that inequality rather than the manipulated independent variable. A good way to make the groups equivalent is to assign the parents *randomly*—that is, in a manner that excludes the possibility of bias—to the conditions or groups, such as by using a lottery. By doing this, we distribute fairly evenly across groups the parents' characteristics, such as their tendency to use physical punishment or be unresponsive to the child's needs. We would also want to make sure that the children in the two groups are equal in aggressive behavior (which might be hard to assess at 10 months of age) and evenly distributed by sex. Girls tend to achieve toileting success somewhat earlier than boys.

After we provide the instruction to the experimental group, we would check to make sure the parents in that group are using the moderate toilet training procedures during the next year or so. We might also collect information on the control group parents' procedures to see if they were in fact harsh. When the children were, say, 5 years of age, we would assess their aggressiveness—for example, by observing them in school. On the basis of Freud's theory, we'd predict that the children whose parents were in the control group would show more aggression than those whose parents were in the experimental group. Figure 1.1 shows how the study would be carried out and results that would support the theory if the difference between groups is substantial and reliable. We would conclude from these results that harsh toilet training can cause children to become aggressive.

You may have noticed that our conclusion used the word *cause:* harsh toilet training can *cause* children to become aggressive. To make *cause–effect* conclusions from research results, it must be clear that *all three of the following criteria* have been met:

- *Covariation of variables*—as one variable (the independent variable) changes, the other (dependent variable) changes in a systematic and corresponding manner.
- *Causal time sequence*—causes precede effects. It should be clear from the methods in the research that the presumed cause occurred before its effect.
- *Elimination of other plausible causes*—all variables not manipulated that could affect variations in the dependent variable have been controlled.

Our research meets these three criteria because toilet training procedures and aggression varied together in the expected direction, toilet training

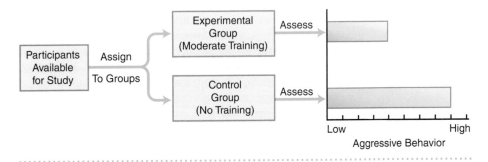

FIGURE 1.1

The left-hand portion of this diagram shows how the study would be carried out. Each parent who pretested as likely to provide harsh toilet training is assigned with the child to either the *experimental group,* which receives instruction in moderate toilet training, or the *control group,* which receives no special instruction. After toilet training procedures have been in effect for a suitable period of time, the researcher assesses the children's aggression. On the right are graphical results that would support the theory that harsh training leads children to become aggressive.

(the cause) preceded differences in aggression, and other plausible causal variables, such as characteristics of the parents and the child's sex, were equated for the two conditions. Keep in mind, as we noted earlier, demonstrating a causal relationship between harsh toilet training and aggression does not necessarily mean that Freud's constructs regarding anal fixation are correct.

We can also see the experimental strategy in the exercise you did on memorizing words, but it was used differently. Instead of having two separate groups of people, the participants (you) learned two sets of words—conceptually related and unrelated—mixed together in a single list. Our method meets the three criteria for cause–effect, allowing us to conclude that word relatedness, the manipulated independent variable, causes greater recall, the dependent variable. When I have used this exercise in my classes, the students' performance has always shown covariation of variables: They recalled more related than unrelated words. The method contained the causal time sequence because the relatedness of the words existed in the list before the participants were tested. How did the method eliminate other causal variables? Let's look at a few ways. First, the participants who learned the related and unrelated words were equated by being the same people. We'll see in Chapter 8 that this approach has more than one name: *repeated measures* and *within subjects,* for example. Second, the related and unrelated words were chosen to be fairly equal on average in length and familiarity. Third, the words were ordered randomly in the list, rather than having a pattern that might make it easier to memorize one or the other type.

The remaining strategies we will discuss use *nonexperimental* approaches that meet only *part* of the criteria for cause–effect conclusions. Nonexperimental research may, for instance, not manipulate an independent variable, not have equivalent groups, or not be able to control other plausible variables that could affect the dependent variable. These approaches are still very valuable. Sometimes the goal of a study requires only that an association between variables be shown, such as in finding that people with certain personality characteristics or behavior patterns are more likely than others to develop a particular disease. And sometimes it is simply not possible or feasible to assign people randomly and manipulate the variables of interest, as happens when we want to study the role of people's sex or age on social relationships, for instance. Figure 1.2 presents a diagram of the four research strategies, giving the likelihood that a well-designed study using each strategy would meet the three criteria for cause-effect conclusions.

The Quasi-Experimental Strategy

Research using the **quasi-experimental strategy** looks for differences between specific conditions or groups but fails to meet one or more criteria for concluding that an independent variable caused any variations in the dependent variable. This failure usually occurs because the study did not manipulate the independent variable(s) *or* did not create equivalent groups, such as by randomly assigning participants to conditions. Cook and Campbell (1979) have

Research Strategy	Criteria of Cause–Effect Conclusions		
	Covariation of Variables	Causal Time Sequence	Elimination of Other Plausible Causes
Experimental	Yes	Yes	Yes
Quasi-experimental	Yes	Sometimes	Rarely
Correlational	Yes	Rarely	Almost Never
Descriptive	Sometimes	Rarely	Never

FIGURE 1.2

Diagram indicating whether a well-designed and executed study using each research strategy is likely to meet each of the three criteria for cause-effect conclusions for the relevant independent variable. Because it is so unlikely that a nonexperimental strategy would yield results that meet all three criteria, researchers usually presume that it will not and require a strong argument for concluding that a causal relationship exists.

described several forms of quasi-experimental research, and we'll describe two. One form uses "nonequivalent groups that receive different treatments or no explicit treatment at all" (p. 95). Another form "uses naturally occurring variability for defining the independent variable" (p. 344), such as comparing ex-convicts who found jobs with others who did not (the independent variable) for subsequent arrest records (the dependent variable). Psychology studies often use naturally occurring characteristics of the individuals tested—such as their age, sex, or level of intelligence or anxiety—as independent variables. For example, we might study differences between males and females in social relationships. These strategies are called *quasi*-experimental because the studies *look* superficially like they might be using an experimental strategy since they test separate groups of individuals, but they lack important methods of control.

How might we use the quasi-experimental strategy to study the prediction from Freud's theory about harsh toilet training and aggression? We could recruit parents from the pediatrician's office who have just begun toilet training their child and separate them into two groups on the basis of their answers in an interview about the methods they are using in their training. On the basis of the theory, we would expect that the children of parents using harsh training procedures would be more aggressive later when they enter school than those of parents using moderate procedures. If we found the expected difference in aggression (the dependent variable), we could not conclude that the toileting procedures caused it. One reason we couldn't is that we cannot be sure that other causal variables, such as other parental characteristics, are not responsible. That finding would be consistent with predictions from the theory, but would lend only weak support for it.

The Correlational Strategy

The term *correlation* refers to the *co* or joint relation between variables: changes in one variable correspond with changes in the other. It is the same as covariation, but it is usually reflected statistically as a **correlation coefficient,** which can range from +1.00 through .00 to −1.00. The sign (+ or −) of the coefficient indicates the *direction* of the relationship. A plus sign means that the association is "positive": high scores on one variable, say, harshness of maternal toilet training procedures, tend to occur with high scores on another variable, such as the child's aggressiveness. Conversely, a minus sign means that the association is "negative": *high* scores on one variable tend to occur with *low* scores on the other variable. Disregarding the sign of the coefficient, its absolute value indicates the *strength* of association between variables. The higher the absolute value (that is, the closer to either +1.00 or −1.00), the stronger the correlation. A coefficient approximating .00 means that the variables are not related. We'll discuss correlations in much more detail in Chapter 6.

The **correlational strategy** in research assesses the degree and direction of statistical association between variables. Freud's theory predicts a positive correlation between two variables: the harsher the toilet training practices, the more aggressive behavior the child should show later. To use the correlational strategy to study this prediction, we would need to measure the parents' harshness in toilet training and the children's aggressiveness. Suppose we measured both variables when the children are, say, 5 years old by assessing aggression in school and having the parents recollect the training methods they used. We would then calculate the correlation coefficient between the two variables; if it is positive and strong, it would be consistent with the prediction and lend some support for the theory. But it would meet mainly the covariation criterion for making cause–effect conclusions. The causal time sequence would be unclear because the toilet training practices were measured years later.

The Descriptive Strategy

The **descriptive strategy** simply involves observing events or phenomena to detail or categorize them or to chart their course. For example, researchers might observe toilet training practices or aggressive behavior in different societies or at different ages and describe what these events are like. This research might show that aggression takes different forms in different cultures or at different ages. Studies using the descriptive strategy can be important in the process of testing the association between toilet training and aggression in at least two ways. First, we may notice an indirect association between the two variables—for instance, cultures with harsher toilet training practices seem to have more aggressive children. Second, descriptive studies can tell us exactly what behaviors to look for when assessing these variables in research with correlational, quasi-experimental, or experimental strategies.

In summary, scientists can coordinate their use of descriptive, correlational, quasi-experimental, or experimental strategies to match their research goals. Two other issues should be mentioned. First, researchers can have *more than one goal and use more than one strategy* in a single study. For example, they could use the experimental strategy to assign participants and manipulate toilet training as we discussed earlier, but could also examine with the quasi-experimental strategy differences between boys and girls in the effects of harsh toilet training. Second, although the experimental strategy is typically the approach best suited to examining cause–effect relationships, we can structure research designs that use quasi-experimental and correlational strategies in ways that *enhance the plausibility of a causal link* between the variables. We will discuss both of these issues in later chapters.

SUMMARY

Science is a system of knowledge and process for acquiring knowledge through objective empirical methods. Although scientists may acquire knowledge and fix beliefs through methods of tenacity, authority, and intuition, they strive instead to employ rationalism and empiricism. Scientists assume events are lawful, conduct tests of empirical questions by observing events systematically and collecting data, and try to apply control and be objective in their tests, often by using a blind procedure. The replication process enables science to be self-correcting. In contrast to science, pseudoscience refers to a "sham science" that develops knowledge mainly through tenacity, authority, and intuition, with very little rationalism and empiricism.

Although important elements of the scientific approach appeared in ancient Greek and Arab cultures, it did not flourish until the Renaissance. Researchers devised strategies for testing predictions, important sources of which are explanations of phenomena, that is, theories and their subclasses, models and hypotheses. Theories are good, or useful, if they are well organized, parsimonious, and stated clearly enough to be falsifiable. To design a study, scientists coordinate the strategies they employ to match their goals for conducting it. The experimental strategy is well suited for determining if variations in an independent variable cause changes in a dependent variable; this strategy meets three important criteria: covariation of variables, causal time sequence, and elimination of other plausible causes. Nonexperimental approaches lack at least part of these criteria. The quasi-experimental strategy either does not manipulate the independent variable or does not equate the groups, such as by assigning participants randomly. The correlational strategy uses the correlation coefficient to assess the degree and direction of association between variables. And the descriptive strategy uses observational methods to detail, categorize, or chart the course of events or phenomena.

KEY TERMS

science	blind	research strategy
tenacity	self-correcting	independent variable
authority	replication	dependent variable
intuition	pseudoscience	experimental strategy
rationalism	introspection	quasi-experimental
empiricism	theory	strategy
lawful	parsimonious	correlation coefficient
empirical questions	constructs	correlational strategy
data	falsifiability	descriptive strategy
control	model	
objective	hypothesis	

REVIEW QUESTIONS

1. Distinguish among *tenacity, authority,* and *intuition* as ways of gaining knowledge and fixing beliefs.
2. Define in detail *rationalism* and *empiricism,* and indicate why these approaches are better suited for acquiring valid knowledge than tenacity, authority, and intuition.
3. Why is *systematic observation* better than *casual observation* in gaining knowledge?
4. What are the main characteristics of science?
5. What are *empirical questions?* Give an example of one regarding the role of different parenting characteristics and infants' reactions to being placed temporarily in a room separate from their parents.
6. What is meant by the term *data?* How do researchers collect data?
7. How do scientists apply *control* and endeavor to be *objective* in conducting research?
8. What does it mean to say that science is *self-correcting?*
9. Outline the phases in doing scientific research.
10. What are *pseudosciences,* and how do they try to seem like sciences?
11. Why is learning about the scientific approach useful for psychology students and in their future careers?
12. What is the main shortcoming of *introspection* as a way of observation?
13. Describe the characteristics of good theories, including the concepts of *parsimony, constructs,* and *falsifiability* in your answer.
14. Define and distinguish among the terms *theory, model,* and *hypothesis.*
15. What are the four main goals scientists can pursue in research?
16. What are *independent variables* and *dependent variables* in research?

17. What is the *experimental strategy* in conducting research, and what are the three criteria it meets in drawing cause–effect conclusions?

18. Compare and contrast the *experimental, quasi-experimental, correlational,* and *descriptive* strategies in scientific research.

RESOURCES

BOOKS, CHAPTERS, AND ARTICLES

Ainsworth, M. D. S. (1979). Infant-mother attachment. *American Psychologist, 34,* 932–937.

Ainsworth, M. D. S., & Bell, S. M. (1970). Attachment, exploration, and separation: Illustrated by the behavior of one-year-olds in a strange situation. *Child Development, 41,* 49–67.

Berscheid, E. (1985). Interpersonal attraction. In G. Lindzey & E. Aronson (Eds.), *The handbook of social psychology* (3rd ed., pp. 110–168). New York: Random House.

Berscheid, E., & Lopes, J. (1997). A temporal view of satisfaction, stability, and the environmental context of relationships. In R. J. Sternberg & M. Hojjat (Eds.), *Satisfaction in close relationships* (pp. 129–159). New York: Guilford.

Garcia, J., & Koelling, R. A. (1966). Relation of cue to consequence in avoidance learning. *Psychonomic Science, 4,* 123–124.

Garcia, J., Hankins, W. G., & Rusiniak, K. W. (1974). Behavioral regulation of the milieu interne in man and rat. *Science, 185,* 824–831.

Lazarus, R. S., & Folkman, S. (1984). *Stress, appraisal, and coping.* New York: Springer.

Lazarus, R. S., & Launier, R. (1978). Stress-related transactions between person and environment. In L. A. Pervin & M. Lewis (Eds.), *Perspectives in interactional psychology* (pp. 287–327). New York: Plenum.

Skinner, B. F. (1938). *The behavior of organisms.* New York: Appleton-Century Crofts.

Skinner, B. F. (1953). *Science and human behavior.* New York: Macmillan.

Squire, L. R. (1992). Declarative and nondeclarative memory: Multiple brain systems supporting learning and memory. *Journal of Cognitive Neuroscience, 4,* 232–243.

Squire, L. R., Haist, F., & Shimamura, A. P. (1989). The neurology of memory: Quantitative assessment of retrograde amnesia in two groups of amnesic patients. *Journal of Neuroscience, 9,* 828–839.

INTERNET SITES

http://www.apa.org This is the American Psychological Association (APA) Website, which gives information about the organization, recent psychology findings, and issues relevant to psychology students.

http://www.psychologicalscience.org This is the American Psychological Society (APS) Website, which gives information about the organization, recent psychology findings, and issues relevant to psychology students.

APPLICATION ACTIVITIES

ACTIVITY 1–1: LEARNING AND MEMORY EXERCISE

Instructions *(continued)* OK, remember that you will read the nouns one at a time with about 2 seconds between words, starting first at the top of the leftmost column and then using the reverse order for the second reading, beginning at the bottom of the rightmost column. Now remove the paper and use your finger to point at each word as you read it.

APPLE	SOCK	BIRD	TREE
SHIRT	PHONE	DRESS	PIN
BRUSH	CHERRY	BANK	GRAPE
PEACH	DISH	LEMON	BICYCLE
TABLE	HORSE	CAMERA	SHELL
PANTS	PENCIL	FISH	SHOE
HAMMER	CAT	ORANGE	ELBOW
DOG	TAPE	CARD	MOTOR
BOOK	BELT	RADIO	SHEEP

Immediately after the second reading, turn the book over and write on the paper as many words as you can remember in any order you wish. Allow about 2 minutes for this.

Scoring   Half of the words in the list are *conceptually related* to other words in the list—they can be categorized as fruit, clothing, or animals—and the rest are *conceptually unrelated* to other words in the list. To complete the exercise, you'll need to count up separately the number of correctly recalled:

- *Conceptually related words:* apple, peach, cherry, lemon, orange, grape, shirt, pants, sock, belt, dress, shoe, dog, horse, cat, bird, fish, and sheep.
- *Conceptually unrelated words:* brush, table, hammer, book, phone, dish, pencil, tape, bank, camera, card, radio, tree, pin, bicycle, shell, elbow, and motor.

Then return to page 16.

ACTIVITY 1–2: THE AMERICAN PSYCHOLOGICAL ASSOCIATION WEBSITE

If you have access to the Internet at home or on campus, contact the APA Website at the address given under Resources. The home page has links to information specifically for students, about timely research findings ("Today's Headlines" and "Press Releases"), and about each of the more than 50 divisions of APA. Click on five of the links. Describe the information in each that was the most interesting to you.

ACTIVITY 1–3: APPLICATION QUESTIONS

1. Sir Francis Galton, a 19th-century scholar, decided to test the commonly held belief that "prayers work" (see Webb, Campbell, Schwartz, & Sechrest, 2000). He reasoned that if prayers are effective, they should protect people who are frequent objects of prayer—particularly kings, queens, and other royalty—and help them live longer. He examined longevity data and found that the mean age at death was 64.04 years for royalty and 70.22 for upper-class individuals. Which ways of acquiring knowledge and beliefs do you think were responsible for the belief that prayers work? Do these same ways apply to this belief today? Describe whether and why you think Galton's reasoning was sound.

2. Describe a possible example of illusory correlation or confirmatory bias that you have seen occur in your own thinking, the behavior or thinking of a friend or relative, or on TV.

3. Think about the following four nonempirical questions: (a) Does God exist? (b) Are people born either "good" or "evil"? (c) Are women basically "good" and men "evil"? (d) Does the mind of a newborn contain some knowledge, or is it entirely a "tabula rasa" (blank slate)? Generate from each of the four questions one *empirical question* that could be tested, with the results having a bearing on the answer to the nonempirical question.

4. For each of the following empirical questions, indicate which research strategy—experimental, quasi-experimental, correlational, or descriptive—would be the best one to use to answer it. (a) What percentage of college students drink heavily, and how has the percentage changed over the past 20 years? (b) Are the length and severity of patients' chronic back pain related to their feelings of depression? (c) Do 10-year-old children learn concepts more easily than 5-year-olds? (d) Do food additives cause asthma attacks? (e) Does graduating from college make people happier? (f) Do laws restricting driving to people 16 years of age or older save lives?

PROLOGUE

You probably know of instances when two people witnessed the same event but recalled details of it differently. Maybe that actually happened to you, or maybe you heard about a criminal case in which witnesses disagreed or a conviction was overturned when the real perpetrator was found. Why do errors occur in eyewitness recall? Elizabeth Loftus (1975) decided to study this question because she knew of instances from everyday life and from research in which different people recalled the same events differently and was aware that most theories of memory assumed that memories correspond very closely to reality. In her research report, she described four experiments to test whether information we receive after an original experience can alter our memory of it. Let's look at one of them.

In the experiment, 150 college students watched a short videotape of a white sports car traveling on a country road and having an accident; then they answered a questionnaire with 10 questions about what they had seen. All questions were the same except one that was critical and had two versions, which constituted the independent variable. For half of the students it read, "How fast was the white sports car going while traveling along the country road?" For the remaining students it read, "How fast was the white sports car going when it passed the barn while traveling along the country road?" Notice that the second version has the words *when it passed the barn*. That was the only difference between the two questions, and the tape had *no barn*. Loftus had added the misleading phrase to see how it would affect the participants' recall of what they had seen. The students returned a week later and answered a different questionnaire about the accident in the tape. As the final item, they answered "yes" or "no" to the question, "Did you see a barn?" This was the dependent variable.

What did the results reveal? Of the 75 participants in each condition, 13 (17.3%) of those with the misleading phrase in the earlier critical question said in the second test that they had seen a barn in the tape, but only 2 (2.7%) of those without the misleading phrase said they had seen one. The false assumption of a barn in the initial question lead many participants to incorporate a barn's existence into their memories. This and other findings from Loftus' research have enhanced our knowledge about memory processes, indicating that people unconsciously "reconstruct" their memories by filling in gaps with inferences or altering stored material based on new information (Loftus & Ketcham, 1991).

This chapter is designed to help you understand how to solve the initial problems in doing research: coming up with research ideas and a basic outline of the methodology you could use. Chances are you will be required to design and conduct a study in this or a subsequent research course. Don't be disheartened if you don't come up with an idea immediately. Students typically need to *look* for possibilities, and this is hard to do just from scanning your memory. Scanning alone often leads to the anxious conclusion, "I can't think of anything." The story of how Loftus came to her research idea gives some hints about useful approaches that we will examine in this chapter. By using these approaches, you can come up with more possibilities than you'll need.

SOURCES OF RESEARCH IDEAS

What sources did Loftus use in developing the idea to study how misleading information affects memory? There were three sources: everyday experience and knowledge, prior research findings, and existing theories.

USING GENERAL EXPERIENCE AND KNOWLEDGE

Loftus knew from her general knowledge that errors of memory occur: witnesses of the same event often disagree about what they saw or heard, and people have been convicted of crimes because of incorrect witnesses' memories. She became curious about why these errors occur.

Another example of general knowledge as a source of research ideas comes from social psychology. In the 1960s, American news media described the shocking case of the stabbing murder of a woman named Kitty Genovese in Queens, New York. Dozens of residents heard the commotion, which took place outside their homes that night in three attacks during half an hour. With each attack, the commotion aroused the residents to turn on their lights, causing the attacker to flee. Although he returned after each of the first two attacks to stab her again, no one called the police during the episode, and only one person called after she was dead. Because of this incident, researchers began to study why bystanders don't help. Darley and Latané (1968) used the experimental strategy by placing individually in a small room students who thought they would simply take turns talking about personal issues with either one, two, or five others in separate rooms through a telecom. During each student's speaking time, the others' microphones would not work. Actually, only one student was tested at a time; the other "speakers" were tape recordings. At one point, a tape-recorded speaker sounded like he was having a seizure and pleaded for help. Did the actual participants run out quickly for help? The answer depends on how many other students they thought were listening: the larger the number, the less likely and slower they were to act. All students who thought they were the only ones listening acted. But only about two thirds of those who thought five others were listening ever intervened, and most of them took more than a minute to act.

Students in my research methods course often generate research ideas from their general experience and knowledge. Here are a couple of examples:

■ A student wondered whether students' religiousness (conviction and participation), feelings of optimism, and perceived stress were associated. Using a correlational strategy, she found a strong negative correlation between survey scores of optimism and stress, but no correlation between religiousness and either optimism or stress.

■ A student expected that adolescents who realize they are homosexual would have a more difficult time coming to terms with their sexual feelings than heterosexuals would. By comparing survey responses using a quasi-experimental strategy, he found that homosexuals reported having experienced much stronger negative emotions, such as fear and guilt, and discomfort regarding their sexuality in adolescence than heterosexuals did.

The studies we have discussed of psychologists and students clearly show that general experience and knowledge can be a useful source of research ideas, which may lead to very interesting and important findings.

How can you identify possible research ideas from your own experience and knowledge? A good way is to *brainstorm,* scanning your memory for different categories of knowledge. One category is clichés or common beliefs, such as "Opposites attract," or "You can't teach an old dog new tricks," or "Two heads are better than one." These beliefs were established through the processes of tenacity, intuition, and authority, which we examined in Chapter 1. Another category is differences among people you know, such as family and friends. Have you noticed in them personality or behavioral differences about which you either suspect a cause or wonder about what it might be? For each category, write down as many ideas as you can, regardless of their quality. After completing the lists, evaluate each idea's usefulness. Keep the best ones in mind as you review the rest of this chapter and the next two, which deal with ethics and measurement in research.

Using Prior Research Findings

Prior findings are another source of research ideas. When Loftus designed her research demonstrating that subsequent misleading information can change witnesses' memory of an event, she was aware of relevant prior research showing that memory often does not correspond exactly to reality. For example, Bartlett (1932) had series of participants examine an abstract drawing with a label, such as "portrait of a woman," and then copy it after it was taken away. The first participant examined the original drawing to make the first copy. Subsequent participants used the preceding copy to make the next one, and so on across several participants. The results showed that succeeding copies came to look less like the original abstraction and more like representations of the label, such as a woman's face. Using a similar method, Allport and Postman (1947) showed participants a picture of a subway scene with several seated passengers and two who were standing: a black man and a white man who was holding a razor. Each participant who saw the picture then described it to a second participant who had not seen it. The second participant then communicated the description to the next one, and so on through several descriptions. In more than half of the final descriptions, the black man, not the white man, held the razor, and many contained embellishments, such as where the train was headed or that the razor was used threateningly, even though the picture did not objectively show these things. Findings like these led Loftus to predict that misleading information after an event could alter people's memory of the event.

Students who use research findings to generate ideas for their studies have usually learned about the findings in prior courses. They recall the research spontaneously or find it by searching through past textbooks or class notes. Here are a couple of examples:

■ A student had read that children develop notions about sex roles at early ages. She examined this issue with experimental and quasi-experimental strategies by having male and female kindergartners rate with happy faces how "good" or "bad" boys were who were portrayed in stories as performing gender-stereotypical or gender-atypical activities. She found that the participants, particularly the males, rated the atypical behaviors more negatively than stereotypical behaviors.

■ A student who was working with chemically dependent urban adolescents had read of findings indicating that people who abuse substances, such as alcohol, have low self-esteem and difficulty coping with stress. By using a correlational strategy and having the adolescents fill out surveys, he found very strong associations between the degree of alcohol abuse and the extent to which they reported having low self-esteem and needing to use alcohol to cope.

As you can see, previously conducted studies provide a useful source of research ideas. Often the methodologies and findings replicate those of the earlier studies, but they can also provide new knowledge by using somewhat different participants or measures of variables than those used in prior research.

USING THEORIES

Loftus also used theories as sources of her idea that providing misleading information would affect memory. At that time, the main theories of memory assumed that errors and forgetting occurred because of decay from nonuse of the material, interference from other learned material, or poor cues to elicit the memory (Hulse, Deese, & Egeth, 1975). Those theories either assumed memory is otherwise accurate or did not address the possibility that it is not. Many theorists thought that inaccuracies and disagreements in people's recall resulted more from differences in their perceptions of events, rather than memory changes. Loftus wanted to test these theories and, perhaps, disprove them. To do this, she used deductive reasoning—something like, "If it is true that misleading information can change memories, participants who receive misleading information after witnessing an event should subsequently have a greater incidence of errors than those who do not get that information, assuming their perceptions were equal." How could she make their perceptions equal? The best way was to use an experimental strategy and assign the participants randomly to either an experimental group (who would get the misleading information) or a control group.

Although theory is an important and useful source of research ideas, only a few of my students in a semester propose testing a theory initially, perhaps because they don't think they understand theories well enough. But when presented with a theory and asked to design a study to test it, they generally do well. For example, my students have designed and conducted studies based on predictions of a theory called the health belief model (Becker & Rosenstock, 1984). This theory describes a series of cognitive events that leads to a decision about whether to take preventive action against an illness or injury. According to the model, the greater the person's *perceived threat* (worry or concern) regarding the health problem and sum of the *benefits* minus *barriers* (pros and cons) the person perceives in taking action, the greater the likelihood of taking preventive action. These assessments depend on many factors, including information and knowledge the person has accumulated about the health problem, such as from the mass media. Here are a couple of examples of research my students have done to test the health belief model with respect to the health problem of sexually transmitted diseases (STDs).

- Students had other students rate in a survey their awareness of media information about STDs and how threatened they felt about contracting these diseases. Statistical analysis revealed a strong positive correlation between media awareness and perceived threat regarding STDs, as the health belief model predicts.
- Students surveyed female undergraduates regarding two specific STDs: herpes, a well-known STD, and trichomoniasis, a less well known one. The researchers reasoned that the health belief model would predict that participants would feel greater perceived threat for herpes than for trichomoniasis because of their greater knowledge of the familiar STD. Statistical analysis confirmed this prediction.

Theories provide professionals and students with a rich source of ideas for research projects.

REVIEWING RELEVANT LITERATURE

Once you have identified one or more ideas to study, you will need to examine relevant literature to clarify your ideas, find out what research has already been done on the topic, and learn more about the methods that have been used in prior studies. This information will help you construct a **research design**—a format for carrying out a research strategy that identifies the number of variables being studied, the number of conditions in which each subject will be tested, and whether data for the individuals tested will be grouped or examined individually.

Although useful literature materials will be mostly journal articles, they can also include books and electronic materials. The literature available can be classified on the basis of two dimensions: *scholarly versus general* sources and *primary versus secondary* sources. A **scholarly source** is intended for professionals and students. Its authors are experts or researchers in the field and typically cite references for their statements. In contrast, general sources are intended for the general public and prepared by writers, such as for popular magazines. How can you tell scholarly from general sources? One way is to look at the materials for advertisements: whereas general sources usually have advertisements for everyday products, such as soaps or cars, scholarly sources do not. A **primary source** is the original, firsthand statement or description, such as of an idea or investigation. Secondary sources provide secondhand information, usually derived from primary sources directly.

When designing research, use general and secondary sources mainly to organize or develop ideas. Although they are fairly easy to read and understand, they are less useful than primary scholarly sources for two reasons: They typically give less-detailed information and sometimes contain errors in fact or interpretation about what a primary source reported. When gathering literature, follow this rule of thumb: After generating your research idea, *use only primary scholarly sources whenever possible,* even if they are inconvenient to get.

BOOKS AND JOURNALS

Books and chapters in edited books can serve two purposes in a literature review. First, a book or chapter can be a primary scholarly source, such as of a theory. For example, Piaget (1952) presented a full description of his theory of cognitive development in a book. Second, books and chapters often present secondhand descriptions of research and theory, with references to the primary sources, which you can then obtain. Textbooks can be used in this way.

Scientific *journals* are periodicals that present two main types of scholarly articles: research reports and reviews. A research report is a primary source for one or more empirical studies that it describes fully and in great detail; it usually describes prior studies briefly and is a secondary source for those. A review article presents brief descriptions of many studies on a specific topic and an overall interpretation of their findings; it is a secondary source for all of those studies. The articles in most scientific journals are *peer reviewed,* which means that experts on the topic of a manuscript (typed report) read and recommended its publication before the journal editor formally accepts it. Because journals can publish only a limited number of pages each year, most manuscripts are not accepted. Journals that are peer reviewed usually present higher quality articles. If you have browsed in the periodicals section of your college library, you may have noticed that most journals specialize on certain topics. The areas of specialization are often reflected in their titles—for example, *Behavior Therapy, Child Development, Cognitive Psychology, Health Psychology, Journal of Personality and Social Psychology, Journal of Sex Research,* and *Physiology and Behavior.* (Go to **Box 2.1**)

Box 2.1   CONTENT OF A RESEARCH REPORT

Scientific research reports usually have five major sections, some of which may be divided into subsections. Our description of the sections will use the format for journal articles given in the *Publication Manual* of the APA (2001), which is described in detail in Appendix A of this book.

Abstract

The first section of a research report is the *Abstract*—a summary, giving a very brief description of the purpose of the study, the participants, the methods used to study the variables, and the outcome. The Abstract is a very useful starting point that gives an overview of the research. If this research appears relevant for your interests, you'll need to read the entire report, beginning with the Introduction.

Introduction

The *Introduction* outlines the problem studied, indicating why the research was done and how relevant past research and theory provide a basis for the design and each hypothesis of the study. You should find an explicit statement of each hypothesis toward the end of the Introduction, usually in the last paragraph. In journals following the APA format, you will not see a title ("Introduction") printed; the section just appears after the abstract.

Method

The *Method* section is usually divided into three subsections: Participants, Apparatus or Materials, and Procedure. This section must give very detailed information so that other researchers will know and be able to replicate precisely what was done in the study. The *Participants* or *Subjects* subsection should state all relevant details about the individuals tested in the research. Current APA guidelines state that **participants** is the preferred term to refer to people tested in research (*respondents* can be used for people who complete surveys in research); **subjects** is an equivalent term used to refer to animals or when the individuals could be either animals or people. Note that the APA introduced this distinction fairly recently—you'll find all early psychology articles and some current ones referring to humans and animals as subjects. The *Apparatus* or *Materials* subsection should specify all laboratory equipment (apparatus items) and stimuli or psychological tests (materials) used, describing them in detail if they were constructed specially for the study. The *Procedure* describes the steps in executing the study and collecting the data, including exactly how the variables were manipulated, controlled, and observed. As you read the Procedure, try to imagine what the participants experienced and did. Sometimes there are variations to this structure. For instance, there may be an additional subsection describing an overview of a very complex research design to help the reader understand the rest of the method. From the information in the Method section, you should be able to identify all research strategies (experimental, quasi-experimental, correlational, or descriptive) and independent and dependent variables used.

Results

The *Results* section presents all statistical outcomes needed to justify the conclusions drawn from the data. Sometimes there are subsections if the design is very complex. Even if you do not know and understand all of the statistical terms and symbols in a Results section, you can expect to understand the gist of the findings from the narrative material and graphs or tables of data.

Discussion

The *Discussion* summarizes the findings and states whether they support each hypothesis and how they relate to the past research and theory mentioned in the Introduction. When the results contradict a hypothesis or some past research or theory, this section should try to explain in detail why. The Discussion should also evaluate the adequacy of the method and design, pointing out the strengths and weaknesses, describe the extent to which the results might apply to other situations or participants, and give specific ideas for future research based on this study's outcome. Following the Discussion, a complete list of references is given.

ABSTRACTS AND ELECTRONIC DATABASES

Abstracts of scientific writings have been available in hardbound volumes for many decades. The APA's monthly *Psychological Abstracts* is an example. Until recently, students and researchers searched the literature by using an index in each hardbound volume to find abstracts, which then enabled them to decide whether to get a copy of the actual material. This very cumbersome and tedious process is now obsolete and has been streamlined enormously through electronic databases.

Three electronic databases for abstracts are especially useful for psychology research. The most important one is the electronic version of *Psychological Abstracts,* which is updated monthly and is available through college libraries either as the Web-based **PsycINFO** or as a CD-ROM version, called *PsycLIT* (accessed through a library workstation). *MEDLINE* is a database of abstracts for medical literature and is accessible on the Internet, and the *Web of Science* covers a variety of fields, including social and natural sciences and arts and humanities. These databases cover thousands of journals, add information about many thousands of new research articles and other items each month, and focus on scholarly sources, not popular magazines or newspapers. If you have used Internet search engines, such as Yahoo or Google, you will see many similarities in the procedures for doing a search with the databases we will describe.

PsycINFO

Libraries provide electronic versions of *Psychological Abstracts* by subscribing through one of several commercial services or formats. Depending on the service they subscribe to, there can be minor differences in the look and function of the various PsycINFO and PsycLIT systems. For our discussion and examples, we will use the PsycINFO process because Web-based versions are supplanting the CD-ROM versions. Whichever system your library uses, they can subscribe for all available years (from 1887 to present) or for only some, such as the last 3 years. Although the abstracts in PsycINFO are mostly of journal articles, they also include other materials, such as scholarly books and chapters in edited books.

At the beginning of a search, you will be asked to specify which of your library's subscription years you would like included. You will then click on a button (for example, "Start Search"), which takes you to a search page where you can type in a word or phrase in the search window and launch the search. If you type in a more than one word with hyphens in between, the system will search for the words together as a phrase; if you type them separated with spaces, the system will search for each word individually and then in combination. On that page, you'll also see that there is a list of "Search Hints" and some options you can choose, such as to place limits on the search, which we will consider later. When you click on "Search," the search output will be listed below as a series of "records" that appear in the default "display" format by year of publication, with the most recent ones first. You'll also see the number of records the search yielded and that you can change the display format and the years chosen to search.

Figure 2.1 shows the search output for the term "eyewitness memory" for the years 1996–1998 (using the WebSPIRS subscription service that my college library uses; others will be very similar). Look first at the upper portion of the

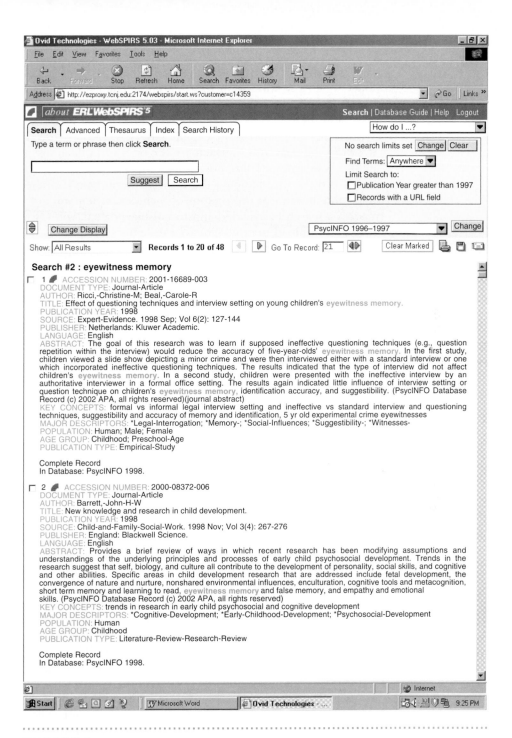

A PsycINFO user screen showing the first page of the search output for the term "eyewitness memory" for the years 1996–1998. This output uses the *default format,* giving the title, author, source, abstract, and other fields. You can reduce the number of fields by clicking on "Change Display" to use a different format, such as *titles only* or *citation and abstract.*

page and notice three buttons labeled "Suggest," "Thesaurus," and "Change" limits, which you will use in your searches. Then scan down to the number of records found, the opportunities to change the display format and the search years, and then the records found. Notice that each record consists of a list of "fields" that are labeled in capital letters, including the *TITLE, AUTHOR, SOURCE,* and *ABSTRACT,* which are the ones you will almost always need to examine. As we will see later, most of the other fields will be useful in refining your search process. By changing the display format, you can alter the number of fields and amount of information it includes. When you are satisfied with the records a search has yielded and the display format, you will want a copy of it. You can download the outcome to a diskette, e-mail it to yourself, or print the records you mark in a box to the left of each record. The copy will have a "search history" that consists of a list of search terms used and the number of records found for each term.

The abstracts provide the most critical information for the next phase of reviewing the literature. They will enable you to decide whether the article or book is relevant for your project and whether to examine the entire item. There are four ways of obtaining an article or book. First, your library may have it. Second, another nearby library may have it and allow you to photocopy or borrow it. Third, you can order it through your library's interlibrary loan process. Fourth, Web-based versions of *Psychological Abstracts* often offer procedures at the end of a record for acquiring a *full-text copy* of the item you want.

At the end of this chapter is an "Application Activity" (Activity 2–1), which gives you a step-by-step example of a search with several "tips" on ways to make a search most effective and efficient. Do the entire exercise by taking this book with you to a computer that has access to PsycINFO or PsycLIT and performing each step.

Other Electronic Databases

Several other electronic databases are available for retrieving abstracts of materials for psychological research, particularly in disciplines outside psychology that relate to its subfields, such as health, educational, or social psychology. One of the most useful of these is *MEDLINE,* which functions a lot like PsycINFO, but covers medical journals as well as nonmedical journals that are related to medicine. For instance, it has abstracts for articles published in health psychology, genetics, and physical therapy journals. The U.S. National Library of Medicine (a division of the National Institutes of Health) publishes MEDLINE and makes it available to everyone anywhere in the world free of charge on the Internet (at http://www.nlm.nih.gov).

Four other useful sources of abstracts that relate to psychology research require subscriptions and may be available through your college library. One of these is *ERIC,* a database of the Education Resource Information Center, which has abstracts of research articles and other materials on education and human development. Another of these your library may offer is *ABI/Inform,* which covers the business-related literature, such as on advertising and personnel management. The *Web of Science* (WoS, which includes and offers separately its *Social*

Science Citation Index) allows searches in various disciplines for particular authors or topics, using keywords or phrases. A unique feature of the WoS is that, once you have identified a key article or book, you can find subsequent materials that used that item in their reference lists. This approach allows you trace the literature that follows up on the topic of the key article or book. Lastly, various services, such as *Lexis-Nexis,* provide databases of the general nonscholarly media, such as magazines and newspapers.

ONLINE MATERIALS

The Internet can provide materials other than abstracts that may be of use in a literature search. A growing and often very valuable Internet service is the online publication of journal articles. Many respected journals are making the articles they publish available online, either directly from their own Websites or through a service, such as EBSCOhost. If you are using a service, you should be careful to choose sources that are scholarly. In EBSCOhost, for instance, you can use "Advanced Search" and click on "Scholarly (Peer Reviewed) Journals" to eliminate nonscholarly materials.

Other kinds of material available on the Internet include data, surveys, and papers. There are two main problems with these materials. First, the information they provide is often purged periodically and then is no longer available. If this happens, it is a problem because someone who reads your work would not be able to consult the source you cited. Second, the information on Websites is often unreliable or invalid. Anyone can set up a Website, and there are no filters, such as librarians or a peer-review process, to separate the wheat from the chaff. A simple way to evaluate information from the Internet is to look at the Website address to "consider the source." A dot-com or dot-net Website is less likely to have reliable information than a dot-org, dot-edu, or dot-gov. Dot-org, dot-edu, and dot-gov Websites are typically maintained by respected organizations, such as the American Cancer Society or the Centers for Disease Control; dot-coms and dot-nets often are not. In addition, you should be very wary of information on Websites belonging to individuals, businesses, and political or advocacy organizations. These sites typically have a point of view or profit motive they want to promote.

One final point in doing a literature search: don't expect to find an article that describes a study that is identical to what you want to do. If you do the same study, it will be a replication. Researchers rarely want to do a study that is purely a replication because it would simply confirm or disconfirm prior results and not advance our knowledge very much. Instead, they are more likely to use one of three approaches: They might change the methodology a prior study used, replicate part of a prior study or add other independent or dependent variables, or conduct an entirely new study. Loftus did an entirely new study in her research on the effects of misleading information on memory. With any of these approaches, the planned research is unique in some way, and the researchers would not find a study in the literature that did exactly the same thing.

AFTER YOU IDENTIFY IMPORTANT MATERIALS

After you have identified the most important articles and books on the topic you want to study, you need to get copies of them and read them carefully. Although scholarly books are more likely to be primary sources for theories than for research, journal articles can be primary sources for both theories and research. If you are planning to test a theory, read a primary source of it to find out exactly what it proposes so that you can figure out what it would predict for the variables you are planning to study. When preparing to read the articles, find a strategy that will help you to organize and understand the material so that you can make decisions about the hypotheses and methods for your investigation. Here's a strategy I recommend:

1. Before reading journal articles, use the abstracts to separate them on the basis of what they found; some may have found opposing results. Try to identify and keep track of the research strategy—experimental, quasi-experimental, correlational, or descriptive—they used.

2. Read the Introductions, looking to see if they mention theories that you weren't aware of so you can consider them (you'll find sources listed in the References). Also see how they defined or conceptualized the variables they examined. Ask yourself, "Did studies with opposing results conceptualize variables differently?" If so, you may want to get information about the way the variables were conceptualized and use it in designing your research.

3. Read the Discussions, looking for statements about strengths and weaknesses of the methods they used and about ideas for future research or applications. These statements can help you specify more clearly what you want to study and the methods you will want to use.

4. Next read the articles' Method sections. Ask yourself, "Do the subjects, materials, or procedures for the studies with opposing results differ in important ways that may account for the different results?" Your answer may help you determine what to study and the methods to use. Even if the results of those studies have been consistent, you should identify aspects of the methods in those articles you might use and aspects you might want to change for your research design. Using deductive reasoning to decide on changes to make can increase the likelihood of finding interesting and important results. For example, you might decide to use older or younger participants than in the prior studies because other research on related topics has found that age affects performance. As an illustration, consider the Loftus research again: The participants were college students. Given the large improvements research has found in memory and cognition as children develop, we might expect that misleading information would have an even greater influence on children's memory of events they witness.

After having examined the literature in a systematic way, you should be ready to generate possible hypotheses to test and the methods to use.

FORMING HYPOTHESES AND CHOOSING METHODS

Most often, doing a literature search on a topic of interest to you will lead to several ideas for a research project that you might do. If so, you can choose from among them on the basis of your degree of interest and the feasibility of the methods. How do methods differ in feasibility? Here are several examples of feasibility problems.

- You're interested in studying children of different ages, but the schools in your area will take too long to give permission to do the study or will not give permission at all.
- The materials or apparatus you will need are not available to you or would cost too much to purchase.
- Conducting the research would require laboratory or classroom space that you may not be able schedule.
- Testing the number of participants you will need for the study will take more time than you can devote.
- You may lack needed expertise and credentials, such as to conduct therapy.
- The procedures of the research may be ethically questionable, such as if they involve some risk of physical or psychological harm to the participants. We'll discuss research ethics in Chapter 3.

Although professionals may have fewer problems like these to deal with than students, they still must consider feasibility when designing research. Your instructor can help you determine the feasibility of the ideas you generate and may even be able to suggest some changes in the method you are considering that can increase the feasibility of a project.

FORMULATING SCIENTIFIC HYPOTHESES

Once you have some research ideas that seem interesting to you and feasible to conduct, you will need to develop good scientific hypotheses for them. What makes hypotheses good? The criteria are like those we considered in Chapter 1 for good theories. First, good hypotheses state *explicit predictions* for the variables to be examined. For instance, suppose we were interested in studying connections between anxiety and nervous behaviors, such as nail biting, and expected that nervous behaviors would be "a function of"—that is, would depend on and vary with—anxiety. This is an interesting idea, but it is not explicit enough. For example, we would need to indicate the direction of the association, such as, "the greater the anxiety, the more nervous behavior people will display" or "people under high anxiety will display more nervous behavior than people under low anxiety."

Second, good hypotheses are *testable and falsifiable*. For a hypothesis to be testable, we must be able to measure the occurrence of the variables it includes. A hypothesis regarding the content of infants' dreams would not be testable because we cannot get verbal descriptions from babies. In fact, even demonstrating convincingly that babies have dreams would be difficult, if not impossible at this time. The wording of a hypothesis determines whether it is falsifiable. It must be stated such that failing to find the predicted relationship would be clear evidence that the hypothesis is incorrect. For the most part, this means the hypothesis should not contain "weasel words." For example, the hypothesis, "Alcoholics Anonymous (AA) helps people stop drinking if they really, deep down, want to stop" contains the weasel words "really, deep down, want to stop." If our research then found (a) only about 20% of those in an AA group and in a control group succeeded in stopping drinking and (b) no difference in success for those who claimed an "extremely strong" versus a "moderately strong" desire to quit, would our findings falsify the hypothesis? No, because we did not show, and probably *could not* show clearly, that the drinkers "really, deep down" wanted to quit. If the wording enables rational thinkers to explain away any opposing findings, the hypothesis is not falsifiable.

Third, good hypotheses provide *clear definitions* of the variables. In our example on studying anxiety and nervous behaviors, what do we mean by anxiety? We can examine anxiety by actually manipulating it—for instance, by creating a situation that arouses people's feelings of anxiety—or by measuring it, such as with a questionnaire. If we just measure it, we would also need to decide whether we want to assess people's usual levels of anxiety or their levels at the time of testing. Some questionnaires assess *trait anxiety,* or characteristic levels of the variable, and other questionnaires assess *state anxiety,* or current levels of it (Rosenhan & Seligman, 1984). In addition, which nervous behaviors will we examine, and how will we measure them? Nervous behaviors can take many forms. They can be motor, such as nail biting or foot tapping, or verbal, such as saying "um," for instance. And they can vary in the frequency and magnitude with which they occur and the amount of time the person engages in them. Each of these decisions enables us to define the variable "operationally." An **operational definition** specifies the meaning of a variable in terms of the methods (operations) used to measure or produce different levels of it. All variables examined in scientific research should be operationally defined in the research report, usually in the Introduction before the hypotheses are stated. Operational definitions tell other researchers exactly what our variables were so they can understand and replicate them precisely.

MATCHING HYPOTHESES WITH STRATEGIES

We just saw that good scientific hypotheses make explicit predictions. Part of this issue is the match between the prediction and the research strategy we plan to use. Recall from Chapter 1 that researchers can use experimental, quasi-experimental, correlational, and descriptive strategies that should be coordinated with the goals of the research. The exact wording of the hypothesis makes the match between the prediction and the strategy. Let's see how with our example of studying connections between anxiety and nervous behaviors, assuming that we decided to define nervous behaviors as the frequency of nail or cuticle biting.

Researchers use the *experimental strategy* to determine whether variations in an independent variable cause differences in a dependent variable. To use the experimental strategy for the anxiety and nervous behavior study, we would test only people who bite their nails or cuticles at least occasionally. We would then manipulate anxiety by randomly assigning the participants to an experimental group that will get the anxiety-arousing situation and a control group that is tested in exactly the same way but without the anxiety situation. During testing, someone who is blind to the purpose of the study would assess nail/cuticle biting. This strategy meets all three essential criteria for making cause–effect conclusions:

- Covariation of variables—it can show that nail/cuticle biting, the dependent variable, varies with anxiety, the independent variable.
- Causal time sequence—the independent variable will precede the dependent variable.
- Elimination of other plausible causes, by randomly assigning the participants and treating them identically except for the pressure-arousing situation.

The hypothesis to match the experimental strategy should state outright or clearly imply a causal relationship, such as, "The pressure-arousing situation will produce a greater frequency of nail/cuticle biting than the control condition."

Nonexperimental strategies typically lack one or more of the criteria for making causal conclusions, and their hypotheses would be worded differently. In research using the *quasi-experimental strategy,* for instance, we might not manipulate the independent variable (anxiety) or have equivalent groups. An example of using a quasi-experimental strategy would be to have participants who bite their nails/cuticles at least occasionally fill out a questionnaire to measure their usual anxiety levels (trait anxiety) and use these scores to form nonequivalent groups, people with high and low anxiety. We would then assess their nail biting in one or more of several ways. For instance, we could have them rate on a scale the frequency with which they bite their nails/cuticles. Or we could have someone who is blind to the purpose examine their nails and cuticles or observe their nail/cuticle biting under a specific condition, such as while they watch a videotaped documentary on TV. The hypothesis to match this strategy should specify a relationship that will be found, but *not* a causal one. If we used the video test, for example, the hypothesis might state, "Participants with high levels of anxiety will bite their nails or cuticles more frequently during the video than those with low anxiety levels." Notice that the hypothesis states the direction of the connection—those with high anxiety will bite more—but does not imply that anxiety causes the nervous behavior. Notice also that we could turn the design around; we could identify people who do and do not bite their nails or cuticles and assess their usual levels of anxiety. With this quasi-experimental design, our hypothesis would be, "Participants who bite their nails or cuticles will have higher anxiety scores than those who do not."

If we used the *correlational strategy,* we would not separate the participants into groups. We would simply assess each participant's anxiety level and nail/cuticle biting and compute a correlation coefficient for the two variables. Although the easiest way to make these assessments would be by questionnaire, we could use other approaches, such as by having someone who is blind to the purpose of the study observe and give scores for their behavior during standard testing situations. In either case, the hypothesis would be stated to reflect what the coefficient should indicate. For instance, if we used questionnaires, we might state that "respondents' self-reports will show that the greater their anxiety, the more nail or cuticle biting they perform" or "their self-reports will be positively correlated: the higher their anxiety, the more nail or cuticle biting they do."

The *descriptive strategy* is used simply to detail or categorize events or to chart their course, usually because there is insufficient theory or prior research to provide a basis for predictions. As a result, hypotheses are likely to be less specific or even absent in descriptive research. For example, researchers using this approach might observe schoolchildren to determine whether there are differences in signs of anxiety at different ages or in different societies. This research might find that children show their anxiety in different ways in different societies and that nail/cuticle biting doesn't exist in some societies, but in other societies it begins very early and increases as children get older. Knowing about these findings would be important for researchers who later want to use correlational, quasi-experimental, and experimental strategies to examine anxiety and nervous behaviors.

DECISIONS ABOUT SUBJECTS

Researchers have many decisions to make about the individuals who will be tested in a study. We start by identifying the study's **population,** or entire set of people or animals of interest, from which we will select a **sample,** or subset of individuals who will be tested as representatives of the population. This process requires that we answer several questions. For example, will the subjects be humans or animals? What characteristics must they have—for instance, in terms of age, sex, cultural background, personality, or behavior habits, such as being nail biters. How will they be recruited? How many subjects will be needed? If they will be separated into groups, will the assignment process use a random (unbiased) method or a method based on an existing characteristic, such as age or sex? The answers to these questions should correspond with the planned topic, goals, and research strategy of the study. For example, if we plan to use an experimental strategy, the subjects must be assigned in a manner that is likely to produce equivalent groups, such as by random assignment. Obviously, the subjects must be available to the researcher to test; if not, the project is not feasible. We'll describe methods for sampling and assignment to groups in Chapters 5 and 10.

DECISIONS ABOUT MATERIALS AND PROCEDURES

The research materials (or apparatus) and procedures are the backbone of the testing situation and usually define operationally the independent and dependent variables. As a result, decisions about which materials and procedures to use and how to schedule them for the testing situation are critical and must be made with great care.

Let's use the anxiety and nervous behavior research in our examples again. Suppose we were using an experimental strategy to study these variables by presenting an anxiety-arousing situation for participants in the experimental group. That situation might make use of an apparatus, such as to present a cognitive task with false feedback that the participants were doing poorly while peers watched. We would need to select or design a task that would arouse anxiety and then decide what the control group would do during their testing session. Would they perform the same task with real feedback or do something else? How much time would they spend on the task? Would the task need to leave the participants' hands free so they could bite their nails or cuticles during testing? These are some of the many decisions we would need to make, and some of them could have a great influence on the success of the experiment. For instance, if the task does not arouse enough anxiety or is not performed for enough time, we would find little difference in nervous behavior between the experimental and control groups.

In contrast, suppose we were using a quasi-experimental, correlational, or descriptive strategy and would need to measure the participants' anxiety levels, using a questionnaire as materials. Should it assess trait or state anxiety, and which of several available instruments would we use? Which nervous behavior would we assess, and how and when would we measure it? If we had the respondents report both their usual anxiety levels and nail or cuticle biting in a questionnaire, would it matter which assessment came first—that is, would filling out one affect how they answer the other? Once again, the decisions we make regarding the materials and procedures we use could influence the study's outcome.

RESEARCH VARIETIES

Once we have identified one or more hypotheses for our research and chosen the methods to use in the study, we should consider what the results of the research will mean if they turn out as expected. Will the results be important or interesting simply because they satisfy our curiosity or test a theory, or will they have some practical application? Are the methods we will use very artificial, or will they represent or relate to situations or processes in "real life"? The answers to these questions enable us to classify research on the basis of two dimensions—applied versus basic research and laboratory versus field research—and help us see what the results will mean.

APPLIED VERSUS BASIC RESEARCH

Scientists in all fields can have many purposes for conducting research. When scientists do **applied research,** their intention is to provide evidence that is directly relevant for solving an existing practical problem. In the field of chemistry, applied research might be conducted to find a substance that would enable farmers to increase their yield of corn, for example. Here are a few examples of applied research in psychology.

- To reduce the hazards in mining jobs, leading to hundreds of deaths and thousands of injuries each year in the United States, Fox, Hopkins, and

Anger (1987) designed and tested a program of rewards to improve worker safety behaviors. After the program was introduced, work-related injuries dropped sharply and remained relatively low during the years when the program was in effect.

◼ Because high anxiety in hospitalized people impairs recovery and increases medical costs, Gruen (1975) provided psychological counseling to reduce the anxiety of heart attack patients. Compared with a control group that received only standard hospital care, those who got the counseling developed fewer heart complications and spent 1.2 fewer days in intensive care and 2.4 fewer days in the hospital.

◼ To improve the effectiveness of using computers to coach students through a series of lessons, Kritch and Bostow (1998) compared computer programs that differed in the levels of activity they required. This research found that programs requiring very high levels of active participation were more effective than those requiring less-active participation.

Each of these studies was designed and conducted to produce evidence that could have direct and immediate real-world application. When the purpose of a study involves applied issues, the researcher typically addresses them in the Introduction and Discussion sections of the research report.

In contrast, **basic research** is designed and conducted to answer fundamental or theoretical questions about phenomena, without focusing on a specific practical purpose for the outcome. The main focus of basic research is to add to our body of knowledge and understanding. Here are some examples of basic research in psychology.

◼ To test the theoretical view that children learn grammar mainly through corrective feedback from adults for mistakes, researchers observed parent–child conversations (Brown, Cazden, & Bellugi-Klima, 1969). They found that as children first begin to talk, parents focus their feedback on the correctness of the content or meaning of the child's statement rather than its grammatical form. For instance, when a girl pointed to her mother and said, "He is a girl," her mother answered, "That's right."

◼ Researchers examined the role of stress reactions on memory by having people watch a series of pictures while listening to a story about a boy and his mother who go to a hospital (Cahill, Prins, Weber, & McGaugh, 1994). For some participants, the story was emotional: An accident had severed the boy's feet, which surgeons reattached. The other participants heard a neutral story about the boy at the hospital. Before hearing the story, half of the people in each condition received a drug that limits physiological reactions to stress. A test a week later showed that the drug impaired the memory of story details for the emotional story, but not the neutral one. These findings suggest that heightened physiological reactions enhance the memory of stress experiences.

◼ Latané, Williams, and Harkins (1979) conducted a study of a phenomenon called social loafing in which individuals work less hard when in groups than when alone. They tested participants in group sizes of one, two, four, and six people and found that the degree of social loafing increased with group size.

These examples describe studies that were not conducted to solve practical problems and produced important outcomes without direct or immediate application.

Do all studies fit neatly into the categories of applied and basic research? No, and there are three reasons to think of applied and basic research as ends of a continuum rather than a pair of separate categories. First, some studies have purposes or outcomes that are both applied and basic. The experiment by Loftus on the effect of misleading information on memory is an example: She tested the theoretical view that memory errors and forgetting occur because of decay from nonuse of the material, interference from other learned material, or poor cues to elicit the memory. Inaccuracies and disagreements in people's recall were thought to result from differences in their perceptions of events, rather than memory changes. But she also knew that her findings might have implications for views and processes in legal cases involving eyewitness testimony. Another example comes from the results of studies on stress and cigarette smoking: smoking appears to reduce stress temporarily, but may increase stress in the long run (Parrott, 1999). These findings increase our understanding of why people smoke and also suggest that training in ways to reduce stress might help smokers quit. Second, much applied research is based on the results of basic research, such as on perception and cognition. For instance, using the Loftus research and findings from basic research on cognition, researchers designed a "cognitive interview" technique and demonstrated that it improves eyewitness memory (Fisher, McCauley, & Geiselman, 1994). Third, the outcomes of many studies that were done without intending to discover a solution to a practical problem or that seemed to have little practical use were eventually applied to solve real-world problems (Nickerson, 1999). Applied and basic research varieties are interdependent.

LABORATORY VERSUS FIELD RESEARCH

The setting for research has important implications for the methods and strategies that we can use in conducting an investigation. In **laboratory research,** the study is conducted in a setting that allows the researcher a high degree of control over who is present, how data are collected, and exactly what the participants experience at any given time. Usually, but not always, the participants realize they are being tested. Although people tend to think of laboratories as places with institutional furniture, test tubes, and researchers in white lab coats, any environment that allows a high degree of control fits our definition. Thus, a classroom, a therapist's office, or a production room in industry could be a laboratory if there is sufficient control during the study. In contrast, **field research** occurs in a real-life setting, usually with less opportunity for the researcher to control the environment, but the participants often do not realize they are being tested while data are collected. Field research is especially useful in studies of social processes, such as aggressive or helping behavior.

Although laboratory research is sometimes criticized as using "artificial" situations that have little similarity to everyday life, field research can be contrived, too, depending on how it is structured and carried out. Humans, and many animals, have quite a variety of experiences in a wide range of situations, many of which are in laboratories, such as in hospitals. If the research situation is artificial or contrived, such as by having events occur at exact intervals, often all we need to do is get accustomed to it, and then it becomes "natural" to us. The critical issue is the extent to which the laboratory or field situation has two kinds of realism: mundane and experimental (Aronson, Brewer, & Carlsmith, 1985). **Mundane realism** refers to the resemblance of the research situation to the subjects' real-world experiences. In contrast, **experimental realism** has to do with whether the research situation has an impact on the subjects and gets them involved in the procedures and ready to take the experience seriously. Recall the experiment by Darley and Latané (1968) we discussed earlier on bystander intervention: The participants were in separate rooms, speaking through a telecom, when one speaker seemed to be having a seizure and asked for help. The participants' likelihood of running out for help decreased as the number of other people they thought were listening increased. The situation in this study has a fairly low degree of mundane realism and a very high degree of experimental realism. Although the procedure in laboratory research and field research may be high in one type of realism and low in the other, having experimental realism is probably more important than mundane realism.

Like applied and basic research, laboratory and field research can be seen as ends of a continuum, rather than separate categories. The amount of control researchers have can be higher in some field research than in some laboratory research, and both can be high in experimental realism. Perhaps the more important issue is whether laboratory and field research on the same topics produce different results. There is evidence that they do not: researchers looked at a large number of research reports on various topics in social psychology, matched up studies conducted in laboratory and field settings on the same topics, and found similar outcomes for the laboratory and field studies (Anderson, Lindsay, & Bushman, 1999). This finding indicates that the criticisms of artificiality in laboratory research and of the lack of controls in field research are exaggerated. Well-designed and conducted laboratory and field studies tend to produce similar results.

WILL THE OUTCOME GENERALIZE?

The extent to which results obtained under the circumstances of a particular study can *generalize*, or would be found under a different set of circumstances, is called **external validity.** Would the same outcome occur with subjects with different characteristics, in other situations, or at other time periods? When scientists plan research, they have in mind how far they would like the results to generalize. The greatest degree of external validity occurs when the research results can be generalized broadly across large populations of individuals, different situations, and different time periods.

Generalizing Across Individuals

The individuals tested in psychological research can differ in many ways, including their species (much research in psychology is conducted with animals), cultural background, gender, age, personality traits, and cognitive abilities. Generalizing to humans from data obtained by testing animals can be justified, but the researcher needs to present rational arguments to make a convincing case. Thus, if the research is on physiological processes, for instance, the researcher can describe how the organs or chemistry is similar across species. If the research is on learning processes, the researcher can cite studies showing that related processes are similar across species.

If we use college students as our participants, as so many psychology studies do, will the results generalize to people of different ages, from other social classes, and with lesser cognitive abilities? Depending on the topic being studied, the extent to which researchers are justified in generalizing to a larger population from a sample of college students can vary. Let's consider two studies we have already discussed: the Loftus study on the effects of misleading information on memory of events and the Darley and Latané study on the effects of the number of people present on the likelihood of bystander intervention. Chances are that misleading information has similar, but not necessarily identical, effects on eyewitness memory for almost all people, regardless of their characteristics (although the effect may be even greater for children). But the effects of variables on bystander intervention might differ considerably across cultural groups, ages, and gender. Social processes often vary greatly across these characteristics.

The characteristics of the sample in a study will be determined by the method used to obtain them. Will we recruit them from a limited population, such as at a college in a particular course? Will we use a *random* process for recruiting participants, making sure that all individuals in the population have an equal chance of being asked to take part in the study? Will the individuals be required to participate or enticed with money or course credit? Will participants be recruited by using announcements, such as in class or on posters or the Internet? People who volunteer to participate in research often differ from those who do not (Rosenthal & Rosnow, 1975). Research volunteers tend to be better educated, higher in social class, more sociable, and higher in need for social approval than nonvolunteers. In Chapter 10, we will examine in more detail the strengths and weaknesses of different methods for obtaining participants.

Generalizing Across Situations and Time Periods

We've already seen that social psychology studies in laboratory and field settings tend to produce similar results—that is, the results from laboratory research generalize nicely to real-life situations. Still, some aspects of the situation in which participants are tested may affect external validity. For instance, if you were doing a study of people's attitudes on social issues, such as abortion, on the grounds of a church, the participants might give different answers than they would if tested in another location. The testing situation also includes the researcher who collects the data, and this person's gender may influence the participants' behavior, such as in an interview about their current romantic relationships. What's more, variables can be defined and measured in different ways. For example, people's sensation of pain can be assessed by having them fill out a rating scale, by observing how much discomfort they display, and by using physiological measures, such as of heart rate (which increases with pain). Studies of pain sometimes find different results with different measures (Chapman et al., 1985). These examples suggest that the data collected under certain circumstances may not generalize well to other situations.

Many variables in psychological research change over time. Some of them change in cycles during the day or across a week, month, or year. For example, many people feel tired at certain daytime hours, most people begin their work or school week on Mondays and end it on Fridays, women have monthly menstrual cycles, and many people have more negative mood states, such as depression, in the winter months. In addition, some variables, such as social attitudes or behavior, change relatively permanently over time. Sexual attitudes and behavior provide many examples, such as people's attitudes about homosexuality, casual sex, and sex before marriage. Researchers should consider whether their results can be generalized across time or are bound by time.

Deciding How Far to Generalize

In the process of deciding how far research results can generalize, psychologists usually begin with a **continuity assumption**—that is, psychological or behavioral processes are likely to be similar across the dimensions of subjects, situations, and time periods unless there are reasons to assume otherwise (Underwood & Shaughnessy, 1975). Then they use rational thinking and evidence to decide whether there are "reasons to assume otherwise." This is usually done by arriving at a consensus among experts in the discipline. If logic and prior related findings suggest that the processes are similar across all three dimensions, they decide to stick with the continuity assumption and generalize broadly. But if there are reasons to assume the processes are different across dimensions, they decide to restrict the generality of the results to appropriate subjects, situations, and time periods.

The best way to test the limits of generality of research results is to do research with a variety of subjects, situations, or time periods. Sometimes the limits are discovered by replicating all or part of the study while varying the dimension of concern, such as the subjects' ages. An example of how research can clarify the limits of generality comes from an experiment by Melamed and Siegel (1975) with 4- to 12-year-old children who were in the hospital awaiting elective surgery, such to remove their tonsils. The children were assigned to two groups: the experimental group saw a film showing a boy in the hospital being somewhat afraid but coping with the procedures; the control group saw a film about a boy going on a nature trip. The children in the experimental group subsequently showed less anxiety than those in the control group. But other studies found that the effect of a film or video to prepare children for surgery depends on the child's age and previous medical history. Specifically, children under 7 years of age more so than older ones may be made more anxious by the preparation if they have had prior difficult experiences with medical procedures (Melamed & Bush, 1985; Miller & Green, 1984).

Designing research is a complicated process that begins by examining relevant resources and literature. Researchers use this information to form hypotheses and decide on the methods to test them. Research decisions regarding methods and strategies will influence what the results will mean and the degree to which they generalize to subjects, situations, and time periods that were not actually tested in the study.

SUMMARY

Generating research ideas starts with looking for possibilities, using various sources. Our general experience and knowledge can provide a good source for research ideas if we brainstorm, scanning our memory for ideas that relate to concepts that interest us. Prior research findings that we come across in textbooks or the news media are another good source. And existing theories, such as the health belief model, are very useful because they outline predictions regarding relationships between variables that we may find interesting to test in research.

The next step is to search relevant literature, focusing mainly on scholarly sources rather than general ones and on primary sources rather than secondary ones. Scientific books and peer-reviewed journals are the most important primary scholarly sources to seek out and obtain to consult in developing a research design and writing a report for the study. Some useful ways to find this literature include looking through textbooks, which are secondary sources, using abstracts and electronic databases, especially PsycINFO (or PsycLIT), MEDLINE, and Web of Science. Online materials are convenient, but their information can be invalid or unreliable, especially if it comes from a dot-com or dot-net Website.

The literature you obtain will help you formulate scientific hypotheses that are explicit, testable, and falsifiable and that provide clear definitions of the variables to be studied. An operational definition gives a variable's meaning by specifying the methods used to measure or produce different levels of it. The exact wording of a hypothesis should match the research strategy—experimental, quasi-experimental, correlational, or descriptive—that will be applied to test it. Only hypotheses to be tested with experimental strategies should state or imply a cause–effect relationship between the independent and dependent variables. Decisions to be made in designing a study include selecting a population and sample. The research strategy will influence decisions about the subjects to be tested and the materials and procedures that will be used.

Although applied research is conducted to help provide a solution to a practical problem, the main goal of basic research is to answer fundamental or theoretical questions. The setting for research is important. Laboratory research allows the researcher a high degree of control over the situation, but field research is done in a real-life setting, often with less control. Although laboratory research has been criticized as being artificial, a more important issue is the extent to which the research methodology has mundane realism and experimental realism. Laboratory and field research appear to produce very similar outcomes for research on the same variables.

The results from research with a high degree of external validity can generalize broadly across large populations, different situations, and other time periods. Researchers in psychology usually decide how far research results can generalize by starting with the continuity assumption and then determining through logic or evidence whether reasons exist to assume that the psychological or behavioral processes are likely to be different for different people, situations, or time periods.

KEY TERMS

research design	operational definition	field research
scholarly source	population	mundane realism
primary source	sample	experimental realism
participants	applied research	external validity
subjects	basic research	continuity assumption
PsycINFO	laboratory research	

REVIEW QUESTIONS

1. Describe the Loftus study on the effects of misleading information on eyewitness memory.
2. How can everyday experience and knowledge, prior research findings, and existing theories be useful sources of research ideas?
3. What are the differences between *scholarly and general sources* and between *primary and secondary sources* as types of literature one could find? Give an example of each type of source that you have used or read.
4. What are *peer-reviewed journals,* and why do they provide especially good scholarly sources?
5. Describe the five major sections of a research report.
6. What is *PsycINFO,* and what information does it contain?
7. What are the two main problems with using online materials as sources of information?
8. Describe the characteristics of good hypotheses.
9. Give two different operational definitions each of *anxiety* and *intelligence.*
10. Look back at the examples of *applied and basic research.* Why is the Gruen study an example of applied research, and why is the study by Cahill et al. an example of basic research?
11. Discuss the criticism of *laboratory research* that it uses artificial situations. Include the issue of *mundane versus experimental realism* in your answer.
12. What is *external validity,* and how do researchers use the *continuity assumption* in deciding how far to generalize?

RESORCES

BOOKS, CHAPTERS, AND ARTICLES

Kardas, E. P. (1999). *Psychology resources on the World Wide Web.* Pacific Grove, CA: Brooks/Cole.

Koch, C. (1997). Learning the research process on the World Wide Web. *Council on Undergraduate Research Quarterly, 18,* 27–29, 48–49.

INTERNET SITES

http://library.albany.edu/internet/searchnet.html This Website describes how to do efficient searches on the Internet.

http://www.lib.berkeley.edu/teachinglib/guides/internet/findinfo.html A Website that teaches people who are unfamiliar with the Web how to use it.

http://www.psychwww.com This Website has information about and links to psychology journals and other resources.

http://www.indiana.edu:80/~iuepsyc/psycjump.html This Website has information about and links to psychology journals and other resources.

APPLICATION ACTIVITIES

ACTIVITY 2–1: PsycINFO STEPS AND TIPS

For this exercise, suppose you want to make a thorough review of the research literature on the effectiveness of different types of psychotherapy in treating emotional problems in people who have suffered great trauma, such as in war. Although as a student, you would not be conducting research by providing therapy, you might need to do a term paper on the topic. You would start by accessing the PsycINFO database (PsycLIT will be very similar) through your library and selecting the publication year(s) you want to search. In this exercise when you see the word **Do** and an action in brackets, such as [**Do:** Type the word "trauma."], carry out the action. Here are some useful steps and tips on conducting a search:

1. *Use the help screens.* Before doing your first search, it's a good idea to work through the help screens quickly. [**Do:** Try out the help screens.] Use them during a search when stumped.

2. *Choosing the years.* Start with all years available through your library to get a sense of the amount of available literature. [**Do:** Access PsycINFO and request all years.] You can narrow the range later, before saving or printing the records you find.

3. *Initial limits of the search.* Limit the search initially to include only items written in English (and other languages you speak well) and exclude dissertations and technical reports because they are difficult to get and typically not peer-reviewed. [**Do:** Click on "Change" search limits. Then set the lan-

guage limits and choose "journal-article" in *document type*.] Although searching only for journal articles may be too restrictive for many searches, you can revise these limits at any point or retain them throughout the search you do.

4. *Choosing the best search terms.* Two very common problems occur in identifying the search terms to enter. One is not knowing what to call the concept you are searching for, and the other is not realizing that terms other than the one you know may also apply or be even better. Three approaches can help. First, look through textbooks or notes to find one or more terms that may apply. Second, after typing into the search window the best term or concept you can think of, use the "Suggest" button and the electronic *thesaurus*. [**Do:** Type in the search window "trauma." Use the "Suggest" button and then the thesaurus. Repeat these actions for the term "shell-shock" (a common term for emotional difficulty resulting from trauma).] These procedures will provide lists of related terms you could consider. In the lists you'll find some terms that are fairly broad (such as "life-experiences") and other terms that are narrower (such as "child-abuse"). By hyphenating words in a term, you require that the search find the words together in the exact sequence, not separated. [**Do:** Notice that the lists include the official term for the search topic: *posttraumatic-stress-disorder*. Type it (with hyphens) in the search window.] Third, because the database will search for exact matches, use an asterisk (*) to "truncate," or shorten, words that could be written with different endings. For instance, therap* will find "therapy," "therapies," and "therapeutic;" and trauma* will find "trauma," "traumatic," and "traumatized." You should get a greater number of relevant records with the truncated version. If you want to combine two or more terms, connect them with "AND" (in capital letters) if all must be present in the record for it to qualify or with "OR" if any of the terms can be present for a record to qualify.

5. *Do a trial search.* Once you have identified the search terms you want to use, do a trial search to see how many records you get with the initial limits. [**Do:** Type in the search window "posttraumatic-stress-disorder AND psychotherap*" and click on "Search."] The trial search may produce a very large number of records, sometimes thousands (I got more than 500 in 2002). [**Do:** Mark a few of the more recent records this action produced, and print them as hard copy. The icons for *print, save,* and *e-mail* are at the top of the search output.]

6. *Broadening the search.* If a trial search produces too few records or not enough that are really relevant, you may need to broaden the search by lifting some of the limits, changing an "AND" conjunction to an "OR," or using a different term, such as "therap*" or "treatment" in addition to "psychotherap*." [**Do:** Change in the search window "psychotherap*" to "(psychotherap* OR therap* OR treatment*)" and click on "Search."] This should produce more records (I got more than 1,800) than you had previously because it will accept records with any terms that begin with the truncated forms we entered.

7. *Narrowing the search.* If you find in a trial search that there are too many records or if many of them are not relevant to your needs, you may want to narrow your search. You can do this by searching a smaller range of years, such as only the past 20 years, or by setting additional limits, such as the *population* (human, animal, female, male, inpatient, outpatient) or *age group.* You can also limit the *publication type*—of the many types, empirical-study, literature-review-research-review, and meta-analysis (a procedure that pools the results of many studies) are the most useful. [**Do:** Retain the same terms but set new limits: for population, choose human; for publication type, choose literature-review-research-review and meta-analysis. Click on "Search."] Setting additional limits should reduce the number of records (I got 131). [**Do:** Mark a few of the more recent records this action produced, and print them as hard copy.] Review articles, particularly in the journals *Psychological Review* and *Psychological Bulletin,* are very useful *secondary sources* for the topic of interest. They give an overview of the findings of many studies and have extensive reference lists that you can use to find primary sources for your research.

8. *Finalize the search.* By testing a variety of terms and limits, you should be able to find the right balance to get a reasonable number of relevant records. Keep in mind that you should *not* expect to find a record with exactly the study you want to do. In fact, most researchers don't want to find the identical study because that would mean that their study would be a replication, not an original investigation. [**Do:** Change the limits for our topic—"posttraumatic-stress-disorder AND (psychotherap* OR therap* OR treatment*)"—so that you end up with between *30 and 100 records of journal articles,* not books or dissertations, for this exercise.] [**Do:** Mark six records, a couple at the beginning, in the middle, and toward the end of the search output, and save the six to diskette or e-mail them to yourself.]

9. *Review the records found.* In a real search, you would examine the abstracts carefully to make sure you have found enough relevant records and to identify the ones most likely to be useful for your needs. Then you would get copies of those articles.

ACTIVITY 2–2: READING A RESEARCH REPORT

Read the research report (Naquin & Paulson, 2003) in the Companion Website (www.prenhall.com/sarafino) for this book, using the strategy described in this chapter to help you organize and understand the material it presents. Answer the following questions.

1. Does the report mention any theories or define in some way the variables the study examined? If so, describe the theories or definitions briefly.

2. What strengths or weaknesses of the study and ideas for future research or application does the report describe in the Discussion?

3. From reading the Method section, describe three changes you could make to design a follow-up study. Using your current knowledge, why would you expect each of these changes might lead to interesting findings?

4. Indicate which research strategy—experimental, quasi-experimental, correlational, or descriptive—the study used and why you think so.

ACTIVITY 2–3: APPLICATION QUESTIONS

1. We saw earlier that we can develop research ideas from clichés or commonly held beliefs, such as "Opposites attract," "You can't teach old dogs new tricks," and "Two heads are better than one." Think of two more examples, giving a total of five. Then for each of the five examples, develop a "good" hypothesis that the belief suggests, match it with a research strategy—experimental, quasi-experimental, correlational, or descriptive—and state why you think they match.

2. Here are three psychological constructs: learning, anger, and hunger. For each construct, generate two operational definitions—one that specifies how to measure it and one that specifies how to produce different levels of it.

3. Suppose you conducted a study with a survey that your participants could find on the Internet. What could you do to attract them to the Website and to participate? Think about generalization issues. Discuss whether the results of a survey conducted on the Internet have a higher or a lower degree of external validity than a survey distributed on paper to college students or to people at a shopping center near where you live.

4. Look at the Method section of the research report (Naquin & Paulson, 2003) in the Companion Website (www.prenhall.com/sarafino) for this book. Rate the method for its mundane realism and experimental realism on a scale from 1 (very low) to 10 (very high). Justify each of the two ratings you give.

CHAPTER 3

ETHICS IN CONDUCTING RESEARCH AND REPORTING OUTCOMES

PROLOGUE

In the early 1900s, John B. Watson was one of the founders of the school of thought in psychology called *behaviorism*, which proposed that nearly all behavior is the product of experience. Because one of his interests was in the development of emotions and there was no research showing that emotional reactions

can be learned, he decided to study the acquisition of a fear through conditioning (Watson & Rayner, 1920/2000). He and his coauthor chose an 11-month-
old infant now known as "Little Albert" to serve as the participant. The boy was
available at a hospital because his mother was a wet nurse there. In pretests, the
boy had shown interest in and no dislike of a variety of items, including a white
rat, a rabbit, and a bunch of cotton, but showed distress to a sharp, loud noise.
The researchers stated two justifications for the method they used with Albert:
he seemed otherwise emotionally very stable, so that "we felt we could do him
relatively little harm" (2000, p. 313), and they thought he would have had fear-
producing experiences at home.

The conditioning trials were designed to establish a fear of a white rat
and carried out in a well-lit room while Albert sat on a table that was covered with a mattress. On the first trial, the rat was placed on the mattress
in front of him, and he reached for it. Just as he touched it, behind his
head a researcher struck a metal bar with a hammer, which made a sharp,
loud noise. Albert "jumped violently and fell forward, burying his face in
the mattress. He did not cry, however" (2000, p. 314). He experienced a
second identical trial on the same day and reacted by falling forward and
whimpering. A week later, he had five additional trials pairing the rat with the
noise on one day. Although he did not cry on the first trials, he did on the last.
Then the researchers placed the rat on the mattress without using the noise,
and the boy

> began to cry. Almost instantly he turned sharply to the left, fell over on left side,
> raised himself on all fours and began to crawl away so rapidly that he was caught
> with great difficulty before reaching the edge of the table. (2000, p. 314)

Several days later, he experienced a series of trials without the noise, testing his
reaction to the rat and objects like it, such as a rabbit, a dog, and a Santa Claus
mask. In all cases, he showed negative reactions, such as turning away from the
object or crying. Several days after that, tests with the rat alone produced mild
reactions, so he received two trials with the noise to "freshen up" his reaction.
Weekly tests showed continued but lessened negative reactions to the rat and
other animals during the next month, when he was taken from the hospital. Although the researchers described several methods they had planned to try to reduce Albert's fear, he was no longer available to them. Studies since then have
shown that some methods they proposed are effective in reducing fears
(Sarafino, 2001).

Were the researchers ethically justified in creating a fear in Albert? If you
answer *yes*, should they have deleted the two later trials to "freshen up" the fear
as it weakened and made sure to provide the methods they had planned for reducing the fear? Although Watson and Rayner's findings are very important and
widely cited, the ethics of doing their study has received a great deal of criticism.
Examining the ethical issues involved in the way we design, conduct, and report
scientific investigations serves as a good bridge between finding topics to study,
which we considered in Chapter 2, and beginning to collect data on behavior,
which we'll discuss in Chapter 4.

CODES OF ETHICS

The term **ethics** refers to a set of moral principles or values to govern people's conduct, such as in their work activities. When Watson and Rayner published their study in 1920, no ethical guidelines existed for conducting research. The first published guidelines for psychologists was a document of the American Psychological Association (APA, 1953), but it was geared mainly for the professional practice of psychology, such as in clinical and counseling activities. Over the intervening years, several new versions appeared. In 1982, the APA published ethical codes specifically for psychology researchers, and the latest version published in 2002 gives a detailed set of ethical principles and codes of conduct to guide the behavior of psychologists in nearly all facets of their work. Thus, for psychologists who provide therapy, there are specific standards for explaining the results of diagnostic assessments to the client, maintaining confidentiality, and many other issues. For psychologists engaged in research, the focus is on safeguarding participants' rights and protecting them from harm or discomfort, providing humane care for animal subjects, and being scrupulously honest in reporting the findings of research.

GENERAL PRINCIPLES

Because psychologists work in many settings and roles, the APA (2002) ethics code is divided into two sets of guidelines: general principles and ethical standards. The *general principles* constitute aspirations toward which psychologists should strive; the *ethical standards* are specific guidelines for conduct that the APA can enforce with sanctions. Five general principles apply broadly:

- *Beneficence and Nonmaleficence.* Psychologists try to benefit and do no harm to the individuals with whom they work or for whom they provide services.
- *Fidelity and Responsibility.* Psychologists strive to establish trusting and consultative relationships with colleagues, clients, and others with whom they work in an effort to serve the interests of those individuals and to prevent unethical conduct.
- *Integrity.* Psychologists strive to be honest and fair toward others and in describing their qualifications, in their research, and in other activities.
- *Justice.* Psychologists oppose injustice in the distribution and quality of psychological services and procedures for all individuals.
- *Respect for People's Rights and Dignity.* Psychologists respect people's rights to privacy, confidentiality, and autonomy and try to be aware of and sensitive to cultural and individual differences, including those related to "age, gender, gender identity, race, ethnicity, culture, national origin, religion, sexual orientation, disability, language, and socioeconomic status" (p. 1063).

The journal article in which these principles are presented also gives dozens of specific, detailed ethical standards, many of which are quoted at various points later.

Research in all scientific disciplines has the potential for producing benefits and risks. In medicine, for example, we see benefits of research reported in the mass media weekly, such as new procedures for clearing clogged arteries without requiring surgery and drugs that reduce "bad" cholesterol, thereby preventing heart disease. In psychology, research has demonstrated that therapy techniques like those Watson and Rayner planned to use with Little Albert are effective in reducing people's intense fear of social situations and are more effective than a drug (atenolol) commonly prescribed for that purpose (Turner, Beidel, & Jacob, 1994). And a study demonstrating that children awaiting surgery who watched a 22-minute videotape of a hospitalized child coping with medical procedures showed less anxiety before surgery and faster recovery after than children who received standard preparation (Pinto & Hollandsworth, 1989). Not all of the findings of research can be applied to benefit people—some major benefits involve demonstrating important processes or answering theoretical questions, as Watson and Rayner's study did. As we saw in Chapter 2, the benefits from science can come from applied research or basic research.

What about risks of harm or discomfort to participants in research? Some of the most dramatic cases come from *physically harmful* medical and military research, and we'll describe a few. In widely known examples, Nazi scientists carried out horrendous experiments, such as immersing people in freezing water to see how long they would survive and infecting people with malaria and other diseases to observe the course of the illness or to test treatments for it (Kimmel, 1996). The participants did not volunteer or give their consent. Could this have happened in a society that is not fascist? Yes. Two examples, also from the 1930s and 1940s, occurred in the United States. In one study, 18 patients, mostly from a Rochester, New York, hospital, were not informed that they were injected with high levels of plutonium-239, a radioactive substance, as part of a government study to test how long plutonium lasts in the body (Watson et al., 1993).

Another harmful study, begun in 1932 by the U.S. Public Health Service (PHS) in and near the city of Tuskegee, Alabama, examined the course of untreated syphilis (Bell, 2000; Brandt, 2000). Why? A prior study in Norway that was stopped when treatment became available had found that 70% of untreated patients who were followed for many years suffered no serious effects (of course, 30% did: the long-term effects include brain and cardiovascular damage and death!). The PHS recruited about 400 poor, semiliterate black men with syphilis and a control group of 200 similar men without syphilis; those in the control group who became infected later were added to the syphilis group. The men with the disease were told they had "bad blood," a colloquialism for syphilis in the South, and would receive free treatment if they participated. Instead of providing treatment, the PHS gave them ineffective substances, such as "spring water" and aspirin, when they came for medical visits and actually convinced other physicians in the area not to treat the men by claiming the PHS was giving treatment and evaluating it. The PHS also gave inducements, such as hot meals, money, and free transportation, to get participants to come to medical visits, where they would give blood samples and, at least once, had a painful, medically unnecessary spinal tap to test for neural effects. To make sure the men would have an autopsy for the study when they died, the PHS offered to pay the men's funeral expenses if they came to the hospital when severely ill. This study continued for 40 years, until the American news media learned of it and published stories criticizing it.

Psychological Harm

Although some psychology research with humans can produce physical harm, such as when studying the perception of pain, the more likely risks are of psychological discomfort or harm. Most individuals who learn of the study with Little Albert probably feel that it produced at least some short-term harm to the boy. Although we don't know what happened to him, Watson and Rayner (1920/2000) stated that they thought the fear would persist to some degree, perhaps into adulthood.

Another well-known psychology study in which participants experienced intense distress examined people's obedience to commands to administer strong pain to another person. Milgram (1963) used advertisements to recruit 40 men of various backgrounds to participate in a study, falsely described as testing learning processes, with the promise of earning a good wage just for coming to the laboratory. Each session used one participant who experienced a well-orchestrated ruse. Upon arrival for the study, he met a man who was introduced as another subject but was actually an accomplice, and the two of them were told that the study concerned the effect of punishment on learning. The men were shown a shock apparatus for delivering punishment, and their supposed roles in the study—one as the "learner" and one as the "teacher"—was decided by rigged drawing straws.

The ruse continued. The men were taken to an adjacent room, where the learner (the accomplice) had his arms strapped to a chair to prevent movement and had electrodes attached to his wrist. The men were told that even when the shocks are painful, they would cause no permanent injury. The teacher then went back to the room with the shock apparatus and was shown how to use a microphone to communicate with the learner in the other room and how to use the apparatus. He also tried out the apparatus on himself as a "test," actually getting a moderate shock; he didn't know that no shocks would actually be administered to the learner. Once the learning task began, the teacher read word lists that the learner could hear through a speaker and then tested him. If the learner made an error, the teacher would press a switch to deliver the supposed shock, which the apparatus would confirm by turning on a red light and buzzer. The shocks would start at a very weak level, but each time the learner made another error, the teacher would deliver the next strongest shock. During the learning task, the learner (accomplice) became a critical part of the ruse. Using a set of predetermined responses, the learner would make errors deliberately. When the shocks supposedly reached fairly high levels, the learner protested the shocks vocally, made pounding sounds with his feet, and stopped giving answers to the tests, which would earn more shocks. No teacher had stopped the process until that point. If a teacher balked at continuing to give shocks, the researcher used statements as prods, with the strongest being, "You have no other choice, you *must* go on."

Did the teachers go on, as commanded? Most did. Only a few stopped after the protests began, and 26 of the 40 (65%) of the men continued delivering the shocks all the way to the end of the scale, marked "Danger: Severe Shock"! Were the teachers distressed? Yes, extremely so, and Milgram provided examples. One of those who quit before the end said, "Oh, I can't go on with this; no, this isn't right. It's a hell of an experiment. The guy is suffering in there" (p. 376). Many teachers who continued after the learner started to protest began to sweat profusely, tremble, and stutter. An observer of one session noted that within 20 minutes the initially calm participant

> was reduced to a twitching, stuttering wreck, who was rapidly approaching a point of nervous collapse. He constantly pulled on his earlobe, and twisted his hands. At one point he pushed his fist into his forehead and muttered: "Oh, God, let's stop it." And yet he continued . . . and obeyed to the end." (p. 377)

This man and other participants were extremely conflicted, probably feeling trapped into violating societal norms and their own internalized standards of behavior but realizing no serious consequence would befall them for disobeying. They surely never thought they were capable of hurting someone so easily. In fact, other people generally don't expect individuals to be so obedient: in a survey that described the study, Milgram found that students and colleagues thought only a tiny minority of participants would keep on giving the shocks to the end.

Degrees of Risk

When researchers design studies, they often face ethical dilemmas and choices. In these situations, they need to *balance* the potential scientific or applied benefits of doing the study against the possible risks it may pose to the participants. The degree of risk research methods present for participants varies, and many psychology studies present virtually *no risk* at all. When risks exist, they can be classified with rules outlined by the U.S. Department of Health and Human Services (USDHHS, 1982) into two categories:

- **Minimal risk** means that there is some risk, but the likelihood and magnitude of harm or discomfort are no greater than "ordinarily encountered in daily life or during the performance of routine physical or psychological examinations or tests" (p. 6).
- **Risk** means any likelihood or magnitude of harm or discomfort greater than minimal risk.

Methods with minimal or more risk need to be evaluated for ways to reduce the potential for harm or discomfort. If risk still exists, the next decision is whether the likely benefits of the study outweigh the risks to the participants. All of the studies with risk of harm or discomfort we've discussed so far were done many years ago, before clear codes existed for making these judgments, so researchers used their own criteria. For instance, Watson and Rayner thought Little Albert would not be seriously harmed because he was so well adjusted. As we'll see ahead, professional and governmental guidelines now require that impartial professionals approve research plans before the study is conducted.

ETHICS IN PSYCHOLOGY RESEARCH WITH HUMANS

Ethical considerations in psychological research have two viewpoints at their core. First, all participants, regardless of their ages or other characteristics, have rights that supersede those of the researcher and should be defended against harm and discomfort. Second, because the scientific search for knowledge produces great benefits and is essential to the future of society, researchers need a reasonable degree of latitude in making decisions about what to study and how to study it. In this section, we will examine methodological issues that can present ethical problems in psychological research with humans and see how researchers can reduce risks and increase the benefits from their work.

POTENTIAL ETHICAL ISSUES

Milgram's (1963) study sparked a strong debate on the appropriateness of commonly used procedures in psychological research. Both the procedures he used and the strong emotional impact they had on the participants were criticized (Kimmel, 1996). Soon after, the APA set up a committee to examine research ethics in depth.

The most current version of the ethical codes that APA (2002) developed to guide psychology researchers' decisions covers a wide range of potential professional activities. These codes are available in a journal article and presented in the format of an outline, with each section or issue numbered. As we consider ethical codes for researchers, you'll find quoted sections (with corresponding section numbers) from the APA article to give you the exact words. The first codes we'll consider deal with general responsibilities in planning and conducting any research project.

General Responsibilities

In any study, researchers are responsible for making sure that the individuals who have contact with participants are competent and sensitive to the needs of diverse populations, that the procedures do not violate laws or professional standards, and that the methods used have received appropriate approval. Some APA codes relating to theses issues apply to all psychologists, and others apply only to those doing research.

> **(SECTION 2.01a)** *Boundaries of Competence*
>
> Psychologists provide services, teach, and conduct research with populations and in areas only within their boundaries of competence, based on their education, training, supervised experience, consultation, study, or professional experience.

> **(SECTION 2.05)** *Delegation of Work to Others*
>
> Psychologists who delegate work to employees, supervisees, or research or teaching assistants . . . authorize only those responsibilities that such persons can be expected to perform competently . . . and . . . see that such persons perform these services competently.

(SECTION 3.04) *Avoiding Harm*

Psychologists take reasonable steps to avoid harming their clients/patients, students, supervisees, research participants, organizational clients, and others with whom they work, and to minimize harm where it is foreseeable and unavoidable.

(SECTION 8.01) *Institutional Approval*

When institutional approval is required, psychologists provide accurate information about their research proposals and obtain approval prior to conducting the research. They conduct the research in accordance with the approved research protocol.

Although no set of standards can anticipate every ethical problem that could possibly happen, the APA guidelines deal with the most widely encountered and troublesome ones in psychological research. One research procedure that can present ethical problems is the use of deception.

Deception

What was the most prominent procedure in Milgram's methodology that enabled him to carry out the study? Lies, of course: he created an elaborate ruse to deceive participants. In research methods, **deception** refers to the act of misleading, deluding, or withholding information to give a false impression for the purpose of hiding or creating a variable. For instance, Milgram deceived the participants about the purpose of the study, the identity of the learner, and the transmission of electric shock from the apparatus to make participants think falsely that the study was about the use of shock as punishment for errors. The current APA expressly discourages or limits the use of deception:

(SECTION 8.07) *Deception in Research*

a. Psychologists do not conduct a study involving deception unless they have determined that the use of deceptive techniques is justified by the study's prospective scientific, educational, or applied value and that effective non-deceptive alternative procedures are not feasible.

b. Psychologists do not deceive prospective participants about research that is reasonably expected to cause physical pain or severe emotional distress.

c. Psychologists explain any deception that is an integral feature of the design and conduct of an experiment to participants as early as is feasible, preferably at the conclusion of their participation, but no later than at the conclusion of the data collection, and permit participants to withdraw their data.

Why do researchers use deception? Most commonly, it's because they want to study unbiased "natural" behavior, such as in social or emotional situations. For instance, people who know that some feature of their behavior is being observed may modify how they behave so they will look good (Kimmel, 1996). If you had been a participant in the teacher's role of Milgram's research, would you have given much shock if he had told you he was studying people's obedience to authority by assessing how much pain you would inflict on another person when asked to give punishment for errors? Probably not. Or consider the study by Darley and Latané (1968) we discussed in Chapter 2 in which participants were deceived into thinking an emergency situation was happening: Someone was having a seizure. If the participants had known the situation was faked, would they have responded at all? And if they did, would the time it took to respond have increased, as it did, with number of other individuals who were also aware of the incident? These fascinating and important findings probably would not have been discovered without deception or with other methods, such as a survey or role-playing. Recall that Milgram conducted a survey of students and colleagues to determine their predictions for the number of participants who would keep on giving the shocks to the end. They thought only a tiny minority would. Still, alternative methods sometimes produce similar outcomes to studies that use deception and should be considered when designing research (Kimmel, 1996).

Are there different types of deception, and are some types worse than others? Some deception in research occurs in an *active* manner: The researchers give misleading information in an effort to create an untrue impression, such as by lying about the study's purpose or claiming to a participant that an accomplice is also a participant (Kimmel, 1996). Other deception occurs in a *passive* manner: The researchers withhold information. For example, they may not say that a shocking event will occur or that their study is comparing different age groups. Or they may give a broad but accurate title to a survey that has a specific purpose, such as giving the title, "Survey of Everyday Happenings" to a survey that measures stress from daily hassles. But the active or passive feature is not a critical issue in deciding whether deception is ethical. The critical issue is the degree to which the deception increases the likelihood or magnitude of harm or discomfort—the greater the increase, the less ethical it is.

Researchers and others who oppose the use of deception generally cite three concerns (Baumrind, 1964, 1985; Christensen, 1988; Kimmel, 1996). First, lying is morally wrong and degrades society. Second, deceiving participants provides an avenue for harm to occur. Third, people who serve as participants may become upset at having been deceived—feeling gullible, angry, or embarrassed—and less trustful of psychologists and other professionals. The first two concerns may be addressed and reduced by restricting the use of deception and requiring researchers to get approval of the research design by impartial professionals to safeguard the rights and welfare of the participants. The APA codes specified earlier do these things. The third concern has been examined in research that found consistently that participants deceived in research do not mind that they were misled or feel that they were in any way harmed (Christensen, 1988). For example, the participants in a study on alcohol and aggression that used deception and had some risk of physical and mental stress were contacted by phone to ask if they would fill out a survey about their experience (Pihl, Zacchia, & Zeichner, 1981). The survey asked about aspects of the study that may have bothered them. About 19% claimed that an aspect of the study troubled them. What bothered them? Only 4% said they were troubled by the deception; boredom during participation was more bothersome than deception. The most distress the participants reported concerned the alcohol consumed—mainly its type, its amount, or the speed with which they consumed it. Deception does not seem to produce bad feelings, probably because participants understand why it was needed.

The APA codes call for restricting the use of deception to research in which it is truly necessary. Concealing important information from participants or deceiving them should be avoided whenever possible. If deception is necessary to carry out the study, researchers should consider how extensive the deception must be—the less, the better—and its possible impact on the participants. The more extensive it is and the greater the impact, the harder it is to justify or to balance against the benefits of the study.

Privacy, Anonymity, and Confidentiality

Participants have the same rights within a research situation as they do elsewhere in free societies. Three of these rights involve people's expectations of privacy, anonymity, and confidentiality. In research, **privacy** refers to participants' freedom from unauthorized intrusions on or assessments of their feelings, thoughts, or behavior in situations when people reasonably expect that these variables are restricted from observation. This is of particular concern when observations are done unobtrusively, such as by watching people at a shopping mall from a concealed position or rummaging through their garbage. The setting of the research and the sensitivity of the information collected influence whether people can reasonably expect privacy. Most behaviors that occur in most public places are not private. For instance, at a baseball game, people's attendance or the words they shout would not be private, but what they whisper to a friend is. In public restrooms, however, eliminative and grooming behaviors would be considered private.

Anonymity means that the identity of participants is unknown or masked. Researchers can maintain anonymity in two ways. First, they can simply not collect or keep records of the participants' names or other personal identifiers. In a survey, for example, the materials would not ask for names and might state clearly that respondents should not provide any. Second, if collecting identifiers is necessary, such as to provide credit or payment for participation, identifying information should be separated from the research data and linked only through a code or other technique. For instance, to provide credit for participation in a survey, the researcher might have participants put a code on the survey materials and on a separate list of participants. The code might be the name of their course instructor and the last four digits of their home phone number.

Confidentiality means that any information obtained about individual research participants is not divulged to others, unless it is authorized by the participant or required by law. A relevant APA standard states:

(Section 4.07) *Use of Confidential Information for Didactic or Other Purposes*

Psychologists do not disclose in their writings, lectures, or other public media, confidential, personally identifiable information concerning their clients/patients, students, research participants, organizational clients, or other recipients of their services that they obtained during the course of their work, unless (1) they take reasonable steps to disguise the person or organization, (2) the person or organization has consented in writing, or (3) there is legal authorization for doing so.

Thus, confidential research information about a participant can be disclosed for scientific or professional purposes if the participant cannot be identified. Gossiping clearly does not qualify! Keep in mind that simply telling others that an individual participated could be damaging to that person—for example, if the study was on a deviant behavior, and the person's friends and family strongly disapproved of just discussing the topic. Maintaining confidentiality requires self-discipline by all research staff, and they should be informed of the APA guidelines. Very similar guidelines specified in the 1996 Health Portability and Accountability Act (HIPAA) went into effect in the United States in 2003 to protect the privacy, anonymity, and confidentiality of health information (USDHHS, 2003).

Informed Consent

Perhaps the most serious ethical failure in the medical and military research we described earlier that produced physical harm is that the participants were not told accurately what would happen to them or given a fair and free opportunity to decline to take part in the studies. The horrific Nazi research is an example, and the eventual convictions of the scientists at the Nuremberg trials led to the development of a principle called informed consent. By **informed consent** we mean that individuals should be told in advance all features, positive and negative, that might influence their willingness to participate in a study and told that they may decline or discontinue participation freely at any time. This principle is addressed in multiple APA standards, including the following:

(Section 8.02) *Informed Consent to Research*

a. When obtaining informed consent . . . , psychologists inform participants about (1) the purpose of the research, expected duration, and procedures; (2) their right to decline to participate and to withdraw from the research once participation has begun; (3) the foreseeable consequences of declining or withdrawing; (4) reasonably foreseeable factors that may be expected to affect their willingness to participate, such as potential risks, discomfort, or adverse effects; (5) any prospective research benefits; (6) limits of confidentiality; (7) incentives for participation; and (8) whom to contact for questions about the research and research participants' rights.

b. Psychologists conducting intervention research involving the use of experimental treatments clarify to participants at the outset of the research (1) the experimental nature of the treatment; (2) the services that will or will not be available to the control group(s) if appropriate; (3) the means by which assignment to treatment and control groups will be made; (4) available treatment alternatives if an individual does not wish to participate in the research or wishes to withdraw once a study has begun; (5) compensation or monetary costs of participating including, if appropriate, whether reimbursement from the participant or a third-party payor will be sought.

(SECTION 8.04) *Client/Patient, Student, and Subordinate Research Participants*

a. When psychologists conduct research with clients/patients, students, or subordinates as participants, psychologists take steps to protect the prospective participants from adverse consequences of declining or withdrawing from participation.

b. When research participation is a course requirement or opportunity for extra credit, the prospective participant is given the choice of equitable alternative activities.

The first of these sections is fairly straightforward. It means basically that researchers should be honest about the research experience and not apply sanctions to individuals who decline or withdraw from participation.

Part of the second section deals with research participation as a requirement of or an extra credit opportunity for students in psychology courses, especially introductory psychology. This issue is more complicated than it may seem. Many college psychology departments have established a *participant* (or *subject*) *pool* system by which students "volunteer" to be participants in research, thereby meeting a requirement or getting credit toward their grades in certain courses. Proponents of this system say that participation has educational value for the students. But critics say the research experience is often boring and not very educational, and the alternative activities from which students can choose are frequently very burdensome, so participation is not really voluntary (Kimmel, 1996). How can departments address these criticisms? To increase the educational value of participating in studies, many researchers talk with the students after they participate, telling them what the study is about and how it relates to specific material they have been learning in their course. To make the alternative activities more equitable, departments should make sure the activities take a similar amount of time as participating in research. Examples of reasonable tasks that can serve as alternatives include attending and taking notes on a research presentation, assisting in collecting data for an ongoing project, and writing a summary of a journal article the student can choose from a predetermined set (Kimmel, 1996).

What should a researcher do if the participants are incapable of giving permission, such as young children and people with intellectual or emotional disabilities? Let's consider the case of children: Informed consent should be obtained, preferably in writing, from their parents or individuals who can reasonably act *in loco parentis* (teachers or directors of institutions, for example). Individuals giving consent should be informed of all features of the research that may affect their willingness to consent. At the time of testing, each child should be asked if he or she is willing to do the task and be allowed freely to decline.

For some types of research, getting informed consent may not be necessary. An APA standard covers this possibility and gives examples:

(SECTION 8.05) *Dispensing with Informed Consent for Research*

Psychologists may dispense with informed consent only (1) where research would not reasonably be assumed to create distress or harm and involves (a) the study of normal educational practices, curricula, or classroom management methods conducted in educational settings; (b) only anonymous questionnaires, naturalistic observations, or archival research for which disclosures of responses would not place participants at risk of criminal or civil liability or damage their financial standing, employability, or reputation, and confidentiality is protected; or (c) the study of factors related to job or organization effectiveness conducted in organizational settings for which there is no risk to participants' employability, and confidentiality is protected or (2) where otherwise permitted by law or federal or institutional regulations.

In using archival data or observing public behavior in public places, privacy is usually not a problem, but anonymity and confidentiality should be maintained. With surveys, it's hard to imagine cases in which receiving informed consent is not at least implied by the fact that the people filled the surveys out. To guard against the possibility of people completing a survey against their will, the instructions should tell respondents the topic of the survey, features of the task that might affect their willingness to participate, and that they should feel free to decide not to complete it. A simple way to get an explicit record of consent for a survey while maintaining anonymity is to have respondents simply check a box to indicate their agreement to participate before filling out the materials.

Psychologists sometimes use technological devices to collect data, such as by tape recording the behavior of participants. The APA codes address the need for informed consent when filming or recording behavior:

(SECTION 8.03) *Informed Consent for Recording Voices and Images in Research*

Psychologists obtain informed consent from research participants prior to recording their voices or images for data collection unless (1) the research involves simply naturalistic observations in public places, and it is not anticipated that the recording will be used in a manner that could cause personal identification or harm, or (2) the research design includes deception, and consent for the use of recording is obtained during debriefing.

What about data collection using the Internet? In most cases, researchers who collect data on the Internet can require that participants indicate their informed consent before starting the task. An example of a controversial situation comes from a study by Stern and Faber (1997). The researchers adapted for e-mail processes a classic social psychology method called the *lost-letter technique* in which stamped envelopes preaddressed to organizations with opposing goals are deliberately "dropped" and left for people to find and mail. The addresses on the envelopes are actually the researchers', and the measure of interest is the number of envelopes received in the mail. People are more likely to return envelopes to organizations they like than to those they dislike. In the Internet study, e-mails were sent to randomly selected addresses in the United States and were seemingly misdirected and for someone named "Steve." The e-mails asked for help in "fund-raising," but only one stated specifically the recipient of the funds: Ross Perot, as a 1996 presidential candidate. The researchers counted and content analyzed the replies, finding that 52% expressed an unfavorable attitude of Perot, and none expressed a positive attitude. The issue here is that the research did not use an informed consent procedure and could not make replies anonymous (replies have return addresses), except "by blocking part of the screen" (p. 263). Do you think this research procedure is ethical?

When informed consent is needed, researchers typically *get the consent in writing* by having the person sign a form that provides all pertinent information about the study. Actions to protect participants should begin before the research data collection starts and continue during and after testing. Let's look at efforts researchers can use at each stage. (Go to **Box 3.1**)

BOX 3.1　　**THE CONTENT OF INFORMED CONSENT**

When researchers seek informed consent from a prospective participant or guardian, they usually have the person read a form that provides all the relevant information, ask any questions he or she may have, and sign and date the form if he or she consents. The form should describe the participant's experience with the following information:

1. *Topic.* Give the study a title that indicates the general or obvious topic. Avoid using jargon or "charged" words when describing the topic. For example, in a study of stress, you might use the title "Study of Everyday Irritations," if that is accurate.

2. *Affiliation and contact.* Indicate your affiliation—for instance, "I am a student at [name of college] who is conducting a study for a psychology course I am taking."—and give a phone number or e-mail address by which participants can contact you.

3. *Task.* Describe the task the participants will experience, without giving away the independent variable or the expected outcome (hypothesis) of the study.

4. *Benefits and risks.* Describe any benefits the participants may get, such as payment or course credit, and any risks of harm or discomfort. If the task involves a sensitive topic, such as the participant's sexual behavior or attitudes about abortion, state this feature clearly and unambiguously. You must describe all features of the study that might reasonably influence people's willingness to participate.

5. *Place and time.* Indicate where and when participation will occur and the amount of time it will take. Don't just guess the time; test it.

6. *Anonymity and confidentiality.* State, "Do *not* put your name on the materials" (if participation is anonymous) and "All information I gather from your participation will be kept strictly confidential." If necessary, have the participants submit their completed materials in a sealed envelope or at another location to assure anonymity.

7. *Freedom to decline or quit.* You must state clearly that the person should feel free to decide (a) not to participate, (b) not to complete any part of the task, or (c) to discontinue participation. Do not try to coerce people to participate.

8. *Questions.* Offer to answer all questions the person may have; answer truthfully, of course.

9. *Consent.* Specifically ask the person (or guardian) to indicate that he/she understands what participation will entail and consents to participate. In most cases, you should get the person's signature; in some cases, the person can just sign initials or check a box affirming willingness to participate.

10. *Feedback.* An opportunity to receive a full explanation of the study should be offered. If the person wants the feedback, indicate when and how this will be arranged and get contact information if you will need to reach participants later.

An example of a formal informed consent form is presented in Chapter 10 (Figure 10.1). Sometimes the consent procedure includes instructions for completing the task. If your procedure does this, you may need to describe in some detail where and when the task will be done; what the task will consist of; what the participant will do, such as how to answer questions in a survey; and what to do when finished.

PROTECTING PARTICIPANTS BEFORE THE RESEARCH

The process of protecting participants begins with the original planning of the study. As scientists generate ideas for their research topics and methods, they can keep in mind the issues and guidelines we've discussed and try to identify alternative ideas when they see possible ethical problems. If researchers are uncertain of the meaning of a particular APA standard, whether a possible problem exists, or how to eliminate a problem, they should consult with colleagues or relevant organizations.

Institutional Review Boards

A formal process of having impartial committees review research proposals for ethical problems and to protect participants from harm and discomfort has been available since the late 1960s (Kimmel, 1996). In the early 1990s, the U.S. Department of Health and Human Services (USDHHS, 1991) updated and specified the review procedure and required that research with human participants at colleges, schools, hospitals, and other institutions that receive U.S. federal funds, such as from grants, undergo review before being conducted. The procedure requires each institution to establish an **Institutional Review Board** (IRB) that consists of at least five members whose backgrounds enable them to review scientific proposals and be sensitive to the needs of special subgroups, such as children or minority groups. The membership must include at least one person who is employed by the institution and one who is not, and one person who is a scientist and one who is not. The IRB is charged with judging research proposals on two bases: the ethical appropriateness of the method and a **risk–benefit analysis,** which assesses the balance between the potential scientific or applied benefits of doing the study against the possible risks it may pose to the participants. As Figure 3.1 diagrams, studies with high benefits and low risks are likely to be approved. The IRB can approve a study or require that it be redesigned or abandoned.

Do all planned studies go through the same IRB procedure? No—the USDHHS guidelines describe three variations for the procedure. First, studies of specific types are *exempt* from review. They include

1. "Research conducted in established or commonly accepted educational settings, involving normal educational practices," such as to test the effectiveness of teaching methods.
2. "Research involving the use of standard educational tests (cognitive, diagnostic, aptitude, achievement), survey procedures, interview procedures or observation of public behavior," assuming that the data are anonymous and that if a person's data were somehow disclosed, no "criminal or civil liability" or impaired "financial standing, employability, or reputation" would result.
3. "Research involving the collection or study of existing data, documents, records, pathological specimens, or diagnostic specimens," if they are public materials or the participants are anonymous. (USDHHS, 1991, p. 5)

These types of studies are exempt from IRB review because they present virtually no risk of harm or discomfort to participants.

All other research requires review, and the IRB can decide to have two levels of examination—*expedited review* and *full review*—depending on the degree of risk the study presents to participants. Expedited reviews are carried out by only some of the IRB members, usually the chairperson or designees who are experienced reviewers, and are reserved for research that pose no more than *minimal risk,* as we defined earlier, to the participants. All studies that appear to present

---

FIGURE 3.1

Diagram (called a "decision plane") illustrating how a proposed study's risks and benefits influence the decision of whether to approve it. When a risk–benefit analysis places a study in the upper-left region, it is likely to be rejected. When a risk–benefit analysis places a study in the lower-right region, it is likely to be approved. When a risk–benefit analysis places a study near the diagonal, the decision is very difficult to make.

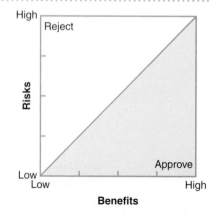

more than minimal risk must receive the full review by the entire IRB. In addition to risk of harm or discomfort, the IRB process examines whether the risks are as low as possible and are outweighed by the benefits of doing the study, privacy and confidentiality will be maintained, participants are free to decline or withdraw, and full informed consent will be used. The IRB can waive the informed consent requirement if the study cannot be carried out without the wavier, the method poses no more than minimal risk to the participants, and the participants will receive a full explanation of the study and any deception afterwards (USDHHS, 1991).

Let's look at the likely IRB process for an experiment with a methodology that presented some ethical problems and risk for participants. Researchers recruited college students and had them fill out questionnaires and undergo several medical tests, such as for blood pressure and eyesight, with the pretext of assessing the health characteristics of undergraduates (Jemmott, Ditto, & Croyle, 1986). The research used deception and no informed consent. One medical test, called the "Thioamine Acetylase Saliva Reaction Test," was false and purportedly assessed an enzyme deficiency that could lead to a disorder of the pancreas. Each student was shown the results of the test, indicating that he or she had the deficiency, and told either that the deficiency was rare or that it was very common. The students then filled out a survey that included items asking them to rate the seriousness of various diseases, including "thioamine acetylase deficiency." As soon as they completed the survey, they were given a full explanation of the study and deception so they would understand that they were not ill, the disease was fictitious, and the test results were fabricated. The study revealed that those students who were told that the deficiency was rare rated it as being more serious than those who were told that it was common. How would an IRB decide to approve this research? Because the method posed somewhat more than minimal risk, they would probably use a full review. They would take into account that there is a need for information about how people think about their health status, that the study could not be done convincingly without the deception, and that the students would get a full explanation right after participating. They might judge the benefits as moderate, perhaps halfway along the horizontal axis of Figure 3.1, and the risk of psychological discomfort as low to moderate, perhaps a quarter of the way along the vertical axis. The risk–benefit analysis, would place the research in the shaded area of the diagram, below the diagonal line, indicating the IRB would approve the project.

Difficulties with the IRB Process

Although the IRB process is an excellent system for protecting the rights and welfare of research participants, many researchers have offered criticisms of it, focusing on four problems (Kimmel, 1996; Landrum & Chastain, 1999; Wiederman, 1999). First, the process sometimes takes longer than it should and delays the start of the research. This can be a serious problem if access to participants or conditions of the study depend on the timing. Second, the methodological techniques used in research can be very specialized, and nonspecialists may not understand their function or need. When this happens, an IRB may reject the project or recommend changes that would undermine the quality of the research. Third, some researchers feel that IRB processes are biased against basic research in favor of applied research. This problem and the prior one can be reduced in two ways: the IRB can provide training or information to members, and the researcher can try to anticipate the need for information and provide it in the proposal or as an attachment. Fourth, because the membership varies from one IRB to another and in the same IRB over time, there can be inconsistencies in decisions they make. Many researchers feel that some IRBs are too zealous in trying to protect participants. For instance, some IRBs are very restrictive in the use of surveys that deal with sexual topics. They consider the topics to be sensitive, producing discomfort. Other IRBs disagree. Studies of sexuality that have people fill out a survey anonymously and use full informed consent procedures would qualify as exempt from review in many, but not all, IRBs. The problem of inconsistency in IRB judgments might be reduced if the review system had an appeal process outside the host institution's IRB. Currently, appeals occur only within the original IRB, and its members may be quite stubborn. (Go to **Box 3.2**)

Box 3.2   ETHICS ASSESSMENT IN STUDENT RESEARCH

Years ago, a research methods student proposed doing a study in my course on the effects of smoking marijuana while studying on students' memory during exams. I told him that it was an interesting issue, but there were serious ethical and practical issues to consider, not the least of which was that I had plans for my life that didn't include prison. When students conduct research, the student and the supervising instructor are both responsible for making sure the participants are protected. As always, the researchers are the first line of defense for participants (and in this case, for ourselves, too!). In many psychology departments, the instructor serves as the ethics evaluator of his or her students' projects, usually with the permission of the IRB to act as a member doing an expedited review when the project poses no more than minimal risk. The student submits a proposal for the research to the instructor who may send it to the appropriate person or committee (we'll discuss the content of research proposals in Chapter 10).

Some college departments have a research ethics committee that functions with links to the institution's IRB. The relationship between the two bodies can vary from one college to the next, and either body may receive a student's proposal from the instructor. One way the two bodies can work together is for the departmental committee to prescreen student proposals, reviewing with the IRB's permission only the minimal risk projects and sending all proposals for studies with more than minimal risk to the IRB for their full review. The outcome of any level of review for students' projects can be to approve, reject, or require alterations to the plans before collecting data.

Think back to the Milgram obedience study. What did the researcher do if the "teacher" balked at having to continue giving shocks after the "learner" had begun to protest and stopped giving answers to the tests? The researcher used a series of prods. The first time the teacher indicated an unwillingness to continue, the researcher said, "Please continue." For additional hesitations, the researcher said, "The experiment requires that you continue," then, "It is absolutely essential that you continue," and finally, "You have no other choice, you *must* go on."

Milgram did not want participants to withdraw easily because in real life, people experience pressure to obey when they are inclined otherwise. To encourage obedience, he used **coercion,** the process of compelling a person's act or choice by applying pressure, such as through threats, force, or other inappropriate inducements. The APA codes state

(SECTION 8.06) Offering Inducements for Research Participation

a. Psychologists make reasonable efforts to avoid offering excessive or inappropriate financial or other inducements for research participation when such inducements are likely to coerce participation.

b. When offering professional services as an inducement for research participation, psychologists clarify the nature of the services, as well as the risks, obligations, and limitations.

Remember also that informed consent procedures include telling participants that they should feel free to decline to take part in or to withdraw from the study. Keep in mind that pleading with people to participate ("Please do it. I'll flunk the project if I don't get data.") is also coercive and violates the freedom to decline aspect of informed consent. Researchers should respect the person's freedom to choose *not* to participate in the research or to discontinue participation at any time without undue coercion to reconsider such decisions.

Another ethical issue that can arise during testing is when research procedures result in unforeseen undesirable circumstances for the participant. If this happens, the researcher should take immediate action to correct the circumstances, including any long-term effects they may have on the participant. What should Milgram have done once he could see that the men in the "teacher" role were in intense distress: sweating, trembling, and stuttering? Some psychologists would say he should have stopped the experiment (see, for example, Baumrind, 1964). But what about the opposite situation—unforeseen *desirable* circumstances? Sometimes they can present an ethical issue, as we can see in a study that involved the use of punishment as therapy for a 14-year-old boy's frequent and chronic coughing that had become so severe he was expelled from school (Creer, Chai, & Hoffman, 1977). After trying several other therapies without success, the boy and his parents agreed to allow the therapist use mild electric shock (for real!) as punishment for coughing. The researchers had planned to conduct the study in four phases—no shock, shock each time he coughed, no shock, shock each time he coughed—each of which would last for at least one 1-hour session. The purpose of the first no-shock phase was to collect data (called "baseline") on the amount of coughing he normally did, and the purpose of the second no-shock phase was to see if the cough returned when punishment did not occur. During the 1-hour baseline session, he coughed 22 times. In the initial phase with shock, the boy coughed once, which resulted in his receiving mild shock to the forearm. But he did not cough again for the rest of the hour or during the next 2 hours. Because the punishment worked much faster than the researchers expected, they needed to decide what to do about the rest of the planned study. They cancelled it, and follow-ups over the next 2 ½ years showed that the boy's chronic cough did not recur.

The researchers' responsibilities usually do not end once testing is over. Three subsequent activities are part of the APA code. First, researchers carry out an educational function after testing: explaining what the study was about or communicating the study's outcome, especially if the participants indicated an interest in learning what the research finds or are students fulfilling a course requirement to take part in research. This is part of a process called **debriefing,** in which the researcher describes the nature and purpose of the study, explains the methods used, asks if the participant has questions, and corrects misconceptions, if any. Second, if the study used deception by misleading participants or withholding important information, the researcher *must* provide debriefing and include **dehoaxing,** which involves detailing the deceptions used and the need for them. A main purpose of dehoaxing is to convince the participants that what they were led to believe is not true. For instance, in the study in which students were falsely told they had a disease (an enzyme deficiency) a researcher met with each participant immediately after testing and explained that the disease does not exist and the saliva test was a trick (Jemmott et al., 1986). Third, if the study had the potential for producing psychological discomfort, the debriefing *must* check for these effects and, if present, include **desensitizing,** a counseling process aimed at eliminating or reducing any negative emotional states the research produced. Milgram's obedience study had debriefing sessions with dehoaxing and desensitizing, using "procedures . . . to assure that the subject would leave the laboratory in a state of well being" (1963, p. 374). Research findings indicate that both dehoaxing and desensitizing are generally effective in achieving their goals (Holmes, 1976a, 1976b).

Debriefing procedures can benefit the researchers, too. Researchers can ask participants questions to get information that can help in interpreting the findings of the current study and planning future research. Most questions would be open-ended. Some questions can help researchers find out how participants perceived the conditions they experienced and whether they thought they noticed or used any demand characteristics. Asking the participants what they were thinking at various points in the study may help the researchers to interpret what the findings mean and whether the methodology worked. Simply asking for participants' views on ways to improve the methods they experienced can yield valuable information for use in future research.

The ethical standards for protecting participants in research are obviously more stringent than for protecting individuals in many other situations. For example, TV "reality" shows and *Candid Camera* often involve deception and violations of privacy and anonymity without obtaining advanced informed consent. Could the benefits of these activities outweigh the risks? Is it likely that an IRB would approve such activities?

ETHICS IN CONDUCTING RESEARCH WITH ANIMALS

Think back to the six award-winning psychologists whose portraits were presented in a box in Chapter 1. For three of them—B. F. Skinner, John Garcia, and Larry Squire—the research they conducted was mainly with animal subjects. Do many psychology studies use animals? No, only about 7% of psychology articles in the late 1970s used animals, mostly rats, mice, and birds (Gallup & Suarez, 1985), and the use of animals declined markedly through the 1980s (Thomas & Blackman, 1992). The fact that psychologists who used animals in most of their research have won APA awards for their contributions to the discipline suggests that their work with animals produced important findings.

PROS AND CONS OF USING ANIMAL SUBJECTS

Why do psychologists and other scientists use animals as subjects? Scientists who use animals in their research do so for several reasons; they can

- Carefully control the experiences of each animal in the laboratory during testing and in its general living situation.
- Study the same animal during any or all portion(s) of its entire life after conception, testing the subject as often as needed. Most species used in laboratory research reach "old age" normally in a few years or less.
- Examine in detail the role of genetics because most animals can be selectively bred and reproduce frequently, often starting only months or a few years after birth.
- Monitor the animal's behavior or physical status continuously each day.
- Examine variables, such as chemical or physiological manipulations, that would be judged too harmful for use with humans. Many body mechanisms in humans, such as of large internal organs, nerve synapses, and genetic transmission, are very similar to those in many other species, including rats, birds, and sometimes insects.
- Study certain animals simply to understand the physiology and behavior of those species. Doing so can answer theoretical questions and, perhaps, lead to knowledge that may benefit the species themselves, such as by improving veterinary medicine or animal care of other types.

These advantages in using animals in research have enabled scientists to make important advances in their knowledge, theoretical concepts, and applications that benefit humans and animals. Medical research provides some of the more well-known examples, such as in the development of chemotherapy and surgical techniques for treating cancer.

In psychology, animal studies have been particularly important in developing knowledge on two topics: learning processes and physiological mechanisms. Most of the early research on learning tested animals to understand how motivation and aspects of the task influence the speed with which learning occurs and the strength and persistence of the resulting behavior. Skinner's work on the role of reinforcement in learning provides an obvious example: the knowledge he gained from animal research on the consequences of behavior became the basis for testing how variations in the types and patterning of reinforcement affect human behavior. Professionals apply this knowledge widely today in schools, industry, and therapy to help people function better (Sarafino, 2001). In studying physiological mechanisms, psychologists have sometimes needed to perform surgery on subjects, such as to stimulate or disconnect specific areas of the brain to find out what they do and how they work. This research led to Squire's work on memory impairments in people with amnesia and in identifying areas of the brain that are involved in different types of memory. Noninvasive techniques, such as brain imaging, are now available that enable researchers to study many of these issues in humans, thereby reducing the need to use animals in physiological research (Buckner & Logan, 2001; Kimmel, 1996).

But a great deal of controversy exists regarding the use of animals in research, despite the benefits people have gained. Animal rights activists have joined together in sociopolitical groups, such as People for the Ethical Treatment of Animals (PETA) and the Animal Liberation Front (ALF), claiming that researchers mistreat and cause great suffering in laboratory animals, which has led to emotional debates in the news media and the courts. These groups argue that individuals who conduct or support research with animal subjects practice a form of discrimination called **speciesism,** a term chosen to link with sexism and racism, in which humans neglect the rights and welfare of animals with the justification that we are more valuable (Kimmel, 1996). They point out that animals feel pain, and their lives are often severely restricted and destroyed in research, which, of course, is true. They are also correct in saying that animals cannot be informed of and consent to the risks in research. Unfortunately, some of these activists have beliefs that do not allow for compromise and have engaged in extreme behaviors, including breaking into research centers to free laboratory animals and destroy equipment. And many examples have been found of exaggerated descriptions of laboratory conditions and of staged photographs of research animals that they have presented as real. In the long run, these acts are likely to harm their cause of protecting animals.

Do research conditions produce pain or discomfort in animals? A good deal of medical research certainly does, such as when studying the effects of painful diseases or procedures to reduce pain, but very few psychological studies do (Miller, 1984). And the focus of animal rights activists on research conditions is odd, given that animals suffer much more pain, discomfort, and abuse from pet owners and food producers than from researchers. Interestingly, a survey of 574 individuals attending an animal rights rally revealed two relevant findings (Plous, 1991). First, 37% of the respondents reported that they eat meat, poultry, or seafood at least occasionally. Second, more than twice as many respondents said that the main focus of the movement should be on protecting animals used for research (54% of the respondents) rather than for food

(24%). These contrasts reveal a double standard that is hard to reconcile. Another inconsistency probably exists with respect to having pets. Many individuals who feel strongly about protecting animals have pets. Did these animals volunteer or give their permission to be pets? Perhaps these people would defend having pets by saying that their pets are treated very well and love their owners. But the issue is, would the animals choose a different life situation if they could? Pet owners probably believe the animals would not.

Most of the controversy about animal rights boils down to a difference in beliefs about what is morally right. Is it morally acceptable to conduct research on animals now, under conditions as humane as possible, so that we can improve the lives of and reduce pain and suffering in many millions of humans and animals in generations to come? If we were to ask this question of scientists and animal rights activists, we would get sharply different answers. Did you ever see the wonderful movie *Sophie's Choice*? It's about a mother forced by Nazis to make this decision: Both of your children are scheduled to die, but you may choose one to save. She made the wrenching decision, saving one, but was haunted by her choice thereafter. Was she right to choose at all? Many scientists liken society's choice to hers. We can choose to do animal research to expand our knowledge and protect future humans and animals, or we can choose not to make that choice and allow future pain and suffering to occur. Most scientists feel that society should choose to allow the research, but many animal rights activists feel otherwise.

CARE AND TREATMENT OF RESEARCH ANIMALS

Many activists have views that are moderate, recognizing the value of and need for some research with animals. They focus on eliminating research conditions that inflict needless suffering on animals, especially when there may be alternative methods to produce similar advances in knowledge. But there are currently only a few adequate alternatives, such as brain imaging (Kimmel, 1996; Mondics, 2002). As a result, the emphasis is on establishing standards to restrict the pain and discomfort of animals in research and promote their humane care and treatment in research. This is where animal rights groups have had their most positive and constructive effects.

Strict regulations now exist in some nations to safeguard the rights and welfare of research animals (Kimmel, 1996). The United States provides a good example, where laws and regulations have four specific provisions that cover institutions in which animal research is done. First, researchers must provide animals with proper health care, feeding, housing, and cleanliness. Second, researchers should avoid subjecting animals to cruel or unnecessarily painful conditions. Third, a governmental agency will conduct periodic, unannounced inspections of animal research facilities. Fourth, the institution must have an **Animal Care and Use Committee** (ACUC) to review proposed research procedures and ensure that the laws and regulations are followed. The committee members should include a veterinarian, an animal researcher, a nonscientist, and a person from outside the institution. In addition, psychology research with animals is subject to the following APA standards:

(SECTION 8.09) Humane Care and Use of Animals in Research

a. Psychologists acquire, care for, use, and dispose of animals in compliance with current federal and local laws and regulations, and with professional standards.

b. Psychologists trained in research methods and experienced in the care of laboratory animals supervise all procedures involving animals and are responsible for ensuring appropriate consideration of their comfort, health, and humane treatment.

c. Psychologists ensure that all individuals using animals under their supervision have received instruction in research methods and in the care, maintenance, and handling of the species being used, to the extent appropriate to their role.

d. Psychologists make reasonable efforts to minimize the discomfort, infection, illness, and pain of animal subjects.

e. Psychologists use a procedure subjecting animals to pain, stress, or privation only when an alternative procedure is unavailable and the goal is justified by its prospective scientific, educational, or applied value.

f. Psychologists perform surgical procedures under appropriate anesthesia and follow techniques to avoid infection and minimize pain during and after surgery.

g. When it is appropriate that the animal's life be terminated, psychologists proceed rapidly, with an effort to minimize pain, and in accordance with accepted procedures.

The APA standards apply to situations in which animals are used for scientific research and for educational purposes, such as in demonstrations of reinforcement in operant conditioning.

ETHICS IN REPORTING RESEARCH OUTCOMES

Science has a noble goal: to seek truth. Misrepresentations of data collected or analyzed or of the source or authorship of materials published are incompatible with that goal. On occasion, we hear of professionals or students who are accused of fabricating data or of taking credit for authoring material that belongs intellectually to others. Although these acts do not seem to occur very frequently and appear to occur more often among students than professionals, they happen often enough to be a concern (Swazey, Anderson, & Lewis, 1993). The reason for these ethical violations can usually be found in the rewards the perpetrators receive for their work: course grades, academic degrees, status in the scientific community, and, if the perpetrator has an academic position, promotion and tenure. Let's examine the ethical issues in reporting research outcomes.

FALSIFYING DATA

One of the most serious ethical violations researchers can make is in **falsifying data,** deliberately fabricating or altering data from research. The false data may have been newly created or modified to achieve a desired goal. A widely cited example of falsifying data is the case of an early 1900s psychologist, Sir Cyril Burt, who had died a few years before discovery (Kimmel, 1996). He had conducted research on the role of heredity in people's development of intelligence, using data collected on identical twins who were either reared together or apart. Another researcher, named Leon Kamin, discovered many inaccurate and implausible aspects to Burt's data. For example, in papers written years apart with substantial additions of new participants over time, key correlation coefficients remained exactly the same (reported to three decimal places)—an extremely improbable event. Although this and other specific evidence led some scientists and historians to conclude that Burt falsified data, others attribute the evidence to his sloppiness. We will never know with absolute certainty one way or the other because he could not respond to the charges, and much of his records were discarded after his death.

The Burt case and others prompted the APA to include in their code of ethics the following standards of conduct regarding errors in reporting data.

(SECTION 8.10) *Reporting Research Results*

a. Psychologists do not fabricate data.
b. If psychologists discover significant errors in their published data, they take reasonable steps to correct such errors in a correction, retraction, erratum, or other appropriate publication means.

Errors in data, whether accidental or deliberate, need to be found and corrected. We saw in Chapter 1 that science is a self-correcting enterprise, and replication studies help us find the errors because of discrepancies in the results of different studies. But if falsified data are consistent with data from other studies, we may never realize the false data are erroneous. To keep science advancing toward truth, we must be extremely careful about reporting real and accurate data from our research.

PLAGIARISM

Another troublesome ethical issue in reporting research is **plagiarism**—using the words or ideas of others in ways or formats that suggest the material is your own creation. This issue is addressed in the APA standard:

(SECTION 8.11) *Plagiarism*

Psychologists do not present portions of another's work or data as their own, even if the other work or data source is cited occasionally.

The act *does not have to be deliberate* to be plagiarism; oversights count. Paraphrasing or using exactly another person's words or ideas *without giving credit to the source with the correct format* is plagiarism. It is true that intentional plagiarism is worse than accidental plagiarism (like first-degree murder is worse than second-degree) but both are plagiarism and unacceptable.

Let's consider an example from one of my courses some years ago: a paper on eating disorders. Although there was extensive plagiarism, we'll look at only a little of it, taken from one journal article (Mazzeo, 1999, p. 42). The first of these two quotations comes from the tail end of one paragraph in the article, and the second comes from the upper half of a nearby paragraph. (Note: The underlines were not in the original article; they are there to show the parts used in the student paper word for word.)

> . . . Moreover, <u>body image disturbance is a significant factor in both the development and outcome of clinical and subclinical eating disorders</u> (Attie & Brooks-Gunn, 1989; Freeman, Beach, Davis, & Solyom, 1985).
>
> Body image has been variously defined and operationalized. <u>Extant measures of body image assess a wide variety of areas including perception</u> (e.g., Ruff & Barrios, 1986), <u>attitudes</u> (e.g., Franzoi & Shields, 1984), <u>and preoccupation (Cooper, Taylor, Cooper, & Fairburn, 1987).</u> However the relevance of each of these aspects of body image to disordered eating behaviors remains unclear. <u>The earliest measures of body image were measures of body image perception. These measures assess the accuracy with which an individual estimates her size</u> (e.g., Ruff & Barrios, 1986). However, previous research . . .

Now look at a portion of a paragraph from the student paper, which is presented here exactly as it was, except that it wasn't indented (I indented because I am quoting from the student's paper).

> . . . Body image disturbance is a significant factor in both the development and outcome of clinical and subclinical eating disorders (Mazzeo, 1999). Body image has been defined in various ways. Extant measures of body image assess a wide variety of areas including perception, attitudes, and preoccupation (Cooper, Taylor, Cooper, & Fairburn, 1987). The earliest measures of body image were measures of body image perception. These measures assess the accuracy with which an individual estimates his/her size. One measure . . .

Notice that there are no quotation marks around the word-for-word parts from the original article. Maybe the student thought that giving the source "(Mazzeo, 1999)" or leaving out some words makes it okay. Neither does; it's still plagiarism. This was all explained in class and in a handout, but it happened anyway!

What are the correct formats to avoid plagiarizing? If you are *paraphrasing*, using your own words to present another's words or ideas, just citing the *author(s) and date* is fine. So, if the student had not used word-for-word material, the "(Mazzeo, 1999)" would have worked. If *word-for-word* material contains more than a few words, you should treat that string of words as a *quotation* and format it in one of two ways. If the quotation is fairly *short*, simply type it into a regular paragraph, put quotation marks around it, and cite the author(s), date, and page number(s). For example, the student could have written: Mazzeo has pointed out that "body image disturbance is a significant factor in both the development and outcome of clinical and subclinical eating disorders" (1999, p. 42). If the quotation is *long*, present it as an indented paragraph, like the preceding quotations from the Mazzeo article, making sure to give name(s), date, and page number(s).

Actually writers should almost never use word-for-word material at all in research articles. They should use their own words. Quoting is only appropriate when exact words need to be presented so that some really critical material retains its "flavor" or meaning, such as a hard-to-grasp theoretical statement. When instructors ask students to write a paper, they mean "write" *not* "copy and type." Maybe they should tell their students, as I have, "If you quote a lot, I'll give that part of your possible grade to the actual author(s), not you." Sometimes finding plagiarism in papers is difficult, but it's getting easier using the Internet (Silverman, 2002). Instructors can type some suspect material into a search engine, and up comes the original if it's in the database!

PUBLICATION PROCESSES

Research reports submitted for publication undergo a review process. To be accepted, they must be appropriate in content, meet methodological and ethical standards, and be prepared according to the stylistic guidelines of the journal (most journals that publish research in psychology use APA style, which we will examine in Appendix A). The ethical codes we've considered so far do, in fact, influence whether a paper will be published. In addition, there are issues that relate to the authorship on the paper. The APA standards on these issues are

(SECTION 8.12) *Publication Credit*

a. Psychologists take responsibility and credit, including authorship credit, only for work they have actually performed or to which they have substantially contributed.

b. Principal authorship and other publication credits accurately reflect the relative scientific or professional contributions of the individuals involved, regardless of their relative status. Mere possession of an institution position, such as department chair does not justify authorship credit. Minor contributions to the research or to the writing for publications are acknowledged appropriately, such as in footnotes or in an introductory statement.

c. Except under unusual circumstances, a student is listed as principal author on any multiple-authored article that is substantially based on the student's doctoral dissertation.

Gaining authorship and the order of authorship in published articles with multiple authors should be based on each person's contributions. Individuals who contribute substantially to the project's design, execution, data analysis, interpretation, and writing should receive authorship, and those who contribute more should receive appropriate authorship credit.

SANCTIONS FOR VIOLATIONS

Individuals who violate ethical standards in research are subject to sanctions from the organization that established and monitors adherence to the standards. Students who violate ethical codes can receive a lower grade on the project, a lower grade in the course, expulsion from college, or some combination of these events. As we have just seen, one important sanction comes from journals, which can deny publication of the report that results from the offending research. Other sanctions are specific to professionals and their institutions. For example,

- ▪ If violations in USDHHS codes occur at an institution that receives U.S. federal funds, those funds can be withdrawn.
- ▪ Research facilities that violate animal welfare codes can be shut down.
- ▪ Psychologists that violate APA ethical standards for research or other professional activity can be censured or expelled from the organization.

In addition, the reputation of the researcher and the institution are impaired when their violations become known, making it more difficult in the future for them to receive grants or to publish. The bottom-line message: Be ethical!

SUMMARY

The research by Watson and Rayner on conditioning a fear in an infant and by Milgram on obedience provide prime examples of ethical issues in psychological studies that have since been addressed in research guidelines, such as from the APA and the USDHHS. The APA codes include five general principles that are aspirations and dozens of ethical standards, which the APA can enforce with sanctions. Although scientific research produces many benefits, it can create situations with risk or minimal risk of physical and psychological harm or discomfort.

One ethical concern in research is the use of deception for the purpose of hiding or creating a variable. Active deception involves providing misleading information to participants, and passive deception involves withholding information. Using deception can increase the likelihood or magnitude of harm or discomfort; the greater the increase, the less ethical it is. Other ethical concerns include research methods that intrude on people's privacy or that do not maintain anonymity and confidentiality with regard to information about the participants. One of the most serious ethical issues of many studies was the lack of informed consent, the procedure of telling prospective participants all the positive and negative features of the study that might influence their willingness to take part. The USDHHS requires each institution that receives federal funds to establish an Institutional Review Board that conducts a risk–benefit analysis for research proposals to safeguard the rights and welfare of participants. Although certain categories of planned research with virtually no risk to participants are exempt from review, studies with risk or minimal risk must receive either a full review or an expedited review. Finally, researchers should not apply coercion to get participants to agree to participate and should give some type of debriefing after, that must include dehoaxing if deception was used in the study and desensitizing if there was some potential for psychological discomfort.

The use of animal subjects in research is controversial, with many animal rights activists opposing the practice entirely and calling people's support for animal research speciesism. Partly in response to these concerns, some nations have developed standards for the care and treatment of animal subjects. In the U.S., institutions that use animals for research must have an Animal Care and

Use Committee. Other ethical concerns pertain to professionals and students falsifying data and engaging in plagiarism in reporting their research.

KEY TERMS

ethics	informed consent	desensitizing
minimal risk	Institutional Review	speciesism
risk	Board	Animal Care and Use
deception	risk–benefit analysis	Committee
privacy	coercion	falsifying data
anonymity	debriefing	plagiarism
confidentiality	dehoaxing	

REVIEW QUESTIONS

1. Describe the Watson and Rayner (1920) and Milgram (1963) studies in detail, pointing out aspects of their methods that may be ethically questionable.
2. Describe the six general principles in the APA codes.
3. What is *deception,* and why do researchers use it sometimes?
4. Define and discuss the issues of *privacy, anonymity,* and *confidentiality* in research ethics.
5. Define *informed consent,* and describe fully the APA standards pertaining to it.
6. What is an Institutional Review Board?
7. Using the process of risk–benefit analysis, indicate the differences between *no risk, minimal risk,* and *risk.*
8. What are *debriefing, dehoaxing,* and *desensitizing,* and when should they be used?
9. Describe the pros and cons of using animals in research and the procedures now used in the U.S. regarding the care and treatment of animals subjects.
10. Describe exactly what *plagiarism* is and the correct formats for presenting words and ideas of others.

RESOURCES

BOOKS, CHAPTERS, AND ARTICLES

APA (American Psychological Association). (1992). *Ethical principles of psychologists and code of conduct.* Washington, DC: Author.

Chastain, G., & Landrum, R. E. (Eds.). (1999). *Protecting human subjects: Department subject pools and Institutional Review Boards.* Washington, DC: American Psychological Association.

Kimmel, A. J. (1996). *Ethical issues in behavioral research: A survey.* Cambridge, MA: Blackwell.

Reverby, S. M. (Ed.). (2000). *Tuskegee's truths: Rethinking the Tuskegee Syphilis Study.* Chapel Hill: University of North Carolina Press.

USDHHS (United States Department of Health and Human Services). (1991). *Protection of human subjects.* Washington, DC: U.S. Government Printing Office.

INTERNET SITES

http://www.apa.org/ethics/ This Website has the current version of the APA standards for ethical conduct of psychologists.

http://www.apa.org/science/anguide.html A site that has the current version of the APA standards for the care and treatment of animal subjects.

http://ohrp.osophs.dhhs.gov/irb/irb_guidebook.htm This USDHHS site gives the IRB Guidebook in a detailed, yet readable, form.

APPLICATION ACTIVITIES

ACTIVITY 3–1: A REAL-LIFE ETHICAL DILEMMA

Suppose an epidemic of a highly infectious disease has broken out, and the government has only enough vaccine to inoculate half the uninfected people in the country. Although most cases are in 10 states, there are some in every state. How should the government distribute the vaccine? One approach is to choose at random, giving all people who want the vaccine in the country an equal chance of getting it. Another approach is to distribute it only to the states with the most infections on the grounds that the people in those states are at greatest risk of infection. Which of these approaches do you think is best or fairest, and why? Can you think of a better approach?

ACTIVITY 3–2: EVALUATING ETHICAL VIOLATIONS

Alex wants to conduct a survey on students' past stealing behavior to see if there are gender and ethnic differences. Suppose you are her instructor and are reviewing her research proposal, which reveals the following aspects to the method. The informed consent materials say that the study is on stealing, but doesn't say the participants will report on their own acts and doesn't say that gender and ethnic comparisons will be made. The materials also say that it is really important that they participate, otherwise she will not be able to complete her course. In order to contact the participants for debriefing, Alex will have them put their names on the questionnaire. What problems do you see, and what would you ask her to do instead?

ACTIVITY 3–3: WRITING AN INFORMED CONSENT FORM

Write an informed consent form for the Watson and Rayner (1920) study, using the material in Box 3.1 as a guide. Who would have to sign it?

ACTIVITY 3–4: PARAPHRASING (NOT PLAGIARIZING)

Pick a paragraph from this chapter that describes the Milgram (1963) method and is more than 10 lines in length. Suppose you were writing a paper about Milgram's research in which you were allowed to cite a secondary source (as this textbook is). Paraphrase the paragraph you chose, presenting it exactly as you would in the paper.

DATA: MEASUREMENT AND ANALYSIS

PROLOGUE

Measuring *overt* (outward) behavior and *covert* internal variables, such as feelings and physical states, are critical aspects of doing research in psychology. How do researchers decide what to measure and how to do it? An example comes from a study I conducted some years ago at a day care center to compare the social behavior of infants (mean age = 16.0 months) and toddlers (mean age = 27.1 months) with continuous day care experience since 3 months of age (Sarafino, 1985). Age was an independent variable in this research, and social behaviors were dependent variables. Although early research had found that children's social behavior is very limited in infancy and progresses with age, the results of later studies suggested that infants are more interested and competent in social interactions with peers than was once thought.

Given the limited language and motor skills of the children, a major challenge in designing the research was to determine exactly what to look for in their behavior and how to structure the observations. I first examined the research literature to devise precise operational definitions of specific types of behavior that can be classified as nonsocial, marginally social, and social behaviors. Here is one example of each:

- *Facing Away/Toys* (nonsocial). Child plays with toys alone, independently, and facing away from the peer, apparently unconcerned with and unaffected by what the peer is doing.
- *Facing Peer/Toys* (marginally social). Same as Facing Away/Toys, but the child is near and facing in the direction of the peer.
- *Social Interest/No Toys* (social). Child is not playing with toys, but is looking at the peer; may try to initiate interaction by touching, vocalizing, smiling, or waving, but the peer does not respond.

These are three of nine behavior categories that were defined to include all activities that the children could engage in during testing. Two student researchers who had spent time playing with the children on previous occasions but were unaware of the purpose of the study or the relevant literature on social behavior observed 13 pairs of children.

How was testing structured? For each session, the two researchers placed a pair of similar-age children in a playpen with day care toys in a familiar room. They observed the children for 15 minutes with no distractions while sitting a few feet away, not interacting with them in any way. Each session was divided into 60 15-second intervals, signaled to the researchers by means of tape-recorded signals conveyed through earphones. During the first 10 seconds of each interval, the researchers recorded letter codes they had been trained to use to keep a continuous log of the occurrence of each of the nine behaviors; the last 5 seconds were used for checking or completing these records. For the first half of the session, each child in a pair was observed by one of the two researchers, who then switched to watching the opposite child for the rest of the session. Thus, each researcher collected half of the data for every child. The results revealed that the infants displayed almost as much social behavior as the toddlers, and little of that was antisocial, such as fighting. But the toddlers showed more positive social behavior and more sustained social interchanges than the infants.

This prologue illustrates how precisely we can and should define the variables we measure and carry out data collection. Given the operational definitions of the behaviors, wouldn't you be able to assess these variables precisely with some practice? Systematic observation requires careful measurement. This chapter describes methods by which we can measure independent and dependent variables, make the measurements precise, evaluate the degree of precision obtained, and interpret the data we collect.

WHAT AND HOW TO MEASURE

Deciding exactly what to measure and how to do it often involves conflicting choices, including whether to measure overt behavior or covert processes. For instance, suppose you wanted to study people's current levels of stress. What overt behaviors would reflect stress? Would it be better to measure stress as a covert variable? Let's suppose you chose to assess it as a covert variable. One way to do this is to examine people's physiological arousal, such as heart rate or blood pressure, which are known to increase in stressful situations. Physiological arousal can be assessed with a device called a *polygraph*. If you had access to the equipment, which physiological measure would you use? Let's suppose you chose heart rate. Would you want to assess it in a laboratory or in people's everyday life activities? Most polygraphs are cumbersome, but miniature versions are available that can fit in a person's pocket.

Other ways to assess stress use questionnaires, usually measuring people's past experience of life events or of daily hassles. *Life events* are major happenings, such as losing a loved one or a job, that require substantial psychological adjustments; *daily hassles* are everyday pressures or annoyances, such as having too much work to do or being stuck in traffic. Life events are very different from daily hassles, and so are their effects—for instance, people's health status seems to be more closely related to hassles than to life events (DeLongis, Coyne, Dakof, Folkman, & Lazarus, 1982). What's more, the specific hassles people experience are likely to depend on their life situations: the hassles of college students and same-age nonstudents are likely to differ, and specialized questionnaires have been developed for students (Sarafino & Ewing, 1999). If you were using a questionnaire to measure stress, you would need to decide which one to use based mainly on how you conceptualize the construct.

The method we use to assess a variable becomes our operational definition of it and can affect the study's results. For example, descriptive research to estimate the need for mental health treatment among American adults have used different ways to assess the yearly prevalence of mental and addictive disorders and found very different results. Early estimates that about 30% of adults need treatment were based only on whether survey respondents had experienced emotional or addictive symptoms in the past year. By using a different measure in which respondents must also report that the symptoms interfered substantially with their lives or led them to talk to a professional or take medication, researchers found that the percentage of adults who need treatment decreased to 18.5% (Narrow, Rae, Robins, & Regier, 2002). Having participants report experiences, feelings, or attitudes involves indirect assessment methods because the researcher does not observe these variables directly.

In the next few sections, we will examine many of the almost limitless varieties of direct and indirect assessment procedures for measuring overt and covert variables in psychological research. As you read about these procedures, keep in mind that they can be used to assess either independent or dependent variables.

Observing Overt Behavior

Overt behaviors are open to view or direct assessment and can be of two types: verbal and motor. Verbal behaviors are actions that require the use of language. Motor behaviors involve body movement, without requiring the use of language; they include gross motor actions that use the body broadly, such as running or pushing, and fine motor actions that require precise and coordinated movements, such as threading a needle or playing tennis or golf at an expert level. Many social, emotional, and cognitive activities involve actions with both verbal and motor components. For example, filling out a crossword puzzle is a cognitive activity that requires both verbal and motor actions.

Learning and Cognition: Action, Correctness, and Speed

When observing overt behavior to study learning and cognition, we can assess whether an action occurred and, if it did, its correctness and speed. Let's look at some examples.

The perception of depth is an important cognitive ability, even in early infancy when babies begin to crawl and risk accident, such as falling down stairs. Do infants perceive depth? Gibson and Walk (1960) studied this issue using an ingenious apparatus called the "visual cliff," shown in Figure 4.1, that had a sheet of thick glass spanning two flat areas with a checkerboard pattern covering the apparatus floors. One area under the glass was deeper than the other: the floor was immediately below the glass for the "shallow" area and a foot or more below the glass for the "deep" area. Although the glass provided the same physical support for both areas, one side looked deeper. Separating the two areas was

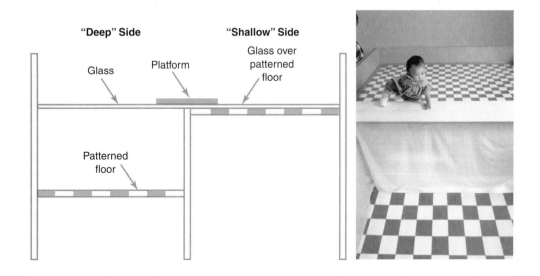

FIGURE 4.1

The visual cliff. The drawing shows a cross section of the apparatus; the depth of the floor on the deep side is adjustable. The photograph shows a baby leaving the platform on the shallow side.

a slightly raised platform. The researchers placed each 6- to 14-month-old baby on the platform and observed what happened when the mother encouraged her infant to approach her while stationed first across the deep area and then across the shallow area. When the mother was on the deep side, only 3 of the 36 babies crept onto the glass toward her; of the others, some went away from her toward the shallow side, and some stayed on the platform and cried. The infants' overt actions showed that they can perceive depth.

Correctness is often measured when we want to determine *how much* people or animals have learned or *how well* they can discriminate between stimuli. We can record the number of correct (or incorrect) responses the subjects make, and if the number of opportunities to respond differs across subjects, we can calculate the percentage of correct (or incorrect) responses. For instance, we can assess how many words in a list people can recall, as we did in an activity in Chapter 1. When testing animals, we can assess their learning a discrimination by putting them individually in a simple maze with a critical choice point. Turning toward one path—which is painted with, say, horizontal stripes—leads to a chamber with a reward, but taking the path painted differently, such as with vertical stripes, leads to an empty chamber (Woodworth & Schlosberg, 1965). After the animals receive training for several days and begin to learn the discrimination, we would see that the percentage of correct turns—taking the path painted with horizontal stripes—increases across days.

Speed is another measure of learning and cognition that we can observe in overt behavior. It can reflect a variety of constructs, such as how well people and animals have learned a task, the motivation they have to perform it, and the cognitive processes needed to do a task. One way speed can be used assesses the time it takes to learn some task to a specified level of mastery, such as with no errors on two successive trials. This is called the *learning-time* method (Woodworth & Schlosberg, 1965). An example of the learning-time method comes from one of the earliest and most thorough tests of human learning and forgetting ever reported. Ebbinghaus (1885/1964), serving as his own participant, spent many hours memorizing long lists of *nonsense syllables*—nonwords that consist of a consonant, a vowel, and another consonant. In one of the many studies he reported, he learned and then relearned several lists of syllables, timing how long each learning session took. He assessed how much he remembered from the first session by calculating the difference in time spent for first and second learning, which reflects the "savings" in time for second learning as a result of remembering from first learning. If the learner took 10 minutes for first learning and 5 minutes for second learning, 5 minutes (or 50%) was saved. Subsequent research using this approach has tested many participants in each study (Hall, 1966). When we use speed in this way, we are measuring correctness to some extent because faster mastery usually reflects fewer errors.

Performance speed, such as the distance traversed or the number of items completed per unit of time, can be used to study the effects of motivation on learning and performance of learned responses. For instance, we could randomly assign children who have not learned mathematics to a group that receives a reward or a group that receives no reward for doing math problems and assess how many problems they complete per hour. Or, we could assess how fast athletes run in miles per hour or feet per minute under certain motivational conditions. As a research example, an experiment used running speed as a measure of the incentive that food reward variations provided for hungry rats who were tested across many weeks (Campbell, Batsche, & Batsche, 1972). Each day each rat had one *trial*—that is, a single full testing: The animal was placed at the start of a runway with walls and a transparent top and allowed to move freely to the end, where it could turn and find a food reward. For two of the groups, the food reward was always either one large pellet or many smaller pellets (that in total weighed the same amount as the large pellet). After the first weeks while the rats' speeds increased as they learned that running leads to reward, running speed, measured with electrical devices, began to stabilize and stayed faster for the many pellets reward than for the one large reward thereafter. Why did the many pellets produce faster running? One interpretation is that the many pellets reward looks like a larger amount than the one large reward.

Another speed measure is *reaction time,* or the time it takes the subject to get the response started (Woodworth & Schlosberg, 1965). Although reaction time can be used to examine many issues, it is often used in studying cognitive processes that end in an overt response, such as giving an answer. Let's look at three examples. First, Stroop (1935/1992) measured the amount of time people took to name the ink colors used in printing 100 names of colors, such as RED. In one condition, the ink colors and names matched (for example, RED was printed in red ink); in another condition, the colors and names didn't match (for example, RED was printed in blue). The results showed that total reaction time in naming the ink colors for all 100 names was far shorter if the colors and names matched than if they didn't match. Why? Reading is an automatic process for most readers, which probably made it interfere with the conscious decision making involved in identifying ink colors. Second, Shepard and Metzler (1971) asked people to examine pairs of line drawings like those in Figure 4.2 and decide as quickly as possible whether the drawings in a pair are of the same object

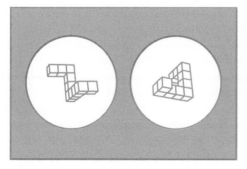
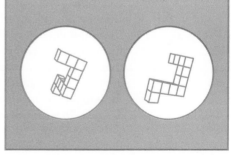

FIGURE 4.2

Examples of pairs of line drawings used by Shepard and Metzler (1971, Figure 1B and C). The drawings in the pair on the left are of the *same* object and differ only in rotation (they differ by 80 degrees). The drawings on the right are of *different* objects: if you examine them very closely, you'll see that they are not exactly the same when you rotate them in your mind.

rotated or different objects. The researchers varied systematically the degree of rotation of one drawing from the other in a pair across 1,600 pairs and found that the greater the rotation, the greater the reaction time. This finding suggests that people make such decisions by actually rotating images of objects in their heads. Third, Haber and Haber (1982) wanted to find out if people articulate words in their minds as they read silently. The researchers hypothesized that if silent reading involves articulating sentences in the mind, reading would take longer if the sentences are tongue twisters than if they are not. They had college students signal immediately upon finishing reading silently each of 20 sentences: 10 tongue twisters (such as, She sells seashells by the seashore) and 10 control sentences (He finds string beans by the small barn) that were equivalent for grammatical complexity and number of syllables. Reaction times were much greater for the tongue twisters than for the control sentences, suggesting that people articulate words in the mind as they read silently.

Sensory Attention, Habituation, and Experience

Parents and teachers who are trying to teach a young child new skills are often frustrated by what they call "the child's inability to concentrate" or "short attention span." Paying attention is essential to learning because it allows the individual to take in information and store it in memory. Although all five senses can attend to information, we will focus our discussion on the overt behavior of eye movements in *visual scanning*. Essentially right from birth, human infants visually scan their worlds (Salapatek, 1968). When a geometric pattern, such as a triangle, is placed in the center of babies' visual fields, they fix their gaze on it and begin to scan the perimeter rather than the center. How do we know what they are scanning? We can record their eye movements precisely with a photographic device, such as a video camera that peeks through a small opening in the center of the pattern. As children get older, their scanning becomes more efficient, and they do not need to spend as much time scanning items to discriminate correctly between them (Nodine & Simmons, 1974).

A similar method with a video camera can be used to measure visual *habituation,* the decline in attention with continued exposure to the same stimulus. Because individuals who scan efficiently get all the information they need quickly from stimuli, they are likely to habituate to stimuli faster than individuals who scan less efficiently. Using this reasoning, Ruddy and Bornstein (1979) hypothesized that babies who habituate quickly in early infancy should show stronger cognitive ability in later infancy than babies who habituate slowly. They tested 4-month-olds for habituation in a laboratory by placing each one in an infant seat and presenting 15 trials. In each trial, a pattern of vertical stripes was projected on a screen in their field of vision for 10 seconds; eye movements were videotaped for later scoring. Habituation was defined as the decline in looking time from the first two to the last two trials. At 12 months of age, the infants were assessed at home for cognitive abilities using a standardized test. Consistent with the hypothesis, the greater the infants' habituation, the higher their cognitive ability scores months later.

Another way to use overt behavior to assess visual attention is to give participants a task that requires vigilance. Dittmar, Berch, and Warm (1982) used this approach to test whether people who are deaf maintain visual attention better than people who hear. The participants sat in a small sound-attenuated booth and watched a bar of red light move repeatedly across a screen for 45 minutes, looking for a blip that was easily detectable if they were paying attention. When they saw a blip, they pressed a button. The individuals who were deaf correctly detected more blips than those who could hear, particularly in the last 15 minutes. One explanation for the better visual vigilance of people who are deaf is that they compensate for their lack of hearing as a source of information by using their visual systems more efficiently and persistently.

Because physical stimuli are the basis of experience, many psychologists study the ability to detect and discriminate between stimuli. The field of **psychophysics** is the study of functional relations between physical stimuli and subjects' perceptions of and reactions to them (Woodworth & Schlosberg, 1965). When testing the ability to detect stimuli, researchers often measure the **absolute threshold,** or minimum intensity that can produce a sensation. Using loudness as our example, the procedure is like the hearing tests you've experienced in which one stimulus at a time is presented. Absolute threshold testing involves a series of trials that can be arranged in different ways, one of which is called the *method of limits:* On alternate trials the sound intensities gradually *ascend,* starting with intensities that are below the threshold, or *descend,* starting from well above threshold. For each stimulus, the individuals are asked whether they hear it. The researcher calculates the absolute threshold by averaging across trials the minimum intensities at which the individual could hear a sound.

When testing the ability to discriminate between stimuli, researchers often assess the **difference threshold,** or the minimum variation that can be sensed between stimuli. To test for the difference threshold, the researcher presents two stimuli at a time and asks whether they are the same or different. Trials can be arranged with the methods of limits or another pattern, but the participants judge on each trial whether or not they notice a difference. The score on each trial is the minimum degree of difference in the stimuli that the person could sense. The researcher can then determine the *just noticeable difference* (jnd), the minimum degree of variation at which the stimuli were recognized as different on half of the trials. These procedures can assess absolute and difference thresholds for all five senses: hearing, vision, taste, smell, and touch.

Social and Emotional Behavior

Because overt social and emotional behaviors happen all around us, it's easy to think that everyone will know what behavior we observed if we simply name it, such as social play. But as we saw in the opening story, defining social behaviors is not so simple. For one thing, we need to take into account the *age* of the participant. The operational definitions I used in that study were specific to infants and toddlers and would not be appropriate for older children, who would initiate interaction differently, almost always with language and more elaborate motor behavior.

In addition, definitions of social and emotional behavior should reflect the *culture* of the individuals observed: these behaviors depend strongly on people's cultural history and customs. Sometimes a class of behavior may be expressed in different ways, and we may need to identify its subclasses. For example, aggression can include physical and verbal acts, such as hitting or shoving versus name-calling or threatening (Hartup, 1974). And it may reflect different purposes: The aim of hostile aggression is to injure or damage, whereas the aim of instrumental aggression is to acquire a goal, such as a toy (Feshbach, 1964). We can distinguish physical and verbal aggression directly in the overt behavior, but hostile and instrumental aggression must be identified on the basis of the context in which it happens. These subclasses are important in studying age, gender, and cultural differences in aggression. For instance, verbal and hostile aggression increase in early childhood, and boys perform more hostile aggression than girls in the United States (Hartup, 1974).

When conducting descriptive research, we may need to define the behavior in a broad or flexible way and collect data on as many variations as possible so that we can give rich details about it and categorize it or chart its course carefully, which we can illustrate with two studies. First, Festinger, Riecken, and Schachter (1956) had read a news story about a doomsday prediction that led them to do a social psychology study. In the story, a Mrs. Keech claimed to have learned from aliens from a planet called Clarion that a flood would occur months later, on December 21, and wipe out her community and much of North and South America. Given that the event was not likely to occur, the researchers wanted to observe how she and her quasi-religious group of followers would react when the catastrophe didn't happen, but they didn't know exactly what the people would do. So they pretended to join the group and simply took notes secretly on what the followers did and said. The finding was fascinating: The group didn't decide that the prediction was wrong; their belief was instead strengthened when Mrs. Keech announced at 4:45 A.M. on December 22 that God had spared the world because the group's efforts had created "such a force of Good and light" (p. 169). This study was done before the APA developed ethical codes on deception and privacy in research—would the methods be questioned today?

Second, Hall and Veccia (1990) studied interpersonal touching behavior in Boston area public places but were uncertain exactly the forms it would take. So they decided to record a variety of variables, such as the toucher's sex, whether or not the touch appeared to be intentional, a description of the touch (for example, arms linked), and the touch's apparent function (such as, affectionate, controlling, or attention getting). Five observers went to a variety of public places, secretly watched the behavior of pairs of individuals, and recorded verbally into a small tape recorder the preceding variables for each instance of touching they saw. By doing this, they were able to provide rich detail in their descriptions of touching behavior. For instance, linking arms was more likely to be initiated by females than males in mixed-sex touching, occurred fairly often in female–female touching, and did not occur in male–male touching.

You may have noticed that the observations in the last two studies were done secretly—or *unobtrusively*—without the subjects' awareness. Why? Because people's social behavior can be very different and not natural if they know their acts are being observed and recorded. Animals' behavior is affected in similar ways if they detect the presence of an observer. The influence of the observer's presence on behavior is called **reactivity.** We can also make unobtrusive observations by using equipment, such as hidden cameras—Have you seen the *Candid Camera* television show?—or cameras with false lenses. In reflex cameras, the image the photographer sees in the viewfinder comes through the lens. Eibl-Eibesfeldt (1972) used a reflex camera that appeared normal, but the real lens actually pointed to the side rather than forward. When he used this camera, he could avoid reactivity because the subjects probably thought he was photographing something else. As we saw in the last chapter, using unobtrusive observation can present ethical problems.

Overt emotional behavior can occur socially or when alone and can be assessed accurately when people display certain facial expressions, particularly for the emotions of sadness, enjoyment, fear, anger, and disgust (Ekman, 1993). Each emotion when strongly expressed has specific facial characteristics, such as the mouth open or closed and the brows raised or lowered, as shown in Figure 4.3 for three emotions. People around the world use basically the same facial expressions for emotions. Babies in early infancy do, too (Izard, 1979; Sroufe, 1979). One way to examine social and emotional behaviors is to place the person in a *structured situation* that should elicit them—for example, putting a bitter tasting food in a baby's mouth elicits the expression of disgust. Likewise, we can elicit and measure *Type A behavior* in a standardized interview designed to encourage its characteristics—competitiveness, impatience, and hostility—by interrupting the person and asking questions in a rude or challenging manner (Rosenman, Swan, & Carmelli, 1988).

We've now seen a variety of measures in psychological research that involve observing overt behavior, but many important variables we might want to study are not displayed outwardly. They involve covert behavior.

OBSERVING COVERT BEHAVIOR

People's attitudes, feelings, memories of past experiences, and current physical states, are covert, not directly observable. How can we measure them? We'll examine two approaches, taking *physiological measures,* which involve fairly direct assessment, and *self-report measures,* which are indirect.

Physiological Measures

Physical states can be assessed in a variety of ways that almost always require specialized equipment. For example, a polygraph and simpler devices can measure heart rate, blood pressure, respiration rate, the galvanic skin response (skin conductivity), brain electrical activity, muscle tension, and body temperature. Other methods involve analysis of the blood or urine to measure its levels of specific cells or chemicals, such as hormones the body releases during stress. A study using these approaches tested Type A and Type B (opposite of Type A) individuals in a competitive and harassing situation and found greater increases in blood pressure, heart rate, and stress hormones in Type A than Type B participants (Glass et al., 1980). Methods that use very complex equipment, such as *positron emission tomography* (PET), can measure brain activity by assessing the blood flow and oxygen content in specific regions of the brain, such as while trying to solve a cognitive problem (Buckner & Logan, 2001). A PET scan produces an image that appears in color; red regions have higher blood flow and are the most active.

Brain electrical activity can be measured with an *electroencephalograph* (EEG). When the sensory system detects a stimulus, such as a clicking sound, the signal to

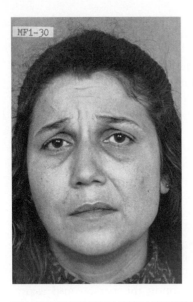  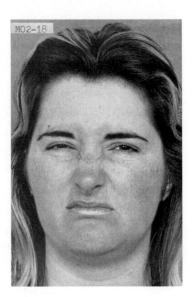

FIGURE 4.3

Facial expressions reflecting the emotions of sadness, enjoyment (happiness), and disgust. Notice the detailed characteristics of each.

the brain produces a change in voltage that the EEG detects from sensors that touch the subject's scalp. The EEG output is a graph of the electrical activity, which shows as a spike called an *evoked potential* that is time-locked to the occurrence of the stimulus in a trial. The strength of these evoked potentials can be averaged across many trials to give a more stable measure called the *event-related potential* (ERP). Leynes and Bink (2002) used ERPs to study physiological processes in people's memory for actions that they had either actually performed or only imagined performing. In the first phase of the study, the participants saw on a computer screen dozens of commands, such as "bend the wire," one at a time, and either performed the action or imagined performing it. About an hour later during ERP testing, each command was presented on a screen, and the participants had to decide whether they had performed it before or imagined doing it. The results showed differences in ERP data for the performed versus the imagined actions, suggesting that enacted and imagined behaviors create distinctly different memory traces in the brain.

Self-Report Measures

Because researchers cannot actually observe most current or past attitudes or feelings and past experiences of individuals, they often use indirect assessment approaches, especially *self-reports,* to measure these variables. In the **self-report** method, participants disclose their attitudes, feelings, or experiences by responding to a **survey**—that is, a series of questions or statements—presented in an oral *interview* (in person or on the phone) or in a *written questionnaire.* Using self-report measures has two principal advantages. First, they may provide the only way of collecting data on certain types of covert variables. Second, they enable researchers to collect data relatively efficiently, generally requiring less time and other resources than other methods. But self-reports can also have some disadvantages, especially with respect to their accuracy, because they rely on respondents' perceptions and memories, which may be vague or incorrect.

Surveys can include closed- and open-ended items. **Closed-ended items** restrict the person's response to a fixed set of options, such as yes/no, true/false, or a set of alternatives. For example, three closed-ended items that surveys on worrying might use are

Do you worry that your family may split up?

　　　YES　　　　　NO

I worry more than most people I know.

　　　TRUE　　　　FALSE

I spend a lot of time worrying about schoolwork and tests.

　　Agree　　Mildly agree　　Mildly disagree　　Disagree

Open-ended items ask for information but allow the person to respond freely, without restriction. Two open-ended items that could be used in a survey on worrying are

Name the five things that worry you most.

Look at this picture of a girl worrying. What do you think she's worrying about?

Researchers can choose between closed- and open-ended items to get factual information, such as the person's age, gender, and ethnic background. To assess ethnic background, for instance, a closed-ended item might present alternatives (such as Caucasian, African American, Hispanic, and Asian) and ask the person to circle one; an open-ended item would ask the person to state his or her ethnicity or write it in a particular space.

Which type of item is best? Both can be very useful, and it's not uncommon for surveys to include some of each. The main advantages of closed-ended items is that they are easy to score, convert directly to statistical data, and keep the respondent from giving answers that are irrelevant or off the mark. Open-ended items lack these qualities, but they do not impose a particular point of view on the respondent, and freely given answers may provide useful information the researcher hadn't considered. As a result, open-ended items may be especially useful in studying a topic that has not yet been investigated very much. When open- and closed-ended items are used for a block of questions in the same survey, they are often arranged so that the open-ended items appear first because they can ask for broader information. In organizing items on a topic, there is a "funneling" rule of thumb: just as a funnel has a broad opening and becomes more and more narrow, broad questions on the topic should come first, with subsequent items becoming increasingly specific or detailed.

Many questionnaires use closed-ended items that are rating scales, like the one earlier that has respondents rate their agreement with a statement about worrying. A researcher named Likert (1932) introduced this general approach using 3- and 5-point scales, with the ends representing distinct opposites. We'll illustrate his approach using a 5-point scale of agreement for a statement on worrying:

I worry a lot.

Strongly agree   Agree   Undecided   Disagree   Strongly disagree.

The respondent would circle the appropriate answer, which the researcher would score using predetermined points—for example, strongly agree = 5 to strongly disagree = 1. Although researchers can examine the data for each individual item, the scores across multiple items in a questionnaire are usually *summed* or *averaged.* If some statements are phrased oppositely to others ("I worry a lot" versus "I worry very little"), adjustments are made before adding scores so that all measurements are in the same direction. To do this, the items phrased in one direction will need to be *reverse-scored* (for instance, strongly agree would get a score of 1 instead of 5). Scales using this general approach are usually called **Likert scales,** or *Likert-type scales,* even if they use different numbers of labels for the alternatives. The alternatives can assess a wide variety of dimensions other than agreement, such as *approval* (for instance, strongly approve to strongly disapprove), *likelihood* (very likely to very unlikely), or *frequency* (very often to almost never). Using "undecided" as one of the alternatives is often of little value (Schuman & Presser, 1996). Many researchers prefer middle alternatives that nudge respondents off the fence, as "slightly agree" and "slightly disagree" would do.

Other rating scales label in words only the ends of the continuum, again using distinct opposites. We'll consider three variations. First, in **graphic rating scales,** people indicate their ratings by placing a mark at the corresponding point along a continuous line of a standard length, usually 100 millimeters, as in the following scale to measure pain as a symptom of illness:

The mark shows that the rating is of more than moderate pain. The researcher obtains the score by measuring with a ruler the distance from the "no-pain" end.

Second, **segmented rating scales** (sometimes called *semantic differential scales*) have people indicate their ratings by marking the appropriate segment in a continuum. The segments are often separated with lines or colons, as in this 6-point scale in which a rating for loneliness was entered:

How lonely do you feel?

:_____: _X_: _____: _____: _____: _____:

Not lonely   Very lonely

The mark indicates that the person was only a little lonely. The researcher predetermines the score for each segment; in this example, if "not lonely" = 0 and "very lonely" = 5, the score would be 1 point.

Third, **numerical rating scales** have numbers spanning the continuum between endpoints, and the respondents give their ratings by circling the appropriate one. In the following scale to assess the desirability of money as a reward, a rating was entered that indicates money would be a fairly strong reward for that person:

How desirable is money to you as a reward when you do something well?

0   1   2   3   4   5   6   ⑦   8   9

Not   Very
desirable   desirable

The circled number is the score the person would receive for that item in the survey. The Likert scales and the graphic, segmented, and numerical ratings scales we've examined are some of the many closed-ended approaches researchers can use to obtain self-reports of covert behaviors, and each of these approaches can vary in the labels it uses and the number of alternatives it presents.

The labels that researchers choose in constructing rating scales can influence the way respondents interpret and answer closed-ended items (Schwarz, 1999). As an example, let's consider labels that refer to the frequency of people's recent experiences or behaviors—say, how often they felt irritated. We could construct labels that reflect a low frequency ("less than once a year" to "more than once a month") or a high frequency ("less than once a week" to "more than once a day"). The low-frequency labels would produce very different responses than the high-frequency labels and would suggest to respondents that the irritations the researcher is studying occur rarely and are therefore relatively intense. In a study of people's daily time spent watching TV, researchers compared data from two scales in six half-hour increments with different labels (Schwarz, 1999). One scale ranged from "up to ½ hour" to "more than 2½ hours" and the other ranged from "up to 2½ hours" to "more than 4½ hours." The respondents' data showed that 16.2% of those using the former scale and 37.5% of those using the latter scale said they watched more than 2½ hours of TV. One way to avoid these problems is to use an open-ended item instead—for example, "How many hours a day do you watch TV?" (Go to **Box 4.1**)

REMNANT MEASURES OF BEHAVIOR

The word *remnant* means a part, member, or trace of an object or event that remains at a later time. **Remnant measures** use existing remains, products, or evidence of behavior to infer or explain past events or states of affairs. Because we do not observe the actual behavior, these measures use relatively indirect assessment methods. Although remnant measures are often applied because the behavior occurred long ago, they can be used with current behavior, too. One advantage of remnant measures is that they generally are *unobtrusive*—that is, as-

BOX 4.1   COMPOSING A SURVEY

Even though there are hundreds, maybe thousands, of published psychological surveys available in the literature, researchers (including students) sometimes decide to construct their own. They generally do this because there are no existing surveys on the topic of interest, or the ones available are problematic, such as by using an operational definition that is different from the one the researcher has in mind or being too long or difficult to score. If you decide to compose a survey, here are some tips you should consider.

1. Decide and write down in advance exactly your idea of what you want to measure. How would you define it conceptually, including all elements it must contain?

2. Decide on the characteristics of the individuals that could be tested with the survey. Their genders, age groups, ethnic backgrounds, or special abilities could affect the phrasing and structure of items you use.

3. Write items you'll need for describing the participants' demographic characteristics in a report. This information should include their age, gender, and ethnicity; depending on the topic being studied, you may also need to specify other information, such as their income, employment or marital status, or number of children. Some of these can be closed-ended items, but when the answer is a specific number, such as age, it is usually best to use open-ended items and have respondents fill in the data. It's usually not a good idea to use ranges in closed-ended items for numerical data—such as, "Age (circle): 17–22, 23–28, 29–34"—because you will not have the exact data and cannot calculate means or other statistics you may need. If no computations will be done on a set of data, using ranges may be useful if you think participants would not want to give exact data, such as of annual income.

4. Ask questions only on what you need to know. Don't ask for unnecessary detail or use items as a "fishing expedition."

5. Word each item very carefully, using five rules. First, make each item as *simple and straightforward* as possible, avoiding jargon and other words people might not understand. You may know what *reinforcement* or *introverted* are, but your participants may not. Second, make the *wording very precise;* vague or ambiguous words lead to misinterpretations. For example, what does the phrase "in the past few months" mean? People's interpretations will vary, with some saying about 3 months and others saying 7. Third, *avoid negatively phrased items,* such as "The city council should not approve the proposed homeless shelter." Agreeing with this statement means that the person disagrees with the proposal, which is confusing. Fourth, *avoid double-barreled items* that tap more than one issue with just one response, such as "To what extent do you support funding for the arts and for scientific research?" If people support each differently, what

answer should they give? If they decide to give the "average," how will you know that's what they did? Fifth, *avoid loaded items,* which bias individuals to respond in a particular way, as in "Most people favor the president's budget. Do you support it?" and "Do you approve of teens engaging in immoral sexual behavior?" The former item suggests that opposing the budget is unpopular, and the latter uses an emotionally charged word that conveys a negative meaning to the issue of sexual behavior.

6. When using closed-ended items, use a set of responses that spans in even increments the full range of answers people are likely to give and gives enough alternatives to allow respondents to express themselves accurately. Rating scales with four to six alternatives are very common, but more alternatives can be used if there is reason to expect that respondents will be able to discriminate among them well. Dichotomous answers (yes/no, agree/disagree) can be used, but can be difficult to answer and less precise because people's beliefs and feelings usually involve "shades of gray" rather than absolutes.

7. In closed-ended items, make sure the answers in each item match the statement or question asked. For example, don't use a rating scale of "strongly agree" to "strongly disagree" for the question, "Do you approve of the job your senator is doing?"

8. Decide on a statistical analysis plan in advance. If you will be summing scores from multiple items, make sure the scales you will need to sum have comparable data that you can combine meaningfully. If some items are closed-ended and others are open-ended or if the closed-ended scales vary in their labels or the number of alternatives, you may not be able to combine data from them in a meaningful way. If possible, use the identical format across all items to be combined.

9. Pretest the survey with friends who will not be in your actual study, and have them think aloud with you present as they fill it out. Use friends who will give constructive criticism, not just praise. Do they seem to interpret items as you do? Interview them after. Do they have suggestions to improve the survey? Do they think each item is clear? Do the response alternatives span the full range that other people would use? Are the response formats easy to use? Apply their feedback when revising the survey.

10. Make the survey look professional. Format the fonts and printing so that each item is clearly presented, with distinct separations between items, easy-to-use responses, and no typographical errors.

Students usually begin the process of constructing a survey with the thought, "This'll be a piece of cake." It isn't. Chapter 10 describes how to find an existing survey.

sessments are made without the subject's awareness. As a result, they reduce the problem of reactivity (Webb, Campbell, Schwartz, & Sechrest, 2000). We will discuss two types of remnant measures: physical traces and archival data.

Physical Traces

When detectives go about solving a crime, they look for evidence of the presence and actions of the perpetrator, such as fingerprints, hair and DNA samples, or weapons left behind. These are remnants of the criminal behavior that are **physical traces,** or material signs or evidence of the past event. Physical traces can involve *erosion,* or selective wear on or depletion of an object, and *accretion,* or the deposit of material (Webb et al., 2000).

Physical traces involving erosion can include the reduced amount of cereal in a box as a measure of eating behavior, the wear on people's shoes as a measure of activity, and the wear on library reference books as a measure of use. As an example, researchers found ancient skulls with coin-sized circular holes that could not have been battle wounds and concluded that the holes were made for superstitious reasons, such as to allow demons to leave the body (Stone, 1979). Physical traces involving accretion can include fingerprints, dust on books, and food or beverage containers in people's garbage as measures of use. Let's look at two very different examples of studies using accretion evidence. First, Newhagen and Ancell (1995) examined people's use of bumper stickers as physical traces of their emotional expression. By observing and keeping track of the stickers on cars parked in specific residential areas in Washington, DC, they found that emotional expression varied with ethnicity and income. There were a greater number of stickers per vehicle in low-income than high-income neighborhoods and the stickers had relatively intense and positive messages in high-income White neighborhoods and very subdued messages in high-income Black neighborhoods. Second, researchers examined the remains of bodies from the 18th and 19th centuries in New England (Sledzik & Bellantoni, 1994). Accretion evidence revealed that people had dug up a body after it had decomposed and rearranged the skeleton into a symbol of death, suggesting that they performed vampire rituals in the belief that they could stop the dead from draining life forces from the living.

Archival Data

Not all traces of behavior, past events, or states of affairs are material; some are in an abstracted form, such as in written records, databases, or pictures. The term *archives* refers to recorded information or the places where they are stored. Thus, **archival data** are abstracted traces of variables that are recorded in hard copy or electronic formats. Some of the more common sources of archival data are newspapers and magazines, video and audio libraries, government or institutional records, telephone directories, research data collected previously for other purposes, and Internet sites for organizations (see the list under Resources at the end of this chapter). A student of mine conducted a study using archival data to compare sexism in commercials during children's TV shows from 1985 and 1995. His family had made and saved videotapes of the earlier shows, and he made the newer ones for comparable shows. He then scored the amount of time people of each gender appeared and found that males were on screen more than females in both years. Let's look at other interesting outcomes from some published studies that have used archival data from different sources.

Berkowitz and Macaulay (1971) conducted a series of studies examining whether highly publicized violent crimes are infectious, prompting subsequent increases in violent crimes. The archival data were obtained from news media and the FBI monthly counts of specific types of crime for each of 40 American cities for the years 1960 to 1966. One of the analyses they conducted was on crimes of aggravated assault in the month following each of two highly publicized crimes, the assassination of President John F. Kennedy in 1963 and Richard Speck's murder of eight nurses in 1966. The researchers checked in the month after each of those crimes to see whether there was an increase in assaults beyond the usual number for the same month of the remaining years of the study. In each case, there was an unusual and very large increase in aggravated assaults, supporting the hypothesis that sensationalized crimes breed similar crimes.

Another study using archival data examined the hospital records of patients who had gall bladder surgery and were assigned rooms with or without a view of a natural setting through their window (Ulrich, 1984). Of patients during the months when trees have leaves, 23 had been assigned to rooms with a scenic view of trees and 23 had been assigned to rooms with a view of a brick wall. The rooms were equivalent in all other respects, including their size and the ease with which patients could see out the window from the bed. The patients were selected so that the two groups could be matched for important health-relevant variables, such as age, sex, weight, and smoking history. The patients' records revealed that those with a scenic view remained in the hospital a shorter time after surgery and used fewer doses of narcotic pain medication.

Using archival data from previously conducted research can also be fruitful. In 1921, Lewis Terman began a well-known, long-term study of over 1,500 preadolescent boys and girls who were very bright and virtually all of Caucasian background (Terman & Oden, 1947). Data on a wide variety of psychological, social, and physical variables have been collected on the participants, nicknamed the "Termites," at 5- to 10-year intervals ever since, and many researchers have gotten access to these data over the years. Because by the mid-1990s about half the Termites had died, researchers could study the role of psychological and social factors in the longevity and causes of death of these individuals. We'll consider three findings from two of these studies (Friedman et al., 1995; Tucker, Friedman, Wingard, & Schwartz, 1996). First, the stronger the personality traits of dependability and conscientiousness the Termites had in childhood, the longer they lived. Second, the risk of dying by age 80 was the same for Termites who did and did not marry by midlife. Third, Termites who smoked cigarettes or drank heavily died at younger ages than those who did neither.

Limitations of Remnant Measures

Although remnant measures have the advantages of allowing researchers to study events that cannot be observed directly or happened long ago and of reducing reactivity during assessment, they also have some important limitations. Probably the most important limitation is that the researcher can only use whatever remnant measures are available. Sometimes the data needed to investigate a topic simply do not exist. And sometimes the physical traces and archival data exist, but are biased. Remnant measures can be biased through two processes, selective deposit and selective survival (Webb et al., 2000).

In *selective deposit,* some pertinent traces or data are not established or entered. Let's consider a couple of examples. Suppose you wanted to compare the physical activity of men and women by measuring the wear on their shoes, but women more than men do a lot of activities while barefoot. The erosion traces would be biased, with the wear on women's shoes understating their activity. Or suppose you were using police records to study criminal behavior, such as sexual abuse of children. Two difficulties in using these archival data are that many sex crimes are never reported to the police, and authorities in some communities deliberately misclassify child sexual abuse to spare families the ordeal of testifying about incest (Sarafino, 1979). In *selective survival,* some traces or data that existed are removed. In the shoe wear example, if women discard shoes more readily than men do, the data would be biased. Similarly, archives may be purged, sometimes in the interest of saving space, and the choice of which data to remove may be biased.

We've noted that remnant measures reduce reactivity during assessment, but that does not mean reactivity did not influence the production of physical traces and archival data when they were established or entered. Individuals may alter the way they behave when people other than researchers are watching them. For instance, suppose you were using quotations from political speeches reported in newspaper articles as a source of archival data to compare the views of two candidates for president. Certainly, people giving speeches know they are being observed, and they adjust their statements or choose their words carefully, perhaps saying very different things to different audiences. As a result, their behavior is reactive, but not to a researcher's presence. Researchers who use archival data need to keep in mind behavioral influences of these kinds, look for ways to clarify or corroborate data that are suspect, and adapt their interpretation of the study's outcome accordingly.

In summary, we have discussed a wide variety of ways to collect data through observing overt behavior, observing covert behavior, and using remnant measures of behavior. Each of these approaches can be used to study topics in almost any area of psychology and can be applied in research employing experimental, quasi-experimental, correlational, and descriptive strategies. Often researchers find it useful to use more than one approach to measure behavior in a study, either because different measurement approaches may reveal different facets of the phenomenon or because similar findings with different measurement approaches can clarify or strengthen conclusions from the study. (Go to **Box 4.2**)

COLLECTING DATA ON NATURALLY OCCURRING BEHAVIOR

Most studies are structured so that all the data obtained in each observation are used in analyses. For instance, when testing rats in a maze, running speed data for each trial is used. When people fill out a survey about their current feelings or attitudes, all the relevant data they provide are used. But psychologists often study ongoing or naturally occurring behaviors for which complete records cannot be obtained, such as because the behavior occurs spontaneously, too infrequently, in

BOX 4.2   USING COMPUTERS TO COLLECT DATA

Researchers began using electrical devices to collect data decades ago for two main reasons: precision and objectivity. Electrical devices enable researchers to present stimuli, such as words, at a precise, standardized pace and measure behavior exactly, especially when assessing performance speed, reaction time, and visual scanning. In addition, observation that uses electrical devices is objective, eliminating the possibility of bias in the researcher's observations. Over the years, these devices have become increasingly sophisticated and precise, and today they often involve computers, which have the added advantage of being able to score the behavior and enter the data into a statistical database. Although the computers are usually stand-alone units in laboratories, we'll focus this discussion on collecting data over the Internet.

For the many topics of psychology that can be studied on the Internet, Birnbaum (2001) has described procedures to create programs to collect data for three areas:

- *Psychophysics* (the study of the correspondence between perception and physical stimulation): Suppose you wanted to assess people's ability to discriminate between gray squares of varying darkness. You could present a series of two squares at a time on the monitor and ask participants to identify with the mouse which of the pair is darker. The computer could keep track of the correctness of the answers and even the degree of difference in darkness for each pair.
- *Logical thinking:* You could present a series of logical problems, each of which has a correct answer—as a number, for instance. The participants would type their answers to each problem in a box. The computer could keep track of the correctness of the answers and other variables, such as the difficulty of the problem.
- *Personality and social psychology:* You could type into the program a survey with closed-ended items to assess a personality trait or attitude, using a Likert scale. The respondents would use their mouse to choose their answers. The computer would keep track of the answer to each item and calculate totals or means across items.

Special problems must be addressed when doing research on the Internet. We'll consider just three (see Birnbaum, 2001, for more information). First, it's possible for the same person to participate more than once, particularly because researchers often have people participate anonymously. If you use an anonymous procedure, you can ask people to participate only once. Use demographic information to match up likely cases of multiple submissions and discard extras. Second, recruiting participants can be a challenge. You can encourage participation by publicizing the study by submitting your Website to a popular search engine; using e-mail or conventional advertising means, such as posters and announcements; and getting an organization to put an announcement for your study on their site. Third, if you have a deadline for collecting your data, you'll need a backup plan in case you don't get enough participants.

a rapid stream of activity that is difficult to follow, or mainly under certain circumstances. In these cases, researchers need to make decisions in advance about scheduling the observations, and two timing approaches are especially useful.

One of these timing approaches is called **event sampling,** which involves making observations of the behavior only when a predetermined situation occurs. For example, if we were studying nervous behavior among boys and girls at school, we might arrange for observations of overt behaviors only on days when major exams are scheduled. If we are using a survey to study whether people usually drink alcohol alone or socially when they feel depressed, we might specify the emotional circumstance and ask questions about any drinking episodes and people present. If we were studying the form of children's aggression at a playground by videotaping episodes, we might turn on the recorder only when a fight was about to happen. In these examples, data collection is contingent on the occurrence of an event. Researchers often use event sampling when they expect that the behavior will occur infrequently or mainly under certain circumstances, but sometimes it is used to define exactly when to start an observation or which individuals to observe.

In another timing approach, called **time sampling,** the researchers collect data only during predetermined intervals of time within one or more observation periods. One way to do this is to divide each observation period into subperiods of equal length (say, 30 seconds) and designate a short interval (say, 10 seconds) at the start of each subperiod for collecting data. The intervals for collecting data can be selected systematically—as in our example, always the first 10 seconds of each subperiod—or randomly; either way, the goal is to get a sample of behavior that is representative of its total occurrence. Time sampling is a particularly useful method when the behavior occurs too frequently or as a rapid stream of activity that is difficult to follow. Recall back to the opening story about the study of infant and toddler play in which researchers observed each pair of children for a 15-minute period, divided into 60 15-second subperiods, and collected data only during the first 10 seconds of each subperiod. A time sampling method was used because of the complexity of the observation task. The researchers were scoring nine different behaviors that often occurred quickly as a stream of actions.

The study on interpersonal touching in public places by Hall and Veccia (1990) that we discussed earlier used both event and time sampling methods. The observers used event sampling to decide which people to observe, choosing the pair of individuals at the public place, such as a shopping mall, who was nearest to a preselected landmark when a timing device signaled through an earphone the start of an observation interval. For time sampling, the researchers divided the observation period into 20-second subperiods, allocating the first 10 seconds of each as the observation interval. If more than one touch occurred in an interval, the researchers recorded verbally on an audiotape information about only the first touch. The information included an estimate of the people's ages, whether or not touching occurred, the body parts involved in a touch, and the sex of the giver and receiver of a touch. The extra time in each subperiod could be used to complete the recording and prepare to observe the next pair of individuals.

TYPES OF DATA

When researchers design a study, they must decide what type(s) of data to collect, based on three factors: the exact variables specified in the research hypothesis, the methods they will use to assess the behavior, and the statistical procedures they plan to use in analyzing the data. In this section, we will examine variations in the types of data they can collect.

QUANTITATIVE AND QUALITATIVE DATA

The data that subjects provide can be *quantitative*—that is, already in or easily converted into numerical form—or *qualitative,* usually in narrative form. The large majority of psychology studies collect quantitative data.

Quantitative Data

For quantitative data, sometimes the researcher simply records whether a given behavior did or did not occur, as we saw in the study of infants tested for their depth perception on the visual cliff apparatus. They either crawled off the platform toward the mother or they did not. This is a *discrete* variable—the data simply classify the behavior into distinct categories, which can be easily converted into numbers: crawled = 1, did not crawl = 0. In contrast, *continuous* variables produce quantitative data with uninterrupted gradations from low to high. Most quantitative data for continuous variables are of three types: frequency (how often), duration (how long), and magnitude (how strongly/much). Let's look at how each type of data can be used in measuring behavior.

- **Frequency** data refer to the number of times a behavior occurred. For example, the study we've discussed on infant and toddler play assessed the frequency of social behaviors. Other behaviors that can be assessed with frequency data include attending school classes, biting nails, taking medication on schedule, smoking cigarettes, doing specific exercises, hitting classmates in school, and thinking anxious thoughts.
- **Duration** data express the length of time a behavior lasts from start to end. As an example, a study assessed the amount of time children engaged in simple social acts, such as rolling balls to each other (Whitman, Mercurio, & Caponigri, 1970). Other behaviors often assessed with duration data include watching television, visual scanning, exercising, sitting in one's seat, and feeling depressed.
- **Magnitude** data describe the behavior's intensity, degree, or size. For instance, a study of rats' alcohol intake assessed the volumes of liquid consumed (Martinetti, Andrzejewski, Hineline, & Lewis, 2000). Other behaviors that can be assessed with magnitude data include survey ratings (such as, the degree of approval or agreement) of attitudes or personality, concentration in studying, exercise, calories consumed, speed of running, reaction time, EEG evoked potentials, and loudness of speech.

Sometimes these types of data are expressed as a *rate*—that is, per unit of time—as in "the number of hours spent watching TV *per week*" or "the amount consumed *per hour*."

Qualitative Data

The narratives in qualitative data are oral or written descriptions of personal experience, often conveying the concepts or phenomena more richly than a questionnaire could. For instance, a report on women's coping with breast cancer by rethinking their attitudes and priorities described one participant's stated view:

> I have much more enjoyment each day, each moment. I am not so worried about what is or isn't or what I wish I had. All those things you get entangled with don't seem to be part of my life right now. (Taylor, 1983, p. 1163)

When used in purely descriptive research, no effort is made to quantify the information the person provided. A clear and sensitive statement speaks for itself.

In other research, qualitative data are collected from participants or selected from archives with the intention of converting it to quantitative data, enabling statistical analyses. How do researchers convert the data? They use **content analysis,** a process in which narrative information is classified into categories or rated on specified dimensions (Smith, 2000). To promote accuracy and objectivity in the conversion, the *coders* who perform it are trained to apply the classification or rating criteria carefully and kept blind to the purpose of the study. Suppose we were conducting a content analysis of sexism in children's books. One step would be to select a representative sample of books and perhaps only parts of them, such as even numbered or randomly selected pages. Sampling may be necessary because of the huge number of books available and amount of time content analysis takes; if the amount of relevant materials is manageable, we would use them all. Other decisions need to be made. How large should the units of analysis be—would the coders look for and analyze individual words, themes, pictures, or some other aspect? Would the coders just classify the units (for example, sexist versus nonsexist) or rate them, such as on a 6-point scale from "extremely sexist" to "not at all sexist." Also, the researcher must specify exactly the rules the coders will use to classify or rate the units.

Content analysis has been used to study issues as varied as language acquisition, creativity, emotional expression, self-help groups, suicide, stereotypes, and propaganda (Smith, 2000). Let's look at two examples of studies that used content analysis with archival data, one that classified the narratives and one that rated them. The first study analyzed gay males' and females' personal advertisements placed in gay-oriented publications in the Chicago area (Bailey, Kim, Hills, & Linsenmeier, 1997, Study 1). After examining many gay and lesbian ads and talking with the publications' staffs, the researchers compiled a list of specific terms typically used in the ads. These terms were used to classify the advertiser's characteristics and partner preferences in more than 3,500 ads along several dimensions, some of which were sexual (such as, "top," "bottom," and "dominant") and some were nonsexual ("masculine," "feminine," and "athletic"). Two findings from the statistical analyses were that men advertisers used the term "masculine" more than "feminine" to describe themselves and the partners they preferred, and women advertisers used the term "feminine" more than "masculine" to describe themselves and their preferred partners.

The second study examined race relations on prime-time television in the United States in the late 1970s (Weigel, Loomis, & Soja, 1980). The researchers videotaped 3 consecutive hours of broadcasts, including commercials, each night for a full week on the three networks. To assess race relations in the programs, they constructed 5-point scales that coders used in rating interpersonal interactions on several qualities, such as the level of intimacy and shared decision making, among characters that were black or white. The researchers compared the ratings for interactions involving black and white characters with interactions involving only white characters. Statistical analyses revealed that the black–white interactions showed less intimacy and shared decision making than the white–white interactions.

Although researchers often develop their own coding system for content analyses in their studies, it can be efficient to search the literature for one that already exists that may match their needs. Several computer programs that conduct content analyses are now available. For instance, Pennebaker, Mayne, and Francis (1997) used a program to code interviews of men who had lost a partner to AIDS and evaluated their psychological adjustment a year later. The data revealed that the more words they used in the interview reflecting insightful thinking the better their adjustment a year later, but the more words they used involving death, the poorer their adjustment later.

SCALES OF MEASUREMENT

Once we have determined what we want to measure and possible ways to measure it, we need to coordinate these ideas in with the possible statistical procedures we can apply to analyze the data. Doing this before collecting the data enables us to know that we will be able to do the analyses we want to do. A critical step in this coordination is to classify the type of data we would collect into one of four different *scales of measurement:* nominal, ordinal, interval, and ratio (Stevens, 1951). But keep in mind that a study can have more than one type of data.

Nominal and Ordinal Scales

In a **nominal scale,** the data we collect contrasts subjects by classifying each into one of two or more categories based on the individual's behavior or other characteristics. For this reason, nominal data are sometimes called *categorical.* The data we collect are not "scores," but the number or percentage of individuals classified in each category. In the visual cliff study of depth perception (Gibson & Walk, 1960), the infants were classified as having crawled or not crawled off the platform when the mother was on the deep side: 3 crawled and 33 did not. The infants are contrasted only by the *name* of the category—"crawler" or "noncrawler"—which is why the scale is called *nominal.* In the study of gay and lesbian personal ads (Bailey et al., 1997), the researchers classified ads according to the gender of the advertisers and the different terms they used to describe themselves and their partner preferences: masculine or feminine, for instance. Other examples of nominal scales are political party affiliation, marital status, whether a person is or is not receiving therapy, and whether a person claims to exercise regularly.

An **ordinal scale** differentiates only by a rank ordering. It has all the properties of a nominal scale, but also expresses *magnitude* (greater than and less than) relationships among subjects for the underlying variable, as occurs in rankings of students in scholastic performance and of sports teams in win–loss records. But the distances between adjacent ranks on the underlying variable, such as scholastic performance, are probably not equal. For instance, suppose the grade point averages of the five top-ranked students at a school were 4.00, 3.99, 3.59, 3.39, and 3.34. Using ranks with these data would mask the fact that some distances are tiny, others are large, and no two are exactly the same. Other examples of ordinal scales are the rankings for winners of a spelling bee, sales of popular music CDs, military level (such as sergeant, corporal, and private), and socioeconomic class (lower, middle, and upper class).

Because nominal and ordinal scales lack important numerical properties, such as equal distances on the underlying variable, the data they produce cannot logically be used in arithmetic operations—they can't be meaningfully added, subtracted, multiplied, or divided. We'll see that this feature will have implications for the statistical analyses in which data on these scales can be used.

Interval and Ratio Scales

In an **interval scale,** consecutive scale values *represent equal distances* in the underlying variable. The distance between the scores 1 and 2 is the same as the distance between 4 and 5. Interval scales have all the properties of ordinal scales and go a step further. Some examples of interval scales are temperature (such as degrees centigrade), grade point average, IQ, and scores on attitude and personality surveys that use Likert scales. Actually, some researchers would disagree with some of these examples, claiming that grade point average, IQ, and survey scores really use ordinal scales because we cannot know for sure that the distances between consecutive scale values are equal. But most psychologists view these distances as being approximately equal, justifying their being classified as interval scales.

A **ratio scale** has all the properties of interval scales, including equal distances in the underlying variable, plus an *absolute or "true" zero point.* The zero is important for two reasons: It indicates the absence of the attribute being assessed, and it allows us to see the scores as *ratios* of one to another—for example, a score of 8 is four times as much as 2. This is a useful feature when interpreting research data. For instance, in the study on infant and toddler social behavior in this chapter's opening story, it was possible to say in the research report that a specific type of play occurred "only about half as frequently" among the older than the younger children (Sarafino, 1985, p. 26). If the data were on an interval scale, we couldn't specify a ratio. Other examples of ratio scales are the number correct on a test, amount of time spent at work, speed of running, and an object's height or weight. A zero on each of these scales means there is none or there can't be less. You may be wondering why temperature is not a ratio scale; a thermometer has a zero point. It's because zero centigrade does not mean there is no temperature; it means, pure water freezes at that temperature. What's more, although 80 degrees is a lot warmer than 20, it's not four times as warm.

An important feature of interval and ratio scales is that their consecutive values represent equal distances in the underlying variable. As a result, the data they produce can be meaningfully added, subtracted, multiplied, and divided.

CRITICAL ASPECTS OF DATA

Good examples of data collection we see in everyday life occur in sports contests in which the behavior of individual athletes, such as swimmers or figure skaters, receives scores. We'll use examples from individual sports to illustrate three critical aspects of data that affect the quality and interpretation of research. These aspects are the variance, reliability, and validity of the data.

VARIANCE

In swimming contests for speed, each athlete gets a different score for the time from start to finish. The scores vary from one swimmer to the next and for one swimmer across contests. Variation is essential in research data; without it, we would see no relationships or differences between variables. Some data show little variance, and some show a lot. Is all variation desirable in research? No, and the desirability depends on its source.

To discuss sources of variation, we will define the term **variance** conceptually as the degree to which scores in a set of data deviate from the mean. Statistically, we can calculate the variance by finding the *average* deviation in four steps: subtract each score from the mean (M, or $\overline{X}$) to get its deviation, square each deviation, sum the squares, and divide by the number of scores minus 1. The formula is

$$\text{Variance} = s^2 = \frac{\sum (X - M)^2}{n - 1}$$

Some variance in a study's data is *systematic*—that is, it is concentrated consistently in certain research conditions. Other variance is *nonsystematic*, affecting the scores randomly and fairly evenly across all conditions in the study. With these definitions in mind, we can describe three sources of variation in research data, using a hypothetical experiment comparing the swimming speed (the dependent variable) of swimmers who do and do not receive a counseling program (the independent variable) designed to increase the motivation to win.

▪ *Systematic Variance from the Independent Variable.* If the motivational counseling improved performance, the swimmers' scores in the experimental group would be higher than in the control group. Thus, some of the variation in research data for the full sample of participants results from operation of the independent variable. Any effective independent variable would have this effect. In the opening story about the study on social play, age as the independent variable increased the variation in the dependent variable: toddlers had higher levels of some social components of play than infants did.

▪ *Systematic Variance from Extraneous Variables.* In Chapter 1, we discussed how scientists try to apply *control* to eliminate unwanted or extraneous factors that might bias the outcome of their research. An **extraneous variable** is an uncontrolled factor in a study that can affect one condition differently from another, rendering the effect of the independent variable unclear. The swimmers' performance might show systematic variation from an extraneous variable if an influential factor was not controlled because of an oversight in the design or because control was not possible. For example, suppose that the researcher could not randomly assign the swimmers to groups or equate the groups in some other way, and the experimental group was already more motivated than the control group before counseling began. Or suppose the groups were tested on different days, and the swimmers in the experimental group were more rested since the last contest than those in the control group. If the experimental group swam faster than the control group, some of this variation would probably be due to the extraneous variable: the original difference in motivation or the amount of rest. How much of the observed difference was due to the motivational counseling, and how much was due to the extraneous variable? Keep in mind that the effect of the extraneous variable can be opposite to that of the independent variable. For instance, if original motivation was higher in the control group and the counseling raised the motivation of the experimental group, the groups might perform equally.

▪ *Nonsystematic, "Error" Variance.* Conceptually, the term **error variance** refers to variation in data that results from factors whose effects are nonsystematic, or random: these factors affect the data in all conditions of the study, usually somewhat equally, and are as likely to increase as decrease scores. Statistically speaking, error variance is a measure of all the variation that is not associated with the conditions of the study (it is sometimes called *within-groups variance*). What factors produce error variance? A main source of error variance is *individual differences* among subjects—for instance, in their intellectual ability, personality traits, and motivation to do well. It also occurs if subjects differ in alertness during testing, respondents interpret items in a survey differently, the apparatus functions differently on occasion, and the researcher's behavior varies during testing. Error variance increases when chance determines the distribution of these circumstances across conditions.

Factors that produce either systematic or nonsystematic effects raise the overall variance of the data and can affect the mean scores for the different conditions of the study.

We've already seen that systematic variance affects the means: the swimmers swam faster in one condition than the other. How can nonsystematic variance affect the means? By chance: Suppose the researcher randomly assigned the swimmers to the experimental and control groups. Because random assignment is nonsystematic, it *usually* produces fairly equal groups, especially when each group has a substantial number of subjects, say, more than 25. But random procedures sometimes distribute factors less equally—for example, one of the groups of swimmers may be *by chance* more motivated or just stronger. In other words, variance is rarely distributed in a perfectly nonsystematic manner across groups, and error variance almost always affects the numerical differences between groups at least a little. As we'll see later, this is the reason researchers need to do statistical analyses of their data.

We said earlier that some variance is more desirable than others. In designing studies, researchers choose and apply methods with an eye toward *maximizing* systematic variance from the independent variable and *minimizing* variance from the other sources, extraneous variables, and error variance. We'll discuss in later chapters the methods that researchers can apply to achieve these goals.

RELIABILITY

Suppose Beth is a swimmer who's trying to control her weight so that she will have less mass to move during contests. The old scale she uses at home gives unreliable readings: when she got on and off the scale three times in a row without doing anything to change her true weight, the readings were 138, 142, and 139. And none of these readings is the same as the 140 reading she got from another scale at home she tried immediately after. This example illustrates that measurement unreliability can be seen within the same scale and in comparison with another one. The **reliability** of a measurement procedure refers to the degree of consistency or dependability of the data it produces. If the true value has not changed, a reliable measurement procedure should produce the same outcome when applied repeatedly or applied by another observer.

Measurements of behavior are almost never perfectly reliable. Scientists assume that a measure consists of two components: the *true score* and *measurement error*. Beth's old scale clearly had a lot of measurement error. In most cases, measurement error is less when assessments are made with electronic or mechanical devices than when made by people. This contrast can be seen in speed and ratings data in sports: Elapsed time data in swimming or downhill skiing is very precise and consistent, but qualitative ratings of figure skating vary a good deal, especially across judges (Bragg, 2002). Researchers can assess the reliability of their measurement procedures in several ways, and we'll consider a few.

One approach involves examining the records collected independently by two observers of the same behavior to ascertain their degree of consistency, which is called **interobserver reliability** (or *interrater reliability* or *interobserver agreement*). If the data represent the frequency of behavior, researchers usually calculate the reliability with the *sessions total method*, summing the data for a session for each observer, dividing the smaller total by the larger, and multiplying by 100 to get the percentage of agreement. An average is calculated across sessions and subjects. The general rule of thumb is that 80% agreement is the minimum acceptable level (Sulzer & Mayer, 1972). Similar approaches can be used to assess the coders' reliability in content analyses of archival data. When the data are of duration or magnitude, researchers often use a *correlation method* to calculate interobserver reliability: The data for each observer are entered in a correlational analysis. The higher the correlation coefficient, the more reliable the assessment. For instance, in a study we described earlier on infants' habituation to visual stimuli, two observers scored the babies' scanning time from a videotape (Ruddy & Bornstein, 1979). The correlational analysis produced a coefficient of .88, and .80 is usually considered the minimum level for acceptable reliability.

Correlational approaches are also used for establishing the reliability of a survey. One method retests people, usually days or weeks apart, using the same survey; another separates the items of a survey into two sets. In either case, the procedure yields two scores for each of the individuals tested, and these data are entered in a correlational analysis. A coefficient of .70 is usually the cutoff for acceptable reliability. We will examine these methods in detail in Chapter 6 when we discuss correlational strategies in research.

VALIDITY

Suppose judges of figure skating assessed the complexity and precision of each jump or other feat to score the *artistic merit* of the performance. Even if this assessment is reliable, it would not be very valid because it is measuring another construct, technical skill. The **validity** of a measurement procedure is the degree to which it actually assesses what it is intended or claims to measure. If you were doing a study of stress from life events and used a scale of daily hassles, your measurement would have low validity.

How can we tell whether a measurement procedure is valid? Several approaches are used. The simplest, called **face validity,** evaluates whether the procedure *looks like* it measures what it is supposed to assess. This approach is not as sophisticated as others. It involves judging subjectively whether the procedure appears "on the face of it" to assess the construct. Suppose you wanted to find a survey that measures stress from life events and came across two surveys, each purporting to measure stress. One asks about the person's experience of major situations, such as a divorce or illness of a family member, and the other asks about having too much work to do, being stuck in traffic, or having an argument with a clerk. The former survey has a good deal of face validity for assessing life events, and the latter does not. Although face validity is useful in deciding whether a survey should receive further consideration in your selection, it is usually not a sufficient method for making the final decision. Other more sophisticated approaches use statistical analyses, particularly correlational methods, to describe the validity of measures more precisely. We will examine these methods when we discuss nonexperimental strategies in Chapter 6.

For measurement procedures to be useful in science, they must be reasonably reliable and valid. Because the scores from a highly reliable measure are consistent, we can have confidence that they are close to the true value. If a measure is highly valid, we can be confident that it measures the intended construct. These features are important when selecting measurement procedures to use in a study and when interpreting the results of past studies.

MEASUREMENT BIAS

All studies have the potential for *measurement bias*—that is, incorrect assessments with a consistent pattern—and the source of bias can be the participant or the observer. Probably in most cases the bias occurs unconsciously, rather than deliberately. Measurement bias usually has a bigger impact on the data's validity than on their variance or reliability.

Bias from the Participants

If you were a research participant, wouldn't you try to figure out what the study is about and is attempting to find? People do that. Aspects of the study that participants employ to determine its purpose are called **demand characteristics** (Orne, 1962). To the extent that individuals think they've figured it out, their behavior may be affected. For example, if they think they know the purpose, rightly or wrongly, and want to "help" the researcher, they may try to behave in ways they think will support the research hypothesis. This is one way participants can be the source of measurement error.

A biasing process relating to demand characteristics is called social desirability. In **social desirability bias,** individuals behave in ways they think are socially acceptable. For instance, when filling out a survey, they overreport their good qualities or behaviors and underreport their bad ones. They answer as they think they "should," hesitating to reveal that they perform certain behaviors, hold particular beliefs or attitudes, or have certain problems. Studies comparing self-reports and archival records of actual behavior have found that substantially more people claim to go to church regularly and to have given to charity than is actually the case (Hadaway, Marler, & Chaves, 1993; Parry & Crossley, 1950). Some evidence indicates that enhancing people's perception of privacy can reduce social desirability bias. Researchers randomly assigned male teenagers to respond on paper or on a computer to an anonymous survey on HIV-risk sexual behavior, such as engaging in male–male sex and sex with an intravenous drug user. The results showed far higher reports of risky behavior among those who responded on computer (Turner, Ku, Rogers, Lindberg, & Pleck, 1998).

Participants in survey research can produce measurement error in another way called response set bias. If people use **response set bias,** they give similar answers or ratings—high, low, or somewhere in the middle—across most or all items in a survey, regardless of the meaning of each question. For instance, some people seem to be *yea-sayers,* acquiescing to almost any statement: They agree to both pro and con statements on an issue, such as their approval of abortion (*naysayers* would do the opposite). Other people give almost all answers near the middle, seeming to avoid giving very high or low ratings. Three methods can be used to reduce response set bias. First, include items that are phrased in positive and negative directions, such as "I worry a lot about . . ." and "I almost never worry about . . ." (some items will need to be reverse-scored). Doing this makes it more difficult to be a yea- or naysayer. Second, using a rating scale with an even number of alternatives eliminates the option of choosing the exact middle score. Third, using a rating scale with a large range, say, more than 6 points, sometimes reduces each type of response set bias by making high and low scores "too extreme" and giving respondents room in the middle to spread out their ratings. It's a good idea to decide in advance how you will deal with surveys with suspected response set bias. Appendix B discusses ways to identify and deal with erroneous data.

Bias from the Observer

A classic study had research confederates go to psychiatric hospitals, posing as possible patients who claimed only one symptom of mental illness: They heard a voice that said "dull," "empty," and "thud" (Rosenhan, 1973). They tried to behave otherwise in their normal ways. They were diagnosed as schizophrenic, and thereafter, the hospital staff interpreted their normal behavior, such as taking notes on their experiences, as evidence of their illness. The fact that the confederates were admitted to the hospital and diagnosed produced expectations in the staff, coloring their observations. **Observer bias** refers to measurement error that results from observers' expectations of what they will perceive.

How can researchers reduce or prevent observer bias? We will discuss two ways, both of which we've seen before. First, researchers can automate data collection, using electronic or mechanical devices to measure the behavior. Second, they can limit the information about the study that they give to the observers. We saw a method in Chapter 1 called a *blind* procedure in which the observer is unaware of the goals of the study or the purpose of the observations. This method was used in the study in the opening story of the present chapter: the observers of the infant and toddler play behaviors did not know that the purpose of the research was to examine age differences in social behavior. By being blind to the purpose of the study, the observers were unlikely to have biased expectations of the social behavior they would see in the infants and the toddlers.

DATA ANALYSIS: THE BASICS

Some students wonder, "Why do we need to analyze data? Won't the outcome of our study be obvious just by looking at the data?" Occasionally it is, but usually it's not. For instance, as students look through the "raw data," the unanalyzed scores they collected, they rarely think they found the effects they hoped to find. Without the aid of statistical analyses, people often misperceive research findings, either seeing patterns that don't exist or not seeing patterns that do. Statistical analyses help us see clearly what we have and have not found. These analyses involve both *descriptive statistics* and *inferential statistics*

DESCRIPTIVE STATISTICS

One step in clarifying our findings is seeing how the data are distributed in each *data grouping*, or set of data for a specific research condition. **Descriptive statistics** provide an abstract picture of the distribution of data in a grouping in terms of its central tendency and variability. We discussed variability earlier when we introduced the concept of variance, a measure of how diverse the scores are. The **standard deviation** (*SD*) is the most commonly reported descriptive statistic for variability; it is calculated by taking the square root of the variance. A simpler and less useful measure of variability is the **range,** or the span between the lowest and highest scores.

The term *central tendency* refers to the area of the range where the data tend to be concentrated. There are three commonly used measures of central tendency. The **mean** is the arithmetic average of a data grouping, which is calculated by dividing the sum of the scores by the number of scores: *M,* or $\overline{X} = (\sum X) \div n$. The mean is the most commonly cited measure of central tendency. The **median** is the middlemost score when the data are arranged from lowest to highest (if there is an even number of scores, it is the average of the middle two). The median is used mainly when the data include a few extreme scores at the high or low end of the scale, because the mean misrepresents the central tendency under those circumstances. The **mode** is the most frequently occurring score in a set of data.

INFERENTIAL STATISTICS

We conduct research to test a hypothesis that groupings of data are either related to or different from each other. Once we know statistically what the distribution of each data grouping looks like, we want to decide whether they support the hypothesis. Making this decision must take into account the possibility that the relationship or difference the data distributions portray is really just a chance happening. Although we can never be 100% certain that the relationship or difference our data show is real, we can calculate the *probability that we would obtain these distributions when no relationship or difference actually exists.* This calculation is done with **inferential statistics**—mathematical procedures for determining the probability that relationships or differences in our data actually exist in the population from which our sample of subjects was drawn. Inferential statistics also tell us whether the magnitude of a relationship or difference is so large that it is not likely to have resulted from chance alone.

There are two types of inferential statistics. **Parametric statistics** test hypotheses based on data that allow us to estimate the *parameters*—that is, the descriptive statistics, such as the mean or standard deviation—of the population from which the research sample of subjects was drawn. Thus, to use parametric statistics the data we analyze must be on an *interval* or *ratio* scale, and the variable should have an approximately *normal distribution* (bell shaped) in the population. **Nonparametric statistics** test hypotheses that do not involve parameters; nonparametric statistics are used when the data are on a *nominal* or *ordinal* scale or the data are *not normally distributed.* The type of data we collect determines whether we use parametric or nonparametric inferential statistics to test our hypotheses.

The *purpose* of the statistical analysis and the *number of data groupings* being analyzed are other critical factors that affect which statistics researchers use. Statistical analyses are done with one of two purposes: to *assess the relationship* and to *assess the difference* between data groupings. Table 4.1 shows how the purpose of

TABLE 4.1

Parametric and Nonparametric Statistical Tests to Assess Relationships and Differences for Two Groupings of Data and More Than (>) Two Groupings (all tests can be performed on SPSS)

Purpose and type of test	No. of data groupings	Paired groupings[a]	Name of test
Assessing relationships			
Parametric statistics (interval or ratio scales)	2	Yes	Pearson r
	> 2	Yes	Pearson r if testing each grouping against each other
	> 2	Yes	Multiple regression testing if two or more groupings predict another grouping
Nonparametric statistics (nominal or ordinal scales)	2	Yes	Spearman (rho) rank correlation (ordinal scale)[b]
Assessing differences			
Parametric statistics (interval or ratio scales)	2	Yes/no	Paired/independent t test
	> 2	Yes/no	Analysis of variance (ANOVA)
Nonparametric statistics (nominal or ordinal scales)	2	Yes	McNemar test (nominal scale) Wilcoxon matched-pairs signed-ranks test (ordinal scale)
	2	No	Chi-square (χ^2, nominal scale) Mann-Whitney U (ordinal scale)
	>2[c]	Yes	Cochran Q test (nominal scale) Friedman χ^2 (ordinal scale)
	> 2[c]	No	Chi-square (χ^2, nominal scale) Kruskal-Wallis H or k-sample median test (ordinal scale)

[a]Other names for paired data groupings are dependent groups, matched groups, related samples, repeated measures, and within-subjects testing. Yes/no means that versions of the test will accept either paired or independent data groupings.

[b]The table does not include nonparametric statistics for assessing relationships with *nominal* data (*phi coefficient* or *point biserial correlation* tests) because they are used mainly to assess effect size.

[c]If the design is a factorial—that is, it combines more than one independent variable (see Chapter 9), nonparametric statistics provide only an incomplete or fragmented analysis.

Sources: Siegel (1956) and Tabachnick & Fidell (2001)

the analysis affects the parametric (shaded sections) and nonparametric statistics we can use to analyze two or more data groupings. To use the table to identify the statistical test to use for an analysis, you will need to make four decisions:

1. Do you want to assess a relationship or differences between your data groupings?

2. Are your data on interval or ratio scales (use parametric statistics) or on nominal or ordinal scales (nonparametric)?

3. How many data groupings will be included in the analysis?
4. Are the data in the groupings paired—that is, does each subject you tested have a score in more than one grouping in the analysis?

We will discuss each of the statistical tests in the table in detail in chapters that cover the corresponding research designs.

STATISTICAL SIGNIFICANCE

Calculating inferential statistics enables us to decide whether a relationship or difference in two or more data groupings is statistically **significant**—that is, it is sufficiently great that it probably didn't happen just by chance. The term *significant* refers to a mathematical concept and doesn't mean "important." If an outcome is statistically significant, we can reject the *null hypothesis* (null means "not any" from the Latin *nullus*) that there is no relationship or difference in favor of the research hypothesis that the study is testing. How do we decide whether the outcome is significant? The process is in some ways like a jury's decision in a criminal trial. They decide that the defendant is guilty if it seems extremely unlikely ("beyond a reasonable doubt") that he or she is innocent, which in research is like the null hypothesis: the independent variable had no effect.

Calculating inferential statistics leads to two numerical figures. One figure is the *statistical value*, such as the *r* value from a correlational analysis and the *t* and *F* values from the *t* test and analysis of variance (ANOVA), respectively. The second figure states the *probability* of obtaining the pattern of data in the analysis when no relationship or difference actually exists. In other words, the probability figure expresses the likelihood that we would be making an error (called *Type I error*) in rejecting the null hypothesis. As the statistical value increases in absolute terms—that is, disregarding + or − signs—the probability of making a Type I error decreases. Thus, the probability figure reflects the *confidence* we can have that a significant outcome is real, not just due to chance. This is like "beyond a reasonable doubt." Suppose we calculated a *t* test to assess reaction time differences between an experimental group and a control group, each with 30 subjects. If the statistical value (*t*) were 2.01, the difference would be significant at the .05 level of confidence, and if the *t* were 3.47, the difference would be significant at the .001 level of confidence. Notice that as the *t* value increased, the probability of making an error in rejecting the null hypothesis decreased from 5 chances in 100 to 1 chance in 1000. Although the traditional, and arbitrary, minimum confidence level (called *alpha*) for rejecting the null hypothesis is .05, researchers often report the exact probability level their statistical program gives for the analysis. Because researchers do studies in an effort to reject the null hypothesis, they hope the analysis testing their research hypothesis will produce a high statistical value and a low probability of making a Type I error.

What determines the magnitude of the statistical value? To answer this question, we'll use the *t* test example we just discussed and our previous discussion of variance in research data—systematic variance due to the independent variable, systematic variance due to extraneous variables, and error variance.

Conceptually, the statistical value that we calculate in inferential statistics, such as *t* tests, is a ratio of systematic and error variance:

t (statistical value) = (systematic variance + error variance) ÷ error variance

The systematic variance can be due to the independent variable and extraneous variables. In well-controlled experiments, researchers maximize the amount of systematic variance due to the independent variable and minimize extraneous and error variance. We'll see in Chapter 5 how researchers can control variance.

Is it possible to not reject the null hypothesis when in fact it is false, that is, when a relationship or difference really exists? Yes, and this is called *Type II error.* Sometimes a statistical test has too much **power,** or the sensitivity of a statistical procedure to detect a relationship or difference. The type of statistic used and the research design can affect the power—for example, parametric tests are generally more powerful than nonparametric tests, so it is a good idea to make assessments on interval or ratio scales. But the size of the sample can play an especially big role. Having too few subjects risks Type I error; having too many risks Type II error. Sometimes researchers find significant outcomes when the actual relationship or difference between data groupings is nonexistent or trivial because they had hundreds of participants when dozens should have been enough and would have given a fairer statistical test. For this reason, the *Publication Manual* of the APA (2001) recently began to require that for main analyses researchers report an additional statistic called **effect size,** a form of correlation reflecting in standard units the amount of variation in the dependent variable that is linked to the independent variable. For most measures of effect size, a value of .51 reveals that the independent variable accounts for about half the variation in the dependent variable, whereas .10 and .90 indicate, respectively, that the independent variable accounts for very little and almost all the variance in the dependent variable. Sample size does not affect effect size.

Statistical significance and effect size are complementary issues in understanding and interpreting research results. A significant outcome tells us that a study found a reliable relationship or difference in the variables tested, and effect size tells us its magnitude. The knowledge presented in this chapter can help you decide how to measure variables, make your measurements precise, and interpret the meaning of the data you collect. This knowledge will help you to examine research reports more critically and to design sound research of your own.

SUMMARY

Deciding exactly what to measure and how to measure it are extremely important aspects of research design that form the operational definition of the concept we are studying. If we collect data by observing overt behavior, such as by measuring the absolute threshold and difference threshold in studies of psychophysics, we need to make sure reactivity does not bias the subjects' behavior. Observing covert behavior is often done by taking physiological measures or by using self-report measures. Surveys may include closed-ended and open-ended items, which may take the form of Likert scales, graphic rating scales, segmented rating scales, and numerical rating scales.

Unobtrusive approaches for collecting data often use remnant measures, particularly physical traces and archival data. When collecting data on naturally occurring behavior, researchers can use event sampling and time sampling to obtain representative data if it is not possible to get complete records of the behavior. Quantitative data include frequency, duration, and magnitude measures. Because qualitative data are in narrative form, researchers must use content analysis to convert them into numbers if statistical analyses are planned. The data we collect can be on a nominal, ordinal, interval, or ratio scale.

Some data show little variance, and some show a lot. The variance we find in our data can include systematic variance from independent variables, systematic variance from extraneous variables, and error variance. Researchers try to maximize the reliability and validity of their data, such as by assessing interobserver reliability and face validity. All approaches for assessing behavior have the potential for biased measurement. Bias from the participants can include demand characteristics, social desirability bias, and response set bias. By fostering the participants' perception of privacy and by structuring surveys to discourage response sets, researchers can reduce bias from the participants. Keeping the observer blind to the study's purpose and goals can prevent observer bias.

Statistical analyses help us see what a study has and has not found. Descriptive statistics include measures of variability (standard deviation and range) and of central tendency (mean, median, and mode). Researchers can analyze their data with two types of inferential statistics—parametric and nonparametric—to discover whether they have found a significant relationship or difference between two or more data groupings. The power of the statistical test and the effect size affect the likelihood of a significant outcome.

KEY TERMS

psychophysics	time sampling	demand characteristics
absolute threshold	frequency	social desirability bias
difference threshold	duration	response set bias
reactivity	magnitude	observer bias
self-report	content analysis	descriptive statistics
survey	nominal scale	standard deviation
closed-ended items	ordinal scale	range
open-ended items	interval scale	mean
Likert scales	ratio scale	median
graphic rating scales	variance	mode
segmented rating scales	extraneous variable	inferential statistics
numerical rating scales	error variance	parametric statistics
remnant measures	reliability	nonparametric statistics
physical traces	interobserver reliability	significant
archival data	validity	power
event sampling	face validity	effect size

REVIEW QUESTIONS

1. Describe the Gibson and Walk (1960) study of infant depth perception and the data they collected.

2. What are performance *speed, reaction time,* and *habituation* measures?

3. How are the *method of limits, method of constant stimuli,* and *method of adjustment* used in determining absolute and difference thresholds?

4. Describe some concerns and problems in collecting data on social and emotional behavior.

5. Define the measure called the *event-related potential* and the findings of Leynes and Bink (2002) on people's memory for actions.

6. Describe the various forms of rating scales used in surveys.

7. Describe the recommended tips for composing a survey.

8. Define the remnant measures called *physical traces* and *archival data,* giving two examples of each. What are the pros and cons in using remnant measures?

9. What are *event sampling* and *time sampling,* and why are they used?

10. What are the three types of quantitative data?

11. What is *content analysis,* and why is it used with qualitative data?

12. Define and give two examples each of the four scales of measurement.

13. Describe in detail the three critical aspects of data: *variance, reliability,* and *validity.*

14. What types of measurement bias in research data can come from the subjects?

15. Describe in detail what *descriptive* and *inferential statistics* are.

16. What does the term statistically *significant* mean, and how are *power* and *effect size* important?

RESOURCES

BOOKS, CHAPTERS, AND ARTICLES

Birnbaum, M. H. (2001). *Introduction to behavioral research on the Internet.* Upper Saddle River, NJ: Prentice Hall.

Goldstein, G., & Herson, M. (Eds.). (1990). *Handbook of psychological assessment* (2nd ed.). New York: Pergamon.

Schmidt, W. C. (1997a). World-Wide-Web survey research: Benefits, potential problems, and solutions. *Behavior Research Methods, Instruments, & Computers, 29,* 274–279.

Schmidt, W. C. (1997b). World-Wide-Web survey research made easy with WWW Survey Assistant. *Behavior Research Methods, Instruments, & Computers, 29,* 303–304.

INTERNET SITES

http://psych.fullerton.edu/mbirnbaum/programs/surveyWiz.htm This Website gives a program for making simple surveys to use on the Internet, which may be used free of charge for noncommercial scholarly endeavors.

http://psych.hanover.edu/Research/exponnet.html An APS Website that lists studies that are collecting data on the Internet.

http://survey.psy.buffalo.edu/ This site gives a program for making surveys to use on the Internet, which may be used free of charge for noncommercial scholarly endeavors.

http://www.unl.edu/buros/ A site of the Buros Institute of Mental Measurements with links to thousands of social science tests.

http://www.zoomerang.com An online program for constructing and administering surveys on the Internet.

ARCHIVAL DATA SOURCES ON THE INTERNET

http://americanheart.org The American Heart Association site with data about heart disease and stroke and information on their causes and treatment.

http://www.cancer.org The American Cancer Society site with data about cancer and information on its causes and treatment.

http://www.census.gov The Website of the U.S. Bureau of the Census with population data for the United States.

http://www.cdc.gov/nchs The U.S. Centers for Disease Control site (National Center for Health Statistics) with data on the prevalence of illnesses in the United States.

http://www.samsa.gov The Website of the National Clearinghouse for Alcohol and Drug Information in the United States.

http://who.org The World Health Organization site with data about worldwide illnesses and causes of death.

APPLICATION ACTIVITIES

ACTIVITY 4–1: OBSERVING OVERT BEHAVIOR

Go to a public place where students spend time, such as the campus library or student center, and pick out a student who is at least several feet away to observe without his or her knowing. Count and keep a tally of the frequency of the person touching his or her head or hair during each of 10 consecutive minutes. If the person leaves before the time limit, pick another student and start over. Be sure to have a watch, piece of paper, and pen or pencil available. What difficulties did you find in collecting the data?

ACTIVITY 4–2: COMPOSING CLOSED-ENDED ITEMS

Write closed-ended items for a survey to assess daily hassles. Start by writing four items that have flaws and then rewrite them so that one you think they are "good." What were the flaws in the first four items, and why are the "good" versions better?

Go online to one of the two Websites listed in Internet Sites under Resources that provide programs for composing an Internet survey. Consult Box 4.1 (Composing a Survey) and then construct a brief Internet survey of several items on any psychology topic you wish. Also have items to get demographic information.

ACTIVITY 4–4: SCALES OF MEASUREMENT

For each of the following examples of data, indicate which of the four scales of measurement is being used.

1. Blindfolded participants taste a few potato chips from each of four bags and move the bags so that they are in order from best to worst.
2. Blindfolded participants taste three different colas and rate how good each one tastes.
3. Observers watch subway riders and measure with a stopwatch how long they look at any other person during a 5-minute period.
4. A survey asks individuals to state their religious affiliation.
5. A survey asks respondents to state their height.
6. A teacher counts the number of correctly spelled words on a spelling test.

ACTIVITY 4–5: DESCRIPTIVE STATISTICS

Using the ten scores—2, 8, 6, 5, 7, 1, 4, 2, 2, 3—determine the values of the following descriptive statistics:

1. Mean
2. Median
3. Mode
4. Range

CHAPTER 5
EXPERIMENTAL STRATEGIES

PROLOGUE

Can psychotherapy reduce nightmares? If so, what aspects of treatment are responsible for the improvement? These are the questions William Miller and Marina DiPilato (1983) pursued in a study with 32 adults, mostly women recruited through advertisements, who had suffered for many years from frequent nightmares that would awaken them from sleep. These people received an initial interview to assess the history, frequency, and intensity of their nightmares; they also filled out surveys to assess emotional and personality adjustment and dream content. They were then randomly assigned to one of three therapy conditions that formed the independent variable:

- *Relaxation training.* Six weekly 45-minute sessions of training in progressive muscle relaxation, in which individual clients would sit or lie quietly and focus their attention on specific muscle groups while alternately tightening and relaxing those muscles.
- *Systematic desensitization.* Six weekly 75-minute sessions in which individual clients were trained in and applied relaxation to calm themselves while imagining nightmare scenes that have increasingly distressing content.
- *Delayed treatment.* Participants were informed that they would receive treatment, but it would be delayed for 4 months. When they received treatment, half got relaxation training and half got systematic desensitization.

Prior research had found preliminary evidence for the value of relaxation training and of desensitization in treating nightmares. But because systematic desensitization procedures include relaxation, it was possible that only relaxation was responsible. Having a delayed treatment condition enabled the researchers to compare the relaxation and desensitization treatments against no treatment for the first few months. The main dependent variables were the frequency and intensity of the nightmares.

The schedule for the experiment was as follows. For the first 6 weeks, the clients in the relaxation and desensitization conditions received treatment. From weeks 6 to 15, participants in all three conditions mailed in sleep and dream diaries. At about week 15, all participants were interviewed individually to collect data on nightmare frequency and intensity; the delayed treatment began soon after and continued for 6 weeks. At week 25, clients in all three conditions were interviewed about the frequency and intensity of their nightmares. Data analysis revealed that at week 15, nightmares for the treated groups had declined in frequency by nearly 80% (from a mean of 9.4 per week to 2.0) and intensity by about 32%; the delayed treatment group showed no change. Nightmare frequency, but not intensity, was significantly lower at week 15 with each type of treatment than with no (that is, delayed) treatment. By week 25, all three groups had received therapy and had much lower nightmare frequencies than at the start of the study, and the desensitization group showed continued declines in nightmare intensity, which was now significantly lower than in the other conditions. These results suggest that relaxation and systematic desensitization can reduce nightmare frequency and that improvements in intensity continue and are greater with desensitization than with relaxation alone in the weeks after treatment.

In this part of the book, we discuss the most commonly used research strategies in psychology. This chapter covers experimental strategies; the next covers nonexperimental strategies. The Miller and DiPilato (1983) research on treating nightmares used an experimental strategy. What methodological features did it have that qualify it as an experiment? We'll answer this question at various points in this chapter after reviewing the characteristics of experiments.

The noun *experiment* has more than one meaning: a careful test of a hypothesis under controlled conditions, for instance, or a tentative trying out of a procedure or idea—as in, "I added some nutmeg to the recipe as an experiment." Scientists generally have the former meaning in mind when they refer to an experiment, and they sometimes call it a "true" experiment to clarify their meaning.

CHARACTERISTICS OF "TRUE" EXPERIMENTAL STRATEGIES

Chapter 1 introduced the concept of experimental strategies in research and described some basic characteristics that distinguish experimental from nonexperimental strategies. Research using an experimental strategy typically:

- *Manipulates,* or systematically controls the levels of, an *independent variable* to test its potential or suspected influence on a *dependent variable* that the researcher assesses to see if its value corresponds to variations in the independent variable. In Miller and DiPilato's experiment on treating nightmares, the researchers manipulated the therapy conditions (the independent variable) the clients received to see how these variations influenced nightmare frequency and intensity (the dependent variables).
- *Compares the dependent variable under at least two situations,* usually by separating subjects into experimental and control groups or conditions. An **experimental group** receives a special, manipulated level of the independent variable. A **control group** is used as a baseline for comparison—in its most common form, it is kept at its usual, unmanipulated level of the independent variable. In the study on treating nightmares, the experimental groups were the relaxation training and systematic desensitization conditions, and the control group was the delayed treatment condition.
- *Equates the subjects in the different conditions* before the manipulation, usually by randomly assigning individuals to conditions. The participants in the experiment on treating nightmares were randomly assigned to groups.
- *Controls unwanted effects of extraneous variables* on the dependent variable(s). We'll see later that the Miller and DiPilato study controlled for several possible extraneous variables, but we can cite one example now that pertains to the skills of the therapists who administered the relaxation training and systematic desensitization. Therapists' skills can differ. If they do, it is possible that inadvertently the "good" therapists might be assigned to give one type of therapy, and the "not so good" ones might give the other. If this were to occur, an extraneous variable would exist that "confounds," or renders unclear, the effect of the independent variable. Miller and DiPilato tried to prevent this problem: they reported that "every therapist treated clients within both relaxation and desensitization conditions" (p. 872), which would spread the therapists across conditions and reduce the possibility of confounding.

Confounding refers to the situation in which the effect of an independent variable is rendered unclear because extraneous variable may have affected the dependent variable. Experimental strategies have an advantage over nonexperimental strategies of affording a high degree of control, which gives researchers the opportunity to eliminate confounding. Because well-designed studies using experimental strategies have these characteristics, their results allow researchers to make cause-effect conclusions.

CAUSAL INFERENCE

A conclusion that one circumstance or event causes another is called a **causal inference.** In science, a researcher's causal inference involves a rational process and specifies that variations in an independent variable had an effect on, or produced corresponding changes in, a dependent variable. We saw in Chapter 1 that research can lead to *cause-effect* conclusions if it clearly meets *all three* of the following criteria:

- *Covariation of variables*—as the independent variable changed, the dependent variable changed in a systematic and corresponding manner.
- *Causal time sequence*—it should be clear from the methods in the research that the presumed cause occurred before its effect.
- *Elimination of other plausible causes*—the methods in the research controlled all extraneous variables that could affect the dependent variable.

The diagram in Figure 1.2, which is reproduced on the inside of the front cover so that you can find and consult it more easily, compares the likelihood that well-designed and executed studies using experimental and nonexperimental strategies would meet each of the criteria for causal inference. The diagram indicates that studies using experimental strategies are far more likely to meet all three criteria than those using nonexperimental strategies. We will examine cause-effect issues in research using quasi-experimental, correlational, and descriptive strategies in later chapters.

The Miller and DiPilato (1983) research on treating nightmares meets the criteria for making cause-effect conclusions. It demonstrated *covariation of variables* by showing that nightmare frequency and intensity (the dependent variables) changed with the clients' treatment status—that is, whether they had gotten or not yet gotten relaxation training or desensitization. It established a *causal time sequence* because the relaxation and desensitization treatments occurred before changes in nightmare frequency and intensity; the dependent variables did not change until after the clients received treatment. And it addressed *other plausible causes,* or extraneous variables, by randomly assigning participants to conditions to make the groups equal before the manipulation and by using several other methods that we'll see later.

Being able to determine that certain variables cause changes in other variables is a critical feature in two of the goals of science, understanding and application. Having a full understanding of events or phenomena requires that we know why and under what conditions they occur. Applications of existing knowledge to benefit people and societies are far more likely succeed if we have a good understanding of the events or phenomena we want to change. The Miller and DiPilato results expanded our knowledge of why and under what conditions nightmares can be reduced, indicating that relaxation is helpful for decreasing the frequency of nightmares, but desensitization may be needed to reduce their intensity. In contrast, applications of scientific knowledge to help people eat low-fat diets to avoid getting colon cancer are not very sophisticated or effective yet. We lack a strong understanding of the processes that determine what people eat, or even the causes of colon cancer, partly because almost all of the relevant research has employed nonexperimental strategies. As a result, we know, for example, that people who eat high-fat diets are more likely than other people to develop colon cancer, which establishes a covariation of variables and causal time sequence. But we don't know that high-fat diets *cause* cancer because other plausible causes have not yet been eliminated—for instance, people who eat high-fat diets may also fail to eat *protective* vegetables, which may be the actual cause.

VARIABLES AND VARIANCE

Variables and variance are intertwined: to the extent that variables change in quantity or quality, they display variance. Researchers want some variables in their studies to display or produce a lot of variance and other variables to display or produce little or no variance. When using an experimental strategy, researchers hope the independent variable will be responsible for a lot of variance in the dependent variable, making the data for one group significantly different from another.

SYSTEMATIC VARIANCE FROM AN INDEPENDENT VARIABLE

Levels of the independent variable form the basis for separate groups or conditions in an experimental strategy. The variance an independent variable produces is intended to be *systematic*—it is expected to affect the data in one condition differently than in another. As a result, the mean scores for the dependent variable should be markedly different for these conditions if the independent variable is effective. Conceptually, we can think of the control group as having a "zero" level of the independent variable because it is not changed from its usual level and each experimental group as having more or less than zero, which may result in a higher or lower mean than the control condition.

How can the level be less than zero? Sometimes researchers want to see what happens when the level of the independent variable is less than usual. For example, an experiment arranged for healthy young adults, who usually engaged in little physical activity, to experience different activity levels for each of four consecutive months (Jennings et al., 1986). The four levels consisted of the people's usual activity (the control condition); below-normal activity, which included 2 weeks of rest in a hospital setting; and two above-normal activity levels in which they engaged in scheduled exercise. The dependent variables were physiological assessments taken at the end of each month. Compared with data for the usual (control) activity level, the participants' heart rate and blood pressure were significantly lower after months with above-normal activity. Below-normal activity did not alter heart rate or blood pressure, probably because the people's usual lives were already pretty sedentary. How much less activity can one get?

Researchers try to maximize the effect of an independent variable by using levels they expect will have markedly different effects on the dependent variable. How they manipulate and maximize the effects of an independent variable depends in part on the type of variable it is.

Types of Manipulated Independent Variables

When researchers manipulate an independent variable, they determine or control the level of the variable that each subject in each condition will experience in the experiment. In nonexperimental research strategies, independent variables are usually not manipulated, but in experimental strategies, they are. Whether researchers can manipulate a variable and how they do it depends on the type of variable it is. Although the range of factors that can be manipulated as independent variables is virtually limitless, most of them can be classified individually as belonging mainly in one of four categories: environmental, instructional, task or activity, and invasive variables.

Environmental variables involve physical or social features of the surroundings or situation the subject experiences during testing. One example we saw in earlier chapters is the study that manipulated the number of bystanders present (the independent variable) during an emergency and found that the greater the number of bystanders, the slower and less likely the participants were to act (the dependent variables). For other environmental variables, researchers might manipulate the amount of background noise to test its effects on hearing sounds accurately, the amount of reinforcement to see its effects on a child's learning, and the color of a laboratory room to test its effects on people's moods.

Instructional variables refer to variations in the directions or other information participants receive before having an experience or being tested. For example, a study that had people with asthma inhale several doses of a neutral (*placebo*) substance, but told them that succeeding doses had more and more of an allergic chemical, found that nearly half the people developed symptoms, some as full asthma attacks (Luparello, Lyons, Bleecker, & McFadden, 1968). Other instructional variables might include giving participants different instructions regarding how difficult the cognitive task they will perform will be or the strategies they should use in memorizing the list of nouns they will learn in the study.

Task or activity variables entail varying the quantity or quality of the actions or mission the subjects will engage in during the study. We've seen in this chapter two examples of research that varied the participants' task or activity as the independent variable. The Miller and DiPilato (1983) study had people with nightmares engage in different therapy conditions and the Jennings et al. (1986) study had individuals engage in different levels of physical activity. For other task or activity variables, researchers might manipulate the complexity of arithmetic or logical problems to solve, amount of frustration an activity produces, or the degree of similarity between stimuli in a visual discrimination task.

Invasive variables involve physical changes in the subject's body produced by administering drugs or performing surgery. For example, a researcher might want to see how much relief depressed patients get from different amounts of an antidepressant drug or how much pain reduction patients with chronic pain get from surgical techniques on their nervous systems.

With each type of independent variable, researchers typically would use at least one experimental and one control group or condition. For example, in a study with the environmental variable of reinforcement, the children in the experimental group would receive rewards for their performance, but those in the control group would not. With the instructional variable of asking participants to use specific memorization strategies, one experimental group might be told to form a visual image for each noun, another might be told to think of a rhyme for each noun, and a control group would simply be asked to learn the words. With the task or activity variable of problem complexity, the control group might be a very simple level of complexity. And with the invasive variable of using drugs to reduce depression, the study would have a control group that would not receive the drug or have a delay—of, say, several weeks—before receiving it.

Maximizing an Independent Variable's Effect

In the study on treating nightmares, the researchers manipulated the independent variable by setting up three conditions and determining which condition each participant would experience by applying a random assignment method. To maximize the likelihood that the conditions would have different effects on the dependent variables, they designed the three conditions to be as different from each other as possible.

Another example of maximizing an independent variable's effect comes from an experiment on people's memory for events that lead to a mentally shocking event (Loftus & Burns, 1982). The researchers showed college students a short video of a bank robbery in which a lone robber holds up a teller and runs with two men in pursuit into a parking lot, passing two boys who were playing. The video had two identical versions, except for the ending: the last 15 seconds was either violent or nonviolent. In the violent version, the robber fires a gun, and the "shot hits one of the boys in the face and he falls to the ground bleeding, his hands clutching his face" (p. 319). The nonviolent version ended by simply showing what was occurring in the bank: "the manager is informing the employees and customers about what has happened and asking everyone to stay calm." In a test of the students' memory, those who saw the violent version remembered fewer details relating to the robbery, such as the color of the robber's eyes or the large number on the football jersey of one of the boys, than those who saw the nonviolent version. Notice how the shocking nature of the violence was maximized: the person injured was a child, and he was shot in the face and bleeding. If he had been a man shot in the leg with pants covering the blood, it wouldn't have been so shocking. The nonviolent version is the control condition, and the contrast between the two levels of the independent variable is stark.

How can we maximize the effects of other types of independent variables? Let's look again at examples we used earlier. For instance, in a study with the environmental variable of reinforcement, when children in the experimental group perform well, we would give them rewards they like a lot, rather than weaker reinforcers. If the study used the instructional variable of asking participants to use specific memorization strategies, we might describe and have the participants practice how to form visual images for words or how to find rhymes. If we used the task or activity variable of problem complexity, we would select difficulty levels that were quite different between groups. And if the study used the invasive variable of antidepressant drugs, we would choose amounts that are very different, probably including one that is close to the maximum that is medically safe to take. How would we know before doing the study what levels to use? Sometimes our intuition will suffice, as in the study on the effects of mental shock on memory. But more often, we would examine relevant literature for guidance or clues and do pretests. For instance, to find out what rewards specific children would like a lot, we could interview them or have them or their parents fill out a survey on the child's reinforcer preferences (Sarafino, 2001).

To determine whether the levels an independent variable are different enough and affect the participants differently, researchers often apply a **manipulation check**—a test to verify the intended differential action of the independent variable's levels. Although manipulation checks can be applied during the study, they are usually conducted after the dependent variable has been measured. For example, in the Loftus and Burns experiment on people's memory for events that precede a mentally shocking event, the questions the researchers asked the participants after they saw the video of the bank robbery included one to assess how upsetting it was to watch the video. The ratings the participants gave were significantly higher, nearly twice as high, for the violent than the nonviolent version of the videotape. This suggests that the violent video was in fact more mentally shocking than the nonviolent version, confirming the state that the researchers proposed would lead to impaired memory.

Deciding on the levels of the independent variable to use in a study is a critical aspect of the design process. When researchers maximize an independent variable's effect, they move scores of the dependent variable from the different conditions farther apart. By moving the scores apart, they increase the systematic variance in the data they collect *and* the likelihood of finding a significant effect. Other sources of variance should be minimized because they reduce the likelihood of finding a significant effect or a clear, unconfounded cause-effect relationship.

Unwanted Sources of Variance

Two types of variance are undesirable, and researchers try to minimize them. One of them is systematic variance from extraneous variables, and the other is nonsystematic, "error" variance.

Systematic Variance from Extraneous Variables

If a factor other than the independent variable affects the data consistently in one research condition more than in another, that factor is an extraneous variable that is affecting the data in a systematic fashion. Extraneous variables threaten the internal validity of the research, confounding the effect of the independent variable. By **internal validity** we mean the degree to which the research results can be attributed to variations in the independent variable, rather than some other factor. The greater the internal validity, the more certain we can be that the independent variable *caused* whatever variation was found in the dependent variable. Experimental strategies produce high levels of internal validity, which is essential for meeting the three cause-effect criteria.

We'll examine a variety of extraneous variables later in this chapter that can threaten the internal validity of research, but we'll discuss one now. We've seen that a defining feature of the experimental strategy is that the subjects in different conditions of the study are equivalent before manipulation of the independent variable. If the subjects are not equivalent, confounding exists and compromises the study's internal validity. Sometimes nonequivalent groups are formed accidently and may go undetected for some time. One such case was a widely reported study of monkeys who developed ulcers after being in a stressful situation for several hours a day (Brady, 1958; Brady, Porter, Conrad, & Mason, 1958). Two monkeys were tested while sitting side by side in chairs that kept their bodies in place, but allowed them to move their heads, arms, and legs. Both monkeys would receive painful electric shocks periodically unless one of them, called the "executive," prevented the shock by pressing a lever; the other's lever did not work. For each pair, the executive was selected for that role on the basis of a pretest in which it responded at a high rate to avoid shocks. After a few weeks of this experience, executive monkeys, but not the others, began to die, and autopsies revealed that they had ulcers. The researchers concluded that the psychological stress of having to control the shock caused the ulcers.

How were the groups nonequivalent? Researchers began to suspect a problem in the design when attempts to replicate the findings failed. In addition, a replication with rats as subjects found the opposite effect: the animals that could not control the shock developed more ulcers than those that could (Weiss, 1968). Subsequent research revealed that the Brady research had a confounding from the way the subjects were assigned to the conditions (Weiss, 1977). It turns out that the likelihood of animals developing ulcers in long-term avoidance tasks increases with their rate of responding to prevent the aversive stimulus (such as shock), regardless of whether they can or cannot control it. Recall that the executive monkeys were the ones that responded at high rates in a pretest.

Four points can be made about this case and the formation of nonequivalent groups in general. First, we can see the self-correcting aspect of science at work. Replications failed to support Brady's findings, and researchers worked to find out why. Second, extraneous variables are not always easy to spot and may go undetected for a long time. Third, these studies were done before ethical guidelines existed for conducting research with animals. A review by an Animal Care and Use Committee might reject a proposal to do this type of research today or require alterations in the methods. Fourth, nonexperimental studies that use a quasi-experimental strategy often use nonequivalent groups deliberately, such as by forming separate groups of males and females or of people of different ages, to examine gender or developmental differences.

Nonsystematic, "Error" Variance

Nonsystematic variance has random effects, being as likely to increase as decrease scores in any research group or condition. As a result, it affects the data across conditions fairly equally and tends to increase the variance—that is, disperse the data—within each group or condition, without pulling the means apart. We saw in Chapter 4 that the calculated value from inferential statistics, such as the *t* test and analysis of variance, is a ratio of systematic and error variance (also called within-groups variance): the denominator in the calculation consists entirely of error variance. In addition, the higher the calculated value, the greater the likelihood of finding a significant difference. This means that the greater the error variance in the data, the lower the likelihood of finding a significant difference between conditions. Heightened error variance reduces the power of the statistical tests researchers use. In virtually all studies, researchers want to minimize nonsystematic, error variance. What produces error variance?

Most of the error variance in a study usually comes from *individual differences* among the subjects. Before people or animals enter a research project, they already differ in a great number of ways, such as their learning ability, prior experiences, physiological processes, emotionality, and sociopolitical views. They are individuals, and no two are exactly alike. You can see this more concretely by looking at Figure 5.1, which presents two sets of 30 boxes with numbers in them. The boxes represent hypothetical individual participants who were assigned to two research conditions, relaxation and desensitization therapy, and the numbers in each box are their scores on tests of four personality or motivational traits, such as conscientiousness or optimism, assessed before they started therapy. The scores in the same position (with the same font style) in the boxes represent the same trait. Now look at only the lower left scores (in bold font) and notice how they vary: They range from 15 to 83 in the relaxation group and 19 to 80 in the desensitization group, and few are the same. And if you look at each set of four scores, you will find no two identical sets. As a result of the preexisting differences among individuals, they are likely to be affected in different ways by the same level of the independent variable.

An example of the role of individual differences in the effect of an independent variable comes from the Miller and DiPilato (1983) experiment on treating nightmares. Interviews with the clients at week 25 indicated that there were differences in outcomes: in the relaxation group, for example, 37% reported having no more nightmares, 45% reported at least an 80% reduction, and 18% reported no change. Some individuals received a great deal of benefit from relaxation, and others got little benefit. What's more, in the desensitization group, 78% reported no more nightmares, and in the delayed treatment group, 20% said their nightmares were *worse* than before therapy. Much of this variation in outcomes resulted from individual differences. For instance, correlations revealed that the personality traits of the clients assessed before treatment were related to the degree of improvement they reported.

Other sources of error variance are *transient internal and external states* that the subjects or researchers may experience. When human or animal subjects are tested, some will be feeling especially well or in a very good mood, and others

Relaxation   **Desensitization**

51	35	53	54	44	55	83	54	26	38	40	78
37	25	28	58	58	55	60	58	34	59	37	64

13	78	42	84	49	71	61	48	42	77	66	64
61	93	83	59	54	62	27	46	57	48	80	84

48	61	29	47	84	77	47	83	35	57	30	43
22	66	35	62	59	87	78	91	67	56	21	27

63	58	67	37	57	35	47	79	11	36	55	37
77	70	38	82	79	56	53	68	37	57	36	45

28	79	32	42	37	63	49	62	51	73	29	59
38	43	59	48	67	44	76	72	58	88	59	58

54	75	69	23	39	52	63	89	46	74	31	38
73	26	44	29	35	70	44	34	71	31	38	42

65	36	38	88	35	38	69	46	39	23	38	19
72	76	81	72	39	31	41	74	34	91	63	32

46	87	67	45	26	72	52	47	67	37	55	85
16	32	42	92	41	53	40	77	52	46	68	52

35	41	56	38	39	46	24	38	65	76	35	54
46	88	15	41	53	52	20	55	80	28	73	72

68	18	59	75	33	54	58	39	36	72	33	53
68	30	26	45	64	44	25	33	45	89	19	47

FIGURE 5.1

Illustration of individual differences for 60 participants, represented by boxes with numbers in them, assigned to two research conditions, relaxation and desensitization therapy. The numbers in each box are scores on tests of four personality or motivational traits. The scores in the same position (with the same font style) in the boxes represent the same trait. The data for each trait show a great deal of variation within each group, and there are no two identical sets of data.

will not. Some will be alert, and others will be unusually tired. Some may be tested when construction noises from another room are a little distracting, and others will be tested in total quiet. These factors are transient, occurring for a short period of time or for only some individuals, and are likely to happen on a random schedule and have nonsystematic effects on the data. Also, the researchers may treat some subjects differently from others because of their own transient states, such as being tired, in a hurry, or in a bad mood at one time and not at another. Although the differences in treatment are likely to be fairly subtle, they may have large effects on the way the subjects behave. For instance, a researcher who works with rats as subjects may usually pet or stroke the animals while transporting them from their home cages to the testing apparatus, which may calm the subjects and make them less wary or emotional. If the researcher doesn't do this all the time, some animals will be more wary or emotional during testing than others, and this can affect how they react to stimuli or other features of the task. Similarly, a researcher may be friendlier to human participants or more precise in giving instructions at some times than at others, and this may alter the people's behavior.

Last, *measurement error* can be a source of nonsystematic variance, and we can illustrate its role with two examples. First, suppose you were conducting a study and measuring performance speed or reaction time as the dependent variable. If the measurements were made manually with a stopwatch, they might vary more and be less accurate than if they were made automatically with an electronic timing device. Why? There are many possible reasons. One reason could involve the accuracy of the apparatus itself: The stopwatch may be a less-accurate instrument than the electronic timing device. Another reason might be that manual activation of the stopwatch can involve human error, such as if the researcher is distracted momentarily. If one measurement approach is less consistent than another, it is a *less-reliable* measure. Second, suppose you were testing people with a survey, perhaps having them rate their agreement with several statements. If the statements contain words that are uncommon or have more than one meaning, for instance, the respondents will not know exactly what is being asked. This will affect their interpretations of the items and the ratings they give, with people who would have given the same ratings to a clearly phrased statement now giving different ratings. Once again, the reliability of the measurement would be compromised. If measurement errors affect the data in each condition of the study similarly, as they usually do, they tend to increase nonsystematic variance.

How can researchers control unwanted variance? The rest of this chapter addresses this question, examining the sources of the variance and how to minimize them.

CONTROLLING UNWANTED SYSTEMATIC VARIANCE

Controlling systematic variance in an experimental strategy involves maintaining equal groups of subjects across the research conditions and treating subjects in all conditions exactly the same except for the different levels of the independent variable(s). Research that employs tight control has a high degree of internal validity and is in a better position to draw definitive cause-effect conclusions. The following sections describe methods for controlling extraneous variables, beginning with ways to create and maintain equivalent groups of subjects.

CREATING AND MAINTAINING EQUAL GROUPS

We've seen that extraneous variables confound, or render unclear, the effect of different levels of the independent variable on the dependent variable, and that a critical source of confounding in an experiment is nonequivalent groups. Unplanned nonequivalent groups can occur in two ways. First, the groups may have been unequal from the start because of the way the subjects were placed in the groups, as happened in the "executive monkey" study described earlier. Second, groups that were originally equal may become unequal because some individuals may drop out before the study ends.

We will examine methods to prevent or control these problems, starting with the approach called random assignment. What does the term *random* mean? In everyday usage, it can have several meanings, including "accidental" or "without a definite plan, method, or aim." In science the term has a narrow meaning: **Random** refers to a process or event that occurs strictly by chance, with no possibility of bias. Random does not mean "haphazard" or "casual," which involve a lack of care, deliberation, or intention.

Random Assignment

Studies often compare two or more separate groups of subjects who have different levels of the independent variable and for this reason are described as using a **between-subjects** or **independent-groups design.** The most common and desirable method for creating equal groups in between-subjects designs before the independent variable is manipulated is random assignment. In **random assignment,** procedures are used to ensure that each subject to be tested has an equal and unbiased chance of being placed in each group or condition to be compared in the study. Independent-groups designs in which subjects are randomly assigned to conditions are called *randomized groups designs.*

People often assume that simply "intending" or "trying" to be unbiased is sufficient to randomize subjects and equalize groups, but it is not. For instance, some people might think a researcher could create equal groups by assigning participants to research conditions on the basis of where they choose to sit in the classroom in which they are tested. Those sitting on the left side are in one condition, and those on the right are in the other condition. But classroom seating is surely associated with personality and intellectual characteristics that might be extraneous variables. What about assigning participants alphabetically by last name—would that create equal groups? Probably not—for example, some first letters of last names tend to be disproportionately associated with certain ethnic groups. These methods are examples of haphazard or casual assignment, not random assignment

The mechanics underlying random assignment in independent-groups designs are based on the lottery procedure of "drawing lots," so that the outcome is determined by chance alone, which is unbiased. Although researchers can randomly assign subjects to conditions in several ways, we will describe three of the most common methods. The *simple random assignment* method just involves conducting an unbiased lottery. For example, in the Miller and DiPilato report on treating nightmares, the researchers described how they assigned clients to three conditions—relaxation, desensitization, and delayed treatment—in the following way:

> Randomization was accomplished by the second author drawing slips of paper without replacement from a total pool of 45 (15 slips naming each of the three groups). These slips were then sealed in individual envelopes and placed in files, which were assigned to clients according to their successive order of intake. (1983, p. 872)

In the typical lottery procedure, the person draws lots, such as labeled slips of paper or chips, from a container and cannot tell in advance from vision or touch which condition each lot designates. The term *without replacement* in the quotation means that each slip (or other lot) is not placed back in the container. If the drawing is done with replacement, the same slip could be drawn again. Flipping a coin to assign individuals to one of two conditions is another example of simple random assignment with replacement. Drawing lots with replacement usually produces groups with different numbers of subjects. A major advantage of random assignment by drawing lots without replacement is that the researcher can equalize the number of lots designating each condition, thereby keeping the number of subjects exactly or nearly the same across conditions, as Miller and DiPilato did.

An extension of the simple random assignment is the *block random assignment* method that adds a structure called "blocks," where a block consists of one slot for each condition in the experiment. The researcher carries out block random assignment in a stepwise sequence, filling all slots in each block with subjects, using a simple random assignment method without replacement, before moving to the next block. For example, if the study will have four groups of subjects, the researcher would make up four slips, one for each condition, and put them in a container. When the first subject arrives, the researcher would reach into the container and draw one slip, which identifies the group for this individual. The researcher draws from the three remaining slips for the second subject and from the two remaining slips for the third subject, assigning the fourth subject to the last remaining group by default. At that point one block is filled. For the next block, all four slips are again put in the container, and the procedure is repeated for the fifth through eighth subjects, filling that block. The procedure is repeated until all the planned blocks are filled. Block random assignment has two advantages. First, it yields the same number of subjects in each condition. Second, if the experiment takes a long time to complete because the subjects are tested individually, events that happen outside the experiment will not affect one condition differently from another because each block is filled at about the same time. In a college setting, for instance, student participants have more knowledge and different experiences as a semester progresses and across semesters, but these changes are not likely to confound the independent variable's effects because they will be spread across conditions, affecting each similarly. As a result, any changes like these that occur would tend to increase nonsystematic instead of systematic variance.

The *random distribution* method for assigning subjects to conditions involves simply organizing research materials randomly, usually just by shuffling them in a stack, before distributing them to the participants. For example, you might conduct a survey that used two different sets of instructions as the independent variable to see how they would affect the ratings the participants would give. If you know approximately how many participants you will test, you can make sure that the stack of materials contains the same number of surveys with each set of instructions, thereby allowing you to keep the number of participants in each condition the same or similar. A student in my research methods course used this approach in an experiment in which other students were asked to read a resume of a male applicant for a job in computer programming and rate his likely job performance. There were actually three versions of the resume that were identical except for the applicant's ethnic background—Caucasian, Asian, or African American—as indicated only by his name, place of part-time employment, and presidency of an ethnic organization. The researcher made 20 copies of each version, stapled one version to the survey, shuffled the stack several times, and distributed them to 60 participants in the shuffled order. Statistical analysis revealed a stereotypical prejudice: the Asian American had significantly higher job performance ratings than the two other applicants, which did not differ.

Sometimes researchers can streamline the lottery process by generating a list of random numbers in a computer program (Excel and SPSS have this feature, for example) or using a *table of random numbers,* like the one in Appendix B. The following is a brief version of a table of random numbers, with the digits presented in sets of three columns:

	Columns							
Rows	*1–3*	*4–6*	*7–9*	*10–12*	*13–15*	*16–18*	*19–21*	*22–24*
1	760	289	415	345	762	901	385	847
2	069	321	852	316	709	412	079	864
3	354	053	782	916	342	178	056	985
4	671	430	296	872	413	590	237	694
5	501	806	384	197	239	741	802	656

A table of random numbers is a list of digits that are arranged randomly by a special computer program that selects the digit for each position by conducting a lottery from the numbers 0 to 9. As a result, each digit has an equal chance of being in any position in the table, and the placement of successive digits is independent in every direction. This means that we can use single digits or any combination of digits, such as three- or five-digit sets, in any direction and starting from any position in the table. To use the table, you would need to decide in advance the number of digits to group and the direction you will use from an arbitrarily chosen starting point. For our examples, we'll begin at row 2, column 4 (the digit is 3, printed in color so you can find it easily) and move to the right, one row at a time.

Suppose we were assigning participants to two groups. We could use one digit at a time, dividing the possible numbers in half, such as by using even numbers (0 included) or 0 to 4 for experimental group and odd numbers or 5 to 9 for the control group. If we used the odd–even approach in the simple random assignment method, the first person to be tested would have the digit 3 and be in the control group. Moving to the right in the table, the digits (and groups) for the next 11 subjects in order would be: 2 (experimental), 1 (control), 8 (experimental), 5 (control), 2 (experimental), 3 (control), 1 (control), 6 (experimental), 7 (control), 0 (experimental), and 9 (control). Notice that the groups so far do not contain an equal number of participants—there are five experimental and seven control subjects. Because the computer draws each digit with replacement, always from a pool consisting of 0 to 9, the same digit can appear close together and be used again. To assign all the participants we will need, we would continue moving to the right and then down to additional rows. In Activity 5-2 at the end of this chapter, you can try out block randomization (which produces an equal number of subjects in each group) and randomizing for more than two groups.

Does random assignment create equivalent groups? It usually does, and its likely success increases with the number of subjects in the groups. Suppose we assign five participants to each of two therapy groups with the block random assignment method, and a pretest showed that they varied in a personality variable, such as optimism. Their scores in the order in which they were tested were: 31, 22, 62, 80, 68, 39, 50, 75, 47, and 53. Now, suppose we used the same odd–even approach we applied earlier with the same starting point in the table of random numbers. The block random assignment method would put the people with optimism scores of 31, 80, 68, 75, and 47 in the control group and those with scores of 22, 62, 39, 50, and 53 in the experimental group. By calculating the respective means (60.2 and 45.2), we see a higher numerical value for optimism in the control group than in the experimental group. With only five participants per group, the likelihood that random assignment will equalize groups is not high.

When the number of subjects per group is much higher—20 to 40—the likelihood that random assignment will equalize groups is quite high (Hsu, 1989). We can illustrate the success in equalizing larger groups by looking back at the data in Figure 5.1, which presents data generated by using a table of random numbers as hypothetical scores for four personality or motivational traits. Recall that each box represents a participant, and scores in boxes in the same position (with the same font style) represent the same trait. Are the traits fairly equal for the two groups? Let's look at the means for the relaxation and desensitization groups, respectively. For the scores in the upper left corners of the boxes (regular font), the means are 47.53 and 46.10; for the upper right (underlined), they are 55.47 and 55.93; for the lower left (bold) they are 50.33 and 49.77, and for the lower right (italic) they are 56.37 and 57.47. The means are fairly close for each of the traits. In addition, if we total the data in each box to give a composite score and compute the mean for each group, we see that these means (209.70 and 209.27) are quite close. If actual participants had gotten these scores and were randomly assigned to the conditions, the two groups would be equalized nicely before the researcher manipulated the independent variable. This is the kind of outcome researchers hope random assignment will produce.

Is it possible to test whether random assignment worked before carrying out a study? Most often researchers just assume the groups are equalized because they have a sufficient number of subjects, but if relevant data are available, it is useful to do a test to give greater credence to a causal inference, especially if the number of subjects is small. The procedure for doing the test simply involves performing a statistical analysis, such as a *t* test, on the data for the relevant variable. A nonsignificant outcome suggests that the groups are not markedly different (but we can't conclude they are the same). In the Miller and DiPilato (1983) study on treating nightmares, the researchers collected data on the participants' nightmare frequency and intensity history before assigning them to groups. Statistical analysis revealed no significant difference between relaxation, desensitization, and delayed treatment groups on these variables, supporting the researchers' view that the groups were not substantially different.

Matching

You may be thinking, "If we want groups to be equivalent, why don't we just match the subjects, one-for-one?" Actually, researchers sometimes match subjects as a way to equate groups. For instance, Bandura, Ross, and Ross (1963) conducted an experiment on the role of modeled aggression on children's aggressive behavior. The researchers formed four groups, each with 12 boys and 12 girls, by matching the children for ratings of the amount of aggression they displayed in nursery school interactions. Three experimental groups watched a real-life person, a filmed person, or a cartoon character performing distinctive aggressive acts against a Bobo doll; the control group did not see aggression. Before being given the opportunity to play individually with several toys, including the Bobo doll, the children experienced a mildly frustrating situation. Then, when allowed to play with the toys, the children who had seen aggression against the Bobo doll showed significantly more of the same acts they had witnessed. Studies that compare two or more matched groups of subjects who have different levels of the independent variable are described as using a **matched-subjects** (or *matched-groups*) **design.**

In the technique of **matching,** the researcher forms sets of subjects who are very similar on some characteristic, with each set containing the same number of subjects as there are conditions in the study. Each individual in each set is then assigned to a group, usually by random assignment without replacement. The characteristic that forms the basis for matching is called the *matching variable*, and it is typically known or expected to be strongly related to the dependent variable. For instance, suppose we were studying the effectiveness of two programs to prevent drug abuse in 11-year-olds at their school. We might want to match the children in the two programs and a control group on some variable that would relate strongly to their likely use of drugs in the future, such as their ratings of the availability of drugs in their neighborhoods. Availability is strongly related to use (Stein, Newcomb, & Bentler, 1987). We would take the three children with the highest ratings of availability and randomly assign them to the three groups. Then we would take the next three highest and randomly assign them, and so on. If the matching variable is not related to the dependent variable, the groups will not be equalized in any important way, and the procedure will be of little value. Often the matching variable and dependent variable are very similar or the same, such as when the study on modeling and aggression used measures of aggressive behavior as the matching variable and dependent variable. All of this assumes that there is a practical way of assessing the matching variable, which is essential, of course.

So far, matching sounds like an ideal way to equalize groups, but it isn't. The most critical problems with matching relate to choosing matching variables. Yes, drug availability is strongly related to future use, but so are other variables, such as whether the person's friends and family members use mood-altering substances, the person's commitment to religion, and personality traits, such as rebelliousness and impulsiveness (Sarafino, 2002). Which of these variables should be the matching variable? How about using more than one? There are two problems with using more matching variables. First, with each additional variable, the difficulty coordinating the use of data from each of them increases dramatically. For instance, what if a possible participant has a high level of one matching variable but a low level of another? Often such individuals are simply not used. Second, we are rarely sure when we have used all of the important variables. As one researcher has pointed out, experience has shown that even after matching carefully for one variable, participants

> were often still markedly different with respect to another; and once they were matched with respect to a second, there was still another way in which they differed, and so on—always the subjects seemed to be different, and different in a way which could very well have an effect on the results. (Helmstadter, 1970, p. 115)

As a result of these problems, matching to create equivalent groups is generally reserved for two circumstances. First, the researcher has access to only a small number of subjects. We saw earlier that random assignment methods are less successful with small than with large numbers of subjects. Second, the researcher wants to be sure that the groups are equivalent for a particularly important variable. For example, although the study by Bandura et al. (1963) on modeling and aggression had a substantial number of participants, they used matching. They probably did because they could identify one really important matching variable—the children's usual aggressive behavior—and wanted to ensure that the groups did not differ on it.

An important feature of matching variables is that some are easier to use than others. Some can be assessed without actually testing individuals, such as just by looking at him or her to determine the gender of the person or animal and by consulting school records to estimate the person's academic ability. Some variables are dichotomous, having only two values, such as gender, which makes them easier to coordinate with another matching variable. In the study by Bandura et al. (1963) on modeling and aggression, the researchers made sure that each group had 12 boys and 12 girls as they matched them for ratings of usual aggressive behavior. And some variables can be matched across groups by using only individuals with a particular characteristic, such as being a certain age or having a certain medical condition. But keep in mind that using this last approach can limit the external validity—that is, the ability to generalize the results to individuals without this characteristic.

One last point about matching is that researchers generally do not expect that the groups will be perfectly matched, even on the matching variable, unless the variable is dichotomous, such as gender. Assessments of almost all personality or behavioral variables usually have a good deal of variance, and the means for different groups may be close but are almost never identical. Keep in mind that random assignment does not make separate groups of individuals exactly equal either, but it usually becomes the preferred approach as the number of subjects per group increases. (Go to **Box 5.1**)

Box 5.1   STEPS IN THE MATCHING PROCEDURE

Suppose we were doing a study to test the effectiveness of using computerized tutorials, like those available with this book, to teach mathematics to 16 third graders who are not doing well in that subject, having grades of D or less. We would assign the students to two groups that would use their 1-hour study period at the school each day to learn math concepts and procedures either with computers or with standard workbooks, the control condition. The sample consists of eight boys and eight girls, but the boys have generally gotten higher grades. Because of the small number of participants, we'd use a matching procedure to equalize the two groups. Here are five steps we might use.

1. *Select the matching variable(s).* The most important way to select matching variables involves doing a literature search to find out what factors are strongly associated with the dependent variable, learning math. Let's suppose that our search revealed two factors are most important: gender (boys tend to do better in math than girls, which is reflected in our students' grades) and intellectual ability, as measured by intelligence (IQ) tests.

2. *Assess the matching variable(s).* Both of these variables are easy to assess, especially because the school already has recent IQ scores for all of the third graders. If another variable was chosen or the school didn't have the data, we would need to identify a way to measure the variable and carry out the assessment to obtain scores.

3. *List the numerical matching variable with names.* List the numerical scores, the IQs, keeping track of the individual's gender and which student has which score—in this case, by using the child's name.

102 F (Sue)	78 F (Patty)	93 F (Lori)	86 F (Kim)
84 F (Gina)	94 F (Ana)	96 M (Joe)	89 F (Jane)
94 M (Bob)	109 M (Rick)	105 M (Jim)	80 M (Sam)
104 F (Meg)	84 M (Matt)	89 M (Leo)	95 M (Hal)

4. *Form sets of scores.* Each set should contain the same number of subjects as there are conditions in the study (ours has two conditions) and should have scores that are adjacent in magnitude. A study with, say, four conditions would have four subjects in each set. If we had

continued

only one numerical matching variable, we would just list the sets in descending (or ascending) order of scores. But because we need to match two variables, we will list the IQ sets within gender, starting with the girls. This will enable us to make sure each group will have the same number of males and females.

Set 1: 104 F (Meg) and 102 F (Sue)   *Set 5:* 109 M (Rick) and 105 M (Jim)
Set 2: 94 F (Ana) and 93 F (Lori)   *Set 6:* 96 M (Joe) and 95 M (Hal)
Set 3: 89 F (Jane) and 86 F (Kim)   *Set 7:* 94 M (Bob) and 89 M (Leo)
Set 4: 84 F (Gina) and 78 F (Patty)   *Set 8:* 84 M (Matt) and 80 M (Sam)

5. *For each set, randomly assign subjects to groups.* By drawing lots, we place one participant from each set in the tutorial (experimental) group and one in the workbook (control) group. Look above at Set 1 that contains the girls with the two highest IQ scores. Now look below and see that random assignment placed Sue in the tutorial group and Meg in the workbook group. Looking at each set above, you can see how random assignment distributed these individuals below.

Tutorial group		Workbook group	
102 F (Sue)	109 M (Rick)	104 F (Meg)	105 M (Jim)
94 F (Ana)	95 M (Hal)	93 F (Lori)	96 M (Joe)
89 F (Jane)	89 M (Leo)	86 F (Kim)	94 M (Bob)
78 F (Patty)	80 M (Sam)	84 F (Gina)	84 M (Matt)

Did we equalize the groups on the matching variables? Yes, pretty well. There are four boys and four girls in each group, and the mean IQ scores are 92.00 for the tutorial group and 93.25 for the workbook group. The means are close, and it's actually a good thing that the mean is a little higher in the workbook group: If we find that the students learned better with the tutorials, it would be clear that it wasn't because they had higher IQs.

Repeated Measurement

So far, our discussion on ways to equalize subjects in different conditions has focused on studies with different individuals in separate groups, using between-subjects or matched-subjects designs. Another approach tests the same subjects in more than one condition of the study. Studies that test individuals under each level of an independent variable use a **within-subjects** (or *repeated measures*) **design.** Each subject is measured more than once on the dependent variable. Because the within-subjects design can be applied with experimental and quasi-experimental strategies, we'll use the term **controlled within-subjects design** to refer to a true experiment that involves repeated measurement.

Within-subjects (repeated measures) designs match closely the subjects in different research conditions because they are the same individuals. This eliminates the need to use random assignment or matching procedures to equate the subjects. Controlled within-subjects designs have several advantages, one of which is that they are efficient, requiring fewer subjects and less time to carry out the study. But they can be more complex than between-subjects designs to plan and run because the researcher usually must apply special control procedures to prevent potential confounding: Having been tested in one condition may affect the subjects' performance in another condition. These control procedures are complicated and will be described in detail in Chapter 8.

Controls Against Differential Attrition

Once we have created equivalent groups, we also need to ensure that the groups remain equalized throughout the study, except for variations from the independent variable. But a problem can arise from *attrition*—a reduction in the number of subjects during the course of a study (which is often called "mortality"). Subjects sometimes do not complete a study—for instance, participants may find the experience or task too emotionally or physically painful, difficult to do, embarrassing, or boring. If individuals are tested or followed over a long period of time—weeks or even years—they may lose interest, move away, or die, especially if they were being studied because they had a serious medical illness. When attrition occurs equally across conditions, it generally has little effect on the study's internal validity but may reduce the external validity if those who drop out share some characteristic, such as being older, poorer, or more anxious, than those who continue in the study.

Differential attrition refers to the situation in which subjects fail to complete the study at a much higher rate in some research conditions than in others. This becomes a problem if it results from an aspect of the independent variable, such as if one condition is more unpleasant than another; this aspect can lead to attrition by itself or combined with a characteristic of the subjects. For instance, suppose three types of psychotherapy were being tested against each other and a control condition, but one of the therapies involved deriding the clients, such as by calling their ideas "nutty." People might be more inclined to drop out of that condition than the others because they find the experience offensive, especially if they have low self-esteem. When differential attrition happens, the original equivalence of groups may be lost, producing a confounding that renders the independent variable's effects unclear.

How can researchers control against differential attrition? If they suspect that it may occur and know why, they can administer a pretest to assess the factor that would produce the differential attrition; in the example on therapies, they might measure the clients' self-esteem. They would use the measure of the factor in one of two ways. First, they could restrict participation to only individuals who score above or below a certain level of that factor, making it less likely that attrition would occur. Second, they could use the measure of the factor to equate the groups later: if a subject is lost in one group, a subject in each other group with a similar score on that factor would be dropped, thereby equating the groups on that factor. These approaches might reduce the study's external validity, but can protect its internal validity. If the researchers do not have access to a measure of the factor responsible for the loss or cannot identify the factor, there is little they can do to address the confounding if differential attrition occurs. (Go to **Box 5.2**)

Box 5.2 STATISTICAL CONTROL

If researchers know a confounding exists, can identify the factor responsible for it, and have access to a measure of that factor, they may be able to take that factor into account by applying statistical control. Using statistical methods, they can remove from the data the variability associated with that factor and conduct the statistical analysis without it. For example, in our study on using computer tutorials to improve students' math skills in which we matched the two groups on IQ, suppose that subsequent math scores were significantly higher in the children who got the tutorials than those with the workbook. But additional analyses revealed another difference: The prior overall grade point average (GPA) was higher in the students in the tutorials group than in the workbook group. It may be that factors other than IQ produced the GPA differences and are responsible for the difference in math performance. Statistical procedures can partial out the variability in math scores associated with GPA and then examine group differences in the remaining variability. If the tutorials group still has significantly higher math scores after applying statistical control, we can rule out the factors underlying GPA variation as the cause of the differences in math performance. Although the procedures that accomplish statistical control are complex and beyond the scope of this book, it is important to be aware that they are available.

PREVENTING PRE- AND POSTTESTING PROBLEMS

Other methods in controlling extraneous variables pertain to studies that compare pretest and posttest data. Imagine that you read about two studies in which participants are pretested, given some training, and then posttested. In one study, researchers tested the swimming skills of many 2½-year-olds, provided monthly swimming training for 6 months for the 30 who had the poorest skills, found that the children's skills were far greater then than at the original test, and concluded that the training enhanced the swimming skills. In the other study, researchers tested how well 8-year-olds cope with dental fears, asking them if they have thoughts like, "This is going to hurt" or "I hate shots," which suggests poor coping, or "Be brave" or "It won't be so bad," which reflects good coping. The 20 children who scored lowest then received training in relaxation for several months. The researchers tested the children's coping in a similar way at a dental visit 2 years later, found that their coping improved greatly, and concluded that training in relaxation enhanced coping. Are these conclusions justified? No, because the studies failed to control several other factors that could be responsible for the improvements the participants showed from pretest to posttest (see Campbell & Stanley, 1963). After we describe these factors, we'll see how researchers can control for them.

History and Maturation

Because time passes between administration of a pretest and a posttest, the participants may undergo changes from factors outside the research, especially if the amount of time separating the tests is large, such as months or years. One of these factors, called **history,** refers to experiences that occur during the course of a study and may affect the dependent variable but are not part of the independent variable. For example, suppose that in the intervening months of the study we just described on children's coping, a very popular TV show described how thinking positive thoughts can be helpful when afraid. If some of the children saw the show, that experience could be responsible for their improved coping and would be a potential confounding. Note that "history" does *not* pertain to events prior to the study.

Another factor that can operate during the time between pretest and posttest is developmental **maturation**—the process of physical and psychological growth in which genetics plays a dominant role. During infancy and early childhood, for instance, children around the world show large gains in motor and cognitive skills without formal training. In the swimming skills study, it is possible that the improvements the children showed as they reached 3 years of age resulted mostly from maturation, rather than the training they received. Although children have great difficulty learning to swim before 2 years of age, they learn fairly easily by 3 (Sarafino & Armstrong, 1986).

Regression to the Mean

The word *regress* means to move back. **Regression to the mean** refers to the tendency of individuals who score initially very high or low when tested or observed to score more toward the middle of the distribution when reassessed. For example, a basketball player who normally averages 20 points (baskets) in a game, gets either 35 or 7 points when we observe for the first time. If we observe a game a week later, the player is likely to shoot more toward his or her average. The difference in performance results from sources that are nonsystematic, such as how the player feels, how the opposing team plays, or how the fans behave. As a result, it contributes to error variance.

Factors like these can also affect the performance of subjects in research. Many subjects who score unusually low or high in a pretest, will score more toward the middle of the distribution in a posttest as a result of regression to the mean. This becomes a possible confounding when subjects are selected for their very high or low scores, as in the swimming and coping studies. Because many of the children probably scored lower on the pretest than their usual level of swimming or coping, we would expect them to score higher on the posttest regardless of the training. The children's improvements in swimming and coping may have resulted from regression to the mean rather than the training they received.

Testing Changes and Sensitization

Because using a pretest and a posttest involves repeated measurements, something about the testing may change from the first assessment to the second or the subject may change as a result of being tested the first time. The former situation is called **testing changes** and refers to alterations in the way data are collected in one test than in another. Testing changes occur if the pretest and posttest instruments or procedures are different, such as if two different tests are used to measure a trait—for example, coping skills—or if the researcher gains more skill at assessing the dependent variable or becomes bored with the activity. In **pretest sensitization,** the pretest experience changes the subjects, such as by making them more skilled in the task, giving away a hidden purpose of the study, or altering their attitudes, perceptions, or knowledge in ways that affect how they score on the posttest. If the factors involved in testing changes or pretest sensitization raise or lower scores on the dependent variable in a systematic way, a confounding exists—the effect of the independent variable in causing any difference between pretest and posttest scores becomes unclear.

Solutions to Pre- and Posttesting Problems

Researchers can resolve confounding problems associated with pre- and posttesting by including control conditions in the experimental design. Of course, when using a control condition, the researchers must randomly assign or match individuals to the groups they will compare. To eliminate the confounding factors of history, maturation, and regression to the mean, researchers use a control group that does not receive the experimental treatment—in our examples, the training in swimming or relaxation. If the experimental and control groups differ significantly on the dependent variable scores, the researchers can conclude that the experimental treatment caused the difference. The experiments by Miller and DiPilato (1983) on treating nightmares and Bandura et al. (1963) on modeling and aggression used control groups in this way.

To rule out the effects of testing changes or pretest sensitization, researchers can include a control condition within the experimental group: Some subjects would take the pretest, and others would not. If the individuals who did and did not take the pretest do not perform differently on the posttest, the researchers can conclude that no effects of testing changes or pretest sensitization occurred.

EQUATING METHODOLOGICAL DETAILS

Other methods for controlling extraneous variables are used when methodological details can be the source of confounding. Designing and carrying out research are complicated processes that involve lots of details in decision making and action. When using an experimental strategy, researchers must prevent confounding by making certain that the subjects in each of the groups are treated exactly the same way, except for manipulation of the independent variable. Treating subjects the same requires that researchers identify all methodological details that need to be equalized. This is not easy to do because not all details need to be equalized, and some details are so "obvious" that we may fail to notice them. To decide which details need to be equalized, researchers look for factors that might possibly influence the performance of the subjects. The color of the researcher's shirt is not likely to be an important factor, but many other factors will be—for example, the time of day of testing, specific questions in a test, and length of the materials the subjects must read will probably need to be controlled.

Researchers can equate methodological details across groups in two ways. First, they can use the strategy of **holding conditions constant**—that is, by making all details of the methodology identical for all groups, except for manipulations of the independent variable. We can consider some examples by referring back to studies described earlier. In the experiment my student did on the effect of a job applicant's ethnic background on ratings of his likely job performance, the instructions and survey the respondents read were exactly the same. The three versions of the resume were also identical, except for three clues of the applicant's Caucasian, Asian, or African-American background. These clues gave his name (John Smith, Lee Chow, or Tyrone Jackson), workplace (Mike's American Grill, Hunan Kitchen, or Maxine's Soul Food Restaurant), and organization for which he served as president (Circle K, Asian-American Club, or African-American Club). In the experiment Loftus and Burns (1982) conducted on people's memory for events that precede a mentally shocking event, the videotape of a bank robbery had two identical versions, except for the ending: the last 15 seconds was either violent (a shooting) or nonviolent. The participants in both conditions were tested in small groups, got course credit for participating, received the same instructions at the beginning of the study, and filled out the same survey after watching the video.

When a potential extraneous variable is not held constant, researchers can use the strategy of **balancing,** or making sure that the variation occurs to the same degree in each condition. Characteristics of the subjects provide a common example of variables that are usually balanced rather than held constant. For instance, researchers match or randomly assign subjects to conditions in an effort to balance a variety of characteristics across groups. For some characteristics, especially gender or age, we can be more deliberate: suppose 70% of the participants in a study are females; we would balance for gender by making sure each group has the same ratio of females to males. Although it is possible to hold gender constant by testing only one gender, doing so might limit the external validity, or generalization, of the results. We'll discuss in Chapter 8 special balancing methods that are applied when repeated measures are used.

ELIMINATING BIASES

The last methods we'll consider for controlling extraneous variables are used to reduce biases in measurement. We've seen in earlier chapters that the source of measurement bias can be either the participant or the observer. If the bias raises or lowers scores in one group more than another, it contributes systematic variance and creates a confounding, affecting the likelihood of finding a significant difference between research conditions. Depending on which group's scores are raised or lowered, the bias can either increase or decrease the difference between the means of the groups. Like any confounding, biased measurement that contributes systematic variance renders the effects of the independent variable unclear.

Sources of Bias

The most common sources of measurement bias in research using experimental strategies are the expectancies of the participants and observers (the researchers). The participants' performance may reflect their use of *demand charac-*

teristics, aspects of the study that affect people's ideas about its purpose, and *social desirability bias,* in which people tend to behave in ways they think are socially acceptable. Biased measurement can arise from the observer's expectations if they affect how he or she interprets and scores behavior. If the observer expects to see more of a specific behavior, such as aggression, in one group than in another, he or she may tend to interpret behaviors that are borderline or unclearly hostile as aggressive for participants in that group. Expectancies are a feature of being human and tend to operate without the participant's or the observer's awareness. Biases in research are typically not deliberate. (Go to **Box 5.3**)

Box 5.3   PARTICIPANT BIAS IN THE "HAWTHORNE EFFECT"?

A series of studies was begun in the 1920s to examine the effects of job conditions, such as working hours, bonus pay, and room lighting, on worker productivity at the Hawthorne plant of the Western Electric Company in Illinois (see Bramel & Friend, 1981; Gillespie, 1988; Parsons, 1974). The participants in the experimental group were six women, five who assembled electrical relays and one who delivered parts to them. They were asked to work in a separate room under varying conditions, and their productivity was compared with that of the other workers at the plant (the control group) who had the standard working conditions. The data analysis revealed an unexpected outcome: productivity was heightened in the six women, even when the changed condition was unfavorable, such as when rest periods were discontinued or when the amount of lighting in their room was less than that of the general plant.

How can these results be explained? For many years, researchers concluded that the improved performance resulted from participant bias: the women expected that the changes should increase output and felt that the attention they received meant that the company was interested in them. This conclusion was so widely accepted and stated in books and articles that this type of participant bias was given a name: the *Hawthorne effect.* But the conclusion from the research is now in doubt because careful examination of its methodology has revealed important confounding factors (Bramel & Friend, 1981; Gillespie, 1988; Parsons, 1974), for example:

- The participants in the experimental and control groups were not equated.
- Two of the original five assemblers were replaced because of insubordination and low productivity. One of the replacements was a woman whose output was among the plant's highest.
- Participants in the experimental group received more feedback about their work and more bonus pay than those in the control group.

Although it is possible that the type of bias described by the Hawthorne effect did occur in the original research, its existence is currently unclear.

Controlling Systematic Biasing

Researchers can build methods into the research design to eliminate or reduce systematic bias arising from the expectations of the participants and observers. We'll start with a few useful methods for reducing participant bias. To reduce social desirability bias, we can try to enhance participants' perceptions of the privacy and anonymity of their behavior or responses, such as by having survey respondents seal their completed materials in an envelope and drop it in a box. To reduce bias from demand characteristics, we can try to mask the variables by using *deception* or a *blind* procedure. Recall from Chapter 3 that using deception can present ethical problems, but it can be used if an IRB approves the methodology. The blind procedure simply keeps the participants in the dark as much as possible about the purpose and hypothesis of the study and which research condition they are experiencing.

Other methods can be used to assess the likely presence of participant bias in the research data. One approach involves using part of a *debriefing* session to inquire about what the participants thought was happening in the study or how they interpreted their experience. Another approach incorporates in the design a group that receives a *placebo* condition, which applies a neutral or inactive procedure that appears like it could be real. Experiments on the effects of drugs often do this by having a group that receives a pill or injection that contains an inert, harmless substance. To the extent that participants in the placebo condition react to the substance, their expectancies affected their behavior. If the placebo condition has the same reaction as a group that gets the real drug, the researchers conclude that the substance in the drug is not effective.

Observer bias can be reduced in a few ways. First, a researcher can apply a *blind* procedure to the observers who will actually collect the data by limiting the information they receive so they are unaware of the study's goals or the purpose of the observations. A **double-blind** procedure prevents both the participant and the observer from knowing which condition the person is receiving. Second, the researcher can automate data collection by using electronic or mechanical devices to assess the subjects' behavior. Third, to increase the accuracy of the observers' data, the researcher can inform them about *interobserver reliability* procedures that will be used to compare the consistency in their data records.

CONTROLLING ERROR VARIANCE

Because high levels of error variance impair the ability to find a significant statistical outcome, researchers try to minimize sources of nonsystematic variance. We will consider three approaches for controlling error variance that researchers often use.

One way to reduce error variance is to recruit a sample of subjects that are as homogeneous as possible—for example, by using animals who are all of the same genetic strain or using people who share important characteristics, such as gender, age, or educational background. Doing this reduces the individual differences among the subjects, which is a major source of error variance. Although this approach may also limit the external validity of the results, this is not necessarily problem for two reasons. First, as we saw in Chapter 2, researchers usually subscribe to the *continuity assumption,* that the processes underlying behavior can be viewed as similar across a wide range of individuals unless there is evidence to assume otherwise. Second, basic research tests hypotheses that do not focus on specific application to real-world issues (Mook, 1983). External validity is more likely to be important for applied research.

Another approach for controlling error variance is simply to make sure that all subjects are treated in much the same way in each condition except for manipulation of the independent variable. Researchers can do this by training observers very carefully, standardizing the procedures they use, and holding constant all laboratory environmental conditions, such as temperature and lighting.

The third approach for minimizing error variance is to use reliable measurement procedures. When conducting research in which observers score overt behavior as the dependent variable, the researcher should evaluate the data with interobserver reliability procedures. If automated methods are used to assess the dependent variable, the devices should be selected on the basis of their tested reliability. Similarly, when using survey methods, the instruments researchers employ should be selected in part on the basis of evidence of their reliability. We will examine methods for establishing the reliability of instruments in the next chapter.

SUMMARY

In experimental strategies, researchers manipulate an independent variable, comparing experimental and control groups for differences in one or more dependent variables. To use an experimental strategy, researchers must equate subjects in different conditions and control the effects of extraneous variables that can produce a confounding, rendering the effects of the independent variable unclear. Researchers can make causal inferences about the effects of the independent variable if the groups differ significantly in measures of the dependent variables and if extraneous variables have been controlled.

Researchers using experimental strategies manipulate levels of an independent variable to produce systematic variance in the dependent variable. Not all independent variables can be manipulated; those that can include environmental, instructional, task or activity, and invasive variables. Researchers can conduct a manipulation check to verify the intended function of the independent variable.

Systematic variance from extraneous variables reduces the internal validity of the research by confounding the effect of the independent variable. An important type of confounding occurs when the groups or conditions in the study are not equivalent before manipulation of the independent variable occurs. Other types of unwanted variance have nonsystematic effects on the dependent variable, contributing to error variance and reducing the likelihood of finding a significant difference between groups.

The preferred way to reduce the likelihood of having nonequivalent groups in an independent-groups (between-subjects) design is random assignment. Between-subjects designs that assign subjects to groups on the basis of chance—using simple random assignment, block random assignment, or random distribution—are called randomized groups designs. Another way to equalize groups is through the technique of matching in which the researcher identifies sets of individuals who are very similar on a characteristic that is related to the dependent variable and then randomly assigns each subject in each set to groups. A third way to equalize groups is to use repeated measurements on the same individuals in a within-subjects design. During the course of an experiment, differential attrition can occur, making previously equivalent groups unequal. Researchers can collect and use pretest scores to control against differential attrition.

Studies comparing pretest and posttest scores can guard against confounding from history, maturation, and regression to the mean by including control groups. To rule out the effects of testing changes and pretest sensitization, researchers can compare posttest scores for subjects in the experimental group who were specifically assigned to take or not take the pretest. Equating methodological details can be accomplished by holding conditions constant and balancing. Researchers also need to control nonsystematic error variance and biased measurement that arises from expectations of the participants and observers.

KEY TERMS

experimental group
control group
confounding
causal inference
manipulation check
internal validity
random
between-subjects design
independent-groups
   design

random assignment
matched-subjects
   design
matching
within-subjects design
controlled within-
   subjects design
differential attrition
history
maturation

regression to the mean
testing changes
pretest sensitization
holding conditions
   constant
balancing
double-blind

REVIEW QUESTIONS

1. Describe the methodology of the Miller and DiPilato (1983) experiment on treating people's nightmares.

2. Describe the main characteristics of experimental strategies and how they relate to the researcher's ability to make causal inferences.

3. Define and give one example (not in the book) each of the four types of manipulated independent variables: environmental, instructional, task or activity, and invasive.

4. Describe and give one example (not in the book) of the type of variance researchers want to maximize and the two types of variance they want to minimize. Discuss how one type of variance results from manipulating the independent variable.

5. How can nonequivalent groups confound the results of an experiment?

6. What is *random assignment?* Describe how to carry out *simple random assignment, block random assignment,* and *random distribution* methods.

7. Describe in detail the procedure and purpose of *matching.*

8. What is the difference between an *independent-groups (between-subjects) design* and a *within-subjects design?*

9. How can *history, maturation,* and *regression to the mean* be confounding factors in studies comparing pretest and posttest scores? How can these problems be prevented?

10. Define and give one example (not in the book) each of *holding conditions constant* and *balancing* to equate methodological details of research.

11. How can researchers control biased measurement arising from the participants and observers?

12. How can researchers minimize nonsystematic, "error" variance?

RESOURCES

BOOKS, CHAPTERS, AND ARTICLES

Campbell, D. T., & Stanley, J. C. (1963). *Experimental and quasi-experimental designs for research.* Boston: Houghton Mifflin.

Keppel, G. (1991). *Design and analysis: A researcher's handbook* (3rd ed.). Englewood Cliffs, NJ: Prentice Hall.

INTERNET SITE

http://trochim.human.cornell.edu This Website has links to information about several experimental design issues discussed in this chapter.

APPLICATION ACTIVITIES

ACTIVITY 5–1: FIND THE CONFOUNDING

Suppose that your instructor had each student in your class write a detailed proposal of an experiment and swap it with another student so that each can give and receive feedback on possible confounding factors before doing the study toward the end of the semester. Here's the proposal you must critique:

> My hypothesis is that a woman's being overweight lowers others' liking of and judgments about her. I plan to ask students in my classes if they would complete a survey in which they will examine a color photograph of a young woman, rate statements about her, and return the materials to me at the next class meeting. Three of my classes will be used, one for each photograph. All the photos are ones I have of relatives who live far from the college; each woman is shown engaging in a recreational activity; the upper three-quarters of her body nearly fills

the long side of the 4″ by 6″ photo. The photos picture: (1) an obese woman with dark hair waiting to catch a baseball, (2) a slightly overweight woman with red hair throwing a basketball, and (3) a thin woman with blonde hair hitting a tennis ball with a racquet. I will make up a survey in which respondents will rate on a 6-point scale (1 = strongly disagree; 6 = strongly agree) several statements, such as "I think I would like her as a friend" and "I think she has a lot of self-control."

Write your answers to the following questions about the proposal. (1) What are the intended independent and dependent variables? (2) The proposal has several problems in methodology. Describe four likely confounding factors in the design, indicating exactly how each would affect the scores in the different groups. (3) Describe an aspect of the method that would probably increase the error variance of the data. (4) How would you suggest that the student redesign the experiment before running it?

ACTIVITY 5–2: USING A TABLE OF RANDOM NUMBERS

Appendix B has a table of random numbers that we can use for this activity that has two parts. First, we'll use the table with the block random assignment method to place equal numbers of subjects in two groups, experimental and control, using even numbers for the experimental group and odd numbers for the control group. Each block would have two slots, one for each group. We'd only need to use the table of random numbers for the first assignment in each block because the second assignment would be filled by default. Go to the table in Appendix B, decide the path you will follow to get digits, arbitrarily select the starting digit, and begin a list that states the group for each succeeding subject. For the first block, the starting digit determines the group for the first subject (if the digit is odd, the subject is the control group, and the next subject would be in the experimental group automatically). Put these outcomes in the list. Do the same process for the second block and so on until all the planned blocks (we'll do 10 blocks) are filled. Notice that the number of participants in each group is equal as each block is filled.

Second, use the table of random numbers with more than two groups. We'll use four groups here that we'll designate simply as A, B, C, and D. Deciding which numbers will designate which groups requires some creativity; one approach might be to use only the single digits 1 to 4, and disregard other digits we encounter. Go to the table of random numbers, decide the path you will follow to get digits, arbitrarily select the starting digit, and begin a list that states the group for each succeeding subject. To get the same number of subjects per group, we'll use the block random assignment method, where each block consists of a slot for each group—A, B, C, and D—which we'll designate with the digits 1, 2, 3, and 4, respectively. If the starting digit is between 1 and 4, we'll use it to place the first subject in a group. Then continue in the path to the next digit between 1 and 4 to place the next subject, skipping any digit that refills a slot in a block before the entire block is filled. Use this same procedure with each succeeding subject until all planned blocks are filled (we'll do 10 blocks again). You should have 10 subjects in each group.

ACTIVITY 5–3: EQUALIZING GROUPS WITH
MATCHING AND RANDOM ASSIGNMENT

Suppose you are conducting an experiment with separate groups of participants on the ability of undergraduates to solve complex logic problems when under three different levels of time pressure: high, moderate, and low. You want to ensure that the participants in each group are equated for logical ability. Let's see how matching and random assignment methods work, starting with matching on their scores on a standardized test of logical ability that you already administered. High scores mean high ability. The 30 students' scores (and initials) are

56 (IM)	96 (ES)	54 (NT)	73 (VM)	66 (GR)	76 (PK)
75 (AD)	88 (JA)	77 (AY)	67 (KP)	77 (BY)	69 (SE)
43 (SQ)	39 (RG)	91 (CC)	85 (UB)	90 (SW)	88 (VB)
71 (ZL)	63 (HL)	72 (DV)	54 (WS)	57 (DA)	73 (TN)
83 (WV)	68 (CE)	81 (YB)	89 (FL)	79 (LH)	49 (XL)

Apply a matching procedure to equalize the three groups. Then redo the process with the random assignment method, using the table of random numbers in Appendix B. Answer the following questions. (1) Describe how you used the table of random numbers. (2) How successful were the methods? Calculate the mean logical ability score for each of the three groups. Did one method equalize the groups much better than the other? (3) If the random assignment approach was less successful, suggest a likely reason.

ACTIVITY 5–4: HISTORY, MATURATION,
AND REGRESSION TO THE MEAN

Design three studies that compare scores on a pretest and posttest on any topic you wish. Make each confounded: one with history, one with maturation, and one with regression to the mean. How could you change the design to control for these confounding factors?

NONEXPERIMENTAL STRATEGIES

PROLOGUE

What's life like for elderly people in a nursing home? Two things you may know are that residents in nursing homes show declines in activity and health after they begin living there and have few responsibilities or opportunities to influence their everyday lives. Could it be that their declines in activity and health result in part from their dependency and loss of "personal control" there? Ellen Langer and Judith Rodin (1976) studied this issue by manipulating the amount of responsibility and choice allowed residents of two floors of a modern, high-quality nursing home. Theory and the results of prior research had suggested to these researchers that long-term loss of responsibility and choice might lead to psychological difficulties and impaired health.

The researchers randomly selected one of the floors to be the experimental group, which was given enhanced responsibility and control—for example, they were given small plants to care for and encouraged to make decisions about participating in activities and rearranging furniture. The residents of the other floor served as the control group and continued to have standard care with little responsibility or choice: They were assigned to activities, and when given plants, they were told that the staff would take care of them. Notice that the individual participants in the two groups were not randomly assigned or matched, so there is a question of whether the groups were equal. The researchers could not treat some individuals one way and some another on the same floor because the participants would notice the discrepancy, but the residents had always had little contact with people of other floors, so the floors could be treated differently. The researchers also could not move residents to different floors, as random assignment and matching procedures would require, because of ethical and logistical concerns.

The participants and nursing staff filled out surveys before the manipulation and again 3 weeks later to assess the residents' happiness, activity, and alertness. The self-report and nursing staff pretest and posttest survey data revealed that all three dependent variables improved significantly among residents in the experimental group relative to the control group, who actually decreased somewhat on these variables. What's more, the influence of the enhanced responsibility and choice continued: after 18 months, residents in the experimental group were more happy, active, and alert than in the control group (Rodin & Langer, 1977). And comparisons of health data showed that the residents in the experimental group were healthier in the intervening months and had half the rate of death than those in the control group. Can we conclude that the manipulation *caused* these differences? Not really, and we'll examine why in this chapter.

Many very important questions cannot be investigated with "true" experimental strategies because of ethical, practical, or logistical problems in manipulating a variable or equating groups. Under these circumstances, researchers turn to a nonexperimental approach instead, as Langer and Rodin did, because they could not equate the groups of residents fully. A nonexperimental strategy may also be the most appropriate approach if the goal or hypothesis of the research simply involves a description or prediction of events or phenomena. When using a nonexperimental strategy, researchers try to make the methodology as tightly controlled as possible. This chapter describes a variety of nonexperimental approaches, their benefits and limitations, and ways to maximize their internal validity and control unwanted variance.

OVERVIEW

Chapter 1 introduced you to the distinction between experimental and nonexperimental research and described that the latter can use *quasi-experimental, correlational,* and *descriptive* strategies.

TYPES OF NONEXPERIMENTAL RESEARCH

The three types of nonexperimental research are really quite different from each other. To refresh your memory of their strategies, we'll define each type again:

- **Quasi-experimental strategy**—the researcher looks for differences between groups or conditions, but either does not manipulate the independent variable(s) or does not create equivalent groups, such as by randomly assigning subjects to conditions.
- **Correlational strategy**—the study assesses the degree and direction of statistical association between variables in a single group of subjects.
- **Descriptive strategy**—the researcher simply observes events or phenomena to detail or categorize them or to chart their course.

If you look back at the diagram in Figure 1.2 (see inside front cover), you'll see that well-designed and executed nonexperimental studies typically do not enable researchers to make causal inferences. This is because they meet only part of the three criteria for a cause–effect conclusion. These criteria are *covariation* of the independent and dependent variables, *causal time sequence* (demonstrating clearly that the cause preceded the effect), and *elimination of other plausible causes* (confounding factors) that might have affected the dependent variable.

You can also see in the diagram that the three strategies differ in their likelihood of meeting the criteria for cause–effect conclusions, with the likelihood decreasing from quasi-experimental to correlational, and then to descriptive strategies. We will focus in this chapter on quasi-experimental and correlational strategies. A detailed discussion of descriptive strategies will wait until Chapter 12 because students rarely use this approach in their projects.

VARIANCE IN NONEXPERIMENTAL METHODS

Why are quasi-experimental strategies more likely than correlational strategies to meet criteria for causal inference? The answer has to do with their ability to control systematic variance from two sources, the independent variable and extraneous variables. Let's look first at the criterion of causal time sequence. Some types of quasi-experimental research have an advantage in being able to demonstrate a causal time sequence because they involve manipulating an independent variable, as Langer and Rodin did by enhancing the responsibility and choice of residents on one of the floors. To maximize the effect of the independent variable, the researchers described to the experimental group several ways by which they would now have choices. For instance, they could decide which plant to take (or none) and take care of, how they wanted the furniture in their rooms arranged, which activities to engage in, and when and where to visit with other residents. This manipulation of the independent variable was designed to increase systematic variance in the data in a favorable way, pulling the means of the groups apart on the dependent variables.

Second, quasi-experimental strategies are more likely than correlational strategies to provide opportunities for researchers to control extraneous variables with the methods of holding conditions constant or balancing. We can see several examples of this control in the Langer and Rodin study. First, the two floors had little contact, so the possibility of communication across groups was slight. Second, the floors were selected from four on the basis of similarity of the people living there: They had similar male to female ratios, lengths of time at the home, and staff evaluations of their physical and psychological health and prior socioeconomic status. Third, although the researchers could not match individual participants or assign them to the groups, they did randomly select which floor would receive the experimental condition. Fourth, pretest self-report and staff ratings of happiness, activity, and alertness were compared for the two groups, and none showed a significant difference. Fifth, the groups were treated similarly, except for manipulation of the independent variable. An administrator called a group meeting for each floor and talked about the nursing home and positive features that exist there; the experimental group was told about opportunities for responsibility and choice; the control group was told of the staff's interest in and responsibility for them. Sixth, the nurses who provided evaluations of residents and other data were unaware of the research conditions.

In addition to controlling systematic variance nicely, Langer and Rodin reduced error variance by restricting the sample to residents who were between the ages of 65 and 90 and were physically able to get around and communicate with others. Their study is a fine example of quasi-experimental research that is tightly controlled, having a very high degree of internal validity and falling just short of fully meeting the criteria for causal inference. Although the researchers provided a great deal of evidence that the groups were very similar on several measures, they pointed out that "we simply cannot know everything about the equivalency of these subjects prior to the intervention" (Rodin & Langer, 1977, p. 900). It may be that the participants differed on one or more extraneous variables that were not measured. Still, the methodology comes about as close to the experimental strategy as a quasi-experimental study can, which enhances the likelihood that its results reflect cause–effect.

PREPARING TO DO A NONEXPERIMENTAL STUDY

Conducting research takes a good deal of preparation, including making many decisions about methodological details. Chapter 10 gives explicit instructions and checklists to help you prepare to carry out various types of research designs. If you know that you will be using a nonexperimental strategy in a study, look over that chapter now to see the kind of information it contains and how it can help you.

QUASI-EXPERIMENTAL STRATEGIES

"More Orgasms, More Years of Life?" was the title of a newspaper article in the *New York Times* that described medical research findings on sex and death (Altman, 1997). The study of nearly 1,000 middle-aged men across 10 years had found that the death rate of men who reported having sex twice a week or more was half that of men who reported having sex only once a month. Does that mean people should have lots of sex to improve their health and longevity? I'm sorry to disappoint some of you, but it doesn't. The study used a quasi-experimental strategy that had few controls: Although it showed covariation of variables (sex and death rates), it neither manipulated the independent variable (sex frequency) nor eliminated important extraneous variables, such as the men's health or marital status during the 10 years. A cause–effect conclusion on the link between sex and death is not justified. It also tested only men, thereby limiting external validity. I wonder how many people read the same news article and arrived at a wishful-thinking conclusion!

QUASI EXPERIMENTS WITH MANIPULATED INDEPENDENT VARIABLES

In the research on sex and death, we see once again that a quasi-experimental study was done when researchers could not randomly assign participants to groups. The study also could not manipulate the independent variable (sex frequency). But quasi experiments *can* manipulate independent variables and even apply strong controls against extraneous variables, as we saw with the Langer and Rodin (1976) study. Some quasi-experimental strategies manipulate an independent variable, using between- or within-subjects designs, and others do not (Cook & Campbell, 1979); we'll consider first the ones that do.

Nonequivalent Control Group Design

The **nonequivalent control group design** uses separate experimental and control groups, without using random assignment or matching to equate them, and only the experimental group receives a particular experience or treatment (Cook & Campbell, 1979). Because of the way the groups were formed, we assume they are not equal, although the researchers can provide evidence of their similarity. Usually, but not always, pretest and posttest observations are made: All subjects are tested before the experimental group has had the treatment and again after.

Table 6.1 diagrams on the left side the pattern of conditions the nonequivalent control group design usually uses and gives data on the right side from the Langer and Rodin study, an excellent example of this design. Notice two aspects of the data: The mean scores for happiness increased among participants in the experimental group and decreased in the control group and that pretest–posttest *difference scores* were calculated. Statistical analyses in nonequivalent control group designs usually compare difference scores, which assesses whether the changes from pretest to posttest are significantly different for the two groups. By comparing difference scores, researchers use pretest scores as a "baseline," thereby taking into account to some degree the initial inequalities between the groups. In the Langer and Rodin study, the residents' changes in happiness were significantly different for the experimental and control groups.

Why does this design include a control group? Recall back to the discussion in Chapter 5 on preventing pretest–posttest confounding problems. Having a control group can help researchers rule out possible confounding effects of *history* (experiences that happen between the tests that are not part of the research), developmental *maturation,* and *regression to the mean* (the tendency for very high or low pretest scores to be more toward the middle of the distribution

TABLE 6.1

The Pattern of Conditions Across Time in Typical Nonequivalent Control Group Designs and Example Pretest and Posttest Data of Happiness Ratings of Nursing Home Residents

	Pattern of conditions			Happiness ratings data[a]		
Group	Pretest →	Treatment →	Posttest	Pretest	Posttest	Difference
Experimental	Yes	Yes	Yes	5.16	5.44	+ .28
Control	Yes	No	Yes	4.90	4.78	−.12

[a] From Langer and Rodin (1976) Table 1, representing the residents' mean self-report ratings of happiness. Residents in the experimental group received the treatment (enhanced opportunities for responsibility and choice); those in the control group did not.

when retested). But a control group is an advantage only if the groups do not differ in the likelihood that history, maturation, or regression to the mean would affect their data. How might the likelihood differ? If the control group in the nursing home study had had very low pretest scores for happiness, say, a mean of 2.30 instead of 4.90, regression to the mean would have been likely at the posttest. Or if new nursing staff had started working on the floor of the control group right after the pretest, and they were very nasty, a history confounding might have existed.

The outcomes of research using a nonequivalent control group design do not always reveal the means going up at posttest for one group and going down for the other. All sorts of patterns are possible. Let's look at a study in which the researchers expected that the dependent variable would decrease from pretest to posttest in the experimental group. Morier and Keeports (1994) tested the effectiveness of an interdisciplinary course called "Science and Pseudoscience" (S&P) in decreasing students' beliefs in paranormal events. The psychologist and chemist instructors presented material on logic, statistics, and scientific reasoning and used that information to discuss the validity of paranormal and pseudoscience beliefs, such as of clairvoyance, biorhythms, and astrology. Students in this course served as the experimental group, and those in a course called "Psychology and Law," which did not cover the scientific method, served as the control group. Each course was a seminar with mainly nonscience majors. In a pretest early in the semester and a posttest on the last day of class, the students filled out a survey called the Belief in the Paranormal Scale, yielding scores that could range from 24 (low belief) to 120 points. A graph of the results is presented in Figure 6.1a. Although beliefs in the paranormal were a bit higher for students in the experimental group (S&P course) at pretest, the groups did not differ significantly. By the end of the semester, paranormal beliefs had declined for students in the S&P course and were now significantly lower than those of students in the control group.

How else could the study have turned out? The figure shows three other possible outcomes, each of which depicts lowered beliefs in the experimental group. Although it is possible that beliefs in the paranormal might increase at posttest—for instance, if students reacted against an instructor who seemed very

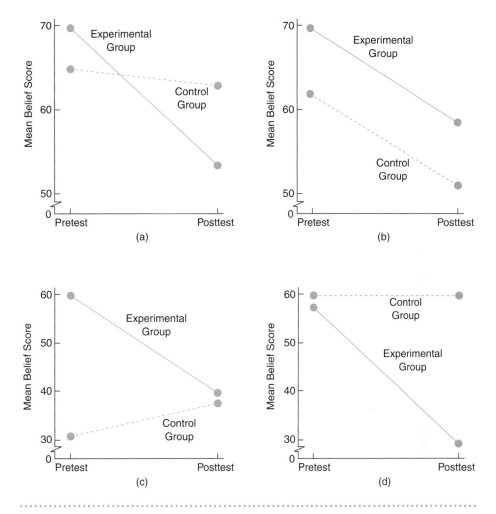

FIGURE 6.1

Graphical illustrations of the actual outcome (graph *a*) for the Morier and Keeports (1994, data from Table 1) study with a nonequivalent control group design and three hypothetical outcomes (graphs *b*, *c*, and *d*) the study might have produced instead.

biased and heavy handed—such outcomes aren't likely. Let's look at the graph in Figure 6.1b: paranormal beliefs declined in both groups, and they were markedly higher in the experimental group at pretest. This pattern of data suggests that something other than the course was responsible for the variations in beliefs. Perhaps students in the S&P course enrolled in it precisely because they believed in the paranormal and wanted a chance to defend those beliefs. Then why did they and the students in the control group have lower scores at posttest? A likely possibility is a *history* factor—for instance, suppose a very popular TV show debunked such beliefs convincingly midway during the semester, and most of the participants saw it.

Figure 6.1c presents a different possible outcome: paranormal beliefs were far higher among students in the S&P course than in the control course at pretest, and they declined in the experimental group but increased somewhat in the control group. This pattern suggests three possible processes. First, the difference between groups at pretest may have occurred for a reason like the one discussed for Figure 6.1b—maybe students in the S&P course enrolled because they believed in the paranormal. Second, the increase in paranormal belief scores among students in the control course may have resulted from regression to the mean because they had pretest scores that were extremely low, almost as low as they can get on the scale. Third, the role of the S&P course in changing beliefs is unclear because history could have been involved. For example, suppose the popular TV show debunked the beliefs, and many students in both groups watched it. The show would reduce the beliefs in the experimental group, but what would happen to the control group's beliefs? Their beliefs were already near rock bottom, so the show could not have reduced them much, if at all, and regression to the mean may have moved them up somewhat.

In Figure 6.1d, students' paranormal beliefs were very similar in the two courses at pretest and declined markedly among those in the S&P course, but did not change in the control course. This sounds pretty good, and it's a lot like the pattern in Figure 6.1a. The data in both of these graphs support the effectiveness of the course better than the data in other two graphs, but they all have the shortcoming of all nonequivalent control group designs: The groups were not equalized before the researchers manipulated the independent variable, the courses. And whatever unequal factors there were may have influenced the likelihood that history would affect the beliefs in each group differently. For example, suppose part of the inequality between students in the two groups was that those in the S&P course watched a lot more TV than those in the control course. If so, there's a greater likelihood that the popular TV show debunking paranormal beliefs would have been seen by and affected the posttest scores of students in the S&P course than in the control course.

Although there are shortcomings to nonequivalent control group designs, they are often the only way to study some topics in psychology. Moreover, sometimes when using a nonequivalent control group, it may not be possible to collect pretest data—for example, when studying the psychological effects of an unpredictable major event or disaster, such as an earthquake. In cases like this, researchers don't actually manipulate the independent variable, the occurrence of the event or disaster, but they know exactly when, where, and how strongly it occurred. Thus, they have much of the critical knowledge that manipulation would provide. One such study was begun about a week after the 1989 Loma Prieta earthquake in the San Francisco Bay area and examined people's experience of nightmares (Wood, Bootzin, Rosenhan, Nolen-Hoeksema, & Jourden, 1992). The participants were recruited mainly from undergraduate psychology classes. The students in the experimental group were from Stanford and San Jose State Universities, which are very near the epicenter of the earthquake; those in the control group were from the University of Arizona, which is about 750 miles away. Only students who had been in the region of their university at the time of the earthquake were allowed to take part. The participants filled out a survey at the start of the study and then kept daily logs for 3 weeks on the experience and content of dreams.

Let's look at three interesting findings from this research. First, over the 3 weeks, between 53% and 75% of the students at each university reported at least one nightmare, but 40% the San Francisco area students and only 5% of the Arizona students had at least one nightmare about an earthquake. Second, the mean number of nightmares was 1.8 times higher for students in the San Francisco area than those in Arizona. Third, positive correlations were found between anxiety and dreams: The greater the anxiety the students felt during the quake, the greater the number of nightmares they reported. These findings make sense and are important, but the ability to make causal inferences is impaired by aspects of the design that could not be avoided under the circumstances. For one thing, the groups did, in fact, differ in three potentially important ways: The San Francisco area sample was older, contained a higher percentage of females, and had more attrition. Also, the lack of a pretest means that the researchers cannot rule out the possibility that people normally have more nightmares about earthquakes in the San Francisco area than in Arizona, even when none has occurred recently, because California is prone to quakes. Although the researchers addressed these problems well with statistical analyses and logic, we still do not know the degree to which these or other inequalities between the groups may have been responsible for the important relationships they observed.

Time-Series Designs

The term *time series* refers to taking multiple assessments over time (Cook & Campbell, 1979). Some quasi-experimental strategies use time-series data collected in a within-subjects design with pretest and posttest assessments. In the **interrupted time-series design,** researchers take a series of assessments before and after a major event occurs or a treatment condition begins and compare the pretest and posttest data. The time series is "interrupted" by the event or condition. Researchers can use this approach when they can manipulate the event or treatment, predict that an event or condition will occur, or have access to archival time-series data from before and after an event or condition already occurred. Taking a series of assessments allows researchers to examine patterns in the variable to see how stable the behavior has been and its normal fluctuations. We'll soon see that examining patterns in the data offers important advantages.

The simplest form of interrupted time-series design does not have a control group, as in a study by Fox, Hopkins, and Anger (1987) that manipulated conditions at two open-pit mines to reduce their high number of worker injuries. In 1975, the researchers began a program that rewarded workers at a coal mine with trading stamps monthly for not having had injuries requiring a physician's care and for making safety suggestions. The workers could redeem the stamps at stores for hundreds of different items, such as a bowling ball, microwave oven, and gas-fired barbecue grill. The data on worker injury came from the mining company, which kept records in compliance with U.S. government regulations. Figure 6.2 presents data on the yearly costs of injuries as an index of their number and seriousness. As you can see, the data for several years before and after the start of the program show an abrupt and stable drop in injury costs. Although

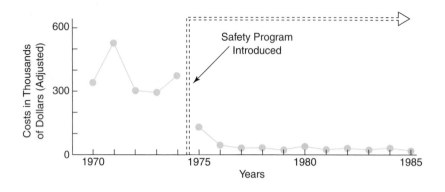

Time-series data on injury costs at a coal mine from the 5 years before a worker safety program was introduced and the next 10 years while the program was still in force (from Fox, Hopkins, & Anger, 1987, Figure 3). The yearly costs are adjusted for inflation and the number of hours worked.

part of this drop may reflect a lower willingness to report injuries due to the resulting loss of stamps, this factor probably had only a small impact because the data for number of injuries and days lost showed a very similar pattern.

Notice how stable the worker injury data are, especially after the safety program was introduced. The stability may have resulted from the researchers and workplace having good control over factors that might otherwise add to nonsystematic variance. For example, hiring practices and work rules may have reduced individual differences among participants, and the safety program may have made the workers more attentive to their behavior. One advantage in having multiple assessments is that we can see the stability in the data, which suggests that whatever difference exists is unlikely to have resulted from chance factors. Other advantages in having multiple assessments relate to the absence of a control group, with the possibility of confounding from extraneous factors when pretest and posttest data are compared. Patterns in time-series data may argue against the effects of history, maturation, and regression to the mean in the outcome. For instance, to check whether regression to the mean might have been responsible, we would look at the pretest time-series data. Because regression to the mean is likely when scores are unusually high or low at pretest, we would look to see if the safety program began when injuries were unusually high. Looking at Figure 6.2, we can see that injuries were at a moderate level when the program began, and we could rule out that confounding.

Now, to help you see the importance of patterns in time-series data, let's compare the data from the mine safety research and another study that used an interrupted time-series design. Researchers conducted a time-series study to see if a newspaper's policy of printing the names of people convicted of shoplifting and other crimes decreased the frequency of those crimes (Ross & White, 1987). The researchers used judicial records as archival data, spanning 30 months before to 18 months after the policy was implemented, and did not manipulate the independent variable or use a control group. Figure 6.3 gives the

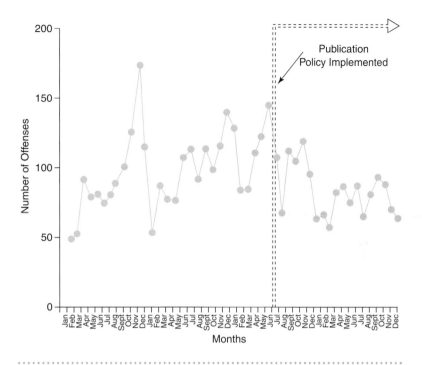

FIGURE 6.3
Monthly data (1982–85) from judicial records on the number of shoplifting
offenses in the community served by a newspaper that began a policy of
publishing the names of individuals convicted of shoplifting and other
offenses (from Ross & White, 1987, Figure 1). Implementation of the policy
began in June of 1984.

data for shoplifting. Statistical analysis revealed fewer shoplifting offenses after
the newspaper began publishing the names. But notice how variable the data
are, rising and falling repeatedly. Part of the reason for the variability is that the
data are charted per month, not per year, as in the mine safety study. Now compare pretest and posttest data for shoplifting and look at the patterns or trends
in each. Are the numbers of offenses markedly different in pretest and posttest?
After the newspaper implemented the policy, are the data stable enough to rule
out some temporary history factor? Did implementation begin when offenses
were at a moderate level? The answer is *no* to all these questions. It is more difficult to rule out confounding in this study than in the mine safety study.

Researchers can add features to the basic interrupted time-series design to
bolster the internal validity of the study and increase the clarity of the effects of
the independent variable. One feature they can add is a control group, even if it
is not equivalent to the experimental group. Another useful feature is to add
more dependent variables—some that would and some that would not be expected to change after the event occurs or treatment condition begins. A study
incorporated both these features to test the effectiveness of a law in New York

State to reduce litter by requiring buyers of certain beverages to pay a deposit on each bottle and can container (Levitt & Leventhal, 1986). These containers are called returnable; other bottles and cans are nonreturnable. A main way the researchers measured littering was to count the number of cans and bottles discarded along highway exit ramps, one each in New York and New Jersey. The two exits were similar in use patterns, and the one in New Jersey was used as a control group because that state did not have a comparable law. The researchers counted both returnable and nonreturnable containers, using the nonreturnable items as a dependent variable that should not be affected by the law. Because the implementation date for the law was announced well in advance, the researchers could begin observations many weeks before, making seven pretest and seven posttest observations, spaced 2 weeks apart. The number of returnable bottles and cans decreased in posttest observations by 44% in New York, and only 3% in New Jersey; this difference was statistically significant. The number of nonreturnable containers did not decrease, actually showing a nonsignificant increase, in both locations. By including a control group and an extra dependent variable, the researchers enhanced their ability to conclude that the law was responsible for the change in littering.

QUASI EXPERIMENTS WITH NONMANIPULATED INDEPENDENT VARIABLES

"Where Children Learn How to Learn: Inner-City Pupils in Catholic Schools" is the title of a *New York Times* newspaper article that describes research showing that children who attend American Catholic schools do better academically than those in public schools (Chira, 1991). One study found, for example, that Catholic school students consistently score from 3% to 6% higher on math proficiency tests than public school students. The article argues that this difference is due to differences in the educational process, which is possible. But studies on such issues are almost always quasi-experimental—they do not manipulate the educational processes or equate the groups. As a result, they fail to control important extraneous variables, particularly the income levels and home environments of the children's families and the ability of private schools to exclude problem students, either through admissions or expulsion procedures. Most people who learn of research findings through the mass media probably do not realize the importance of controlling extraneous variables, even when they are told that those factors existed in a study.

Many studies in psychology compare individuals who can be classified on the basis of having a measurable characteristic, which is called a **subject variable.** Examples of subject variables include age, gender, ethnic background, socioeconomic status, height, weight, college major, personality traits, behavior patterns, and psychological disorders. We use these existing, naturally occurring factors to assign individuals to groups (Cook & Campbell, 1979). As a result, quasi experiments with subject variables as independent variables are often called **natural-groups designs.** Subject variables exist at the start of the study and are not manipulated. Groups formed in this way are not equivalent and can differ on many factors other than the specific subject variable by which individuals were assigned. Matching procedures can be used to make the groups similar on one or more of these factors, which would strengthen the design, but as we saw in Chapter 5, matching is not likely to equate the groups completely.

Gender and Age Differences

Two of the most common subject variables studied in psychological research are gender (sex) and age. In testing for gender differences, researchers assign males and females to separate groups on the basis of their sex classification and compare their scores on a dependent variable, such as aggression or a cognitive ability. If statistical analysis reveals a significant difference, it is described as a *gender* (or sex) *difference.* Studies using this approach have found gender differences on several variables (Schau, 1987). On average, for instance, boys have better skills than girls in visual-spatial tasks, such as constructing block designs, and girls have better skills than boys in verbal tasks, such as spelling and verbal analogies. These differences may not be very large, but they are fairly consistently found. The causes of the gender differences found in psychological variables are unclear because the research is quasi-experimental. The results of other research suggest that the causes for gender differences probably involve both inborn, physiological factors and learned, experiential factors that differ for males and females.

A principal goal in developmental psychology is to predict and understand normal patterns of growth and maturation. To achieve this goal, researchers work to discover *age differences* in physical, motor, intellectual, social, and personality variables. Because they cannot randomly assign subjects to age groups or manipulate their ages, they select and assign individuals to groups on the basis of age. The choice of the specific age levels of the independent variable is critical: The ages often coincide with theoretical predictions or prior findings and must be spaced far enough apart that differences could be found. Two basic approaches are used in studying age differences. When researchers use a **cross-sectional design,** they observe different individuals of different ages at about the same time; when they use a **longitudinal design,** they observe the *same* individuals repeatedly over a long period of time. Cross-sectional research uses an independent-groups design; longitudinal research uses a within-subjects design. Suppose an investigator wants to examine age-related changes in children's "dependency behavior" when their parents are not present. If the researcher uses the *cross-sectional design,* a sample of perhaps 30 children at each of three ages (say, 2, 6, and 10) might be observed for their efforts to get help and attention from adults at their day care center or school. If the researcher uses the *longitudinal design* instead to study the same measure of dependency, 30 2-year-olds would be selected and assessed at 2, 6, and 10 years of age. Although this research would take 8 years to complete, longitudinal studies can span less time.

Obviously the longitudinal approach is costly in both time and money. Also, the longer a study lasts, the greater the likelihood of attrition—individuals in the sample may move away, lose interest in participating, or become ill or die, for example. Despite these difficulties, it is a valuable research approach that is unique in its ability to see *individual changes* and the *stability of characteristics* across time. For instance, a longitudinal study will tell us if a child who was highly dependent at an early age continues at later ages to be more dependent than most children. The cross-sectional design has two disadvantages. First, it loses sight of stability and individual changes. Second, it has the potential for a special type of extraneous variable: Although the age groups may differ in normal growth and maturation, they may also differ in *history* because the groups passed through each age during different time periods. Children at age 2 today are passing through their third year of life in a different time period than children who were 2 years old 8 years ago. These children are from different cohorts, where a **cohort** is a group of individuals who were born at about the same time and, for that reason, probably experienced historical events in society that were similar, such as the presence of war, high divorce rates, or popular TV shows. In general, the greater the difference in age, the more likely it is that differences in history will produce a confounding called a *cohort effect,* the influence of having been born at different times.

To illustrate how cohort effects can produce very different outcomes in cross-sectional and longitudinal studies, let's look at some census data on religious affiliation among women in the Netherlands across several decades (Hagenaars & Cobben, 1978). Because the amount of data the researchers presented is so large, we will consider only four of the 10-year age groups and four of the census years. Figure 6.4 gives in a matrix and graph the percentages of religious *nonaffiliation* for seven cohorts who formed the age groups at the 1909, 1929, 1949, and 1969 census years. Look first at the matrix in which each cell

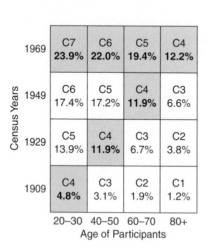
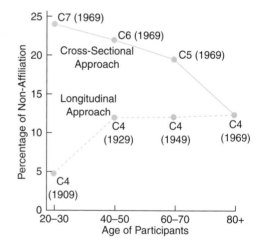

FIGURE 6.4

Census data presented in a matrix and a graph to illustrate different outcomes in cross-sectional and longitudinal approaches resulting from cohort effects. The data represent percentages of religious nonaffiliation among women in the Netherlands and were taken from the census records for 1909, 1929, 1949, and 1969. The full data set includes additional age groups and census years (from Hagenaars & Cobben, 1978, Table 1). Each cell in the matrix and data point in the graph gives the cohort number: C4, C5, C6, and C7 are the cohorts 4, 5, 6, and 7.

gives a cohort number (for example, C4 means the fourth cohort) and the percentage of nonaffiliation. Let's focus on three features of the matrix. First, notice that each cohort, such as C4, moves upward in the matrix on a diagonal. These are the same people being assessed repeatedly—except that some were surely lost to attrition across census years, of course—and would be the participants if the study were done with a longitudinal design. Second, look at the cells running horizontally. These are different people being assessed with a cross-sectional approach in a single census year. Third, look at the cells running vertically: The percentage of nonaffiliation increased steadily across census years, suggesting that history is likely to be an extraneous variable in the cross-sectional data.

Now look only at the shaded cells with data in boldface font. These are the data plotted in the graph with the vertical axis representing the percentages of religious nonaffiliation, the dependent variable, and the horizontal axis representing the ages of the participants, the independent variable. The upper graph line gives the cross-sectional data for 1969. If these were the only data we had, we would conclude that nonaffiliation *decreased* (or, affiliation increased) steadily with age among women in the Netherlands. The lower graph line gives the longitudinal data, and if these were the only data we had, we'd conclude that nonaffiliation *increased* (or affiliation decreased) from young adulthood to middle age and stayed much the same thereafter. These are very different outcomes, and cohort effects, probably from societal changes across decades, are almost certainly the reason for the difference.

Not all cross-sectional data are confounded with cohort effects. Researchers need to be aware of the possibility for confounding and address it when designing the study or interpreting the results. One way to design a study to take cohort effects into account is to combine the approaches (Buss, 1973; Schaie, 1965). Looking back at the study of dependency behavior in 2-, 6-, and 10-year-old children, the combined approach would have us select and test 2- and 6-year-olds initially. So far the study is cross-sectional, but we then test longitudinally these same children. That is, 4 years later we retest these children when they are 6 and 10 years old. Doing this would allow us to assess cohort effects. For example, if we compared the two sets of data from 6-year-olds and found a significant difference, we would conclude that a cohort effect occurred and use that information to interpret other age-related differences.

Behavioral, Experiential, and Personality Differences

The Insurance Institute for Highway Safety (IIHS, 2002) publishes data on the death rates from car accidents in the United States, separated by the size of the car. For example, the death rates in 1999 per million registered passenger vehicles for cars 1 to 3 years old were 249 for mini cars, 161 for small cars, 127 for midsize cars, and 122 for large and very large cars. To study this phenomenon and analyze the data, we would separate the people who died into groups, based on the size of the car they were riding in. If we found a significant difference between the mini and small cars and between the small and midsize to very large cars in the number of deaths, would that mean smaller cars are less safe than larger cars? If so, are they less safe because of poor handling, or braking, or safety features like air bags? Are owner/drivers of smaller and larger cars different from each other, such as in their age, gender, need to drive in bad weather, or tendency to take risks? In this quasi experiment, many uncontrolled factors would make it difficult to identify a cause for the effect.

A very common method for forming groups based on behavior or personality variables is to identify individuals who do and do not have a specific characteristic and compare those groups. For example, many studies have compared people who do and do not exercise regularly and found that those who exercise report less anxiety, tension, and depression in their lives (Dishman, 1986). In other research, the children of mothers who smoke cigarettes were compared: Those with mothers who smoked at least a pack a day had far more behavioral problems, such as anxiety, depression, and disobedience, than those whose mothers smoked less than a pack a day (Weitzman, Gortmaker, & Sobol, 1992). Most studies that use this approach to form groups do not equate them, except by age and gender of the participants, but sometimes they apply statistical control procedures. The study of children of smoking mothers partialled out the effects of many other potential extraneous variables, including health, intelligence, and family income factors.

In another study that used this method to form groups, researchers identified elderly people who had been caring an average of 5 years for a spouse with Alzheimer's disease, a brain disorder in which intellectual and personality functions deteriorate (Kiecolt-Glaser, Dura, Speicher, Trask, & Glaser, 1991). The control group consisted of people who had not been caregivers; the groups were matched on age, sex, education, and income. Assessments of emotional status and health-related dependent variables were made at intake and again after about 13 months. The results revealed that compared with the control groups during those months, the caregivers showed significantly greater depression, days of infectious illness, and biochemical decrements in immune function. Notice an important feature in the methodology of this study: The researchers formed the groups and examined physiological and emotional changes in the following year or so. This is a **prospective approach** in which researchers study whether differences in a variable—in this case, caregiving—at one point in time are related to differences in one or more other variables at a *later* time. Most quasi experiments use a **retrospective approach,** assessing the independent and dependent variables by looking back in the recent or distant lives of the participants. For instance, in the studies of the emotional status of people who do and do not exercise, the researchers usually had participants report their exercise and emotion for the recent past. The prospective approach gives greater plausibility to a causal link than the retrospective approach does because the causal time sequence is clearer: In the caregiving study, caregiving preceded the assessed levels of immune function, health, and emotion.

So far in our discussion of comparing groups that differ on behavior or personality, we've focused on forming groups based on *dichotomous* (or discrete) variables: the person is a caregiver or not, or exercises regularly or not. But researchers can also form groups on the basis or behavior or personality measured as a *continuous* variable, such as the degree of aggressiveness, cell phone or

Internet usage, political or religious conviction, self-esteem, optimism, anxiety, and stress. How do researchers form groups then? They usually use one of two procedures. In the **median-split method,** researchers identify the median score—that is, the middle score in the distribution—on the assessment and assign those above the median to one group and those below to another. In the **extreme-groups method,** researchers use only individuals who score on a test at the upper and lower ends of the distribution—say, the upper and lower 25% or 30%. These methods can only work with a two-group study. For more groups, researchers can modify the extreme-groups method, using percentages that divide the scores into the number of needed groups, such as using the upper, middle, and lower thirds. Keep in mind that with any of these approaches the participants' scores are high or low *relative to the distribution,* not necessarily in an absolute sense. Suppose we want to separate individuals who exercise regularly into high and low levels based on self-reported minutes per week of exercise, but all participants claim between 30 and 150 minutes. We can separate them into high and low groups in a relative sense, but 150 minutes is not a great deal of exercise.

Genetic Differences

Studies have found evidence for the role of genetics in a wide variety of behaviors and personality traits, such as alcohol abuse and Type A behavior patterns (Sarafino, 2002). How do researchers do these studies? The methods are based on a distinction between two types of twins: *monozygotic,* or identical, twins who have the same genetic inheritance and *dizygotic,* or fraternal, twins who are no more genetically similar than any singly born siblings of the same parents. When psychologists do **twin studies,** they separate the twins by type into two groups (the independent variable), assess the behavior or personality (the dependent variable) of each member of each twin pair, and compare the groups for similarities and differences on the dependent variable within the pairs. Notice that this is a quasi-experimental strategy: We do not manipulate genetic inheritance and do not randomly assign individuals or pairs to groups.

The rationale for making these comparisons is logically straightforward. Because the two members of a monozygotic pair are genetically identical, we can assume that differences between them on the dependent variable are environmentally determined. Thus, the greater the similarity between these twins, the more likely that the behavior or personality is genetically influenced. Differences between dizygotic twins, on the other hand, are due to both genetic and environmental factors, even when they are the same sex. If both members of each monozygotic pair and same-sex dizygotic pair have had equal environmental experiences, we would be able to measure genetic influence simply by subtracting the differences for the monozygotic twins from the differences for the dizygotic twins. But the degree of environmental equality is not always very high, especially for dizygotic twins, and inferential statistical analyses are needed to test whether the differences are significant. If the dependent variable is discrete—that is, each person is classified as either having or not having the behavioral or personality characteristic—the analysis compares the *concordance* rates: If both members of a twin pair have the characteristic, they are concordant for it. Suppose we were studying twins in which at least one has alcoholism. If both members have alcoholism, they are concordant for alcoholism; if one has alcoholism and the other doesn't, they are not concordant. If the dependent variable is a continuous variable, the analysis typically uses the assessed score.

Testing for Group Differences

In quasi experiments, we use statistical tests to determine whether the difference between groups is significant. We saw in Chapter 4 that the scale of measurement we use to assess a dependent variable affects our choice of the test to use. Some dependent variables simply place individuals in categories—for instance, the person has alcoholism or does not, or has a Type A behavior pattern or does not, and so on—which constitutes a *nominal scale* of measurement. A continuous variable usually yields data on an *interval scale* or a *ratio scale* of measurement. To find an appropriate statistical test, we'd consult Table 4.1 (see inside front cover). We'd first ask, "Do we want to assess a relationship or a difference?" We've already established that quasi experiments test for differences. If we have interval or ratio data, we'd focus on *parametric* statistics in the shaded area of the lower portion of the table; if we have nominal or ordinal data (ranks), we'd consider the *nonparametric* tests in the nonshaded area. Because other aspects of the research design, particularly its number and pairing of data groupings, influence the specific choice of a statistic, we'll finish describing the decision-making process when we discuss corresponding designs in Chapters 7 to 9. For now, just remember that the calculated value from the test will determine whether and at what level the difference is *significant*. If the *probability* of obtaining that value by chance— that is, when no difference actually exists—is less than .05, we can conclude that this large a difference is significant and not likely to have occurred by chance alone.

One final point about quasi-experimental strategies: Researchers often refer to the results of quasi-experimental designs as "correlational" because the results demonstrate covariation but lack a clear causal time sequence, elimination of other possible causal variables, or both. In that sense, a study can test for differences between groups and still yield a correlational outcome or conclusion. For example, in the study that found higher levels of children's behavior problems if their mothers smoked more than pack a day than if they smoked less, the researchers could have conducted the study with a correlational strategy. That is, they could have used the actual number of cigarettes the mothers smoked per day and assessed relationships to the children's scores for behavior problems with correlational statistics. If we found a significant correlation, would the conclusion be different? Not really. We'd still know that maternal smoking is associated with children's problems, and we'd still *not* know the cause. The statistical test applied does not always tell you the research strategy the researcher used or the degree to which a causal inference is justified. (Go to **Box 6.1**)

Box 6.1 JOURNAL ARTICLE TITLES THAT SAY "THE EFFECT OF . . ."

The journal article for the study we described earlier on nightmares following an earthquake had the title, "Effects of the 1989 San Francisco Earthquake on Frequency and Content of Nightmares" (Wood et al., 1992). Do the words *effects of* mean that the researchers used an experimental strategy and demonstrated a clear and unambiguous cause–effect relationship? No, the study was a nicely controlled quasi experiment, but they did not equate the experimental and control groups. Then why does the title say "effects of"?

Many journal articles for nonexperimental studies have titles that include the phrase "the effect of" or "effects of." Here are a couple of other examples:

- "Effects of Gender in Social Control of Smoking Cessation"—a quasi experiment comparing males' and females' self-reports of the influence of friends and family on their ability to quit smoking cigarettes (Westmaas, Wild, & Ferrence, 2002).
- "The Effect of Accuracy of Perceptions of Dietary-Fat Intake on Perceived Risk and Intentions to Change"—a quasi experiment comparing individuals who overestimate, underestimate, or accurately estimate the fat content of their diets. The dependent variables included perceived heath risks from diet and intentions to change their diets (O'Brien, Fries, & Bowen, 2000).

The main reason the titles use the word *effect* is that the research outcome is consistent with a cause–effect process, even though it may only provide evidence for covariation. In many cases, *relationship* or *role* may be a better word in the titles.

CORRELATIONAL STRATEGIES

Researchers use correlational strategies when they want to assess the degree and direction of statistical association between variables. Sometimes they use these strategies when their research goal is to predict one variable from another, such as predicting students' likely success in college from Scholastic Achievement Test (SAT) scores. Other times they use correlational strategies when experimental and quasi-experimental strategies are not feasible to conduct for ethical or logistic reasons, and finding that the variables are significantly related would be consistent with a cause–effect process. Looking back at Figure 1.2 (see inside front cover), you can see that correlational strategies are somewhat less likely than quasi-experimental strategies to meet the cause–effect criteria of a clear causal time sequence and elimination of other plausible causes.

CORRELATIONAL ANALYSIS

It was in the mid-to-late 1800s when Sir Francis Galton, a scientist with wide-ranging interests, formulated the concept of "co-relations" (Fancher, 1979). He was studying the inheritance of human characteristics, such as height and intelligence, and noticed, for instance, that tall parents tended to have tall children and that there were many exceptions to this rule. In biology and psychology, relationships between variables are imperfect—the links are partial or incomplete. To grapple with this problem and visualize imperfect relationships, Galton came on the idea of plotting one set of data against the other, as in Figure 6.5, which shows a matrix he developed when he plotted the heights of 314 adults and their parents. The numbers in each cell represent the number of parent–child pairs with the corresponding heights. Plots like this one helped Galton make some important discoveries. For example, he noticed a *trend* in the data—as one variable increased, so did the other, which he called a "co-relation."

Galton also discovered the phenomenon of *regression to the mean*—the tendency for individuals with extreme scores at one observation to have more mod-

Children's Heights (Mean = 68.0")

Parents' Heights (Mean = 68.1")	63"–64"	64"–65"	65"–66"	66"–67"	67"–68"	68"–69"	69"–70"	70"–71"	71"–72"	72"–73"
72"–71"						1	2	2	2	1
71"–70"				2	4	5	5	4	3	1
70"–69"	1	2	3	5	8	9	9	8	5	3
69"–68"	2	3	6	10	12	12	2	10	6	3
68"–67"	3	7	11	13	14	13	10	7	3	1
67"–66"	3	6	8	11	11	8	6	3	1	
66"–65"	2	3	4	6	4	3	2			
Mean Height of Parents in Each Column	67.2	67.3	67.4	67.6	67.9	68.2	68.4	68.8	69.1	69.3

FIGURE 6.5

A matrix Galton developed to show the relationship of parent and child heights (from Fancher, 1979, Figure 7–3). The shading is added here to clarify patterns: Cells with darker shading have the highest numbers (10–14) of parent–child pairs, cells with lighter shading have moderate numbers (5–9), and cells with no shading have low numbers (1–4). Cells with no data mean no pairs with these heights were observed in the sample.

erate scores when observed again. When we discussed regression to the mean in Chapter 5, we were considering types of confounding in studies that compare pretest and posttest data. But regression to the mean can occur in other research situations, particularly when observations are made on related individuals and compared, such as across generations. Figure 6.5 provides examples: Look, for instance, at data corresponding to parents who were among the shortest in the sample, 65 to 66 inches tall. Of their 24 children, only 9 were as short or shorter than they; 13 were taller, more toward the sample mean of about 68 inches. Why would regression occur across generations? Remember that it results from nonsystematic sources. The combinations of genes in the process of conception occur in a random manner from the genetic materials the father and mother contribute. If an observed characteristic that results from inheritance is of an unusually high or low level in one of these individuals—for instance, the father is very short—the genes this person transmits to an offspring are likely to be ones that yield a more moderate level of the characteristic.

Scatterplots

Look again at Figure 6.5, especially the geometric form of the shaded area. It roughly forms an oval that reveals the co-relation Galton saw in the overall data: As the parents' heights increased, so did the children's. This diagram is the forerunner to the modern-day **scatterplot**—a graph that consists of data points, shown as dots or other symbols, for paired values for the two variables being analyzed. To see examples of scatterplots, look at Figure 6.6, which presents three hypothetical sets of data and the corresponding scatterplots for the same two variables, psychological depression and sociopolitical attitudes. Think of these data as coming from three different studies, each with 15 participants, that had different outcomes because they used different surveys.

Notice in each data set in this figure that each participant has two scores, one for depression and one for sociopolitical attitudes. These are the variables being analyzed. The arrows leading from a pair of scores in each data set show where the corresponding plotted data point would be placed. Looking at the study 1 data and graph, for example, we would find 51 on the vertical axis and 26 on the horizontal axis, follow a perpendicular line from each point to the intersect, and plot the paired value. Now, let's compare the patterns of data points in the three scatterplots. The data for studies 1 and 3 show trends. In study 1, as sociopolitical scores increase, depression scores tend to increase, too. This pattern reflects a *positive correlation* between the two variables. In study 3, as sociopolitical scores increase, depression scores *decrease*, reflecting a *negative correlation*. In study 2, the data do not show any pattern—depression appears just as likely to increase as decrease with increases in sociopolitical attitudes. This lack of pattern reflects no correlation between variables.

These trends can be seen more clearly in the slopes of the dashed lines that pass through the data points. These lines are called regression lines. A **regression line** is a straight line that best "fits" or represents the data points, depicting how changes in one variable relate to changes in the other. Although the slope of a regression line is actually computed so that it represents the path that minimizes the summed squared deviations of the data points, we'll illustrate

Three Data Sets

	Study 1: *r* = +.87			Study 2: *r* = .00			Study 3: *r* = −.75	
	D1	**SP1**		**D2**	**SP2**		**D3**	**SP3**
1	61	26	1	57	24	1	51	13
2	65	22	2	62	12	2	64	9
3	46	17	3	46	13	3	46	14
4	26	12	4	26	22	4	23	23
5	29	9	5	50	10	5	31	20
6	36	19	6	38	16	6	50	19
7	38	13	7	31	20	7	38	14
8	30	12	8	36	11	8	33	26
9	36	14	9	59	15	9	37	25
10	59	24	10	48	26	10	60	10
11	51	26	11	53	22	11	57	15
12	41	14	12	32	24	12	26	24
13	51	18	13	63	19	13	62	13
14	52	22	14	27	9	14	49	23
15	46	20	15	41	20	15	48	10

Three Scatter plots

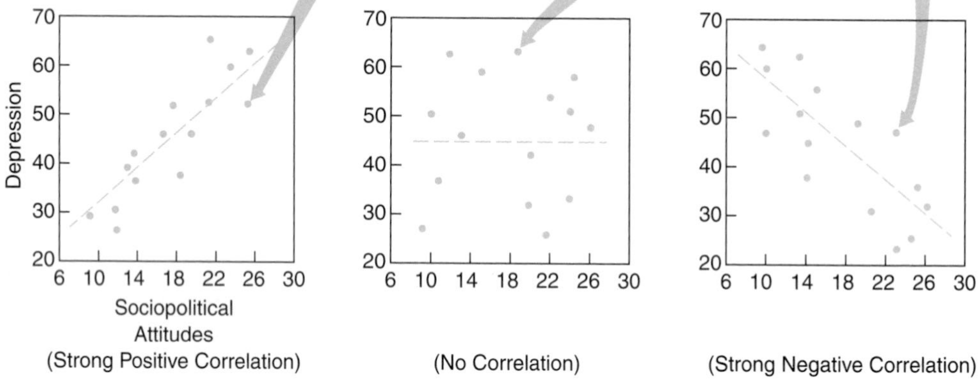

(Strong Positive Correlation)   (No Correlation)   (Strong Negative Correlation)

FIGURE 6.6

Three hypothetical data sets and corresponding scatterplots for the same two variables, psychological depression (D) and sociopolitical attitudes (SP), that might be found in three different studies, each using different surveys with 15 participants. Notice three things. First, each participant has two scores in a data set, one for D and one for SP. Second, the arrows leading from a pair of scores in each data set show where each plotted data point would be placed (at the intersect of the scores from the horizontal and vertical axes). Third, the scatterplots for studies 1 and 3 show trends in the data: in study 1, D increases with increases in SP; in study 3, D decreases with increases in SP. These trends can be seen in the slopes of the dashed lines that pass through the data points. The calculated correlations are given at the top of each data set.

its meaning in a conceptual way with the study 1 scatterplot. Look at the pattern of data points but imagine that the regression line is not there; you can see an overall trend and can visualize fairly well a line that could go through the center of the trend. That line would cut the data points about in half, with roughly the same number of points above as below it. Galton plotted regression lines and realized that the *slope* of a line represented the *strength* of the relationship between the two variables: the steeper the slope, the stronger the relationship. The slope also shows the *direction* of the relationship: In our scatterplots, if the line slopes from the lower left to the upper right, the correlation is positive; if the line slopes from the upper left to the lower right, the correlation is negative. Notice that the regression line in the study 2 data is horizontal; these data have a zero correlation. For Galton's data on parent–child heights in Figure 6.5, trying to visualize the regression line is a bit more difficult because there are no dots for the data points. Still, if you examine the pattern, you'll notice that the line would slope moderately from the lower left to the upper right, but not be as steep as in the study 1 data in Figure 6.6.

Scatterplots are almost never presented in journal articles or other research reports, unless there is something unusual about the pattern of data. But they can be very useful. Researchers use scatterplots to clarify what they found. For instance, the pattern of data in a scatterplot may help them understand why no correlation was found for variables that should be related. We'll consider what they would look for after we discuss correlation coefficients.

The Concept of Correlation Coefficients

Galton made enormous contributions to our understanding of the nature of statistical associations, and his work inspired Pearson to take the next step, to *quantify* the strength and direction of correlations (Fancher, 1979). Pearson devised a procedure called the *Pearson product-moment correlation* (or just *Pearson's r*) that calculates the regression line for the variables and the amount by which the scores deviate from the line. This procedure yields a **correlation coefficient** (symbolized as r) that can range along a continuum from +1.00 to +.01 for a positive correlation and from −.01 to −1.00 for a negative correlation. The strength of a positive or negative association is given in the absolute value of the calculated r: disregarding the positive or negative sign, the closer the r is to an absolute value of 1.00, the stronger the correlation between the two variables.

For the data sets in Figure 6.6, the r values were +.87 for study 1, .00 for study 2, and −.75 for study 3. Coefficients with absolute values greater than about .60 are usually described as strong or very strong; those between about .30 and .60 are moderate, and those below .30 are weak. When researchers describe a correlation as strong, moderate, or weak, they are referring to the degree of association between variables and the ability to predict the value or level of one variable if we know a specific value of the other. For example, suppose we could assume that the outcome of study 1 in the figure would generalize well and I told you that I just took the sociopolitical attitude survey and got a score of 16. You could predict with a high degree of accuracy that I would get a score around 41 or so on the depression scale. How? You'd go to the scatterplot, find 16 on the horizontal axis, run a perpendicular line to the regression line, and from that point run a line perpendicular to the vertical axis—at 41 points! When variables are only moderately related, predictions like this one are less accurate. Although Pearson's r is the most widely used statistical test for assessing the strength of a relationship, it is not the only one, as we'll soon see.

Calculating a Correlation Coefficient

The Pearson product-moment correlation is a parametric statistic that can be used only with data that are on an interval or ratio scale, as Table 4.1 indicates (see inside front cover). If the data we are analyzing include at least one variable on a nominal or ordinal scale, we will need to use a nonparametric statistic to calculate a correlation coefficient. We can determine the correct statistic to use in the same way as we did earlier in this chapter. Look at Table 4.1 and ask three questions:

1. Is the purpose of the test to *assess differences* or *assess a relationship?* Answer: Relationship; we would focus on the upper portion of the table.
2. Are the data on a *nominal* or *ordinal* scale, or an *interval* or *ratio* scale? Answer: If the data for both variables are on an interval or ratio scale, we'd focus now on parametric statistics (the shaded area of the upper portion); otherwise, we would consider the nonparametric statistics.
3. Are we assessing relationships among *more than two data groupings?* Answer: If no, we would focus now only on statistics in the upper portion of the table corresponding to "2" data groupings; if yes, we would focus on the portion corresponding to "> 2" data groupings.

Because in correlational analyses, the data groupings are always paired, we would be ready to make our decision. If the data for both variables are on interval or ratio scales, we would use Pearson's *r*, but if at least one variable is ordinal and the other is ordinal, interval, or ratio, the Spearman (rho) rank correlation should be our choice. In either case, the analysis is described as *bivariate* because it involves two variables. Because parametric statistics are typically more powerful than nonparametric statistics, it is preferable to design studies that take measurements on an interval or ratio scale. *Appendix B of this book gives step-by-step instructions* for calculating Pearson and Spearman correlations with an SPSS computer program and a manual formula for Pearson's *r*.

Regardless of which statistical test we choose to calculate a correlation, the coefficient has much the same meaning and will determine whether and at what level the relationship is significant. Along with the coefficient, the computer program we use to perform the analysis will also give the *probability* of obtaining that value by chance—that is, when no association actually exists. If that probability is less than .05, we can conclude that the association we found is not likely to have occurred by chance alone. I calculated the Pearson's *r* for Galton's data on parent–child heights in Figure 6.5, using the midpoint for each cell—for instance, 68.5″ for a cell that ranges from 68″ to 69″—because the actual data were not available. The correlation is significant: $r(312) = +.38$, $p < .001$. Let's examine this shorthand statement, which is the standard way to express the statistical outcome of a correlational analysis in narrative form in research reports.

▪ We first specify the statistical test: *r* is the symbol for the coefficient in a Pearson product-moment correlation. If I had needed to use the Spearman rank correlation, the coefficient would have r_s as the symbol.

- The number in parenthesis is the degrees of freedom (*df*), which equals the number of pairs of scores minus 2 (*df* = *N* − 2) for a Pearson's *r* analysis. If several analyses all have the same *df*, that can be stated once.

- The calculated value of *r* is +.38, a moderately strong correlation; the calculated values from statistics are rounded to *two decimal places*.

- The *p* is the symbol for the probability of Type I error, and it is less than .001 for these data. Because the *p* refers to the likelihood that we would be *wrong* in rejecting the null hypothesis (that there is no relationship), we typically want the *p* to be very low. In this example, the risk of a Type I error would be less than 1 chance in 1,000. Values of *p* are usually rounded to *two decimal places*, but journals often report three decimal places if the precision reflects a stronger confidence level. The *p* values can be expressed either as *equal to* (using an = sign) or as *less than* (<) or *greater than* (>) the stated level. You will see all of these variations used in this book and in journal articles.

Notice also that this coefficient and the slope of the regression line that you tried to visualize earlier correspond—both are moderate. Galton was correct when he realized that the slope of a regression line reflected the strength of a relationship.

To illustrate and clarify the meaning and application of correlation coefficients, let's look at an example study. Researchers used the correlational strategy to test a theory underlying the use of cognitive therapy in treating depression (Seligman et al., 1988). Cognitive therapy is a treatment approach that is designed to help people change maladaptive automatic thoughts that they apply in everyday life. According to one theory of depression, some automatic thoughts lead people to feel helpless and hopeless and to have low self-esteem—which are defining features of depression. One category of automatic thoughts that lead to depression involves applying a pessimistic viewpoint to explain everyday events. If applying a pessimistic viewpoint automatically and habitually leads to depression, depressed individuals in cognitive therapy should show corresponding declines in both their depressive symptoms and their use of pessimistic automatic thoughts. The researchers assessed the depressive symptoms and tendency to apply pessimistic automatic thoughts of depressed clients before clients received cognitive therapy (at pretest), at posttest, and a year later. There were three main findings. First, the clients' symptoms and automatic thoughts decreased significantly from pretest to posttest. Second, correlational analyses revealed that the greater the depressive symptoms of these people, the greater their tendency to use pessimistic automatic thoughts at pretest, $r(37) = +.56$, $p < .001$; at posttest, $r(29) = +.57$, $p < .001$; and a year later, $r(25) = +.64$, $p < .001$. Third, the change scores from pretest to posttest were significantly correlated, $r(31) = +.65$, $p < .001$. The researchers concluded that depression symptoms improved "in lockstep" (p. 17) with pessimistic explanations of events.

Students in my research methods courses sometimes choose correlational strategies when they design and conduct projects. Here are two examples, each of which used survey methods with college students as respondents.

▪ A student studied associations among scores on established tests of religious commitment, stress, and optimism and found a significant negative correlation between optimism and stress levels ($r = +.68$, $p < .001$), but no correlation between religious commitment and either optimism ($r = .+16$, $p > .20$) or stress ($r = -.20$, $p = .13$), with all $dfs = 58$.

▪ A student tested the relationships between students' self-ratings of political ideology (degree of liberalism or conservatism) and their ratings of the ideologies of friends and parents. The ratings of their own political ideology and their scores on an established test of political ideology were significantly correlated ($r = +.46$, $p = .002$); their self-ratings were also correlated with their ratings of the ideologies of their friends ($r = +.32$, $p < .04$) and parents ($r = +.49$, $p = .001$), with all $dfs = 44$.

Look at the relationship between the r and p values in these examples: As the absolute value of r increases, the p value decreases. Notice also that the nonsignificant coefficients are low, and their corresponding p values are greater than .05.

Is it necessary to calculate an *effect size* for a correlational analysis? No, because an effect size is simply an estimate of the association between the variables examined, and the correlation coefficient already indicates the strength of the relationship.

Coefficient of Determination

When students learn about correlation, they often assume incorrectly (as I did for a while) that correlation coefficients form a ratio scale—for instance, an r of .80 is twice as strong as an r of .40. That is, we can predict one variable from another twice as accurately with an r of .80 than .40. Not so. To help you understand correlation correctly, we need to refer back to the topic of *variance.* We saw earlier in this chapter that the Pearson product-moment correlation test calculates the regression line and the amount by which scores deviate from it—the deviation is variance. We have also seen in this and prior chapters that variance can be systematic and nonsystematic (error variance). The mathematics of statistics can partition, or separate, these two types of variance. In a correlational test, systematic variance is the portion of the total variance that is shared by the variables being tested—that is, it is the amount of variability in a variable that can be "determined," or accounted for, by variation in the other variable. The regression line essentially plots the path of systematic variance graphically. Variance that is unrelated to those variables is nonsystematic error variance and is reflected in scores that deviate from the line. When all scores fall close to the regression line, there is little error variance, and the correlation coefficient is high. You can see contrasting degrees of variance in the scatterplots in Figure 6.6: Scores are fairly close to the regression line when the correlation is high, but they are far from the line when the correlation is low.

Although the correlation coefficient reflects systematic variance, it is actually the square root of a better measure of it. If we square the correlation coefficient, we get the **coefficient of determination** (r^2), or the proportion of the variance of one variable that can be accounted for by variation in the other variable. The r^2 for a correlation of +.80 (or −.80) is .64, which means that one variable accounts for 64% of the variance of the other. Although a correlation of .40 is numerically half of .80, the r^2 is only .16, or 16%. My student's study of political ideology, described earlier, found that the participants' ideologies correlated with those of their parents and friends at +.49 and +.32, respectively. Looking at the corresponding values of r^2, we see that 24% ($.49^2 = .24$) of the variance in the participants' ideologies can be accounted for by their parents' views, which is more than twice the amount ($.32^2 = .10$, or 10%) that can be accounted for by their friends' views. If you think about all the factors that can influence people's ideologies, a single factor accounting for 24% of the variance is quite a lot.

INTERPRETING CORRELATIONS

A nicely designed study using a correlational strategy with over 1,500 American adults examined relationships between their self-reported health and emotional or personality characteristics (Lubin et al., 1988). The health data included self-ratings from very poor to excellent and the numbers of prescription medications ("meds") and nonprescription meds they were currently using. The emotional and personality variables were anxiety (A), depression (D), hostility (H), positive affect (PA, such as feeling happy or pleased), and sensation seeking (SS). Although the researchers analyzed each variable individually, to simplify things, we'll look only at analyses that combined variables by adding scores: A+D+H and PA+SS. The Pearson's r and p values the researchers reported for A+D+H and PA+SS with health variables are

Health variables	*r* and *p* for A+D+H	*r* and *p* for PA+SS
Self-ratings of health	−.16 ($p < .001$)	+.25 ($p < .001$)
Prescription meds used	+.07 ($p < .01$)	−.07 ($p < .01$)
Nonprescription meds used	+.05 ($p < .05$)	−.02 ($p > .05$)

In looking over these correlations, three questions come to mind. First, even though almost all the correlations are significant, they are quite low—how can they be significant? Second, how do we interpret low, significant correlations? Third, regardless of the absolute value of the r, what does a significant correlation tell us about whether one variable causes changes in another?

Low Correlation Coefficients

How can a low correlation be significant? Let's consider three reasons. First, there may be very little error variance in the data. Second, think back to Chapter 4 where we discussed the concept of *power*—the sensitivity of a statistical procedure to detect a relationship or difference. An analysis with extremely high power can detect a weak relationship and calculate that the probability of being wrong (making a Type I error) in concluding it actually exists is very slight, less than 5 chances in 100, for instance. Extremely high power often results from having a very large number of subjects. Third, some studies involve large numbers of analyses: Of every 100 analyses, 5 are likely to be significant just by chance alone. When a study uses a large number of analyses, researchers often choose a more stringent *alpha*—that is, the minimum level of *p* to qualify as "significant"—such as by setting alpha at .01 instead of the usual .05. The study on emotions and health had over 1,500 participants and involved dozens of analyses. To interpret its low, significant correlations, we can apply coefficients of determination. For instance, the A+D+H and PA+SS variables each correlated significantly at an absolute value of .07 with prescription meds. The corresponding value of r^2 is .0049, which means that knowing the levels of either A+D+H or PA+SS would enable us to be just 0.49% more accurate on average in predicting prescription meds use than we would be without considering A+D+H or PA+SS.

Sometimes features of the data or the research methodology can mask or distort associations between variables, reduce the power of a statistical analysis, and produce a low correlation when the actual relationship is much stronger. To illustrate four of these problematic features, look again at the scatterplots in Figure 6.6 and maintain your place there because we'll be using the diagrams for a while. One of these features occurs when a study uses measures of one or both variables that have *low reliability*. We saw in Chapter 4 that measures with low reliability produce inconsistent data that increase error variability. That is, even when the true value of the variable has not changed, an unreliable measure will yield varying data. In the scatterplot for the study 2 data, there is no pattern to the data. The data points just seem to be scattered about in a nonsystematic fashion. This outcome could result entirely or partly from using a very unreliable measurement procedure.

Another feature that can distort a correlation is a **curvilinear relationship** between the variables—that is, the data points form a pattern that is not *linear*, and the trend does not follow a straight line. For example, look again at the data in the study 2 scatterplot and imagine that the four dots in the lower right region were shifted to the right so that the sociopolitical scores were, say, 4 points higher. The linear regression line would probably stay in about the same position, and there would still be a zero correlation. But in your visual image, don't you see a pattern to the dots? It forms an upside-down U and has a name: an *inverted-U* pattern. The relationships between some variables have an inverted-U pattern. For instance, people perform best on moderately difficult tasks when their emotional arousal, such as from anxiety, is at a medium level and perform much less well when their arousal is at a very low or very high level (Anderson, 1990). Other shapes of curvilinear patterns can also occur. Underlying the Pearson's *r* is the assumption that the pattern of data points for the variables is basically linear. If researchers have reason to expect a fairly strong correlation and find a weak one, they often look at the scatterplot to see if the pattern has a curvilinear form.

A third feature that can distort an association is a **restricted range,** or a narrow span of scores. Look again at the scatterplot patterns in Figure 6.6. For each set of data, imagine that the data points were moved so that the regression line still passes through the middle, but the points form a ball-shaped or slightly oval pattern somewhere along the line. Because the cluster of scores is so restricted, the shape of the distribution does not extend along a clearly defined line. As a result, the correlational mathematics can't identify the slope of the line accurately, thereby producing a lower coefficient. Correlational analyses need at least a moderately broad range of scores on both variables to identify the regression line and its slope accurately. Once again, examining the scatterplot for the variables can help researchers determine if a restricted range may have been responsible for a weak correlation.

The last feature that can distort a correlation is the occurrence of **outliers,** which refer to one or a few scores that are clearly outside the main distribution of the data. Look again at Figure 6.6, but just the scatterplot for study 1. Imagine that an extra data point has been added, either in the far regions of the upper left corner or in the lower right corner. The rest of the data seem to form a fairly clear oval, following the regression line; the one added in one of the corners sticks out like a "sore thumb." This extra score would lower the correlation because it is far from the regression line. Outliers can also occur at a far end of the regression line. For instance, notice that there are three data points in the lower left corner. Now use your finger to cover the two dots that represent the sociopolitical score of 12, leaving the data for the person with very low scores on depression and sociopolitical attitudes. That score would be an example of an outlier, and it would distort to some degree the correlation coefficient. Sometimes researchers decide that outliers are flukes and exclude them from analyses or use a mathematical rule to bring them closer to the rest of the distribution, but doing this after the fact can introduce bias in the data. Appendix B describes ways for dealing with outliers.

Directionality and Causal Inference

A student of mine wanted to study the role of exposure to media aimed at women, such as TV soap operas and fashion magazines, on college females' body image and found a very strong negative correlation: the higher the exposure, the lower or more negative the body image, $r(98) = -.79$, $p = .01$. What does this finding mean? Does the very high correlation mean that variations in one of the variables probably caused changes in the other? No, the correlation's strength does not suggest anything about cause. Given that the student wanted to study the role of media in body image, does the significant correlation mean women's exposure to the media aimed at women lowers their body image? We can't make a causal inference from just a correlation because the design did not demonstrate a clear causal time sequence or eliminate other plausible causes. In fact, if there is a causal relationship between these variables, it could operate in the other direction: having a low body image leads women to have more exposure to the media aimed at them. What we know from the correlation is simply that the two variables are strongly associated. The fact that a causal relationship between variables could operate in either direction is a basic problem in correlational outcomes called **directionality.**

A classic example of the directionality problem is in the relationship between watching a lot of violence on TV and being aggressive. Does watching TV violence *cause* individuals to become aggressive, or does being aggressive *cause* people to prefer watching violence? Because researchers cannot manipulate the TV shows people watch across months or years, most studies of this issue have used correlational strategies and shown simply that the two variables are related. Is it possible to use correlational methods and produce results that convincingly demonstrate that watching a lot of TV violence causes aggression, and not the other way around? Yes. Doing the research is very difficult to design and carry out, but it has been done. One especially fine study used correlational procedures in a longitudinal design (Eron, Huesmann, Lefkowitz, & Walder, 1972). The study began in 1960 when the researchers collected data on 875 third graders' aggressiveness, preferences for violent TV shows, and a variety of family characteristics. Aggressiveness was assessed through peer ratings in school. In assessing the children's preferences for violent TV, the researchers had the parents list their child's three favorite TV shows, classified the shows as violent or nonviolent, and scored the child on the basis of the number of violent shows in his or her list. After 10 years (which the researchers "for convenience" called "13th grade") when the participants were 19 years old, the researchers were able to locate and interview 211 of the boys and 216 of the girls and to collect peer ratings of the aggressiveness these participants had shown in high school. The participants' current preferences for TV violence were measured in much the same way as 10 years earlier, except that the participants provided their own lists of favorite shows during the interview.

Preliminary statistical analyses showed that the boys in the study scored much higher on aggressiveness and preferences for TV violence than the girls, which is consistent with almost all studies of aggressive behavior. Perhaps because of a restricted range in the girls' data, correlations between aggressiveness and preferences were relatively weak for them, and the researchers focused on analyses of the boys' data. The researchers addressed the problem of directionality by using a statistical approach called **cross-lagged panel correlations,** in which correlations between the two variables are calculated across two or more points in time (Cook & Campbell, 1979). Because of the large number of correlations in this and other analyses, the researchers raised the minimum level of p to qualify as significant from .05 to .01. Figure 6.7 diagrams the approach and presents the cross-lagged panel correlations for aggressiveness and preference for TV violence. The most important correlations are along the diagonals: there was no association ($r = +.01$) between aggressiveness in the third grade and watching violent TV years later, but there was a significant, moderately strong positive correlation between watching violent TV and later aggressiveness. This outcome suggests that if there is an underlying causal relationship between the two variables, we have evidence of its direction: watching violent TV is more likely to lead to aggression than the other way around.

Notice also the correlations along the vertical and horizontal lines. Preferences for violent TV at the 13th grade were not significantly related to preferences at the 3rd grade or to concurrent aggression. If aggressive people are attracted to watching violence, these correlations would both be positive and much stronger. And what does the significant correlation between 3rd- and 13th-grade aggression mean? Aggressiveness is a fairly stable behavioral pattern, and many non-TV factors influence it, including people's personal experiences and heredity. Although using cross-lagged panel correlations to demonstrate cause-effect can have limitations (Cook & Campbell, 1979), the pattern of signif-

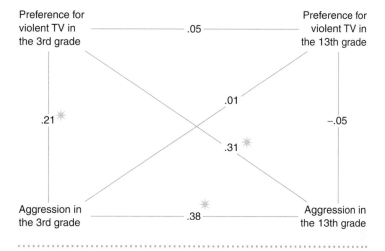

FIGURE 6.7

All possible cross-lagged panel correlations between aggressiveness and preference for TV violence across a 10-year period for 211 boys (an asterisk means the *r* is significant). The most important correlations are along the diagonal lines. (From Eron et al., 1972, Figure 1)

icant and nonsignificant correlations in this study tells us the direction of any causal influence that may exist between aggression and watching violent TV.

Third Variables and Causal Inference

Suppose someone told you that the shoe size of schoolchildren correlates with their reading or math ability. Would you advise your friends and relatives who are parents to stretch their children's feet to improve their academic performance? Of course not. Given that the correlation is real, you'd try to think of a reason for it—for instance, foot size and reading or math ability increase with age! In other words, age or development is an extraneous "third variable" in this relationship. Because we cannot directly control many potential extraneous variables in correlational research, there is always the possibility that a relationship reflects the effects of a **third variable,** an uncontrolled factor that is responsible for the variations in both of the correlated variables. Third variables are not always obvious or easy to discover. For example, some years ago I read that marketing researchers found a significant correlation between the number of frying pans in the home and the IQs of the residents: the more frying pans, the higher the IQs. Because you realize there must be a third variable operating here (and you won't run out and buy frying pans before your next exam), what might it be? My guess is household income: IQ correlates moderately with income, and people with high incomes can afford to own more pans.

Could there have been one or more third variables operating in the study by Eron and his colleagues on aggressiveness and watching violent TV? Yes, but the researchers used an ingenious approach to rule out many possible extraneous variables. They used a statistical technique called a **partial correlation,** which removes or "partials out" the variance associated with a third variable and recalculates the correlation between the two research variables. If the correlation coefficient is about the same with the partial correlation procedure as with the regular correlation procedure, that possible third variable can be ruled out as being responsible for the original correlation. But if the correlations are different, that third variable may have been responsible. For example, suppose in the frying pan study the original (regular) correlation with IQ was +.40; if the correlation drops to only +.15 when we partial out income, we'd conclude that income was probably responsible for at least part of the original correlation. To use the partial correlation technique, we must have data on the potential third variable. Fortunately, Eron et al. (1972) collected data on family characteristics and other factors at both the 3rd- and 13th-grade testing. Using the data for 12 possible third variables, they recalculated the important correlation (+.31) between 3rd-grade aggressiveness and 13th-grade preference for violent TV 12 times, each time removing the variance for one of the extraneous variables. Table 6.2 presents the partial correlation for each potential third variable (the statistically "controlled variable," as they called it). As you look down the table, notice two features. First, the variables tested were chosen carefully, with each being a logically compelling possible third variable. Second, no partial correlation differs much from the original +.31, indicating that none of the factors tested contributed substantially to the original correlation.

TABLE 6.2

Partial Correlations Between Preference for Violent TV at 3rd Grade (VTV3) and Aggressiveness at 13th Grade (AGG13), Statistically Controlling for 12 Possible Third Variables, for Comparison Against the Original Correlation (+.31)

Controlled (third) variable	Partial correlation between VTV3 and AGG13
3rd-grade variables	
Peer-rated aggression	.25
Father's occupational status	.31
Participant's (child) IQ	.28
Father's aggressiveness	.30
Mother's aggressiveness	.31
Parents' punishment administered	.31
Parents' aspirations for child	.30
Parents' mobility orientation	.31
Participant's hours of television watched	.30
13th-grade variables	
Father's occupational status	.28
Participant's aspirations	.28
Participant's hours of television watched	.30
None (original correlation for comparison)	.31

Note: All coefficients are positive. The numbers of participants across analyses varied (mean = 166), probably due to missing data.

Source: Adapted from Eron et al. (1972), Table 4.

By combining the outcomes of the cross-lagged panel correlation and the partial correlation procedures, these researchers have provided rather strong evidence from correlational strategies that watching violent TV can cause aggressiveness, at least in boys. Of course, there is always the possibility that they neglected to test a third variable that was, in fact, responsible for the original +.31 correlation, but this seems unlikely, given the lack of influence of the 12 compelling factors they did test. The design and analyses they used take their research about as close to meeting all three of the criteria for causal inference as a correlational strategy can get. (Go to **Box 6.2**)

BOX 6.2

INFERRING CAUSES FROM VARIED RESEARCH STRATEGIES

We have seen that sometimes it is not logistically or ethically feasible to manipulate independent variables and randomly assign subjects to groups to demonstrate cause-effect relationships. Often the preferred types of evidence are not available, and professionals must make judgments about likely causes and effects, particularly when developing theories or in applied situations, such as clinical practice (Meehl, 1993). Two approaches can help in these circumstances. First, they can try to base their thinking and decisions as much as possible on the results of quasi-experimental and correlational research with human participants that used careful methodological and statistical controls. Second, they can formulate a rational justification for causal inference by weaving together the outcomes of experimental research with animal subjects and nonexperimental research with humans. Let's look at an example of the latter approach.

After reviewing the results of dozens of studies on the role of stress in memory and brain structure, Bremner and Narayan (1998) proposed a theory to explain how long-term, intense stress leads to impaired memory ability. Here are some highlights of the findings they reviewed.

- Animal research with experimental strategies had shown that intense stress increases the release of hormones called glucocorticoids from endocrine glands, and high levels of these hormones cause damage to and reduce the size of the hippocampus, an area of the brain that is involved in memory processes. Some of these experiments also demonstrated learning and memory deficits in animals after stress-induced damage to the hippocampus.

- Research had found that increases in glucocorticoid levels are correlated with the degree of memory impairments in elderly adults.

continued

■ Quasi experiments compared people who had the psychiatric condition called posttraumatic stress disorder (PTSD) with control participants who were matched for several factors, including age, race, alcohol use, and education. PTSD results from intense stress, such as in war or child abuse. Participants with PTSD had poorer memory function and smaller hippocampus sizes (measured with radiological imaging methods called MRI) than the control participants. These associations alone do not demonstrate cause–effect because of a directionality problem: People with PTSD may have been born with smaller hippocampus sizes, which may have made them more likely to perceive stressful events as highly intense and, therefore, to develop PTSD.

Putting these findings together, Bremner and Narayan proposed that long-term, stress-produced high levels of glucocorticoids damage the hippocampus, causing impaired memory processes in humans.

REGRESSION AND MULTIPLE REGRESSION ANALYSIS

Remember when we discussed how we could use the regression line in a scatterplot to make a rough prediction of a person's score on one variable if we knew his or her score on a correlated variable? Predicting scores on one variable from scores on another can be done mathematically and is called **regression analysis.** The process of regression analysis plots a regression line mathematically and more precisely than people can do visually, by applying the standard equation for a straight line that you may have learned in an earlier math class:

$$Y = a + bX$$

where Y is the score we want to predict (we'll assume on the vertical axis), a is the value where the extended regression line would cross the vertical axis, b is an index of the line's slope, and X is the score we already know (on the horizontal axis). With the calculated regression line as its basis, a regression analysis "draws" mathematically a vertical line from the horizontal axis (at the score we already know) to the regression line. Then from the intersection on the regression line, it "draws" a horizontal line to the vertical axis, intersecting at the score we are trying to predict.

Researchers and professionals can use regression analysis to predict a variety of outcomes, such as a person's future college grades from an SAT score, job performance from an aptitude test score, heart disease from blood cholesterol levels, and speed of running from the volume of oxygen consumed during physical exertion. These examples describe analyses of *simple linear regression,* which tests only two variables (bivariate) and assumes that the data points are linear in a scatterplot. The variable with the score to be predicted (Y in the formula) is the called the **criterion variable;** the variable with the score we already know (X)

is the **predictor variable.** In addition to predicting a value on the criterion variable, a regression analysis yields a correlation coefficient symbolized as capital R to distinguish it from r, even though they are statistically alike. The analysis also gives an R^2, which is like the coefficient of determination (r^2) and indicates the proportion of variance of one variable that is accounted for by the other. The reason for the capital letters is that regression analyses are usually computed with more than two variables.

An extension of simple linear regression is **multiple regression,** in which the prediction for a criterion variable (Y) is made from a linear combination of two or more predictor variables (X_1, X_2, and so on). The regression equation with two predictor variables would now become, $Y = a + b_1X_1 + b_2X_2$, for example. There are two main reasons for using multiple regression instead of simple linear regression. First, the prediction for a criterion variable may be more accurate with more than one predictor variable. For example, predicting a student's college grades may be more accurate if, in addition to SAT scores, we include high school grades and a rating of his or her "maturity" that might be made by evaluating information in an essay the student wrote and letters of recommendation. Running a multiple regression on data for a large number of students will tell us whether using three predictor variables accounts for significantly more of the variance in the criterion variable than just two or just one predictor variable. Second, multiple regression can be used to control statistically for and rule out the effects of potential third variables in research. For example, in the study of TV and aggression, Eron et al. (1972) performed a multiple regression using aggressiveness at 13th grade as the criterion variable and the 3rd-grade scores for watching violent TV and for each possible third variable as the predictor variables. Watching violent TV at third grade accounted for significantly more of the variance in 13th-grade aggressiveness than any of the other variables, and all the other variables combined accounted for very little additional variance.

SPECIAL-PURPOSE CORRELATIONAL USES

Correlational statistics are applied in all areas of psychology and have many uses beyond the ones we've seen so far. We'll consider some other uses.

Testing the Role of Genetics

In the hypothetical twin study on alcoholism we discussed earlier, we used a discrete variable (classifying individuals as having alcoholism or not) and analyzed concordance data for differences. How would we handle the data if we measured alcohol abuse as a continuous variable, such as the number of drinks consumed per day? Many twin studies apply correlational statistics with the logic that if heredity plays an important role in the appearance or level of a characteristic, the correlation coefficient for that variable in pairs of twins should increase as the degree of genetic relationship increases. The level of the characteristic should correlate more highly among pairs of identical than same-sex fraternal twins. This approach has produced evidence in dozens of studies for the role of genetics for many psychological characteristics. For example, the average correlation coefficients across many studies are, respectively for identical and fraternal twins, +.82 and +.59 for general intelligence, +.52 and +.25 for the extraversion-introversion personality traits, and +.51 and +.22 for neuroticism (Scarr & Kidd, 1983). In each case, the correlation is much higher for identical than fraternal twins.

Testing Tests for Reliability and Validity

We discussed in Chapter 4 that the measurements scientists make in research should be both reliable and valid. If a measurement procedure is *reliable,* the data it produces are consistent and dependable across time, assuming that the variable it measures has not changed. The more consistent its outcome, the more reliable the measure. A *valid* measurement procedure assesses what it intends or claims to assess. Measurements in psychological research often rely on surveys or tests. A major focus of the field of *psychometrics* is to provide evidence for the reliability and validity of these instruments, and this evidence is usually based on correlational analyses.

Researchers use basically two approaches to assess the reliability of an instrument. One approach, called **test-retest reliability,** examines the consistency of responses by the same people with the same instrument at two testing sessions, usually spaced a few weeks apart. Suppose we had composed a new instrument to measure people's anxiety and wanted to assess its reliability with the test-retest approach. If we tested a large number of people, we should find that each person's scores are similar at the two sessions. We wouldn't expect all individuals to score exactly the same at both sessions, but their scores should be close. To quantify the consistency of the scores, we would run a correlation on the two data groupings, test and retest: the higher the coefficient, the more reliable is the instrument. As a general rule of thumb, researchers consider an instrument to be reliable if it yields a coefficient of at least +.70 (and very reliable above .80) in a test-retest evaluation, recognizing that the correlation is likely to decline if the time between testing sessions increases beyond a month or so. Figure 6.8 presents two diagrams, one illustrating high test-retest reliability and one illustrating low reliability.

The second approach, called **inter-item reliability,** uses a single testing session, splitting the items in the instrument in half and performing a correlation between the scores on each half, which can be carried out in two ways. One way is called the **split-half method** and involves dividing the items into two sets, such as by separating odd- and even-numbered items or by random assignment, adding the scores for each set for each participant, and then calculating the correlation between the two sets. A problem with this method is that the specific items that happen to end up in the two sets may affect the correlation. The second method overcomes this problem: the **internal-consistency method** involves splitting the items randomly into two sets over and over, running a correlation each time, and then averaging the coefficients. The most commonly used statistical procedure for calculating internal consistency is **Cronbach's alpha** (Streiner, 2003). It yields a single coefficient, *alpha* (this name does not relate to the term you recall in connection with Type I error). Computer programs can do the internal-consistency method and calculate Cronbach's alpha if you input each and every item score for each participant, which is tedious but worth it.

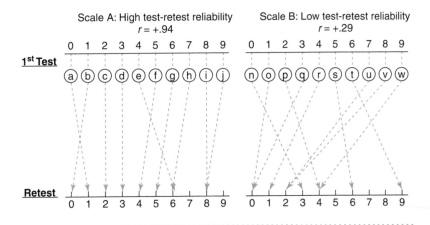

FIGURE 6.8

Diagrams of high and low test-retest reliability for Scale A and Scale B for assessing, for instance, people's anxiety. Each of the 10 hypothetical participants with each scale (**a** to **j** for Scale A and **n** to **w** for Scale B) got a different score, 0 through 9, at the first testing. One month later they were retested on the same scale. As the diagrams depict, scores on the test and retest were very consistent across time on Scale A but not on Scale B. Pearson's *r* analyses on the data yielded a high coefficient for Scale A and a low coefficient for Scale B.

(To access the procedure in SPSS, click on *Analyze,* then *Scale,* and then *Reliability Analysis.*) A coefficient of at least +.80 in a split-half or internal-consistency method indicates that the instrument is very reliable, but +.70 is often acceptable. There are two limiting factors in inter-item reliability methods: all items in the analysis must be intended to measure the same variable, and the coefficient is likely to be reduced if the number of items in the instrument is small, say, below 15 or 20.

There are several types of validity, and each is assessed differently. In Chapter 4, we defined *face validity* as whether the measurement "looks like" it measures what is intended to assess. We might see face validity, for example, if an instrument to measure depression asked about feelings of sadness, hopelessness, and being unable to cope with and control undesirable events. Our earlier discussion stated that face validity is the simplest method for judging validity and that we would discuss more complex approaches later. Here's where we do that, and we'll examine two broad approaches, criterion validity and construct validity, each with two methods for evaluating it.

By **criterion validity,** researchers mean the degree to which an instrument's scores correlate with an existing standard or predict a future event or variable. The existing standard or the future event serves as the "criterion" for the measure's validity. One method for assessing an instrument's criterion validity is to test its **concurrent validity,** or the degree to which its scores correlate with scores from an established, already validated instrument. If we were developing a new instrument to measure intelligence (IQ)—for instance, a brief form that has 30 items—we would have participants take the new test and one that is already known to measure IQ well, such as the Stanford-Binet IQ test. The higher the correlation between the two sets of data, the greater the concurrent validity of the new instrument. Another method for assessing an instrument's criterion validity is to test its **predictive validity**—the degree to which its scores forecast a future variable. To validate our new IQ test, for example, we would correlate its scores with the participants' academic grades in the following year. The greater the concurrent and predictive validity of an instrument, the greater its criterion validity.

By **construct validity,** researchers mean the degree to which the scores on an instrument are consistent with the construct(s) it is supposed to measure or the theory that was used as the basis for its development. Suppose we are developing a test of the *authoritarian personality,* the tendency of some people to submit blindly to authority and be rigid and dogmatic in their beliefs. We can assess an instrument's construct validity in two ways. First, we can examine its **convergent validity**—the degree to which its scores correlate with scores from validated instruments that assess *conceptually similar,* but not identical, variables. To test the convergent validity of the authoritarian personality scale, we could have participants fill it out along with established scales of political and religious conservatism. If the authoritarian and conservatism scores correlate highly, we have evidence of convergent validity. Second, we can test the instrument's **discriminant validity** (or *divergent validity*) by demonstrating that its scores *do not* correlate with established scales of very dissimilar or conceptually unrelated constructs. For example, we should find low correlations between authoritarian personality and scores on scales of depression and self-esteem. Because there can be so many conceptually similar and dissimilar variables for the construct an instrument assesses, establishing a measure's construct validity usually takes considerable time as evidence accumulates over many studies.

Factor Analysis

Factor analysis refers to a class of complex correlational techniques to assess interrelationships among a large set of variables to identify the underlying constructs or dimensions, called "factors," that link the variables into subsets or clusters. Computing a factor analysis requires each and every item score for each participant be input into the analysis. What purposes do factor analyses serve?

One common reason for doing a factor analysis is to confirm the intended structure of a psychological test. For example, Scheier and Carver (1985) developed an instrument to measure people's optimism. It has 12 items, four each that are phrased in a positive direction (for instance, "In uncertain times, I usually expect the best."), phrased in a negative direction ("If something can go wrong for me, it will."), and unrelated "filler" items. Respondents rate their agreement with each statement on a Likert scale, and negatively phrased items are reversed-scored prior to totaling the ratings. The researchers performed a factor analysis with data from over 600 undergraduates to show that the positive and negative items were perceived and responded to differently, and Table 6.3 presents the outcome. The coefficients in the table are called *factor loadings* and reflect the correlations of each item with the factor as a whole. Notice the items with high loadings (shaded) on each factor: Half of the items load strongly on one factor, and half load on the other. None loads strongly on both. The items that load in factor 1 are the ones that were phrased in the negative direction; those with loading in factor 2 were phrased in the positive direction. By looking at the items that load on each factor, the researcher tries to determine what the factor means. In this case, the decision is easy and obvious. Factor analyses don't always turn out so clearly and often yield several factors rather than just two.

Another reason for doing a factor analysis is to test a theory that describes a construct that has more than one component to it, and theories can vary in the number of factors they propose that the construct contains. For instance, a theory by Spearman (1904) claims that intelligence involves a dominant factor, general intelligence (*g*), and secondary factors for specific topics; other theories claim and describe several factors and no general one. If Spearman was correct, factor analyses should reveal a single factor on which most items in intelligence tests would load, and some secondary factors that correspond to the topics of the questions, such as math. Studies that have included factor analyses have tested each theory, sometimes finding support for one theory over others. Although no theory has received full support, factor analyses seem to confirm the idea of a general intelligence factor, but the number of other factors in intelligence is still unresolved.

TABLE 6.3

Factor Loadings for Items a Test of Optimism Phrased in Positive or Negative Directions

Item number	Factor 1	Factor 2
1	−.06	+.56
3	+.62	+.02
4	+.01	+.72
5	+.09	+.61
8	+.83	−.03
9	+.68	−.02
11	+.01	+.66
12	+.53	+.04

Note: Items 2, 6, 7, and 10 were not included because they were filler items.

Source: Scheier and Carver (1985), Table 2.

SUMMARY

When researchers have a goal other than demonstrating cause–effect for a study or experimental strategies are not feasible, they turn to a nonexperimental approach, using a quasi-experimental, correlational, or descriptive strategy. Quasi experiments use manipulated independent variables in the nonequivalent control group design and the interrupted time-series design. Other types of quasi experiments use natural-groups designs in which the independent variables are subject variables, such as gender, age, behavior or personality characteristics, and genetic relationship. In examining age differences, researchers can use the cross-sectional approach, the longitudinal approach, or a combination of the two. To study behavior or personality characteristics as independent variables, researchers can use prospective or retrospective approaches, often forming groups by using the median-split method or the extreme-groups method. Twin studies are used in examining genetic differences.

When a goal of a study is to assess the degree and direction of statistical association between variables, researchers use correlational strategies. If the data analyzed in correlational analyses are graphed in a scatterplot as paired values for the research variables, we can visualize roughly where a regression line would go, showing the trend of the data points. The Pearson's correlational analysis yields a correlation coefficient (r), ranging from +1.00 to –1.00, reflecting the degree and direction of statistical association. Squaring that coefficient gives the coefficient of determination (r^2), which indicates the amount of variance in one variable accounted for or explained by the other variable. A correlation can sometimes be masked or distorted by features of the data or research methodology, such as low reliability of measurement, curvilinear relationship, restricted range, or outliers. The problem of directionality in correlational interpretation can be addressed by using cross-lagged panel correlations. Using a partial correlation technique can reduce the problem of third variables by controlling for the variance associated with an extraneous variable.

Regression analysis and multiple regression are statistical procedures that enable researchers to predict the level of a criterion variable from values along a predictor variable. Researchers can also use correlational techniques with other purposes, such as in testing the role of genetics in behavior, assessing the reliability and validity of surveys, assessing interrelationships among many variables, and testing models. Psychometric research can assess an instrument's test-retest reliability and inter-item reliability; the latter is done by the split-half method or by the internal-consistency method with Cronbach's alpha statistical procedure. An instrument's criterion validity can be evaluated with concurrent validity and predictive validity methods, and its construct validity can be tested with convergent validity and discriminant validity methods. Factor analysis tests a large set of variables for their interrelationships, allowing researchers to identify underlying constructs or dimensions.

KEY TERMS

quasi-experimental strategy
correlational strategy
descriptive strategy
nonequivalent control group design
interrupted time-series design
subject variable
natural-groups design
cross-sectional design
longitudinal design
cohort
prospective approach
retrospective approach
median-split method

extreme-groups method
twin studies
scatterplot
regression line
correlation coefficient
coefficient of determination
curvilinear relationship
restricted range
outliers
directionality
cross-lagged panel correlations
third variable
partial correlation
regression analysis

criterion variable
predictor variable
multiple regression
test-retest reliability
inter-item reliability
split-half method
internal-consistency method
Cronbach's alpha
criterion validity
concurrent validity
predictive validity
construct validity
convergent validity
discriminant validity
factor analysis

REVIEW QUESTIONS

1. Describe the methodology and results of the Rodin and Langer study on the role of personal control in psychological and health variables.

2. How is the control of systematic variance involved in the greater ability of quasi-experimental than correlational strategies to meet the criteria for cause–effect?

3. Describe the main characteristics of the *nonequivalent control group design* and a few possible outcomes that were not found in the Morier and Keeports study on beliefs in paranormal events.

4. Describe the main characteristics of the *interrupted time-series design* and the difference in clarity of outcomes between the Fox, Hopkins, and Anger study on mine safety and the Ross and White study on publishing the names of lawbreakers in a newspaper.

5. Define the *cross-sectional design,* the *longitudinal design,* and the concept of *cohort effects* in developmental research.

6. Give one example each of using the *median-split method* and *extreme-groups method* to create two groups on the basis of a subject variable.

7. What are *scatterplots* and *regression lines?* When are scatterplots useful for researchers?

8. Describe how to use Table 4.1 (see inside front cover) to decide which statistical test to use to calculate a correlation coefficient.

9. What is the *coefficient of determination,* and how is it related to the *correlation coefficient?*

10. What data and methodological factors can distort associations between variables and lead to low correlation coefficients?

11. Describe in detail the Eron et al. study on watching violent TV and later aggressiveness and how the researchers applied *cross-lagged panel correlations* and *partial correlations* to address the problems of *directionality* and *third variables.*

12. What are *regression analysis* and *multiple regression,* and why are they useful?

13. Define and discuss the various forms of correlation-based reliability and validity assessment methods for psychological surveys and tests.

14. What is *factor analysis,* and why is it useful?

RESOURCES

BOOKS, CHAPTERS, AND ARTICLES

Cook, R. D., & Campbell, D. T. (1979). *Quasi-experimentation: Design & analysis issues for field settings.* Chicago: Rand McNally.

Goldstein, G., & Herson, M. (Eds.). (1990). *Handbook of psychological assessment* (2nd ed.). New York: Pergamon.

INTERNET SITES

http://www.ericfacility.net/ericdigests421483.htm This Website distinguishes between experimental and quasi-experimental design strategies.

http://www.fammed.ouhsc.edu/tutor/qexpdes.htm Website with descriptions and research examples of quasi-experimental designs.

http://www.burns.com/wcbspurcorl.htm A Website with examples of spurious correlations—variables that are statistically but not causally related.

APPLICATION ACTIVITIES

APPLICATION 6–1: DESIGNING QUASI EXPERIMENTS

Imagine that your college is planning to introduce a program for all entering freshmen to reduce student interpersonal conflicts by participating in a video and discussion series during the entire month of October to enhance their appreciation of diversity. Design two quasi experiments, one using a nonequivalent control groups design and one using an interrupted time-series design, to evaluate the program's success in reducing the recent high levels of conflicts. What extraneous variables could threaten the internal validity of each study? What could be done to decrease those threats and produce clearer outcomes?

APPLICATION 6–2: INTERPRETING CORRELATIONS

Suppose you read a research article with the following statistical outcome for two variables, stress and drinking alcohol, in a correlational analysis: $r(28) = -.46$, $p = .01$. What does each number and symbol in this shorthand statement represent? How would you interpret the outcome of the study?

For each of the following research outcomes from bivariate correlational analyses, describe the directionality problem in interpreting the results and a likely third variable that may be responsible for the finding. In each case, assume the participants were college students, and the relationship found was significant ($p < .05$).

1. A study of individuals who were currently in romantic relationships found a positive correlation between the degree of satisfaction with the relationship and the amount of communication the participants felt existed in the relationship.

2. A study of women revealed a negative correlation between their levels of body satisfaction and eating-disordered behavior.

3. A study of students found a negative correlation between their levels of self-esteem and anxiety in taking tests.

4. A study of students revealed a positive correlation between their levels of alcohol consumption and their parents' levels of authoritarianism.

5. A study found a positive correlation between levels of stress and of motivation for scholastic achievement.

6. A study found that the amount of time individuals spend on the Internet is negatively correlated with their GPA.

CHAPTER 7
SINGLE-FACTOR, INDEPENDENT-GROUPS DESIGNS

Picture on a table in front of you three glasses that can hold the same volume of liquid. Two of them have a large diameter and are short (they are identical), and the other one has a small diameter and is tall. The two short glasses have equal amounts of cola, which you confirm visually and adjust with an eyedropper if necessary. The tall glass is empty. A friend pours the cola from one of the short glasses into the tall one, sets the now empty short glass aside, and asks, "Do the two remaining glasses have the same amount of cola, or does one have more?" You answer, "They have the same amount, of course." This answer shows that you can "conserve," or recognize that an object's quantity doesn't change just because its shape changes. Jean Piaget (1929, 1952) used this and similar tests with children and found that those who were younger than about 7 years of age could not conserve. For example, they'd usually say that one of the glasses had more and justify the choice by saying something like, "because it's taller" if they chose the tall one, or "because it's fatter" if they chose the short one. From tests like this, Piaget proposed his highly regarded theory that describes four stages of cognitive development that unfold with maturation in childhood and can be accelerated only modestly by deliberate training.

Was Piaget correct that training would produce small, superficial gains? Dorothy Field (1981) tested this issue with 3- and 4-year-old children who in pretests showed no evidence that they could conserve with five very different conservation problems. Field randomly assigned the children to an experimental and a control group, making sure they were similar in intellectual ability, age, and gender distribution. The experimental group received 1½ hours of training on two conservation problems over a few sessions; the training was structured like games, and the children received feedback for their answers and small rewards for correct answers. The control group received no training, but played irrelevant games with the researcher and received rewards. Did the training work? Yes, very well. A week after the last training session, the children were tested again on the five conservation problems; the experimental group correctly answered significantly more problems—6.52 times as many—than the control group. Two other findings indicate that the trained children's superiority was not limited to the conservation problems on which they were trained and was durable. First, close to 40% of the trained children could solve at least one type of problem for which they were *not* trained. Second, when tested again a few months later, the trained children continued to outperform the controls, getting 4.14 times as many problems correct. The beneficial effect of training on cognitive ability has been replicated in many studies with children of different ages and cultures (Dasen & Heron, 1981).

In Field's study, we can see a fine example of the type of research discussed in Chapter 5 called the **independent-groups** or **between-subjects design,** in which the researcher compares two or more separate groups of subjects who have different levels of a single factor, the independent variable. Each subject participates in only one research condition, and the researcher looks for *differences* in the dependent variable between data groupings. In this chapter, we focus on between-subjects designs that test a single *factor,* or independent variable, for differences in the dependent variable. You've seen the term "factor" before with a very different meaning in the correlational technique called *factor analysis*. Try not to confuse the two terms.

HYPOTHESIS TESTING AND RESEARCH DESIGN

How do researchers decide which research design to use? They begin by looking at the hypothesis they want to test. In the case of Field's research, she knew she wanted to test the hypothesis that training would accelerate young children's ability to solve cognitive problems through logical thinking. This hypothesis proposes a cause—training, which she could manipulate—and an effect: accelerated cognitive ability.

FROM HYPOTHESIS TO DESIGN

With this goal, Field knew she'd need to use an experimental strategy. The simplest design in an experimental strategy would involve two independent groups, one that does and one that does not get training, and that are equated by random assignment. She decided on this approach, but made sure the groups were balanced for a few critical variables. To see how she probably arrived at her research design and strategy, let's look at the path of questions and answers in Figure 7.1, starting at the upper left and following the arrows. Field decided to

Questions and answers			Designs and strategies	
Ss in conditions of IV are independent?	IV manipulated?	Equated Ss in groups?	Research design (where covered)*	Research strategy
YES (independent groups)	YES	YES	Randomized groups (Ch. 5)	Experimental
	YES	NO	Nonequivalent control group (6)	Quasi-experimental
	NO (events occur on own)	NO	Nonequivalent control group (6)	Quasi-experimental
	NO (IV is a S variable)	NO	Natural groups (6)	Quasi-experimental
NO (dependent groups)	YES	YES (same Ss)	Controlled within-Ss (5)	Experimental
	YES	YES (matched)	Matched-Ss (5)	Experimental
	NO (IV is a S variable)	YES (same Ss)	Longitudinal (6)	Quasi-experimental
	NO (events occur on own)	YES (same Ss)	Time-series (6)	Quasi-experimental

*Chapter numbers where the research designs are covered are given in parentheses. For additional information about each design, use the index to find the exact pages and check the glossary (at back of book) to find definitions.

FIGURE 7.1

Diagram with questions and answers about a study's independent variable (IV) and subjects (Ss) to determine the type of research design and research strategy (follow arrows) it uses.

1. Use independent groups—that is, she answered *yes* for the first question: The children tested in each level of the independent variable, the experimental and control groups, would be separate, or "independent," people. As a result of this decision, we'll find the design she used in the shaded, upper portion of the figure.

2. Manipulate the independent variable—in this case, by providing training for some children, but not others. Thus, she answered *yes* to the second question, and we'll find her design in the top two rows of the shaded portion of the figure.

3. Equate the groups, mainly through random assignment.

As you can see in the figure, Field used a randomized-groups design and experimental strategy. If she had not made these three decisions, she would have used some other design. Researchers choose a design that is appropriate for and likely to be successful in testing the specific hypothesis. For example, if researchers want to compare independent groups but cannot equate them beforehand or manipulate the independent variable, such as the subjects' past experience or gender, they can apply a nonequivalent control groups design or a natural-groups design that uses a quasi-experimental strategy.

What is the lower portion of Figure 7.1 about? Notice that the answer is *no* to the first question: In all of the designs in this portion of the figure the subjects tested at the different levels of the independent variable are *not* independent, the groups or conditions they form are "dependent." Let's see what the word *dependent* means here. Sometimes researchers need or want to test the subjects in all conditions or levels of the independent variable, using a within-subjects (or repeated measures) design. Or they may decide to equate groups by the technique of matching, whereby the subjects who are most similar on a variable that is strongly related to the dependent variable of the study are randomly assigned to conditions. Thus, in a study with two conditions, for each pair of subjects who are very similar on the matching variable, one would be in one condition and one in the other condition. To the extent that the matching variable is related to the dependent variable, we'd expect that performance scores on the dependent variable would be correlated for the two groups. Similarly in within-subjects designs, because the same subjects are in all conditions, we'd expect their scores on the dependent variable to be related to some degree. If scores are correlated, they are not independent of one another. This is why studies that use repeated measures or matching to equate groups are classified as using a **dependent-groups design.** We will examine dependent-groups designs in the next chapter.

Some research designs are basically flawed from the start, and researchers try not to use them. We saw one of these designs in Chapter 5 when we considered ways to prevent pre–post testing problems, such as the extraneous variables of history, maturation, and regression to the mean. One example we discussed was of a hypothetical study in which 2½-year-old children who were pretested as having poor swimming skills received 6 months of swimming training and showed great improvement at the end of training. This type of study uses a *one-group pretest–posttest design,* which lacks a control group to rule out the influence of extraneous variables. No matter how much improvement the children showed, we could not justify concluding that the swimming training was responsible for it. Another flawed design is the *one-group posttest-only design,* which not only lacks a control group but doesn't even have pretest data for comparison. For instance, suppose we provided a program to enhance the self-esteem of freshmen high school students and find that almost all of them report that they have higher self-esteem at the end of the academic year than they had at the start of the year. What would that mean? We wouldn't have a control group to rule out the possibility that their self-esteem might have improved on its own, and we wouldn't even know for sure that their self-esteem had been lower! It's rare for these research designs to produce useful data. Early studies in clinical psychology often used these designs, and many of their findings have either been disconfirmed by better research or are ignored today because confounding variables obscure their meaning.

PREPARING TO DO A SINGLE-FACTOR STUDY

Because conducting research takes lots of preparation and careful decisions, Chapter 10 gives explicit instructions and checklists to help you prepare to carry out various types of research designs. If you know that you will be using a single-factor, independent-groups design, look over that chapter now to see the kind of information it contains and how it can help you.

TWO-LEVEL, SINGLE-FACTOR STUDIES

The simplest independent-groups designs to test a single factor involve just two levels of the independent variable, and researchers look for differences in the dependent variable that correspond to these levels. Usually, a control group represents one of the two levels. We'll examine some variations in two-level, single-factor studies, based on whether the independent variable is manipulated and whether there is a control group.

TWO MANIPULATED LEVELS WITH A CONTROL GROUP

Field's (1981) experiment on training cognitive skills in young children is a fine example of a study with two levels of a manipulated independent variable that includes a control group. In Chapter 2, we saw another one: the experiment of Loftus (1975) on eyewitness memory. In that study, college students watched a video of a white sports car traveling on a country road and eventually having an accident. Then they filled out a questionnaire on what they had witnessed. For half of the students—the control group—a question asked, "How fast was the white sports car going while traveling along the country road?" For the remaining students—the experimental group—the words "when it passed the barn" were inserted after the word "going" in the same question. There had been no barn in the video. Loftus had manipulated the presence of the misleading phrase about the barn. A week later when the students were asked if they had seen a barn in the video, many of those in the experimental group, but few in the control group, said they had seen a barn.

TWO MANIPULATED LEVELS WITHOUT A CONTROL GROUP

Sometimes researchers manipulate an independent variable, but do not include a control group. The absence of a control group is usually considered a weakness in the design because it can limit the conclusions the researcher can make. We'll consider two studies of this type, each of which examined a single factor with two independent groups. You'll see that the absence of a control group is much less problematic in the first study than in the second.

Chances are that you've seen in a prior course the diagram in Figure 7.2, which shows a kitten in an unusual apparatus that was used in testing the influence of early experience on the development of the visual system (Blakemore

FIGURE 7.2

Apparatus for research to test the role of experience on the development of the visual system. It consists of a tall cylinder with black-and-white stripes painted on the inside surface, a clear glass platform mounted partway up, and a cone-shaped collar for the kitten to wear. Some kittens had vertical stripes (as shown) on the inside surface, and others had horizontal stripes. (From Blakemore & Cooper, 1970, Figure 1)

& Cooper, 1970). The kitten is wearing a cone-shaped collar to block vision of its own body and is standing on a clear glass platform mounted partway up a tall cylinder with vertical black-and-white stripes painted on the inside. The purpose of the apparatus was to limit the visual field to a specific stimulus environment: the kittens either saw vertical stripes, as in the figure, or horizontal stripes, the second level of the independent variable. There was no control group with kittens in a visually varied environment. From birth onward, the kittens were housed in a dark room, but beginning at 2 weeks, each kitten was placed in the lighted apparatus for 5 hours each day; the only visual experience they had was of exclusively vertical or horizontal lines for the first 5 months of life.

Over the next weeks, the cats were tested in a lighted room furnished with tables and chairs and showed visual deficits. The kittens raised in the vertical environment had trouble perceiving horizontal lines, and those raised in the horizontal environment had trouble perceiving vertical lines. Some deficits recovered quickly. For example, after 10 hours of testing they no longer failed to show a startle response when a researcher thrust an object toward them or were frightened when they reached the edge of a table on which they were standing. Other visual deficits were permanent—for instance, cats raised with horizontal stripes kept bumping into table legs. Physiological assessments revealed that the visual cortex of the cats' brains had failed to develop specialized cells to detect the type of stimuli they had lacked in their early experience. For example, cats that had seen only horizontal lines had specialized cells for those stimuli, but not for vertical lines.

The second study with two levels of an independent variable and no control group examined the role of hearing good news and bad news on people's attitudes and feelings (Holloway & Hornstein, 1976). When the participants arrived to take part individually in the study, they were asked to sit in a waiting room for a while. In the room, the person could hear a radio playing music. Soon an "announcer" interrupted the music to make a news announcement, which was a ruse and consisted of either good news or bad news. Some participants heard the good news of a man whose life would be spared by receiving a kidney transplant from a kind donor, but the others heard the bad news of a woman who was murdered, presumably by a respected clergyman who knew her well. Soon after the news item, the researcher turned off the radio and had the participant answer questions about the morals of other people, such as "What percentage of people are basically honest?" The participants who heard the bad news gave lower estimates—that is, they felt that fewer people in general had high morals—than those who heard the good news. The participants' attitudes about other people's morals were more negative among those who heard the bad news than among those who heard the good news.

Why is the lack of a control group more problematic for the second study than the first? In the research on the development of the visual system, a control group would have consisted of cats with usual experiences. Researchers already knew the perceptual behavior and physiology of normal laboratory cats, and the contrasting and corresponding differences after carefully controlled, specific perceptual experiences provide convincing evidence that the visual deficits resulted from the different experiences. Looking at the outcome now, a control group probably would not alter the outcome or interpretation of the study. But in the second study, the lack of a control group limited the researchers' conclusions. Although they could justify stating that good and bad news have different effects on attitudes about other people's morals, they could not say whether good news raises the attitudes or bad news lowers the attitudes relative to no news at all. Would the attitudes of people with no news fall in between, or somewhere else? Is the adage, "no news is good news" correct? Having a control group when using an experimental strategy is virtually always good scientific practice. In hindsight, we can see that the absence of a control group in the research on visual development did not impair interpretation of the outcome, but researchers don't know in advance exactly what the outcome of their study will be.

USING A NONMANIPULATED INDEPENDENT VARIABLE

Looking back at Figure 7.1, you can see in the lower rows of the shaded area that using an independent variable that is not manipulated characterizes certain designs; the specific design depends on whether the factor is a nonmanipulated *event* or *subject variable.* We discussed research in Chapter 6 that used two levels of a nonmanipulated independent variable. For instance, in studying nonmanipulated events, some research we discussed compared the academic skills of students in Catholic schools and public schools and found higher skill levels in the Catholic schools. If we consider the type of school as a long-term "event," following the arrows in the figure reveals that this research used a nonequivalent control groups design (public schools are the control group; they provide the standard system of education in the United States). As an example of research with subject variables, we saw that studies comparing males and females have found gender differences in math and verbal abilities. Following the arrows in the figure, we see that this research used a natural-groups design. Nonequivalent control groups and natural-groups designs use quasi-experimental strategies: the independent variables are not manipulated, and the individuals in the two groups are not equated.

Many of my research methods students have done projects that used two levels of a nonmanipulated independent variable, often investigating the role of gender, age, or personality characteristics in people's behavior. For instance, a student used surveys to assess gender differences in four dependent variables among college students: their levels of stress and use of three ways of coping with stress. The coping methods were emotion focused (that is, trying to regulate one's own emotional responses), problem focused (trying to reduce the demands of the situation or increase one's ability to deal with them), and seeking social support. By using more than one dependent variable, the student made the study and the results more interesting. She found that although males and females did not differ in their levels of stress and use of emotion-focused coping methods, females used more problem-focused coping and social support when feeling stress.

MANAGING WANTED AND UNWANTED VARIANCE

We've seen in earlier chapters that researchers try to maximize variance in data that arises from levels of the independent variable and to minimize variance of two other types: systematic variance from extraneous variables and nonsystematic, error variance. When reading a report of past research, we must rely on the information given in the research report to decide how effectively the researchers managed wanted and unwanted variance. That information is usually there, but sometimes it isn't—for example, in the study on development of the visual system in kittens by Blakemore and Cooper (1970), the journal article doesn't say specifically that the kittens were randomly assigned to the vertical and horizontal stripes experience.

Research reports should provide all relevant information so that the reader will understand exactly what the levels of the independent variable were, what the dependent variables were, and how effectively extraneous and error variance were controlled. For example, Blagrove (1996) conducted a series of studies on the role of sleep deprivation on suggestibility and wanted to illustrate how similar the sleep-deprived and control participants were on age, gender, and amount of sleep they usually got. He collected data on the relevant subject variables and presented those data in the Participants section of the report. As an example, for Study 3, he said (pp. 49–50):

> In the sleep-loss group, ages ranged from 18 to 21 years, with a mean age of 19.3 years ($SD = 1.2$). There were 7 men and 8 women, with a mean usual sleep time of 8.4 hr ($SD = 0.6$). Controls ranged in age from 18 to 23 years, with a mean age of 19.8 ($SD = 1.4$). There were 8 men and 8 women, with a mean usual sleep time of 8.1 hr ($SD = 0.4$).

This description is very precise, allowing us to know exactly how similar the two groups were on these critical variables. We can see that these three factors were well controlled and not likely to confound the effects of the independent variables in this study.

Maximizing Variance from the Independent Variable

To maximize the variance from the independent variable, researchers manipulate or select levels of that factor they believe will be associated with markedly different scores on the dependent variable. Often, this simply translates into making levels of the independent variable as different from each other as is feasible to do. Let's consider three examples. First, studies focusing on subject variables usually compare very different levels of those factors. For instance, we saw in Chapter 6 that research on the role of personality on behavior often compares people with high and low levels of the personality characteristic, generally using the median-split or extreme-groups methods to form the groups. Second, in the research on visual development, Blakemore and Cooper (1970) wanted to contrast two very different visual patterns of straight lines that the kittens would see exclusively for 5 months. In terms of the angular relationship of lines, horizontal and vertical are as different as straight lines can be, and that's what they used. Any spatial orientation other than perpendicular would make the lines less different in their angular relationship.

Third, in the experiment on sleep deprivation, Blagrove (1996) advertised the opportunity to participate for pay in a study on sleep deprivation and memory. The participants in the control group were told to sleep at home each night of the study, and those in the experimental group had to remain awake continuously at the laboratory, monitored by research assistants; in Study 3, the experimental group was awake for 43 hours. The researcher assessed the participants' suggestibility by presenting a story to them, asking them leading questions about its details, telling them their answers were wrong, and asking them to recall again. The researcher scored suggestibility by summing instances of being led astray by leading questions and changing answers after negative feedback. The results revealed that suggestibility was significantly greater for participants in the experimental group after sleep deprivation than in the control group. In Studies 1 and 2, sleep deprivation involved only 21 hours, and the effects were not significant. Using 43 hours is about as long as is feasible to do for sleep deprivation, and comparing that condition against no deprivation maximized the effects of the independent variable.

But making levels of the independent variable as different as possible from each other is not the only way researchers decide which levels of the independent variable to use in a study. They use their knowledge of prior research findings, logic and common sense, and predictions from theories. Suppose we decide from these sources that the relationship between the independent and dependent variables may follow an inverted-U pattern—that is, scores on the dependent variable are highest at moderate levels of the independent variable. For example, you've probably heard someone account for the high risk taking of adolescents by saying that they have higher feelings of invulnerability than people of younger and older age groups—a notion from a theory by Elkind (1974). If we were interested in testing developmental differences in feelings of invulnerability, we wouldn't use an extreme-groups method to form age groups, such as comparing children against middle-aged adults. On the basis of the theory, we wouldn't expect very much difference in the dependent variable: both would be low in invulnerability. Instead, we'd include a group of adolescents—that is, people with a moderate level of the independent variable, age—to contrast with an older or younger group, or both. Now our research hypothesis can predict a difference between the groups.

Minimizing Extraneous and Error Variability

We have discussed the importance of minimizing extraneous and error variability in prior chapters. Extraneous variables can produce systematic variance that differentially affects the dependent variable in different research conditions; this threatens the internal validity of the research, confounding and rendering unclear the effect of the independent variable. Excessive error variance reduces statistical power and, therefore, the likelihood of finding a significant difference between groups. Because we have already discussed methods to minimize these types of variability in Chapter 5, we will only summarize them here.

The methods researchers use in controlling unwanted systematic variance from extraneous variables depend on the intended purposes for using them:

■ To create equal groups, researchers use random assignment, matching, or repeated measurement (within-subjects) techniques.

- To control against differential attrition, if they know why it may occur, they can administer a pretest and use the scores to restrict participation to subjects that are likely to complete the study or to equate the groups after attrition has occurred.

- To control the influence of a confounding that already exists, if they know what the factor is and have a measure of it, they may be able to apply statistical control.

- To prevent the problems of history, maturation, and regression to the mean in pretest and posttest comparisons, they include a control group.

- To equate methodological details of the study, researchers use the methods of holding conditions constant or balancing their influence across groups.

- To control against participant bias, researchers may use deception (which can produce ethical problems) or a blind procedure. Debriefing methods and placebo conditions can be used to assess the presence of participant bias.

- To control against observer bias, they may tell observers of interobserver reliability measures that will be made or use a blind procedure or automated devices in data collection.

Researchers can control nonsystematic error variance using a fairly homogeneous sample of subjects, collecting data with reliable instruments and procedures, and making sure all subjects are treated identically except for manipulation of the independent variable.

VARIETIES OF CONTROL GROUPS

Our discussions of control groups so far have focused mainly on the standard type, which is kept at its usual, unmanipulated level of the independent variable to serve as a baseline for comparison. In general, the experimental group receives a special treatment, and the control group does not. But there are other types of control groups that do not follow the standard pattern, and we've alluded to or mentioned briefly a couple of them in prior chapters. We'll examine three of the more commonly used of these other control groups: the placebo, waiting list, and yoked control groups.

PLACEBO CONTROL GROUPS

Imagine this story. A pharmaceutical company developed a new painkiller, conducted an experiment with headache sufferers, found that people who took the drug reported less pain than those in a control group that did not get the drug, marketed the painkiller, and found that people stopped buying it because it didn't really work. If the drug didn't work, why did the research participants who took the drug (the experimental group) report less pain than the controls? Probably, they thought they had less pain because they knew they were taking a drug for pain and *expected* it would help. This story reports a real situation that occurred repeatedly before researchers knew that *placebos*—that is, inert, or inactive, substances or procedures—can alter people's perceptions and behavior by influencing their expectations. Remember from Chapter 5 that participants' expectancies, such as demand characteristics, can be a source of confounding that biases the data researchers collect. Any influence a placebo has on the dependent variable is called a **placebo effect** (Roberts, 1995).

If researchers suspect that placebo effects may occur, they can include in their research design a **placebo control group** that receives a condition that looks like an active substance or procedure but is not. Using a placebo condition enables the participants to develop false expectations. Experiments today to test the effects of drugs and many other medical and psychological treatments generally include a placebo control group. In this type of research, people in the experimental and placebo control groups are usually told in advance that some participants will get the "investigation treatment" and others will not. For example, researchers testing a painkiller might give all participants in both groups identical looking pills and tell them "this may or may not reduce your pain" (notice that this is not deception). If the data from the two groups do not differ, the researchers would conclude that the real treatment had no actual effect because the experimental and the placebo control groups should have had the same expectations. But if the groups differ significantly, the researchers would conclude that the treatment did have an effect over and above any effect of the placebo.

What would a placebo condition be like for a psychology experiment? We'll consider three examples. First, psychologists and medical professionals sometimes work together to test the effects of drugs for relieving emotional problems, such as anxiety or depression, and use methods like those just mentioned. Second, many clinical health psychologists conduct research on the effectiveness of psychological treatments in relieving pain, such as from severe headaches (Sarafino, 2002). One of these treatments is *biofeedback*, a process by which individuals can learn to control a physiological function, such as heart rate or muscle tension, by monitoring its status with an electromechanical device. For instance, a device to measure muscle tension (an electromyograph) assesses the electrical activity of muscles as they contract. To treat the condition of muscle-contraction (or tension-type) headache, sensors from the device are attached with adhesive to the skin, usually on the forehead, and the level of tension is reported to the patient, such as with loudness of a tone from a speaker. To create a placebo control condition, researchers attach the sensors and provide false feedback, typically by playing a tape recording of tone changes that are not linked to the person's performance. Researchers who averaged the data on pain across many studies found that patients report 43.5% improvement in the experimental group (real biofeedback) and 18.5% improvement in the placebo condition (Holroyd & Penzien, 1986).

Third, researchers wanted to evaluate the effectiveness of audiotapes of music or other sounds with embedded messages at subliminal levels (people cannot hear them consciously) that are designed to help people lose weight (Merikle & Skanes, 1992). The participants were women who wanted to lose weight and thought subliminal messages could work. They were randomly assigned to an experimental group that received a commercially available tape with subliminal weight-loss messages and a placebo control group, which got a tape in identical packaging that contained subliminal messages to help relieve people's dental anxiety. All these participants were asked to listen to their tapes for 1 to 3 hours a day, which they could do while engaging in other activities. The results revealed that both groups lost a modest amount of weight over a 5-week period, but the amounts lost were almost identical, indicating that subliminal weight-loss messages are not effective in helping people lose weight. (Go to **Box 7.1**)

BOX 7.1 WHY PLACEBOS RELIEVE PAIN

Do people's expectations of relief from a placebo treatment for pain simply fool them into not noticing the pain? Not necessarily—there's another explanation: Expectations of pain relief may lead the body to release substances called *endogenous opioids,* which are opiatelike chemicals the body produces naturally to reduce the sensation of pain. An experiment with dental patients who had had impacted wisdom teeth removed found evidence for this explanation (Levine, Gordon, & Fields, 1978). Patients who volunteered to participate in the study all received nitrous oxide anesthetic at the start of surgery and two injections, one 2 hours later and another 3 hours after that. All participants were told the substance in each injection might increase, decrease, or have no effect on the pain. The substance in the injections formed the independent variable: it was either naloxone, which blocks the effects of opiate narcotics and opiatelike substances, or a placebo. The researchers determined whether a particular injection would contain the naloxone or the placebo by *random assignment* and used a *double-blind procedure* to ensure that neither the participant nor the researcher knew which treatment the patient was receiving.

The dependent variable was the participant's pain ratings, which were taken several times during the study. The results revealed two important findings. First, the patients reported much more pain after receiving the naloxone than the placebo, which means that the endogenous opioids' effects were being blocked. Second, of the patients who received the placebo as the first injection and naloxone as the second, those who reported pain relief after the placebo reported increased pain after the naloxone, but those who did not react to the placebo showed no change in their pain with the naloxone. This finding suggests that the people who had gotten pain relief from the placebo may have expected relief and then released endogenous opioids, and the effects of these substances were blocked later when the naloxone was given. People who did not react to the placebo may not have expected relief or released endogenous opioids at that time, so their levels of pain were high after both injections.

YOKED CONTROL GROUPS

Do you know what a *yoke* is? It's a frame that joins or links two animals at the neck to equalize their events and pace while working together, such as in pulling a wagon. For a **yoked control group,** each of its members is paired and tested simultaneously with a member of the experimental group so that they both experience exactly the same events at the same time, except for the critical feature of the independent variable. For example, suppose we were conducting a study on the effectiveness of biofeedback in treating headaches and wanted to be sure that the experimental and control participants receive exactly the same feedback at exactly the same time. We would test one participant from each group together but in adjoining rooms, and they would both get simultaneously the exact same feedback for any changes in muscle tension of the person in the experimental group, irrespective of the status of muscle tension of the control participant.

How do the yoked and placebo methods differ? A yoked control group ensures that the subjects in both groups experience the same events at the same pace; a placebo condition does not. When the exact timing of events is a critical issue to be controlled, the yoked procedure is preferred. In Chapter 5, we discussed a study of ulcers in "executive" monkeys (Brady, 1958). Although nonequivalent groups confounded the outcome, this research still provides an example of a nicely designed yoked control group. Two monkeys sitting side by side would receive painful electric shocks unless the one in the experimental group prevented the shock by pressing a lever. The monkey that could not prevent the shocks was in the yoked control group. That study found that the monkeys in the experimental group, but not the yoked control group, developed ulcers and died. Subsequent unconfounded experiments used a similar yoked control condition with rats as subjects and found the opposite results: animals in the yoked control group (that could not control the shock) developed more ulcers than the ones in the experimental group (Weiss, 1968, 1977).

WAITING LIST CONTROL GROUPS

Think back to the research on treating nightmares described in the prologue for Chapter 5 in which Miller and DePilato (1983) tested two forms of therapy, relaxation training and systematic desensitization, against a "delayed treatment" condition. A delayed condition in which individuals do not receive the experimental treatment initially but will later is called a **waiting list control group.** Usually the researcher gives the participants in that group a reason for the delay, such as that there aren't enough therapists or materials for everyone who would like the treatment, which may be false. Waiting list control groups are commonly used in clinical psychology and in many applied research areas, such as in medicine and health promotion, to provide evidence for the effectiveness of a treatment method. Using a waiting list control group has two purposes. First, it allows researchers to compare the effects of a treatment or condition against a no-treatment condition that is like a standard control group. Because the controls expect that they will eventually get the treatment, the researchers can ask them to provide data at the same times as the experimental group does. Second, using a waiting list control group addresses the ethical issue of providing beneficial therapy for one group and not another—all of them will have the treatment at some point.

Some people might still object ethically to making people who need therapy wait, but some justifications can be made for doing so. First, studies with waiting list control groups are usually done without clear evidence that the experimental treatment will be effective. Providing that evidence is the purpose of the research. Sometimes researchers stop the delay and give the waiting list controls the treatment early if it becomes clear before the planned end of the study that it works. Second, people in a waiting list control group do not have anything taken away that they would normally get. For instance, when testing a psychological treatment for a medical condition, such as headache pain, people in both the experimental and the waiting list control groups would continue to receive standard medical treatment. Third, participants typically know when they sign up for a study with a waiting list control group that there may be a delay in receiving treatment. Fourth, the treatments in research are expensive to provide and usually given for free if untested, and sometimes participants are even paid to take part.

MULTILEVEL, SINGLE-FACTOR STUDIES

So far in this chapter, we've focused on single-factor designs with two levels of the independent variable forming the basis for two separate groups of subjects. This is the simplest research design with independent groups, particularly if the researcher assesses only one dependent variable. Most researchers (and journal editors) prefer designs that are more complex because the outcomes are typically more informative. One way to make a design more complex is to add levels of the independent variable, which makes it a *multilevel* design. For example, the research by Miller and DiPilato (1983) on treating nightmares had three treatment groups: relaxation training, systematic desensitization, and delayed treatment (waiting list control group). All of the information we discussed on control groups, managing wanted and unwanted variance, and manipulating levels of the independent variable with two-level designs applies to multilevel designs, too.

WHY RESEARCHERS USE MULTILEVEL DESIGNS

There are two main reasons for using more than two levels of an independent variable. First, multilevel designs enable researchers to test for or demonstrate nonlinear relationships between independent and dependent variables. For example, research reported by Perin (1942) tested the effects of the amount of prior reinforcement (reward) on responding during extinction—that is, when the response is no longer reinforced. Rats that were deprived of food for 23 hours were trained to make lever-pressing responses in a Skinner box (or "operant chamber"), receiving a food pellet as the reinforcer for each lever press. The training session for each subject ended when it had been reinforced a predetermined number of times: 5, 10, 30, or 90 times, which constituted the four levels of the independent variable. On a subsequent day after 22 hours of food deprivation, each animal was placed in the Skinner box again and tested for the number of lever presses it would make without reinforcement (during extinction). Figure 7.3 shows two important outcomes. The number of responses in extinction increased with the number of times the subjects had been reinforced, and the relationship between the two variables is not linear. If it were linear, the data points would fall along a single straight line. This relationship is curvilinear, following a *negatively accelerated function:* The graph rises sharply at first, but the rate of increase in the dependent variable decreases as the level of the independent variable increases. Thus, increasing the number of times lever pressing is reinforced in training beyond 20 or 30 adds less and less to the behavior's persistence when reward is no longer provided. Suppose we had done a similar study with only two levels of prior reinforcement—say, 10 and 30 times in training. We'd have found a fairly sharp increase in persistence (23 versus 43 responses), but we would not know that the rate of increase in persistence becomes smaller and smaller.

Second, having more than two levels may be necessary to support the research hypothesis clearly or unambiguously. In the research on treating nightmares, Miller and DiPilato wanted to compare two treatment approaches against each other and against a control group, which required a design with three groups. By contrast, another study we considered earlier might have benefited from adding one or more groups. In the research by Holloway and Hornstein (1976), participants were listening to music, heard good news or bad news,

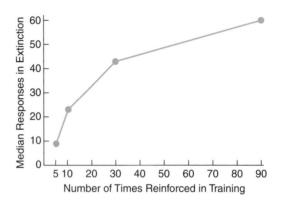

FIGURE 7.3

Median number of lever-pressing responses of rats during an extinction session (that is, reinforcement is no longer given) after having been reinforced with food pellets for lever pressing 5, 10, 30, or 90 times during training. The animals had been deprived of food for 23 hours for the training session and for 22 hours for the extinction session. (Data from a study by Williams, as reported in and adapted from Perin, 1942, Figure 4.)

and then made judgments about other people's morals. Their attitudes about other people's morals were more negative after hearing bad news than after good news. But because no control groups were used, the researchers could not say whether good news raised the attitudes or bad news lowered the attitudes relative to no news at all or neutral news. The design would be stronger with two additional groups, one that hears no news interruption in the music and one that hears neutral news. The independent variable would now have four levels: good news, bad news, neutral news, and no news.

As a matter of efficiency, researchers try to use the simplest design that will test the research hypothesis clearly and fully. The main issue in deciding to make a design more complex is whether there is something important to be gained in the clarity or completeness of the findings by doing so. A good strategy in making this decision is to sketch out as graphs all of the possible outcomes, think about what each outcome would mean regarding the hypothesis, and then consider how the meaning might be clearer by including other conditions in the design.

CHOOSING THE LEVELS

As we saw in our discussion of research with only two levels of the independent variable, researchers choose the levels to study that are as different as possible from each other and by using information from prior research, logic and common sense, and predictions from theories. For example, if we decide from these sources that the relationship between the independent and dependent variables may follow an inverted-U pattern, we may want to include in our design three levels of the independent variable—low, moderate, and high. Let's look at a couple of examples of processes researchers might use in choosing levels of the independent variable.

Bransford and Johnson (1972) performed a well-known experiment in which high school students were asked to listen to a paragraph, rate its ease of comprehension on a 7-point scale (1 = very difficult, 7 = very easy), and recall as much of it as they could. Here is the paragraph; read it and rate its ease of comprehension:

> If the balloons popped, the sound wouldn't be able to carry since everything would be too far away from the correct floor. A closed window would also prevent the sound from carrying, since most buildings tend to be well insulated. Since the whole operation depends on a steady flow of electricity, a break in the middle of the wire would also cause problems. Of course, the fellow could shout, but the human voice is not loud enough to carry that far. An additional problem is that a string could break on the instrument. Then there could be no accompaniment to the message. It is clear that the best situation would involve less distance. Then there would be fewer potential problems. With face to face contact, the least number of things can go wrong. (p. 719)

In rating the ease of comprehension, you probably thought, "I haven't a clue of what this paragraph means" and rated it hard to comprehend, around a 3 or so. The paragraph was designed to be hard to understand without some context; the mean ratings the research participants gave were between 2 and 4 if they had insufficient context.

The purpose of this study was to test the hypothesis that grasping the context of information is essential for people to process and understand material. The researchers manipulated the context for the paragraph you read, which the students heard as a tape recording. Each of five separate groups of 10 students listened to the paragraph under the following context conditions, which formed the levels of the independent variable:

- *No context:* The participants simply heard the paragraph presented once. This was simply a control group.
- *No context (2):* The students heard the paragraph twice. The purpose of this condition was to see if hearing the material the first time would give context to the information and enhance comprehension and recall. No other group heard the material more than once.
- *Context before:* Just before hearing the paragraph, the participants examined for 30 seconds the drawing presented in Figure 7.4a. (After you look

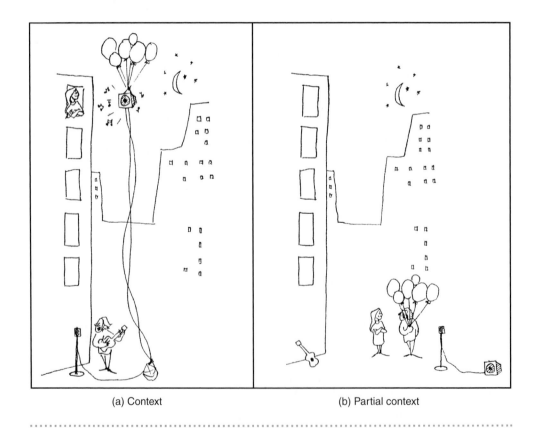

(a) Context   (b) Partial context

FIGURE 7.4

Two drawings used in the Bransford and Johnson (1972, Figures 1 and 2) experiment to provide (a) context and (b) partial context to the paragraph the participants heard.

at the drawing, scan the paragraph and see how the drawing gives context to the material and adds to its comprehension.)

- *Context after:* The students heard the paragraph first, and then saw for 30 seconds the drawing in Figure 7.4a.
- *Partial context:* Just before hearing the paragraph, the participants examined for 30 seconds the drawing in Figure 7.4b, which contains all of the elements of Figure 7.4a but their positions are rearranged so that the drawing adds little to the meaning of the paragraph.

After hearing the paragraph and rating its ease of comprehension, the students were given 7 minutes to write as much of the paragraph as they could recall, even if the ideas they wrote were not word for word. The researchers scored each student's written recall by counting the number of "idea units," or basic propositions, it contained of the 14 in the actual paragraph.

Notice in the research design the different levels of the independent variable the researchers chose to include, particularly the *no context (2)*, *context after*, and *partial context* conditions. These groups were included to demonstrate that the context must be available and meaningful when people process information and to rule out other explanations for the better recall the researchers expected when comparing the *context before* and *no context* conditions. For the context before condition, the mean scores were 6.10 for ease of comprehension and 8.00 for number of idea units recalled; for the other conditions, the means ranged from 2.30 to 3.70 for comprehension and 3.60 to 4.00 for recall. Statistical analyses revealed significantly higher comprehension and recall scores in the context before condition than the other conditions. Because the researchers chose logically and carefully the conditions to include in the design, they were able to conclude that context enhances people's understanding of material, but only if it is available and meaningful when they process the information.

Other researchers designed a study to test whether participant biases, such as demand characteristics, might be responsible for the findings of prior research that people who are hypnotized can be induced to perform antisocial and harmful acts they otherwise would not do (Orne & Evans, 1965). The acts in these studies were handling a venomous snake, putting one's hand in acid to retrieve a coin, and throwing acid at a person. The researcher who tested the participants made the situations look real and dangerous, but they were actually tricks. Consider the coin in acid situation, for instance. The participant watched a coin dissolving in a beaker of acid, was distracted while a harmless solution was substituted with a partially dissolved coin in it, retrieved the coin very quickly with a bare hand, and plunged the hand immediately into a basin of soapy water. Presumably, the quickness of the act and the hand washing prevented injury. The researchers clearly used deception; doing this research today could be problematic because an IRB might reject the methodology for ethical reasons.

When testing participants, the researcher in each condition stressed the dangers involved in the action and did not know whether or not a participant was hypnotized (that is, the study used a blind procedure). Like the study on context and comprehension, this research had five conditions:

- *Real hypnosis*—the researcher told hypnotized individuals to perform each act, one at a time, conveying implicitly the expectation that the person would comply and trying to persuade anyone who hesitated.

- *Waking control (convey refusal)*—nonhypnotized participants who were aware that the study was on hypnosis were asked to perform each action, one at a time. The researcher conveyed implicitly, by tone of voice and the like, an expectation that the person would *refuse* to comply and tried weakly to persuade anyone who hesitated.

- *Waking control (convey compliance)*—nonhypnotized individuals, aware that the study was on hypnosis, were told to perform each act, one at a time. The researcher carried out the same procedure as in the real hypnosis condition, conveying implicitly the expectation that the person would comply and trying to persuade anyone who hesitated.

- *Simulated hypnosis*—nonhypnotized participants were asked to act as if they were hypnotized. The researcher carried out the same procedure as in the real hypnosis condition, conveying implicitly the expectation that the person would comply and trying to persuade anyone who hesitated.

- *Unaware control*—nonhypnotized individuals who were not aware that the study was on hypnosis were told to perform one act at a time. The researcher conveyed the expectation that the person would comply and tried to persuade anyone who didn't.

The first two conditions replicated those used in studies that produced results suggesting that hypnotized people would do these acts: participants were far more likely to perform the acts if they were in the real hypnosis condition than in the waking control (convey refusal) condition. Orne and Evans included the three other conditions in their study to test possible explanations of the prior findings. For instance, it may be that just being asked to comply in a research setting or people's beliefs about how to behave when hypnotized is responsible for the willingness of hypnotized people to perform such acts. Table 7.1 presents the

TABLE 7.1

Percentage of Individuals Who Attempted to Perform the Three Dangerous Acts: Grasping a Venomous Snake, Putting Hand in Acid to Retrieve a Coin, and Throwing Acid at a Person

	Act		
Condition	Grasp snake	Hand in acid	Throw acid
Real hypnosis	83.3	83.3	83.3
Waking control (convey refusal)	50.0	16.7	16.7
Waking control (convey compliance)	50.0	83.3	83.3
Simulated hypnosis	100.0	100.0	100.0
Unaware control	50.0	50.0	33.3

Source: From data in Orne and Evans (1965), Table 2

study's outcome, showing that the percentages of individuals who attempted to perform the acts were similar for the real hypnosis, simulated hypnosis, and waking control (convey compliance) conditions, suggesting that hypnosis does not affect people's willingness to perform dangerous acts.

These two studies illustrate how valuable additional groups in a study can be and how researchers choose the levels of the independent variable by using information from prior research or theory and their own logic and common sense.

ANALYZING DATA FROM SINGLE-FACTOR, INDEPENDENT-GROUPS DESIGNS

The main statistical analyses for single-factor, independent-groups designs involve assessing differences between data groupings. We've seen in earlier chapters that researchers use inferential statistics to determine whether the data from subjects tested at contrasting levels of the independent variable are significantly different—that is, the difference is great enough that it probably did not happen by chance alone. We've also seen that by using Table 4.1 (see inside front cover) we can choose the appropriate statistical test to assess group differences by answering a few simple questions about the research design. In the remainder of this chapter, we'll discuss the statistical tests for *assessing differences between independent groups* when the research design involves a *single factor* and the research strategy is either *experimental or quasi-experimental*.

As we discuss data analyses, keep in mind two points. First, sometimes studies with one independent variable have more that one dependent variable. For example, a study using three levels of psychological stress might examine the effects of stress on blood pressure, heart rate, and self-reported feelings of stress. If there is more than one dependent variable, each is usually analyzed with a separate test. Second, you will find *step-by-step instructions in Appendix B* for using an SPSS statistics computer program to calculate each of the statistical tests we discuss and formulas for calculating some of them manually.

TWO-LEVEL DESIGNS

In a two-level design, we compare two groups of subjects for differences in a dependent variable. Let's see what statistic to use for the experiment by Field (1981) in the opening story in which children in an experimental group received training in cognitive tasks and those in a control group did not. By looking at Table 4.1 (see inside front cover), we can identify the statistical test to do by starting at the left column of the table and answering four questions:

1. Is the purpose of the test to *assess differences* or *assess relationships?* Answer: We want to assess differences. As a result, we would focus on the lower portion of the table.

2. Are the data on a *nominal* or *ordinal* scale, or an *interval* or *ratio* scale? Answer: The dependent variable was the number of cognitive problems the children solved, which is a ratio scale. Because the dependent variable con-

sists of interval or ratio data, we'd focus on the shaded area (parametric statistics). If our dependent variable had just categorized or ranked individuals, we'd have nominal or ordinal data and would focus on the non-shaded area of the lower portion of the table (nonparametric statistics).

3. Are we assessing differences between *more than two data groupings?* Answer: No, we have two groups. Looking at the column labeled "No. of data groupings," we will focus now only on the shaded portion of the table for "2" data groupings.

4. Are the data from the two sets *paired* with each other (that is, matched or collected with a repeated-measures or within-subjects design)? Answer: No, we're considering an independent-groups design. Looking at the column labeled "Paired sets," we can focus only on the portion of the table corresponding to "No," which leads us to one parametric statistic, the *t* test.

Researchers generally prefer to use parametric analyses because they have more power than nonparametric analyses. Because parametric statistics use the data collected in the research to estimate parameters, such as the mean or standard deviation, of the population from which the data were drawn, they lose some power when the data fail to meet two criteria. The data distribution should be similar to a normal curve, and the amount of variance in each data grouping analyzed should be similar. Statistical tests can detect whether the data depart markedly from these criteria; if they do, we can apply statistically accepted adjustments in the analysis or use a nonparametric analysis instead.

Parametric Analysis

Interval scales have approximately equal distances between consecutive scale values of the underlying variable; ratio scales have that property and two others: a true zero point and a ratio relationship between scale values. Earlier in this chapter, we considered a study by a student of mine who examined gender differences (the independent variable) in four dependent variables, measured with interval scales. Her study used Likert rating scales to assess undergraduate males' and females' levels of stress and use of three ways of coping with stress. Because she used interval measurement for each variable, she knew that each analysis would use a parametric statistic.

She'd have used Table 4.1 (inside front cover) to determine the statistical analyses as we did previously. How many data groupings are compared in each analysis? The answer is two: males versus females. Are the data groupings "paired"—that is, did the study use a dependent-groups design (either within-subjects or matched groups)? The answer is "no," it used an independent-groups (between-subjects) design. Following these answers in the table across to the right-hand column, we see that the analysis should use a *t* **test,** which assesses differences between two groups. In this case, my student used an independent-samples *t* test because she had an independent-groups design.

How did my student's analysis turn out? Table 7.2 gives the descriptive statistics (means and standard deviations) and outcomes of her four *t* tests. Using a table to present statistical outcomes is appropriate if it summarizes the results of several analyses, saves space, and makes the findings easier to comprehend. We've

TABLE 7.2

Descriptive Statistics and t Test Outcomes Comparing Males and Females for their Levels of Stress and Use of Three Coping Methods for Dealing with Stress (all dfs = 99)

Variable[a]	Mean (SD)		t	p[b]
	Males	Females		
Stress	10.67 (4.41)	11.03 (3.92)	.45	> .60
Emotion-focused coping	9.30 (2.79)	10.01 (2.53)	.15	> .80
Problem-focused coping	9.24 (2.12)	10.00 (2.27)	1.85	< .06
Seeking social support	1.58 (0.74)	2.04 (0.86)	2.73	< .01

[a] Stress = daily hassles; emotion-focused coping = trying to regulate one's own emotional responses; problem-focused coping = trying to reduce the demands of the situation or increase one's ability to deal with them; and seeking social support = talking with friends, relatives, or others.

[b] All *p*s are two-tailed values.

seen in prior chapters that we decide if an outcome is significant on the basis of the value of *p*, or the likelihood that a difference as large as we found might have resulted if no difference actually exists. If our *p* is less than .05, we can reject the null hypothesis that the difference is due to chance and conclude that the difference is real because there are fewer than 5 chances in 100 that this conclusion is wrong. Looking at the *p* values in the right-hand column, you can see that males and females did not differ (*p* > .60 and .80) in their levels of stress and use of emotion-focused coping methods. But females used more problem-focused coping (a "marginally significant" difference, because the *p* value is very close to .05) and social support (*p* < 0.01) when feeling stress. One thing to keep in mind about calculated *t* values is that they can be negative, having a minus sign. The sign has no effect on the strength or interpretation of the outcome—*it's the absolute value that counts*. The only reason for the negative *t* is that the scores of the group with the larger mean were subtracted from those of the group with the smaller mean to calculate the difference between means in the *t* test formula.

Now, notice four features of the data in the table. First, the *p* values decline as the *t* values increase. In general, as the absolute value of *t* increases, the likelihood that the difference is due to chance (or Type I error) decreases, giving us more confidence that the difference is real. Second, the *t* value is a function of the absolute difference between the means and the amount of error variance (the *SD* is the square root of the calculated error variance). Look, for instance, at the data for the variables of stress and seeking social support. For stress, the means are very close and the *SD*s are fairly high, yielding a very low *t* value that is not statistically significant. For seeking social support, the females' mean is nearly 30% higher than the males', the *SD*s are fairly low, and the *t* value is significant. The larger the difference in the means and the lower the error variability, the higher *t* value. Third, the means tell us which group had the higher scores. Fourth, as the note states, the *p* values represent two-tailed tests. (Go to **Box 7.2**)

Box 7.2   ONE TAIL, TWO TAILS, AND POWER

In a *t* test analysis comparing two sets of data to determine whether a difference between conditions is statistically significant, researchers can choose to apply a one-tailed or a two-tailed test. This choice can affect the test's power—that is, its sensitivity to detect a difference. To see what the "tails" are, look at Figure 7.5, which shows two graphs of the frequency distribution of all possible differences that would occur if the null hypothesis is correct and we repeated a study with different samples of subjects, say, 100 times. The horizontal axes plot the sizes of group differences in *SD* units; both graphs are identical except for the placement of the rejection regions (shaded areas) for the null hypothesis in the tails, or ends where very low frequencies occur. Because the null hypothesis is true, we would expect most replications would produce small differences between groups—as the graphs show, most of the outcomes fall in the middle region within 1 *SD* of zero.

The graph on the left depicts the distribution with a *one-tailed test* in which one end has all five of the times we would make a Type I error, wrongly rejecting the null hypothesis, in the 100 replications. The graph on the right shows the distribution with a *two-tailed test,* with each tail having one half of the five times we would make a Type I error. Notice in the one-tailed test that because all the Type I errors are clustered at one end, the critical value for rejecting the null hypothesis is lower than in a two-tailed test. This means that with a one-tailed test we can reject the null hypothesis with a smaller difference between groups than with a two-tailed test—in other words, one-tailed tests have more power. For example, look back at my student's data in Table 7.2 using a two-tailed test for the variable of problem-focused coping. The *t* value of 1.85 was just short of the critical value, and was described as "marginally significant." If she had been able to use a one-tailed test, that *t* would have been significant at the .05 level of confidence.

How do researchers decide whether to use a one- or two-tailed test? To use a one-tailed test, we must be reasonably sure which of the two groups or conditions will have the higher mean, either because of logic or the results of prior research. Look again at Figure 7.5: If we were sure that whatever difference we find will be on the right-hand side of the graph, why would we need a rejection region on the left side? Having part of the rejection region there would make the statistical test too conservative. My student used two-tailed tests for problem-focused coping (and the other dependent variables) because she wasn't sure whether females would report more or less of the variable than males. A major difficulty researchers have in making the decision to use a one-tailed test is not knowing how sure they are about the direction of the difference they will find.

Very few statistical tests provide the option of choosing one- or two-tailed tests, and the most commonly used ones that do are the *t* test and Pearson's *r*, because their values can be either positive or negative (Keppel, 1991). Some statistical tests, such as analysis of variance (ANOVA) and chi-square, produce calculated values (F and χ^2) that can only be positive and, thus, are by design one-tailed tests.

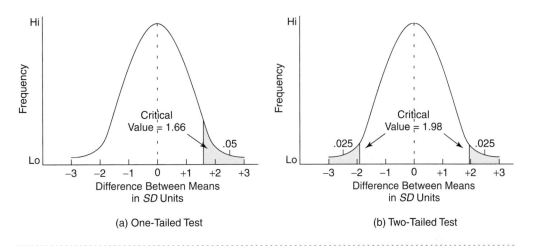

(a) One-Tailed Test   (b) Two-Tailed Test

FIGURE 7.5

Two graphs of the frequency distribution of all possible differences that would occur if the null hypothesis is correct and we repeated the study 100 times, each time with, say, 50 subjects in each of two groups. The graph on the left shows a one-tailed test: the rejection region is at one end, which has all 5 of the times that we would make a Type I error at $p = .05$, and the critical value of *t* for rejecting the null hypothesis is 1.66. The graph on the right shows a two-tailed test: the .05 rejection region is split in half, and the critical value of *t* is 1.98.

Nonparametric Analysis

Researchers use nominal or ordinal data for two reasons. First, sometimes the dependent variable can best be expressed in a categorical manner, such as yes/no or political party affiliation, or as a rank ordering of individuals, respectively yielding nominal or ordinal data. Second, the data the researchers will analyze are not normally distributed or fail in some other way to meet the criteria for using parametric statistics. To select the statistic for nominal or ordinal data in a two-level independent-groups design, we'd consult Table 4.1 (see inside front cover) again. We'd still be assessing differences, of course, but we'd be using a nonparametric analysis and would again ask two questions. How many data groupings are compared in each analysis? The answer is two. Are the data groupings "paired"—that is, did the study use a dependent-groups design? The answer is "no," it's an independent-groups design. Following these answers in the table across to the right-hand column, we see that the analysis to choose would depend on whether the data are nominal or ordinal.

If the data are on a nominal scale of measurement, we'd typically use a **chi-square** (χ^2) test, which evaluates whether the observed frequencies of individuals in one category versus another are significantly different from the frequencies expected on the basis of either chance alone or a theory's prediction. Usually, the expectation is based on chance, and the null hypothesis is that the frequencies are equal across categories. For example, the research of Loftus (1975) on eyewitness memory in which students watched a video of a sports car traveling on a country road and eventually having an accident used a chi-square test in which equal frequencies constituted the null. Recall that the control group was asked, "How fast was the white sports car going while traveling along the country road?"; the experimental group was asked the same question with the misleading phrase "when it passed the barn" inserted after the word "going." The frequencies involved the number of students in each group who answered "yes" or "no" when asked later whether they had seen a barn. To see the distribution of the frequencies in that study, we can draw a *contingency table,* with the independent variable on one side and the dependent variable along the top:

	Saw barn?	
	"Yes"	"No"
Experimental group	13	62
Control group	2	73

If the misleading phrase has no effect and the null hypothesis is correct, we'd expect the number of individuals who answered "yes" to be equal and very low for both groups. A chi-square was calculated and revealed that the frequencies were significantly different for the experimental and control groups, $\chi^2 (1, N = 150) = 8.96, p < .01$ (note: with χ^2, we must give the N). The experimental group had more participants who said they had seen the barn and fewer who said they did not see one than the control group.

If the data are on an ordinal measurement scale, an easy to use and powerful nonparametric statistic is the **Mann-Whitney *U*** test. The data in the analysis must be ranked across both groups combined; if the scores are on an interval or ratio scale, they must be converted to rank scores, which SPSS will do automatically. The Mann-Whitney *U* calculates the average rank for each group and then assesses whether the ranks for the two groups are significantly different; it can be done as a one-tailed or two-tailed test. The outcome is usually expressed as a standardized *z* score. Two complications can occur with this test: First, there can be tied ranks, which is usually handled by averaging the range of ranks the scores would use and assigning the average to each of the tied subjects. Second, if you calculate the Mann-Whitney *U* without a computer program, different procedures must be used for small and large samples (Siegel, 1956).

Estimates of Effect Size

Statistics that estimate effect size are based on correlational analyses, which enable them to assess the degree of association between variations in the independent and dependent variables. Effect size statistics for between-subjects designs usually apply codes for the levels of the independent variable, such as the experimental group = 1 and the control group = 0, and then calculate a correlation coefficient or similar statistic between the independent and dependent variables. SPSS offers few statistical procedures for calculating effect size for two-level, independent-groups designs.

Fortunately, calculating an effect size for two independent groups is easy to do manually with the formulas given in Table 7.3. Let's consider two examples. First, using the formula for $r_{es:t}$ (where the subscript *es:t* refers to "effect size

TABLE 7.3

Statistics to Estimate Effect Sizes for Two-Level Independent-Groups Designs with Different Analyses and the Meaning of the Calculated Size of the Effect

Effect size statistic and formula		Size meaning		
		Small	Medium	Large
For *t* test analysis[a]				
$r_{es:t} =$	$\sqrt{\dfrac{t^2}{t^2 + df}}$	.10	.30	.50
or				
Cohen's $d =$	$\dfrac{t(n_1 + n_2)}{\left(\sqrt{df}\right)\sqrt{n_1 n_2}}$	.20	.50	.80
For chi-square (χ^2) analysis				
Cramér's $V =$	$\sqrt{\dfrac{\chi^2}{N_{tot}(k - 1)}}$ where k is the smaller of the numbers of rows and columns	.10	.30	.50
For Mann-Whitney *U* analysis and other tests that yield a *z* score				
$r_{es:z} =$	$z/\sqrt{N}$ where N is the total number of subjects in the comparison	.10	.30	.50

[a] An important difference between the two formulas is that Cohen's *d* is measured in standard deviation units: $d = .5$ indicates that the means differ by .5 of an *SD*.

Sources: Clark-Carter (1997), Cohen (1988), and Rosenthal & Rosnow (1984)

for *t*"), we'll calculate the effect sizes for two of the *t* values in my student's study of gender differences in stress and coping methods. We saw in Table 7.2 that the *t* values for the dependent variables of problem-focused coping and seeking social support were 1.85, which was marginally significant, and 2.73, respectively; both *df*s were 99. Plugging the relevant data into the formula, we find small-to-medium effect sizes: $r_{es:t} = .18$ for problem-focused coping and .26 for seeking social support. Second, using the formula for Cramér's *V*, we can compute the effect size for the Loftus (1975) study on eyewitness memory: we would divide the χ^2 value (8.96) by the total number of participants (150) and take its square root. To present effect size values in a report, researchers can simply add them at the end of the statistical outcome data—for instance, $\chi^2 (1, N = 150) = 8.96, p < .01$, Cramér's $V = .24$—or, if reporting outcome data in a table, add a separate column. In Table 7.2, for example, a column for effect size might go at the extreme right side.

MULTILEVEL DESIGNS

A multilevel design has three or more levels of an independent variable. Its statistical analysis is described as *one-way* if it has only a single factor—that is, it tests for differences along only one independent variable. We examined two examples of multilevel, single-factor designs in this chapter, each with five levels. One example was the Bransford and Johnson study on the role of the context of information in people's ability to process and understand material, and the other was the Orne and Evans study of the effects of hypnosis on people's willingness to perform dangerous acts. How do we analyze data when the design has more than two independent groups?

One approach some people might suggest would be to apply a series of two-level tests—t, χ^2, or U tests—for all possible pairs of groups. Let's see how this would play out in the Orne and Evans study by looking at the groups listed in Table 7.1. We would test real hypnosis versus each of the other groups, which would be four tests; waking control (convey refusal) versus each of the remaining groups, which would be three tests; waking control (convey compliance) versus each remaining group, two tests; and the simulated hypnosis versus unaware control groups. That comes to 10 tests. But there's a problem in doing multiple tests on data from the same study. Researchers use a minimum confidence level for rejecting the null hypothesis for a single test; this level is called *alpha* (α) and is usually set at .05. But each additional test increases the chances of wrongly rejecting the null—making a Type I error—in at least one of the tests. We can calculate the influence of additional tests on the likelihood of making a Type I error with the formula:

$$1 - (1 - \alpha)^c, \text{ where } c = \text{the number of tests computed}$$

Thus, for a study with five groups ($c = 10$ tests) and $\alpha = .05$, $(1 - \alpha)^c$ would equal .60, and the chances of making a Type I error would be .40. In contrast, the chances of a Type 1 error at $\alpha = .05$ would be .14 for a study with three groups ($c = 3$ tests) and .76 for a study with eight groups ($c = 28$ tests).

One method to deal with the problem of inflated risk of Type I error with multiple tests is to apply the **Bonferroni adjustment,** in which we divide the desired alpha level (usually .05) by the number of tests we would perform, producing a more rigorous alpha level for each test. Thus, to maintain a .05 alpha level across 10 tests, we would require a p of .005 (.05 ÷ 10 = .005) to reject the null hypothesis for each test. A problem with using this approach is that when we use a large number of tests, we risk inflating Type II error, failing to reject the null when it is false, because meeting the more rigorous alpha level requires each pair of means to differ by a greater margin. As a result, researchers tend to use multiple tests with the Bonferroni adjustment when they plan to do only a few tests. For example, with five tests, they would require a p of .01 (.05 / 5) for each.

But the preferred approach for analyzing data for multilevel designs is to use statistics that are specifically designed to hold the desired alpha level constant (usually at .05), regardless of the number of groups or conditions being compared. The rest of this chapter describes parametric and nonparametric statistics for multilevel, single-factor designs.

Parametric Analysis

Looking again at Table 4.1 (see inside front cover), you can see that if we are assessing differences with parametric statistics and more than two data sets (groups), we would use an **analysis of variance** (ANOVA). Although there are several versions of ANOVA, each being appropriate for research designs with specific characteristics, they all partition the variance in the data into two types: *between-groups variability*, which consists of systematic plus nonsystematic (error) variance, and *within-groups variability*, which consists only of error variance. Then they calculate the ratio of the two, dividing between-groups variability by within-groups variability, to get an *F* value. The process is in many ways like the *t* test—in fact, if you were to calculate a *t* and an *F* for the same data from two groups of subjects, you'd find that the *F* value is the square of the *t* value. We will focus in this chapter on the *one-way ANOVA*, which assesses differences among more than two levels of one independent variable and produces only one *F* value. We'll see in Chapter 9 that ANOVAs for designs with two or more independent variables yield additional *F* values.

To calculate the two types of variability, the ANOVA starts by computing two forms of squared deviations from the mean—the basis in calculating variance—each of which is called a **sum of squares** (*SS*) for short. To calculate the **sum of squares within groups** (SS_{wg}), the procedure subtracts the mean (*M*, or $\overline{X}$) from each score (*X*) for a group, squares that value, sums the squared values for each group, and then adds together the sums for all groups. The formula is (subscripts for *M* and *X* indicate the group):

$$SS_{wg} = \Sigma(X_1 - M_1)^2 + \Sigma(X_2 - M_2)^2 + \Sigma(X_3 - M_3)^2 \ldots, \text{ and so on for all groups}$$

To calculate the **sum of squares between groups** (SS_{bg}), the procedure first computes a *grand mean* (M_G), or the average of all of the group means. It then subtracts the M_G from each group mean, squares that value, multiplies each squared value by the number of subjects in the corresponding group, and sums across groups. The formula is (subscripts for *n* and *M* indicate the group):

$$SS_{bg} = \Sigma(n_1[M_1 - M_G]^2) + \Sigma(n_2[M_2 - M_G]^2) + \Sigma(n_3[M_3 - M_G]^2) \ldots, \text{ and so on}$$

The rationale for using the grand mean is that if the null hypothesis is true, the means for each of the groups would be close to the grand mean, and no difference would be found. But if the different levels of the independent variable have spread the means apart, some or all of the means should differ from the grand mean and from each other.

Because variance is an *average* of the deviations from the mean, the procedure for calculating the between-groups and within-groups variability needs to take into account the number of units (subjects or groups) that went into their corresponding means. This is where the *degrees of freedom* come in. For between-groups variability, the df_{bg} equals the number of groups or conditions (*k*) reflected in the grand mean (M_G) minus 1 ($df_{bg} = k - 1$); for within-groups variability, the df_{wg} equals the total number of subjects minus the number of groups ($df_{wg} = N_{tot} - k$). So, once the sums of squares are computed, the procedure divides each by the associated *df*, which gives quantities called *mean squares*. The **mean squares between groups** (MS_{bg}) is the estimate of the between-groups variability and will be the numerator in the ratio that yields the *F* value. The **mean squares within groups** (MS_{wg}) is the estimate of the within-groups variability and will be the denominator in the *F* ratio. If the analysis is done with a computer statistics program, these outcomes are reported in an ANOVA summary table. Table 7.4 shows an ANOVA table for a one-way analysis for independent groups with hypothetical data for a study comparing four age groups. Let's see how to read the table one column at a time, starting at the left.

- ▪ *Source:* As a source of variance, *between conditions,* or groups, refers mainly to the independent variable; *within conditions,* or groups, refers to error variability.
- ▪ *SS:* Notice that there are sums of squares for between conditions (SS_{bg}) and within conditions (SS_{wg}). We can usually ignore the totals.
- ▪ *df:* The $df_{bg} = 3$ because the study had four groups (*k*, and $df_{bg} = k - 1$); $df_{wg} = 76$ because there were 80 participants in the study ($df_{wg} = N_{tot} - k$).
- ▪ *MS:* Each $MS = SS \div df$.
- ▪ *F:* The $F = MS_{bg} \div MS_{wg}$.
- ▪ *p:* The *p* (sometimes labeled "Sig" in computer outputs) tells us whether the *F* is significant. In these data, it is, at the .01 level of confidence.

When reporting the outcome of an ANOVA in a sentence, we include both *df*s, usually in parentheses after the *F* value. For instance, for the single-factor design in Table 7.4 with four independent groups and 80 participants, we might report: $F(3, 76) = 4.05$, $p = .01$, followed by the effect size estimate (which we'll consider a little later).

What does the significant *F* tell us? To answer this question we need to discuss the concept of an **omnibus test**—any analysis that compares more than two levels of an independent variable(s) at one time. A significant outcome of an omnibus test simply tells us "something is different in there," but it doesn't say which conditions are different or how many differences there are. As a result, we may need follow-up analyses to *compare two conditions at a time.* Researchers can choose from two types of analyses, depending on whether they had made a

---

TABLE 7.4

An Example ANOVA Summary Table for a One-Way Design with Four Independent Groups

Source	SS	df	MS	F	p
Between conditions (age)	240.93	3	80.31	4.05	.01
Within conditions (error)	1507.08	76	19.83		
Total	1748.01	79			

specific research hypothesis for the two conditions *prior to* starting the study. If researchers *had a prior hypothesis* for the two conditions, they use a follow-up analysis called a **contrast** (or *planned comparison* or *a priori test*) that simply involves doing a *t* test for the two conditions. If the researchers *had no prior hypothesis* for the conditions and decided to do an analysis after inspecting the data, they use **post hoc comparisons,** special analyses that test for differences between all possible pairs of means and take the number of comparisons into account. There are several statistics for doing post hoc comparisons (or *unplanned comparison, multiple comparisons,* or *a posteriori tests*), including the *Scheffé, Tukey, Duncan,* and *Dunnett's* tests. An important and practical distinction between the types of follow-up analyses is that a *post hoc comparison can be done only if a significant F was found,* but a contrast can be done without a significant *F* because a difference was predicted and a comparison was planned in advance. Contrasts and post hoc comparisons can be performed along with the ANOVA in SPSS and other programs.

A nice example of a one-way analysis with post hoc comparisons comes from a study of age differences in toddlers' ability to exercise self-control, such as in complying with requests to wait when something they want is delayed (Vaughn, Kopp, & Krakow, 1984). As part of the study, each 18-, 24-, or 30-month-old child was seated at a table with his or her mother, who simply sat reading a magazine. A researcher placed an unusual telephone on the table, showed the child some of its features, and then left the room after stating clearly, "Sit right there and *don't touch* the phone while I'm gone!" How long did the toddlers wait before touching the phone? The mean waiting times from youngest to oldest, were 10.26, 69.70, and 113.05 seconds, which produced a significant *F* value ($F(2, 69) = 19.84, p < .001$). Because the researchers had predicted only that waiting times would increase with age without specifically stating which ages would differ, they did post hoc comparisons, which revealed that each age group was significantly different from every other age group.

Nonparametric Analysis

As Table 4.1 (see inside front cover) shows, if we assess differences with nonparametric statistics and have more than two independent data groupings, we would use a **chi-square** (χ^2) for nominal data or either the **Kruskal-Wallis *H*** or the ***k*-sample median test** for ordinal data. The chi-square test is the same one as we considered earlier, which can be used with more than two groups. The Kruskall-Wallis and *k*-sample median tests use rank-ordered data across all groups and evaluate whether the distribution of ranks differs significantly from equality. These two tests can be used with two or more groups and yield a χ^2 value.

Let's look at an example of a nonparametric analysis of nominal data from a study on deaths from heroin use (Siegel, Hinson, Krank, & McCully, 1982). In the course of becoming addicted, the body develops a "tolerance" for the drug, requiring more and more of it to achieve the same psychoactive effects, so that the addict now regularly takes doses that would ordinarily kill individuals who had never or rarely used it. Tolerance seems to involve physiological reactions to protect the body from the drug's physical effects. But addicts sometimes die from taking their normal heroin dose—normal, that is, in terms of the amount and purity. Why should this be? The researchers reasoned that these deaths happen when the tolerance effect fails temporarily because the usual stimuli that have come to elicit the protective reaction are not there, say, if the addict took the drug in a new environment. To test this hypothesis, they conducted an experiment, assigning 107 rats to three groups. The two experimental groups were injected with heroin in a specific room (which we'll call the "drug room") every other day with increasing doses until they acquired a high level of tolerance; on alternate days, they received a sugar-water injection in a distinctly different room. The control group received daily injections of sugar water, alternating the place between the same two rooms. Then the each group received a large dose: one experimental group received it in the drug room, the other experimental group got it in the different room (where they had gotten sugar water), and the control group got it in either of the rooms. If the drug room environment could elicit the protective reaction, fewer rats in the drug room group should die from the dose than in the other groups. The results confirmed this expectation: 32.4% of the animals in the drug room group died, compared with 64.3% of the different room group and 96.4% of the control group. A chi-square analysis revealed that these percentages differed significantly among the groups.

Because overall analyses of more than two groups are omnibus tests, follow-up tests to compare two conditions at a time are needed. With chi-square, Kruskal-Wallis, and *k*-sample median tests, probably the best way to make these comparisons is to repeat the same test for each pair of groups (these tests can be used with just two groups), using the Bonferroni adjustment for the alpha level if many tests will be done. The follow-up tests can be done as contrasts or post hoc comparisons, but the latter is only appropriate if the omnibus test was significant. In the heroin experiment, the follow-up tests were contrasts because they were planned in advance and revealed that the death rates in each group differed significantly from the death rates in each other group.

Estimates of Effect Size

The unfocused nature of an omnibus test usually renders an effect size computed directly from its outcome of limited use in understanding the strength of the association. A better approach is to calculate effect sizes for a multilevel, single-factor design from the outcomes of follow-up comparisons of two groups at a time. We'll examine effect size procedures for parametric analyses first.

After conducting a one-way ANOVA, follow-up analyses can involve contrasts or post hoc comparisons. If they are contrasts, they would be *t* tests, and the corresponding effect sizes would be calculated with either of the formulas in Table 7.3. We would then interpret them as small, medium, or large effect sizes according to the information in the table. For post hoc comparisons we have a problem: there are no procedures available to calculate effect sizes from their outcomes. There are two ways to deal with this problem. First, we can use an effect size statistic called eta squared (η^2) that is calculated from the omnibus ANOVA test with the formula:

$$\eta^2 = \frac{F(df_{bg})}{[F(df_{bg})] + df_{wg}}$$

Second, we can calculate t tests for each pair of groups just to get the t values to use in the formulas in Table 7.3 and then compute effect sizes from those data.

For nonparametric analyses of multilevel, single-factor designs, recall that the chi-square, Kruskal-Wallis, and k-samples median tests all yield a χ^2 value. Thus, the Cramér's V test in Table 7.3 can be calculated with the χ^2 value from the overall test and from each follow-up comparison.

SUMMARY

When studying the role of different levels of an independent variable, researchers use an independent-groups (between subjects) design if they compare two or more separate groups of subjects who have different levels of the factor. If researchers match the subjects in the groups or test the same subjects in different conditions, they use a dependent-groups design.

Two-level, single-factor studies test just two levels of one independent variable that can be either manipulated or nonmanipulated and often includes a control group. Researchers can use three types of control groups other than the standard type. A placebo control group is included to control for placebo effects that can arise from participants' expectancies. A yoked control group is used to ensure that simultaneously tested experimental and control subjects receive exactly the same experiences except for a critical aspect of the independent variable. And a waiting list control group simply delays the experimental condition; it is like a standard control group but addresses ethical issues when the experimental group receives a beneficial treatment condition. Multilevel, single-factor studies have more than two groups with one independent variable to test for or demonstrate a curvilinear relationship between the independent and dependent variables and to ensure that the results will be clear and unambiguous.

When performing analyses to assess differences between groups or conditions, the choice of statistical tests depends on the answers to three questions. First, are the data for the dependent variable measured on a nominal or ordinal measurement scale or on an interval or ratio scale? The answer determines whether the appropriate analyses will use parametric or nonparametric tests. Second, how many data groupings will be compared? Third, are the data groupings paired? For two-level designs, a parametric analysis involves the t test and a nonparametric analysis uses the chi-square test for nominal data or the Mann-Whitney U test for ordinal data. For multilevel, single-factor designs, using multiple two-level tests, such as t, χ^2, or U, can inflate the likelihood of Type I error, unless the Bonferroni adjustment is applied. A better approach for a parametric analysis involves the one-way analysis of variance, which calculates the sum of squares between groups and sum of squares within groups, which when divided by the degrees of freedom yield the mean squares. Dividing the mean squares between groups by the mean squares within groups yields the F. For a nonparametric analysis, the chi-square test is used for nominal data and the k-sample median test is used for ordinal data, both of which yield a χ^2 value. Because in multilevel designs the one-way ANOVA, chi-square, Kruskal-Wallis, and k-sample median statistics are omnibus tests, they are usually followed by contrast or post hoc comparison tests. Effect sizes can be calculated to assess the degree to which variations in the independent variable can account for the differences between groups in the dependent variable.

KEY TERMS

independent-groups design
between-subjects design
dependent-groups design
placebo effect
placebo control group
yoked control group
waiting list control group
t test

chi-square (χ^2)
Mann-Whitney U
Bonferroni adjustment
analysis of variance (ANOVA)
sum of squares (SS)
sum of squares within groups (SS_{wg})
sum of squares between groups (SS_{bg})

mean squares between groups (MS_{bg})
mean squares within groups (MS_{wg})
omnibus test
contrast
post hoc comparisons
Kruskal-Wallis H
k-sample median test

REVIEW QUESTIONS

1. Describe Field's (1981) study on the role of training on children's cognitive abilities and how her hypothesis influenced her design.
2. How do the *independent-groups design* and *dependent-groups design* differ?
3. Describe two research designs that researchers try to avoid because they are basically flawed from the start.
4. Describe the Blakemore and Cooper (1970) and Holloway and Hornstein (1976) studies and discuss why the absence of a control group is a greater problem for the latter.
5. Discuss how researchers maximize variance from the independent variable and minimize extraneous and error variability.
6. What are the three types of control groups, other than the standard type, the book describes, and why are they used?
7. Discuss why researchers use multilevel designs and how they choose levels of the independent variable, using the Bransford and Johnson (1972) and Orne and Evans (1965) studies as examples.
8. Describe how to use Table 4.1 (see inside front cover) to choose the appropriate parametric or nonparametric statistical test for a single-factor design with two independent groups. Which statistic would you use with nominal or ordinal data, and with interval or ratio data?
9. What are *one-tailed* and *two-tailed tests*?

10. How can we estimate effect size after performing a *t* test or chi-square test for a two-level design?

11. Why is it not a good idea to analyze a multilevel design with multiple two-level tests, and how can we correct for the inflated risk of Type I error?

12. Describe the one-way ANOVA procedure.

13. What is an *omnibus test,* and why are *contrast* and *post hoc comparison* tests used?

14. Describe how to analyze nominal and ordinal data from a multilevel design.

RESOURCES

BOOKS, CHAPTERS, AND ARTICLES

Cohen, J. (1988). *Statistical power analysis for the behavioral sciences* (2nd ed.). Hillsdale, NJ: Erlbaum.

Keppel, G. (1991). *Design and analysis: A researcher's handbook* (3rd ed.). Englewood Cliffs, NJ: Prentice Hall.

Siegel, S. (1956). *Nonparametric statistics for the behavioral sciences.* New York: McGraw-Hill.

Winer, B. J. (1962). *Statistical principles in experimental design.* New York: McGraw-Hill.

INTERNET SITES

http://trochim.human.cornell.edu This Website has links to information about several experimental design issues discussed in this chapter.

http://www/ruf.rice.edu/~lane/stat_sim/index.html This Website is the Rice Virtual Lab that gives statistics tutorials. For instance, by clicking on *ANOVA* and then *one-way ANOVA,* you can see how the statistic partitions the sum of squares for a data set. By clicking on *chi-square* and then *2 × 2 contingency tables,* you can see how changes in the data affect the statistical outcome.

APPLICATION ACTIVITIES

APPLICATION 7–1: WANTED AND UNWANTED VARIANCE

Suppose we were designing an experiment on the effects of two propaganda messages on college students' attitudes about gun control. Describe specific aspects of the design that you would suggest for maximizing variance from the independent variable and for minimizing extraneous and error variability.

APPLICATION 7–2: DESIGN AN EXPERIMENT

Studies have shown that people's estimates of their own blood pressure are inaccurate (Sarafino, 2002). Suppose we wanted to test the hypothesis that biofeedback training for blood pressure can help people estimate their blood pressure status more accurately. Design *two* single-factor "true" experiments, one with *two levels* and one with *three levels* of the independent variable to test this hypothesis, and answer the following questions about each experiment:

a. Would you use one or more control groups? If so, state the type(s) and why.
b. How would you assign participants to groups?
c. Describe the dependent variable and state the type of measurement scale: nominal, ordinal, interval, or ratio.
d. State the statistical analyses you would do and explain how you chose them.

APPLICATION 7–3: EFFECT SIZES

Calculate the effect sizes (see Table 7.3) for the following statistical outcomes from single-factor designs with two independent groups, each with 30 subjects:

a. $r_{es:t}$ for the outcome: $t(59) = 2.68$, $p < .01$ (two-tailed).
b. Cohen's d for the same outcome ($t(59) = 2.68$, $p < .01$).
c. Cramér's $V =$ for the outcome: $\chi^2(1) = 4.02$, $p < .05$.

Are the effect sizes small, medium, or large?

APPLICATION 7–4: STATISTICAL DECISIONS

Suppose we used a survey with 3rd, 7th, and 11th graders to test the hypothesis that self-esteem increases with years in school and found the following ANOVA outcome: $F(2, 117) = 7.45$, $p < .001$.

a. Is the result statistically significant? If yes, at what level of confidence?
b. Can we conclude that the research hypothesis is true?
c. Can we say that the 3rd and 7th graders or the 7th and 11th graders differed? If not, how could we test for these differences?
d. What effect size estimate could we calculate with only the F value and df?
e. What would be a better way to test for effect sizes in this study?

CHAPTER 3

SINGLE-FACTOR, DEPENDENT-GROUPS DESIGNS

PROLOGUE

"Davy Crockett meets organizational behavior management" could be a playful title for an experiment by Lise Saari and Gary Latham (1982) on the effects of different payment schedules on the productivity of beaver trappers who were working for a forest products company in northwestern United States. The researchers were aware that animal subjects perform behaviors at higher rates when reinforced on a *variable ratio* schedule than on a *continuous* schedule if the number of rewards received is equated for the two conditions (Ferster & Skinner,

1957). But this effect had not always been demonstrated in research with humans in work situations, probably because of methodological problems.

Let's define these two reinforcement schedules and see how they were applied with the beaver trappers as an extra incentive beyond their base hourly pay during the 12-week trapping season.

- *Continuous reinforcement* (CRF)—a reinforcer is given for each and every instance of the behavior. Under the CRF condition, in addition to the trappers' base pay, they received $1.00 for each beaver they caught.
- *Variable ratio reinforcement* (VR)—the number of responses that must be made for each instance of reward changes and is unpredictable from one instance to another. Under the VR condition, whether or not the trappers would receive extra pay when they brought in a beaver depended on their predicting correctly twice whether a roll of a die would produce an odd or even number. If both predictions were right, they'd get $4.00; but if not, they'd get no extra pay.

Because on average, the trappers in the VR condition should predict two rolls of the die correctly one of four times, the overall pay rate ($1.00 per beaver) should be equal to that in the CRF condition across the 12 weeks.

The researchers decided to carry out the study as a *controlled within-subjects design* in which each of 12 trappers would experience in alternate weeks either the CRF or VR condition. The trappers were randomly assigned so that half would start with CRF and half would start with VR. The experiment revealed that the number of beavers caught per hour of work was much higher (nearly 40% higher) under the VR condition than the CRF condition, and this difference was significant, $t(11) = 3.15$, $p < .01$ (I calculated the effect size, $r_{es:t} = .69$, which is quite strong). This finding is consistent with the results of studies with animal subjects, such as rats and pigeons. Response rate is higher with VR than CRF schedules of reinforcement.

This chapter examines the methodology and analysis of research using single-factor, dependent-groups designs, with an emphasis on within-subjects, or repeated measures, designs in which each subject is tested in more than one condition of the study. We introduced the concept of within-subjects designs in Chapter 5 as a way of equating groups of subjects because the same individuals serve in each level of an independent variable. We will discuss these designs in greater detail here and see that within-subjects designs often require special techniques to control for a potential confounding: having been tested in one condition, or level of an independent variable, may affect the subjects' performance in another condition.

TYPES OF DEPENDENT-GROUPS DESIGNS

The lower portion of Figure 7.1 (see inside back cover) outlines four types of dependent-groups designs and the research strategies they use. The main defining feature of these designs is that the subjects' performance is likely to be correlated across levels of the independent variable, which is why they're called "dependent." This is not the case in independent-groups (between-subjects) designs. In independent- and dependent-groups designs, researchers can opt to use experimental or quasi-experimental strategies. Recall that research using an experimental strategy can lead to a cause–effect conclusion if it meets three criteria: (a) *covariation of variables,* (b) *causal time sequence* in which the cause clearly precedes the effect, and (c) *elimination of other plausible causes* so that extraneous variables do not confound the results.

We saw in Chapter 5 that there are two ways by which methods applied to create equivalent groups can produce correlated scores for the dependent variable. One way is when researchers use a *within-subjects design,* taking *repeated measures* on the same subjects across levels of the independent variable. The other way is when researchers use a *matching* technique to equate separate groups of subjects.

WITHIN-SUBJECTS DESIGNS

Because within-subjects designs test individuals more than once across levels of an independent variable, they are often called repeated-measures designs. As Figure 7.1 indicates, researchers can use repeated measures across levels of an independent variable that is being tested with experimental or quasi-experimental strategies.

One issue to keep in mind about repeated measures is that the procedure and statistical implications are different from taking measurements more than once within a condition to obtain a stable and reliable measure of the behavior. As an example of the latter procedure, researchers who are studying people's reaction time to a visual stimulus might present it repeatedly in a session and use the participants' average reaction time as the person's score for that stimulus. In this case, the person is tested in only *one condition* of the study, and the reaction time data are combined for an accurate measure.

Controlled Within-Subjects Designs

Like all studies using an experimental strategy, controlled within-subjects designs that are conducted well apply methods that meet all three of the criteria mentioned earlier, allowing researchers to make causal inferences from the results. The experiment by Saari and Latham (1982) on pay schedules for beaver trappers is a straightforward example. Each of the 12 trappers served in both pay conditions, alternating weekly between the CRF and VR schedules of reinforcement. Thus, the participants in the two conditions were equated because they were the same individuals. In addition, the rate of pay per beaver was held constant—$1.00 per beaver—across the two conditions. The only factor the researchers wisely did not hold constant was the order in which the trappers experienced the pay schedules—that is, whether the first schedule would be the CRF or the VR, followed by the alternating. Instead, the researchers used both orders and *balanced* them so that half of the trappers started with the CRF and half started with the VR schedule. Why? If, for instance, all the trappers had started with CRF, the reason for the superiority of the VR schedule might have been an "order effect," such as the trappers somehow finding the CRF schedule less desirable because it was first. By controlling for all these potential extraneous variables, the researchers could conclude that the reinforcement schedules caused the difference in performance.

Quasi-Experimental Within-Subjects Designs

Researchers often apply within-subjects designs with a quasi-experimental strategy when they cannot create equivalent groups or manipulate the independent variable. We have discussed in earlier chapters some of these methodologies, including the:

- *Longitudinal design,* which tests the same individuals more than once over a long period of time, and age is the independent variable.
- *One-group pretest–posttest design,* in which researchers take one measurement on the subjects before and one after an event or treatment occurs. The time frame relative to the event or treatment is the independent variable. This design lacks a control group to rule out the role of extraneous factors, such as maturation or history.
- *Interrupted time-series design,* in which researchers take a series of measurements on the same subjects before and after an event occurs or a treatment condition begins, and the time frame relative to the event is the independent variable. This design is like the pretest–posttest design, but by taking a *series* of measurements, researchers may be able to use patterns of data to rule out the influence of certain extraneous variables.

In all these designs, repeated measurements are taken over time on the same subjects, and the scores from the different time periods are compared. Like all quasi-experimental research, these designs can meet only one or two of the three criteria needed for causal inference.

MATCHED-SUBJECTS DESIGNS

In matched-subjects designs, researchers equate separate groups of subjects for one or more matching variables that they know or expect will be strongly related to scores on the dependent variable. We saw in Chapter 5 that to carry out this process, researchers must:

- Select each matching variable and have a reliable and valid way to assess it.
- Measure the matching variable and form sets of subjects who are very similar on that variable. Each set should contain the same number of subjects as there are conditions in the study.
- Assign the subjects from each set to groups randomly.

Because the subjects are matched on at least one variable that is related to the dependent variable, we would expect their performance to be correlated to some degree. Thus, studies with matched groups are dependent-groups designs.

Let's look briefly at three studies that used matched-subjects designs. First, an experiment on the role of modeled aggression on children's aggressive behavior assigned 3- to 5-year-olds to four groups that were matched for ratings of the aggression they had displayed in interactions at their nursery school (Bandura, Ross, & Ross, 1963). Each child in three groups watched aggressive acts performed; the fourth group did not. Then each child was tested for aggression. Because ratings of the children's usual aggression would be expected to correlate with the aggression they would show when tested, those ratings could be an appropriate matching variable. Second, a study used hospital records as archival data to test whether patients who had been assigned rooms with or without a view of a natural setting tended to recover sooner and use less medication (Ulrich, 1984). The patients in the two groups were matched for several variables that relate to health, including their age, sex, weight, and smoking history. Third, an experiment tested whether rats that could or could not avoid or escape electric shocks by performing a simple response would differ in subsequent physical characteristics, such as their weight and development of ulcers (Weiss, 1968). Three rats at a time were placed in adjoining compartments and tested in three conditions: An experimental rat could prevent or turn off periodic shocks, a yoked control rat got shocks if the experimental rat failed to respond, and a control rat never received a shock. The subjects were matched for weight before being assigned to groups.

ORDER EFFECTS AND CONTROL METHODS

When using repeated measures across conditions of a study, the conditions will occur in some order or sequence for each subject. Suppose the study on pay schedules of beaver trappers had been done differently: All trappers received the CRF schedule ($1.00 per beaver) for the first week and the VR schedule ($4.00 if they won the die toss) second, and alternated the two schedules for the remaining 10 weeks. Suppose also that all the trappers were new employees, and their skill in beaver trapping would improve gradually across the first few months. If so, for each alternation of CRF and VR, the trappers would have been somewhat more skilled during the VR week than the CRF week. Thus, part or all of the reason for the superiority of the VR schedule would be the trappers' greater skills. If these circumstances had occurred, the *order* of the conditions would have had a differential effect favoring the VR condition, which means that the effects of the pay schedules, the independent variable, would be confounded. This is an example of a phenomenon called *order effects* that can occur whenever researchers use within-subjects designs.

WHAT ARE ORDER EFFECTS?

The term **order effects** (or *sequence effects*) refers to the circumstance in which a study's outcome appears to have been influenced by the order in which a series of conditions was administered. Order effects are not always undesirable, and they may be an independent variable in research—for example, in studying learning processes, researchers often test subjects repeatedly after more and more experience with a task. In such cases, changes with practice are wanted. But if order effects confound, or render unclear, the effects of an independent variable, they are a source of unwanted systematic variance and must be avoided or controlled. The remainder of our discussion of order effects assumes that they are unwanted and would confound the research results if left uncontrolled.

TABLE 8.1

Types of Order Effects and Ways to Reduce Their Unwanted Impact

Type of effect	Definition (and example)	How to minimize impact
Practice effect	Improvements in task performance due to learning or warming up. (Novice golfer hits balls more and more accurately over time of practice.)	Give subjects practice on the task before introducing the research conditions.
Fatigue effect	Decrements in task performance due to becoming tired or bored. (Accuracy in a repetitive clerical activity declines after an hour with no rest.)	Make the task as brief and interesting as possible.
Carryover effect	The influence of a treatment or condition extends long enough to affect behavior in a subsequent condition. Can improve or impair performance. (Effect of a drug in one condition continues into the next.)	Allow enough time after each condition for its influence to wear off.

Table 8.1 defines three types of order effects, shows that they can either improve or impair performance, and describes ways to minimize their impact. But minimizing the impact of order effects is typically not sufficient. Researchers also need to control the remaining order effects by balancing or equalizing them across all potentially affected research conditions. To guard against unwanted order effects, researchers apply some form of **counterbalancing,** which involves varying the orders with which subjects experience the levels of the independent variable. Ideally, counterbalancing arranges the orders so that each condition appears equally often in each ordinal position. Researchers can choose from several methods of counterbalancing. To contrast the counterbalancing methods we'll examine, we will apply each one to variations of a study testing people's preferences for three brands of cola beverages: Coca-Cola, Pepsi-Cola, and Royal Crown (also called "RC"; some aspects of the method are based on research by Thumin, 1962). For all the study variations, assume that the participants were

- Told the names of the colas that would be included in the study (we'll abbreviate the names: Coca-Cola = *C,* Pepsi-Cola = *P,* and Royal Crown = *R*)
- Asked to taste a series of colas in tiny cups, each containing exactly .25 ounce (½ of a tablespoon) of liquid
- Asked on each *trial,* or single full testing, to rate each beverage they tasted on a scale (1 = poor and 10 = excellent) right after each taste, rinse thoroughly with water, spit the water into a sink directly beside them, and then wait 10 seconds before tasting the next cola
- Tested in a dimly lighted room to reduce visual cues that might help them identify the cola brand in each cup

As we discuss the different counterbalancing methods, we'll see that they can equalize the order effects either for *each individual subject* or for *each overall condition* across subjects.

When using an *individual counterbalancing* approach, researchers *test each subject more than once per condition* in an effort to distribute the order effects equally in each of the conditions the individual experiences. Two commonly used individual counterbalancing approaches are *reverse counterbalancing* and *block randomization.*

Reverse Counterbalancing

The simplest method for equalizing order effects is **reverse counterbalancing,** in which the researcher presents the different conditions to each subject in one sequence and then presents them again in the opposite order. In the cola-tasting study, if the original order is Pepsi, Coke, and Royal Crown (P–C–R), the reverse order would be R–C–P. As you can see, each participant would have more than one trial with each cola. Reversing the sequence helps ensure that any practice, fatigue, or carryover effects will be distributed evenly across the three conditions. Reverse counterbalancing is sometimes called *ABBA counterbalancing,* where the A and B refer to different conditions in the study. Although the name ABBA suggests that there are only two conditions, it actually applies to studies with any number of conditions.

The basic format for reverse counterbalancing can be modified or extended in at least two ways. First, although we can keep the original and reverse orders the same for all subjects, it is usually better to vary the original order, and therefore the reverse order, across the subjects. For example, some participants in the cola preference study might taste P–C–R, R–C–P, and others might taste R–C–P, P–C–R. Or we could use a random assignment procedure for the colas in the original order, and the reverse sequence would follow from that. Second, we may want to test each subject in each condition more than twice, especially if we want to make sure we get a stable and reliable measure of the behavior, such as when testing perceptual phenomena or using reaction time measures. For example, a participant in the cola preference study might taste each cola six times for a total of 18 trials, such as:

P–C–R, R–C–P; P–C–R, R–C–P; P–C–R, R–C–P or
R–C–P, P–C–R; R–C–P, P–C–R; R–C–P, P–C–R

When researchers have more than one assessment for one condition of the study, they usually combine the data, such as by calculating the mean, for a more accurate measure.

Reverse counterbalancing is most likely to be used in studies that involve a fairly small number of conditions and number of assessments per condition. Two problems can occur with ABBA counterbalancing. First, participants may detect the reversal pattern and then apply expectations that may affect their performance in the next condition(s) they experience. For instance, in the cola preference study, suppose the person could tell which cola was which, noticed the reversal pattern after having tasted P–C–R, R–C–P; P–C–R, R–C, guessed correctly that the next cola would be P, and thought, "Oh, good. The next one is Pepsi, my favorite." The person's expectations could bias the next tasting. The more frequently the reversal pattern is repeated, the more likely participants will detect it and apply expectations. Second, the impact of order effects in one sequence, such as A–B, may be different from the impact in the opposite direction, B–A; if so, the order effects will not be balanced. If we expect this could happen, we can alternate ABBA with BAAB sequences to balance inequities. After collecting the data, we can assess whether an imbalance existed by comparing absolute difference scores between A and B for the A–B and B–A sequences, probably with a *t* test. If the difference scores are significantly larger for one of the directions than the other, the counterbalancing didn't work.

Some of my research methods students have used reverse counterbalancing when conducting studies with within-subjects designs. In one example, a student examined the degree to which children found two riddle types funny. Riddles start with a question, such as "Why was the little strawberry worried?" One type of riddle has an incompatible ending, and another type has a compatible ending. For the "little strawberry" riddle, an incompatible ending is, "Because his mom and dad were in a jam," and a compatible ending is, "Because he couldn't find his mother." The student used a tape recorder to present a series of riddles to the children, using ABBA counterbalancing for the two riddle types, and found that the children rated as funnier the riddles with incompatible endings than compatible endings.

Randomization Methods

Another way to balance order effects across conditions is to present the conditions in a randomly determined sequence, using procedures like those for random assignment of subjects to groups. Although a single randomized sequence may balance order effects well if each subject will experience each condition many times, a more effective method is to apply a different random order for each subject. Let's look at one example of each method my students used:

- A student researcher read aloud a list of words naming 20 negative personality traits, such as "gossipy" and "lazy," and 20 positive traits, such as "sincere" and "heroic," to 45 participants twice in a single random order before asking them to recall the words. Although the positive and negative traits appeared to be evenly distributed in the list, simply randomizing the order might have produced a biased distribution, with most of the positive traits presented at the beginning or end, for example. To guard against possible order effects, she could have used a different order for the second reading.

- A student researcher had participants solve 12 five-letter anagrams, each printed on an index card in a deck of 12 cards that he shuffled in advance to make a different random order for each of 30 individuals. He interrupted the solution process for some of the anagrams and gave the answer to see if the participants would recall more of the solutions for the completed anagrams than the interrupted anagrams.

When researchers plan to present each condition to each subject many times and want to randomize the order, they usually structure the process with a procedure called *block randomization*. This procedure is like *block random assignment,* which we discussed in Chapter 5, that researchers often use to create equal groups.

To counterbalance order effects with **block randomization,** each subject receives many trials for each condition that are divided into *blocks,* where a block consists of one trial for each condition, arranged in a random order. Thus, the size of a block equals the number of conditions in the study. In the cola preference study, for example, a block would consist of one taste each of C, P, and R in a random order. When researchers use a block randomization procedure, each subject experiences a series of blocks and must do each entire block before moving to the next block. The number of blocks will equal the number of presentations planned for each condition. If we planned for 12 presentations of each cola, the randomized orders within blocks might be

Block 1:	C–P–R	Block 7:	P–C–R
Block 2:	R–P–C	Block 8:	R–P–C
Block 3:	R–P–C	Block 9:	C–P–R
Block 4:	C–R–P	Block 10:	C–R–P
Block 5:	P–C–R	Block 11:	P–C–R
Block 6:	P–R–C	Block 12:	R–C–P

In this example, each participant would have 36 tastes of cola. When each trial takes only a short time, the total number of presentations can be very large. For instance, researchers who test brain processing of information may have each participant make quick decisions about visual stimuli with many hundreds of trials per person (Ludwig, Jeeves, Norman, & DeWitt, 1993; Shepard & Metzler, 1971). But if the number of planned trials is small, the likelihood that block randomization will equate order effects across conditions is reduced, and some other counterbalancing method should be chosen.

Because individual counterbalancing methods require each subject to experience each research condition more than once and, perhaps, many times, they may have two drawbacks. First, if each trial takes a lot of time to complete, the procedure may be very time consuming and expensive to carry out, the participants may object and drop out, and fatigue effects may occur. Second, experiencing all the conditions more than once may tip off the participants to the purpose of the research with some independent variables and lead to participant bias in their performance.

CONTROL BY OVERALL COUNTERBALANCING

Methods that can provide alternatives to individual counterbalancing attempt to equalize order effects by *administering each condition to each individual only once,* varying the order across subjects to achieve an *overall balancing.* These procedures distribute order effects in patterns that should make the *average* effects the same for all conditions of the study. Two commonly used procedures for overall counterbalancing in within-subjects designs are the *all possible orders* and *Latin square* methods.

All Possible Orders

The procedure called **all possible orders** or **complete counterbalancing** equalizes order effects by using every possible sequence of the research conditions the same number of times, with each subject receiving only one of the sequences. When applying the method of all possible orders, we would make a list of all of the possible sequences the conditions can take and then randomly assign subjects to each of these sequences. We can determine in advance the number of possible orders by calculating *K!* (pronounced "K factorial"), where *K* is the number of conditions to be balanced and *factorial* means the cumulative product of *K* and all successive integers smaller than it. For the cola preference study with three colas, *K!* would be: $3 \times 2 \times 1 = 6$, or six possible orders. These orders are

C–P–R	P–C–R	R–C–P
C–R–P	P–R–C	R–P–C

Each participant would have just three trials, one with each cola. Because we'd probably want more than one participant for each sequence, we'd use the same set of sequences and randomly assign additional individuals to each new set in a "block" fashion, filling a set entirely before starting another new set. Notice two features of the method of all possible orders. First, order effects are perfectly balanced because each of the possible sequences is represented the same number of times in the study. Second, the total number of participants will be some multiple of the number of possible orders.

Although researchers prefer the all possible orders method when using the overall balancing approach for eliminating order effects, this method has an important limitation: it becomes *unwieldy when the number of conditions exceeds four or five.* Why? The number of possible orders increases exponentially with the number of conditions, as indicated in these calculations of *K!*:

$$2! = 2 \text{ orders} \quad 3! = 6 \quad 4! = 24 \quad 5! = 120 \quad 6! = 720 \quad 7! = 5040$$

To use complete counterbalancing with six conditions, the number of possible sequences would be 720, and the number of subjects would be some multiple of that; with seven conditions, the number of sequences and subjects would be 5,040. Clearly, we'd want to use a different approach when there are many conditions to counterbalance.

Researchers sometimes extend the complete counterbalancing approach by having each subject repeat the sequence more than once. Let's consider two examples. First, the study on pay schedules for beaver trappers we discussed earlier had two conditions, CRF and VR pay schedules, that were alternated weekly. There were two possible orders, CRF–VR and VR–CRF, and the number of trappers was 12, a multiple of two. Across the 12 weeks of the trapping season, the orders were repeated six times, with half of the trappers having one order and half having the other. Notice that the order effects are perfectly balanced because each sequence was represented the same number of times.

Photograph of
Experimental Situation

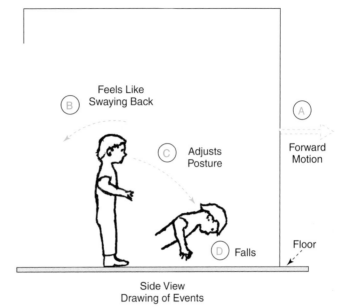

Side View
Drawing of Events

FIGURE 8.1

Photograph of the experimental situation and a side-view drawing of events during testing of an infant. The drawing depicts that the forward motion of the walls and ceiling (A) would make the infant feel like the body is swaying backward (B), leading the infant to adjust its posture (C) to counteract the felt sway, and, perhaps, fall forward (D). The opposite events should happen if the walls and ceiling moved backward. (From Lee and Aronson, 1974, Figure 1 and Figure 2 [adapted].)

Second, an experiment used a similar counterbalancing approach in testing 13- to 16-month-old infants in one session for their reaction to visual sensations that they are losing balance while standing upright (Lee & Aronson, 1974). As the photograph in Figure 8.1 shows, an infant stood facing its seated parents in the experimental situation. Although the floor was fixed, a researcher could move the walls and ceiling forward or backward, and that visual stimulation should suggest a loss of balance to the infant, as diagrammed in the same figure. When, for instance, the walls and ceiling moved forward, the infant should feel like it was falling backward and would adjust its posture, perhaps falling forward. The opposite events would happen if the walls and ceiling were moved backward. To equate order effects for the forward and backward trials, the researchers had some of the infants start with the forward movement, and some with the backward, and then alternated the direction for a total of 20 trials in the session. You may be wondering whether it was a good idea to alternate backward and forward trials because the participants might notice the pattern, predict the next condition, and protect their balance in advance. There are two reasons to conclude that this was not a confounding. First, the participants were so young and probably wouldn't have noticed the pattern. Second, most infants *did* lose balance, as the researchers expected, so any efforts they may have used to protect their balance did not work anyway.

Latin Square Method

The Latin square method is an alternative to all possible orders that is frequently used for overall counterbalancing when the number of conditions is large. In a **Latin square,** the conditions in a within-subjects design are arranged systematically into a matrix so that each condition (a) appears in each ordinal position one time and (b) precedes and follows each other condition once. In the matrix ("square"), each row constitutes a full sequence. The term Latin square comes from an ancient Roman puzzle that required for its solution that these characteristics be met. Once we have constructed the matrix of conditions, each subject is randomly assigned to receive one sequence (row). If we want more than one subject for each sequence, we would use the same matrix repeatedly and assign additional individuals in a "block" fashion, filling all rows before starting another matrix. The total number of subjects the design requires will be some multiple of the number of conditions. Go to **Box 8.1** to see the full procedure for constructing a Latin square.

A within-subjects design that applied the Latin square method to counterbalance order effects manipulated four conditions of physical activity with 19- to 27-year-old men who had been leading sedentary lifestyles (Jennings et al., 1986). Over a 4-month period, physiological measurements, such as of blood pressure, were taken at the end of each month that each man spent at his normal level of activity and at below normal, above normal, and much above normal activity. For the Latin square, the researchers used a 4×4 matrix to determine the sequence of 1-month periods in which the men experienced one of the four activity conditions. The number of individuals tested in the experiment was 12, a multiple of four. The men's blood pressures were significantly lower after a month of above normal and much above normal activity than after normal and below normal activity.

We have examined two methods each for individual counterbalancing and overall counterbalancing of potential order effects when researchers test different levels of an independent variable in within-subjects designs. Two additional points should be made about counterbalancing. First, other counterbalancing methods exist for achieving an individual or overall balancing of order effects, and sometimes researchers apply a blend of methods if that seems likely to work best. Second, counterbalancing may be desirable for repeated measurements that are not taken across levels of an independent variable. For example, a student of mine conducted a correlational study to validate a survey that measures stress. She administered to the same participants four other surveys that were expected to produce scores that would correlate highly with stress. Because of concerns about order effects among the four validation surveys, she used the method of all possible orders to counterbalance the sequence in which those surveys were filled out.

To illustrate how to construct a Latin square, we'll extend the cola preference study to include the "diet" versions of the beverages so that there are
six conditions: C, P, R, Cd, Pd, and Rd (d = diet). We would start by drawing a blank K × K matrix, where K is the number of conditions—in this
case, six. Then we would perform the following steps:

1. After arranging the conditions in a random order, pair them in sequence to a series of digits, beginning with 1. For example, the random order of conditions with the paired digits might be: P–1, Rd–2,
   C–3, Cd–4, Pd–5, and R–6.

2. Generate the first row in the matrix—that is, the first sequence of
   conditions—with the digits we just generated, using the formula: 1,
   2, K, 3, $(K-1)$, 4. This formula can be used with any even-numbered
   K; it can be shortened for fewer conditions, and it can be extended
   by adding "$(K-2)$, 5" for eight conditions, adding to that "$(K-3)$, 6"
   for ten conditions, and so on.

3. Our formula for six conditions would yield the digits 1, 2, 6, 3, 5, and
   4. Plug those digits sequentially into the first row of the blank matrix
   and convert the digits to the symbols for the conditions (1 = P, 2 =
   Rd, 6 = R, 3 = C, 5 = Pd, 4 = Cd). See the way these data were entered
   in the first row in the following matrix, which has the conditions symbols in bold font so you can see how the conversion identifies the sequence of conditions. A person assigned the first row will taste P, Rd,
   R, C, Pd, and then Cd.

4. Generate succeeding rows by adding 1 to each number in the preceding row, using the rule that $K + 1 = 1$. The shaded boxes allow you
   to follow a condition (in this case, regular Coca-Cola) to see that the
   design meets the criteria that each condition appear once in each
   position and is preceded and followed by each other condition once.

1 = **P**	2 = **Rd**	6 = **R**	3 = **C**	5 = **Pd**	4 = **Cd**
2 = **Rd**	3 = **C**	1 = **P**	4 = **Cd**	6 = **R**	5 = **Pd**
3 = **C**	4 = **Cd**	2 = **Rd**	5 = **Pd**	1 = **P**	6 = **R**
4 = **Cd**	5 = **Pd**	3 = **C**	6 = **R**	2 = **Rd**	1 = **P**
5 = **Pd**	6 = **R**	4 = **Cd**	1 = **P**	3 = **C**	2 = **Rd**
6 = **R**	1 = **P**	5 = **Pd**	2 = **Rd**	4 = **Cd**	3 = **C**

These same steps apply for any Latin square design with an even number
of conditions. If we have an odd number of conditions, the procedure is
more complex and would require us to make and coordinate two matrixes
(see Winer, 1962 for the procedure). If you plan to use the Latin square
method, keep in mind that the number of subjects you'll need for the
study must be some multiple of K.

DECIDING TO USE A
DEPENDENT-GROUPS DESIGN

How do researchers decide whether to use a dependent-groups or independent-groups design? Given the difficulties in finding and applying matching variables for matched-subjects designs and in controlling order effects in within-subjects designs, the elegance and simplicity of independent groups seems very appealing. We'll focus this discussion mainly on within-subjects designs because, by testing the same individuals at more than one level of the independent variable, they are distinctly different from approaches that use separate groups of subjects and offer several very important and unique advantages.

WHY TO USE OR NOT USE A WITHIN-SUBJECTS DESIGN

Researchers consider the potential for several benefits in choosing to test subjects with repeated measures. First, within-subjects designs guarantee *equivalent subjects* in each level of the independent variable at the start of the research. Given that the subjects are the same individuals, they couldn't be more similar. Thus, the possibility of having unequal groups as a confounding is eliminated. In between-subjects designs, although we may be able to randomly assign subjects to conditions in an effort to equalize individual differences across groups, there is always some chance that the procedure will create unequal groups. Matched-subjects designs can help to reduce nonequivalence, but the subjects are almost never perfectly matched.

Second, within-subjects designs require *fewer subjects* because we would test the same individuals across levels of the independent variable. For example, a study with three independent or matched groups with 25 participants in each condition will require a total of 75 subjects, but essentially the same study conducted with repeated measures will require only 25. This is a distinct advantage and may be the sole option when only a small number of individuals is available—for instance, if the subjects must be animals that are hard to acquire or must be people with special characteristics, such as an unusual psychological or physical disorder.

Third, using repeated measures across conditions is typically more *convenient and efficient* than using independent-groups or matched-subjects designs. As we've already seen, within-subjects designs use fewer subjects, which saves the researcher's time in testing them and, perhaps, resources, such as money if the participants or assistants are paid. Also, if the participants' task would be very brief in a between-subjects design, it would be wasteful to have them come in for just a short time, such as to give ratings about stimuli presented in a few minutes. More data could be obtained with repeated measures in a longer testing session for more conditions. In addition, recruiting participants, setting up the tasks, giving instructions, and other preparation activities take time that could be reduced if repeated measures were used.

Fourth, within-subjects designs have *more statistical power*—that is, they are more sensitive in detecting differences in systematic variance from the independent variable—than matched-subjects designs, which are more sensitive than independent-groups designs. Why does repeated measures yield the greatest sensitivity? Recall that the formulas for many statistical tests, such as the *t* test, divide systematic variance by error variance. Most of the error variance in psychology research derives from individual differences among the subjects in different conditions. Using repeated measures reduces error variance because it virtually eliminates the variation that arises from individual differences between subjects, thereby yielding a higher value of the *t* or other statistic. Although matched-subjects designs also reduce error variance resulting from individual differences, the reduction is less than in within-subjects designs because the subjects are usually matched only on one or two potentially relevant measures. The increased power of repeated measures has other advantages. For one thing, when we use a sample with large individual differences, the enhanced power from repeated measures is heightened. Also, because of the greater statistical power of repeated measures, a study conducted as a within-subjects design may need fewer subjects to provide a fair test of the hypothesis. Although reducing the number of subjects reduces power, we can cover this loss with the increase in power from using repeated measures.

Fifth, research *hypotheses often require repeated measurements,* especially when studying changes in behavior over time, such as in longitudinal research, pretest–posttest designs, and research on learning or forgetting. As an example, Campbell, Batsche, and Batsche (1972) studied the effects of food reward on learning in hungry rats. The animals were tested once per day in a runway, each time having the chance to run from one end to the other, where they would find the food. Running speed increased steadily and sharply during the first month or so and then leveled off and continued at this very high level in the weeks thereafter. This description shows the basic properties of a *learning curve:* Performance increases substantially at first and then stabilizes at some high level (Hulse, Deese, & Egeth, 1975). Researchers who study learning expect changes in performance over time and practice, and their studies generally use repeated measurements.

And sixth, *real-life issues* may require that the subjects experience more than one level of the independent variable. We'll consider two of many ways that the benefits of repeated measures can relate to real-life issues. First, it may be useful to have participants experience more than one condition if it seems likely that they will communicate among themselves about their experience. The study on beaver trappers provides an example: If it had used separate groups of trappers (either randomly assigned or matched), with one receiving the CRF pay schedule and the other receiving the VR schedule, wouldn't they have talked to each other about their new pay arrangements? Second, some experiences in real life usually occur as contrasts, such as when comparing two similar items to buy in a store. Marketing researchers might study how the way the items are displayed influence whether people look at or buy them. In such cases, a repeated-measures approach might be more appropriate, especially if the results would generalize better to real-life behavior.

As this discussion suggests, within-subjects designs can have some disadvantages or limitations, too. One problem is that some variables have *long-term carry-over effects* that may be impossible to balance out. For example, people who

TABLE 8.2

Summary of the Relative Value in Using Independent-Groups (Between-Subjects), Matched-Subjects, and Within-Subjects Designs under Different Research Circumstances or Concerns

Research circumstance or concern	Extent each design helps[a]		
	Independent groups	Matched subjects	Within subjects
Subjects/participants are scarce	Low	Moderate	High
Must conserve time or resources	Low	Low	High
High levels of individual differences are likely to impair statistical power markedly	Low	Moderate	High
Independent variable requires measurement of changes over time	Low	Low	High
High likelihood of communication about their experiences among participants	Low	Low	High
Long-term carryover effects are likely	High	High	Low
Participants are likely to balk if repeated measures will take a great deal of their time	High	High	Low
Participant bias is likely from exposure to > one condition or testing for matching variable	High	Low	Low

[a] Low = the design typically helps little or not at all; moderate = the design usually helps somewhat; high = the design typically helps a great deal.

receive therapy to manage stress or training in a sport learn skills. If we designed a study to compare two different therapy or training methods, the first condition each participant experienced would provide some skills, perhaps all that the person would need. Because we can't "erase" a skill, what would be the purpose of providing the second condition? Another problem with using repeated measurements is that some independent variables may require participants to spend a great deal of *time in the study*, which they may balk at doing. The last problem we'll mention is that exposing participants to more than one condition of a study may tip them off to the research purpose or hypothesis, thereby increasing the chance of confounding from *participant bias*. In matched-subjects designs, a similar problem can arise if testing on the matching variable leads to participant bias. Table 8.2 summarizes the relative value of independent-groups, matched-subjects, and within-subjects designs in helping deal with different research circumstances.

Choosing which Counterbalancing Method to Use

If you plan to do a study with a within-subjects design, you'll need to decide which method of counterbalancing to use. One guide in choosing the method is to consult the literature you have collected on the topic you are studying to see the techniques they have used. Chances are those methods would be appropriate for your research, too. In addition, you may find the following rules useful in choosing a counterbalancing method.

■ Use individual counterbalancing methods if you expect large individual differences in the order effects from repeated testing across levels of the independent variable. For example, we might expect great variation in the degree of fatigue and loss of attention among child participants over a half hour of testing. In contrast, adults would show less variation and less pronounced fatigue or loss of attention in the same time period.

■ Do not use reverse (ABBA) counterbalancing if you expect that the size of the order effects will change across testing. Reverse counterbalancing is only suitable when the order effects will be *linear*—that is, if the amount of improvement or decrement in performance remains fairly similar across testing. If you're uncertain of whether the order effects will be linear and decide to use this method, give half the subjects the ABBA order and half a BAAB order.

■ Avoid block randomization and Latin square methods if you expect that there will be carryover effects. Although the balancing these methods provide is fairly thorough, it is not really complete.

These rules involve the researcher's expectations, which are usually based on reasoning and information from the prior research literature. Practical considerations are important, too. For instance, some counterbalancing methods require more subjects than others or a great deal of time to expose each subject repeatedly to all the levels of the independent variable. All these issues can influence the choice of a counterbalancing method to apply. (Go to **Box 8.2**)

Box 8.2   DIFFICULTIES IN BALANCING ORDER EFFECTS

We've seen that nonlinear order effects and carryover effects can influence the choice of counterbalancing methods researchers use. Sometimes carryover effects create problems in the data that can't be counterbalanced at all, as we discussed in the example of people learning sports or stress management skills with two training methods. That is, these people could apply the skills learned with the first training method when they received the second method. The same problem would probably arise even if the participants received the conditions in the opposite sequence, with the second condition first. But what if there were carryover effects that happen more strongly in one sequence than in the opposite sequence? This can happen: In **asymmetric transfer,** the carryover effects in one sequence of conditions are not equal to, or balanced by, the carryover effects in the opposite sequence (Poulton, 1982). Thus, in an ABBA design, for example, the carryover effects of the sequence A–B would not be balanced by B–A.

Let's consider an example of asymmetric transfer. Suppose we were planning a study on the ability to memorize lists of 20 words in which we had just two conditions: The participants will either receive or not receive

continued

instructions to use a specific strategy to memorize the words. The strategy will be to create weird images with the words—so, for the words *dog* and *cigar,* they might imagine a dog smoking a cigar. The procedure will involve showing a complete list of words on a computer monitor for 60 seconds and having the people recall as many words as they can. Suppose also that we were using the method of all possible orders (there would be two orders: A–B and B–A), where A is the instructions condition and B is the no instructions condition. Given that the participants in the A–B sequence receive the instructions to use the strategy for the first condition they experience, would they abandon the strategy when they go to B? Probably not, especially if they thought it worked. And for the B–A sequence, there would be no carryover effects from B (no instructions) to A (instructions to use the strategy). The data for the average number of words recalled with the two sequences might look like this:

	A	B
A–B sequence	17	18
B–A sequence	18	9

Notice that the order effects are not balanced: the number of words recalled is about the same for the A (instructions) condition regardless of the sequence, but for not the B (no instructions) condition. This means that the results are confounded with order effects.

Researchers need to apply reasoning, theory, and information from prior research to predict such problems in advance. If they think carryover effects may not be balanced, they should consider using a between-subjects or matched-subjects design instead of a within-subjects design. Asymmetric transfer can happen in any study with repeated measures, but its likelihood is heightened if the researcher manipulates the independent variable by using different instructions, drugs, training in skills, or methods that arouse emotions (Keppel, 1991). Statistical analyses for within-subjects designs should assess whether asymmetric transfer is present in the data.

PREPARING TO DO A DEPENDENT-GROUPS STUDY

Designing and carrying out research with dependent groups can be very complicated and often takes extra, specialized planning and decisions about methodological details. Chapter 10 gives instructions and checklists to help in these activities. If you know that you will be using a within-subjects or matched-subjects design, look over that chapter now to see the kind of information it contains.

ANALYZING DATA FROM SINGLE-FACTOR, DEPENDENT-GROUPS DESIGNS

Like the analyses for independent-groups designs, inferential statistics for single-factor, dependent-groups designs assess differences between data groupings. The statistical methods are identical for research using matched-subjects and within-subjects designs, and they are similar to the ones we considered for between-subjects designs in Chapter 7. The main distinction between statistics for independent- and dependent-groups designs is that the subjects' performance in the latter is likely to be correlated across levels of the independent variable, which is useful. Statistical analyses for matched-subjects and within-subjects designs can take this correlation into account to increase statistical power.

How do statistical tests for dependent-groups designs use correlations to increase power? Recall the following points we've discussed in this and prior chapters.

- The formulas for many statistical tests, such as the *t* test, divide systematic variance by error variance.
- Most of the error variance in psychology research comes from individual differences among subjects.
- Squaring a correlation coefficient (r^2) gives the *coefficient of determination,* or the proportion of the variance of one variable that can be accounted for by variation in the other variable.
- Because the pairs of scores in a correlation of dependent-groups data come from the same or matched subjects, the correlation coefficient is a very good estimate of the variance resulting from individual differences, or error variance.

Statistical tests for dependent-groups designs, such as the paired-samples *t* test, use this correlation to identify and remove from the calculations the error variance arising from individual differences. Removing that variance still leaves some error variance that results from other factors, such as inaccurate measurement and changes in the subjects' alertness. In calculating a *t* test, for example, having less error variance in the formula's denominator increases the *t* value and the likelihood that the outcome will be significant, which means that the test is more powerful. *Appendix B gives step-by-step procedures* for calculating each of the statistical tests we will discuss for dependent-groups designs when using an SPSS program and formulas for calculating some of them manually.

One other issue should be mentioned about analyses of repeated measures data: It is extremely important to *coordinate the scores from different conditions* carefully. Given that the subjects are tested in more than one condition, and sometimes repeatedly in each condition, we must be certain to keep the corresponding data together. For example, in the cola preference study, some counterbalancing methods would have participants taste and rate each cola many times. We would need to separate scores so that all of the ratings for each cola are kept together. This can be a bit complicated, but it is essential. And when individuals are tested in each condition more than once, we will need to convert the scores into a single score for each individual in each condition. Researchers generally make the conversion by simply calculating the mean of the scores for each individual in the specific condition, which becomes the score that will be used for that subject in the statistical analysis.

TWO-LEVEL DESIGNS

Statistical analyses of two-level designs compare the data for the dependent variable in two conditions of the independent variable. We can use Table 4.1 (see inside front cover) once again to identify the statistical test to use. Because we know we want to assess a difference, not a relationship, between conditions, the tests that apply for a single-factor, dependent-groups design are given in the lower portion of the table. Next we must decide whether to use a parametric or nonparametric test. If our data were assessed on an interval or ratio scale, we would use a parametric test; if we have nominal or ordinal data, we'd use a non-parametric test. But if our interval or ratio data for the two conditions in a study depart markedly from the parametric criteria of having normal distributions and equal variances, we may need to apply statistically accepted adjustments in the analyses or use a nonparametric test.

Parametric Analysis

Let's suppose we have interval or ratio data, so we would use a parametric test. To find the specific test, we would look at Table 4.1 and see that if we want to compare two data groupings, and they are paired, or from a dependent-groups design, we'd use a **paired-samples *t* test.** Although the formula for calculating this form of *t* test differs from that of the independent-samples *t* test, we interpret in exactly the same way the *t* value each test produces.

We can illustrate the application of paired-samples *t* tests to analyze data from dependent-groups designs with two studies. First, the experiment by Saari and Latham (1982) on beaver trappers' pay schedules used a within-subjects design. As we saw earlier, the number of beavers they trapped per hour of work was significantly higher under the VR schedule ($M = 1.08$) than the CRF schedule ($M = 0.78$), $t(11) = 3.15$, $p < .01$. Second, a student in my research methods course conducted a study on the ability of undergraduates to recall information from a paragraph they read once as a function of several variables, such as the amount of sleep they had gotten the night before. The memory tests consisted of 10 fill-in-the-blank questions. Although most of the analyses of the data were correlations, the participants were also tested at two points in time, immediately after reading the paragraph and 4 days later (without rereading the paragraph), and the difference in recall at the two tests could be compared as a test of forgetting. As expected, the number of correctly answered questions was significantly greater at the first testing ($M = 6.61$) than the second ($M = 6.22$), ($t[45] = 2.45$, $p < .02$).

Nonparametric Analysis

If our data are on a nominal or ordinal measurement scale, we would use a nonparametric test. Looking again at the lower portion of Table 4.1, we'll see that if we want to compare two data groupings, and they are paired, or from a dependent-groups design, we'd use either of two tests. The **McNemar test** is used with nominal data, operates like the chi-square, and yields a χ^2 value. The **Wilcoxon matched-pairs signed-ranks test** uses ordinal data by comparing the ranks for each pair of scores; if the scores are on an interval or ratio scale, they must be changed to ranks, which SPSS will do automatically. The procedure assigns a plus sign if the difference in ranks is positive or a minus sign if the difference is negative, weights each pair for the size of the difference, and sums the weighted scores separately for pairs with a plus sign and pairs with a minus sign. The Wilcoxon test compares these two sums by calculating a standardized z score to test the significance of the difference.

Let's consider an example of how the Wilcoxon matched-pairs signed-ranks test was applied on data from research we mentioned earlier in this chapter (Ulrich, 1984). The study used archival data to test whether matched hospital patients who had been assigned rooms with or without a view of a natural setting tended to recover sooner and use less medication. One dependent variable examined was the length of hospitalization from day of surgery to day of discharge, which the researcher decided to score in a rank-ordered manner because counting days (ratio data) was inaccurate as the records didn't give the time of day for surgery or discharge, which varied. Using these ordinal data, the analysis revealed that the patients with a natural view spent significantly less time in the hospital than those without a natural view (their views were of a brick wall), $z = 1.96$, $p < .05$ (note that no df is needed for the z statistic). The analyses of painkiller medication use applied parametric statistics because the data available were on a ratio scale; they found less painkiller use among patients with than without a natural view.

Estimates of Effect Size

We saw in Chapter 7 that estimates of effect size are based on correlational analyses to assess the degree of association between the independent and dependent variables and that they are easy to calculate manually. With two-level, dependent-groups designs, we would apply the formulas given in Table 7.3 (see inside back cover) for independent-groups designs and interpret the outcomes in the same way. For a paired-samples t test analysis, we'd calculate the effect size with either the $r_{es:t}$ formula or Cohen's d formula. As an example, let's consider how effect size could be calculated for the t test analysis in the study that we discussed earlier in which my student found significantly better recall of information when tested immediately versus after 4 days. Plugging the t (2.45) and df (45) into the $r_{es:t}$ formula yields an outcome of .34, which the table indicates represents a medium effect size. So, the complete statement of the statistical outcome for that analysis would include the effect size at the end: $t(45) = 2.45$, $p < .02$, $r_{es:t} = .34$.

For nonparametric analyses, an estimate of effect size is available for analyses that yield or are based on a z score output, including the Wilcoxon matched-pairs signed-ranks test (Clark-Carter, 1997). The formula is the same as that for the Mann-Whitney U test for independent-groups (see Table 7.3, inside back cover). For analyses of two-level, dependent-groups designs that yield or are based on chi-square (χ^2) statistics, such as the McNemar test, we can compute effect sizes by plugging the relevant data into the Cramér's V formula.

MULTILEVEL DESIGNS

As we discussed in Chapter 7, single-factor, multilevel designs have three or more levels of the independent variable, which is true for independent- and dependent-groups designs alike. As in research with independent groups, the preferred statistical tests for analyzing the data from multilevel, dependent-groups designs are specifically designed to hold the desired alpha level constant (usually at .05), regardless of the number of conditions or groups being compared. These statistics are similar to or extensions of the analyses we considered for multilevel, independent-groups designs and can be identified by looking again at the lower portion of Table 4.1 (inside front cover).

Parametric Analysis

As the table shows, if the dependent variable is measured on an interval or ratio scale and we are comparing more than two groups or conditions, we would perform an analysis of variance (ANOVA) to test whether the data groupings differ. With data from studies with matched- or within-subjects designs, the appropriate parametric analysis is called the **repeated-measures ANOVA.** Like an ANOVA with a single-factor, independent-groups design, the repeated-measures ANOVA is described as *one-way* because there is only a single independent variable.

The general conceptual framework and computations for the one-way ANOVA for independent and dependent groups are quite similar. A repeated-measures ANOVA also computes sums of squares, mean squares, and an *F* value that provides an omnibus test of whether a difference exists between two or more of the conditions. The main way by which one-way ANOVAs for independent and dependent groups differ is in the computation of error variance: repeated-measures ANOVAs separate "residual variance" from the rest of error variance. **Residual variance** refers to the amount of variation that remains in the data after subtracting out the systematic variance from the independent variable and the error variance associated with individual differences among the subjects, which is called *between-subjects* variation. Because the ANOVA is an omnibus test, researchers typically do contrast tests if their hypotheses predicted differences between two conditions and post hoc comparisons if they find a significant overall outcome.

If the analysis is done with a computer statistics program, these outcomes are reported in an ANOVA summary table. Table 8.3 shows an ANOVA table for a one-way analysis for dependent groups. Assume that the data are from a within-subjects study on preferences for three brands of cola, and let's see how to read this table one column at a time, starting at the left.

- *Source:* As a source of variance, *between subjects* refers to individual differences, *between conditions,* or groups, refers to the independent variable, and *residual* refers to error variability with between-subjects variability removed. The presence of a row with a label that includes the word *subjects* or *cases* means that the analysis is for repeated measures.
- *SS:* Notice that there are sums of squares for between conditions (SS_{bg}) and residual, or error (SS_{res}). We can usually ignore the between-subjects *SS* and the totals.

TABLE 8.3

An Example ANOVA Summary Table for a Dependent-Groups Design with Three Conditions (Cola Beverages) Tested with Repeated Measures

Source	SS	df	MS	F	p
Between subjects	1535.62	14	109.69		
Between conditions (colas)	796.19	2	398.06	9.31	.001
Residual (error)	1197.28	28	42.76		
Total	3529.09	44			

- *df:* Because the number of conditions (k) is three, the $df_{bg} = 2$ because $df_{bg} = k - 1$, and the $df_{res} = 28$ because there were 15 participants in each condition and $df_{res} = (n - 1)(k - 1)$.
- *MS:* Each $MS = SS \div df$.
- *F:* The $F = MS_{bg} \div MS_{res}$.
- *p:* The p (sometimes labeled "Sig" in statistics programs) tells us whether the F is significant. In these data, it is, at the .001 level of confidence. We can reject the null hypothesis and conclude that the brand of cola is a significant source of systematic variation.

When reporting in a sentence the outcome of an ANOVA, we include both dfs, usually in parentheses after the F value. For instance, for the single-factor design in Table 8.3 with three dependent groups and 45 participants, we might report: $F(2, 28) = 9.31$, $p = .001$, followed by the effect size data (which we'll consider a little later).

An example of a one-way repeated-measures analysis with post hoc comparisons comes from an experiment to test whether the commonly held belief that anxiety impairs males' sexual arousal is correct (Barlow, Sakheim, & Beck, 1983). Researchers recruited 12 young heterosexual men to watch a 9-minute sex video, divided into continuous 3-minute segments that were previously equated as being moderately arousing. To create anxiety, the researchers demonstrated how a moderate level of electric shock to the arm would feel and then explained the meaning of three lights mounted above the TV that would display the video. The lights would signal three anxiety conditions, based on the stated likelihood that shock would be administered to the arm (actually the study used deception and no participant received any shock during the video):

- *Noncontingent-shock threat:* The men were told that if this light is on, there is a 60% chance (supposedly) that they would receive shock.
- *Contingent-shock threat:* They were told that if this light is on, there is a 60% chance (supposedly) of receiving shock *if* their level of *arousal is less than the average* for research participants.
- *No-shock threat:* They were told that this light is irrelevant and would come on just because the computer program governing the lights required that it be on sometimes.

All participants were tested individually and experienced each 3-minute segment with one of the lights being on for 2 minutes and all lights being off for the last minute. The orders of the segments and the lights being on were both counterbalanced. To measure arousal, each man wore a collar on his penis that assessed changes in its circumference. A repeated-measures ANOVA revealed a significant effect of shock threat, $F(2,22) = 3.95$, $p < .05$. Post hoc comparisons with the Duncan multiple range test found less arousal ($p < .05$) in the no-shock threat condition than either of the two shock threat conditions, which did not differ significantly. These results contradict the commonly held view and indicate that anxiety can enhance men's sexual arousal.

Nonparametric Analysis

As Table 4.1 (inside front cover) shows, if we assess differences between conditions with nonparametric statistics and have more than two dependent-groups data sets (conditions), we would use the **Cochran Q** test for nominal data and the **Friedman χ^2** test for ordinal data. (Note: The Friedman is often called a "one-way" or "two-way" ANOVA). Each of these statistics is really a form of chi-square procedure ($Q = \chi^2$). Although these omnibus tests lack accepted contrast and post hoc comparison statistics, we can apply the flawed method of performing multiple two-level McNemar and Wilcoxon tests and adjusting the alpha level.

A study that used nonparametric analyses with three conditions in a within-subjects design examined the kinds of information that help people overcome the memory block called the tip-of-the-tongue state (TOTS; Brennen, Baguley, Bright, & Bruce, 1990). When we experience a TOTS, we know we know something, such as a name; can almost recall it; and feel that we'd recognize it if it were given to us. In one experiment, the researchers constructed a list of 50 questions about famous people, such as "Who is the actor who played the 'Bionic Man'?" [answer: Lee Majors], and tested school and college students. When a participant reported a TOTS for a question, the researcher would give one of three types of cues: the initials of the target person, a photo of the person's face, or just a repeat of the question. The dependent variable was the percentage of correctly resolved TOTSs, and the means were 46.6% for the initials, 14.5% for the photos, and 10.7% for the repeated question. A Friedman test showed that the type of cue had an overall effect, $\chi^2(2) = 14.32$, $p < .001$, and post hoc two-level tests revealed that the initials were more effective cues ($p < .05$) than either the photos or repeated questions, which did not differ.

Estimates of Effect Size

Much of the discussion in Chapter 7 on effect size in multilevel designs applies here, too. Because of the unfocused nature of an omnibus test outcome, it is usually better to calculate effect sizes from contrast or post hoc comparison tests. In a parametric analysis with ANOVA, the contrast statistics would be t tests from which we can calculate an effect size (see Table 7.3, inside back cover). But there are no tests available to compute effect sizes from post hoc comparisons. As we saw in Chapter 7, we can deal with this problem in a one-way analysis in two ways. First, we can use the effect size statistic called eta squared that is calculated from the ANOVA output for repeated measures with the formula (see Tabachnick & Fidell, 2001, for alternative formulas and rationales):

$$\eta^2 = \frac{SS_{bg}}{SS_{bg} + SS_{res}}$$

For the data in Table 8.3, $\eta^2 = 796.19 \div (796.19 + 1197.28) = .40$, reflecting a medium-to-large effect size. SPSS for repeated-measures ANOVA includes eta squared in the printout automatically. Second, we can calculate t tests for each pair of comparisons just to get the t values to use in the formulas for $r_{es:t}$ or Cohen's d in Table 7.3.

For nonparametric analyses of multilevel, single-factor designs with dependent data groupings, the omnibus Cochran and Friedman tests yield χ^2 values. Given that there are no accepted contrast or post hoc comparison tests for these statistics, we have a problem that is similar to the one we just considered for the ANOVA. And the best ways to deal with the problem are also similar. First, we can use the omnibus χ^2 value in the formula in Table 7.3 for Cramér's V to get an overall effect size. Second, we can calculate a McNemar test on each relevant pair of conditions to get the χ^2 value and then compute Cramér's V, giving an estimate of the effect size for each difference. Neither of these procedures is ideal, but each offers at least some evidence for the size of an effect when no other approach is currently available.

SUMMARY

When researchers compare two or more levels of an independent variable by matching subjects in separate groups or testing individuals with repeated measures at more than one level, they use a dependent-groups design. A defining feature of dependent-groups designs is that the subjects' performance is likely to be correlated across levels of the independent variable.

Well-conducted controlled within-subjects designs use repeated measures and meet all three of the criteria for making a causal inference: covariation of variables, causal time sequence, and elimination of other plausible causes of variation in performance. Quasi-experimental within-subjects designs fail to meet at least one of these criteria, usually because they did not manipulate the independent variable or control all extraneous variables that could be plausible causes for the relationship between the independent and dependent variables. In matched-groups designs, the groups of subjects are equated for one or more matching variables that should be strongly related to the dependent variable. Then, individuals who are very similar on the matching variable are randomly assigned to groups.

Using repeated measures can confound the results of research when order effects favor one condition over another. If this type of confounding is a possibility, researchers apply some form of counterbalancing to equalize the order effects across conditions. The simplest approach to equalize order effects is called reverse counterbalancing, or ABBA counterbalancing. Another approach randomizes order effects across conditions, such as with the systematic procedure called block randomization. These two approaches test each subject more than once per condition in an effort to equalize the effects for each and every subject. Other approaches test each subject only once in each condition, managing the orders to make the average effects the same for all conditions, as in the all possible orders (complete counterbalancing) and Latin square methods. One problem that can arise in within-subjects designs is asymmetric transfer. Researchers decide to use within-subjects designs for a variety of reasons, such as their efficiency and statistical power. In addition, some studies have research hypotheses that require repeated measurements, especially if they examine changes over time, such as in studies of learning.

Like research with independent groups, dependent-groups designs, can have a single factor and compare the data for the dependent variable for two or more levels of the independent variable. For two-level designs, parametric analyses apply the paired-samples t test, and nonparametric analyses can use the McNemar test for nominal data and the Wilcoxon matched-pairs signed-ranks test for ordinal data. For multilevel designs, parametric analyses use the repeated-measures ANOVA, which subtracts out the systematic variance and the error variance associated with individual differences among the subjects to yield a residual variance term. Single-factor, multilevel research with nonparametric analyses can apply the Cochran Q test for nominal data or the Friedman χ^2 test for ordinal data. Researchers perform available contrast, post hoc comparison, and effect size statistics to clarify and determine the size of the independent variable's effects.

KEY TERMS

order effects	Latin square	residual variance
counterbalancing	asymmetric transfer	Cochran Q
reverse	paired-samples t test	Friedman χ^2
counterbalancing	McNemar test	
block randomization	Wilcoxon matched-	
all possible orders	pairs signed-ranks test	
complete	repeated-measures	
counterbalancing	ANOVA	

REVIEW QUESTIONS

1. Describe the Saari and Latham (1982) experiment on the role of pay schedules on the productivity of beaver trappers.
2. Describe the two ways for creating equivalent groups in dependent-groups designs and how you could apply each to study the effects of lighting illumination on reading speed.
3. How do controlled- and quasi-experimental within-subjects designs differ?
4. Define *order effects* and *counterbalancing*, and distinguish between the three types of order effects presented in Table 8.1.
5. Define and describe procedures for two types of *individual counterbalancing*.
6. Define and describe procedures for two types of *overall counterbalancing*.

7. In what situations would researchers prefer using a within-subjects design over an independent-groups (between-subjects) design, and what problems with repeated measurement may lead them to use independent groups instead?

8. How is variance treated differently in statistics for dependent- than independent-groups designs?

9. Describe how you would select an appropriate statistical test of differences with ratio or interval data for two-level and multilevel designs, and name the tests you could use. Do the same thing for nominal or ordinal data.

10. Discuss how researchers estimate effect sizes for each of the statistics you named in the previous question and conduct contrast or post hoc comparisons for parametric and nonparametric omnibus tests.

RESORCES

BOOKS, CHAPTERS, AND ARTICLES

Cohen, J. (1988). *Statistical power analysis for the behavioral sciences* (2nd ed.). Hillsdale, NJ: Erlbaum.

Keppel, G. (1991). *Design and analysis: A researcher's handbook* (3rd ed.). Englewood Cliffs, NJ: Prentice Hall.

Siegel, S. (1956). *Nonparametric statistics for the behavioral sciences.* New York: Mcgraw-Hill.

Winer, B. J. (1962). *Statistical principles in experimental design.* New York: McGraw-Hill.

INTERNET SITES

http://trochim.human.cornell.edu This Website has links to information about several experimental design issues discussed in this chapter; it was listed in Chapter 7 for independent-groups designs also, and you may have used it there.

http://www/ruf.rice.edu/~lane/stat_sim/index.html This Website is the Rice Virtual Lab that gives statistics tutorials; it was listed in Chapter 7 for independent-groups designs also, and you may have used it there. You can learn about statistics for dependent-groups designs by clicking on *repeated measures*.

APPLICATION ACTIVITIES

APPLICATION 8–1: MATCHED- VERSUS WITHIN-SUBJECTS DESIGNS

Suppose we were designing a two-level, single-factor study and needed to use either the matched- or within-subjects approach—to be certain that the individuals in the conditions were equated. For each of the following circumstances, describe whether you'd propose using the matched- or within-subjects approach, and why.

1. The study is to compare children's cognitive skills at the beginning and end of the academic year in second grade.
2. The study is to compare how well adolescents resolve interpersonal conflicts set up by the researcher if they are in pairs or in a group of four participants.
3. The study is to compare brain activity when participants are presented with a large variety of specific, very brief stimuli that belong to two different categories.
4. The study is to compare the emotional and cognitive effects of instructions that are distressing versus neutral.

APPLICATION 8–2: USING BLOCK RANDOMIZATION

Suppose that we want to study the effects of brightness of lighting on the ability of people to remember details of very briefly presented (say, for just 5 seconds) complex sentences. We will compare three brightness levels (low, medium, and high), have each participant receive 12 trials with different sentences, have the participants recall five details of each sentence 2 seconds after presentation, and use block randomization to counterbalance order effects of brightness levels. Design a block randomization pattern we could apply.

APPLICATION 8–3: USING A LATIN SQUARE

Suppose that we want to study the effects of a woman's ethnic background—Caucasian, Black, Hispanic, and Asian—on men's judgments of her skills and ability to succeed at a managerial job. We intend to use a within-subjects design, presenting to each man four resumes but using the Latin square method to counterbalance order effects. Design a Latin square for this study and indicate how many participants you'd propose testing.

APPLICATION 8–4: TESTING FOR ASYMMETRIC TRANSFER

Reread the hypothetical study on memory presented in Box 8.2 to illustrate asymmetric transfer. Suppose we conducted this study with a total of 20 participants and then wanted to determine whether the pattern of data shown represents a confounding of asymmetric transfer. One way to test this would be to compare the words recalled with each sequence in just the B condition. What statistic would you use to test this, and what outcome would you need to find to conclude that a significant degree of asymmetric transfer exists?

APPLICATION 8–5: ANALYZING A COUNTERBALANCED DESIGN

The following table presents the order of presentation of three different colas (C = Coca-Cola, P = Pepsi-Cola, and R = Royal Crown) to each of six participants, with the rating of the cola in parenthesis (1 = poor to 10 = excellent) taken immediately after the tasting in each trial. Assume that details of the methodology are the same as we discussed earlier in the section called "What Are Order Effects?"

Participant	Order of Presentation of Colas					
1	C (6)	P (6)	R (9)	R (9)	P (7)	C (6)
2	R (9)	P (7)	C (7)	C (7)	P (7)	R (8)
3	C (6)	P (7)	R (8)	R (9)	P (6)	C (7)
4	R (8)	P (7)	C (6)	C (7)	P (6)	R (9)
5	C (7)	P (7)	R (9)	R (8)	P (6)	C (6)
6	R (9)	P (7)	C (6)	C (7)	P (6)	R (9)

On the basis of information in the table, answer:

1. What counterbalancing method was used to equalize order effects?
2. What are the mean ratings for Coca-Cola, Pepsi-Cola, and Royal Crown across the six participants?
3. If the omnibus ANOVA test revealed a significant effect ($p < .01$), exactly what could we conclude about the colas?
4. Specifically what additional analyses would you still need to do? And just by looking at the means, what do you suppose those analyses are likely to reveal?

FACTORIAL DESIGNS

You've probably seen movies in which a character is helpless in the face of imminent danger, as in the classic early 1900s situation of a woman tied across railroad tracks as a train rapidly approaches. This scene has two elements that should influence the fear a person feels in a dangerous situation: the person's awareness of a "looming" danger—that is, an imminent and fast-moving risk—and an inability to prevent harm. These elements form the basis for two theories of the role of cognition in fear. One theory, the *harm-looming model*, proposes that people's fear increases as their belief that danger is getting closer increases. In *self-efficacy theory*, people's fear increases as their belief that they have the ability to prevent harm decreases.

John Riskind and James Maddux (1993) tested these theories in an experiment by manipulating the looming nature of a danger and the helplessness the participants would feel in preventing harm. Volunteer college students watched brief videos of a tarantula in a high-looming condition, moving quickly toward them, and a low-looming condition in which the spider was still or moved away. Self-efficacy was manipulated by asking each student to imagine being alone in a room under either high or low self-efficacy conditions with the tarantula on the floor. The participants in the low self-efficacy condition were asked to imagine that:

- The door to the room was locked.
- They were strapped in a chair and could not move their arms or legs.
- No one would hear them if they screamed for help.
- In their laps "is a large rolled-up magazine with which you could strike the spider, if you could only move your arms. But you cannot move at all." (pp. 77–78)

The students in the high self-efficacy condition were asked to imagine a similar situation, but the door was not locked, and they could move freely to get away or to strike the spider with the magazine. Immediately after watching the high-looming or low-looming video, they rated on a 7-point Likert scale the degree of fear they felt. The results supported both theories: ratings of fear were significantly higher in the high- than low-looming condition and in the low than high self-efficacy condition.

This brief outline of this research and findings give an example of a study that is more complex than the research we've examined so far in this book because it used more than one independent variable: the degree of looming and of self-efficacy. We'll see later that the design of this experiment was more intricate than the outline presents, and the results were more complex and interesting than can be found by testing only one independent variable at a time.

THE CONCEPT OF FACTORIAL RESEARCH

In earlier chapters, we focused on single-factor studies, describing how to design research to test for differences in a dependent variable at two or more levels of one independent variable. We saw that we can examine the impact of different levels of the independent variable either by assigning the subjects to separate groups for each level—that is, in between-subjects or matched-subjects designs—or by testing each subject at each level with repeated measures in within-subjects designs. These designs are outlined in Figure 7.1 (see inside back cover). Matched- and within-subjects designs are classified as dependent-groups designs because the subjects' scores on the dependent variable in the different conditions are likely to be correlated to some degree. In between-subjects designs, the scores in the different conditions will not be correlated because the subjects in the groups are unrelated; as a result, they are described as independent-groups designs. All the principles we've discussed for designing and conducting single-factor dependent- and independent-groups designs also apply to research with more than one independent variable, particularly with regard to assigning subjects to conditions and controlling extraneous variables.

MORE THAN ONE INDEPENDENT VARIABLE

Pick any behavior you'd like and list in your mind the factors that can cause it to change or vary in its occurrence and strength across and within people. You'll come up with at least a few ideas, such as the behavior's consequences, the environmental temperature or lighting, and each person's genetics, personality, thoughts and beliefs about the behavior, and frequency of having performed the behavior in the past. Many factors affect the expression of each behavior, and their influences in everyday life occur together in some combination. The study on fear of spiders tested the influence of two factors: people's perceptions of whether harm was looming and whether they could prevent the potential harm. You might think of other factors that were not tested in that study that could be included in another study. To arrive at a complete explanation for behavioral variations in a behavior pattern, researchers must examine the impact of many different factors singly and in combination.

Although single-factor experiments can demonstrate a cause of a behavior, that factor is not likely to be the only cause and may not be the most powerful one. Because many factors play a role, each independent variable may account for, or explain, only a small portion of the variance in the dependent variable. Researchers usually want to study variables that account for a large portion of the variance. But accounting for a small amount of variation does not always mean that an independent variable is not important, particularly when the findings have implications for the likelihood of a serious or crucial outcome, such as having a heart attack. Rosenthal (1990) described a study on the effect of aspirin in preventing heart attacks in nearly 22,000 physicians that was ended early for ethical reasons. Why? The physicians were randomly assigned to take either aspirin or a placebo pill, under double-blind procedures, and soon the data were showing clearly that the aspirin was effective: 104 of the physicians taking aspirin and 189 of those taking the placebo had had a heart attack in the intervening time. Was the effect size large? No. Aspirin taking accounted for less than 1% of the variance in the occurrence of a heart attack, but that amounted to a difference of 85 people having heart attacks that could be prevented. It was deemed unethical to allow the remaining physicians who were taking the placebo to continue to do so. Although other factors—such as family history of heart disease, diet, exercise, and cigarette smoking—may have more powerful effects on the occurrence of heart attacks, a finding with a small effect size may still be important.

When researchers examine two or more independent variables at the same time, they usually choose variables that should, in combination, account for a large amount of variance. And they structure the research as a **factorial design,** which means that subjects are tested under all possible combinations of levels of each *factor,* or independent variable. Each of the study's groups or conditions tests subjects at one level of each factor, and each level of a factor is paired with each level of each other factor. As a result, the number of conditions in the study equals the product of the number of levels of each independent variable. If we used two levels of each of two independent variables, we'd have four conditions in the study, as diagrammed in Figure 9.1. You may recall having seen the term *factorial* before in the context of counterbalancing order effects, but it had a different meaning: the product of all positive integers from 1 to *k,* the number of levels of an independent variable. Try not to confuse the two terms.

THE IDEAS OF MAIN EFFECTS AND INTERACTIONS

A principal feature of factorial designs is that they can assess the *separate* influence of each independent variable and their *combined* influence on the dependent variable. As a result, factorial designs provide more information than two single-factor studies, giving a richer, more complete picture of the relationships between independent and dependent variables. The separate influence of a single factor on a dependent variable in a factorial design is called a **main effect.** A main effect is assessed for each independent variable in a factorial design. When we assess a main effect, we consider at that time only the one independent variable and essentially ignore for the moment the fact that some variation in the dependent variable results from the other independent variable(s) in the study. In the experiment on people's fear of spiders, the researchers assessed a main effect of looming (while ignoring self-efficacy) and a main effect of self-efficacy (ignoring looming).

	Self-efficacy	
	High	Low
Looming High	High self-efficacy High looming	Low self-efficacy High looming
Low	High self-efficacy Low looming	Low self-efficacy Low looming

FIGURE 9.1

Diagram of the factorial design for Riskind and Maddux's (1993) experiment on people's feelings of fear of spiders when tested under two levels of looming and self-efficacy. Each cell in the matrix represents a group or condition. Notice that each level of each factor (independent variable) is paired with each level of the other factor.

The combined influence of two or more factors on a dependent variable is often more interesting than the main effects, especially when the influence of one independent variable "interacts" with that of another. An **interaction** exists when the influence of an independent variable changes across levels of another independent variable. In other words, the influence of a factor on a dependent variable is different at one level of the other factor than it is at another level of that factor. Let's consider a couple of examples, starting with an everyday experience you may have had. Suppose your friend teases you in a good-natured way occasionally, deriding two of your characteristics: your intellect and your appearance. When you're feeling anxious about your future or past academic performance, you get upset at the teasing about your intellect but not your appearance, and when you're feeling down because you haven't had a date for months, you get upset at the teasing about your appearance but not your intellect. The effect of the type of teasing on your behavior depends on your specific emotional state.

Another example of an interaction comes from an analysis of factors that appear to play a role in childhood psychiatric disorders. In reviewing the research literature, Rutter (1979) found that children who had just one source of severe, chronic stress in the family, such as poverty or marital discord, were no more likely to develop a disorder than children with no chronic stress. But,

> when any two stresses occurred together, the risk went up no less than fourfold. With three or four concurrent stresses, the risk went up several times further still. It is clear that the combination of chronic stresses provided very much more than an additive effect. There was an *interactive effect* such that the risk which attended several concurrent stresses was much more than the sum of the effects of the stresses considered individually. (p. 295, italics added)

Thus, children in families with high levels of marital discord *and* poverty were far more likely to develop a psychiatric disorder than children with high levels of only one of these factors, who had about the same risk as children with low levels of both marital discord and poverty.

WHY USE FACTORIAL DESIGNS?

Although factorial designs are more complex and usually require more subjects and materials than single-factor designs, researchers prefer them for examining differences between research groups or conditions for four reasons. First, because many factors combine to affect behavior in everyday life, conducting research with more than one independent variable enhances the *external validity*, or generality, of the findings. Second, using factorial designs is *more efficient* than doing separate single-factor studies on the same factors. Adding one or more factors to make a factorial design will usually require more resources than testing only one factor, but doing separate single-factor studies on a topic will require much more resources and produce less information because we would still not know whether the factors interact.

Third, the *opportunity to test for an interaction* between two factors is a great advantage that is not available in single-factor research. Finding an interaction tells us that the effect of an independent variable may vary or have exceptions—

being muted or pronounced—that depend on the level of the other factor. For instance, with regard to the likelihood that a child will develop a psychiatric disorder, marital discord and poverty by themselves confer little risk of developing a disorder, but when these factors are present in combination, the risk surges. Researchers often do factorial research principally to study interactions between independent variables.

Fourth, factorial designs offer special opportunities for *controlling systematic and nonsystematic variance*. For example, having a sample of participants who differ in one or more characteristics, such as age or gender, adds to the error variance in the dependent variable. By treating a characteristic of this type as an independent variable, we can turn some of that variation from nonsystematic to systematic variance. Doing this yields two important advantages: it allows us to test for an interaction between the subject variable and the other independent variable(s), and it makes the statistical analysis more powerful. It enhances statistical power because the analysis removes from the error variance the variation the subject variable produces. We've seen in earlier chapters that decreasing error variance increases statistical power and the likelihood of finding a significant difference.

Another way by which factorial designs help in our efforts to control variance is by enabling us to test for potential confounding variables. We saw in Chapters 5 and 8, for instance, that pretest–posttest studies can have the potential extraneous variables of history, maturation, regression to the mean, and testing changes and sensitization. One solution to this problem we mentioned involves using control groups. As an example, let's examine the **Solomon four-group design,** which has four conditions arranged as a factorial (Solomon, 1949). As Figure 9.2 diagrams, one factor is the presence or absence of a pretest, and the other factor is the presence or absence of an intervening treatment, such as training in a skill; all subjects are randomly assigned to the four groups and receive a posttest. By using this design, researchers can not only assess the effect of the treatment but also the effect of the pretest and the interaction between the two factors. If there is a confounding from history or maturation, we should find a difference between the posttest data for Group N (no pretest or

	Pretest Yes	Pretest No
Treatment Yes	Group PT Pretest + treatment	Group T Treatment only
Treatment No	Group P Pretest only	Group N No pretest or treatment

FIGURE 9.2

Diagram of the Solomon four-group design for examining the possible effects of extraneous variables in pretest–posttest research. All subjects receive the posttest, but only one group receives both the pretest and the treatment before the posttest.

treatment) and the pretest data for the PT (pretest plus treatment) and P (pretest only) groups. If pretest sensitization occurred, we should find a difference in the posttest data for Groups P and N, for instance. Because of the extra resources this design requires, it is usually reserved for pretest–posttest studies in which the potential for confounding seems high or an interaction is likely between the pretest and treatment factors.

One issue to keep in mind in designing a factorial study is that it is *important to measure the main dependent variable(s) on an interval or ratio scale.* As we'll see later, factorial designs are usually analyzed with parametric (ANOVA) procedures. If the data are on a nominal or ordinal scale, we would need to use nonparametric tests, which provide a less satisfactory and complete analysis.

THE SIMPLEST FACTORIAL: 2 × 2

Keeping in mind that we are discussing complex designs in this chapter, the simplest of the factorial designs involves two independent variables with two levels of each, like the designs we've seen so far. The study on fear of spiders had two levels (high and low) of looming and of self-efficacy, and the Solomon four-group study had two levels (presence or absence) of the pretest and of the treatment (training). We'll look first at how to describe a factorial design using diagrams and specific phrases or terminology, focusing on the simplest factorial.

DESCRIBING THE DESIGN

Using a matrix, as presented in Figures 9.1 and 9.2, is the best way to diagram a factorial design. The columns and rows represent the levels of the independent variables, and each cell represents a condition with a specific pairing of the levels so that there is a cell for each of the possible pairings of levels. In the simplest factorial design, the matrix will have two rows and two columns. Drawing the matrix really helps in conceptualizing how the different conditions relate to each other. It will also serve a practical function: It will help in organizing the data for the statistical analysis, keeping track of which data belong with which condition.

Researchers use special terminology in describing a factorial design. Just as a single-factor design can be called a *one-way* design, a factorial with two independent variables is often called a *two-way* design. The "way" refers to the factors, or the dimensions on the matrix. In addition, researchers describe individual factorials with a numerical format or code, such as 2 × 2, in which the × is read as "by." Each number in the code represents one factor, and its value indicates the number of levels of that factor. So, the code for two levels of two independent variables is read "two by two." We'll see later that these ways of describing a factorial can be extended for increasingly complex designs. For example, you might come across a 4 × 5 × 2 ("four by five by two") design, which means that the study has three independent variables with four levels of one, five levels of another, and two levels of another. Because it has three factors, it may be described as a *three-way* design. The code also tells us how many conditions, or cells in the matrix, the design contains if we treat the × as a multiplication sign: 2 × 2 = 4 conditions and 4 × 5 × 2 = 40.

I usually advise students who do their first factorial study to keep it relatively simple by using a two-way design, preferably a 2 × 2. Here are examples of 2 × 2 studies two of my research methods students conducted with surveys.

- ▪ A student examined college students' willingness to provide help to individuals as a function of two factors, the degree of familiarity with the person needing help and the personal cost of providing the help. She constructed four versions of a survey that described requests for help from either a high- or low-familiar person (friend versus classmate) and involving either high or low personal cost in five situations, such as lending money and tutoring for a test. She shuffled the survey materials to use a random distribution method to assign students to conditions.

- ▪ A student examined the effects of two independent variables, social influence and gender-specific tasks, on the conformity of 100 female college participants in making estimates of the cost of a haircut (with blow dry). The survey form had spaces for 15 participants to write their names and estimates, but in reality each participant got a new copy. For the gender-specific factor, the surveys had the participants estimate the cost for either a man's or a woman's haircut. For the social influence factor, the researcher forged bogus names and high estimates (averaging about one third too high) of male students as the first three "participants" for half of the surveys; the rest of the surveys had no prior estimates. She made 25 copies of each of the four survey versions (man's haircut with or without social influence; woman's haircut with or without social influence) and shuffled them to use a random distribution method to assign students to conditions.

We'll see later what my students found in these research projects.

TESTING FOR MAIN EFFECTS

We've seen that a main effect in a factorial design is the separate influence of one factor on a dependent variable, ignoring the other factor(s) in the study. The statistical analysis in Riskind and Maddux's (1993) research on people's fear of spiders revealed significant main effects for both factors: Ratings of fear were higher in the high- than low-looming condition and in the low than high self-efficacy condition.

How does the statistical test "ignore" a factor? It *pools the data* across the levels of that factor. Let's look at Figure 9.3 to see how this works. The figure shows the mean ratings for participants in each of the conditions, formed by pairing high and low looming and self-efficacy. To assess the main effect of looming, the analysis would pool the data across the two levels of self-efficacy, as the horizontal ovals and arrows illustrate, to arrive at *marginal means*—that is, the means for all subjects at specific levels of an independent variable. Notice that the marginal mean is far higher (44% higher) under the high-looming condition than the low-looming condition. Similarly, to assess the main effect of self-efficacy, the analysis would pool the data across the two levels of looming to get the marginal means, as the vertical ovals and arrows show. The marginal mean is far

| Looming | Self-efficacy | | *Marginal* means: main effect of looming |
	High	Low	
High	2.64	4.50	3.57
Low	2.24	2.73	2.48
Marginal means: main effect of looming	2.44	3.61	

....

FIGURE 9.3

Mean ratings of fear for participants in each condition (lightly shaded area) of Riskind and Maddux's (1993) 2 × 2 factorial experiment on the effects of looming and self-efficacy. The marginal means pool the data in the corresponding rows or columns, as the ovals and arrows show. If, as in this study, each condition contains the same number of subjects, we can calculate each mean by simply averaging the means in the respective rows or columns.

higher (48% higher) under the low self-efficacy condition than the high self-efficacy condition. These differences were statistically significant, which means that the greater the looming of a threat or the lower the self-efficacy in preventing harm, the more fear people feel.

The way in which we interpret a main effect depends on whether that factor was tested with an experimental or a nonexperimental strategy. If we used a well-designed and conducted experimental strategy with that variable and find a significant main effect, we can conclude that our manipulation of the independent variable *caused* the corresponding variations in the dependent variable. This is because true experiments can meet all three criteria for causal inference: co-variation of variables, causal time sequence, and elimination of other possible causes, or confounding. If we used a nonexperimental strategy with a variable, we cannot make a causal inference for that factor. Many factorial studies in psychology use an **E × N design**, having at least one experimental (E) and one nonexperimental (N) independent variable. These studies test at least one factor with an experimental strategy, randomly assigning subjects to conditions and manipulating the independent variable, and another factor with a nonexperimental strategy—for instance, by using a subject variable, such as the individuals' age or gender. In these cases, the same rule applies. *We can make a causal inference for a main effect tested with an experimental strategy, but not for a main effect tested with a nonexperimental strategy.*

TESTING FOR INTERACTIONS

If an interaction exists when the influence of a factor on a dependent variable changes across levels of another factor, what might the pattern of data look like?

Diagramming an Interaction

Look back at Figure 9.3 at only the central, lightly shaded area where the means are given for each of the conditions in Riskind and Maddux's (1993) research on factors affecting the fear of spiders (disregard the marginal means). Three of the means for each condition are fairly similar, ranging from 2.24 to 2.73, but one is very different, 4.50. The statistical analysis of an interaction does not pool the data across conditions or use marginal means; it uses each mean from each condition. To get a better idea of what an interaction is, let's see what these same data look like in the graph in Figure 9.4. Notice that the two graph lines are *not parallel.* In effect, an ANOVA tests whether the lines are "statistically non-parallel," considering the amount of error variability associated with the means. Before computing a statistical test on the data from a factorial study, it's a good idea to draw a line graph, even freehand, to get a sense of what the analysis will show. Distinctly nonparallel graph lines suggest that the analysis is likely to find a significant interaction; parallel lines suggest that there is no interaction. *Line graphs of interactions always have lines that are not parallel,* which makes the interaction easy to see. Bar graphs can also reflect an interaction, but it's harder to see because we must keep mental track of which bar represents which condition. Whenever we find a significant main effect and an interaction involving that factor in a study, we should *interpret the interaction first* and then interpret the effects of that factor because the interaction is likely to determine the meaning of a main effect.

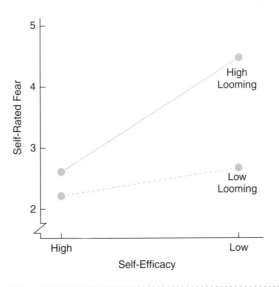

FIGURE 9.4

The interaction in Riskind and Maddux's (1993, Figure 1) experiment on the effects of two factors, looming and self-efficacy, on people's fear of spiders. Notice that the effect of looming is far greater at low than high self-efficacy.

Interpreting Interactions

What does an interaction mean, in words? An interaction affects how we interpret the effects of the independent variables it involves. Let's see how by looking back at Figure 9.4. If the researchers had used only the low-looming condition, they would have found that self-efficacy has only a small effect on feelings of fear of spiders. Or if the study had used only the high-looming condition, they'd have found that self-efficacy has a large effect on fear. Now look at what the high-looming condition adds to the low-looming effects. With high self-efficacy, high looming adds only a little to the fear, but with low self-efficacy, it adds a lot. To describe the effects of a factor that is part of an interaction, we need to say, "It depends." Given the interaction of looming and self-efficacy on fear, our interpretation of the effect of each variable would be that it *depends* on the level of the other. For example, the effect of looming depends on self-efficacy: it has a larger effect when people believe that they have little self-efficacy than when they believe they have enough self-efficacy to prevent harm. Actually, the combined effects of these factors make sense when stated in these words, don't they?

The way in which we phrase our interpretation of an interaction is influenced by whether the design was carried out entirely with experimental strategies or either partly or completely with nonexperimental strategies. The issue is with the phrase, "the effect of." Let's consider two examples. First, in the case of research conducted entirely with experimental strategies, we would be fully justified in saying "the effect of" for any independent variable. So, in the experiment on fear of spiders, we can say that the effect of self-efficacy on fear depends on the level of looming *or* the effect of looming on fear depends on self-efficacy. Either is justified. Second, in the case of factorials using an E × N design, we should try to reserve the phrase "the effect of" for an independent variable tested with an experimental strategy. For instance, suppose we found an interaction in a study using a similar method (an experimental strategy) to study the role of self-efficacy on fear of spiders in a 2 × 2 factorial, with gender (a subject variable) as the other independent variable. It would be better to phrase the interaction as "the effect of self-efficacy depends on gender," rather than "the effect of gender depends on self-efficacy," because we can't make a cause–effect conclusion for a subject variable.

Three other issues also affect the meaning of a significant interaction. First, because an interaction indicates that the role of an independent variable depends on the level of another variable, it shows that the role is not always the same. As a result, it establishes limits for the generalization, or external validity, of findings regarding that variable. For example, a 2 × 2 factorial study tested the effects of time of day on the speed with which young adults and elderly adults read 10 short stories on a computer, which recorded their reading time (May et al., 1993). They were tested either in the morning or late afternoon and told that they should read carefully and would be tested on the material later. Figure 9.5 presents the mean reading speed per word for each of the four groups and depicts a significant interaction, showing that the effect of time of day on reading time depends on the age of the individuals. From these findings we can conclude that time of day has little effect on reading speed for young adults but has a large effect for older adults, who read much more slowly in the morning than in the afternoon.

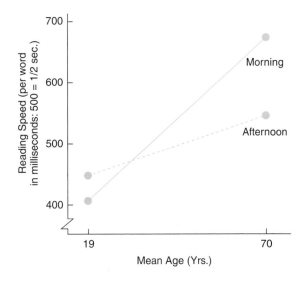

FIGURE 9.5

The interaction between age and time of day on adults' reading speed, given in milliseconds per word (data from May et al., 1993, Table 2). Notice that time of day (about 8:30 A.M. versus 4:30 P.M.) had little effect on reading speed for younger adults, but a large effect for older adults.

Second, interactions can result from artifacts in the task or measurement when the scale does not measure high enough or low enough. If the scale does not measure high enough, it may produce a **ceiling effect** in which performance in one or more conditions is at its maximum and can't go higher. If the scale does not measure low enough, it may produce a **floor effect** in which performance in one or more conditions is at its minimum and can't go lower. In either of these circumstances, the scale can't reflect any further the effects of the independent variable, even if the effects should extend higher or lower. To see how ceiling and floor effects can result in a significant interaction, we'll consider the hypothetical data shown in Figure 9.6 from a 2 × 5 factorial study on math performance in multiplication problems and algebra problems for students ranging in age from 6 to 18 years. Notice that the 12-, 15-, and 18-year-olds were performing perfectly or nearly so on the multiplication problems, indicating a ceiling effect in the data because the task was too easy to reflect further ability improvements. For the 6-, 9-, and 12-year-olds, a floor effect is evident for the algebra problems because the task was too hard, particularly for children at the two youngest ages who have not had any training in algebra. Asking easier algebra questions might have pulled up their performance somewhat, especially among the 12-year-olds. The main issue of concern with interactions resulting from ceiling or floor effects is in their interpretation. For example, we can't be sure that the ability of 12- to 18-year-olds does not improve on multiplication problems, especially on harder ones or in the speed of doing them.

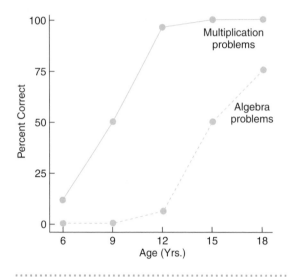

FIGURE 9.6

Hypothetical data from a 2 × 5 factorial showing an interaction—nonparallel lines—resulting from a ceiling effect (performance is at its maximum level) among the older students for the multiplication problems and a floor effect (performance is at its minimum) among the younger students for the algebra problems.

If researchers want to avoid ceiling or floor effects, they must choose tasks and measurement scales to allow changes in the dependent variable to be seen.

Third, the meaning of an interaction should be linked to relevant theories, prior research findings, and the research hypotheses identified in designing the study. Theories often predict whether or not the effects of independent variables should interact, and factorial studies are ideal for testing these predictions. For example, a theory might predict that being overweight has a greater negative effect on the self-esteem of female than male adolescents. If so, we could test the self-esteem of normal weight and very overweight girls and boys and should find an interaction. Linking the meaning of an interaction to prior research is important if those studies had found contradictory results because they used different levels of an interacting variable. For instance, suppose studies had compared the reading speed of adults in the morning and afternoon, but some studies found a difference and others did not. The reason for the contradictory results may have been that different studies tested people of different ages. And researchers should also link the meaning of an interaction to their research hypotheses. Hypotheses for factorial designs should include a *specific prediction for each main effect and interaction* to be tested in the statistical analyses. A good way to generate these predictions is to draw a graph, like those in this chapter, before collecting data to see roughly the position you expect for each mean. Don't try to be exact—just guess the position of each mean relative to each other. Doing this will help you see your expectations of where the differences will be and whether the lines should be parallel or nonparallel in the data you collect.

POSSIBLE OUTCOMES

Eight outcome patterns of significant effects are possible in 2×2 factorial studies. One possible outcome, of course, is that statistical analysis will reveal no significant effects: no main effect for either independent variable, which we'll refer to as *factor A* and *factor B*, and no interaction. The seven other possible outcomes consist of a significant:

1. Main effect for factor A, but not factor B or the interaction
2. Main effect for factor B, but not factor A or the interaction
3. Main effect for factor A and for factor B, but no interaction
4. Main effect for factor A and the interaction, but not factor B
5. Main effect for factor B and the interaction, but not factor A
6. Main effect for factor A and for factor B plus the interaction
7. Interaction, but no main effect for factors A or B

To illustrate these possible outcomes, we'll use as our framework a study on the role of people's hunger cues and weight status—normal weight or overweight—in the amount of food they eat. Because any study can find many different outcome patterns, we'll vary the outcome from the actual one in which the researchers found a significant interaction with no main effects of hunger cues (factor A) or weight status (factor B). As we'll see, these researchers didn't find quite what they expected. (Go to Box 9.1)

Box 9.1   **A SIGNIFICANT INTERACTION WITH NO MAIN EFFECTS?**

How can an analysis reveal a significant interaction if there are no main effects? As we will see, the answer lies in the way the analysis pools the data for a main effect. But first, let's describe the study on hunger cues and weight status (Schachter & Gross, 1968). The researchers recruited male employees of a university who were of normal weight or were overweight by 15% or more and had them come one at a time to a session that began at 5:00 P.M., which would be nearing their dinnertime.

As hunger cues, the researchers manipulated the time shown on a prominent clock that ran either twice or half as fast as normal speed. To help in manipulating the variable of hunger cues, the researchers deceived the men into believing that they were in a study of relationships among physiological and psychological characteristics. When each man arrived at the laboratory, he was seated in a room facing the clock, and elec-

continued

trodes for the physiological measurements were attached with adhesive to his wrists (so that his watch could be removed). He then sat there alone for about half an hour while the equipment was presumably assessing the physiological variables. Then the researcher returned with a long survey for him to fill out alone and a box of crackers, which was left with explicit offers for him to "help yourself . . . you might want some." At this point the fast clock read about 6:15 P.M. (well into dinnertime), and the slow clock read about 5:30 P.M. The researcher returned after 10 minutes with another survey, casually picked up the box of crackers, and left to weigh the box, which had been weighed when full. The difference in weight was used as the measure of the amount eaten, the dependent variable.

The outcome differed from the researchers' expectations, which, for instance, proposed that the obese men with the high hunger cues (fast clock) would eat the most and the normal-weight men with the low cues (slow clock) would eat the least. As you can see in Figure 9.7, the normal weight men with the low cues ate the most. You can also see that the graph lines are clearly nonparallel; the ANOVA confirmed that the interaction between hunger cues and weight status was significant, $F(1, 42) = 11.94$, $p = .002$. But neither main effect was significant, as pointed out earlier, and now we can see why. Look at the marginal means in the rightmost column and lowest row of the tabular data: they are identical for the normal weight and overweight men and are close for the low- and high-cues conditions. Thus, the reason for the absence of main effects is that the pooled means are similar. *When an interaction is present, the absence of a significant main effect does not necessarily mean that an independent variable had no effect.* The pooling may mask the effect in the analysis, but the interaction reflects it. How can we confirm that one or both of these factors had an effect? Remember that the ANOVA is an omnibus test, so a significant interaction simply indicates that two or more conditions in the interaction differ. To find out exactly which ones differ, we would perform contrasts or post hoc comparisons, as we'll see later.

One other thing: When the results disconfirm the original hypotheses, researchers try to explain why in the research report. In this case, Schachter and Gross (1968, p. 171) proposed an "embarrassingly simple" explanation, the role of cognition in deciding what to eat. For example, they described how several normal-weight individuals in the high-cues condition declined the snack, saying, "No thanks, I don't want to spoil my dinner." (Their parents would be so pleased!)

One Main Effect, But No Interaction

We've seen that the study on hunger cues and weight status did not turn out exactly as the researchers expected. As we examine some of the other outcomes that particular study could have had, we'll be referring to Figure 9.8, which depicts four of the possible outcome patterns a 2 × 2 factorial can have. For each outcome, the mean for each condition is presented in a matrix and in a graph, and the marginal means are given along the right side and bottom of the matrix.

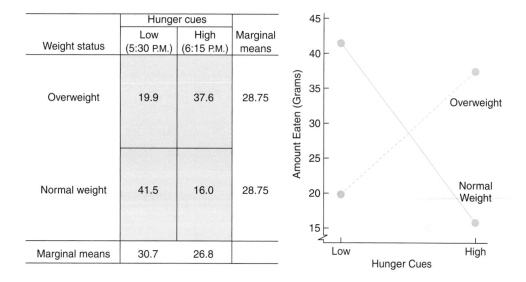

| | Hunger cues | | |
Weight status	Low (5:30 P.M.)	High (6:15 P.M.)	Marginal means
Overweight	19.9	37.6	28.75
Normal weight	41.5	16.0	28.75
Marginal means	30.7	26.8	

FIGURE 9.7

Mean amount eaten (in grams; 30 grams ≅ 1 ounce) by normal weight and overweight partici-pants under high (fast clock, 6:15 P.M.) and low (slow clock, 5:30 P.M.) hunger-cue conditions. (Data from Schachter & Gross, 1968, Table 2)

One type of outcome for a factorial study is to find one significant main effect, but no other main effect and no interaction. In a 2 × 2 factorial, the significant main effect can be for either factor, A or B, as indicated in outcomes 1 and 2 in the preceding list. Figure 9.8a shows an outcome in which overweight participants ate significantly more than the normal-weight people, regardless of hunger cues—that is, the hunger cues main effect and the interaction are not significant. Another outcome like this one would be that the normal-weight individuals ate more than the overweight people; the graph and matrix would look the same, but the "over" and "norm" labels would be swapped. Notice that the graph lines are nearly parallel, indicating that a significant interaction is very unlikely, and the lines are nearly horizontal, indicating that hunger cues had little effect.

Figure 9.8b shows an outcome in which individuals in the high hunger-cues condition ate significantly more than those with low hunger cues, but the weight status main effect and the interaction are not significant. The lines slope, suggesting an effect of hunger cues; the lines are also nearly parallel, suggesting no interaction, and are very close together, indicating little difference in eating patterns between the overweight and normal-weight people. Another outcome like this one might reveal the opposite effect: greater amounts eaten under low than high hunger cues, in which case the lines would slope in the opposite direction.

More than One Main Effect, But No Interaction

A factorial study can also find more than one significant main effect without an interaction, as indicated in outcome 3 in the preceding list and presented in Figure 9.8c. The figure shows that the overweight people ate more than the

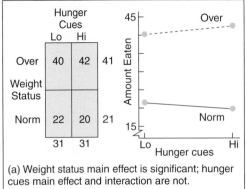

(a) Weight status main effect is significant; hunger cues main effect and interaction are not.

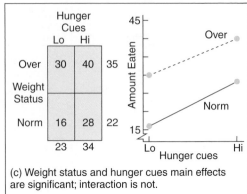

(c) Weight status and hunger cues main effects are significant; interaction is not.

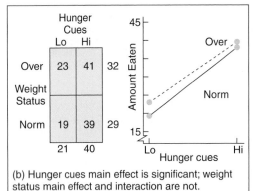

(b) Hunger cues main effect is significant; weight status main effect and interaction are not.

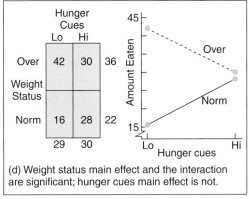

(d) Weight status main effect and the interaction are significant; hunger cues main effect is not.

FIGURE 9.8

Four patterns of possible outcomes a 2×2 factorial can have, each depicted as a matrix and a graph for a study of hunger cues (factor A) and weight status (factor B). Each matrix gives the mean amount eaten (in grams) for each condition, along with the marginal means on the right side and bottom. The marginal means assume that the number of participants is the same in all conditions. Abbreviations: lo, hi = low or high hunger cues; over, norm = overweight or normal weight.

normal-weight individuals, and the hunger cues had similar and substantial effects on eating for both weight groups. Once again, the lines in the graph slope, indicating a main effect of hunger cues, and are nearly parallel, suggesting no interaction. But the lines are far apart, indicating a main effect of weight status. Other outcomes with more than one main effect and no interaction for this study might involve greater eating by the normal-weight people or in the low-cues condition.

I described earlier two 2×2 factorial studies my students conducted. In both cases, the statistical analyses revealed two significant main effects and no interaction, and graphs of their data looked a lot like the one in Figure 9.8c. One of those studies tested people's willingness to provide help to individuals as a function of the degree of familiarity (friend versus classmate) with the person needing help and the personal cost of providing the help. The participants said they'd be more willing to provide help if the person was a friend, as opposed to a classmate, and if the cost was low rather than high. A graph showed nearly parallel lines: the degree to which willingness was reduced by cost was about the same, regardless of whether the person needing help was a friend or just a classmate. The other study examined in a survey the effects of social influence and gender-specific tasks on females' conformity in making estimates of the cost of a haircut. The gender-specific factor involved making estimates of the cost of a man's or a woman's haircut, and social influence was introduced by allowing some participants to see bogus high estimates supposedly given by prior participants. The estimates the actual participants gave were significantly higher if they saw the bogus estimates and for the woman's haircut than the man's (which makes sense because they do really cost more). There was no interaction: The effect of social influence was essentially the same, regardless of whether the participants were estimating the cost of a man's or a woman's haircut.

One or More Main Effects, Plus an Interaction

For outcomes 4, 5, and 6 in the preceding list, statistical analyses would reveal significant differences among one or more main effects *plus* an interaction. Figure 9.8d presents one pattern that this outcome could take: a significant main effect of weight status and an interaction between weight status and hunger cues. The main effect of cues is not significant because the marginal (pooled) means for the low- and high-cues conditions are almost the same, 29 and 30, respectively. Yet the graph of the interaction suggests that hunger cues did play a role, but they had *opposite effects* on eating for overweight and normal-weight participants. If follow-up analyses were to reveal significant differences between the low- and high-cues conditions for the separate weight groups, we could conclude that high cues reduced eating in overweight people and increased eating in normal-weight people.

Two studies we discussed earlier each had an outcome with a significant interaction and one or more main effects, but their outcomes look somewhat different from each other and from the one in Figure 9.8d. Let's look at the means for those studies. Figures 9.3 and 9.4 present the outcome for Riskind and Maddux's (1993) experiment on the role of looming and self-efficacy on people's fear of spiders. Because the marginal means were quite different for the two looming and for the two self-efficacy conditions, each main effect was significant. And the graph lines are distinctly nonparallel, depicting the significant interaction. Figure 9.5 shows the outcome for the May et al. (1993) study on the role that time of day has on the reading speed of young and older adults. The graph clearly shows the significant interaction and main effect of age, with young adults reading faster than elderly adults. But the main effect of time of day was not significant. Although reading speed had a numerically higher marginal mean for the morning ($M = 541.20$) than the afternoon ($M = 495.75$) testing, the difference was too small to reach significance, given the amount of error variance. Yet because the analysis revealed a significant interaction, the researchers could perform follow-up tests showing that time of day had no effect on the reading speed of the younger participants but did affect the reading speed of the elderly individuals, who read significantly slower in the morning than the afternoon.

INDEPENDENT AND DEPENDENT GROUPS IN FACTORIAL DESIGNS

We've seen in earlier chapters that we can have independent or dependent groups in single-factor designs, and we described the advantages, disadvantages, and procedures for each approach. Figure 7.1 (see inside back cover) outlines those designs and the research strategies they use. All of that information applies to each factor in factorial designs as well. We'll see in this section that factorial designs can use all independent groups, all dependent groups, or a mixture of the two.

ALL INDEPENDENT GROUPS

In independent-groups, or between-subjects, designs, we would test a separate group of subjects at each level of an independent variable, and we would not expect their data to be correlated across conditions. Suppose we designed a 2 × 2 factorial study with all independent groups and wanted to have 15 participants in each condition. This design would require four separate, unrelated groups of individuals for a total of 60 participants. An example of an all independent-groups 2 × 2 factorial design is the research we discussed earlier by May et al. (1993) that tested the reading speed of young and elderly adults in the morning and afternoon. The design had two levels of age and two levels of time of day.

How would we assign the participants to the groups? If we were using an experimental strategy with each factor, we would randomly assign the 60 participants to the conditions to equate the groups before manipulating the independent variables. We saw in Chapter 5 that we can get an equal number of subjects in each condition by using the methods of random assignment without replacement, block random assignment, or random distribution. For example, the study my student did on the effects of social influence and gender-specific tasks on females' conformity in making estimates of the cost of a haircut used the random distribution method. The student made enough copies of the survey for each condition and shuffled them in a stack before passing them out to participants. If we were using an E × N design—that is, an experimental strategy for factor A, such as type of reward, and a nonexperimental strategy for factor B, such as gender—we would randomly assign the males and females (factor B) separately to the two levels of reward (factor A). Thus, half the participants of each gender would be in each level of factor A.

MIXED DESIGNS AND ALL DEPENDENT GROUPS

When using dependent-groups designs, we expect the data across conditions to be correlated because we are using within-subjects or matched-subjects methods to equate the groups. Recall that within-subjects designs use repeated measures, testing the same individuals in more than one condition of the study, and matched-subjects designs make sure the individuals in each group are very similar on a matching variable that is strongly related to the dependent variable. When using repeated measures across levels of an independent variable, we may need to eliminate potential confounding from order effects by applying a method of counterbalancing. We saw in Chapter 8 that researchers can control order effects through *individual counterbalancing* methods, such as reverse (ABBA) counterbalancing and randomization techniques, and *overall counterbalancing* methods, such as all possible orders and Latin square techniques.

Mixed Factorials

Research that combines at least one factor tested with independent groups and one factor tested with dependent groups is called a **mixed factorial design.** The dependent-groups factor usually involves repeated measures across levels of that independent variable. An example of a mixed factorial design that we've already seen is the experiment by Riskind and Maddux (1993) on the effects of looming and self-efficacy on fear of spiders. Self-efficacy was tested with independent groups: the participants were asked to imagine being alone in a room with a tarantula on the floor and either being able or unable to move to prevent harm. Looming, the dependent-groups factor, was tested by having each participant watch videos of a tarantula moving quickly toward them (the high-looming condition) and of the spider moving away or being still (the low-looming condition). The researchers counterbalanced the order of the videos. After watching each video, the participants rated the fear they felt.

Another example of a mixed factorial design comes from a study a student of mine did that we considered in Chapter 8 when discussing the reverse counterbalancing procedure. This study used a 2 × 2 design to examine the degree to which children at two age levels (third and fifth graders) found two riddle types funny. The riddle types depended on whether the answer to the riddle question, such as "Why was the little strawberry worried?" is compatible ("Because he couldn't find his mother") or incompatible ("Because his mom and dad were in a jam"). My student presented the riddles in a counterbalanced (ABBA) order. The mean funniness ratings (on a happy-face scale with 4 points) the third and fifth graders gave were, respectively, 3.03 and 3.16 for the incompatible riddles and 2.12 and 1.86 for the compatible riddles. The statistical analysis revealed a significant main effect of riddle type—the children found the riddles with the incompatible answers funnier—but no main effect of age and no interaction.

A common circumstance for using a mixed factorial design in psychology is when one factor is tested with repeated measures taken across chronological time, such as before and after a treatment or longitudinally. In these cases, the hypotheses require repeated measurements, and no counterbalancing is needed, as we saw in Chapter 8. As examples, we'll look at two studies that used 2 × 2 mixed factorial designs. First, researchers conducted an experiment with police officers, about half of whom received training in interviewing skills to help them gather more facts from witnesses of crimes (Fisher, Geiselman, & Amador, 1989). The remaining officers served as a control group. All the officers were pretested by having them tape-record several interviews they conducted. After the training was administered to the experimental group, all officers were again asked to tape-record several interviews. Assistants who were blind to the conditions of the study later transcribed and scored the recordings for the number of facts they contained. The facts were corroborated by other sources of information. The means for the number of facts recorded by officers who did and did not receive training were, respectively, 26.83 and 23.75 at pretest and 39.57 and 24.21 at posttest. Now try to visualize a graph of these means. The line connecting the pretest means would slope slightly, and the line for the posttest means would slope sharply in the same direction. They are not parallel, which suggests that the interaction is significant, and it was: $F(1, 11) = 9.01, p < .05$. Planned comparisons, or contrasts, revealed that the pretest means did not differ and that the trained officers obtained significantly more facts at posttest than at pretest interviews.

Second, a student in my research methods course conducted a 2×2 mixed factorial study comparing the blood pressure of elderly adults before and after receiving a 5-minute back rub at a nursing home where she worked. Half of the 30 participants were characterized as usually calm and alert, and half were usually agitated and disoriented. All of them could maintain a side-lying position for the duration of the back rub, had not taken any medication to reduce anxiety in the prior 24 hours, and had a baseline systolic blood pressure higher than 100, which was measured with an automatic digital device. The mean blood pressures before and after the back rub were, respectively, 134.87 and 128.07 for the calm–alert individuals and 131.07 and 129.00 for the agitated–disoriented individuals. By again visualizing a graph of the means, we can see that the lines connecting the before and after data show that the decline in blood pressure is steeper for the calm–alert than the agitated–disoriented individuals. The statistical analysis revealed that the main effect for the before-to-after decline was significant, as was the interaction: the effect of a back rub on blood pressure depends on a subject variable, whether the people are normally calm–alert versus agitated–disoriented.

All-Dependent-Groups Factorials

Sometimes researchers test the same subjects at *all levels of each independent variable* in a factorial design. Thus, each subject provides data for each and every condition in the study, and all the data groupings are dependent, or expected to be correlated. Dewing and Hetherington (1974) used a 2×3 factorial design with all dependent groups to study the effects of imagery and clues on the time it takes for people to solve anagrams (scrambled letters of words, for example, URTHT can be solved as *truth*). To manipulate imagery, the researchers used solution words that were either concrete nouns—that is, they could produce a mental image (for example, *cabin* and *sugar*)—or abstract nouns, which cannot produce an image, such as *shame* and *truth*. Thus there were two levels of imagery, high and low. For the other independent variable, each anagram had one of three levels of clues for its solution: no clues,

- Structural clues—the first and last letter of the solution word (for example, *s* and *e* for the word *shame*), and
- Semantic clues—the title of the concept to which the noun belongs (for example, *dwelling* for the word *cabin*).

The researchers recruited 72 college student participants and had each solve 12 anagrams, two under each of the six conditions of the study. Each anagram with its clue was printed on a separate card. The dependent variable was the amount of time taken to solve each anagram.

The methodology included a variety of control procedures to eliminate confounding, and we'll describe some. To eliminate order effects, the cards were presented to each participant in a random order, probably by shuffling. To control the effectiveness of the semantic clues across imagery levels, the researchers had other people rate the association of the clues to the high-imagery and low-imagery words and found that the mean ratings did not differ. To minimize potential confounding from the specific order of letters in the anagrams, three different sets of letter orders were randomly generated for each solution word, and they were evenly distributed across conditions. And to equate the anagrams used in the different conditions, the researchers held constant several important features—for example, each item had only one solution word that consisted of five letters and was very commonly used in the English language. The mean time to solution for each condition is presented in a matrix and a graph in Figure 9.9. Consistent with what the figure depicts, the statistical analysis revealed significant main effects of imagery $(F[1, 71] = 64.86, p < .001)$ and clues $(F[2, 142] = 94.15, p < .001)$, and a significant interaction $(F[2, 142] = 5.31, p < .01)$. The interaction shows that the amount of help the structural and semantic clues provided depended on the level of imagery of the solution word.

We saw in Chapter 8 that researchers decide to use within-subjects designs for the several advantages that these designs have. Three of the advantages were particularly important for the anagram study. First, using repeated measures

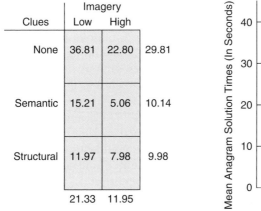
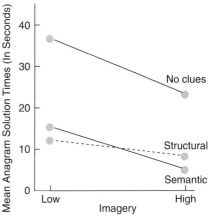

FIGURE 9.9

Mean anagram solution times (in seconds) for high- and low-imagery words with structural, semantic, or no clues (data converted from log-transformed values in Dewing & Hetherington, 1974, Table 1). The data along the right side and bottom of the matrix are the marginal (pooled) means.

guarantees the *equivalence of subjects* tested at those levels of the independent variable. This is an important consideration for a study on solving anagrams because individuals vary greatly in the needed abilities, which can lead to high levels of error variability. Second, using a within-subjects design *increases the statistical power*, which is important when error variability may be high. Third, using repeated measures requires *fewer subjects* than a between-subjects design. If the anagram study had used an independent-groups approach, it would have needed many more than the 72 participants tested.

MORE COMPLEX FACTORIAL DESIGNS

So far in our discussion of complex studies, we've focused mainly on the simplest factorials—that is, 2 × 2 designs—but the research on anagram solution we just described used a 2 × 3 design. That study makes a nice transition to this section on more complex designs because it still had only two independent variables and was still a two-way design. It was a little more complex than a 2 × 2 factorial because it included a third level for one of its factors. Factorial studies become more complex when we increase the number of levels of an independent variable or number of independent variables being examined.

MORE THAN TWO LEVELS OF AN INDEPENDENT VARIABLE

All the material on 2 × 2 factorials that we've discussed applies to two-way designs with more than two levels of one or both factors. Let's look at a few examples of studies with more than two levels of at least one independent variable that differ in the numbers of levels they used and the inclusion of independent and dependent groups.

You've probably heard the concept of "getting away with murder." Sigall and Ostrove (1975) studied people's judgments of the punishment individuals convicted of crimes should receive, depending on the criminal's attractiveness and the nature of the crime. The researchers recruited 120 undergraduates and randomly assigned them to six independent groups in a 3 × 2 design with the restriction that each of the groups have an equal number of males and females. The participants read an account of a crime and biographical information about the convicted individual, "Barbara Helm," and then indicated the prison sentence she should receive, which could range from 1 to 15 years. The information a participant received presented one of three levels for the physical attractiveness factor by including a photo of an attractive woman, a photo of an unattractive woman, or no photo (control group); the crime was either a burglary or a swindle. The researchers hypothesized an interaction: when attractiveness could be used to the criminal's advantage in carrying out a crime, as in a swindle, the participants would suggest a harsher sentence for the attractive woman than the unattractive woman. But when attractiveness is unrelated to a crime, as in a burglary, they'd suggest a more lenient sentence for the attractive woman. The results confirmed the hypothesis of a significant interaction ($F[2, 108] = 4.55$, $p < .025$), but not all details of the hypothesized interaction were upheld in follow-up contrasts. Although attractive Barbara received a significantly lighter sentence than unattractive Barbara for burglary, attractiveness did not affect her sentence for swindle (but the means were in the predicted direction).

Another study used a 3 × 3 mixed factorial design to test the view that people with negative self-concepts tend to behave in ways that increase their likelihood of getting negative feedback (Swann, Wenzlaff, Krull, & Pelham, 1992). The two independent variables involved three levels of depression, the independent-groups factor, and three levels of favorableness of feedback, the dependent-groups factor. The researchers assessed the degree of depression among the undergraduates they recruited and used the scores to separate them into three groups: 13 were classified as depressed, 43 were dysphoric (moderately unhappy), and 28 were nondepressed. Each participant came to the experiment individually, was told that the study was about social impressions, and was asked to fill out a personality survey that three students in another room would evaluate. Once the survey was done, the researcher left with it, supposedly to have the person's personality evaluated, and returned after a while with bogus assessments for seven traits, such as "interesting–uninteresting," rated on a 10-point scale. Of the three evaluations, one was positive (mean rating = 9), one was neutral (rated 6), and one was negative (rated 3); the order in which the evaluations were presented was counterbalanced across participants. After reviewing the feedback, the participant was asked to indicate on a 10-point scale how much he or she would like to meet each of the three evaluators (10 = want to meet very much). The results confirmed the predicted interaction ($F[4, 162] = 6.93, p < .001$), and follow-up contrasts revealed that the nondepressed and dysphoric participants gave far higher ratings for meeting the favorable than the unfavorable evaluator, but the depressed participants gave far higher ratings for meeting the unfavorable evaluator. These results suggested to the researchers that depressed individuals seek out unfavorable appraisals to stabilize their negative self-concepts and make their lives more predictable.

The number of levels that the independent variables can have in a factorial design is, theoretically, unlimited. But practical considerations often restrict the number because the more levels the design includes, the smaller the differences between them become and the greater the number of conditions—and therefore, subjects—that will be needed in the study. One way to reduce the number of subjects with a large number of conditions is to use repeated measures. For example, Jarrard (1963) conducted a 6 × 4 factorial study on the effects of LSD on behavior by administering to rats on separate days one of six different doses of the drug. The rats were tested for lever pressing for food reward on each test day over four successive 30-minute periods to see the drug's effects as it wore off. The test days were separated by several days without the drug to reduce carryover effects, and the order of dose levels was counterbalanced across subjects with the Latin square method. The study found that very small doses of LSD enhanced lever pressing for food, but large doses impaired it. And there was an interaction: As the drug wore off, the rats' lever pressing decreased over time with the small LSD doses and increased with the large doses.

MORE THAN TWO INDEPENDENT VARIABLES

We've seen that two-way factorial designs have two independent variables. If we increase the number of factors in a study, the number of "ways" increases: a *three-way* design has three independent variables, a *four-way* design has four independent variables, and so on. Researchers rarely use independent-groups designs with more than three or four factors, largely because of the increased number of subjects needed. If we planned an independent-groups $2 \times 2 \times 3$ factorial study with 15 subjects in each of the 12 conditions, we'd need 180 subjects. If we added a fourth factor with just two levels, we'd double the number of subjects needed. Adding a fifth factor with two levels (so that we have a $2 \times 2 \times 3 \times 2 \times 2$ design) would require that we recruit and collect and analyze data from 720 subjects! And we'll see later that the number and complexity of possible main effects and interactions with more than four factors become mind-boggling. As a result, we'll limit our discussion of complex factorials to three independent variables.

An example of a three-way factorial design comes from a study of whether people articulate words in their minds as they read silently (Haber & Haber, 1982). Because most adults don't move their lips as they read to themselves, the researchers couldn't simply assess overt behavior. So they proposed that if silent reading involves mental articulation, people would take longer to read material composed of tongue twisters, such as "She sells sea shells by the seashore," than regular sentences, such as "He finds string beans by the small barn." The researchers had students read each of 10 tongue-twister and 10 regular sentences five times in succession and signal immediately upon finishing reading each one. The sentences were printed on separate cards and equated for grammatical complexity and number of syllables. The sentence type—tongue twisters or regular—was one independent variable, and several different sequences of the sentences were used to counterbalance order effects. The second factor was whether the reading was done silently or aloud: half of the students read the first five tongue twisters and regular sentences aloud and then the rest of the sentences silently, and half had the reverse order. The third factor was repetition, the reading of each sentence five times. As you may have figured out, this study was an all dependent-groups $2 \times 2 \times 5$ factorial. All three main effects were significant: the students read faster for regular sentences than tongue twisters, in silent than oral reading, and across repetitions of the same sentence. Only one interaction was significant: across repetitions, reading speed increased more for the regular sentences than the tongue twisters. The three-way interaction of sentence type, silent/aloud reading, and repetition was not significant.

What would a three-way interaction look like and mean? A study of discrimination in hiring decisions was conducted with *five* independent variables, three of which were involved in an interaction (Pingitore, Dugoni, Tindale, & Spring, 1994). The researchers presented videotapes of actors who were supposedly applying for a job. The videos were identical, except for the gender of the applicant and his or her weight status (normal weight or obese), which the researchers manipulated by having the normal weight actors made up to appear 20% heavier (like Jiminy Glick, on TV!). The participants served as evaluators in a mock hiring process and rated the applicant on a 7-point scale, where 1 = definitely not hire and 7 = definitely hire. The design used all independent groups, and each evaluator rated the applicant in only one video. For our purposes, we'll focus on the three factors in the interaction: the gender of the job applicant, the weight status (normal or obese) of the applicant, and the body schema of the evaluator. To assess body schema, the researchers had the evaluators fill out a survey in which they rated their satisfaction with aspects of their own bodies and the importance of each aspect. A median split procedure produced two groups: high and low body schemas. People with high body-schema scores tend to be satisfied with their bodies and feel that their body image is central to their self-concept. The mean hiring ratings were significantly higher for the applicants who were male rather than female and normal weight rather than obese. The main effect body schema was not significant, but that factor was involved in the significant three-way interaction, $F(1, 288) = 10.48$, $p < .01$.

Let's look in some detail at Figure 9.10, which presents the mean hiring ratings as a function of the three factors. The cube gives a three-dimensional diagram

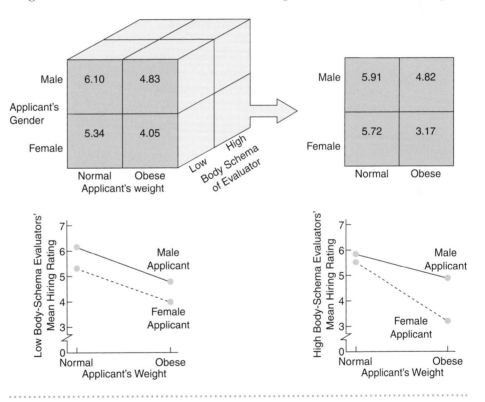

FIGURE 9.10
Diagram with matrices and graphs of a three-way interaction in a study of hiring decisions as a function of the applicant's gender and weight status (normal or obese) and the evaluators' (participants') body schema, or feelings about their own weight (data calculated from Pingitore et al., 1994, Table 2). The cube contains the hiring ratings (7 = definitely hire; 1 = definitely don't hire) for the male and female normal weight and obese applicants in two matrices. The matrix in front (at left) shows the mean ratings from low body schema evaluators, and the one in back (at right) shows the ratings from high body schema evaluators.

of the factors, with two levels each of gender, weight status, and body schema. Think of the cube as consisting of eight blocks, four in the front matrix and four in the rear matrix. Each block represents a condition with one level of each factor—for instance, the upper-left block in the front matrix contains the hiring ratings from low body-schema evaluators of a male normal-weight applicant. The hiring ratings in the front matrix (on the left) come from evaluators with low body schemas, and those in the rear matrix (moved to the right) are from evaluators with high body schemas. Graphs of the low and high body-schema evaluators' data are shown below the corresponding matrices. Notice that the graph lines are parallel for the low body-schema evaluators, but are distinctly nonparallel for the high body-schema evaluators. The statistical analysis revealed a significant two-way interaction of gender and weight status for the high, but not the low, body-schema evaluators. This means that the interaction of an applicant's gender and weight status depends on the body schema of the evaluator, the third independent variable. As a general rule, a three-way interaction indicates that *the interaction of two factors depends on the level of the third factor.* How would we phrase a conclusion from these results? We could say that this study found that evaluators with low body schemas tend to discriminate in hiring decisions against female and obese applicants uniformly, but the discrimination of evaluators with high body schemas against the obese is pronounced if the applicants are females. This is a fascinating finding that could not be demonstrated without conducting a complex factorial study.

PREPARING TO DO A FACTORIAL STUDY

Designing and performing factorial studies can be very complicated, even when the design involves just two independent variables. When counterbalancing is needed for one or more independent variables, the process can become even more complicated. If you think you will be conducting factorial research, keep in mind that Chapter 10 gives instructions and checklists to help you prepare to do research. Consult those materials to make the activities in designing and conducting the study easier, more organized, and more complete.

DATA ANALYSIS IN FACTORIAL DESIGNS

We can determine which statistical analyses to use for factorial designs by looking back at Table 4.1 (see inside front cover), as we've done before. Because factorial designs assess differences between conditions, we would focus on the lower half of the table. If the data were on an interval or ratio scale, we would use a parametric statistic—for factorial designs, it would be an ANOVA because there are more than two data groupings. This choice assumes that the data approximate a normal distribution and the amount of variance is similar in each data grouping. Statistical tests can detect if the data depart markedly from these criteria; if they do, we can apply accepted statistical adjustments in the ANOVA or use a nonparametric test. If the data are on a nominal or ordinal scale, we would use a nonparametric statistic—the chi-square (χ^2) is almost always the test chosen. *Appendix B has step-by-step instructions* for using an SPSS statistics program to calculate each of the statistical tests that we discuss.

PARAMETRIC ANALYSES

One of the main beauties of ANOVA is its versatility. It can be applied for interval or ratio data with as many factors as we want and with independent-groups, dependent-groups, and mixed factorial designs. As we saw in Chapters 7 and 8, the ANOVA is an omnibus test. It doesn't tell us which specific condition or group differs from which others, so we often need to test for specific differences with contrasts or post hoc comparisons, which we'll discuss later in this chapter. We also saw that the one-way ANOVA partitions variance in the data into *between-groups variability,* which consists of systematic and nonsystematic (error) variance, and *within-groups variability,* which consists only of error variance. It does this partitioning by calculating sums of squares, which are divided by the associated degrees of freedom (*df*) to produce mean squares. An *F* statistic is calculated by dividing the mean squares between-groups (MS_{bg}) by the mean square within-groups (MS_{wg}), which is often called an *error term.*

All these procedures occur in ANOVAs for factorial designs, but the partitioning is more finely tuned and detailed. The ANOVA will calculate a sum of squares (*SS*), mean square (*MS*), and *F* for each main effect and interaction and can calculate more than one MS_{wg}, particularly if the study uses dependent groups. For a two-way analysis, the *SS* for the interaction of the independent variables is simply what remains from the total *SS* after the *SS* for factors A and B are subtracted:

$$SS_{A \times B} = SS_{tot} - SS_A - SS_B$$

The ANOVA procedure will calculate all needed *SS*s, *df*s, *MS*s, *F* values, and *p* values, which statistics programs will present in an ANOVA summary table. In the next few sections, we'll examine in detail the procedures and outcomes in analyzing data from two-way and three-way designs with all independent-groups designs or with mixed or all dependent-groups designs.

The Two-Way ANOVA: All Independent-Groups Designs

To analyze the data from a study with two factors and all independent groups, we would apply a two-way **between-subjects factorial ANOVA.** Performing the procedure will produce a summary table like the one in Table 9.1, which gives the output for a 2 × 2 study by one of my research methods students. She used a survey to examine college students' willingness to provide help to individuals as a function of the degree of familiarity with the person needing help and the personal cost of providing help. The survey described requests for help from either a high- or low-familiar person (friend versus classmate) and involving either high or low personal cost, such as in money or time. Looking at the summary table, you see several rows, but you can disregard the rows I've shaded. The rows you'll need are the ones that refer to the main effects (familiar and cost), the interaction (familiar * cost), and the within-groups variability (error).

Although the most important columns in the summary table are the ones labeled *df, F, p* (Sig.), and eta squared, let's look at the mean squares. The ANOVA divides the *MS* for each main effect and interaction by the error *MS* to get each of the three *F* values for an independent-groups design. A two-way ANOVA always has

TABLE 9.1

An Example ANOVA Summary Table for a 2 × 2 Factorial Design with All Independent Groups (Statistics Programs Sometimes Have Additional Rows That Can Be Disregarded).

Source	Sum of squares (*SS*)	*df*[a]	Mean square (*MS*)	*F*	Sig. (*p*)	Eta squared
Corrected model	458.13	3	152.71	11.18	.001	
FAMILIAR	157.50	1	157.50	11.53	.001	.11
COST	297.56	1	297.56	21.79	.001	.18
FAMILIAR * COST	3.06	1	3.06	.22	.637	.00
Error (within-groups)	1311.20	96	13.66			
Total	1769.33	99				

[a] The procedure calculates the *df* values for a two-way, all independent-groups design by plugging into formulas the number of levels of each factor and the total number of subjects (*N*). We'll label as *a* and *b* the number of levels of factors A (familiar) and B (cost). The formulas are: $df_A = a - 1, df_B = b - 1, df_{A*B} = (a - 1)(b - 1),$ and $df_{wg} = N - ab.$

F values for *each main effect and the interaction,* and you'll need to *use all of them.* As usual, the *p* values tell us which of the *F*s is significant. What did my student's study find? The mean ratings of willingness to help for the high- and low-familiarity conditions were, respectively, 17.92 and 15.76 for the high-cost condition and 21.72 and 18.86 for the low-cost condition. The higher the ratings, the more willing they were to help. The ANOVA revealed significant main effects for familiarity $(F[1, 96] = 11.53, p < .001)$ and personal cost $(F[1, 96] < 21.79, p < .001)$, but no significant interaction, $F(1, 96) = .22, p > .05$. An effect size estimate would be added to each statistical notation, as we'll discuss later. By looking at the means, we can see that the participants were more willing to provide help if the person was a friend rather than a classmate and if the cost was low rather than high.

If my student had also found a significant interaction, she'd have done follow-up analyses to locate its source—that is, to determine exactly which means were significantly different from which others—and interpreted the main effects in light of the interaction. In the study on the role of time of day on the reading speed of young and older adults that we described earlier, May et al. (1993) found an interaction of age and time of day and a main effect of age on reading speed, as graphed in Figure 9.5. Follow-up tests showed that time of day had no effect on the reading speed of younger participants but did affect the reading speed of elderly individuals, who read significantly slower in the morning than in the afternoon. A major reason for the main effect of age is that the older individuals read much slower in the morning than in the afternoon.

The Two-Way ANOVA: Mixed or All Dependent-Groups Designs

When a two-way factorial design involves within-subjects or matched groups across levels of one or both independent variables, we'd use a **repeated-measures factorial ANOVA** to analyze interval or ratio data. Earlier in this chapter, we saw examples of mixed or all dependent-groups factorial designs—for example:

- The experiment by Riskind and Maddux (1993) on the effects of looming and self-efficacy on fear of spiders was a 2×2 mixed design with interval data (ratings of fear). Looming (high versus low) was a repeated-measures factor, and self-efficacy (high versus low) was a between-subjects factor.
- The study by Fisher et al. (1989) was a 2×2 mixed design on the effects of training police officers in interviewing skills. Officers who did and did not receive the training (a between-subjects factor) were tested for the number of facts (ratio data) they elicited from crime victims in interviews before and after (a within-subjects factor) the training occurred.
- The research by Dewing and Hetherington (1974) used a 2×3 all within-subjects design to study the effects of imagery (concrete versus abstract nouns as solution words) and clues (either structural, semantic, or none) on the time (ratio data) it takes for people to solve anagrams.
- The experiment by Jarrard (1963) was a 6×4 all within-subjects factorial on the effects of LSD on the number of lever-pressing responses (ratio data) by administering to rats on separate days one of six different doses of the drug. The rats were tested for lever pressing for food reward on each test day over four successive 30-minute periods to see the drug's effects as it wore off.

The researchers who did these studies used repeated-measures factorial ANOVA procedures to analyze the data. As with all two-way ANOVAs, the procedure will compute three F values, one for each main effect and one for the interaction.

Although the ANOVA calculations for factorials that include a dependent-groups factor are different from those that consist of all independent groups, the statistical logic and interpretation are the same. The main difference is in the way the ANOVAs partition the nonsystematic variance, or error variability, and use it to calculate each F value. When the design consists of all *independent* groups, there is only one source of error variability, as shown in Table 9.1, and its MS (error term) is used in calculating each of the three F values. In repeated-measures factorial ANOVA procedures, the nonsystematic variability is partitioned further:

- For a *mixed factorial design,* there are *two* error terms: the $MS_{error:b}$ for calculating the F for main effect of the between-subjects (independent-groups) factor and the $MS_{error:w}$ for calculating the F for the main effect of the within-subjects or matched groups factor and the F for the interaction.
- For an *all dependent-groups factorial design,* there are *three* error terms, one for each main effect ($MS_{error:A}$ and $MS_{error:B}$) and one for the interaction ($MS_{error:A \times B}$).

The repeated-measures factorial ANOVA summary table is divided into two or three parts, based on the error terms used in the calculations. Although the summary tables for two-way ANOVAs are more complex for designs with a dependent-groups factor than designs with all independent groups, there are still only three F values to interpret.

The Three-Way ANOVA

Because three-way designs have three independent variables—factors A, B, and C—the ANOVA will yield *seven F* values. It will produce a separate *F* for each of the three main effects, A, B, and C. It will also produce a separate *F* value for each of the four possible interactions of the factors—three two-way (A × B, A × C, and B × C) and one three-way (A × B × C). For each main effect, the statistic pools the data across the two other factors, and for each two-way interaction it pools the data across the third factor. No pooling is done for the three-way interaction. If the design consists of all independent groups, there will be only one error term that will be divided into each of the *MS*s to yield each of the seven *F* values. But if the design includes one or more dependent-groups factors, there will be additional error terms.

We discussed earlier the need for students to limit the complexity of the factorial designs they use. With each additional independent variable, the number of *F* values in the analysis surges: a two-way design produces three *F* values, and a three-way yields seven. A four-way design produces 15 *F* values, including 11 for interactions: six two-way, four three-way, and one four-way! Interpreting multiple significant interactions is very difficult, especially when each involves more than two factors. Remember that a four-way ANOVA could have five significant interactions involving three or four factors each.

NONPARAMETRIC ANALYSES

Psychology researchers rarely conduct factorial studies with nominal or ordinal data for the dependent variable because available nonparametric statistics provide a less complete and integrated analysis of the data. Instead, they find a way to *measure the dependent variable*, which is usually a behavior, *on an interval or ratio scale so that they can apply an ANOVA* procedure, which provides a more flexible, complete, and powerful test than any available nonparametric statistic can.

What test do they use if this is not possible? Table 4.1 (see inside front cover) lists a few tests that can be used if we assess differences with nonparametric statistics and have more than two data groupings, *but these tests basically perform one-way analyses*. With nominal or ordinal data in factorial designs, researchers rely on chi-square (χ^2) tests, the same ones that we discussed in Chapters 7 and 8 for single-factor designs. When the test is applied across more than one factor, it is an omnibus test yielding only one χ^2 value that examines the interaction, not main effects. To test main effects or differences between any two data groupings, one-way χ^2 tests would be used as follow-up tests. Using multiple tests is awkward and inflates the chances of Type I error, which may require the Bonferroni adjustment for the alpha level if many tests will be done.

FOLLOW-UP AND EFFECT SIZE STATISTICS

Because overall analyses of data from factorial studies are omnibus tests, follow-up tests are often needed, especially when a factor has more than two levels. As we are about to see, effect size estimates are sometimes calculated from the follow-up statistical outcomes and sometimes calculated from the main effects and interaction outcomes.

ANOVA Follow-up and Effect Size Statistics for Factorial Designs

The choice of which follow-up statistics to apply after an ANOVA depends on whether the comparison of separate conditions was planned in advance and whether a significant main effect or interaction was found. If the comparison was planned in advance, we can use a contrast test—either a *t* test or one-way ANOVA—regardless of whether any main effect or interaction was significant, as we saw in Chapters 7 and 8.

If no specific comparisons were planned in advance, we can use follow-up tests within any significant main effect or interaction. To help you see how these tests would work, look back to Figure 9.6 and assume that both main effects (age and type of math problems) and the interaction are significant. *Within a significant main effect* with more than two levels of the factor, in this case, age, we can apply post hoc comparisons to compare each individual level (age) against each other level. For example, we could assess whether the math performance is significantly different for 9- versus 12-year olds and for 12- versus 15-year olds. Post hoc comparisons in factorial designs are essentially the same tests we mentioned in Chapter 7, such as the Scheffé, Tukey, and Duncan tests. *Within a significant interaction* in a two-way design, a common approach is to use a **simple-effects analysis** (often called "simple main effects"), which compares the levels of one factor at just one level of the other factor, using a *t* test or one-way ANOVA. For the means in Figure 9.6, for example, we can compare performance on multiplication versus algebra problems among only the 6-year-olds or only the 12-year-olds. Computer programs, such as SPSS, will calculate any follow-up tests we specify.

A common statistic to estimate effect sizes in an ANOVA is eta squared (η^2) that is calculated with the formula

$$\eta^2 = \frac{F(df_{bg})}{[F(df_{bg})] + df_{wg}}$$

A η^2 can be calculated manually for each *F* in the ANOVA using the corresponding *F* and *df* values for each main effect and interaction; SPSS calculates all of them automatically.

Chi-Square Follow-up and Effect Size Statistics for Factorial Designs

We saw earlier that one-way χ^2 tests can be used as follow-up tests when using chi-square methods to analyze nominal or ordinal data in factorial designs. Adjustments to the alpha level can be made with Bonferroni procedures if there are many comparisons. To estimate effect sizes, we can plug data from the output of χ^2 tests into the formula for the Cramér's *V* statistic, as described in Chapter 7 (Table 7.3, see inside back cover).

SUMMARY

In contrast to single-factor studies, research using a factorial design examines two or more independent variables, or factors, at the same time. Factorial designs have the ability to assess the separate effects of each independent variable, which are called the main effects, and the combined effects, or interaction, of the factors. An interaction is present when the influence of one factor on the dependent variable is different at different levels of another factor in the study—that is, the influence of one independent variable depends on the level of another independent variable. Factorial designs have four advantages over multiple single-factor studies: they can strengthen the study's external validity, are more efficient of time and other resources, offer the opportunity to examine interactions, and provide unique opportunities to control systematic and nonsystematic variance, such as by using the Solomon four-group design.

The simplest factorial design has two independent variables, each with two levels. A factorial with two independent variables is called a two-way design; if it has two levels of each factor, it can be described as a 2×2 factorial design. Each number in the numerical code represents an independent variable, and its value indicates the number of levels of that factor. A $3 \times 2 \times 4$ design is more complex: It has three independent variables, with three levels of one, two levels of another, and four levels of the third factor. Many studies in psychology use an $E \times N$ design, which means that they have at least one factor that uses an experimental strategy (the "E") and one that uses a nonexperimental strategy (the "N"). A factor tested with an experimental strategy can lead to a cause-effect conclusion, but a factor tested with a nonexperimental strategy cannot.

To test for a specific main effect in a factorial design, the statistical test ignores the other factor(s), pooling the data across its levels. If the difference between the pooled, or marginal, means is large relative to the error variability, we are likely to find a significant main effect in the statistical analysis. When a significant interaction between factors exists, a graph of the means for the dependent variable should show distinctly nonparallel lines. Interpreting a significant interaction can be difficult, particularly if it may have resulted from a ceiling effect or a floor effect. Many different statistically significant outcomes are possible in factorial designs. For example, in a two-way factorial study, we can find one main effect, but no interaction; two main effects, but no interaction; one or two main effects, plus an interaction; or no main effects, but an interaction. A factorial design can have all independent groups or all dependent groups, or it can be a blend of the two—a mixed factorial design—with at least one factor using independent groups and one using dependent groups. Researchers increase the complexity of factorial designs by adding levels of one or more independent variable or adding one or more independent variables to the study.

Statistical analyses of data from factorial designs usually involve ANOVA methods because researchers generally want the flexibility and power they provide and the ability to test for interactions. To use these parametric procedures, the data must be on an interval or ratio measurement scale. The between-subjects factorial ANOVA is used for designs in which all the groups are independent, and the repeated-measures factorial ANOVA is applied when one or more factors in the design are tested with dependent groups. The number of *F* values the ANOVA computes depends on the number of independent variables. Analysis of a two-way design yields three *F* values, one for each main effect and one for the interaction, and a three-way ANOVA yields seven *F* values. Occasionally researchers use non-parametric analyses, typically the χ^2, for factorial designs. Researchers perform available contrast tests, post hoc comparisons, and simple-effects analyses as follow-up tests, and they compute effect size statistics to determine the extent of the independent variable's influence on the dependent variable.

KEY TERMS

factorial design	E × N design	between-subjects
main effect	ceiling effect	factorial ANOVA
interaction	floor effect	repeated-measures
Solomon four-group	mixed factorial design	factorial ANOVA
design		simple-effects analysis

REVIEW QUESTIONS

1. Describe the Riskind and Maddux (1993) experiment on the effects of the looming nature of a danger and self-efficacy in dealing with the threat on people's feelings of fear.

2. What are *factorial designs,* and what are their advantages?

3. Consider each of the following research designs: (a) 2 × 3, (b) 2 × 4 × 3, (c) 4 × 6, and (d) 3 × 3 × 4 × 2. Indicate how many factors each study includes, levels of each factor there are, and cells (different conditions) the study has.

4. What do the terms *main effect* and *interaction* mean? How does the statistical analysis for a factorial design calculate the marginal means for a main effect?

5. What is an E × N design, and how does using it affect the ability to make causal inferences?

6. Suppose the mean scores for pessimism in each cell of a 2 × 2 factorial study were 15.0 and 49.2, respectively, for young and old females and 17.5 and 21.8 for young and old males, and the ANOVA revealed a significant interaction and main effect of age. Draw a graph of the means and describe the interaction effects in words.

7. For the example in question 6, explain how these results affect the external validity of the findings.

8. How can ceiling and floor effects lead to finding a significant interaction?

9. Look back at Figure 9.8d and explain why it would be a good idea to interpret the interaction before interpreting the outcome for the main effects of weight status and hunger cues.

10. Using the study by Schachter and Gross (1968), describe how research can find very interesting results, even when there are no significant main effects.

11. Define the term *mixed factorial design* and illustrate how the study by Fisher et al. (1989) qualifies as one.

12. Describe the research by Dewing and Hetherington (1974), and indicate how it is an example of an all-dependent-groups factorial design.

13. Describe the ANOVA procedures for analyzing data from a 2 × 2 factorial with all independent groups and with mixed or all dependent groups.

14. After performing an ANOVA for a factorial design, what other additional statistical procedures do researchers typically need to do, and why?

RESOURCES

BOOKS, CHAPTERS, AND ARTICLES

Keppel, G. (1991). *Design and analysis: A researcher's handbook* (3rd ed.). Englewood Cliffs, NJ: Prentice Hall.

Tabachnick, B. G., & Fidell, L. S. (2001). *Computer-assisted research design and analysis.* Boston: Allyn & Bacon.

Winer, B. J. (1962). *Statistical principles in experimental design.* New York: McGraw-Hill.

INTERNET SITES

http://trochim.human.cornell.edu This Website has links to information about design issues discussed in this chapter. You may have used this site for Chapter 7 or 8.

http://www/ruf.rice.edu/~lane/stat_sim/index.html This Website is the Rice Virtual Lab that gives statistics tutorials on topics that include ANOVA and chi-square. You may have used this site for Chapter 7 or 8, but it also applies here. Click on *ANOVA* and then *Two-way ANOVA*.

APPLICATION ACTIVITIES

APPLICATION 9–1: INTERPRETING ANOVA OUTCOMES

Earlier in this chapter, we discussed a student's 2 × 2 factorial study of the effects of social influence and gender-specific tasks on conformity among female participants in making estimates in a survey of the cost of a haircut (with blow dry). For the gender-specific factor, half of the surveys had the participants estimate the cost for a man and half for a woman. For the social influence factor, the researcher forged the names and high estimates of males as the first three "participants" for half of the surveys; the rest of the surveys had no prior entries. The mean cost estimates the participants gave with and without social influence (prior entries) were, respectively, $17.36 and $12.16 for a man's haircut and $33.48 and $24.76 for a woman's haircut. Graph the means and decide whether you think the main effects and interaction were significant in the ANOVA (two of the *F* values were significant). Then describe in words what the study found.

APPLICATION 9–2: ANOVA GRAPHICAL INTERPRETATION

Suppose researchers studied the effect of arousal on the ability of adults to complete puzzle tasks of different difficulty. The participants were randomly assigned to two arousal conditions: *high*, in which the were given a pharmaceutical that acts as a stimulant (such as, caffeine), and *low*, in which they were given a sedating drug. Each participant was asked to solve two puzzles, one that was *simple* and one that was *complex* in counterbalanced orders. The mean amounts of time (in minutes) to solve the puzzles under the high and low arousal conditions, respectively, were 2.2 and 14.2 for the simple puzzles versus 13.8 and 2.6 for the complex puzzles. Draw a graph of these means and answer the following questions.

a. Pooling the data across puzzle complexity, what was the mean solution time for the *high-arousal* and *low-arousal* participants?

b. Pooling the data across arousal, what was the mean solution time for the *simple* puzzle and the *complex* puzzle?

c. Do you think an ANOVA would find a significant *main effect* of arousal? If so, describe it.

d. Would an ANOVA find a *main effect* of puzzle difficulty? If so, describe it.

e. Would an ANOVA find an *interaction?* If so, describe it; if not, say why you think so.

APPLICATION 9–3: ANOVA MATRICES

a. Suppose you conducted a 2 × 4 factorial study on sexual bias in language. The independent variables are gender (male and female participants) and four words that refer to women—*gal, girl, lady,* and *woman.* You have the participants fill out a survey rating their degree of liking of the words. Construct a matrix of the design and list each of the main effects and interaction(s) the ANOVA would test.

b. Suppose you did the same study, except that you added a third independent variable: words that refer to men—*guy, boy, gentleman,* and *man.* Describe the factorial with the appropriate numerical code. Then construct a matrix of the design and list each of the main effects and interaction(s) the ANOVA would test.

APPLICATION 9–4: INTERPRETING AN ANOVA SUMMARY TABLE

Suppose we did a 2 × 2 factorial study on the self-esteem of high-school students, with the independent variables of grades (high versus low GPA) and year in school (freshmen versus seniors). Scores on the test of self-esteem could range from a low of 10 to a high of 30, and the respective means for the students with low and high grades were 15 and 16 for the freshmen versus 12 and 23 for the seniors. From the following ANOVA summary table, determine what the analysis did and did not find to be significant. Then make a conclusion about each of the main effects and the interaction.

Source	Sum of squares (SS)	df	Mean square (MS)	F	Sig. (p)	Eta squared
Corrected model	431.93	3	143.98	11.85	.001	
GRADES	141.18	1	141.18	11.62	.001	.11
YEAR IN SCHOOL	2.67	1	2.67	.22	.638	.00
GRADES * YEAR	288.08	1	288.08	23.71	.001	.20
Error (within-groups)	1166.40	96	12.15			
Total	1598.33	99				

CHAPTER 10

PREPARING TO CONDUCT A STUDY

Plan the Variables, Design, and Subject Characteristics
Identify the Research Topic and Hypotheses
Determine the Types of Subjects and Availability
Identify How to Manipulate, Select, and Assess Variables
Identify Potential Research Strategies, Designs, and Analyses

Maximize Internal and External Validity
Identify Potential Unwanted Variance Sources and Controls
Identify Limitations on Generalization

Evaluate Ethical Issues
Identify Possible Ethical Risks and Plan Debriefing
Design an Informed Consent Procedure
Submit a Proposal for IRB Approval

Conduct a Trial Run
Do a Pilot Study
Revise the Design

Plan Data Analyses
Specify All Hypotheses
Identify Appropriate Statistical Tests

Finalize the Method and Prepare to Collect Data
Obtain and Set Up Materials and Facilities
Recruit, Assign, and Schedule Subjects
Prepare to Conduct the Procedure

We've seen in prior chapters that researchers can examine the links between independent and dependent variables with a wide array of methods, designs, and strategies. Planning the strategy, method, and design for a study is a complex process, and performing the research takes a good deal of preparation and organized effort. This chapter is designed to help you in this effort by integrating concepts you learned in prior chapters to form step-by-step instructions you can use in preparing to carry out a research project.

To clarify the preparation process, I've selected a research project we've seen before, mainly in Chapter 9, to use as a continuing example in this chapter because it includes a rich variety of methods. The study was conducted by Cynthia May and her colleagues (1993) and examined the effects of time of day on the performance of young adults and elderly adults in a task of reading short stories. Prior research had found that individuals differ in the time of day when they perform best, such as in cognitive tasks. Some people perform best in the morning and are called *morning types,* but others do best later in the day and are called *evening types.* Many people know and can report which types they are. Our earlier descriptions of the May et al. research simplified the project by focusing only on the elements that were relevant to our needs at the time. But now we'll need to consider the full research project. For one thing, the research consisted of two studies, not just the one we discussed:

- *Study 1,* which we did not consider before, used a descriptive strategy. It simply tested with a survey the extent to which 210 young adults (ages 18 to 22 years) and 91 elderly adults (ages 66 to 78 years) were morning types or evening types. The results showed a clear age difference: the scores on the survey indicated that none of the elderly adults were moderately or definitely evening types, and few of the young adults were morning types.
- *Study 2* was a 2×2 factorial with two age levels and two times of testing (about 8:30 A.M. and 4:30 P.M.). This study examined the role of these factors on people's speed of reading 10 short stories and memory of specific statements in the stories. The stories and memory tests were presented on a computer. Our prior discussions of this study dealt only with reading speed as the dependent variable.

Although I haven't yet indicated why the project had two studies or given details of their methods and designs, the decisions the researchers made with respect to these issues will unfold as we use this project as an example of the planning and preparation involved in doing research. In some cases the researchers could describe their decision-making processes explicitly in the research report, but space constraints in journals limit how much detail they can provide. When details were not spelled out, we will infer the processes on the basis of clues in the report or usual research practice.

We will describe the preparation process in roughly chronological order, going through two phases: proposal development and consolidation. The *proposal development phase* starts with initial planning to decide on the research topic, the types of subjects to test, the variables to examine, and appropriate research designs. It also includes steps the researcher can take to maximize the study's internal validity, external validity, and ethical standards, and it culminates in submitting a proposal to an Institutional Review Board (IRB). The *consolidation phase* involves debugging the research procedures, identifying the statistics to use to answer the questions posed in the hypotheses, finalizing the method, and setting up the data collection.

PLAN THE VARIABLES, DESIGN, AND SUBJECT CHARACTERISTICS

The *proposal development phase* in preparing to conduct research consists of a sequence of nine activities that are outlined in Table 10.1, with questions under each activity that form a checklist you can use as you design a study. The chapter numbers at the end of each question indicate where in this book you can find more information about the issue. Each activity in the table corresponds to a

TABLE 10.1

Checklist of Activities for the Proposal Development Phase in Preparing to Conduct a Study (and textbook chapter where the issue is discussed)

A. Identify the Research Topic and Hypotheses
  (1) Have you examined your own or others' beliefs for topic ideas? (Chapter 2)
  (2) Did you search for and consult relevant theories? (Chap. 2)
  (3) Have you searched the relevant literature fully? (Chap. 2)
  (4) What hypotheses have you identified; are they testable and falsifiable? (Chap. 2)
  (5) Are the hypotheses consistent with prior beliefs, theories, and findings? (Chap. 2)

B. Determine the Types of Subjects and Availability
  (1) Will you need human or animal subjects, and what characteristics must they have? (Chap. 2)
  (2) Are subjects likely to be available, and can you get enough? (Chap. 2)
  (3) Can you equate the groups and get demographic data for each subject? (Chap. 5)

C. Identify How to Manipulate, Select, and Assess Variables
  (1) Can you manipulate the independent variable(s)? (Chaps. 1, 5)
  (2) Will the independent variable(s) be nonmanipulated, such as a subject variable? (Chap. 6)
  (3) How can you assess and maximize differences between levels of the independent variable(s)? (Chaps. 5, 6)
  (4) How can you assess the dependent variable(s)? (Chap. 4)
  (5) How will you ensure assessments are reliable and valid? (Chaps. 4, 6)

D. Identify Potential Research Strategies, Designs, and Analyses
  (1) Do any of your hypotheses state a causal relationship between variables? (Chaps. 2, 5, 6)
  (2) Will the research strategy be experimental, quasi-experimental, correlational, or descriptive? (Chaps. 1, 2, 5, 6)
  (3) Should the design include a control group? (Chaps. 5, 7)
  (4) Will the design assess the dependent variable repeatedly to examine differences in the independent variable? (Chap. 8)
  (5) How many data groupings will the design have? (Chaps. 4, 6–9)
  (6) What statistical test(s) can you use to evaluate the main hypotheses? (Chap. 4)

continued

TABLE 10.1 (CONT.)

Checklist of Activities for the Proposal Development Phase in Preparing to Conduct a Study (and textbook chapter where the issue is discussed)

E. Identify Potential Unwanted Variance Sources and Controls
   (1) Will you need to use deception, blind procedures, unobtrusive assessments, or automated data collection to prevent participant or observer bias? (Chaps. 3, 4, 5)
   (2) Will the design need a placebo control group? (Chap. 7)
   (3) How will you create and maintain equal groups? (Chap. 5)
   (4) Will subjects be treated identically except for the independent variable? (Chap. 5)
   (5) How will you control extraneous variables by holding conditions constant or balancing? (Chap. 5)
   (6) Will you need to counterbalance for order effects? (Chaps. 8, 9)
   (7) How will you reduce error variance? (Chaps. 4, 5)

F. Identify Limitations on Generalization
   (1) Will the types of subjects limit the study's external validity? (Chap. 2)
   (2) Will the setting, measures, or time of testing limit the study's external validity? (Chap. 2)
   (3) Does evidence suggest that the continuity assumption is warranted? (Chap. 2)

G. Identify Possible Ethical Risks and Plan Debriefing
   (1) Are there possible physical or psychological risks to subjects that violate APA or USDHHS guidelines? (Chap. 3)
   (2) Can possible risks be eliminated? (Chap. 3)
   (3) Will you provide debriefing? (Chap. 3)

H. Design an Informed Consent Procedure
   (1) Will the study require informed consent? (Chap. 3)
   (2) Should each participant or someone else provide the needed consent? (Chap. 3)
   (3) Will the informed consent procedure use a form that includes all of the features outlined in Box 3.1? (Chap. 3)

I. Submit a Proposal for IRB Approval
   (1) Is it likely that the study will be exempt from IRB review, or will it require a full review or an expedited review? (Chap. 3)
   (2) Have you prepared a research proposal and submitted it to your supervisor (instructor) and IRB? (Chap. 3)

heading for a following section that describes how to carry out that activity. For instance, the title of the next section you'll read is "Identify the Research Topic and Hypotheses," which is the first activity in the table.

IDENTIFY THE RESEARCH TOPIC AND HYPOTHESES

We can generate ideas for research topics and hypotheses by using several sources. One source is the beliefs and notions people develop through their general experiences and knowledge. Researchers often discover ideas by scanning their memories, or an idea is stimulated by an event, such as something they experience or see on TV or by material they read in a book. Second, theories provide a rich source for research ideas and hypotheses. Using a theory as the basis for a study organizes the research program and enhances the value of the research. Whenever possible, link your research hypotheses to one or more theories. Third, the scholarly literature, particularly journal articles, provides a source for research topics and details about the methods to use, such as the best way to measure a variable. Search the literature of the topic of interest fully.

The sources for our topics usually help us clarify our hypotheses, and scholarly articles and books should enable us to determine whether the hypotheses are testable and falsifiable. The hypotheses we develop should be consistent with the beliefs, theoretical predictions, and prior research findings in the literature that form the basis for them. If these sources indicate, for instance, that people should perform better under one reward condition than another, our hypothesis should reflect that relationship.

DETERMINE THE TYPES OF SUBJECTS AND AVAILABILITY

The topic of the research usually affects the types of subjects to test, especially whether they will be humans or animals. But many other decisions about the subjects must also be made, such as their age, sex, cultural background, past experiences, and usual behavior patterns, such as being highly anxious or aggressive. A study on emotions in rats might want to use only young animals that typically behave in an anxious manner. If possible, equate the groups at the start of the research.

In planning a study, we should also determine whether the subjects we will need are easily available in the quantities we'll need. Remember that having too few subjects in a study reduces the power of the statistical analysis and likelihood that it will find a significant difference between conditions. You can get a rough idea of the number of subjects needed by looking at the numbers used in similar or related research. If the subjects we'll need are not available, the study is not feasible. For example, if we want to do a study comparing students in first and fourth grades but cannot get a school to give permission to test them, the study cannot be done, at least in a school. If you use human participants, plan to collect information on demographic variables—especially *age, gender,* and *racial/ethnic background*—even if you are not studying them as independent variables. You'll need that information for the Participants section of the research report.

If your study uses a survey, have the participants give the desired demographic information as part of the questionnaire. But keep in mind that assessing people's racial or ethnic background isn't always as easy as it sounds. A fill-in-the-blank approach can produce illegible answers and combinations, such as "Hispanic and Creole," that you may not know how to classify. Having respondents choose from a list one racial or ethnic background with which they identify most can avoid these problems, but the wording of the items—for example, "Hispanic" versus "Latino," can make a difference in the way people classify themselves (Kirnan, Bragge, Brecher, & Johnson, 2001).

IDENTIFY HOW TO MANIPULATE, SELECT, AND ASSESS VARIABLES

A basic and critical decision is whether the independent variable(s) will be manipulated or nonmanipulated. By using a manipulated independent variable, researchers can control wanted and unwanted systematic variance effectively and use an experimental strategy, allowing them to make causal inferences from the results. Most manipulated independent variables belong to one of four categories: environmental, instructional, task or activity, or invasive variables. A manipulation check can help determine whether an independent variable will have its intended effect. Nonmanipulated independent variables are usually subject variables—such as age, gender, and behavioral or personality characteristics of the participants; we select and assign individuals to groups on the basis of these characteristics. We can maximize the influence of a manipulated or nonmanipulated independent variable by making sure its levels are markedly different from each other.

How can researchers measure behavioral and personality characteristics, either as independent or dependent variables? They can use observations of *overt behaviors,* such as with measures of performance correctness or speed; *covert behaviors,* such as with self-report (survey) or physiological measures; and *remnants* of behavior, such as with archival data. For some types of observation, researchers will need special equipment, such as a polygraph. If the measure will be used to establish the independent variable in a study of group differences, we will need to separate the scores into different levels, such as with the median-split or extreme-groups methods. Regardless of the approach we use for assessment, we should find evidence of its reliability and validity before we use it and provide that evidence in our research report. (Go to **Box 10.1**)

Box 10.1   FINDING AN EXISTING QUESTIONNAIRE

Although researchers sometimes construct surveys specifically for a study they plan to do, they rarely "reinvent the wheel" when suitable instruments have been developed and are available. Existing instruments have usually been tested for reliability and validity, and that evidence typically can be obtained from published research reports. The research described in this chapter's opening story provides an example: The researchers used the Morningness-Eveningness Questionnaire to measure the extent to which the participants were morning or evening types. They stated in their research report (May et al., 1993, p. 326) that:

> Psychometric assessments have shown the questionnaire to have good reliability (Buela Casal, Cabalo, & Cueto, 1990; Smith, Reilly, & Midkiff, 1989), and scores on this test have been shown to correlate with circadian [day–night] variations in oral temperature, sleep-wake behavior, and periods of perceived alertness and performance (Buela Casal, Cabalo, & Cueto, 1990; . . . Smith, Reilly, & Midkiff, 1989).

The correlations with circadian variations constituted construct validity assessments. The May et al. report did not give the actual psychometric data that were provided in the cited references, but it is usually good practice to do so. For example, when saying that the instrument has "good reliability," the researchers could have added that the Smith et al. study found a Cronbach's alpha (internal consistency) of .82, which is pretty strong. If more than one survey is available, the researcher usually makes a choice based mainly on the degree of reliability and validity of the instruments and their length. But sometimes other factors, such as the wording of the items or the cost (some surveys are copyrighted and must be purchased), influence the decision.

How can we find instruments and psychometric data to consider for research we are planning? There are at least five ways:

1. College libraries often have books that are collections of existing surveys, each with citations for primary sources: the original article and psychometric evaluation studies. These books are secondary sources (a few such books are listed in the Resources section at the end of this chapter). If the survey information in the secondary source looks promising, we can get copies of the primary sources.

2. Hard copy directories (such as *Mental Measurements Yearbook* and *Test Critiques*) in most college libraries provide reviews and lists of primary sources for large numbers of instruments.

3. Online databases allow us to search for tests and get information about them. See the Internet sites listed in the Resources section at the end of this chapter.

4. Research reports we gather in our literature search will specify the tests they used and give references to primary sources for the tests and psychometric studies, as May et al. (1993) did.

5. Once we have the names of one or more tests that seem promising, we can search for them in PsycINFO by typing the name of the test in the search window. If we know the year the test was developed, we can limit the search to that far back—otherwise, we'd search as far back as we can. Then we'd look for some of the earliest references to the test because one or more of the early journal articles will probably have the full survey and psychometric data; later articles often have simply used and cited the test.

Finding the full survey we want to use and studies with psychometric data for it usually requires doing more than one or two of these procedures. Keep two cautions in mind when searching for a questionnaire: always *get the primary sources* for a test and its psychometric data and *use instruments with evidence of good reliability and validity* whenever possible. Remember the adage, "Garbage in, garbage out."

IDENTIFY POTENTIAL RESEARCH STRATEGIES, DESIGNS, AND ANALYSES

To identify research strategies to use, we would begin by examining our hypotheses to see whether any states a causal relationship between the independent and dependent variables. If a hypothesis states a causal inference, we will need to use an experimental strategy to test it. But if the study will not meet the criteria for cause-effect (covariation of variables, causal time sequence, and elimination of other possible causes), we must change the hypothesis and use a quasi-experimental, correlational, or descriptive strategy. Using an experimental strategy almost always requires a design with a control group that is equated with the experimental group at the start of the study. We can equate groups by using random assignment in an independent-groups design or using matching or repeated measures in a dependent-groups design.

If the research will use an intrasubject design (see Chapter 11), the data analysis is likely to use graphical rather than inferential statistical procedures. For all other studies, the type of research strategy, design, and statistical tests to use can be determined by applying the answers to questions in Table 10.1 while consulting Table 4.1 and Figure 7.1 (see inside back cover). When planning the statistics, keep in mind that parametric tests (those applied with interval or ratio data) are more powerful than nonparametric tests, and if the design is a factorial, parametric statistics (ANOVAs) provide a much more complete and integrated data analysis than nonparametric tests. Whenever possible, collect the data for dependent variables with interval or ratio, rather than nominal or ordinal, measurement.

MAXIMIZE INTERNAL AND EXTERNAL VALIDITY

When we do research, we want to design it so that the outcome will answer the question underlying the hypothesis as clearly and unambiguously as possible. Having a low degree of internal validity undermines that goal.

IDENTIFY POTENTIAL UNWANTED VARIANCE SOURCES AND CONTROLS

We saw in Chapter 5 that variance in the data that results from the different levels of the independent variable is desirable, but systematic variance from extraneous variables and nonsystematic (error) variance are not. Extraneous variables threaten the internal validity of the research and confound the findings, making the conclusions of the study unclear. Excessive error variance is a problem because it reduces the likelihood of finding statistically significant results, thereby increasing the chances of making a Type II error.

Identifying confounding variables and controlling them are two of the most important activities we can perform in preparing to conduct research. Some extraneous variables in the design to check for are

- Nonequivalent groups
- Differential attrition
- History and maturation
- Regression to the mean
- Pretest sensitization
- Participant bias (demand characteristics and social desirability)

- ■ Observer bias
- ■ Order effects

To design a study with as little confounding as possible, researchers need to consider each of these potential problems carefully (see the material on these issues in Chapters 5 and 8). They must think objectively and systematically about the planned design and ask themselves, "Could any of these problems occur in this study?"

The 2 × 2 factorial study (May et al., 1993) in the opening story of this chapter that tested the effects of time of day on the reading and memory performance of young versus elderly adults used several methods to control extraneous and error variance in the data. Let's look at some of these methods. First, one of the factors in the study was age. Because age is a nonmanipulated subject variable, the two age groups may have differed in other ways. For example, the young adults were introductory psychology students, and the elderly adults were community volunteers for research on aging. To provide evidence that the older group's cognitive ability was probably similar to the younger group's, the researchers noted that the older group had, on average, nearly 17 years of education and a high mean score on a standardized test of verbal ability. By making sure that both groups consisted of people with high intellectual ability, the researchers accomplished two things: they eliminated the possible extraneous variable of reading ability as a cause if the main effect of age were significant and reduced error variability by decreasing individual differences. In addition, the researchers:

- ■ Held constant, across age and time of day conditions, the length and other aspects of the stories by having all participants read the same 10 stories, each with about 250 words.
- ■ Counterbalanced the order in which the stories were presented by using two different orders and making sure that half of the participants in each cell of the factorial matrix had one order and half had the other.
- ■ Balanced the time of day condition across age by testing half of each age group in the morning and half in the late afternoon.
- ■ Balanced the number of incorrect and correct memory items the participants judged and the order in which the items were tested.

To see why this last method for controlling extraneous variables was included, we need to describe the way the participants' memory was tested. Immediately after reading all the stories on a computer, a testing session began in which the participants were asked to recognize whether each of 60 sentences had been in the stories they read. For each story, three sentences were taken word for word and three were fabricated in content and style to look like they were real ones. Testing for each story's sentences occurred in the same order that the stories appeared originally. These balancing methods eliminated the chance that memory would be affected by different numbers of correct and incorrect sentences or the order of the story testing.

IDENTIFY LIMITATIONS ON GENERALIZATION

The greater the external validity of a study's results, the farther they will generalize, such as to subjects with different characteristics and to different settings and time periods. We saw in Chapter 2 that research results often generalize broadly—for instance, the findings on the same topics from research in laboratories and in real-life settings are usually very similar. Even across species, the results of research are often similar. As an example, we'll consider the research, briefly mentioned in Chapter 1, which showed that rats quickly learn to avoid the tastes of foods eaten before getting sick (Garcia & Koelling, 1966). This type of learning has also been demonstrated in other animals, such as cats, birds, and monkeys (Garcia, Hankins, & Rusiniak, 1974), and in human cancer patients, who often become nauseated when they receive chemotherapy treatment (Sarafino, 2002). But not all findings and phenomena generalize well. For example, many psychological processes are different in people who differ in age or sex, and some phenomena, such as attitudes, change markedly over time.

How can we decide how far our results are likely to generalize? Remember from Chapter 2 that researchers usually apply a continuity assumption: that the processes they study are similar across subjects and testing circumstances unless there are reasons to assume otherwise. Two approaches may help us in deciding the likely continuity of our results. First, we can apply logic—does it seem reasonable to assume that the results would be similar with different subjects and circumstances? Second, our literature search may reveal results like those we expect that were found in prior studies with a variety of subjects and circumstances, suggesting that the continuity assumption may be warranted.

EVALUATE ETHICAL ISSUES

Psychologists are obliged to follow specific ethical guidelines for the treatment of human and animal subjects and for reporting research outcomes. The American Psychological Association (APA) and the United States Department of Health and Human Services (USDHHS) have issued ethical codes to serve as guidelines for researchers. Because most psychology research is conducted with people, we will focus here on ethics in research with human participants.

IDENTIFY POSSIBLE ETHICAL RISKS AND PLAN DEBRIEFING

The APA guidelines for research with human participants are designed to protect people who take part in psychology studies. These codes view as potential ethical problems the:

- Risk of physical or psychological harm to participants
- Use of deception
- Violation of privacy
- Failure to maintain anonymity of participants
- Breaches of confidentiality

- Use of coercion
- Failure to use informed consent procedures

Informed consent from the participants is usually required, but can be omitted if the research uses archival data, anonymously filled out surveys on nonsensitive topics, or observations of public behavior that is neither private nor of a sensitive nature. Debriefing is commonly offered to participants and must be provided if the research uses deception or could produce psychological discomfort.

DESIGN AN INFORMED CONSENT PROCEDURE

The procedure for informed consent involves presenting relevant information about the research experience and obtaining the person's written consent to participate. Usually the person reads the information and signs an informed consent form, the elements of which are given in Chapter 3 (Box 3.1). Figure 10.1 gives an example of an informed consent form for a study on gender differences in being able to identify songs from brief (3-second) clips played either with or without some background static. Notice in the form that it does not state the independent variables (gender and static), but describes what the experience will be like.

SUBMIT A PROPOSAL FOR IRB APPROVAL

The last steps in the proposal development phase when preparing to do research involve preparing a proposal and seeking IRB approval to carry out the study. We saw in Chapter 3 that some research is exempt from IRB review, and other research will require a full review or an expedited review. Even if no IRB review is needed, you may still need to prepare a proposal to submit to your instructor before collecting data. Writing a proposal will enable you to organize your ideas better and get useful feedback from your instructor and, perhaps, other students about the procedures you intend to use.

The studies that are exempt from IRB review are essentially the same ones for which informed consent can be omitted because they present virtually no risk of harm or discomfort to participants. In terms of projects that students are likely to perform in a research methods class, those exempt from IRB review would probably include studies involving the use of archival data; educational tests, surveys, or interview procedures; and observations of public behavior. But *to qualify for this exemption, two conditions must exist:*

- The data must be anonymous.
- If somehow data were disclosed that could be linked to a participant, the disclosure would not result in legal difficulties, impaired financial or employment status, or marred reputation for that person.

Most other studies that research methods students might do would require some level of IRB review. To qualify for an expedited review, the study must

---

STUDY ON ABILITY TO IDENTIFY SONGS

DESCRIPTION

This study is being conducted by a psychology student [*name*] under the supervision of Professor [*name*] in the Psychology Department of [*college name*]. If you have questions or concerns about it or your participation, you can reach us at [*phones, e-mail addresses*].

     The research you are asked to participate in will examine the ability to identify popular songs that you've almost certainly heard on the radio or in recordings in recent years because they were big hits. If you participate, you'll listen to very brief clips from 50 hit recordings and be asked to write the name of each song. To be correct for any song, you must give its exact title *OR* give the name of the recording artist and a few words from the song that were not in the clip.

     The study will be conducted in the Social Science Building, Room B18. We will contact you to schedule an appointment. Participation will take about 30 minutes. No information to identify you will be collected on the testing materials, and all information we gather from your participation will be kept strictly confidential. At the end of testing, you will be offered an opportunity to talk about the purpose of the study and to ask questions.

     If you come to the testing and complete at least part of it, you will receive credit to satisfy the research requirement in your introductory psychology course. Remember that you can satisfy the research requirement with another study or with an alternative activity, as indicated in your course syllabus. Please feel free to decline to take part in this study or, if you feel uncomfortable during the testing for any reason, to discontinue participating at any time. There is no penalty for withdrawing.

AFTER READING THE DESCRIPTION, IF YOU AGREE TO PARTICIPATE, FILL IN THE FOLLOWING ITEMS:

1. I agree to participate: _____ _____
                                               Signature   Date

2. After all participants have been tested, I would like to receive an e-mail giving a brief summary of the results (circle):   NO   YES: e-mail address _____

3. _____ _____
          Introductory psychology instructor's name   Class meeting day/time

---

FIGURE 10.1

An example of an informed consent form for a hypothetical study on factors that influence the ability to identify songs from short clips.

present no more than minimal risk of harm or discomfort to participants. All studies that pose more than minimal risk must receive a full IRB review.

     Seeking IRB review requires that the researcher submit a proposal describing the purpose, methods, and expected results of the study. The prior steps in the proposal development phase should provide all the needed information. Although there is no standard format or structure for a research proposal, it is basically a brief, preliminary version of a research report (which we described in Chapter 2), without actually having collected or analyzed data. (Go to **Box 10.2**)

Box 10.2   A RESEARCH PROPOSAL'S CONTENT

We will consider a format for research proposals that can work well, but you'll need to get direction from your own instructor about his or her requirements. A proposal for an undergraduate research project can usually be about three or four double-spaced pages in length, plus an appendix with drafts of materials, such as surveys. The body of the proposal should contain six sections:

1. *Preliminary Title.* Compose the title you think you'll use for the final report.

2. *Purpose.* This section should describe the problem to be studied, the independent and dependent variables (with clear descriptions of each), the research and theoretical bases (with citations of references) for the project, and the hypotheses you have identified.

3. *Proposed Method.* This section should include five types of information, usually in the following order. First, state the research design and strategy you plan to use (see Figure 7.1, inside back cover). Second, give the number and characteristics of the subjects you intend to test, along with a description of their availability. Third, describe the materials, such as surveys or word lists, and any apparatus you expect to use. If you will use existing surveys, give data for their reliability and validity. Drafts of all materials you will use should be appended. Fourth, describe in detail the procedure you plan to use to test subjects, indicating exactly what they will experience and how the independent and dependent variables will be manipulated or assessed. Fifth, indicate where the testing will occur.

4. *Ethical Issues.* State ways by which you will comply with ethical guidelines, such as by using informed consent procedures, collecting data anonymously, and offering a debriefing session. Describe possible ethical violations, such as the use of deception, and present as strong a justification as you can for retaining them in the design (the IRB will need this information).

5. *Anticipated Analysis and Outcome.* Specify the statistical methods you expect to use to evaluate the main hypotheses and the expected findings and implications of the study.

6. *References.* Give all references cited in the preceding sections of the proposal, listing them alphabetically by the authors' names (see Appendix A for the typing format).

CONDUCT A TRIAL RUN

After receiving approvals to conduct the research, we can begin the *consolidation phase* to debug the research procedures and finalize plans for data collection and for the full statistical analysis to test our hypotheses. This phase consists of seven activities that are outlined in Table 10.2, with questions under each activity that

TABLE 10.2

Checklist of Activities for the Consolidation Phase in Preparing to Conduct a Study (and textbook chapter where the issue is discussed)

A. Do a Pilot Study
   (1) Have you obtained the needed materials and facilities to pilot the procedure?
   (2) How much time did the testing take?
   (3) What problems with the materials or procedure did you find?
   (4) If you included a manipulation check, what did it reveal? (Chap. 5)
   (5) Will the subjects need practice trials for the test; how much time will that require?
   (6) Is the range of scores restricted, such as with ceiling or floor effects? (Chaps. 6, 9)

B. Revise the Design
   (1) How can you revise the materials or procedure to solve the problems found in the pilot study?
   (2) If the range of scores is restricted, can you find a different task or measure?

C. Specify All Hypotheses
   (1) Does each hypothesis describe an association between variables or a difference between conditions or groups? (Chap. 4)
   (2) If you do a factorial study, do you have specific hypotheses for each main effect and interaction? (Chap. 9)

D. Identify Appropriate Statistical Tests
   (1) Which descriptive statistics are planned? (Chap. 4)
   (2) Which statistical tests will you use for the main analyses? (Chaps. 4, 6, 7, 8, 9)
   (3) Which secondary analyses (follow-up, effect size, etc.) are you planning to do? (Chaps. 6, 7, 8, 9)

E. Obtain and Set Up Materials and Facilities
   (1) Have you arranged for an appropriate place and the equipment to conduct the study for the full time of the research?
   (2) Have all the changes been made to the materials and procedure?
   (3) Have you determined and practiced the scoring criteria and procedures?
   (4) Are all instructions and materials typed up clearly and completely?
   (5) Will you have a sufficient supply of materials to complete the study?

F. Recruit, Assign, and Schedule Subjects
   (1) Is the sampling method you'll use likely to produce a representative sample?
   (2) Have you determined how many subjects are needed, and are they available?
   (3) How will you assign subjects to conditions; if the study is quasi-experimental or descriptive, will you equate groups for demographic variables? (Chaps. 5, 6)
   (4) Have you made a chart to schedule participants to testing sessions?
   (5) Did you get information to contact (e-mail, phone) participants to remind them of their appointment for testing?

G. Prepare to Conduct the Procedure
   (1) Did you contact the participants to remind them of their appointments?
   (2) Before each testing session, have you checked equipment function and organized all materials?
   (3) Has needed informed consent and demographic data been obtained?
   (4) OK, smile and be courteous—it's show time!

form a new checklist you can use for the remainder of your preparation to conduct a study. Unlike the checklist for the proposal development phase, many of the items do not have chapter numbers because the answers do not need explanation. As before, each activity in the table corresponds to a heading for a following section that describes how to carry out that activity. One of the first activities in this phase is to do a trial run to determine how long the testing procedure will take for each subject and to identify problems that haven't been anticipated.

DO A PILOT STUDY

A **pilot study** is a trial run of the full procedure with subjects that will not be included in the actual study. For our examples, let's assume we are doing a research project like the one by May et al. (1993) on adults' reading speed and memory of stories presented on a computer. But our project will test in the morning and afternoon only one age group, 30- to 40-year-olds, half of whom are morning types and half are evening types. This would be a 2 (time of testing) × 2 (morning–evening types) factorial. Let's also assume that the participants for the actual study will be tested at work during break periods at their desks via the Internet in two sessions, one to determine their morning–evening type and one to test reading speed and memory with the story task.

For the pilot study, we might have several friends at college participate with their own computers. They would fill out the Morningness-Eveningness Questionnaire in one session and do the story task in the second session. By doing this, we can see if there are any problems in the procedure. We could ask them in advance to look for typos and any unclear instructions. By watching their performance or having them think out loud as they work, we can see if they seem to be misinterpreting questions or if they may need a few practice trials to get the hang of the task. We can also interview them after. If we include a manipulation check, we may be able to see if the independent variable had the intended effect. And from the data they provide in the questionnaire or story task, we can see whether the range of scores on the dependent variable is restricted and practice our skills at scoring the data. There's a lot of valuable information to be gained from pilot studies.

REVISE THE DESIGN

Using information from the pilot study and feedback from our proposal, plan the needed changes to the research design, materials or apparatus, and procedure. If the changes will be substantial, we may want to do another trial run, perhaps with fewer participants.

PLAN DATA ANALYSES

We already touched on the issue of statistical analysis in the proposal development phase, but the decision we made was tentative and limited to only the main analyses. Now that the design is firmed up, we are ready to generate a full plan for our data analysis. There are at least two reasons to plan the analysis in advance. First, we need to make sure a statistic is available to test each hypothesis. For example, if we do a factorial study that has one or more main dependent variables measured on nominal or ordinal scales, we'll find no nonparametric statistic that will give a complete and integrated analysis of the main effects and interaction. That would be distressing, right? Second, we should choose our statistical significance level (alpha, which is usually .05) in advance. If we know we will do many statistical tests, such as correlations or *t* tests, in a single study, we may need to apply the Bonferroni adjustment (see Chapter 7) to make the alpha level more stringent and reduce the risk of Type I error.

SPECIFY ALL HYPOTHESES

To identify the statistical tests to use, we'll need to write out clearly and specifically each and every hypothesis we plan to test. Hypotheses that predict an association between variables will need different tests from those that predict a difference between conditions or groups. Each hypothesis will require a statistical analysis. When researchers have more than two data groupings in a study, they usually test more than one hypothesis. If the study will use a factorial design, the researchers should have a hypothesis for each main effect and interaction tested in the analysis.

IDENTIFY APPROPRIATE STATISTICAL TESTS

Some initial decisions to be made relate to choosing the descriptive statistics, which are usually the mean and standard deviation for parametric analyses of data measured on interval or ratio scales. If we have nominal or ordinal data, we cannot use parametric analyses and would not calculate means and standard deviations; instead, we'd simply give frequency counts or percentages for each category in the design.

The Main Analyses

A study's main analyses are done to support or refute the hypotheses that reflect the most prominent or important reasons for conducting the research. To select an appropriate test to analyze the data, we'd use Table 4.1 (see inside front cover) as we've done before and answer a series of questions, narrowing our search to smaller and smaller portions of the table:

1. *Is the purpose of the test to assess relationships or assess differences?* If the purpose of the analysis is to assess relationships, we'd use only the upper portion of the table for the remaining questions, but if the purpose is to assess differences, we'd use the lower portion.
2. *Are the data on an interval or ratio scale, or on a nominal or ordinal scale?* For data assessed on an interval or ratio scale, we'd use a parametric statistic; for nominal or ordinal data, we'd need a nonparametric statistic. Thus, within the portion of the table we chose above (upper or lower), we'd now limit our consideration to only the rows corresponding to parametric or nonparametric statistics.
3. *Does the analysis involve only two data groupings, or more than two?* Staying within the chosen rows, we'd narrow our focus further. If the analysis has only two data groupings, we'd focus only on the rows corresponding to "2"

groupings; but if the analysis has more than two data groupings, we'd consider only the rows for "> 2."

4. *Are the groupings of scores paired—that is, do we have a dependent-groups design?* If we do, we'd look only at the row(s) corresponding to "Yes" to find the appropriate test; if we do not have paired scores, that is, we have an independent-groups design, we'd focus on the "No" row(s). Note that some rows are designated "Yes/no," which means that the statistical test, *t* or ANOVA, has different versions for independent- and dependent-groups designs.

Chapters 7, 8, and 9 describe the different versions of *t* and ANOVA statistics, and Figure 10.2 provides a diagram to identify the specific version of each of these tests to use. The diagram shows that the choice depends on the number of independent variables (factors), number of levels of the factor(s), and whether the analysis has all independent groups or at least one dependent-groups factor.

Secondary Analyses

In addition to the main analyses, researchers typically do secondary analyses, including effect size estimates for each test in the main analyses and, after an ANOVA, follow-up tests: post hoc comparisons or contrasts. Other secondary analyses may be done to test for group equivalence—for example, to show that the groups did not differ significantly on an important variable, such as age or a

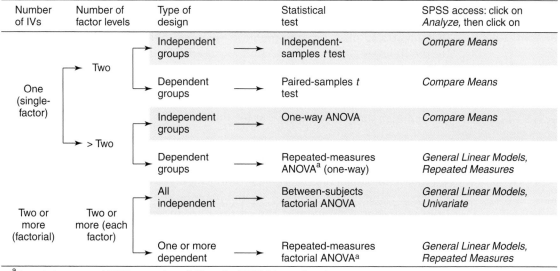

Number of IVs	Number of factor levels	Type of design	Statistical test	SPSS access: click on *Analyze,* then click on
One (single-factor)	Two	Independent groups	Independent-samples *t* test	*Compare Means*
		Dependent groups	Paired-samples *t* test	*Compare Means*
	> Two	Independent groups	One-way ANOVA	*Compare Means*
		Dependent groups	Repeated-measures ANOVA[a] (one-way)	*General Linear Models, Repeated Measures*
Two or more (factorial)	Two or more (each factor)	All independent	Between-subjects factorial ANOVA	*General Linear Models, Univariate*
		One or more dependent	Repeated-measures factorial ANOVA[a]	*General Linear Models, Repeated Measures*

[a]Repeated measures ANOVAs are only available on the SPSS Advanced version.

FIGURE 10.2

Diagram to identify the appropriate *t* test or ANOVA to perform, depending on the number of independent variables (IVs, or factors), the number of levels of the factor(s), and whether the analysis involves a dependent-groups design. See Appendix B for SPSS instructions.

specific trait—or other confounds. For these secondary analyses, effect size estimates are usually not required.

Another purpose for doing a secondary analysis is to see if a manipulation check demonstrated the intended effect of an independent variable. This approach was used in a 3×2 factorial study we considered in Chapter 9 on the effects of the attractiveness of a female criminal and the type of crime she committed on the prison sentence people thought she should receive (Sigall & Ostrove, 1975). As a manipulation check, the researchers had the participants rate her attractiveness on a 9-point scale from the photograph they saw. The mean ratings for the attractive and unattractive photos were, respectively, 7.53 and 3.20 (high ratings = attractive), and an ANOVA revealed that this main effect was significant, confirming the intended effect of the independent variable. The main effect of type of crime and the interaction were not significant.

FINALIZE THE METHOD AND PREPARE TO COLLECT DATA

The last steps in preparing to conduct a psychology study involve getting all materials and procedures ready for collecting the data and arranging for subjects to be available and assigned to the research conditions.

OBTAIN AND SET UP MATERIALS AND FACILITIES

Several very important activities must be completed to get the materials and procedures ready for testing sessions. First, we must make sure as early as possible that any special place or equipment we will need to test subjects will be available for the full time of the study. Second, we need to make all revisions to the materials and procedure that we planned and practice implementing them. Third, we should type up all instructions for participants that we will either read to them or have them read. It's best not to "wing it." Last, we should make sure we have enough materials to carry out the entire study.

RECRUIT, ASSIGN, AND SCHEDULE SUBJECTS

Arranging for subjects to be available and assigned to conditions is the next step in doing a study. When animals are the planned subjects, researchers buy them from professional suppliers or breed the ones they have in their colony. We'll focus on acquiring human participants and assigning them to groups because these processes are usually somewhat more complicated.

Sampling

The process of recruiting and selecting subjects for research is called **sampling.** How do psychologists recruit people for a study? One approach you may be familiar with at your college is a *participant pool,* consisting mostly of introductory psychology students who are required or offered an incentive to take part in the research enterprise. In other cases, researchers recruit participants by knocking on doors of a dorm, using entire classes in school or college, advertising for volunteers in the general community, putting materials and advertisements on the Internet, and getting the support and help of organizations, such as clubs. These are some of the more common methods researchers use to recruit participants.

The way researchers structure the sampling process can have implications for the external validity of the results of their studies. When researchers plan a study, they want to be able to generalize its findings to a *target population,* a large set of individuals that they are interested in and from which they recruited the *sample.* The ability to generalize to the population can depend on the degree to which the sample is *representative* of the population—that is, it is typical of or mirrors the population's characteristics. But we've seen that researchers usually assume that the processes they are studying are similar across subjects and testing circumstances unless there are reasons to assume otherwise; this is called the continuity assumption. So, having a sample with characteristics that mirror those of the target population is not always a critical issue.

When does having a representative sample matter? We'll consider two important factors, with the first being the variables examined. Although the relationships between variables—whether causal or correlational—are usually similar across large segments of the general population, they can be very different across unlike cultures, genders, and people of different ages. Studying cognitive variables offers a good example: Cognitive skills improve dramatically from birth to early adolescence, are fairly stable in adulthood, and then may decline in old age. So, if we study cognitive variables among adults and hope to generalize the findings broadly to adults, we probably won't need a sample with ages and other characteristics that mirror those of the target population. But if we want our results to generalize to all age groups, we'd want to make sure that the sample includes appropriate proportions of children, adults, and elderly people.

The second factor that determines the need for a representative sample is the study's research strategy. We've discussed four research strategies: experimental, quasi-experimental, correlational, and descriptive. Studies using a descriptive strategy are more likely to require a representative sample than research using the other strategies. Large-scale surveys are often designed to describe one or more characteristics of a population, such as their sociopolitical attitudes or their psychological status. For this type of purpose, a representative sample is essential. For example, Goodman and her coworkers (1997) conducted a survey of psychosocial factors in the lives of American 9- to 17-year-olds and their parents. The sample of youths was similar to the national population in age, gender, and ethnic representation. As part of the study, the researchers looked at the data for 535 youths with diagnosed mental disorders to describe differences in psychosocial factors between those that had (13% of the sample) and had not received psychological treatment in the past year. Prior research had used only youths with therapy to describe factors in the lives of youths with psychological disorders. Goodman et al. found that the youths with disorders who did and did not receive treatment differed in several important ways, such as in their ethnic backgrounds and parental monitoring of their behavior. Thus, data on youths with mental disorders that come from research samples of youths in therapy may not be representative of or generalize to the population of all youths with mental disorders, at least for some research topics.

Probability Sampling

In **probability sampling,** participants are recruited in such a way that the odds of any one individual being chosen from the population are known and can be calculated. Thus, if we want to select 100 people from a population of 10,000, and each person has an equal chance of being chosen, we'd know in advance that the odds of any particular individual being chosen would be 1 in 100. Probability sampling procedures usually start with a *sampling frame,* a list of all individuals from which the sample will be drawn. Ideally, the sampling frame will consist of all members of the target population. There is more than one form of probability sampling, but all of them involve a random selection process in some way and, as a result, are likely to produce a representative sample if the number of people who are willing to participate is fairly large. We'll consider three of these forms.

In the most basic form of probability sampling, called **simple random sampling,** each individual in the population has an equal and unbiased chance of being selected. A straightforward way to perform simple random sampling is to write the names of all members of the sampling frame on separate bits of paper, put them in a large box, and select the number we need in an unbiased manner, usually blindfolded. Researchers often use some variation of this procedure. Suppose we wanted a simple random sample of 100 students living in the 1,000 dorm rooms at a particular college; we could put in a box all room numbers for all of the dorms (the sampling frame) and select from those. Or if the room numbers are already available on a printed list, we could choose in a random way one number near the top of the list (among the first 10) and then every tenth room from that point on. Even better, we'd use random numbers, like we did for random assignment in Chapter 5, to make the selections. Keep in mind that if we sample from dorms, we may not be able to generalize our findings on some topics to students living elsewhere. Once again, we could consider whether the continuity assumption is warranted.

Another form of probability sampling is **stratified random sampling,** in which the sampling frame is separated into critical segments before random sampling to ensure that the sample will contain the right proportions of these subgroups. This is a very useful approach if researchers suspect or know in advance that relevant differences are likely to exist among specific segments of the population and want to compare people from those segments. Stratified random sampling involves three steps: separate the sampling frame into "strata," or subgroups; decide the overall sample size and the proportion that should come from each subgroup; and then apply methods of simple random sampling to select the number of individuals needed from each subgroup.

The third form of probability sampling is called **cluster sampling** and begins by identifying a large number of "clusters" (or units) of individuals who have a feature in common, such as being members of the same classroom, organization, or neighborhood. The researcher then randomly selects some of those clusters and attempts to recruit all individuals in each cluster. Thus, suppose we wanted to conduct a study of first-year high school students throughout a large school district and needed a representative sample. We could make a list of all of the homeroom classes, randomly select some of those, and ask all the students in those classes to participate. Researchers tend to use cluster sampling when they cannot construct a sampling frame, such as if the population is huge, or when research procedures would be more efficient if the participants were tested in groups or nearby.

There are two other issues to keep in mind with any of these sampling methods. First, some people we contact to participate will refuse, so researchers often identify a larger number of people to contact than they'll need. Second, there is some possibility that one or more segments of the population will not be as willing or as able to participate as others, which could reduce the representativeness of the sample. For example, people in some socioeconomic groups may be more difficult to contact because they work more hours, have no phone, or have an unlisted number. And if we can contact a representative set of people, some segments may be unwilling to participate because they have less time or find the topic of the study unappealing or even offensive, as might happen in research on attitudes or general behavior relating to political or sexual issues. Researchers need to consider these possibilities if the representativeness of the sample is important. (Go to **Box 10.3**)

Nonprobability Sampling

In **nonprobability sampling,** the researcher cannot identify a sampling frame or estimate the likelihood of any individual from the target population being included in the sample. As a result, the sample is not likely to be representative, or mirror the characteristics, of the population from which it is drawn.

Perhaps the most common sampling procedures in psychological research apply nonprobability methods—mainly **convenience sampling,** a method in which researchers ask for qualified volunteers who are easily available, without making an effort to mirror the population's characteristics. Examples of convenience sampling procedures include requesting volunteers in college classes, dorms, or radio or newspaper advertisements and at worksites or meetings of a club or religious organization. The recruitment procedure is more haphazard than it is random, or unbiased. To illustrate how asking for volunteers can produce a biased sample, think about this common situation: a student organization invites students to send e-mails of ratings of their instructors, which are tallied and listed on an Internet site for prospective students to consult. Who will volunteer? Most will surely be students who liked or disliked a particular instructor a great deal or simply felt it was their duty to respond. These data may be useful for prospective students, but the sample is not representative of the population: all students of that instructor.

Regardless of which sampling method is used, researchers should *specify clearly in the research report the approach they used, the sample's demographic characteristics, and the distribution of these characteristics in the study's groups or conditions.* With this information, other researchers can tell whether the sample was representative of the population and the groups were equal in critical ways. This is why it is important to collect demographic information on each participant.

Box 10.3 **USING RANDOM NUMBERS IN RANDOM SAMPLING**

Suppose we'll need 80 participants from our sampling frame with the names and e-mail addresses of 673 college seniors, but we decide to randomly sample 90 to contact in case some refuse. Random numbers provide a very good basis for random sampling and can be obtained in two ways: by a *computer program* and from a *table of random numbers*. Although computer programs can generate random numbers in Excel and SPSS, a freely accessed online program called *Randomizer* (listed in the Resources section at the end of this chapter) is especially easy to use. You simply fill out a form indicating how many numbers you want (we'd want 90) and the numerical range (1–673 for our example), and it produces a list of random numbers—in a sorted order if you request it!

A table of random numbers, like the one in Appendix B, is a list of randomly generated digits arranged in rows and columns—we will use a brief version (following) that I've reproduced from Chapter 5 to examine how to use the numbers to obtain a random sample. The procedure will have five steps:

1. Assign the numbers 01 to 673 to the individuals in the sampling frame.
2. Decide in advance the number of digits to use as a "unit"—it should be the same as the number of digits in the total number in the sampling frame, in this case, three.
3. Decide the path you'll follow (such as going left to right along rows or up to down along columns), and arbitrarily select a starting point in the table. I've chosen to go across the rows from left to right, starting at 901 (in boldfaced font), and continuing to the succeeding rows.

				Columns				
Rows	**1–3**	**4–6**	**7–9**	**10–12**	**13–15**	**16–18**	**19–21**	**22–24**
1	760	289	415	345	762	**901**	385	847
2	069	321	852	316	709	412	079	864
3	354	053	782	916	342	178	056	985
4	671	430	296	872	413	590	237	694
5	501	806	384	197	239	741	802	656

4. Starting at 901, follow the path, looking at each unit of three digits. Units that fall between 01 and 673 qualify as being in the sampling frame, and I've underlined the 21 shown in this brief table. (Most full tables of random numbers are much longer and have enough digits to do the whole procedure.) We bypass units numerically larger than 673 and any duplicates of ones already used, continuing this search until we have the number of units, 90, we need. At that point, the search ends.
5. After identifying the needed units, find the corresponding numbers in the sampling frame and contact the individuals. If too many of them refuse to participate, we can go back to the table of random numbers and take up where we left off to select more.

How Many Subjects?

Two of the most common questions of research methods students are, "How many pages should the report be?" and "How many subjects do I need?" We'll deal only with the latter question here, and the answer is like a Goldilocks judgment: not too few, and not too many. How can we know how many subjects would be "just right?" Of course, students doing research methods projects often face practical constraints, such as the amount of time they can spend testing subjects and the number of individuals available.

In terms of research design, the most critical issue in determining how many subjects to test is the *power* of the statistical analyses we will apply. If we have too many subjects, we'll have too much power and a heightened risk of incorrectly rejecting the null hypothesis (Type I error). If we have too few subjects, we'll have too little power and a heightened risk of making a Type II error. Either of these two circumstances gives an unfair test of the hypothesis. Researchers can use two approaches to decide the sample size they need to achieve fairness or balance. First, they can consult the literature to determine the number of subjects in prior studies with similar topics and research designs (remember that within-subjects designs have more power and require fewer subjects than between-subjects designs). This can be a simple approach, but often not the best one. Second, they can calculate the sample size needed after making three decisions (Cohen, 1988; Tabachnick & Fidell, 2001):

- The *alpha* level to use in the statistical analysis, which is typically .05.
- The *power* they want for the analysis; .80 is a commonly recommended, but some say overly stringent, level.
- The *effect size* they expect for the variables in the study. Here, they can consult prior research with similar variables to see the effect sizes they found. If the effect sizes are not given (journal articles published before 2001 rarely have them), researchers can calculate those statistics using the formulas in this book.

Although researchers can plug these data into formulas and calculate by hand the number of subjects needed or hunt for sample size tables in statistics books, computer programs are available to do the task more easily. For example, one program called *PiFace* can be accessed on the Internet for free (see the Resources section at the end of this chapter). In any event, keep two practical recommendations in mind: the actual sample size need not be close to the number estimated, and it's best to err on the high side because effect size statistics will show if the effect is small when the analysis had too much power.

Assigning and Scheduling

We can assign participants to the research conditions by random assignment, matching, or repeated measurement to reduce the likelihood of nonequivalent groups. If we are using a quasi-experimental strategy for our research, we should try to balance the groups for as many characteristics as possible, especially demographic variables. Regardless of the method of assignment to conditions, we should try to *make the number of subjects as similar as possible in all groups* because very unequal numbers impair the power of the statistical analysis.

We can organize the scheduling of participants by constructing a chart to keep track of the time slots—those already taken and those still available—for testing, the participants' names, and the condition in which each will serve. We can also write on the chart the scheduled participants' e-mail addresses or phone numbers so we can remind them of their appointments the day before. Reminder contacts greatly reduce the incidence of no-shows and lateness. Using a scheduling chart has another value: we can decrease the chances of a scheduling confounding by making sure that the testing sessions are evenly distributed across times of the day and weeks of the semester. For example, Evans and Donnerstein (1974) found that college students who volunteered to participate early in the term had significantly higher scores on college entrance exams and a test of internal locus of control (people's belief in their ability to influence events in their lives) than those who participated later.

PREPARE TO CONDUCT THE PROCEDURE

If you reminded the participants of their appointment, they'll probably be there. Make sure you are, too! In fact, be there early enough to check that the equipment functions properly and that the materials are organized and ready to use. If you haven't already carried out the informed consent procedure and collected the demographic information, do these activities as soon as each participant arrives. Follow all procedures exactly as they were designed, holding constant for all participants all details of the situation except for variations in the independent variable. Be courteous throughout the session and thank each person for his or her participation.

SUMMARY

Preparing to conduct research requires organized planning and effort. The process consists of many activities that occur in sequence, grouped into two broad phases: proposal development and consolidation. The proposal development phase begins by identifying the research topic and hypotheses, the types of subjects to be tested, and ways to manipulate and assess variables. The activities in this phase then move on to planning the research strategy and design, identifying ways to maximize internal and external validity, and examining the plan for ethical risks. The last steps in this phase involve writing a proposal and submitting it to the research supervisor (instructor) and IRB for approval.

The consolidation phase begins with conducting a pilot study to determine how long the testing will take and identify unanticipated problems. The planning then moves on to specifying hypotheses and appropriate statistical analyses. Many activities are involved in setting up the materials and testing process and in recruiting and assigning subjects to conditions. To recruit subjects, researchers apply sampling procedures that are classified into two types. Probability sampling methods include simple random sampling, stratified random sampling, and cluster sampling. Nonprobability sampling includes convenience sampling. Probability sampling methods involve a random selection process that enhances the likelihood of selecting a sample that is representative of the population. To decide how many subjects to test, researchers can use a number comparable to that used in similar prior studies or calculate the number on the basis of the desired alpha level, the expected statistical power, and the anticipated effect size.

KEY TERMS

pilot study	simple random sampling	cluster sampling
sampling	stratified random	nonprobability sampling
probability sampling	sampling	convenience sampling

REVIEW QUESTIONS

1. Describe the two studies in the research project by May et al. (1993) on the effects of time of day on the cognitive performance of young and elderly adults.
2. Why is it important to collect information on the demographic characteristics of each participant?
3. Describe three sources for finding suitable survey instruments for research.
4. How do researchers decide how far the findings of studies generalize?
5. Describe the content of a research proposal.
6. What are *pilot studies,* and why are they useful?
7. Outline the procedure for selecting appropriate main and secondary statistical analyses.
8. Define each type of probability and nonprobability sampling approach presented in the text.
9. How can you determine how many subjects to test?

RESOURCES

BOOKS, CHAPTERS, AND ARTICLES

Beere, C. A. (1990). *Gender roles: A handbook of tests and measures.* New York: Greenwood Press.

Goldman, B. A., & Mitchell, D. F. (2003). *Directory of unpublished experimental mental measures.* Washington, DC: American Psychological Association.

McDowell, I., & Newell, C. (1996). *Measuring health: A guide to rating scales and questionnaires.* New York: Oxford University Press.

Robinson, J. P., & Shaver, P. R. (1990). *Measures of personality and social psychological attitudes.* Ann Arbor, MI: Survey Research Center, Institute for Social Research.

INTERNET SITES

http://ericae.net Website of the ERIC Clearinghouse on Assessment and Evaluation that gives a long list of instruments if we type the topic, such as "self-esteem," in the search window of the "Test Locator."

http://www.randomizer.org A program that provides tutorials for performing random sampling and assignment and generates lists of random numbers for these processes.

http://www.stat.uiowa.edu/ftp/rlenth/PiFace This Website has a shareware program (PiFace) that works as an add-in module for Microsoft Excel to calculate the number of subjects needed for a study.

http://www.unl.edu/buros This Website of the Buros Institute of Mental Measurements has links to thousands of social science tests.

APPLICATION ACTIVITIES

APPLICATION 10–1: WRITING AN INFORMED CONSENT FORM

Write an informed consent form for Study 1 of the May et al. (1993) project.

APPLICATION 10–2: WRITING A RESEARCH PROPOSAL

Suppose you had been among the May et al. (1993) research team when they planned Study 2 of their project and were asked to write three sections of the research proposal: the proposed method, ethical issues, and anticipated analysis and outcome. Write a draft of those sections.

APPLICATION 10–3: USING A TABLE OF RANDOM NUMBERS FOR SAMPLING

Use the table of random numbers in Appendix B to select a simple random sample of 15 students from a population of 90 undergraduates.

CHAPTER 11

INTRASUBJECT RESEARCH: SMALL-N DESIGNS

PROLOGUE

Think about the last time you got outwardly angry, such as about another person's behavior. Your reaction probably consisted of three dimensions: a *cognitive* component that involved thoughts about, for instance, the person's intentions or unfairness; a *somatic* component with bodily feelings of nervousness or tension; and a *behavioral* component consisting of verbal or physical attack.

Cognitive–behavioral theories in psychology describe this process and suggest ways to reduce people's excessive anger behavior with methods designed to manage each of the three components.

Raymond Novaco (1977) applied a cognitive–behavioral framework to design a program of methods to reduce the anger of a 38-year-old man who was in a psychiatric hospital for severe depression and displayed excessive anger behavior, which he had also shown at work, home, and church. As an example, at home or church, the triggers often involved his children's unruly behavior, and he'd respond impulsively in a physical manner or verbally—such as saying, "I'll knock your goddamn head off." In the first phase of the research, data were collected to determine the frequency and intensity of the man's anger without yet introducing the program to reduce it. This phase lasted only 1 week because of hospital constraints on patients' length of stay. The program was then applied throughout the second phase, until the man's anger was dramatically reduced and stable after $3\frac{1}{2}$ weeks.

The program had two parts: (1) teaching the man about the nature of anger, such as its triggers, early signs of tension and provocation, and differences between justified and unjustified anger and (2) teaching him skills to think about and react differently to triggers. The skills included training in relaxation techniques and alternative thoughts to substitute for angry ones when signs of provocation begin. The design incorporated many dependent variables to measure the man's overt anger behavior before and during the program, and each measure included simultaneous ratings by a clinical psychologist and a psychiatric nurse during observation periods. By having two observers at a time, the researcher could assess interobserver reliability, as we'll see later. The outcome was presented graphically, which showed that his initial high levels of anger declined fairly consistently to zero while his low levels of coping and relaxed appearance increased markedly during the program.

This description presents the full study, which because it had only one participant, is an example of an *intrasubject*—also called *single-subject, single-case,* or *small-N*—research design. The term **intrasubject design** refers to research that manipulates an independent variable and examines its effects on the behavior of a single individual or, at most, a few, usually over time (Hilliard, 1993). If the study has more than one participant, the researcher examines and reports the data for each individual separately, rather than grouping them and presenting the means. Because the data for individuals are kept separate in intrasubject research, data analysis typically involves careful inspection of graphs, rather than inferential statistics, such as *t* tests or ANOVA. When research methods students hear that studies can be done in which they would only test one participant and not do statistical computations, some of them think, "That sounds quick and easy—I'd like to do that type of study for this course." Intrasubject research is not quick and easy to do. Most studies that use intrasubject designs require the researcher to spend huge amounts of time observing each participant over many weeks. And many small-*N* studies in psychology require testing the participant in very tightly controlled conditions with sophisticated equipment, which may take many hours just to configure to the specific need of each study.

With this chapter, we begin the last part of the book and examine several applied, descriptive, and advanced methods that are used less commonly in psychology research than the other methods we've considered so far. Because these types of research appear in the literature fairly often, you may come across them in journal articles. But students in a first course on research methods seldom perform them for two reasons. First, instructors often prefer to have students focus on the more common methods and designs. Second, the applied, descriptive, and advanced methods we'll discuss are often too complex or time consuming for students to do in an introductory-level course. In the present chapter, we'll examine the origins and varieties of intrasubject designs and their advantages and disadvantages. Then we'll consider how researchers analyze the data and evaluate the outcomes from single-subject studies.

ORIGINS OF INTRASUBJECT RESEARCH

To convey how psychologists' use of intrasubject designs began, we'll draw together historical information from prior chapters. In the mid-to-late 1800s, psychology and philosophy were separating, research in psychology was just beginning, and Galton was formulating his concept of correlations. Mathematicians had not yet developed inferential statistics—such as the Pearson's *r*, *t* test, and ANOVA—and this situation would remain well into the 1900s. Because psychology researchers had no way to analyze the results of studies with groups of subjects, they studied and analyzed the data from single individuals, often with introspection procedures in which people would pay close attention to and report their sensations and perceptions under specific stimulus conditions. Let's look briefly as some examples of early psychology research in which data from single subjects were examined without the aid of statistics.

STUDIES OF LEARNING AND MEMORY

In the late 1800s, Ebbinghaus (1885/1964) conducted one of the earliest and most thorough investigations ever done of learning and memory, using himself as the only participant in a series of studies. He described his procedure for some of the studies as follows: they occurred in

> 1879–80 and comprised 163 double tests. Each double test consisted in learning eight series of 13 syllables each . . . and then relearning them after a definite time. The learning was continued until two errorless recitations of the series in question were possible. The relearning was carried to the same point; it occurred at one of the following seven times—namely, after about one third of an hour, after 1 hour, after 9 hours, one day, two days, six days, or 31 days. (pp. 65–66)

As you can gather from this description, the procedure required hours of memorization. By examining data presented in 15 tables on the time it took him to learn or relearn each list of syllables, he was able to show that the amount of forgetting that occurs between learning and relearning sessions increases as the time between them increases.

Another early study of learning that used an intrasubject design was conducted with cats. Thorndike (1898) placed cats, one at a time, in an apparatus called a "puzzle box" that had a latch that would open a door, enabling the animals to leave the box. The cats were hungry and could see food placed outside. By observing each cat's actions very carefully, he noticed two aspects of their behavior that were consistent across cats. First, they seemed more interested in gaining release to escape confinement than to get food. Second, their behavior appeared to follow a pattern of "trial and error" across trials—that is, the time it took each cat to escape decreased gradually from trial to trial. They didn't seem "discover" a solution. Even after several successful escapes, the cats would not run to and trigger the latch immediately but seemed to trigger it eventually while exploring or engaging in other activities.

Our last example of early intrasubject research on learning is the well-known and ethically problematic research by Watson and Rayner (1920/2000) in which they taught an infant named "Little Albert" to fear a white rat. As we saw in Chapter 3, the procedure for a trial involved presenting the rat together with a loud noise that was produced by striking a metal bar with a hammer. Two trials occurred on one day, and several more a week later. Once the fear was learned, the researchers tested its persistence periodically over the next several weeks.

Each of these studies tested one or more subjects across many trials and then examined and reported the behavior for each individual separately, rather than grouping them and calculating means.

STUDIES OF PSYCHOPHYSICS

Research in psychophysics examines the functional relations between physical stimuli and individuals' perceptions of and reactions to them—for example, to determine the minimum intensity of a specific tone for a person to hear it. Psychologists began to study psychophysics in the late 1800s. An example is the work in Germany of Fechner, who developed the basic psychophysical measurement techniques, such as the method of limits, that we discussed in Chapter 4 (Woodworth & Schlosberg, 1965). Using these techniques, he discovered, for instance, that when people experience two equal stimuli in a row, such as in lifting two equivalent weights, and are asked to estimate the magnitude of the second one relative to the first, they tend to overestimate the second stimulus. In the equal-weights example, they claim the second one is heavier. Fechner's studies were intrasubject designs that tested and examined the data for one participant at a time. Some studies in psychophysics today use similar methods and research designs.

CASE STUDIES

A **case study** is a type of research in which a trained professional prepares a systematic biography of a person that can be constructed from records of the participant's history, interviews with a variety of people, and current observations of the person's behavior. Although case studies rarely involve the manipulation of variables, they can be viewed as a type of small-N research because each one pertains to a single individual. Usually, the data they produce are qualitative, rather than numerical, and give a description rather than test a hypothesis. For example, a case study described an abused girl who was discovered in adolescence after being isolated and tied to a chair for most of her life (Curtiss, 1977). Extensive efforts to teach her language skills produced only modest gains.

Case study research can offer useful illustrations and is fairly common in clinical psychology today: It may describe someone with an unusual disorder, a case that contradicts common notions, or a new finding about a common disorder, such as an unusual background for the person or a new treatment method.

Although case studies usually lack control over extraneous variables, making the outcomes difficult to interpret, the information they contain often serves as a source for hypotheses to test with other research methods that offer more opportunities for control to reduce confounding. (Go to **Box 11.1**)

Box 11.1   CASE STUDY OF JOHN'S SEX REASSIGNMENT

In the late 1960s, surgeons performed a routine procedure on an 8-month-old boy's penis, but an accident occurred, and his penis was destroyed. This type of accident occurs very rarely, and the consensus of experts on the course of action to take at the time was to change the child's sex by a process called sex reassignment. To change a boy to a girl involves performing plastic surgery to make a vagina, giving hormone treatments, and raising the child as a girl. The boy's parents consented to these procedures and changed his name to a girl's. Like prior similar cases, follow-up assessments over several years indicated that the child was adjusting well.

In the mid-1990s when the child was an adult, Diamond and Sigmundson (1997) decided to do a long-term follow-up because they had learned that the adjustment had failed: the girl (who they called Joan) was a boy (John) again. After consulting medical records and interviewing the parents and child, they wrote and published a case study on him. Although early assessments suggested Joan was adjusting well, the parents had seen some signs even then that the sexual reassignment wasn't working:

> Girl's toys, clothes, and activities were repeatedly proffered to Joan and most often rejected. Throughout childhood Joan preferred boy's activities and games. . . . Ignoring the toys she was given, she would play with her brother's toys. She preferred to tinker with gadgets and tools, dress up in men's clothing, and take things apart to see what made them tick. . . . Joan did not shun rough and tumble sports or avoid fights. . . . The brother often refused to let Joan play with his toys, so she saved her allowance and bought a truck of her own. (p. 299)

Also, despite not having a penis, she would often stand to urinate, even in restrooms at school. At the age of 12, Joan was required to take estrogen hormones but disliked them because they made her "feel funny," so she'd discard her doses. Eventually, things came to a head when she refused to comply with the medical procedures, began having suicidal thoughts, and prodded her father until he tearfully described what had happened in the early years. The sexual reassignment was then reversed, and by 16 years of age Joan was John again. At the time the case study was conducted, his reconstructed penis did not function quite normally, but he was married to a woman and had adopted her children.

This case study has important implications, and we'll mention two. First, contrary to prior evidence, sexual reassignment methods do not always work well. Second, babies are probably not psychosexually neutral at birth—they seem to be predisposed to some degree to relate to their worlds as a male or female from the start.

STUDIES IN COGNITIVE NEUROSCIENCE

Researchers in *cognitive neuroscience* study the connections between cognitive functions, such as thinking and memory, and physiological processes in the brain. One commonly used approach to study these connections combines case study and experimental methods by comparing the cognitive performance of an individual known to have a brain disorder with that of nondisordered control participants. For example, Moscovitch, Winocur, and Behrmann (1997) conducted 19 experiments, each comparing the performance of a young man, "CK," who had suffered a brain injury in an accident, with control participants. The report describes CK's everyday behavior and functioning in some detail, as a case study would. The tasks involved recognizing famous people from photographs, some of which were altered by adding glasses, for instance, or inverting them. CK's performance was at least as good as that of the control participants at recognizing the people when the faces were upright, even if they were altered in minor ways. But when the faces were inverted or changed markedly, such as with the top and bottom misaligned, his performance was much more impaired than that of the controls. The researchers interpreted the pattern of performance differences between CK and the controls as lending support to some theories of face and object recognition, but not others.

PROS AND CONS OF INTRASUBJECT RESEARCH

Although the great majority of studies in psychology use large sample sizes—that is, more than, say, 20 subjects—small-N designs have some advantages and can be more appropriate than large-sample designs for several types of research problems and situations. Let's look at the advantages of intrasubject designs first, and then consider their disadvantages.

ADVANTAGES OF SMALL-N DESIGNS

Intrasubject designs provide an especially rich set of data about a behavior that is difficult to achieve with large-sample designs for practical reasons. For example, small-N designs are often used to examine behavior intensively—that is, in great detail and over a long period of time—which may be prohibitively time consuming or expensive to do with many subjects. In addition, the availability or cost of subjects may restrict the number of them a researcher can use. For instance, the topic of a study may require animals that are difficult or expensive to obtain or people who have a rare characteristic or disorder, as in the case study we discussed of sex reassignment.

Often intrasubject designs are simply more appropriate than large-sample designs for certain research goals, and we'll discuss three examples. First, if the purpose of a study is simply to demonstrate the existence of a characteristic or phenomenon, as in the sex reassignment case study, a small number of subjects, or just one, may be all that is necessary. Second, if the purpose of a study is to show that a new and untested approach for treating a disorder may have value, a small-N design may be the most reasonable and efficient approach to accomplish the goal. Novaco's (1977) research on reducing a man's anger in the opening story of this chapter is an example of an intrasubject study with this goal. Third, in some types of research, such as in psychophysics, individual differences among participants may be so small and the degree of control of extraneous variables is so strong in the laboratory setting that a small number of participants may be all that is needed to find the expected outcome. Using a large sample in this situation would be inefficient and provide too much power if analyses with inferential statistics are planned.

Another advantage of intrasubject designs is that the individuals' scores are not masked within or misrepresented by group averages, as can occur with large-sample designs. By grouping data and calculating means, researchers run the risk that the data will describe a process or relationship that does not exist in any individual (Sidman, 1960). To see what this means, think back to Thorndike's (1898) study on cats learning to escape from puzzle boxes. He placed each cat in a box and recorded the time it took to escape. Now look at the graph in Figure 11.1a, which presents hypothetical data for the mean speed with which five cats escaped from a box for each of 10 trials. Although Thorndike did not average his data, if he had, he'd have found a similar function: Escape time decreases gradually and consistently across trials. OK, but the question is, does that function describe what each subject did? The answer is, "Not necessarily." Let's see why.

Look again at Figure 11.1, but focus on the two data sets, (b) and (c). Notice that the means for the two data sets are identical and are the same as those in the graph, which shows that either data set could have produced that same graph. Now let's examine the data for the individual cats, starting with the upper set (Figure 11.1b). In that set, escape times fluctuate for any cat across trials, sometimes going up and sometimes down, but the overall trend is down.

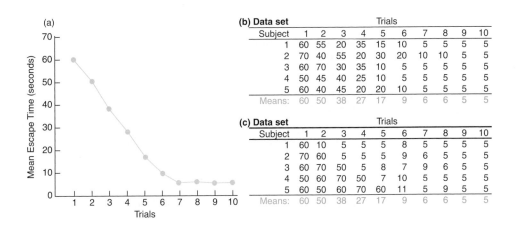

FIGURE 11.1

Illustration of the way grouping individual data can mask or misrepresent the processes studied. The data are hypothetical for five cats, showing their escape time from a puzzle box, and are presented as a graph of the means, (a), and as two possible data sets, (b) and (c), that could have produced those means.

Thorndike's data for individual cats showed this pattern, which suggests they were learning in a gradual, trial-and-error manner, as he concluded. But an alternative view of learning is that it can involve arriving at an "insight" or a discovery of a solution, and the lower data set (Figure 11.1c) illustrates the type of pattern in the cats' escape times we'd expect if this process were correct. Notice that for each cat, escape time plummets all of a sudden and never goes up much from there, which would suggest that each cat discovered the solution. The reason the means for these data produced a gradual decline in the graph is that the plummet occurred in different trials for different cats. If the cats' learning had involved insight, this graph of the means would mislead us to think otherwise. Although Thorndike's results support the view of learning as a gradual process, other intrasubject research with animals and humans has shown that learning can also involve insight, with sudden solutions (Woodworth & Schlosberg, 1965).

DISADVANTAGES OF SMALL-*N* DESIGNS

The most commonly sited disadvantage of intrasubject research is that because only one or a few subjects are studied, there is the possibility of limited external validity, or ability to generalize the findings to a larger population of individuals. This concern has lessened over the years as research demonstrated fairly consistently that the results from small-*N* designs generalize to other people very well for the types of variables investigated with these methods, partly because the variables studied are usually potent, or have strong effect sizes (Kazdin, 2003). Researchers typically consider the likely potency of the variables and generality of the findings before they decide to use an intrasubject design.

Perhaps the most serious disadvantage of intrasubject designs is their difficulty in examining interaction effects, particularly with respect to subject variables, because only one or a few participants are tested (Kazdin, 2003). For example, in the study that opened this chapter on reducing a man's anger, would the effect of the therapy be as strong with women or with individuals of different ages? The therapy's effects are likely to be similar across demographic groups—that is, they'd generalize—but would they reduce anger the same amount in all of those groups? This is a potentially important question, but most single-subject designs can't answer it.

The case study method is a special type of single-subject research and has two additional disadvantages. First, in case studies that report the outcome of therapy or some other intervention, it is difficult or impossible to control for or rule out observer bias. For example, the person who administers the therapy is typically the researcher and observer, and that therapist is likely to believe the intervention will work and have expectations of the behavior changes he or she will see. In this type of case study research, interpretations of the client's behavior are typically based entirely or mainly on the therapist's subjective impressions. Second, case studies generally cannot control for or rule out the effects of extraneous variables, particularly the effects of history, maturation, and regression to the mean. As a result, these studies cannot lead to cause–effect conclusions. But as mentioned earlier, the outcomes can provide the basis for subsequent research that can apply tighter controls.

No single research method can answer all of the types of questions psychologists ask in designing studies, and each method can have a valuable place in scientific efforts to understand behavior. The task of researchers is to choose the most appropriate methods for each study's goals and situation.

BEHAVIOR-ANALYSIS RESEARCH

The topics in psychology that are most likely to be studied with intrasubject designs are in the field of *behavior analysis,* which B. F. Skinner pioneered in the 1930s. Studies in behavior analysis examine the role of learning processes, especially operant conditioning, in the development of behavior. Although studies in behavior analysis often use large-sample designs, most employ small-*N* designs (Kazdin, 2003; Sarafino, 2001). Because of the greater emphasis on intrasubject designs in behavior analysis than in other fields of psychology, we'll focus the rest of our discussion of small-*N* research on the topics, designs, and methods commonly used in that field. But keep in mind that the same designs and methods can be used to study other topics.

OPERANT CONDITIONING

The term *operant conditioning* refers to a learning process in which behavior is changed by the consequences of that behavior. The responses acquired through this learning are called *operant behaviors* because they "operate" on the environment, thereby producing consequences. Skinner (1938, 1953) distinguished between behavioral consequences of two types: reinforcement and punishment. When the consequence that is contingent on a behavior is *reinforcement* (or reward), it produces an increase in the behavior, but when it is *punishment,* it produces a decrease in the behavior.

All behaviors we perform produce consequences, regardless of whether we are consciously aware of them. When we type a word correctly on a computer, there are consequences, such as seeing the correctly typed word on the monitor and being able to move on. We don't really pay much attention to these reinforcing events, but they are there. Our behaviors also have *antecedents,* cues that precede and set the occasion for our action. When driving a car and approaching a traffic light, if it is red, we depress the brake pedal, and if it is green, we depress the gas pedal. The light is the antecedent for our behavior. Our learning to make the correct responses to specific antecedents leads to reinforcement and helps us avoid punishment, such as traffic accidents or unpleasant reactions of other motorists. Variations in the antecedents and consequences of behavior often serve as the independent variables in research on operant conditioning.

BASIC AND APPLIED BEHAVIOR ANALYSIS

We distinguished between basic and applied research in Chapter 2 on the basis of their main focuses. Basic research focuses on answering fundamental or theoretical questions, and applied research focuses on solving an existing real-life problem, such as how best to reduce the occurrence of an inappropriate or maladaptive behavior. Behavior-analysis research began as the field called the **experimental analysis of behavior,** which focuses on conducting basic research on conditioning. Later, the field called **applied behavior analysis** emerged to study ways to apply conditioning methods to solve socially important problems, such as those relating to education, child rearing, and mental illness (Sarafino, 2001).

Once research in behavior analysis identified a system of effective conditioning techniques for changing behavior, professionals organized them into an approach called *behavior modification* in which principles of learning are applied to change specific behaviors, called *target behaviors* (Sarafino, 2001). Professionals can use these principles to increase or decrease a target behavior. They can increase a *behavioral deficit,* an appropriate behavior that the individual does too little (not often enough, long enough, well enough, or strongly enough), or decrease a *behavioral excess,* an inappropriate behavior that the individual does too much. A defining feature of behavior modification is its focus on data collection and analysis. Even before professionals introduce an **intervention**—that is, a program to change a behavior—they use an observational procedure called a *functional analysis* to determine what the usual or everyday antecedents and consequences for that behavior have been. The intervention techniques will be designed to alter the existing antecedents and consequences to modify the behavior. The next step after performing the functional analysis is to collect "baseline" data to determine the behavior's original level.

Researchers in applied behavior analysis collect data on the behavior throughout the baseline and intervention phases of the study. The term **baseline** has two meanings: It can refer to the *data* collected before starting the intervention or the *period of time,* say, 2 weeks, in which those data are collected. For example, we saw at the start of this chapter in the research on reducing a man's anger that the first phase in the study was performed to "determine the frequency and intensity of the man's anger without yet introducing the program to reduce it." That phase was the baseline, and the intervention phase followed immediately and lasted until the behavior had improved markedly. Ideally, the baseline behavior will be *stable*—that is, data on its performance will not fluctuate greatly over time. Researchers try to hold off introducing an intervention until the data appear stable because they will want to compare the data sets: An intervention is successful if the target behavior has improved over baseline levels.

As in all research, the data collected must be valid and reliable. Because research in behavior analysis usually collects data on the target behavior by observing it directly, validity is rarely a concern, and reliability is assessed by comparing the records of two observers of the same behavior, as we discussed in Chapter 4. The method researchers use to assess interobserver reliability depends on the type of data they collect. If the data represent the frequency of a target behavior, researchers typically assess reliability with the *sessions total method* by summing the data for a session for each observer, dividing the smaller total by the larger, and multiplying by 100 to calculate the percentage of agreement. If the data represent the duration or magnitude of each instance of the target behavior, researchers tend to use a *correlation method*—that is, they calculate a Pearson's r statistic for the two observers' data. Novaco's (1977) study on reducing a man's anger had frequency and magnitude (intensity) measures and used both interobserver reliability methods, finding 84.6% agreement for the frequency measures and an *r* of +.86 for the intensity measure. Thus, the measures used in that study were quite reliable.

The information we have considered so far on behavior-analysis research gives a background that applies to most studies in that field of research and to all the designs we are about to examine.

INTRASUBJECT DESIGNS

In our examination of intrasubject designs, we'll see that researchers use a code to name and describe some types of these designs by using the first two letters of the alphabet to signify different phases of the research. The letter *A* indicates a baseline or reversal phase in which the intervention was absent, and the letter *B* symbolizes a phase in which a specific form of intervention was in effect. Other letters, such as *C* or *D*, sometimes are used to indicate phases in which intervention techniques different from those in *B* were in effect. Some of the designs we'll consider employ experimental strategies and qualify as **single-case experiments** because they can meet the criteria for making causal inferences (Kazdin, 2003). They can demonstrate covariation of variables, causal time sequence, and elimination of other plausible causes.

AB Designs

The **AB design** is the simplest type of intrasubject research, consisting of one baseline phase and one intervention phase. The Novaco (1977) study on reducing a man's anger that we've discussed several times is an example. Observers collected data on the man's anger behaviors during baseline and intervention phases, which spanned more than a month and showed large improvements during intervention. But AB designs are not single-case experiments: They are basically one-group pretest–posttest designs and can't rule out other possible causes for the improved behavior, such as history, maturation, and regression to the mean, as we saw in Chapters 5 and 8. In the anger study, for example, factors that were responsible for the man's baseline anger may have changed, such as if a nasty staff member on his ward had been reassigned coincidentally to another ward when the intervention began, making him less angry. Although AB designs are very useful for demonstrating the extent to which behavior changed, they are not ideal for identifying the cause of the change. In a way, they are like case studies in providing preliminary evidence that can be followed up with better-controlled research.

Another example of an AB design is a study by Erhardt and Baker (1990) of the extent to which two 5-year-old hyperactive children would fail to comply with requests before and after their parents received training in behavior modification techniques and began to apply them at home. The techniques included ways to identify antecedents and consequences of the children's noncompliance and to apply reinforcement of appropriate behavior. Noncompliance declined from the baseline levels during the intervention. Once again, factors other than the parents' use of behavior modification techniques may have been responsible for the changes in their children's behavior.

Reversal, ABA or ABAB Designs

In an effort to eliminate some of the problems with AB designs, researchers developed **reversal designs,** which involve a series of phases in which an intervention is alternately present or absent. Two types of reversal designs are commonly used. The **ABA design** consists of three phases: baseline, intervention, and reversal. In a *reversal phase,* the intervention is withdrawn to reinstate the baseline conditions, allowing us to see if the behavioral changes during the intervention revert toward baseline levels. The **ABAB design** contains four phases: baseline, intervention, reversal, and intervention. By reinstating the intervention, we can see whether the behavior responds again to the program's techniques.

Reversal designs have a distinct advantage over AB designs because they can demonstrate repeated increases and decreases in the target behavior that correspond to the presence and absence of the intervention. For example, if the study of noncompliance in hyperactive children had been conducted as an ABAB design, the parents would have used the intervention techniques in the second phase, withdrawn them in the third phase (reversal), and reinstated them in the fourth phase. Chances are, noncompliance would have declined in the first intervention phase, returned to near baseline levels during the reversal, and then declined again when the intervention was in force again. If so, we'd have strong evidence that the intervention *caused* the behavior to change because these changes in noncompliance would correspond to the timing of the presence and absence on the intervention, which would be very unlikely to result from factors other than the conditions in the research. Thus, reversal designs, especially the ABAB design, qualify as single-case experiments.

To illustrate the ABAB design with actual research, we'll consider an intrasubject study with an intervention to reduce the excessive, loud, and abusive statements of Ruth, a woman with mental retardation (Bostow & Bailey, 1969). Her tirades occurred at various times, but they were very severe at mealtimes when she would scream violently when she wanted her tray delivered, her tray removed when she was finished, and so on. To reduce the frequency of her outbursts, the intervention applied two consequences for the target behavior. First, when outbursts occurred, she received a type of punishment called time-out, which involved placing her in a corner of the room and leaving her there for 2 minutes. Second, she received reinforcement (in a pattern abbreviated as DRO) for *not* having an outburst for certain periods of time. The researchers monitored Ruth's target behavior with a tape recorder that had a device to activate it when a sufficiently loud noise occurred. As Figure 11.2 shows, the frequency of her loud vocalizations dropped sharply during both phases in which the intervention was in force and returned to baseline levels during the reversal phase. These data clearly indicate that the combined consequences of time-out and DRO caused her outbursts to decrease. (Go to **Box 11.2**)

Multiple-Baseline Designs

Research using **multiple-baseline designs** basically conduct more than one AB design, with all baselines starting simultaneously and proceeding together for a while. Each baseline period continues for a different length of time before the intervention begins. As a result, multiple-baseline designs have four important

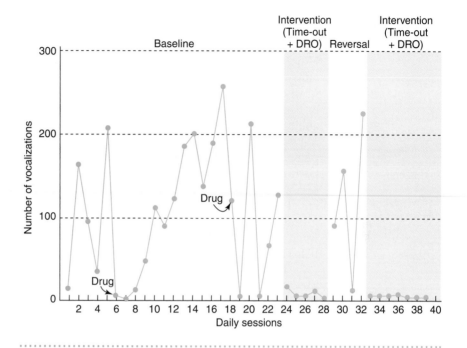

FIGURE 11.2
Number of loud verbal outbursts (vocalizations) a woman named Ruth made in each 1-hour observation session in baseline (or reversal) and intervention phases in a single-case experiment that used an ABAB design. The intervention consisted of time-out punishment for outbursts and reinforcement (with a DRO pattern) for not having an outburst for periods of time. On two occasions (labeled "Drug") during the baseline phase, Ruth was given a tranquilizer because her tirades had been so extreme.

(*Source:* Bostow & Bailey, 1969, Figure 1)

characteristics. First, there are *no reversal* phases. This feature makes multiple-baseline designs useful when the behavior change is permanent or when withdrawing the intervention is undesirable. Second, introduction of the *intervention is staggered* across the separate AB designs. Third, a *baseline* phase in at least one AB design can *overlap an intervention* phase in at least one other design. You can see this overlap in the following multiple-baseline design with three AB designs, where each letter represents a period of time—say, one week—in either the baseline phase (A) or the intervention phase (B):

AB Design #1: **A, A, B, B, B** . . .

AB Design #2: **A, A, A, B, B** . . .

AB Design #3: **A, A, A, A, B** . . .

This overlap enables us to compare the target behavior in baseline with the behavior in the intervention simultaneously within and across designs. We can assess the

Box 11.2   PROBLEMS IN USING REVERSAL DESIGNS

Using reversal designs can present two problems for researchers. First, the effect of the intervention may not be fully or substantially reversible. That is, when the intervention is withdrawn, the behavior sometimes does not or cannot revert back toward baseline levels. Under such conditions, our ability to interpret the results unambiguously is impaired because we cannot be certain why the behavior changed during the first intervention phase. For example, the target behavior may fail to regress because it has been changed permanently by the original intervention phase, as might occur if the participant learned a skill that he or she finds useful in a variety of settings. Thus, tennis players who learn effective strategies for performing excellent forehand and backhand strokes are not likely to stop using these strategies just because their trainers stopped reinforcing that behavior.

Here's an important point: if researchers think that the behavior they plan to change could not be expected to regress when the intervention is withdrawn, they should not use a reversal design. But it is not always possible to predict that an intervention will produce a quick and permanent change in a behavior. For example, therapists used an intervention consisting only of punishment with mild electric shock to reduce a 14-year-old boy's frequent and chronic cough (Creer, Chai, & Hoffman, 1977). The cough had become so severe that his classmates ridiculed the boy, and he was expelled from school at his teachers' request. Various other therapies had been applied without success, so the boy and his parents agreed to try the shock. The researchers planned to use an ABAB design. During the 1-hour baseline period, the boy coughed 22 times. In the initial intervention phase, the boy coughed once, which

> was followed immediately by a mild (5mA) electric shock of 1 second duration to the forearm. . . . Because the boy did not cough again for the remainder of the hour or the next 2 hours, a reversal procedure could not be instituted. (p. 108)

The boy returned to school the next day and experienced no recurrence of the chronic cough in follow-up assessments over a 2 ½-year period.

The second problem researchers can face in using reversal designs is that it may be undesirable or unethical to withdraw an intervention that appears to have produced a beneficial effect. For example, some children with autism perform high levels of self-injurious behaviors, such as head banging or biting their arms hard enough to draw blood. If an intervention successfully reduced these behaviors, it would be neither desirable nor ethically appropriate for the researcher to withdraw the treatment to meet the needs of a research design. Fortunately, other intrasubject research designs do not involve reversal phases and can be used in such situations.

effect of the intervention on the target behavior by making comparisons with baseline data after the introduction of each intervention phase. By making these comparisons, we can see how the intervention selectively affects the behavior in each AB design. Fourth, if the behavior changes only when the intervention begins and not before, we can conclude that the intervention caused the change. This means that multiple-baseline designs are single-case experiments. Multiple-baseline designs can be carried out across different *behaviors,* individual *subjects,* or *situations,* as we are about to see.

The **multiple-baseline, across-behaviors** design uses separate AB designs for each of two or more different *behaviors* for a single individual in a particular setting. In using this research design, we would monitor simultaneously two or more different behaviors—for instance, a factory worker's daily frequency of arriving to work on time, number of items made, and amount of time spent in idle conversation—starting in baseline. Once the baseline data have stabilized for each of the target behaviors, we would apply the intervention techniques, such as reinforcement, to *one* of them. Soon we should see in our graph that this behavior has changed. When the change is clear, we would apply the intervention to the next behavior, and so on. Assuming that the *only* behavior that changes at any given time is the one newly exposed to the intervention, we can infer with strong certainty that applying the techniques caused the change.

An example of a multiple-baseline, across-behaviors design is a study that examined the effects of training to help children with asthma learn to use a device that sprays medication into their airways when an asthma episode has begun (Renne & Creer, 1976). Four 7- to 12-year-olds were having trouble learning to use the device. After baseline, they received training with reinforcement for three behaviors, starting with eye fixation behavior (looking constantly at the device). Then they were trained in facial posturing (inserting the device in the mouth at the right angle and with the lips and nostrils correctly formed), and then diaphragmatic breathing (using the stomach muscles correctly to breathe in the medication). Figure 11.3 depicts the sequencing of training for each behavior and the outcome of the intervention, as reflected in the mean number of inappropriate behaviors the children made. Notice three aspects in the graph. First, like all multiple-baseline designs, the baseline phases started together but lasted for different amounts of time (the baseline lengths increased from the first-, to the second-, to the third-trained behavior). Second, the children's inappropriate behaviors in facial posturing and diaphragmatic breathing did not diminish until each behavior was subjected to the intervention. Third, each behavior responded quickly once the intervention started.

The target behaviors of research using multiple-baseline, across-behaviors designs can vary in the degree to which they are related or unrelated. You can see different degrees of relatedness in the pairs of behaviors in the following examples of studies that have examined the effects of interventions on:

▪ Articulation errors in producing *th* and *z* sounds (Bailey, Timbers, Phillips, & Wolf, 1971)
▪ Classroom behaviors of being out of one's seat and making inappropriate statements or sounds (Calhoun & Lima, 1977)

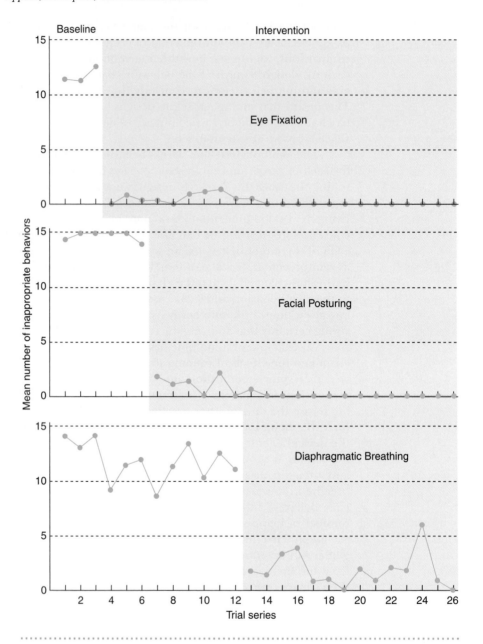

FIGURE 11.3

Mean number of inappropriate behaviors four children made in learning to perform the behaviors of eye fixation, facial posturing, and diaphragmatic breathing when using a device to control asthma episodes. The maximum number of inappropriate behaviors per trial was 15 for each behavior. In this study, the data for the four children were combined rather than presented for each child.

(*Source:* Renne & Creer, 1976, Figure 1)

▪ Sleeping problems of a child not going to sleep on time and entering her sister's bed (Ronen, 1991)

Some of these studies examined several behaviors, not just the two listed, and each specific behavior was observed in a baseline phase and an intervention phase.

The **multiple-baseline, across-subjects** design uses separate AB designs for each of two or more individual *participants* for a particular behavior in a particular setting. In this design, each person receives a baseline phase and an intervention phase for the same target behavior. Once the baseline data have stabilized for each person, the intervention is applied to *one* of these individuals. When data indicate the behavior has changed for this participant, we would apply the intervention to the next individual, and so on. Assuming that the *only* participant whose behavior changes at any given time is the one newly exposed to the intervention, we can infer with strong certainty that applying the intervention techniques caused the change.

A study used a multiple-baseline, across-subjects design to examine the effects of an intervention to prevent HIV (the AIDS human immunodeficiency virus) infection among hospital nurses (DeVries, Burnette, & Redmon, 1991). The target behavior was wearing rubber gloves in hospital activities where there is a high probability of contact with a patient's body fluids. If the patient is infected with HIV, wearing gloves reduces nurses' risk of becoming infected. The intervention, consisting of biweekly performance feedback and encouragement to wear gloves in these activities, was introduced with one nurse first, then another nurse, and so on. Figure 11.4 illustrates the design and results of this study. Notice that the target behavior improved in each nurse only after the intervention was introduced, which indicates that the feedback caused the behavior to change. Other studies have used this type of multiple-baseline design to demonstrate the beneficial effects of interventions to, for example, improve school students' skills in math (Swain & McLaughlin, 1998).

The **multiple-baseline, across-situations** design uses separate AB designs for each of two or more different *situations* for a single individual and a specific behavior. In this design, the participant receives a baseline phase and an intervention phase in each of two or more situations—for example, in different places or with different people present. As with the other multiple baseline designs, the baselines in all situations begin at the same time. Once the baseline data have stabilized in each situation, the intervention is applied in *one* of them. When the change is clear on a graph, the intervention is applied in the next situation, and so on. If the target behavior changes *only* in each situation with the newly presented intervention, we can conclude that applying the techniques caused the change.

As an example of a multiple-baseline, across-situations design, a study tested the effects of an intervention of brief (2-second) time-out punishment procedures on a young man's stuttering (James, 1981). In both the baseline and intervention phases, the client talked while a tape recorder was running in five situations, such as in the laboratory conversing with a researcher, at home talking with an adult, and in various business settings talking with clerks or agents. The results demonstrated that his stuttering decreased in each situation, but only when the time-out consequences were applied there. Similarly, a study used a multiple-baseline,

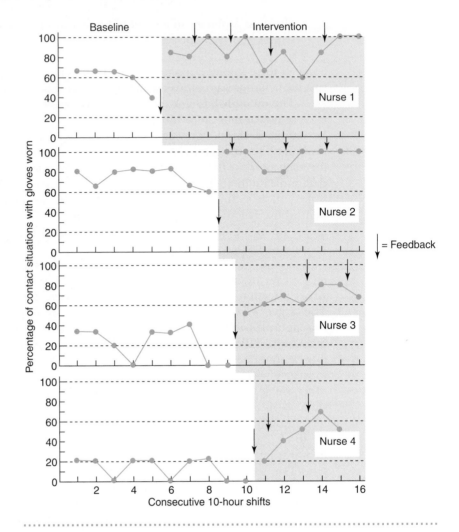

Percentage of cases in which four nurses wore rubber gloves during 16 consecutive 10-hour shifts when contact with a patient's body fluids was likely. The intervention in this multiple-baseline, across-subjects design involved feedback about the nurses' use of gloves and encouragement to wear them more often. The arrows indicate points at which a nurse specializing in reducing the spread of infection in hospitals gave feedback.

(*Source:* DeVries, Burnette, & Redmon, 1991, Figure 1)

across-situations design to demonstrate the effectiveness of an intervention to improve students' on-task behavior in three different settings: language arts, reading, and computer classes (Wood, Murdock, Cronin, Dawson, & Kirby, 1998).

We hinted earlier at a potential problem in using multiple-baseline designs: A target behavior may begin to change during a baseline phase, before the intervention has been introduced. This occurred in a multiple-baseline, across-behaviors design to test the effects of a treatment to reduce a 29-year-old male patient's verbal expression of three delusional beliefs (Lowe & Chadwick, 1990):

- ■ He was to be married to a woman called Amanda, with whom he had not been in contact for many years, and who supposedly was reading his mind and controlling many of the things that happened to him.
- ■ He had been Jesus Christ in a prior life.
- ■ He had been Leonardo da Vinci in a prior life. (p. 466)

The beliefs were treated in the listed sequence. Although the man's statements that he had been Jesus and Leonardo in past lives did not change during the intervention that decreased the Amanda belief, the Leonardo belief began to decline (in baseline) during the intervention that reduced the Jesus belief. When this happens, we can't be certain why the untreated behavior declined—perhaps the decrease in the Leonardo belief resulted because the Jesus and Leonardo beliefs were so similar. But the effects of the treatment would have been clearer if the Leonardo belief had not begun to change in baseline.

Similar problems can arise in other multiple-baseline designs. In the multiple-baseline, across-subjects design, changes in the target behavior for the person receiving the intervention may lead to changes in the behavior of other individuals who are still in baseline. And in the multiple-baseline, across-situations design, changes in the person's behavior in the situation where the intervention was introduced may lead to changes when the person is in other situations still lacking the intervention. But, even though some potential exists for these problems to arise in research, they do not seem to be very common.

Changing-Criterion Designs

Another useful approach for demonstrating that an intervention technique caused changes in a behavior is called the **changing-criterion design.** As the name implies, the criterion for successful performance changes over time, usually becoming more rigorous. For instance, when we start the intervention, we may require a fairly lax level of performance for receiving a reward. After the behavior has stabilized at that level, we may raise the criterion to a higher level—and when the behavior stabilizes again, we may raise the criterion again, and so on. If the behavior increases or decreases in accordance with each change in the criterion, we can conclude that the reward is responsible for the behavioral changes. Thus, research done as a changing-criterion design can qualify as a single-case experiment.

De Luca and Holborn (1992) used a changing-criterion design to study the effects of reinforcement on exercising among 11-year-old obese and nonobese boys. Once each boy's pedaling rate on a stationary bicycle had stabilized in baseline, the researchers began to reinforce pedaling at certain rates in each 30-minute exercise session. As reinforcers for pedaling at the criterion rate, the boys earned "a point"—a bell would ring and a light would go on, announcing the success. The points could be exchanged later for desired rewards. Let's see how the criterion changed. The number of pedaling revolutions required for each instance of reinforcement at the start of the intervention for each boy was set roughly 15% above his average rate in baseline. So, if the boy had pedaled in baseline at the rate of 70 revolutions per minute, the intervention began by requiring an average rate of 80 revolutions per minute. Each subsequent increased criterion was set at 15% above the average pedaling rate he achieved in the preceding phase. Figure 11.5 shows the data for two of the six boys in the study. Notice how their pedaling increased in accordance with each increase in the criterion for reinforcement. This pattern occurred for all six boys. Although the reversal (BL) phase was not necessary in the design, the corresponding decrease in performance makes the effects of the reinforcement clearer.

Alternating-Treatment Designs

Alternating-treatment designs (also called *simultaneous-treatment* or *multielement designs*) examine the effects of two or more treatments, each of which is conducted within the same intervention phase with the same person. Although both treatments are applied in the same phase, they are separated in time and alternated. Thus, each treatment might be applied on different days or at different times during the day throughout the intervention phase. By examining graphs of the data, we can determine if one treatment is consistently more effective than another in changing the person's target behavior.

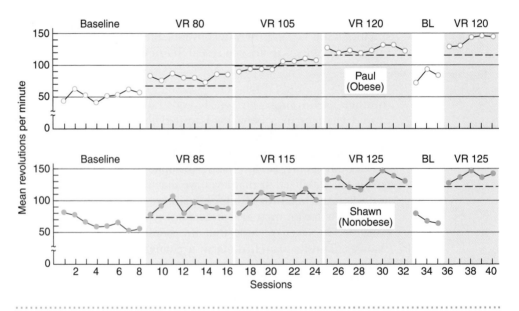

FIGURE 11.5

Mean number of revolutions per minute pedaled on a stationary bicycle by two boys (data for the four other boys, not included here, showed similar patterns) in a changing-criterion design. Each increased criterion (dashed horizontal lines in sections labeled VR) was set at 15% above the average for the previous phase. The BL phase is a baseline (reversal).

(*Source:* De Luca & Holborn, 1992, Figure 1)

Kohler and Greenwood (1990) used an alternating-treatment design to examine the effects of tutoring behaviors of schoolchildren after they were trained in two tutoring procedures to help classmates in spelling. The *standard tutoring procedure* had the tutor give the student reinforcers for correct spellings; for misspellings, the tutor would spell the word once. The *modified tutoring procedure* had the tutor use praise and reinforcers for correct spellings; for misspellings, the tutor would spell the word once as soon as a student gave an incorrect letter. During the intervention, the tutors were told which procedure to apply in each 10-minute tutoring session and observed for instances of a tutoring behavior called "help": spelling a word *more than once* during corrective feedback for an error, which the tutors were not trained to do. Figure 11.6 presents the number of help behaviors per tutoring session by one of the tutors, Karen. Notice that she rarely performed help behaviors in baseline and during the intervention phase when told to use the standard tutoring procedure. But her help behaviors occurred very frequently when she was told to use the modified tutoring procedure during intervention. In the "choice" phase, the tutors were allowed to use the procedure of their choice, and she continued to use help behaviors.

Alternating-treatment designs have two principal advantages. First, as in some other designs, no reversal phases are needed. Second, they can qualify as single-case experiments if care is taken to control extraneous variables, making it unlikely that the outcome would be confounded. If the target behavior shows greater improvement with one of two tested treatments, we can make a causal inference—one treatment caused more improvement than the other did. But a problem can arise in alternating-treatment designs that cannot happen with other

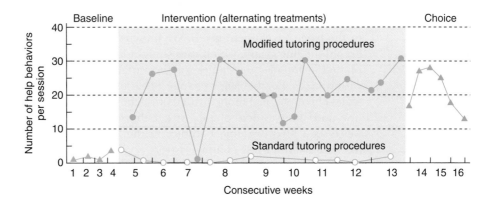

FIGURE 11.6

Number of "help" behaviors a tutor gave per 10-minute tutoring session examined in an alternating-treatment design. The tutor's help behaviors were assessed in baseline, during training in two different tutoring procedures in the intervention phase, and later when the tutor could use either tutoring procedure. (Data for two other tutors, not included here, showed similar patterns.)

(*Source:* Kohler & Greenwood, 1990, Figure 2)

designs: the effects of experiencing one treatment may influence that of another. For example, if a participant receives two treatments, the effect of a treatment may be affected if the person contrasts it with the second treatment (Barlow & Hayes, 1979; Hains & Baer, 1989). If only one of these treatments had been implemented during the intervention, its effects on behavior might have been different.

INTRASUBJECT DATA ANALYSIS

You may be thinking, "OK, intrasubject research has produced important findings and may even be able to maintain a high level of internal validity, but how can we analyze the data if we don't have lots of participants? And how can we tell if the study's conditions, such as baseline and intervention, are significantly different?" These questions create skepticism and discomfort even among some professionals. Let's see how researchers who use small-*N* designs answer them.

DATA ANALYSIS

Almost all researchers who do intrasubject research want to examine individual data to see changes that are obscured by grouping data and computing inferential statistics. The easiest and clearest way to evaluate the degree of change in an individual's behavior is to plot the data for the person in a graph and inspect it visually.

A **graph** is a drawing that depicts variations within a set of data, usually showing how one variable changed with changes in another variable. Although graphs can take several forms, most are constructed with a *horizontal axis* and a *vertical axis*. In graphs of data from behavior-analysis research, the vertical axis typically represents some measure of behavior, such as its frequency or intensity, and the horizontal axis represents another variable, such as chronological time or the type of treatment given. We'll focus on the most commonly used type of graph: the **line graph,** which uses straight lines to connect successive data points plotted at intersecting values for the variables scaled along the horizontal and vertical axes. For behavior change programs, the horizontal axis almost always scales chronological time, divided and labeled to indicate time units across baseline and intervention phases of a behavior change program. All the graphs we've seen for intrasubject studies in the last several pages of this chapter are line graphs with these characteristics.

Graphic Analysis

We can assess behavior changes with line graphs by a procedure called **graphic analysis,** which involves performing a detailed visual evaluation of specific features of the graph. Figure 11.7 illustrates the four features that form the criteria for evaluating the magnitude of change across phases of an intrasubject study. The features to consider are the:

- *Average change* in the overall level of the behavior. Comparing one phase with the next, is the average level of the behavior in each phase markedly different and in the expected direction?

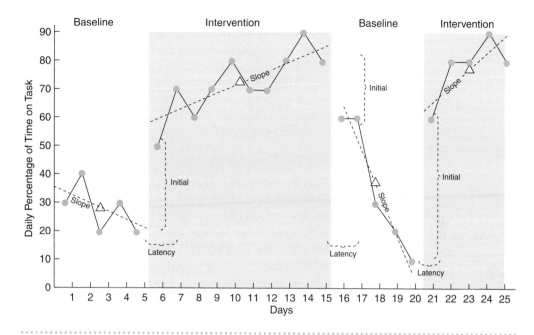

FIGURE 11.7
Graph of hypothetical data in an ABAB design to increase a student's daily percentage of time on academic tasks in school. The figure marks in black what we would try to visualize from the graphed data (colored dots) to see the four features for evaluating the intervention's success: the average change, initial change, slope change, and latency of change. The average percentage for each phase (28%, 72%, 36%, and 78%) is shown with a colored triangle.

- *Initial change* at the start of a new phase. At the point when one phase ends and another begins, is there an abrupt shift in the behavior in the expected direction?

- *Slope change* in the graphs for adjacent phases. Is the direction of slope, or trend, of the graph in one phase very different from the slope in an adjacent phase? A slope close to zero means no substantial change in the behavior occurred over time in that phase.

- *Latency of change* in a new phase. Did it take a short time for change to begin in the intervention? The shorter the time before change begins in the intervention, the more effective the techniques, usually. Strong effects of the intervention may also show up in a longer latency in a reversal phase.

If the answer is affirmative for each of the questions about these features, the effect of the intervention is clear and strong (Kazdin, 2003). Let's look at the graph and see. First, by comparing the averages (triangles) for baseline and intervention phases, we can see that the differences are in the expected direction and quite large. Second, the initial changes from each phase to the next are substantial, the largest coming at the transition from the third to the fourth phases.

Third, the slopes of the graphs in adjacent phases are quite different from each other. Fourth, the latencies for the change in behavior were short in all phases.

These features in the graph indicate that the effects of the intervention were strong. If these features were not very clear, we'd conclude that the program was not effective. Although there is no widely accepted, specific criterion for deciding whether the changes are or are not pronounced enough to reflect a successful intervention, these evaluations require the use of rigorous standards. Only very clear and marked changes should be accepted as reflecting that an intervention was effective.

Problems in Graphic Analyses

Trends in the data in each phase of an intrasubject design may not always be as clear as the trends in Figure 11.7, thereby making a graphic analysis more difficult to interpret. These difficulties can arise from data problems of three types: *excessive variability,* a *decreasing baseline trend* (for a behavioral excess), and an *increasing baseline trend* (for a behavioral deficit). Each type of problem is illustrated graphically in Figure 11.8, using hypothetical data for 1 week of baseline

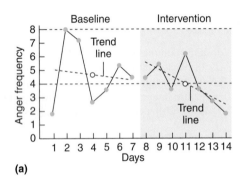

(a)

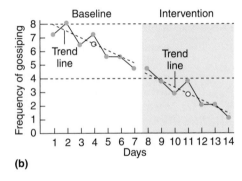

(b)

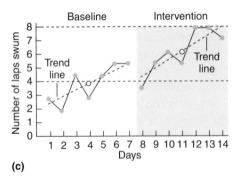

(c)

FIGURE 11.8

Graphs illustrating three types of problem data: (a) excessive variability; (b) decreasing baseline trend for a behavioral excess—that is, a behavior that occurs too much; and (c) increasing baseline trend for a behavioral deficit. The average levels (open circles) and slopes of the trends (dashed lines) for these three sets of hypothetical data are plotted for only 7 days each of baseline and intervention.

and 1 week of intervention. Let's look at these problems by examining the graphs. As we do this, you'll see that the problems illustrated in the graphs are compounded when data are collected for an insufficient amount of time.

Figure 11.8a presents data for the frequency of a person's anger episodes. The excessive variability in baseline makes it difficult to interpret whether any real change occurred in the intervention phase, even though the average level and slopes (trend lines) of the graph suggest that the number of anger episodes per day did decline. This difficulty exists because the baseline data are very unstable, containing sharp fluctuations. Is the declining trend in anger frequency depicted in the intervention data just an extension of the baseline fluctuations, or has the behavior really decreased? Was the high variability an unusual circumstance? If so, collecting baseline data for at least another week might have helped to stabilize the data.

In Figure 11.8b, the data represent a person's frequency of gossiping. Notice that the baseline data for this behavioral excess show a clear decreasing trend that existed before the intervention was introduced to reduce the gossiping behavior. Is the decrease in gossiping after baseline due to the intervention, or is it just a continuation of the existing trend? If the declining trend during the intervention phase had been much sharper than the trend in baseline, we could assume that the difference resulted from the intervention. But the two slopes in this figure are very similar. As a result, we can't determine whether the program was effective or whether the decreasing trends in both phases were due to some other factor, such as a temporary change in the person's general social experiences. Again, collecting baseline data for another week might have clarified the situation, perhaps by showing a reversal in the baseline trend.

Figure 11.8c presents data for the number of laps a person swims in a pool each day. The problem in these data is similar to the one we just saw for the gossiping data. For the swimming behavior, the baseline data for this behavioral deficit depict a clear increasing trend before the intervention was introduced to increase swimming. Once again, the slopes in both phases are not very different, so we can't tell whether the program was effective or whether some other factor is responsible for the increases in swimming in both phases.

In general, whenever baseline data show excessive variability or an increasing or decreasing trend in relation to the treatment goal, researchers should consider delaying the start of the intervention and collecting additional baseline data.

Statistical Analysis of Intrasubject Data

When the outcome from intrasubject research is clear from visual inspection only, the effects can be determined simply with a graphic analysis. But inferential statistics may be useful in two other circumstances. First, when the effects are not so clear visually, statistical tests, such as a single-subject ANOVA, can be applied to clarify the outcome (Anderson, 2002). Second, to demonstrate the general effectiveness of an intervention technique, researchers can combine data from many prior intrasubject studies and perform statistical analyses on those data, complete with effect size estimates (Scruggs & Mastropieri, 1998). Although these statistical procedures are not yet widely applied, they are available.

DIMENSIONS FOR EVALUATING EFFECTS

Professionals commonly evaluate three dimensions of practical considerations for the behavioral changes produced by intervention techniques. The first dimension concerns the *generalization and durability* of the behavioral changes in the person's natural environment. For a behavior change intervention to be viewed as effective and useful, the improved behavior must generalize to the person's natural environment, and it must be durable. Thus, someone who has learned methods to avoid antecedents that lead to an unwanted behavior, such as smoking or drinking, must use these skills in his or her usual environment over a long period of time.

The second dimension for evaluating a program's effectiveness pertains to the *costs and benefits* of the intervention. That is, we can assess its **cost–benefit ratio,** or the extent to which the costs of providing the treatment are outweighed by the money saved in the long run (Jospe, Shueman, & Troy, 1991; Kaplan, 1989). In medical settings, for example, studies have shown that providing behavioral interventions to reduce anxiety enables surgery patients to recover more quickly and use less medication than patients who do not receive these interventions (Sarafino, 2002). The financial savings in medical costs far exceed the costs of administering these interventions.

The third dimension for evaluating a program's effectiveness entails the *amount of change* it produces in the person's behavior and the *importance of the changes* to the person's everyday life and functioning. We can assess these dimensions by considering two outcomes of the behavior change: its clinical significance and its social validity. The concept of **clinical significance** refers to the degree to which the change in behavior is *meaningful* to the person's life and functioning; a meaningful change is one that is *large* and brings the behavior into the *normal range* (Jacobson, Roberts, Berns, & McGlinchey, 1999; Kendall, Marrs-Garcia, Nath, & Sheldrick, 1999). As an example, let's consider a hypothetical case of an 8-year-old boy who stutters, on average, about 10% of the syllables he speaks. Suppose that an intervention reduces his stuttering to 6% of his spoken syllables. This would be a large change, but would the behavior be in the normal range? Actually, no. Now suppose that the intervention was more effective and reduced his stuttering to 3%. This level would represent a clinically significant change because it is both large *and* the behavior is now within the normal range (Gagnon & Ladouceur, 1992). Determining the normal range can be accomplished in two ways. First, research may have previously identified a *norm* for the behavior—that is, its usual level among a large population of individuals of the same age and gender (Trull, Neitzel, & Main, 1988). Second, the researcher may identify and test a control group to assess their average level of the behavior (Dush, Hirt, & Schroeder, 1983).

The term **social validity** refers to the utility and adaptiveness of the behavior change for the person's everyday functioning (Foster & Mash, 1999). We can evaluate an intervention's social validity by collecting data to answer these questions (Wolf, 1978):

■ Are the behavioral goals of the program desired by society and appropriate for the person's life?

▪ Are the person and significant individuals in his or her life—such as relatives, teachers, or coworkers—satisfied with the amount and utility of the behavioral changes the program has produced?

Answers to these questions can be obtained in several ways (Foster & Mash, 1999). For instance, we can ask for assessments or opinions from relevant individuals—the person and people in his or her life who have frequent contact with the person and might be affected by the behavioral changes the program produces. We can also have independent judges make evaluations of the person's behavior after the intervention and other aspects of the program. And we can examine measures of the outcome that show a clear social impact of the changes, such as improved communication and friendships after reductions in stuttering. For a program to modify delinquent behavior, we might assess social impact in terms of the person's future use of drugs or arrests for criminal activity. By evaluating the clinical significance and social validity of behavioral changes, we can get a sense of the degree to which the intervention has made a real difference in the lives of the person, as well as other individuals who are affected by the outcomes of the program. (Go to **Box 11.3**)

Box 11.3   EVALUATING SOCIAL VALIDITY

Hugh had developed muscle tics at the age of 3 and was 11 years old when he entered a treatment program to correct this problem (Finney, Rapoff, Hall, & Christopherson, 1983). In the recent months prior to beginning the program, there had been an increase in the frequency and intensity of four tics: head-shaking, head-jerking, mouth-grimacing, and eye-blinking. The main intervention technique involved having him practice, for 15 minutes a day, behaviors that were the opposite of the tic actions—for example, opening his eyes wider than usual and holding that position for several seconds to reduce eye-blinking. The program produced dramatic reductions in each of these tics within several weeks, and follow-up assessments indicated that these decreases were maintained over the next year.

People commonly seek treatment for tics because of the unusual appearance and social embarrassment these motor behaviors produce. To evaluate the program within a social validity framework, the researchers made videotapes of Hugh during baseline and intervention phases of the treatment. These tapes were rated by two groups of judges: 12 teachers from a junior high school and 36 graduate students in pediatric fields, such as nursing and special education. These judges did not know Hugh, but were chosen because of their regular contact with children of Hugh's age. When the panel rated his tics, using a 7-point scale (1 = not distracting; 7 = very distracting), the average ratings were as follows: about 6.5 for the baseline tapes and 1.6 for the intervention tapes. This assessment of social validity suggests that Hugh's tics became far less embarrassing as a result of this treatment.

PREPARING TO DO AN INTRASUBJECT STUDY

Designing and carrying out intrasubject research is as complicated as doing a study with many participants. The instructions and checklists in Chapter 10 are just as helpful in preparing to conduct small-*N* as for large-sample studies, but the focus of some of the activities would be different. Perhaps the greatest difference would be in the planning of the statistical analyses, which would not be needed for most intrasubject designs. If you know that you will be doing a single-subject study, consult that chapter for information to help in your planning.

SUMMARY

Studies that manipulate an independent variable to examine its effects on a single individual's behavior use an intrasubject (or single-subject, single-case, or small-*N*) design. This type of research originated in early studies on learning, memory, and psychophysics, and in case studies. Small-*N* designs have several advantages—for example, they provide an unusually rich set of data about a behavior that does not mask or misrepresent an individual's scores within group averages. But these designs also have disadvantages, particularly in their difficulty in examining interaction effects with respect to subject variables.

Studies on behavior analysis in the fields of the experimental analysis of behavior and applied behavior analysis are especially likely to use intrasubject designs, usually to examine the effects of variables in operant conditioning. These studies typically examine behavioral changes over time and have at least two phases, with at least one baseline and one intervention phase. AB designs, which consist of a baseline phase (A) and an intervention phase (B), do not indicate unambiguously whether the intervention caused the behavior to change.

Other intrasubject designs qualify as single-case experiments because they apply experimental strategies and can meet the criteria for making cause–effect conclusions. Because reversal designs—ABA designs and ABAB designs—alternate baseline and intervention phases, they can qualify as single-case experiments. It is very unlikely that extraneous variables could be responsible for changes in the behavior if its level varies with and corresponds to the timing of the presence or absence of the intervention. But reversal designs can have two problems: the effect of the intervention may not be fully or substantially reversible, such as if the participant learned a useful skill in the intervention, and withdrawing an intervention may be undesirable or unethical.

Other single-case experiments avoid these problems. Multiple-baseline designs start baselines simultaneously but begin the interventions in sequence, thereby showing patterns of behavior change that correspond to the introduction of the intervention. This approach can be used as three different designs: multiple-baseline, across-behaviors; multiple-baseline, across-subjects; and multiple-baseline, across-situations. In the changing-criterion design, the criterion for success changes, generally by becoming increasingly rigorous. If the behavior increases or decreases in accordance with criterion changes, we can conclude that the intervention is responsible for behavioral changes. Alternating-treatment designs allow the comparison of two or more treatments presented in the same intervention phase.

Data analysis in intrasubject research generally relies on the systematic visual inspection of graphs, typically line graphs, in a process called graphic analysis in which the researcher evaluates the average change, initial change, slope of the change, and latency of change. Other dimensions for evaluating the effects of an intervention include the clinical significance and social validity of the behavior change and the cost–benefit ratio.

KEY TERMS

intrasubject design
case study
experimental analysis
   of behavior
applied behavior analysis
intervention
baseline
single-case experiments
AB design
reversal designs

ABA design
ABAB design
multiple-baseline designs
multiple-baseline,
   across-behaviors
multiple-baseline,
   across-subjects
multiple-baseline,
   across-situations

changing-criterion
   design
alternating-treatment
   designs
graph
line graph
graphic analysis
cost–benefit ratio
clinical significance
social validity

REVIEW QUESTIONS

1. Describe the study by Novaco (1977) on reducing a man's anger behavior.
2. What are intrasubject designs, and how are they different from studies with large samples?
3. Describe how intrasubject designs were used in early research on psychophysics and on learning and memory.
4. What are the advantages and disadvantages of intrasubject designs?
5. Define the terms *baseline* and *intervention* as phases in behavior-analysis research.
6. Define *ABAB designs,* and indicate why they can be superior to *AB designs.*
7. Describe the problems with using reversal designs.
8. Define *multiple-baseline designs,* and indicate how they can be carried out across individuals and situations.
9. Describe the research design and results of the study by DeVries, Burnette, and Redmon (1991) on promoting nurses' glove wearing to reduce HIV infection.
10. What are *alternating-treatment designs* and what are their main advantages?
11. Describe in detail how to conduct a graphic analysis and the problems that can make interpretation difficult.
12. Describe how researchers in applied behavior analysis can demonstrate the clinical significance, social validity, and cost–benefit ratio of their interventions.

RESOURCES

BOOKS, CHAPTERS, AND ARTICLES

Kazdin, A. E. (2003). *Research design in clinical psychology* (4th ed.). Boston: Allyn & Bacon.

Stake, R. (1995). *The art of case study research.* Thousand Oaks, CA: Sage.

INTERNET SITES

http://www.envmed.rochester.edu/wwwrap/behavior/jeab/jeabhome.html
> This is the Website of the *Journal of the Experimental Analysis of Behavior,* which presents abstracts of published small-*N* designs.

APPLICATION ACTIVITIES

APPLICATION 11–1: USING AN ABAB DESIGN

After 25 years of smoking two packs of cigarettes a day, a woman decides she wants to quit. She has read about various methods for quitting and is considering using the widely publicized nicotine patch that she'd affix to her body. A nicotine patch transmits nicotine through the skin to provide some relief for the nicotine withdrawal smokers normally experience upon quitting. Suppose this woman is willing to serve as a participant in a study, allowing you to test the effectiveness of the patch for stopping smoking. Explain how you could use an A-B-A-B design to conduct this test. What measure would you use of her behavior? If the patch worked, what would you expect to see in the data during the four phases of the design? What are the advantages and disadvantages of this type of design?

APPLICATION 11–2: USING A MULTIPLE-BASELINE DESIGN

A teacher is concerned with the disruptive behavior exhibited by one 6-year-old boy in her class. The teacher decides to use a behavior modification program to improve three of this child's behaviors: calling out in class, physically attacking other classmates, and refusing to share toys and materials with other students. Diagram how this teacher could use a multiple-baseline, across-behaviors design to demonstrate that the intervention produced improvements. Draw a graph showing what the data might look like for the three behaviors if the program worked. What are the advantages and disadvantages of using this type of design?

APPLICATION 11–3: DOING A GRAPHIC ANALYSIS

Suppose you conducted a behavior-analysis study with an AB design on techniques to increase a behavioral deficit—performing push-ups—and wanted to do a graphic analysis of the following data that represent the number of push-ups done per day:

> *(33, 31, 35, 37, 38) 39, 41, 48, 53, 55, 61, 56, 71, 79, 73, 81, 78, 85, 77, 83*

The numbers in parenthesis are baseline, and the rest are intervention. Draw a graph of the data and conduct a graphic analysis. Interpret the outcome in terms of the four features to consider when evaluating the magnitude of change in the behavior. Discuss whether there is a possible problem in the baseline trend.

CHAPTER 12

DESCRIPTIVE, PROGRAM EVALUATION, AND ADVANCED METHODS

PROLOGUE

Have you ever seen on TV or in person this situation: two animals of the same species are fighting, and once it is clear which one is winning, the loser makes an appeasement or submissive behavior that ends the fight? Often that submissive behavior makes the loser appear smaller, such as by crouching. In the late 1800s, Darwin proposed that an animal's "making oneself smaller" serves as a stimulus that effectively inhibits further attack from another animal of the same species, and by the mid-1900s, researchers had observed this phenomenon in a wide variety of species (Eibl-Eibesfeldt, 1970).

In the 1970s, researchers decided to study whether humans who were losing fights would also display submissive behaviors (Ginsburg, Pollman, & Wauson, 1977). They chose to study this phenomenon by observing boys on a playground in unstructured and unsupervised activity. The researchers parked a van in a position from which they could videotape a school playground where 28 to 34 boys, 8 to 12 years of age, played during 24 taping sessions, each of which lasted 40 minutes, across 6 weeks. Whenever a fight began, an observer would turn on the video camera to record the event; 72 fights were recorded. A fight was defined as an episode involving "hitting, kicking, pushing, pulling, or jumping upon another child" (p. 417). The camera remained focused on the boys throughout and for a couple of minutes after the episode.

To analyze the video record, the researchers had observers who were blind to the purpose of the study view the recordings and measure with a ruler the losing child's height at the start and just prior to the end of the fight. From these measurements, each observer then judged whether the child's height (from the ground to the top of his head) had decreased at the end of the fight. To test the reliability of these judgments, the researchers randomly selected 12 taped fights for three observers to view and judge. The observers' judgments were in complete agreement for 83% of the fights, demonstrating good interobserver reliability. The results of the study confirmed the hypothesis that humans who are losing a fight would, like animals, display submissive behaviors: Just before the episode ended, the losing boy's height decreased in 58 of the 72 episodes. The specific submissive behavior varied somewhat—for example, some of the losing boys simply showed a bowing of the head with slumping shoulders, but others lay motionless on the ground or knelt down, sometimes tying their shoes!

This study is an example of descriptive research—a type of study that is different from and less common in psychology than most of the other types of research we've examined so far. We'll discuss in this chapter several types of applied, descriptive, and advanced methods and designs that students seldom perform in a research methods class. Because these methods appear in the literature fairly often, you're likely to encounter them in journals and other published material.

DESCRIPTIVE RESEARCH

We saw in Chapter 1 that research using a *descriptive strategy* is designed to detail or categorize events or phenomena, such as the occurrence of a behavior or attitude, or to chart their course. For example, we might conduct a study to demonstrate the existence of a behavior—as the research we just discussed did for submissive behavior by losers of fights—or to characterize the people who display it. As Figure 1.2 (see inside front cover) outlines, descriptive research is very unlikely to meet the criteria for causal inference; it doesn't manipulate independent variables and has little control over extraneous variables. The descriptions that come from this type of research are useful because they provide information that enables professionals to define variables clearly, determine their current levels, and consider how they may relate to other variables. This information often has real-life applications, such as in determining the products an industry will make or the services a government will provide to citizens. We'll examine some of the more common methods used in descriptive research, beginning with surveys.

LARGE-SCALE SURVEYS

Surveys are often conducted to describe the behaviors or other characteristics of a defined population in an accurate and systematic manner. Because of this purpose, it is important to have a large sample that is representative of, or mirrors, the population. To recruit a representative sample, large-scale survey methods generally use some form of probability sampling, which we discussed in Chapter 10. Chapter 4 described how to compose items for and ways to administer a survey—that is, as written or Internet questionnaires or by interviews in person or on the telephone.

Survey methods can have two major problems, nonresponse bias and social desirability bias. In *nonresponse bias,* a substantial number of the individuals selected for recruitment either can't be reached or fail to participate after being contacted. To the extent that the nonresponders are disproportionately from one or a few segments of the population, the final sample may not be representative. This problem is fairly common for written surveys delivered by mail, where participation rates are frequently only 20% if no special efforts are made to enhance the likelihood of return (Mangione, 1998). But participation rates are much higher when researchers send reminders, offer incentives, and keep the survey short and easy to fill out. Participation by 70–85% of the sampling frame is considered very good, but less than 50% is unacceptable for descriptive research because most of the population is not likely to be represented. For face-to-face interviews, participation rates are often 80–90% (van Kammen & Stouthamer-Loeber, 1998). In *social desirability bias,* people answer questions in ways they think are socially acceptable, rather than how they actually feel. This is especially common in surveys of sensitive or embarrassing topics, such as sexual behavior. With either of these problems, any conclusions about the population that researchers make from the survey data are likely to be inaccurate.

We can see a fine example of large-scale survey methods in the yearly research by Johnston, O'Malley, and Bachman (2000) on American adolescents' and young adults' use of various substances, such as cigarettes, alcohol, and illicit drugs. Let's focus only on the surveys of 8th-, 10th-, and 12th-grade students from 1991 to 1999. To recruit a representative sample each year, the researchers used random sampling procedures to select in three stages the: (a) geographic areas across the United States, (b) schools in each area, and (c) students within the schools. Most schools invited to participate agreed to do so, and if any didn't, a similar school was obtained in its place. Student response rates were typically quite high, ranging from 82% to 91% across grades and years, with about 15,500 to 18,300 participants at each grade each year, on average. Because the survey assessed the patterns of use for a very large number of substances, it was divided into parts, each of which was usually administered during a normal class period. The data from this research are amazingly detailed and clear, and it is possible to compare school grades, genders, and ethnic groups at each year and to chart the course of substance use across years with a great degree of confidence in the accuracy of the data. The main limitation to the design is that the sample does not include individuals who drop out of school, which is important to keep in mind when interpreting the data.

How do researchers analyze the data from large-scale surveys? Although they can perform inferential statistics, such as correlations or ANOVAs, for some variables, they often simply report frequencies or percentages if the intention is to describe the target population. The report for the study on substance use presents over 200 pages of tables and graphs describing the frequencies and percentages of students claiming specific patterns of use for each substance. As an example, Table 12.1 presents data from that study giving the percentages of students at each grade level who claimed they drank heavily (five or more alcoholic drinks in a row) certain numbers of times in the prior 2 weeks. Notice that the percentage of students claiming to have drunk heavily at least once was about 15% among eighth graders and increased with grade level. Because this study is repeated each year, data can be compared across years to see if a trend exists—perhaps heavy drinking has increased or decreased steadily during the past several years. As you can see, the outcomes of descriptive research can be extremely important and have clear relevance to decisions people and organizations must make, such as whether and at what ages to offer programs to prevent substance use.

ARCHIVAL DATA METHODS

Other methods for doing descriptive research involve collecting *archival data,* which, as we discussed in Chapter 4, are traces of behavior that exist in hard copy or electronic formats, such as material in newspapers or on Internet sites. Representativeness is also important here: the data sampled should mirror the corresponding population of archival data. For instance, if we are doing a study of topics on Internet chat rooms and want to generalize our findings to all chat rooms, the ones we sample should be representative of the full range.

TABLE 12.1

Percentages of 8th, 10th, and 12th-grade Students Who Claimed the Specified Numbers of Times They Had Drunk Alcohol Heavily. (The question asked, "Think back over the LAST TWO WEEKS. How many times have you had five or more drinks in a row?")

| Number of times | School grade | | |
	8th	10th	12th
None	84.8	74.4	69.2
Once	6.0	8.7	10.2
Twice	4.3	7.0	7.6
3 to 5 times	2.8	6.1	8.7
6 to 9 times	1.2	2.1	2.7
10 or more times	0.9	1.7	1.7

Source: from Johnston, O'Malley, & Bachman (2000, Table 4-4b), the Monitoring the Future Study of the University of Michigan Institute for Social Research.

An example of descriptive research with archival data is a study of sex bias in psychology journal publications (Gannon, Luchetta, Rhodes, Pardie, & Segrist, 1992). At the time these researchers decided to do their study, the APA had had policies for a long time against sex bias in publishing, such as in the use of sexist language in journal articles. The purpose of their study was to describe any changes in sexism in published articles that had occurred in the past 20 years or so. The researchers identified eight journals representing a broad range of psychology areas, such as developmental, physiological, and clinical psychology, and examined all the published articles in those journals from the years 1970, 1975, 1980, 1985, and 1990 (except for one journal that began publishing in 1978). An important strength of this study is the inclusion of journals from diverse fields in psychology, which enhances the representativeness of the sample and the external validity of the findings. The researchers decided in advance to exclude articles reporting case studies and research with animals as subjects, but they still had 4,952 articles to examine!

Each article was read and coded for several forms of sex bias, such as the use of sexist language (for instance, using the pronoun "he" when the sex of the person is undetermined) or inappropriately generalizing from results with participants of one sex to people of both sexes. The data were presented in tables giving the percentages of articles in which there was evidence of each form of sex bias assessed in the study. Table 12.2 gives an example, showing increases in the percentage of articles with nonsexist language in virtually all the journals, with the largest changes occurring by 1980. Changes for most other measures of sex bias were similar, and chi-square analyses comparing the percentages across years revealed significantly less sex bias for most measures over the 20-year span. We can see the descriptive nature of the study's outcome clearly in the authors' conclusion: in published research articles "sexism in psychology has been diminished but not eliminated in the past two decades" (p. 394). This conclusion is a concise description of the change and current status of sex bias in psychology research articles.

TABLE 12.2

Percentage of Studies That Used Nonsexist Language in Each Journal Each Year (J. means "Journal of")

	Year				
Journal	**1970**	**1975**	**1980**	**1985**	**1990**
Developmental Psychology	37	46	97	99	100
Child Development	18	29	79	87	98
J. Abnormal Psychology	41	61	93	100	100
J. Consulting and Clinical Psychology	51	65	92	83	99
Psychophysiology	46	72	84	89	95
J. Behavioral Medicine	—	100[a]	100	96	98
J. Personality and Social Psychology	29	38	81	91	99
J. Experimental Social Psychology	13	31	81	98	99

[a] Data for 1978 (this journal was not published before 1978).

Source: Gannon et al., 1992, Table 5.

NATURALISTIC OBSERVATION METHODS

Another approach for collecting data for descriptive research uses naturalistic observation methods. The term **naturalistic observation** means that the researcher observes subjects' behavior in a "natural," or ordinary, setting without trying to influence or structure it. The goal in using this method is usually to describe the behavior and its normal flow, as it occurs ordinarily. Making sure the setting is ordinary enhances the representativeness of the behavior studied. Often, the researchers will make efforts to be very inconspicuous and unobtrusive, so as not to affect the behavior they observe and record.

The study on submissive behavior of boys in fights that we discussed at the start of this chapter is a good example of descriptive research using the method of naturalistic observation (Ginsburg et al., 1977). The boys' behavior was observed in a natural setting, a playground, while the researchers were unobtrusively stationed in a van parked nearby and did nothing to influence the behaviors they recorded. The outcome of that research was descriptive: The boys showed submissive behaviors, like those of animals, that made them look smaller when losing a fight, and the researchers described variations in the specific behaviors the boys displayed. Other examples of situations in which naturalistic observation might be used in descriptive research include recording the behavior of protesters toward police, schoolchildren when they have a substitute teacher, fish when a potential mate is present, and birds when a new bird of their species comes into their territory. Studies of animal behavior often use naturalistic observation methods and are commonly done in the field of *ethology,* which is closely allied to biology and zoology.

A major drawback can occur with the method of naturalistic observation: The observations can take a great deal of time, sometimes just in waiting for something of interest to happen. Think of the study of boys' submissive behavior at the playground. The observers were cooped up in the van for 16 hours, waiting for fights to break out. Fortunately for the researchers, fights occurred fairly often—72 fights in 16 hours comes to one fight every 13 minutes or so. What if the researchers had observed older boys, or girls? They might have waited much longer for each fight. Another drawback to naturalistic observation is that usually the observer must be concealed, which may not be possible in all situations. Being unobtrusive may be necessary to avoid influencing the behavior. Just the presence of an observer can produce changes in behavior—the phenomenon of *reactivity* that we saw in Chapter 4. One way to prevent these problems is to automate the observations with electronic devices. For example, Mehl and Pennebaker (2003) conducted a study to describe the social environments and natural conversations of undergraduate participants by having them wear computer-controlled tape recorders that recorded 30-second episodes of sounds five times an hour every hour the students were awake during four days of a semester. From these recordings, the researchers were able to describe how and where the students spent time and even the frequencies of their using certain types of words and expressing positive and negative emotions.

In some research situations, the observer must join the individuals who are being observed, which is called *participant observation.* This approach is sometimes used when studying social behaviors in large groups, such as in a club. Sometimes the group can be allowed to know the observer is doing research, but often they cannot know because of their likely reactivity. Three special difficulties can arise with participant observation, especially if the group cannot know the observers are doing research. First, joining a group to do research involves deception, which may be unethical. Second, if observers need to act like participants, how do they avoid influencing the other people's behavior? Third, if the observers cannot take notes or use other ways of collecting data that would reveal their function, how can they keep accurate records of the other people's actions?

STRUCTURED TEST METHODS

Another approach we'll consider for conducting descriptive research involves setting up or structuring the test situation to determine how individuals react to or behave in that situation. By structuring the test situation, the researcher tries to increase the likelihood that the behavior of interest, such as people's helping another person, will occur. Often the purpose of the structuring is to enhance the opportunity to observe the behavior rather than waiting for it to occur naturally. If you wanted to know whether a child knows her home phone number, you could wait until she happens to tell you, or you could just ask! Asking would structure the situation, making the child's stating the number more likely if she knows it. Although methods like these can be used in research that uses an experimental strategy and manipulates an independent variable, we are focusing here on using these methods with descriptive research strategies.

Some of the best-known examples of descriptive research using structured test methods come from Piaget's (1929, 1952, 1977) studies of cognitive development in childhood. He devised many tests of children's ability to use several types of logic in their thinking, and we'll consider two logical operations: reversing and decentering. In *reversing*, people can turn around a sequence of logic or events to restore an original condition or state. One test Piaget used to study reversing involved asking a series of questions, like the following set you might use with a 4-year-old named Bonnie:

> YOU: "Do you have a sister?"
> BONNIE: "Yes."
> YOU: "What's her name?"
> BONNIE: "Josie."
> YOU: "Does Josie have a sister?"
> BONNIE: "No."

To answer correctly, Bonnie would need to reverse the logical sequence, which she didn't do. In *decentering*, people can consider more than one aspect of a situation at a time to arrive at a decision. For example, suppose you take two identical balls of clay and ask Bonnie if they are the same size, and she says they have the same amount. If you then flatten one of the balls and ask her whether they both still have the same amount, she'd probably say "No." Then if you ask her which one has more and why, she points to one and explains, "Because it's taller" if it is the round ball, or "Because it's wider" if it is the flattened one. Note that she is centering on one dimension, either height *or* width, and neglecting the fact that changes in one dimension are compensated by the other. The outcomes of tests like these with children of different ages led Piaget to describe the course of cognitive development as a series of "stages" that correspond to specific age ranges and are characterized by logical abilities that are or are not present.

CASE STUDY METHODS

We saw in Chapter 11 that *case studies* examine single individuals in intrasubject designs with the purpose of providing a biographical description, usually to illustrate an unusual psychological disorder, a new finding about a common disorder, or a situation that contradicts common notions. As such, they constitute descriptive research. One widely reported case study is of a 29-year-old man who suffered substantial losses in memory function after having successful brain surgery to reduce his very severe and frequent epileptic seizures (Scoville & Milner, 1957, case of "H. M."). His memory had been good before the surgery, but deficits were clear at an evaluation a couple of years after. For instance, he couldn't recall having conversed with someone moments earlier, and when asked the current date and his age, he reported a date and corresponding age from before the surgery. This research suggested caution in using surgery to treat epilepsy. In Chapter 11 (Box 11.1) we examined a case study that illustrated the failure of sex reassignment methods with a boy, thereby providing an instance that contradicted the prevailing belief of experts. Although case studies typically lack control over extraneous variables and do not meet the criteria for causal inference, they can have a great deal of impact because they present dramatic and persuasive demonstrations, making the information or issue concrete and poignant rather than abstract (Kazdin, 2003). In fact, researchers and journals probably select to some degree the cases to publish for their likely dramatic force. (Go to **Box 12.1**)

Box 12.1   COMBINING DESCRIPTIVE METHODS

Can we enhance a study's results by combining descriptive methods? Yes, researchers did this in a descriptive study of children's helping behavior, which prior studies with naturalistic observation methods had indicated occurs rarely in children (Peterson, Ridley-Johnson, & Carter, 1984). The basic study involved the observation of day care children with structured test methods in a natural situation in which the opportunity to help was introduced in a creative way. The teacher announced to the children in a play session that she had a new toy, a "super suit," for them to use in turns, each for 4 minutes. Each child would have a chance to wear the "suit"—a colorful smock—over his or her clothes, fastening it with a large button at the back of the neck. But the fastening would require some help: prior testing with similar children had shown that they could fasten the button for other individuals, but not for themselves. The fastening provided a structured test of helping in a very natural situation.

continued

To make sure all children had an opportunity to wear the suit, the teacher drew out of a jar a child's name when it was time for a new child to wear it. Then, the teacher would set a timer (for 4 minutes), put the suit on the new child without buttoning it, and say quietly to the child that she was busy and couldn't button it. An observer who was present started videotaping the child at that point, and the teacher returned to working on classroom materials. All the children were playing freely during testing, and the suited child could deal with the issue of buttoning the smock as he or she wished, such as by asking for help, trying to button it alone, or just holding it in place with a hand. After the testing was over, two observers watched the video recordings independently for instances of several behaviors of the suited child and the other children. For example, the suited child might ask for help or react positively or negatively to another child's offering help. Another child might refuse to help or offer verbally or physically to button the smock either when the suited child asked or gestured for help, called *prompted helping,* or without having been prompted, called *spontaneous helping.* Interobserver reliability for these measures was high, with agreement 91% of the time, on average.

During the more than 3 hours of observation, the children had 56 opportunities to help and showed a great deal of helping: there were 32 instances of spontaneous helping and 13 instances of prompted helping. The authors noted that this amount of helping "is quite an increase over the average of less than once-per-hour rate of helping reported in unstructured naturalistic situations [in prior studies], yet the task was one commonly present in this and similar preschool classrooms" (p. 238). Thus, the structure increased the opportunity to observe the behavior, without making the situation artificial, and showed that preschoolers generally provide help when it is needed. Other observations about the children's behavior were also quite interesting, such as that

> children rarely reinforce one another for altruism. For example, child recipients gave positive consequences for the donor only in six . . . helping opportunities. The recipient was more likely to give neutral consequences when receiving help (i. e., the child who had been helped just walked away). However, more child recipients actually gave negative consequences (e.g., "go away" and a shove in response to another child's attempt to help fasten the suit) than positive consequences for helping. (p. 238)

You can see in this account a richness of the description of the flow of social behavior, in some ways like portions of a case study.

By also incorporating a survey method into the study, the researchers were able to add to the descriptive richness of the findings. They had the children rate on a scale with smiley faces specific social features of a classmate, such as how much they liked to play and work with that child, to assess the social competence of each classmate. From these data, the researchers were able to determine that the three children with the highest social competence ratings gave most of the help and never had their offers of help refused.

PROGRAM EVALUATION

The type of research called **program evaluation** is designed to assess the need for and success of interventions or policies—the "programs"—usually on a large scale, such as for a school or community (Posavac & Carey, 1997). The goals of a program can be quite varied and can include reducing highway speeding, improving rehabilitation programs, aiding people who need medical treatment or welfare assistance, providing job training, and preventing substance use in adolescence. The organizations that provide programs and conduct evaluations can be governments; nonprofit groups, such as the American Heart Association; or for-profit organizations, such as businesses that provide home health care for the aged, wellness programs for employees, or job training.

The outcomes of program evaluations often have political implications, especially when the programs require government approval or funding. Here are some examples of topics studied in the United States in recent years (Passell, 1993; Talbot, 2002):

- Do welfare families who receive allotments of cash instead of food stamps buy less food?
- Does providing home health care services for free to elderly poor people save money in the long run by reducing expenses for nursing home care?
- Do boys and girls learn better in school in sex-segregated than in coed classes?

Each of these issues has political ramifications. Under these circumstances, biases often affect decisions regarding the characteristics of the program to offer and the timing and design of its evaluation. For instance, administrators have vested interests in the results of evaluations of their programs and often want to limit or influence what the studies find and report in press releases and journals. As Campbell (1969) pointed out decades ago:

> Ambiguity, lack of truly comparable comparison bases, and lack of concrete evidence all work to increase the administrator's control over what gets said, or at least to reduce the bite of criticism in the case of actual failure. There is safety under the cloak of ignorance. (pp. 409–410)

These conditions still exist and, along with difficulties in obtaining the funds needed to do carefully controlled research, can undermine the quality of a program evaluation. And these conditions also affect politicians' decisions: would you want to be a public official whom people "blame" for a program that used a lot of time and money, but failed?

The overarching goal of program evaluation research is to provide information and feedback that administrators and public officials can use in deciding what programs to offer and how to structure or improve them. Although program evaluations often focus on assessing the outcomes of policies or interventions, they can have other objectives as well (Posavac & Carey, 1997). We'll examine the most common purposes of program research, beginning with assessing the need for a program in the first place.

NEEDS ANALYSIS

Before designing and implementing a policy or intervention, researchers can conduct a *needs analysis,* a study to identify whether a problem exists, what services or conditions might help reduce the problem, and how many people are likely to be affected by the problem and use a program to correct it. As this definition suggests, needs analyses almost always use descriptive research strategies. Now, suppose we wanted to assess a community's needs regarding public transportation, particularly for elderly people. Data for a needs analysis can be obtained in several ways (Posavac & Carey, 1997). Archival data may be available, such as in census or other public records, which we might use to determine how many elderly people live in the community, for example. Surveys can be conducted with a representative sample, especially of elderly residents, to find out what means of transportation they currently use and how often, at what times, and for what purposes they'd use public transportation, such as busses. We may also want to conduct an inventory of existing transportation services, such as taxis, and to interview some individuals with specialized knowledge, such as social workers or people who work at senior citizen centers.

PROCESS AND OUTCOME ANALYSIS

Once a program has been under way for a while, program evaluations can be done for two other purposes (Posavac & Carey, 1997). A *process analysis* can examine whether the program's services or conditions are known in the target population, are being used or followed by enough people, and are being implemented and structured in the proper manner. As Posavac and Carey (1997) describe,

> Evaluations of process involve checking on the assumptions made while the program was being planned. Do the needs of the organization or community match what was believed during planning? Is there evidence to support the assessment of needs made during the planning stage? Do the activities carried out by the staff match the plans for the program? (pp. 7–8)

We can obtain the data to answer these questions through surveys, records kept by staff, and observations of staff activities. Assessing how the program is being implemented is very important for two reasons. First, if the program activities are not being carried out properly, we can revise them. Second, if the target population is not using or following the program, we would not want to conclude that the planned techniques or design were the reason for the failure if the problem is that they were not applied correctly.

An *outcome analysis* assesses the impact or results of the program. Is the program achieving its goal? For example, in the program to improve transportation for the elderly, has it enabled them to lead active lives and get where they need to go? Whatever the goal, the program evaluation research needs to have a way of measuring the intended changes. In the transportation program for the elderly, we might want to assess how often they leave their homes, whether they missed important appointments because of a lack of transportation, their satisfaction with the new means of getting around, and so on. The outcome measures for programs with other goals would be different, of course. For instance, an outcome analysis for a program to prevent teenagers from starting to use drugs might measure teens' self-reports of drug use, arrest records, or even blood test results. Regardless of the type of goal, the outcome analysis would compare data either from before and after the program for the same individuals or from people who did and did not have the program, which can be done with a descriptive, quasi-experimental, or experimental strategy using the designs outlined in Figure 7.1 (see inside back cover).

Let's consider how a drug prevention program in high schools might apply the different strategies in an outcome analysis. With a *descriptive strategy,* the researchers would present the frequencies or percentages for the measures selected, such as for self-reports of drug use, for teens who did and did not get the program. Because this strategy would not control extraneous variables and not assess the reliability of the differences, it would provide relatively weak evidence for the program's success. If the outcome analysis uses a *quasi-experimental strategy,* it would use inferential statistics, such as *t* tests or ANOVAs, to compare drug use before and after the program without a control group or to compare individuals in the program with a nonequivalent control group, such as students in other schools. Although this approach would provide a stronger test of the program's success, it could not determine unambiguously that the program caused any differences found. In an outcome analysis with an *experimental strategy,* the students in schools would be separated into an experimental (program) and a control group and equated before the program began. One way to equate the groups would be to use cluster sampling (identifying a large number of homeroom classes, for example) and randomly assign those classes to groups. The classes in the experimental group would receive the program, and the others would not. This approach can be difficult to do strategically and politically— for instance, interest groups may lobby public officials or administrators to include certain segments of the students in the experimental group.

When random assignment is not possible, researchers need to be creative to find ways to make the groups as equivalent as possible, as Becker, Rabinowitz, and Seligman (1980) did in an outcome analysis. The program was a new billing plan an electric utility company offered in which residential customers could opt to equalize payments over the year, paying one twelfth the annual total each month rather than amounts that fluctuated with energy use. The concern was whether this plan would increase energy use because consumption would not be tied to the size of each monthly bill. To test this possibility, the researchers wanted to compare energy use for households that did and did not opt for the equal payment plan, but they could not randomly assign households to the conditions. So they decided to compare only adjacent households (not including apartments), those 221 that chose the equal payment plan and 254 next-door neighbors that did not, thereby matching the participants in the two conditions on a variety of relevant variables. Next-door households are likely to be more similar than far-apart households in income, size of houses, and number of occupants, for instance. The final design was a 2 × 2 factorial that compared energy consumption in the summers before and after the plan was offered for households that did and did not opt for it. Figure 12.1 presents the mean energy use for each condition, and an ANOVA revealed that both main effects were significant, but the interaction was not. These results

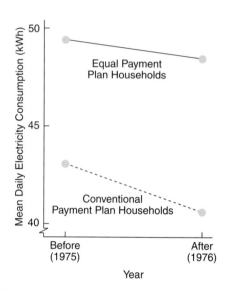

FIGURE 12.1

Mean electricity use in kilowatt–hours (kWh) for households choosing the equal payment plan or the conventional payment plan (paying for the amount consumed each month) in the summers before (that is, in 1975) and after (1976) the billing program was introduced. The second summer was somewhat cooler than the first, which accounts for the decreased consumption. (Data from Becker et al., 1980, Table 1—the PEPCO study)

mean that the equal payment households used more energy than their neighbors did, and both groups used less energy in the second summer than the first. The lack of an interaction between the two factors means that the program had no effect on consumption: If the equal payment plan had affected energy use, the two graph lines would be distinctly nonparallel. (Go to **Box 12.2**)

Efficiency Analysis

Once outcome analyses demonstrate that a program works, program evaluation needs to deal with its efficiency, which usually relates to the issue of costs (Posavac & Carey, 1997). Policy changes and interventions typically cost money, and the organizations that oversee and fund the programs must make choices of how to spend their budgets. They will need to know the program's *efficiency*— that is, its costs relative to its benefits—so they can decide whether to implement or continue it and whether another program might be more efficient. We've seen this issue before, in Chapter 11, where we discussed the *cost–benefit ratio,* the extent to which the costs of providing a program outweigh the money saved in the long run (Jospe et al., 1991; Kaplan, 1989).

A program that costs $100 and saves $1,000 is more efficient than a program that costs $100 and saves $400. But often the costs of providing a program are more easily assessed than its full benefits. At a workplace, for example, what benefits of a wellness program could we assess in dollars to compare with the costs of running it? We might assess worker absenteeism or medical insurance claims, but these variables would reveal only part of the benefits. They wouldn't reflect other important financial gains, such as in workers' improved job satisfaction and resulting increases in productivity. Not taking into account all the benefits will produce a low cost–benefit ratio and, perhaps, lead to a decision not to apply the program. In some settings, such as in managed health care, the costs

BOX 12.2   D.A.R.E.: A PROGRAM THAT HAS FAILED, SO FAR

If you live in the United States, you've probably seen bumper stickers for D.A.R.E., the very popular Drug Abuse Resistance Education program that is conducted in schools by police officers. The officers are specially trained to teach children from kindergarten to 12th grade skills to recognize and resist pressures that lead them to become involved in substance use and violent activities. Is the program effective? The D.A.R.E. Website claims that the program "has proven so successful that it is now being implemented in nearly 75 percent of our nation's school districts and in more than 52 countries around the world" (D.A.R.E., 2000). The widespread use of the program is clear, but that doesn't necessarily mean it is effective. We'll consider what program evaluations have found.

Many outcome analyses have been conducted on the D.A.R.E. program and have revealed little success, so far (Lynam et al., 1999). Most of these studies have compared substance use and related attitudes of students in schools with and without D.A.R.E. programs, and some have evaluated the effects over long periods of time. For example, Lynam et al. (1999) conducted a 10-year follow-up of over 1,000 19- to 21-year-olds who provided data initially while in the sixth grade and had continued to participate by filling out surveys; 76% of them had received D.A.R.E. in school. Of the original 31 schools in the study, 23 had been randomly assigned to receive the program, and the remaining 8 schools served as the control group that received the standard substance information in health education classes. The outcome analysis used surveys to assess the frequency of use of and positive and negative attitudes about cigarettes, alcohol, marijuana, and other illicit drugs. No differences between groups were found for any of the questions about any substance examined. Given the lack of success, why is the program popular among parents and teachers? The authors suggest that the popularity may result from biased perceptions of its success. For example, the parents and teachers correctly see that most students who receive D.A.R.E. do not use drugs in the future, but fail to realize that most students without the program don't use drugs, either.

and benefits of programs can be assessed more easily, such as by using the financial records of a health maintenance organization (HMO) that offers a program. For example, Cronan, Groessl, and Kaplan (1997) studied the benefits and costs to an HMO of programs designed to help arthritis patients adjust to and manage their disease. The researchers randomly assigned the patients to three different interventions and a control condition and examined the program costs and patients' medical expenses for each condition. We'll consider only the data for the least costly program here: compared to the control condition, it saved $315,588 and cost just $27,900 in the first year, saving over $11.30 for each $1 spent.

Science is a creative enterprise that evolves as old questions are answered and people with new perspectives enter the field. As the research questions become more detailed and sophisticated, advances are also made in the methods researchers apply to examine them. Sometimes the advanced methods involve the way data are collected, such as by using electronic devices to help measure behavior during people's everyday lives. For example, a recently developed method called *ecological momentary assessment* allows researchers to collect data repeatedly for participants in their natural activities, such as by using pagers to cue individuals to rate how much stress they are feeling (Shiffman & Stone, 1998). Other advanced methods involve new design or statistical approaches.

Recent advances in research design and statistical procedures will be the focus of the rest of this chapter. Actually, all the methods we've discussed so far were at one time very creative and important scientific advances. For instance, the design of scientific research was transformed after Fisher (1935) published a book describing the logic of experiments and the concepts and procedures for performing analysis of variance. Winer (1962) has described the impact of this work and the intertwining of research design and statistics in the following way:

> The steps from logic to mathematics are small ones. The now classic work on the basic statistical principles underlying experimental design is R. A. Fisher's *The Design of Experiments*. This work includes more than purely mathematical arguments—it probes into the basic logical structure of experiments and examines the manner in which experiments can provide information about problems put to experimental test. Depending on how the experiment is conducted, it may or may not provide information about the issues at question. (p. 3)

If you think back to prior chapters, you'll notice that the analysis of variance is essential in testing for differences among more than two conditions in a study and particularly for factorial designs. Although Fisher's work was originally applied in agricultural research, it was extended to other disciplines and made complex designs possible in psychology. We'll turn now to a description of some advanced research methods that were introduced in the last few decades, are based on creative statistical procedures, and have already produced important findings in psychology.

META-ANALYSIS

A **meta-analysis** is a statistical research method that pools the results of prior studies to create an integrated overview of their findings (Glass, 1976; Rosenthal, 1984; Rosenthal & DiMatteo, 2002; Suls & Swain, 1993). No new data are collected. Researchers who plan to perform a meta-analysis identify a question that has been tested in at least a few past studies and then obtain critical data from those studies, either in published research reports or from the original researchers. The types of data a meta-analysis needs from the studies it includes can vary, depending on its purpose or approach.

Two approaches are commonly used in meta-analyses (Suls & Swain, 1993). In the *combined probability* approach, the purpose of the meta-analysis is to test the overall statistical significance across studies. For this approach, the data we use from the studies must enable us to determine the probability (p) levels for the relevant comparisons so that the statistical methods can test whether the pattern of p values across studies is unlikely to have occurred by chance alone. Thus, we would have a p value representing the overall reliability of the effect across studies. In the *combined estimation* approach, the purpose of the meta-analysis is to estimate the overall effect size of the independent variable across studies. Thus, the data we obtain from the studies must be such that estimates of effect size can be determined for the variables of interest in each study. These data can be as simple as the mean, standard deviation, and number of subjects for each relevant group or condition, but they can also use the outcomes of statistical analyses, such as t or F values. The statistical procedures in the meta-analysis will pool the effect sizes from the studies and calculate an overall effect-size estimate.

Which meta-analysis approach should researchers use? The answer depends on the nature of the question being asked and the data available for the analysis, and a single study can use both approaches (Suls & Swain, 1993). The combined probability approach tests only whether the null hypothesis concerning the variables examined is false across studies. It does not estimate the strength of the relationship. This approach is very useful when an independent variable has been tested in many studies, but some have found significant effects and some have not. The combined estimation approach is especially useful when it is already clear that a variable has a reliable effect, but we want to know how strong the effect is. According to Suls and Swain, combined estimation has more rigorous requirements:

> First, all studies should have similar designs and measure the outcome in a similar way. Second, unlike the probability method in which only the p value is required, combined estimation requires indices of the study effect size which means that information about standard deviations and cell sizes is required. (1993, p. 17)

A problem that often occurs is that published reports may not provide the data needed for the combined estimation approach, and those data may not be available from the original researcher either. In such cases, the meta-analysis may need to discard studies that do not have the required data or rely instead on assessing the combined probability without estimating the overall effect size.

Let's look at an example of a meta-analysis that used both approaches. Fredrikson and Matthews (1990) knew that many studies had found that hypertension (the condition of persistently high blood pressure) and people's physical reactions to stress were related, but other studies had not. In general, when individuals experience stress, they react more strongly if they have hypertension than if they do not. The researchers decided to focus their meta-analysis on the effects of hypertension on cardiovascular reactivity—that is, physiological changes in response to stress that occur in the heart, blood vessels, and blood—such as increased blood pressure and heart rate. They also decided to include only studies that, for instance, tested hypertensive patients who were not currently taking drugs to correct the condition and had a control group consisting of people with normal blood pressure. Then they searched the medical and psychological literature using these and other restrictions, found dozens of studies that qualified, and performed the meta-analysis computations. Because their findings were very complicated, we'll focus on those pertaining to one cardiovascular reactivity measure: systolic blood pressure—the maximum force in the arteries when the heart pumps. The combined probability approach across the studies revealed significantly greater blood pressure reactions to stress among hypertensive than control participants ($p < .001$). And the combined estimation approach yielded moderately strong effect sizes (Cohen's *d*): between .45 and .60, depending on the severity of the patients' hypertension.

An important feature of meta-analysis methods is that they allow researchers to examine the role of *moderator variables*, or factors that can alter the relationship between the independent and dependent variables. Fredrikson and Matthews examined moderator variables and found two previously unknown relationships. First, patients with relatively mild hypertension exhibit cardiovascular reactivity mainly to stressful situations that require them to be active (such as doing arithmetic problems in their heads) rather than passive (watching a stressful film). Second, patients with relatively severe hypertension show high reactivity to both active and passive stressful situations. It seems plausible that many prior studies had found no link between cardiovascular reactivity and hypertension because they tested people with mild hypertension in passive stress situations.

Prior to the development of meta-analysis techniques, the only way to summarize and generalize the findings on a topic was to present a narrative review. For a narrative review, the researcher reads and organizes a large number of studies on a topic, and then tries to draw conclusions about the state of the knowledge in the field and the issues that need more research. Each of these ways of describing the state of knowledge on a topic provides important information from the perspective of one or more experts in the field, is very useful, and complements the other.

MULTIVARIATE ANALYSES

The term **multivariate analysis** usually refers to a category of statistical procedures that involve two or more dependent variables, but it frequently includes correlational methods with one dependent variable and more than one independent variable. We will use the broader definition here and consider the methods of multivariate analysis of variance and structural modeling.

Multivariate Analysis of Variance (MANOVA)

Our earlier discussions of analysis of variance have dealt with the case in which each ANOVA is performed on data for a single dependent variable. But sometimes it is useful or necessary to calculate an analysis of variance for a set of dependent variables all at once, especially if they are conceptually related or aspects of the same construct. The **multivariate analysis of variance** (MANOVA) tests for differences between the means for two or more conditions, using two or more dependent variables simultaneously. For example, suppose we conducted a study to compare people's psychological adjustment after either 2 months of psychotherapy, 2 weeks of therapy, or no therapy (control), with the dependent variables being the clients' self-reports, ratings by a therapist, and ratings by family members. Because the three dependent variables are conceptually related, we might want to use the MANOVA technique to see if the different amounts of therapy affected adjustment overall, across all measures. An advantage to using a MANOVA in these circumstances is that this test maintains the alpha level at .05, whereas performing multiple ANOVAs—that is, one for each dependent variable—increases the likelihood of Type I error.

An example study that used the multivariate analysis approach examined whether age at diagnosis of asthma influences the types of triggers that affect children's asthma episodes (Sarafino, Gates, & DePaulo, 2001). The researchers had parents rate for their child's asthma the impacts of 12 common triggers, eight that are mainly physically based (such as air pollution, allergy problems, and physical activity) and four that are psychosocially mediated (stress or worry, anger, excitement, and laughter). The children in the sample were separated into two groups: those who were diagnosed before 2 years of age and those diagnosed at or after 2. Because at the time of the study the later-diagnosed children were older than the early-diagnosed children, the researchers used a special form of MANOVA that could take the current ages into account; it's called a multiple analysis of *co*variance, or MANCOVA, for short. Two analyses were done, each testing whether the early- and later-diagnosed children differed in trigger impacts; one MANCOVA was performed on the set of physically based triggers, and the other was done on the set of psychosocially mediated triggers. These tests revealed significantly greater impacts of psychosocially mediated triggers for the later-diagnosed than the early-diagnosed children, but no age of diagnosis differences for the physically based triggers.

Once a significant difference is found with a MANOVA (or MANCOVA) for a set of dependent variables, we can perform an individual ANOVA for each variable in the set. The researchers in the asthma triggers study did this and found a significantly greater impact of each psychosocially mediated trigger— stress or worry, anger, excitement, and laughter—for the later-diagnosed than the early-diagnosed children.

Structural Modeling and Path Analysis

A very sophisticated and complex multivariate procedure can be used to enhance the ability to make causal inferences from studies using correlational strategies. In **structural modeling,** researchers test a "model" of the pattern of correlations among variables that would exist if the relationships are causal. The model is usually diagrammed as following a path across time, with each variable having a proposed effect on the next variable in a series. For this reason, the statistical procedure is often called *path analysis,* especially when only one measure of each variable is used.

Figure 12.2 shows a diagram of the model and data from a study of variables that can lead to psychological distress in women with a first degree relative with ovarian cancer (Schwartz, Lerman, Miller, Daly, & Masny, 1995). Look at the arrows in the model, but disregard the data on them for now. The arrows predict that the *monitoring* (that is, high vigilance to threatening cues) of individuals in stressful situations would lead to *intrusive thoughts* (ideas and images about the cues), which would lead to *distress* in a direct path; perceptions of *risk*

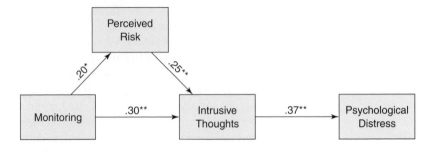

FIGURE 12.2

Diagram of a path model of variables leading to psychological distress of women with a first-degree relative with ovarian cancer. The model indicates that the path from monitoring to the women's distress is direct, through intrusive thoughts; the path through perceived risk is indirect. The coefficients along the arrows were adjusted (controlled) for possible third variables pertaining to the women and their first-degree relatives with cancer (* indicates $p < .05$; ** indicates $p < .01$). (From Schwartz et al., 1995, Figure 1.)

would operate indirectly and not as strongly. Ratings for the four variables were obtained with surveys. The statistical procedure in structural modeling uses regression methods to assess how well the model and the actual data from the study "fit," or correspond. That is, it determines whether the pattern of correlations in the data and model correspond. The correlations should be stronger along the direct path than the indirect path. This is where the coefficients along the arrows are relevant: They show that monitoring predicted the women's intrusive thoughts in direct and indirect (through risk) paths, which then predicted distress. Each significant correlation in the analysis is represented with an arrow. The pattern of correlations shows that the model and the data match well, thereby supporting the model's description of the processes by which monitoring leads to distress. Structural modeling can also be used to compare the success of more than one model, determining which fits the data better.

Keep in mind that structural modeling is a correlational procedure. Although its outcome does not provide a fully unambiguous test of the predicted causes in the model, it does indicate whether the predicted causes are plausible. Because researchers who use path analysis devise the structural model in advance and determine the degree to which the data match the model, the results come closer to meeting the criteria for cause–effect conclusions than correlational studies usually do.

As this final chapter comes to a close, I hope you have enjoyed reading this book and have gained a clear understanding of and appreciation for scientific approaches in studying psychology. Because this information will be important in your future courses and career, you'll probably find the book useful to refer to for many years. To the extent that the information you have learned enables you to think more critically and carefully about evidence and to make contributions in your career, I will have done my job.

SUMMARY

Descriptive research is designed and conducted to detail or classify events or phenomena, or to chart their course, without manipulating an independent variable or controlling extraneous variables rigorously. Several approaches can be used to collect data for descriptive research. In large-scale surveys, researchers try to recruit a large sample that is representative of the population they want to describe. Nonresponse bias and social desirability bias can impair the validity and generality of the findings. Another method for conducting descriptive research involves using naturalistic observation in which researchers monitor behavior in ordinary settings without trying to influence it. Other descriptive research methods use archival data, structured tests, and case studies. These methods can be combined to enhance a study's results.

Program evaluation research is designed to assess the need for and success of policies or interventions that usually apply to large numbers of people, such as an entire school or community. There are four types of program evaluation research, each with a different purpose. A needs analysis is conducted before introducing a program to describe the extent of the problem it would address, one or more programs that could reduce the problem, and the likelihood that people who need the program will use it. The other types of program evaluation occur after the program has been implemented. A process analysis examines whether the target population is aware of and using the program and whether the program is being carried out as designed. An outcome analysis assesses the extent to which the program is achieving its goal, and an efficiency analysis examines the cost of a program relative to its benefits.

Scientific methods and the questions they are designed to answer evolve over time and lead to new and advanced methods, often involving creative statistical procedures. One advanced statistical method, called meta-analysis, combines the results of prior studies, rather than collecting new data, to provide an overview of the findings. A meta-analysis can use a combined probability approach to determine the overall statistical significance of the results across studies and a combined estimation approach to estimate the overall effect size of an independent variable. Other advanced statistical methods are called multivariate analysis, which includes the application of a multivariate analysis of variance (MANOVA) to examine the effects of an independent variable for a set of two or more dependent variables. A multivariate analysis method called structural modeling is a correlational approach in which researchers test a model of the relationships among variables that would exist if the relationships are causal.

KEY TERMS

naturalistic observation	multivariate analysis	structural modeling
program evaluation	multivariate analysis of	
meta-analysis	variance	

REVIEW QUESTIONS

1. Describe the study by Ginsburg et al. (1977) on boys' submissive behaviors when losing a fight.
2. Why is it important to have a representative sample in descriptive research with large-scale survey methods?
3. Describe the problems of *nonresponse bias* and *social desirability bias* in survey research.
4. Describe the strengths of the survey methods used in the Johnston, O'Malley, and Bachman (2000) annual research on adolescent substance use.
5. What are the drawbacks or difficulties in using *naturalistic observation* and *participant observation* methods?
6. Describe the descriptive study of Peterson, Ridley-Johnson, and Carter (1984).
7. Define the type of research called *program evaluation* and its use of *needs analysis, process analysis, outcome analysis,* and *efficiency analysis.*
8. What is a *meta-analysis,* and how is it different from a narrative review?
9. Define the term *multivariate analysis* and the procedures of *multivariate analysis of variance* (MANOVA) and *structural modeling* (path analysis).

RESOURCES

BOOKS, CHAPTERS, AND ARTICLES

Posavac, E. J., & Carey, R. G. (1997). *Program evaluation: Methods and case studies* (5th ed.). Upper Saddle River, NJ: Prentice Hall.

Rosenthal, R. (1984). *Meta-analytic procedures for social research.* Beverly Hills, CA: Sage.

Suls, J., & Swain, A. (1993). Use of meta-analysis in health psychology. In S. Maes, H. Leventhal, & M. Johnston (Eds.), *International review of health psychology* (Vol. 2, pp. 3–28). Chichester, UK: Wiley.

INTERNET SITES

http://www.mapnp.org/library/evaluatn/fnl_eval.htm This Website presents information about planning and implementing program evaluations for nonprofit and for-profit organizations.

http://www.fu-berlin.de/gesund/gesu_engl/meta_e.htm This Website gives a computer program for performing a meta-analysis.

APPLICATION ACTIVITIES

APPLICATION 12–1: DOING DESCRIPTIVE RESEARCH WITH ARCHIVAL DATA

Pick a currently published news magazine, such as *Newsweek* or *Time,* for which your college library has all issues published in the past 20 years and assess whether the use of sexist language has changed in that time. Pick one page from each of the 10 most recent issues and one page from each of 10 issues published 20 years earlier, making sure that each page used contains only text material (no illustrations, such as diagrams or photos). Answer the following questions:

a. How exactly would you decide which qualifying page to use from an issue?
b. What specifically would you look for as evidence of sexism on each page?
c. Collect the data as indicated from the preceding material. How many instances of sexist language did you find for the two time periods?
d. Describe two possible extraneous variables that could be responsible for the pattern of differences (including no differences) you found.

APPLICATION 12–2: PLANNING A PROGRAM EVALUATION PROCESS

Suppose you belong to a club that is considering offering a program to reduce the amount of alcohol the students at your college consume, and you are asked to help design and conduct a program evaluation process. Answer the following questions:

a. Exactly what would you want to find out in a needs analysis?
b. How would you assess drinking and collect the data about it?
c. What would you want to determine in a process analysis, and how would you collect the data?
d. Propose a quasi-experimental design as an outcome analysis to assess whether the program was effective after it has been under way a suitable amount of time.
e. If you were to do an efficiency analysis, how would you measure the program's costs and benefits?

APPLICATION 12–3: PROPOSE A STRUCTURAL MODEL

Propose a model consisting of three variables you believe are probably causally related in a direct path, such that one variable leads to another, which leads to the third (don't use the variables in the book example). Explain what the variables in your model are and the rationale for assuming the sequence of causes.

APPENDIX A

REPORTING THE RESULTS OF RESEARCH

THE PURPOSE AND PROCESS OF COMMUNICATION

A newspaper headline reads, "New Research Finds Children Learn to Write Better with Computers," and the article describes studies comparing second-grade students' writing after being taught writing skills with and without computer tutorials. Scientific research is usually a public enterprise: The outcome of most studies is available to anyone, including scientists and the general public. By communicating the method and outcome of research, the scientist transmits knowledge and enables other researchers to examine critically and in detail exactly what the study did and found. This information can then serve to confirm current theories or be the basis for developing new ideas and questions. In this way, each study plants the seeds for generating future hypotheses and research. The communication can be *written,* such as in a journal article, or *oral,* such as in a speech at a professional convention.

THE GOALS OF COMMUNICATION

Scientific communication has certain basic goals that researchers can meet by conveying four types of information in a written or oral report of a study:

1. *Why the study was done.* The report should outline the practical or theoretical issues and questions the study was intended to test. It should also describe existing research that led to the study's design and state explicit hypotheses.
2. *What the study did.* The report should spell out in detail exactly how the study was conducted.
3. *What the study found.* The report should describe as objectively as possible the results of the study, typically with numerical data that are analyzed with accepted statistical or graphical methods. Some inferential statistics test for differences between groups or conditions, and others test for the degree of relationship between data groupings. In either case, descriptive statistics, particularly the means and standard deviations, for each data grouping should usually be given.
4. *How the study's results relate to current knowledge of the field.* The report should interpret the study's outcome by indicating its theoretical or practical meaning, giving it a context in terms of prior findings, and indicating the strengths and limitations of the method.

You will see more of the details involved in communicating these types of information later in this appendix. For now, keep two points in mind. First, scientific writing is very different from most other types of writing you've done. Second, writing a research report is a very complicated task that is made much easier by being organized. Research reports have a fairly standard structure that is divided into sections, each containing certain types of content. Once you know what types of information go in which sections, the main task is to organize the material within each section. This appendix will help in your writing by giving organizational tips for each section of the report.

PUBLISHING OR PRESENTING A RESEARCH REPORT

Once researchers prepare a research report, the next step is to arrange for communication to be available in professional journals or presentation at a convention. For each of these avenues, researchers must submit a *manuscript* (the typed report) or application for consideration, which may lead to an acceptance or a rejection. The decision to accept or reject a report for publication or presentation is typically made by professionals who are experts in the topic of the study.

Journal Publication

A huge number of journals publish research articles in psychology, and APA publishes many of the most prestigious of these journals. The APA journals include *Behavioral Neuroscience, Developmental Psychology, Health Psychology, Journal of Consulting and Clinical Psychology, Journal of Applied Psychology, Journal of Personality and Social Psychology,* and five *Journals of Experimental Psychology.* As the titles in this short list imply, journals usually specialize on certain topics.

Because publishing costs a great deal of money, journals have budgets that limit the number of pages they can print in a year. This means that journals can't accept for publication all manuscripts they receive, and those they accept must be written concisely. Journals typically make the decision to accept or reject a manuscript on the basis of three criteria, the first of which is the most important:

1. It makes a *significant and original contribution* to a topic of psychology that is within the area of specialization for the journal to which it was submitted.
2. It *communicates clearly* and fully, but as *briefly* as the content permits.
3. It follows the *writing structure and style* that the journal requires.

A manuscript that meets the first criterion but not the others may receive an intermediate decision called "revise and resubmit," which specifies what needs to be changed before the report can be accepted.

The first step in the publication process after writing a full draft of the paper is to select the journal to which it will be submitted. This decision is based mainly on two factors. First, the topic of the manuscript should be within the journal's specialty area. Second, the rigor the journal applies in evaluating the first criterion should be appropriate for the manuscript. For instance, some journals have both a strong preference for manuscripts that present more than one study and very high rejection rates—such as, rejecting over 90% of the manuscripts they receive; others do not prefer manuscripts with more than one study and have rejection rates of about 40–50%. Researchers usually send a manuscript to the most rigorous journal that they think may accept it because placing the article in that journal will add to its prestige and the likelihood that it will be read by other researchers in the field. Information about the topics suitable for a journal and its preferred writing structure and style is available online at the journal's Web site and in at least one printed issue of the journal each year in a section usually called Instructions to Authors. Before submitting the manuscript to a journal for review, researchers often ask colleagues who are familiar with the topic to read the paper and give feedback.

The next step in publishing an article is to submit copies of the manuscript to the journal's editor, who is usually a well-established researcher in the specialty area of the journal. Accompanying the manuscript should be a cover letter that contains information that the journal specifies in the Instructions to Authors—for instance, most journals require a statement that the author(s) will not submit the manuscript to another journal simultaneously. The paper then undergoes *peer review:* the editor recruits about three appropriate researchers who are willing to read the manuscript carefully and evaluate it in writing within a short period of time, such as a month (sometimes it takes much longer). Using these reviews, the editor decides whether the paper should be accepted as is (which is rare), rejected, or revised and resubmitted. Regardless of the decision, the author(s) get a copy of each reviewer's evaluation, presented anonymously. The entire process can take many months or more, especially if it includes revisions. If a manuscript is rejected, authors are free to use the evaluations to revise it and submit it to another journal.

Once a manuscript has been accepted for publication, it is given to a production department where the written material is copyedited for grammar and style, any graphs or diagrams are drawn or copied, and the article is set to print in the journal's format. A manuscript that has been accepted for publication and is in production is described as "in press" (you may see this term occasionally in a reference citation in place of a date of publication). Authors receive a printed draft of the article, called a "proof" (or page proofs), that looks like the final printed version, which they are asked to read carefully for typos and critical errors. A few months later, the article appears in the printed journal. The entire publication process from submitting the manuscript for review to its appearing in print generally takes a year or two.

Presenting Reports at Professional Meetings

The second avenue for communicating the purpose, method, and outcome of research is to present a report at a professional convention or meeting. Scientific organizations hold meetings periodically, such as every August, where researchers can present their recent research. The same research may be communicated later as a journal article, usually in a more detailed or expanded version. This is why some journal articles have a footnote saying that "part of this research" was presented at a convention. The breadth of topics covered at a convention depends on the focus of the organization. Meetings of the APA include presentations on topics that cover the entire discipline, but meetings of more specialized organizations, such as the American Association of Behavior Therapy and the Society for Research on Child Development, cover a more restricted array of topics.

Most organizations require that individuals who want to present research submit an application with a description of its purpose, method, and outcome written briefly, usually in just a few hundred words. A peer-review process is generally used in which researchers evaluate the applications, but the acceptance rate is typically much higher than in journals. Two of the most common formats for presentations are paper sessions and poster sessions. In *paper sessions,* several oral reports are given on related topics, such as on child cognition or operant conditioning, with one researcher from each study doing the presentation with a strict time limit, such as 15 minutes, including time for answering questions from the audience. In *poster sessions,* dozens of researchers display descriptions of their research simultaneously for a period of an hour or two on bulletin boards set up in a large room in many rows. Each poster display has an informative title in large font that passersby can read easily and presents the study's purpose, method, and outcome briefly for interested people to read. At least one of the authors is expected to stand by the poster for the entire session ready to discuss the research with individuals, which is usually a great opportunity for good conversation and getting other people's perspectives about the method and findings. In many cases, students who helped conduct the research and are coauthors of the report do the presentation of the paper or poster.

Tips for Presenting a Paper

Because of the nature of verbal presentations and the short time allowed for the activity, it must be prepared and orchestrated carefully. Here are some tips on presenting a paper paraphrased, expanded, and quoted from the current APA *Publication Manual* (2001):

1. Focus the overall talk around a few main points, and keep reminding the audience of these themes. A valid and simple traditional strategy is, "Tell the audience what you are going to say, say it, and then tell them what you said" (p. 329).

2. Avoid giving too much detail. Don't give the level of detail that would be appropriate for a written report because listeners cannot follow details as easily as readers can. "The audience wants to know (a) what you studied and why, (b) how you went about the research (give a general orientation), (c) what you discovered, and (d) the implications of your results" (p. 329). It's often a good idea to distribute a handout, enabling interested listeners to find details you'll omit orally that they may want to know about.

3. Don't read the presentation. Instead, have written notes to prompt you to say in the best sequence what is important.

4. Rehearse the presentation until you feel comfortable speaking while consulting your notes only for prompts. Rehearse at least once in front of an audience.

5. Make effective use of slides or other visual materials, and be sure they can be read from a distance.

6. Make sure you will finish in time to take questions. The time limit is often strictly followed, with a moderator letting the speaker know how much time is left.

Tips for Presenting a Poster

Each presenter is assigned a numbered bulletin board that has limited space, usually not more than 4 × 8 feet. Because convention attendees will be wandering up and down the many rows of bulletin boards, your poster needs to get their attention and be displayed in a way that is inviting and not confusing. Here are some tips:

1. Print the title in very large font (at least 1½ inches high) as a banner and place it across the top of the board with each author's name and affiliation (college). The title should be very easy to read from several feet away and be informative and concise, so that it conveys the essence of the study's variables and importance.

2. The layout and organization of information is critical and may be determined by the conference organization's guidelines. The information needs to convey an overview of the study and its purpose, method, and outcome in a logical sequence so that it flows from left to right and top to bottom.

3. The poster can be on one large sheet or on separate smaller sheets. The appearance is enhanced and more inviting if the sheets are white or lightly colored and are mounted on a colored cardboard backing. Have with you some pushpins to attach the sheets to the board (there may not be enough, or any, at the convention).

4. The fonts for text material and figures should be fairly large and printed in a dark color (black is fine) so the material is easy to read from 2 or 3 feet away.

5. Don't have a lot of text to read—use a bare-bones approach. People should be able to read the entire display in a minute or two. Bulleted lists with basic information are better than paragraphs.

6. Use graphics when possible and efficient ("a picture is worth a thousand words"), and make them clear and attractive.

7. Have a handout to distribute that gives details that could not be displayed. A good way to prepare the handout is to reduce a full report to two single-spaced pages that focus mainly on the method and results and are printed on two sides of one sheet.

GENERAL GUIDELINES FOR PREPARING RESEARCH REPORTS

Writing a research report is very different from creative writing in which the author may deliberately try to confuse the reader, hold back information to maintain curiosity, or arouse a positive or negative emotion. A research report must present all information needed to understand exactly the purpose, method, and outcome of the study, and the writing style should be "effective." What is effective writing?

Have you heard of Murphy's Law—anything that can go wrong will go wrong? We can reword this observation for writing reports: Anything that can be misunderstood will be misunderstood, at least by some people. We should strive to avoid misunderstandings in our report writing whenever possible, using a proactive, preventive approach. The best way to prevent misunderstandings in reports is to *write effectively,* that is, to write with a style that *is grammatically correct, simple and straightforward, organized, precise, and concise.*

Grammatically Correct, Simple, and Straightforward Writing

Incorrect grammar can mislead people as to our meaning. Let's consider an example of lyrics from a 1960s rock and roll recording of the song *Worst That Could Happen* by a group called the Brooklyn Bridge in which a male singer sings:

> Baby, if he loves you more than me,
> Maybe it's the best thing
> Maybe it's the best thing for you,
> But it's the worst that could happen to me.

What does the first line mean? If we parse that line, the actual grammatical meaning indicates that the triangle includes a gay relationship: if he loves you more than he loves me (the male singer). This is not likely to be what the singer and composer intended. To make the line grammatically correct for the likely intention, the word *me* should be *I,* which would make a different meaning: if he loves you more than I do. You might argue that you and most people would interpret this incorrect grammar correctly because of the context, but I can reply with two points. First, some people might not notice the context. Second, in research reports we seldom have the needed context to clarify our meaning. When writing a research report, we should strive to prevent all misunderstandings. For instance, if a report said "There was a 3 min rest period between each test," would that mean each test was interrupted or that there was a rest period separating adjacent tests? Although the latter meaning is more likely, we can't be sure. We *should* be sure and would be if the grammar were correct.

Many grammatical errors occur in everyday communication, which makes it easy for some people to overlook the errors in their own writing. Here are some examples of common grammatical traps:

- *Affect versus effect.* The meanings of these words depend on whether they are used as a noun or a verb. When used as a noun, *affect* means an emotional condition, as in "Her affect changed when he said . . ."; *effect* means something that results from an event or agent, as in "The psychoactive effect of the drug decreased." When used as a verb, *affect* means to influence, as in "Increasing background noise affected their perception"; *effect* means to bring into being or cause a result, as in "The noise effected a change in perception."

- *Nonsignificant versus insignificant.* In statistical interpretations, use *nonsignificant* to refer to an outcome that does not reach the required p (or α) level; *insignificant* is a related term but connotes unimportance.

- *Number versus amount, and less than versus fewer than.* Use the terms *number* and *fewer than* when referring to countable items, as in "a large number of subjects" or "there were fewer words in one list than the other." *Amount* and *less than* refer to the size or extent of objects or events, such as in their length, volume, or weight.

- *Plurals of words from Latin or Greek.* Many people don't know that the word *data* is the plural for *datum* and requires the plural form of the associated verb. Thus, we should say, for instance, "the data are" or "the data were," not "the data is (or was)." Other common troublesome plurals are *criteria* (plural for *criterion*), *hypotheses* (for *hypothesis*), *phenomena* (for *phenomenon*), and *stimuli* (for *stimulus*).

- *Pronoun agreement with its referent.* Many people use a plural pronoun, such as *they,* to refer to a singular object, as in the sentence, "When *a person* feels guilty, *they* try to defend their egos." Although we hear plural pronouns for singular referents a lot in everyday communication, it is wrong.

- *Pronouns in prepositional phrases or subordinate clauses.* Objective case pronouns, such as *me* and *whom,* should be used after a preposition (as in "to me" or "for whom") and in a subordinate clause ("between you and me").

Writing in a simple and straightforward manner also improves the clarity of a report and reduces misunderstandings. Short words and short sentences are generally easier to understand than long ones that contain several phrases or ideas. Use short words and sentences when the option exists, unless the same word is repeated excessively or the paragraph sounds choppy.

Organized, Precise, and Concise Writing

Each section and the entire report should reflect a coherent and logical progression of ideas. Think in advance about what needs to be said early in a section or report so that later information will be clearer and will flow more easily. For instance, it's a good idea to provide definitions and examples early when discussing a topic so that the remainder of that topic is easier to understand. Any *concepts that people who are likely to read the report may not know should be defined or explained.* For example, if we were writing a report of a study of stress, we might say, "The type of stressors we are investigating are hassles—that is, everyday annoyances or irritations, such as being in a traffic jam."

Precise writing means that we provide accurate and detailed information and choose the specific words that best express each statement we want to make. As an example of choosing the most precise words, the word *thinking* has a broad meaning that encompasses the word *reasoning,* which refers to thinking logically. If we are discussing logical thinking, we should try to call it reasoning or logical or rational thinking, not just thinking. Writing in a concise fashion means that we express ideas economically, leaving out extraneous words. We say exactly what needs to be said in the smallest number of words, and no more.

Judging what does and does not need to be said and whether we are using too many words to say it takes some skill and careful thought.

Writing effectively also requires careful editing. Edit the report as you go along in your writing and across a series of drafts. Students, and probably most professionals, rarely produce an excellent research report in just one draft.

Tips for Effective Writing

Effective report writing requires careful planning and organization. Descriptions written off the top of our heads are likely to be disorganized and imprecise, leading other people to have difficulty understanding what we are trying to say. To avoid these problems, here are some tips to structure the process of writing a report through a series of steps:

1. On a sheet of paper or on a computer, *divide the planned report into the sections* that it will have, usually the Introduction, Method (Participants, Materials/Apparatus, Procedure), Results, and Discussion.

2. *Brainstorm* for each section. What issues and materials that you know about, such as concepts, theories, or other studies, should be included in each section? Jot down a very short reminder—a code, phrase, or sentence—for each item, tossing it in the section in any order for now.

3. Look at all the issues and materials your brainstorming activity produced for each section and *outline* them into a logical progression. In some cases, you may notice gaps in the progression, suggesting that you need more information. You may also want to relocate issues or materials to another section. If an issue or set of materials is complex, you may want to create an outline for it by first brainstorming to identify the essential ideas to be covered and then deciding the order in which to present them.

4. As you write, read and reread carefully each sentence, trying to take the perspective of people who know little about the topic. Could those readers construe the sentence in a way that is different from your intended meaning? Could you state the sentence more precisely or concisely? Is the sentence hard to understand? If you answer *yes* to any of these questions, rework the sentence to eliminate these problems.

5. Use your computer word processor to check the paper for spelling and grammatical errors.

6. When you complete a section or a series of paragraphs, read the material to assess the quality of the organization.

7. After completing your first draft, put it aside for a day or so before rereading it. After revising it for a second draft, have at least one friend or relative who is not highly familiar with the topic of your paper read it to assess its organization and clarity. Is there anything they didn't understand or misinterpreted? If so, find out why and revise the material.

8. For most students, the fourth draft will be about as good as the report will get and can be the final manuscript to turn in to the instructor.

AVOIDING BIAS IN LANGUAGE

Some words or phrases are offensive or insensitive to certain groups of people. The APA *Publication Manual* (2001) states that the organization has adopted a policy to treat individuals and groups fairly and to publish material that is free of demeaning attitudes and biased ideas about people. This means that writing with words or phrases

> that might imply bias against persons on the basis of gender, sexual orientation, racial or ethnic group, disability, or age should be avoided. . . . Just as you have learned to check what you write for spelling, grammar, and wordiness, practice reading over your work for bias. (2001, pp. 61–62).

Using Appropriate Labels

Labels are often used to describe people who share a characteristic, such as ethnicity or sexual orientation, but should only be applied when they are relevant to the design of the study or interpretation of its results. When using labels, authors should "call people what they prefer to be called" (p. 63), recognizing that these preferences change over time and may differ among individuals in a group. For example, currently in the United States and some other places, the terms *Black* and *African American* are both acceptable in referring to persons of African ancestry, and *White* is acceptable in place of *Caucasian*. Because the names of racial and ethnic groups are proper nouns, the labels *Black* and *White* should be capitalized. Other rules for preferred racial or ethnic labels are:

- *Hispanic, Latino,* or *Chicano* may be appropriate, depending on the person's place of origin. Although Hispanic is the broadest of the three terms, it may not be the most appropriate label for the particular participants in a study.
- *Asian* and *Asian American* are preferred over *Oriental* as labels.
- *American Indian* and *Native American* are acceptable labels when referring to people who are indigenous to North America.

In each of these cases, the most appropriate label may be a more specific term, such as *Chinese* or *Vietnamese* instead of *Asian,* if it is accurate and relevant. When using labels to refer to homosexual orientation, although the broad term *gay* can be interpreted to include both males and females, the more specific labels *gay males* and *lesbians* are clearer and often preferred.

Some labels imply a degree equivalence of persons with their psychological or medical conditions or disabilities. This is the case when referring to people as *neurotics, retarded adult, autistic children,* or *cancer patient,* for example. Publishers that follow guidelines of the APA *Publication Manual* prefer phrases that take the form "person(s) with [name of condition or disability]," such as *clients with a neurosis, adult with mental retardation, children with autism,* or *patient with cancer.* Thus, the sentence "There were two groups, autistic children and normal children" would be rephrased as "There were two groups, children with autism and children without autism." The terms *challenged* and *special* are often viewed as euphemistic and usually reserved for participants who prefer them. Although all journals published by APA require reports to follow the guidelines on labeling by conditions or disabilities, some psychological and medical journals do not.

Using Nonsexist Language

Sexist language refers to biased word constructions that reflect or foster stereotypes of gender roles. Sexist language generally takes one of two forms. First, it may incorrectly imply an inequality between males and females, such as referring to the "*men's* and *girl's* swimming teams" or "*all researchers* at the APA convention and their *wives.*" Second, it may involve applying a noun or pronoun generically that has a specific gender reference, usually male, when the individuals referred to are or could be of either sex. A common example is when people use the generic *he* or *man* when the gender of the referents is either unspecified or known to include both males and females, as in the sentences, "A researcher should describe *his* method in detail" and "*Man's* search for truth never ends."

To use *nonsexist* language, we need to start by being sensitive and committed to reducing gender stereotypes in our everyday and formal speaking and writing. We can watch for sexist language as we write a report and edit drafts, substituting gender neutral words or phrases for sexist ones. For example, we can replace *chairman* with *chair* or *chairperson*, *policeman* with *police officer*, and *mailman* with *postal worker*. We can also avoid using masculine pronouns generically by:

- Using plural forms. For instance, change "A researcher should describe *his* method in detail" to "Researchers should describe their methods in detail." In most cases when the singular form is used, the plural is actually more accurate because the author really means to generalize across individuals.
- Rephrasing. As an example, change "If a client practices the techniques, *he* will improve" to "If a client practices the techniques, that person will improve" or "If a client practices the techniques, improvements will occur."
- Dropping the pronoun or replacing it with an article. For instance, change "The therapist must avoid allowing *his* biases affect *his* treatment methods" to "The therapist must avoid allowing biases to affect the treatment methods."

Replacing a singular pronoun with combinations, such as "he or she," "she or he," "s/he," or "he/she," should be done sparingly because they are awkward and distracting.

GRAMMATICAL STYLE AND ABBREVIATIONS

In general, the writing style of a research report is more impersonal than creative writing, which means that researchers try to minimize their use of personal pronouns, such as "I think" or "we did," in their writing. A report can contain personal pronouns, but they should be used sparingly. Other general stylistic issues in report writing include the use of verb tense, active or passive voice, abbreviations, and numbers in report writing.

Tense and Voice

When describing or discussing events or conditions that are known to have occurred at a time period in the past, we use the *past tense* in writing the report. This rule includes our descriptions of existing research and theory and our current data analyses and results. So, we might say, "Armstrong (1996) found that people's beliefs regarding the likelihood of success affected their persistence in a task" and "The data in the current experiment were analyzed with a paired-samples *t* test, which revealed no significant difference." To describe events or conditions that occurred at an indefinite time or began in the past and continues in the present, we use the *present perfect tense,* as in "It has been shown . . ." or "Several studies have applied this method." The Discussion is a section of a research report where the present tense can be appropriate, such as in saying, "These results indicate that . . ."

The term *voice* in grammar refers to the way a sentence expresses the relation of the subject to its verb. In the *active voice,* the subject of the sentence or phrase is the actor, the doer—structurally, the subject precedes the verb, as in:

■ "The participants kept a diary."
■ "The researcher presented the materials."
■ "A computer recorded the responses and reaction times."
■ "Armstrong (1996) conducted a study of the effects of people's beliefs regarding the likelihood of success on their performance."

In the *passive voice,* the subject of the sentence or phrase has something done to it, and the actual actor often follows the verb in a prepositional phrase, as in:

■ "A diary was kept by the participants."
■ "The materials were presented by the researcher."
■ "The responses and reaction times were recorded by a computer."
■ "A study of the effects of people's beliefs regarding the likelihood of success on their performance was conducted by Armstrong (1996)."

In these passive voice sentences, the diary, materials, responses and reaction times, and the study, respectively, are the subjects. The actual actors—the participants, researcher, computer, and Armstrong—have an indirect role. The active voice usually is clearer and has a smoother flow than the passive voice. *Try to use the active voice whenever possible.* The APA *Publication Manual* (2001, p. 42) describes one exception: when we

> want to focus on the object or recipient of the action rather than on the actor. For example, "The speakers [audio] were attached to either side of the chair" emphasizes the placement of the speakers, not who placed them—the more appropriate focus in the Method section.

The decision to use the passive voice should be deliberate and for reasons of clarity or economy of sentence structure.

Using Abbreviations

Abbreviations save space and can improve the clarity of a statement, but they can also be used excessively and impair the writing clarity and flow. The difference in effect depends mainly on whether the abbreviations are standard ones or are created for the particular report. *Standard abbreviations* are in common use and often appear in dictionaries, for example:

- Latin abbreviations for *and so forth* (etc.), *that is* (i.e.,), *versus* (vs.), and *for example* (e.g.,).
- Units of measurement, such as for *hour* (hr), *minute* (min), *second* (s), *millisecond* (ms), *inch* (in), *meter* (m), and *post meridiem* (P.M.). For clarity, don't abbreviate *day, week, month,* or *year.*
- Statistical terms, such as *mean* (*M*) and *standard deviation* (*SD*). Note that statistical abbreviations should be typed in italic font.
- Abbreviations that are accepted as words, such as IQ, ESP, HIV, and AIDS. Plurals of abbreviations simply add an "s" (not italicized) without an apostrophe, as in IQs and *M*s.

Nonstandard abbreviations are shortened notations authors create to replace one or more words, usually to refer to certain variables or procedures. In some cases, these abbreviations appear fairly commonly in the research literature on a topic, such as:

- Conditioned stimulus (CS)
- Minnesota Multiphasic Personality Inventory (MMPI)
- Reaction time (RT)
- Short-term memory (STM)

Whenever we use a nonstandard abbreviation, we must define it the first time we use it in the paper by spelling it out completely and giving the shortened notation in parentheses, as in the preceding examples. Thereafter in the paper, we can just give the abbreviation.

Two problems can occur with nonstandard abbreviations. First, the shortened notation may bear no obvious connection to the term it replaces, making it difficult for the reader to remember what it means. For example, suppose we did a quasi-experimental study of the personality characteristics of children from families of high, middle, and low socioeconomic statuses. If we abbreviated the statuses as Group A, Group B, and Group C, it would be hard to keep track of which is which. But if we used hi-SES, mid-SES, and lo-SES, keeping track would be easy. Second, excessive use of nonstandard abbreviations can impair comprehension. For instance, suppose we defined in our paper the following shortened notations: left hand (LH), right hand (RH), false-positive decision (FP), false-negative decision (FN), and reaction time (RT). Then, in the Discussion, we stated, "The performance advantage of the RH was clear from the RT data, which showed far higher FP and FN rates with the LH." This sentence would be hard to follow. In general, *use nonstandard abbreviations sparingly.*

Rules for Expressing Numbers

Although the rules in the APA *Publication Manual* (2001) for expressing numbers in a manuscript are complicated, the basic rule is to spell out *zero* through *nine* and use digits for 10 and above. But there are many exceptions to the basic rule. For instance, regardless of the magnitudes of the numbers, *use digits to express:*

- All numbers in an Abstract (except if they start a sentence)
- Ages (for example, "5 years old")
- Times or dates (for example, "8:30 A.M.")
- Numbers within arithmetic functions (for example, "a ratio of 4:1" or "divided by 3")
- Percentages (for example, "6%")
- Scores, such as ratings (for example, "a 4-point scale" or "a score of 3 was")
- Numbers that immediately precede a unit of measurement (for example, "3 mg")
- Calculated data (for example, "a mean of 5.27")
- Numbers less than one (for example, "0.76"; note that if the number cannot be greater than one, such as for an r or p value, don't use the zero)

In addition, one exception to the basic rule can override most items in the preceding list: spell out *numbers that start a sentence* anywhere in the report.

TYPING (WORD PROCESSING) AND ASSEMBLING A REPORT

The first point to make about preparing a report should go without saying, but I'll say it anyway: Good research reports should be neatly typed (the word *typing* in this book includes word processing), be free of typographical and spelling errors, and, typically, follow the APA format described in the *Publication Manual.*

General Typing Instructions

The manuscript should be typed on one side of standard 8½ × 11-inch sheets of white bond paper in *12-point font,* preferably in Times Roman or Courier typeface. Use one typeface and font size everywhere. The typing on *all pages* should

- Be *double-spaced throughout*
- Have *margins of at least 1 inch* all around
- Be aligned *flush against the left margin only* ("left justified"). Do not justify both sides of a page.
- Have a *header* with its page number and the first two or three words of the paper's title (the only exceptions are pages with figures, such as graphs or diagrams, which do not use a header).

You can set up all these features in advance of writing so that they occur automatically through your word processor, but you may want to compose in single-space format and convert later. Use *italic font* for material that will be printed in italic, but *do not use bold* font anywhere in the manuscript. Indent (about ½ inch, using the tab function) the first line of each paragraph in the text, but not in the Abstract.

Order of Manuscript Sections

A research report will have several parts, each consisting of at least one page and beginning on a new page. A manuscript can have the following possible parts that are always assembled in the following sequence:

1. Title page. Page 1, containing the paper's title and author name(s) and affiliation(s).
2. Abstract. Page 2, consisting of a short description of the study.
3. Text. Starting on page 3. This is the body of the report and usually contains four sections: Introduction, Method (Participants or Subjects, Materials or Apparatus, and Procedure), Results, and Discussion. The Introduction starts on a new page, but each section of the text thereafter starts on the next line following the preceding section without requiring a page break.
4. References. Starts on a separate page and lists all citations alphabetically by author.
5. Appendixes (if any). Start each on a separate page.
6. Author note (if any). Starts on a separate page.
7. Footnotes (if any). Listed in order, starting on a separate page.
8. Tables (if any). Start each on a separate page.
9. Figure captions (if any). Listed in order, starting on a separate page.
10. Figures (if any). Place each on a separate page.

Notice the "if any" statements—some manuscripts contain none of these parts, and many have only a couple or so. Although the placement of some listed parts, such as footnotes, will be rearranged for the printed article, they must appear in the manuscript in the order listed.

Length of the Report

One question students want answered is, "How many pages should the report be?" This question is hard to answer exactly because instructors often have special requirements for student papers, but we can consider the usual length of manuscripts submitted to journals and to me in my research methods class. First of all, look at the list you just read of parts of a research report: several parts start on a new page and take only a portion of that page, which still counts as "a page." Also, the page, margin, and font sizes are standardized, so that helps define the length. The APA *Publication Manual* (2001, p. 10) gives a rule of thumb: "1 printed page = 4 manuscript pages," including the pages only partly used, such as the title page. If you look through APA journals, you'll see that most articles range in length from roughly 3 to 12 printed pages, and the longer ones typically describe either a series of studies or one very complex study.

Research methods students generally do simple to moderately complex projects. In my experience, the reports I have received that earned at least a "B" grade have ranged from 11 to 21 pages ($M = 14$), not including appendixes. If these reports were published in an APA journal, they would be fairly short ones, occupying 3 to 5 pages, again not counting appendixes.

A SAMPLE RESEARCH REPORT

For the remainder of this appendix, we'll focus on the structure and content of a research report using as an example an article that was published in 2003, which we will call the *sample report*. The reference for that article is:

Naquin, C. E., & Paulson, G. D. (2003). Online bargaining and inter-personal trust. *Journal of Applied Psychology, 88,* 113–120.

If your college library carries the journal in hard copy or subscribes to an "E-Journal" service, such as PsycArticles that offers it, you can look at the printed article or get a copy of it.

THE STRUCTURE AND CONTENT OF A RESEARCH REPORT

If you have already looked through psychology journals, you may have noticed that the structure of the articles can vary somewhat, sometimes quite a lot. There are several reasons for this variation, and we'll describe four.

- Not all psychology journals follow the APA format exactly, so that some may label the sections differently, for example, or use a different system for citing references.
- The format a journal uses for research articles changes over time, even in journals APA publishes. APA revises its *Publication Manual* periodically; the current version was published in 2001 and is the fifth edition. That edition made several changes in manuscript requirements, including a shortened length for Abstracts, a slightly different typing format for references, and the provision of effect size estimates in the Results section. Many decades ago, psychology research articles didn't contain an Abstract section, but sometimes they had a Summary at the end.
- Some journals publish more than one type of article. In addition to the standard research report, a journal might also publish reviews of the literature, papers that propose new theories, and brief reports (research reports that are, perhaps, half of the standard length). These variations affect the structure of the manuscript, such as by combining the Results and Discussion sections.
- Since the 1980s or so, journals have been giving greater and greater preference to publishing research reports containing more than one conceptually related study; some reports describe a series of studies. Some journals now contain mostly articles reporting multiple studies.

Because students in a research methods course are not likely to prepare a report that reflects any of these variations, such as describing more than one study, my task in finding a suitable example report was constrained. I needed to find an article describing a single study that reflects the latest APA requirements and has a rationale, independent and dependent variables, and statistical analyses that are straightforward and reasonably easy for students to understand. The sample report by Naquin and Paulson meets these criteria nicely. As we use the sample report to illustrate the structure and content of a research report, you'll see small portions of the manuscript presented in this appendix as figures. Part of the purpose for these figures is to depict the typing layout, especially for APA requirements in typing headings and the list of references.

When you write a research report, keep this appendix handy to consult as you go. Before writing each section of the report, read over the material in the appendix on that section and examine each of the notes in the figures that pertain. Most of the *notes in the figures* give important tips on how to type details and elements of the section. This appendix also has *many lists that state the order and type of content for a section. Pay close attention to each list and use it as a checklist to outline your writing.*

TITLE PAGE AND ABSTRACT

The title and abstract pages are typed on separate sheets of paper and constitute the first two pages of a research report manuscript.

Title Page

The first page of the manuscript is the title page, and you can see in Figure A.1 that it contains title and author information in a specific format. Looking at the top of the page and working down, you see first the *header* that consists of the first two or three words of the title (excluding the first word if it is an article, such as *The* or *An*), five blank spaces, and the page number. All manuscript pages, except those with figures (such as graphs or diagrams), have a header with this format. The purpose of having a few words of the title on all pages is to enable someone to identify the manuscript to which the pages belong if they become separated, such as if an editor were to drop a stack of several manuscripts down a stairwell accidently.

Moving down the title page, the next element we come to is the *running head,* which is a shortened version of the title. To see how the running head is used, look at an actual published article: the top of every printed page after the first one has some information centered on the same line as the page number. In APA journals, that information is either the name(s) of the author(s), which appears on even numbered pages, or the short version of the title—the running head—which appears on odd numbered pages. Even though the running head appears more than once in the article, the manuscript presents it only once, on the title page. In the manuscript, it is typed in all uppercase letters and can contain no more than 50 characters, including letters, punctuation, and spaces. Position the line flush against the left margin. The only exception to the rule of double spacing between lines in a manuscript is immediately after the running head—line spacing before the title can be more than double.

The *title* should be short and informative, indicating the main variables studied. The APA *Publication Manual* suggests that a title should have a length of about 10 to 12 words and "be a concise statement of the main topic

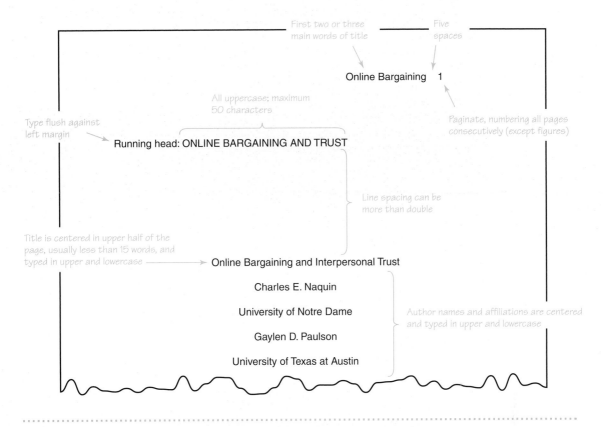

Title page (page 1 in the sample manuscript) with written notes to explain important features. This is a separate page with no additional content. In your word processor, use a hard page break after the last author's institutional affiliation.

and should identify the actual variables or theoretical issues under investigation and the relationship between them" (pp. 10–11). A few examples of good titles are

"Effect of Incorrect Letters in Words on Reading Speed in 8- and 15-Year-Olds"

"Relationships among Job Satisfaction, Self-Esteem, and Depression"

"Toddlers' Memory for Event Details as a Function of Distracting Stimuli"

"Role of Sex and Age in Adult Rats' Physiological Arousal under Stress"

The title may be the most important string of words in the whole report because people are more likely to read and use the title than any other words in an article. Individuals who search the literature or peruse journals look first at the title of an article and then decide whether to read more of it, such as the

Abstract. If the title is not informative, people will skip to another article. When composing a title, avoid excess words, such as "A Study of" or "An Experimental Test of," because they just increase its length and have no useful purpose. Type the title in upper and lowercase letters in the upper half of the page, centered horizontally.

Directly below the title is the *byline,* which consists of the name and institutional affiliation of each author. If there is more than one author, they are listed in the order of the importance of the contributions they made to the study and report. Only individuals who contributed substantially should receive authorship. If all authors have the same affiliation, their names go on one line (or more lines, if many authors), and the name of the institution goes below. Sometimes journals conduct peer reviews of manuscripts in a "masked" manner—that is, without author identification—to prevent any influence of the authors' reputation and enhance the fairness of the process. When using a masked review, the byline is omitted in the title page that the reviewers see.

Abstract

The *Abstract* is a brief summary of the research report with special focus on what was done and what was found. Because it contains elements of the full report, authors usually write it after the rest of the manuscript. Like the title page, the Abstract is typed on a separate sheet of paper (page 2 in the manuscript) and has a great impact on whether people will seek out and read the full article. The Abstract is printed in the published article at the very beginning and is available in electronic databases, such as PsycINFO.

As Figure A.2 shows, the heading "Abstract" (not italic) is centered at the top of the page and is followed by a single paragraph that summarizes the report. Do *not indent* the first line. Although abstracts can vary in the types and order of information they contain, they should not be longer than about *120 words.* They usually have the following elements in this order:

1. A sentence stating the *research question* and *variables.*
2. A brief description of the *participants* (or subjects), indicating their number and relevant characteristics, such as age or gender.
3. A sentence or two describing the *research design and procedure.*
4. A brief description of the *findings,* usually without giving actual data (such as *M*s, *SD*s, or *p* values).
5. A statement of the *conclusions or implications* of the findings.

Fitting all of this information in 120 words requires special efforts at writing concisely.

Two other points about the content of abstracts are also important. First, the material included in an abstract should be *self-contained*—that is, someone reading it should be able to understand every detail without reading the rest of the report. Second, because an abstract summarizes the report, it should not include information that is not in the report.

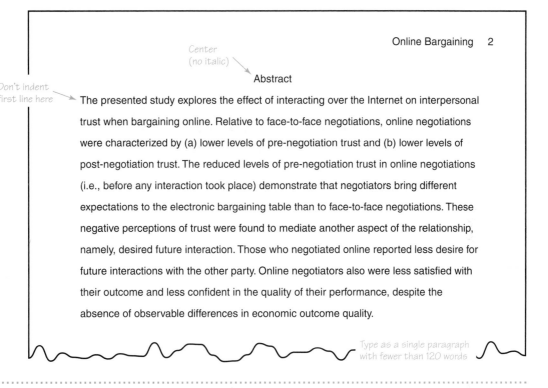

Online Bargaining   2

Center
(no italic)

Abstract

Don't indent
first line here

The presented study explores the effect of interacting over the Internet on interpersonal trust when bargaining online. Relative to face-to-face negotiations, online negotiations were characterized by (a) lower levels of pre-negotiation trust and (b) lower levels of post-negotiation trust. The reduced levels of pre-negotiation trust in online negotiations (i.e., before any interaction took place) demonstrate that negotiators bring different expectations to the electronic bargaining table than to face-to-face negotiations. These negative perceptions of trust were found to mediate another aspect of the relationship, namely, desired future interaction. Those who negotiated online reported less desire for future interactions with the other party. Online negotiators also were less satisfied with their outcome and less confident in the quality of their performance, despite the absence of observable differences in economic outcome quality.

Type as a single paragraph
with fewer than 120 words

FIGURE A.2

Abstract (page 2 in the sample manuscript). Abstracts always occupy page 2, with no other material on that sheet. Use a hard page break at the end of the paragraph.

INTRODUCTION

The first section of the text, or body, of a report is the Introduction, and it begins at the top of page 3 of the manuscript *without* a heading or label announcing "Introduction." Instead, the APA *Publication Manual* requires authors to type the full title of the article centered in the first line of the page (if the title is long, it can use the next line too), as shown in Figure A.3.

Content of an Introduction

The Introduction orients the reader by presenting background information and a context for the study described in the report. It gives the following types of information, usually in this order:

1. *A statement of the research question or problem and its importance.* For example, if your study pertains to a psychological disorder, such as clinical depression, you might indicate how prevalent the disorder is and its impact on people's functioning. If your study examined some theoretical prediction that has not been adequately tested, you would describe the theory and in-

Header continues, and the Introduction starts on a new page

Center article title (no label "Introduction")

Online Bargaining   3

Online Bargaining and Interpersonal Trust

Indent first line for all paragraphs in text

The Internet has significantly influenced the ways in which people communicate and exchange information both within and between organizations (Katsh & Rifkin, 2001; Kiesler & Sproull, 1992). It has been estimated that approximately 80% of business organizations now rely on electronic messaging (e.g., e-mail) as a critical means of communication for everyday operations (Overly, 1999). For example, at Intel (the popular computer chip manufacturer) employees reportedly spend an average of 2.5 hr per day interacting via e-mail, generating over 3 million messages per day (Overholt, 2001). On a broad level, it is clear that with increasing globalization and the emergence of "virtual workplaces" and rapidly changing economic landscapes, e-mail communication represents an indispensable business and managerial tool.

How do these changing modes of communication affect organizations and their members? Recognizing that managers spend a good deal of their time negotiating and dealing with conflicts, it comes as no surprise that practitioners and scholars alike have sought to explore the ramifications of using the Internet when crafting deals and resolving disputes (see Katsh & Rifkin, 2001; Landry, 2000; McKersie & Fonstad, 1997; Thompson, 2001). Conferences and workshops devoted to negotiating and resolving disputes in the online context have been sponsored by such organizations as

Begin with a statement of the problem and its importance

Latin abbreviation

Citation of a single reference

Cite a primary source for data

Alphabetize and put semicolons between citations within the same parentheses

When a citation has more than one author, an ampersand is used if it appears in parentheses; use "and" if it is in the flow of a sentence: "Hall and Ya (1992)"

FIGURE A.3

The beginning of the Introduction (page 3 of the sample manuscript). This first section of an article's text is not labeled, "Introduction," and always starts at the top of page 3.

dicate how testing it would advance our knowledge of the topic or issue. If you did the study to resolve prior contradictory findings, you would state why resolving the issue is important and why your approach could help resolve it. Figure A.3 illustrates how the sample report presented its statement of the problem and importance of the study.

2. *A review of the relevant research literature.* The research you cite should lead in a rational way to your hypotheses, making them reasonable and convincing. Don't expect to cite studies that are the same as yours—and to the extent that they are *different* from yours, you will need to make the connections to your methods and hypotheses clear.

3. *A brief overview of the design and methods.* Give enough information to make clear what the independent and dependent variables are, the type of research strategy you used, and the structure of the design, such as a 3×2 factorial with all independent groups. This discussion should provide only a snapshot to orient the reader; details will be given later in the Method section.

4. *A clear statement of the hypothesis.* Each hypothesis should be stated in detail with no ambiguity. If you're testing for differences between groups, indicate which group should differ from which other, and which should score higher. If you're doing a factorial design, you should have a hypothesis for each factor and interaction tested, and the form of an expected interaction should be clearly described. If you're doing a correlational analysis, indicate for each hypothesis whether you are predicting a positive or negative correlation between variables.

Figure A.4 shows portions of the Introduction from the sample manuscript. Notice three features in the figure. First, it illustrates how to use and cite references for a theory and research on that theory. Sometimes theories and research need to be explained in more detail than in this example, especially if they are complex, and instructors vary in their preferences. Check with your instructor for guidelines on the amount of detail on theories and research he or she wants in the report(s) you write. Second, the figure presents the typing format for headings if subsections will be needed within an Introduction. Most reports don't divide the Introduction, but many do. Third, the figure shows one way to format a hypothesis, but more commonly, hypotheses are simply included in standard paragraphs, often as a series of sentences in the last paragraph of the Introduction.

Format for Citing References in the Text

The references we cite in a research report should be *materials we have actually read.* And as a general rule of thumb, use only *primary sources*—that is, original, firsthand statements or descriptions. It is rarely acceptable to cite secondary sources. Although a report can cite references in any section, the Introduction usually contains more citations than any other section. This is why we will discuss the APA citation format here. Two similar formats can be used in citing references in narrative portions of the report:

- Author's name is part of a sentence, as in "Leynes (1999) found that" or "Ruddy, Paul, Phillips, and Martinetti (2002) conducted a study of . . ."
- Author's name is in parentheses, not included as part of a sentence. For example, "(Vivona, 2001)," "(Breland & Howe, 1996)," or "(Archer, Graham, Waterman, & Hall, 2000)."

analysis. The foundation for this perspective is consistent with social identity theory (Tajfel, 1978; Tajfel & Turner, 1981), which emphasizes the perception of oneness with or belongingness to another. Research in social identity theory suggests that individuals define themselves partly in terms of salient group memberships, such as organizational affiliation, religion, shared interests, and so forth. Such a shared sense of identity among negotiators may promote a deeper understanding of the other individual's thoughts and actions and thereby enhance perceived predictability. In addition, shared identity can create a sense of empathy and concern for the outcomes of the other. In essence, a shared sense of identity yields a more trusting relationship (Lewicki & Wiethoff, 2000; Tyler & Kramer, 1996).

Using theory and research with citations

In both deterrence- and identification-based trust, negotiators seek to eliminate or minimize levels of uncertainty. Although high levels of trust may be hard to attain, attempting to do so from a distance—such as over the Internet—may be especially challenging. We now turn our attention to these challenges.

Trust and the Online Environment

Format for heading if Introduction has subsections

There is a growing stream of research examining the effects of Internet-based communication, such as e-mail, on social interaction and decision making. Because of

Taken together, these three interrelated lines of research suggest that negotiating online encourages the perception that opportunities are ripe for unethical behavior and, as such, the risk for being taken advantage of is high. In essence, the online medium yields significant pre-negotiation cause for concern and leads us to the following prediction:

Statement of a hypothesis

Hypothesis 2: Negotiators who bargain online will exhibit lower levels of prenegotiation trust (i.e., before any interaction) than those who interact face-to-face

FIGURE A.4

Parts of the Introduction (top is from page 7, bottom from page 10, of the sample manuscript) illustrating the use of references for theory and research, a heading for a subsection, and the statement of a hypothesis. Although articles don't usually print hypotheses as separate indented paragraphs, this format is becoming more and more common.

Notice that a citation gives each author's *surname* (not the given name or initials) and the *year* of publication. Variations in these formats can occur in specific circumstances. First, if an author's work is *quoted,* we must *also give the page number* for the quoted material, either in the citation after the year, such as "Davis (2003, p. 32)," or immediately after the quotation. Second, sometimes a citation gives *only the first author's name*—for example, "Kirnan et al. (2002)." This occurs if the reference has six or more authors *or* has three to five authors and was cited earlier in the paper with all authors' names.

METHOD

The Method section begins at the end of the Introduction, on the same page if space permits. Figure A.5 presents the typing format for the start of a Method section: The heading "Method" is centered (no italics), followed on the next line by the heading for a subsection.

The titles and content of Method subsections can vary, depending on features of the study, but the most common subsections are Participants (or Subjects), Materials (or Apparatus), and Procedure. The main rule of thumb in writing each Method subsection is to *make it detailed and clear enough that other researchers could replicate the study* exactly as it was done. Think of the Method section as a complicated recipe: if you write out a recipe for a great cake you make but leave out or describe vaguely an important ingredient or step in the preparation or cooking, the cake will not turn out the same.

Participants/Subjects

The first major subsection of the Method describes the individuals tested in the study. If they are humans, they and this section are called *participants;* if they are animals, they and this section are called *subjects.* The description of participants or subjects is very important in interpreting differences between groups, deciding how far the results should generalize, and making comparisons of findings in other research, such as a replication. The types of information needed depend on whether the individuals tested were humans or animals:

- A Participants section should state the *total number* of participants and information describing the *proportion of males and females,* their *ages* (as a range, a mean, or both), and their *race or ethnicity.* If relevant for interpreting the findings, this section should describe other characteristics, such as socioeconomic status or psychiatric diagnoses.
- A Subjects section should state the *total number* of animals and their *species and strain, age, sex,* and *weight.*

Somewhere in the Method section, perhaps here, the report should indicate how the subjects or participants were *recruited and assigned to conditions,* the *number in each condition,* and the *distribution of characteristics,* such as age or sex, in those conditions. If any participants or subjects did not complete the study, the

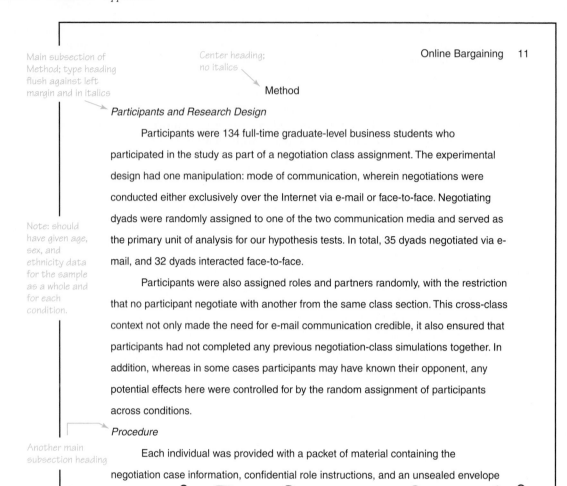

Main subsection of Method; type heading flush against left margin and in italics

Center heading; no italics

Online Bargaining   11

Method

Participants and Research Design

Participants were 134 full-time graduate-level business students who participated in the study as part of a negotiation class assignment. The experimental design had one manipulation: mode of communication, wherein negotiations were conducted either exclusively over the Internet via e-mail or face-to-face. Negotiating dyads were randomly assigned to one of the two communication media and served as the primary unit of analysis for our hypothesis tests. In total, 35 dyads negotiated via e-mail, and 32 dyads interacted face-to-face.

Note: should have given age, sex, and ethnicity data for the sample as a whole and for each condition.

Participants were also assigned roles and partners randomly, with the restriction that no participant negotiate with another from the same class section. This cross-class context not only made the need for e-mail communication credible, it also ensured that participants had not completed any previous negotiation-class simulations together. In addition, whereas in some cases participants may have known their opponent, any potential effects here were controlled for by the random assignment of participants across conditions.

Procedure

Another main subsection heading

Each individual was provided with a packet of material containing the negotiation case information, confidential role instructions, and an unsealed envelope

FIGURE A.5

The beginning of the Method (page 11 of the sample manuscript) appears on the same page as the end of the Introduction (if space permits). The Method generally has three or four main subsections, starting with one describing the participants or subjects.

report should indicate how many and why. Figure A.5 shows the Participants and Research Design section of the sample manuscript. You'll notice a shortcoming of this section of the sample report: it does not give demographics or the distribution of those characteristics to conditions.

Materials/Apparatus

The next major subsection of the Method describes the *materials,* such as surveys or lists of words, or the *apparatus,* such as a computer or blood pressure gauge, that were used in the study. The amount of detail the section should provide depends on the uniqueness of the items. Here are some rules regarding the amount of detail to provide:

- Standard laboratory equipment, such as a stopwatch or table, can be mentioned without giving details.
- If the materials or apparatus used were specialized and obtained from another source, such as a manufacturer or a prior journal article, the report should give an overview of their structure and function, along with information enabling others to obtain the same items. Thus, for equipment, the report should identify the manufacturer and model number of equipment; for a survey, the report should give the reference for the journal article or book that contains the survey.
- If the materials or apparatus were developed specifically for the study, a very detailed description should be given, perhaps including diagrams or a full survey as a figure or appendix.
- If a survey was used in the study, the Materials section should provide evidence of its reliability and validity. The scoring procedure and range of possible scores are often given with the description of a survey.

The Method in the sample report has a subsection called "Dependent Variables," the start of which is presented in Figure A.6. As you examine that figure, notice four things. First, it is essentially a Materials section. Second, it contains secondary subsections with the headings, "Pre- and post-negotiation trust" and "Outcome quality." Note the typing format for these headings. Third, the authors describe in general terms the survey they used, the Organizational Trust Inventory—Short Form, which they adapted from another source. They indicate the changes they made to it, and refer to an appendix that presents the survey as it was actually administered. A journal article is likely to have one or more appendixes if the research developed or applied a new or modified survey or used an unusual apparatus. Fourth, the authors cite a reference for the validity of the survey and present reliability data ("Cronbach's $\alpha = .70$").

Procedure

The Procedure subsection is usually the last part of the Method, and Figure A.5 shows how to type its heading and start its first paragraph. It describes, mainly in chronological order, exactly what the researcher did and the participants or subjects experienced from the beginning to the end of the research sessions. It also specifies all methods of control that were used and any design features of the study that weren't presented earlier. The Procedure usually contains the following information, not necessarily in the listed order:

- A step-by-step description of *exactly what was done,* without being too wordy. How were the stimuli presented? How were groups differentiated operationally? What was the testing environment like?
- *Names for the groups or conditions,* which may be abbreviations. Make the labels meaningful so they are easy to follow and remember.

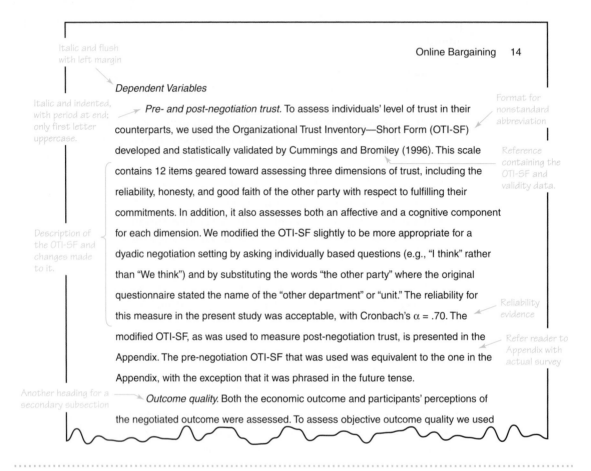

Italic and flush with left margin

Online Bargaining   14

Dependent Variables

Italic and indented, with period at end; only first letter uppercase.

Pre- and post-negotiation trust. To assess individuals' level of trust in their counterparts, we used the Organizational Trust Inventory—Short Form (OTI-SF) developed and statistically validated by Cummings and Bromiley (1996). This scale contains 12 items geared toward assessing three dimensions of trust, including the reliability, honesty, and good faith of the other party with respect to fulfilling their commitments. In addition, it also assesses both an affective and a cognitive component for each dimension. We modified the OTI-SF slightly to be more appropriate for a dyadic negotiation setting by asking individually based questions (e.g., "I think" rather than "We think") and by substituting the words "the other party" where the original questionnaire stated the name of the "other department" or "unit." The reliability for this measure in the present study was acceptable, with Cronbach's α = .70. The modified OTI-SF, as was used to measure post-negotiation trust, is presented in the Appendix. The pre-negotiation OTI-SF that was used was equivalent to the one in the Appendix, with the exception that it was phrased in the future tense.

Outcome quality. Both the economic outcome and participants' perceptions of the negotiated outcome were assessed. To assess objective outcome quality we used

Format for nonstandard abbreviation

Reference containing the OTI-SF and validity data.

Description of the OTI-SF and changes made to it.

Reliability evidence

Refer reader to Appendix with actual survey

Another heading for a secondary subsection

FIGURE A.6

The start of a Method subsection (called "Dependent Variables," page 14 of the sample manuscript) that contains secondary subsections: "Pre- and post-negotiation trust" and "Outcome quality." Using secondary subsections is optional, and many articles don't have any. Note the format for typing the headings of the secondary subsections.

- Any *instructions* to the participants. If verbatim instructions need to be specified, present them as a quotation (indented paragraph) if they are less than, say, 10 lines in length or as an appendix if they are much longer.
- The *researcher's role.* Give his or her characteristics, such as gender or age, only if they are relevant to the study's design or interpretation.
- The complete *research design,* making sure the independent and dependent variables are clear, if not already so.
- *Methods of control*—for example, random selection, random assignment, matching, or counterbalancing—if not already stated.

If any of these issues has been specified earlier, assume that the reader remembers. You may want to refer to prior statements but don't repeat them in any detail.

RESULTS

The next major section of a research report is the Results, which summarizes the data and describes the statistical analyses and their outcomes. Figure A.7 presents portions of the Results section of the sample manuscript, showing that it follows immediately after the last paragraph of the Method and can have subsections if

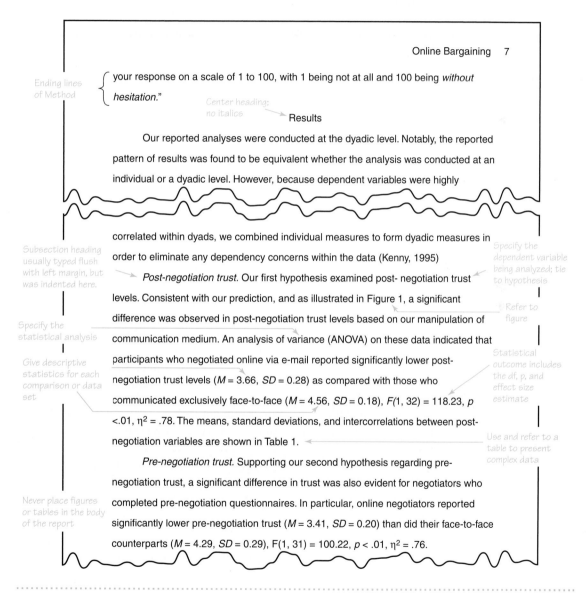

Online Bargaining   7

Ending lines of Method

your response on a scale of 1 to 100, with 1 being not at all and 100 being *without hesitation.*"

Center heading; no italics

Results

Our reported analyses were conducted at the dyadic level. Notably, the reported pattern of results was found to be equivalent whether the analysis was conducted at an individual or a dyadic level. However, because dependent variables were highly

correlated within dyads, we combined individual measures to form dyadic measures in order to eliminate any dependency concerns within the data (Kenny, 1995)

Subsection heading usually typed flush with left margin, but was indented here.

Post-negotiation trust. Our first hypothesis examined post- negotiation trust levels. Consistent with our prediction, and as illustrated in Figure 1, a significant difference was observed in post-negotiation trust levels based on our manipulation of communication medium. An analysis of variance (ANOVA) on these data indicated that participants who negotiated online via e-mail reported significantly lower post-negotiation trust levels ($M = 3.66$, $SD = 0.28$) as compared with those who communicated exclusively face-to-face ($M = 4.56$, $SD = 0.18$), $F(1, 32) = 118.23$, $p <.01$, $\eta^2 = .78$. The means, standard deviations, and intercorrelations between post-negotiation variables are shown in Table 1.

Pre-negotiation trust. Supporting our second hypothesis regarding pre-negotiation trust, a significant difference in trust was also evident for negotiators who completed pre-negotiation questionnaires. In particular, online negotiators reported significantly lower pre-negotiation trust ($M = 3.41$, $SD = 0.20$) than did their face-to-face counterparts ($M = 4.29$, $SD = 0.29$), F(1, 31) = 100.22, $p < .01$, $\eta^2 = .76$.

Specify the dependent variable being analyzed; tie to hypothesis

Refer to figure

Specify the statistical analysis

Statistical outcome includes the df, p, and effect size estimate

Give descriptive statistics for each comparison or data set

Use and refer to a table to present complex data

Never place figures or tables in the body of the report

FIGURE A.7

The start of a Results section (pages 15 and 16 of the sample manuscript) that includes subsections. Although the heading for a primary subsection is usually typed on a separate line in italics, sometimes it is typed as shown if it will be printed like a heading for a secondary subsection to save space.

the study has several variables or hypotheses. If there are no subsections, the "Results" heading is typed as shown, and the paragraphs follow one after another.

The Results section should answer the research questions the report outlined in the Introduction, but it should not try to explain or qualify the findings—interpretations and implications belong in the next section, the Discussion. Here is a list of information that a typical paragraph of the Results should contain, usually in this order:

1. Specify the *dependent variable* and the *purpose of each analysis*—for example, "To test the hypothesis that word familiarity affects memory, the analysis compared the number of familiar and unfamiliar words the students recalled."

2. Give the *descriptive statistics for each data grouping* in the analysis. Do not give individual scores, except if the study used a single-case design or if some anonymous scores are needed to illustrate a point. If the Results will cover many variables, it may be useful to put the descriptive statistics (*M*s and *SD*s), and maybe the outcomes of inferential statistics, in a table. We'll discuss the use and format of tables later in this appendix.

3. If a *table or figure* is used, *refer to it* in words and *point out the main findings* it presents.

4. Give the reasons for any unusual feature in the analysis, such as using an alpha level that is more rigorous than .05 because many analyses were done on the same data.

5. For each inferential analysis, *identify the statistical test* used. Then state whether the outcome is significant and its direction, such as "the experimental group remembered significantly more words than the controls" or "a significant positive correlation was found between anxiety and depression." Give the calculated value (such as the *r*, *t*, or *F*), degrees of freedom (*df*), and *p* value.

6. For the main analyses, especially those that test a hypothesis, also give the estimated *effect size*. Remember that because effect size statistics assess the association between variables, a correlation coefficient already reflects the association, and no separate estimate of effect size is needed. Also recall that the APA *Publication Manual* did not require effect sizes before 2001, so you may not see them in most articles you read.

Do not place a table or figure in the body of the manuscript. Such items go on separate pages toward the end of the report.

DISCUSSION

The Discussion is the last section of the text of a research report, and Figure A.8 shows that it begins immediately after the Results. Its basic purpose and content is described nicely in the APA *Publication Manual* (2001, p. 26):

> After presenting the results, you are in a position to evaluate and interpret their implications, especially with respect to your original hypothesis. You are free to examine, interpret, and qualify the results, as well as to draw inferences from them. Emphasize any theoretical consequences of the results and the validity of your conclusions.

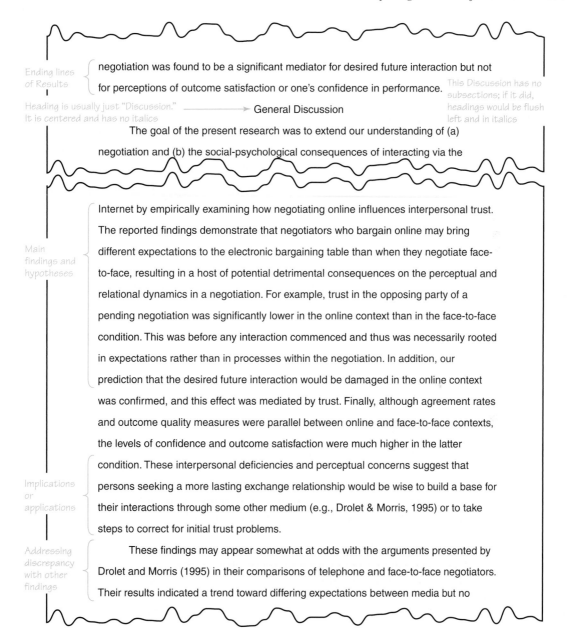

negotiation was found to be a significant mediator for desired future interaction but not for perceptions of outcome satisfaction or one's confidence in performance.

Ending lines of Results

Heading is usually just "Discussion." It is centered and has no italics

This Discussion has no subsections; if it did, headings would be flush left and in italics

General Discussion

The goal of the present research was to extend our understanding of (a) negotiation and (b) the social-psychological consequences of interacting via the

Main findings and hypotheses

Internet by empirically examining how negotiating online influences interpersonal trust. The reported findings demonstrate that negotiators who bargain online may bring different expectations to the electronic bargaining table than when they negotiate face-to-face, resulting in a host of potential detrimental consequences on the perceptual and relational dynamics in a negotiation. For example, trust in the opposing party of a pending negotiation was significantly lower in the online context than in the face-to-face condition. This was before any interaction commenced and thus was necessarily rooted in expectations rather than in processes within the negotiation. In addition, our prediction that the desired future interaction would be damaged in the online context was confirmed, and this effect was mediated by trust. Finally, although agreement rates and outcome quality measures were parallel between online and face-to-face contexts, the levels of confidence and outcome satisfaction were much higher in the latter

Implications or applications

condition. These interpersonal deficiencies and perceptual concerns suggest that persons seeking a more lasting exchange relationship would be wise to build a base for their interactions through some other medium (e.g., Drolet & Morris, 1995) or to take steps to correct for initial trust problems.

Addressing discrepancy with other findings

These findings may appear somewhat at odds with the arguments presented by Drolet and Morris (1995) in their comparisons of telephone and face-to-face negotiators. Their results indicated a trend toward differing expectations between media but no

FIGURE A.8

The start of a Discussion section (pages 9 and 20 of the sample manuscript) for a research report. Typically, the heading is simply "Discussion." Like other sections of a journal article, the Discussion can have subsections, but this article does not.

The Discussion ties together and expands on information stated in the Introduction, Method, and Results. The flow of its content often unfolds in the following sequence:

1. *Summarize the main findings,* particularly with reference to the original *hypotheses and theoretical predictions* stated in the Introduction. Do not state that one group performed better than another group if the means were in that direction but the difference was not statistically significant. If it is important to make a comparison of this type, be sure to state clearly that the difference was nonsignificant.

2. Identify *results that are not consistent with the original hypotheses* and suggest or speculate clearly on reasons for the discrepancies.

3. *Compare the current results with those of other studies,* especially those cited in the Introduction, and try to account for the differences.

4. Identify the *strengths and limitations* of the methods that were used in the current study, particularly in relation to those of other studies. Some topics to consider are the ways by which the independent variable was manipulated, measures used to assess the dependent variable, differences in the characteristics of the samples, and aspects of the statistical analyses. Don't just mention these comparisons; use them to *make a point and consider implications*—for example, are the current findings more or less likely to generalize broadly, or more or less likely to be confounded?

5. Describe *alternative explanations* for the results, such as the possible effects of specific third variables, and explain why one explanation seems most convincing.

6. Address *new considerations.* Are there links between the current findings and other phenomena in psychology or other disciplines, such as biology or sociology? Do the results or the interpretation of them suggest new theories or revisions of old ones on the topic? Do the results or the interpretation of them suggest topics or designs for future research? Might it be possible to apply the results to real-life problems?

The Discussion involves the most intellectually creative writing of a research report. Two approaches can help in this process. First, reread the reports you cited in the Introduction, looking specifically for and keeping track of ideas for the items in the preceding list. Second, take the perspective of a journal reviewer: What criticisms might a reviewer have of your research? Doing this will help you to identify limitations of your study and to address or justify them in the Discussion.

REFERENCES

After the text of the report, *each of the remaining elements of the manuscript will begin on a new page,* and this rule applies to the next section of the report, the References. The references listed here should match those cited in the report: each item cited should have its complete reference listed, alphabetized by authors' names, and there should be no references listed that were not cited earlier in the report.

The APA *Publication Manual* (2001) details the rules for typing the reference for each possible type and variety of source materials, such as journal articles and books. We saw earlier in this book that using online materials can be problematic. If you must use a Web site for a reference, consult the guidelines currently available at the APA Web site (www.apastyle.org/elecref.html). The rules for typing references for online materials are frequently updated. Figure A.9 illustrates how to type references for the most commonly cited types of sources. When typing references, follow the formats you find there regarding what to italicize, where to capitalize, and how to punctuate.

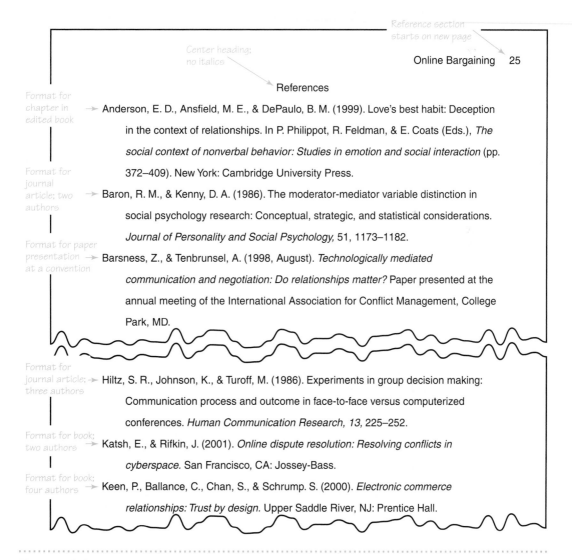

Reference section starts on new page

Center heading; no italics

Online Bargaining   25

References

Format for chapter in edited book
Anderson, E. D., Ansfield, M. E., & DePaulo, B. M. (1999). Love's best habit: Deception in the context of relationships. In P. Philippot, R. Feldman, & E. Coats (Eds.), *The social context of nonverbal behavior: Studies in emotion and social interaction* (pp. 372–409). New York: Cambridge University Press.

Format for journal article; two authors
Baron, R. M., & Kenny, D. A. (1986). The moderator-mediator variable distinction in social psychology research: Conceptual, strategic, and statistical considerations. *Journal of Personality and Social Psychology, 51,* 1173–1182.

Format for paper presentation at a convention
Barsness, Z., & Tenbrunsel, A. (1998, August). *Technologically mediated communication and negotiation: Do relationships matter?* Paper presented at the annual meeting of the International Association for Conflict Management, College Park, MD.

Format for journal article; three authors
Hiltz, S. R., Johnson, K., & Turoff, M. (1986). Experiments in group decision making: Communication process and outcome in face-to-face versus computerized conferences. *Human Communication Research, 13,* 225–252.

Format for book; two authors
Katsh, E., & Rifkin, J. (2001). *Online dispute resolution: Resolving conflicts in cyberspace.* San Francisco, CA: Jossey-Bass.

Format for book; four authors
Keen, P., Ballance, C., Chan, S., & Schrump. S. (2000). *Electronic commerce relationships: Trust by design.* Upper Saddle River, NJ: Prentice Hall.

FIGURE A.9

Parts of the References section (pages 25 and 26 of the sample manuscript), including its beginning at the top of a new page.

Appendixes, Author Notes, and Footnotes

Virtually all journal articles have an author note, but only some have one or more appendixes or footnotes. Student manuscripts for research methods courses often have an appendix, especially if the instructor requires one for presenting the raw data or printouts from statistical computer programs.

Appendix(es)

An Appendix is a part of a report that presents material that would be inappropriate to or distracting from the flow of writing in the text of a report, but would be useful to help the reader understand or replicate the research. If there is more than one Appendix, each title is given a letter (A, B, C, and so on), assigned in order of appearance: "Appendix A" precedes "Appendix B." The report refers to an Appendix if there is one, as we saw in Figure A.6 for the sample manuscript. An Appendix is likely to be used to present a lengthy, previously unpublished survey (as in Figure A.10), a long set of instructions

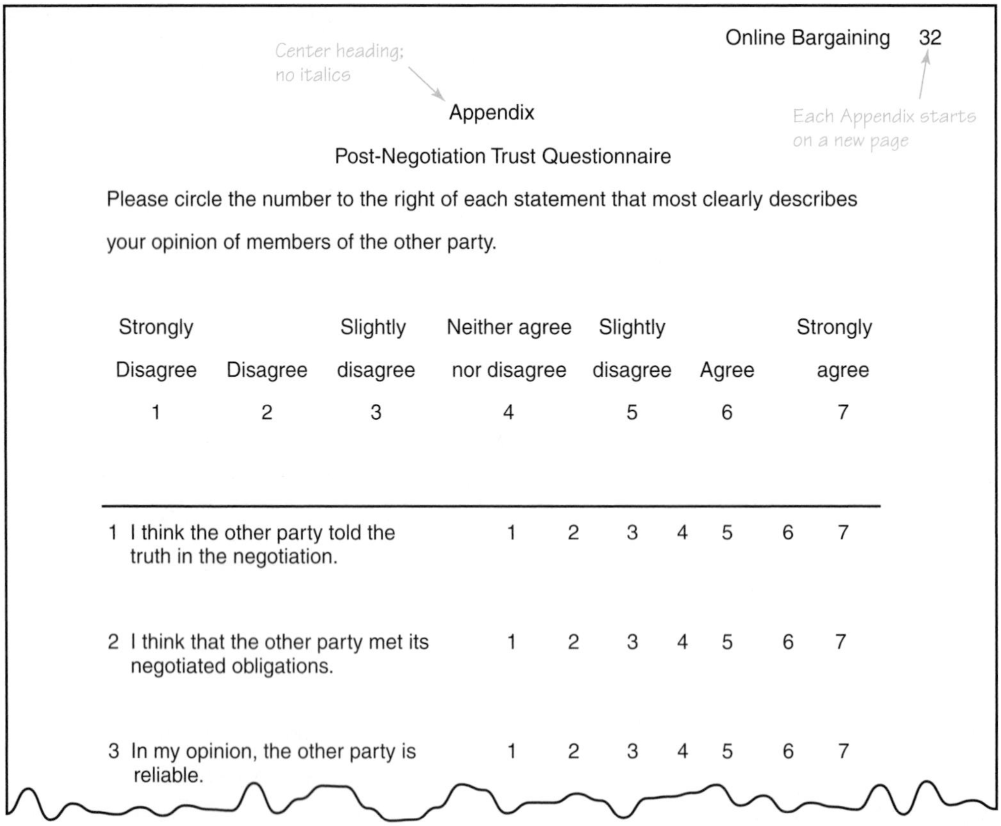

Online Bargaining 32

Appendix

Post-Negotiation Trust Questionnaire

Please circle the number to the right of each statement that most clearly describes your opinion of members of the other party.

Strongly Disagree	Disagree	Slightly disagree	Neither agree nor disagree	Slightly disagree	Agree	Strongly agree
1	2	3	4	5	6	7

1 I think the other party told the truth in the negotiation.	1	2	3	4	5	6	7
2 I think that the other party met its negotiated obligations.	1	2	3	4	5	6	7
3 In my opinion, the other party is reliable.	1	2	3	4	5	6	7

FIGURE A.10
The start of an Appendix (page 32 of the sample manuscript) to present a questionnaire that had 12 items (the figure shows only the first three).

for participants, or a detailed description of an apparatus or set of stimulus materials.

Author Note and Footnote(s)

The Author Note begins on a new page and provides information about the authors and other aspects about the research that they may want to express. Figure A.11 presents an example. Author notes commonly contain the following information:

1. The departmental affiliation of each author.
2. Any acknowledgements to other individuals for contributions to or assistance in the study or the report.
3. A statement of which author to contact (usually with postal and e-mail address) for further information.
4. The sources of financial support for the research.
5. Disclosures, such as having presented part of the report at a convention.

When a manuscript contains one or more *footnotes,* they are typed on a page with the heading, "Footnote" if there is one, or the plural if there are more. Each footnote is identified with a superscript number that is assigned in order of appearance in the report.

Online Bargaining   34

Center heading; no italics

Author Note starts on a new page

Author Note

Charles E. Naquin, Mendoza College of Business, University of Notre Dame; Gaylen D. Paulson, McCombs School of Business, University of Texas at Austin.

Portions of this research were presented at the annual conference of the International Association of Conflict Management, Cergy, France, June 2001. We are indebted to Michael Roloff, James Schmidtke, and Trexler Proffitt for their assistance at various stages of this project.

Correspondence concerning this article should be addressed to Charles E. Naquin, Mendoza College of Business, University of Notre Dame, Notre Dame, Indiana, 46556. E-mail: charles.naquin.1@nd.edu.

FIGURE A.11
An Author Note (page 34 of the sample manuscript).

Tables, Figure Captions, and Figures

Tables and figures often provide an efficient and clear way to present a large amount of data or other information. Each table and figure appears on a separate sheet of paper and is assigned an identifying number ("Table 1," "Table 2," "Figure 1," "Figure 2," and so on) that is used to refer to it in the text. As a general rule, the information in tables or figures should not duplicate each other or restate what is presented in text form elsewhere in the report. See Appendix B for additional instructions on preparing tables and figures.

Tables

A table presents information organized in columns and rows, which are easy to format in word processors. The information can be numerical or verbal (words or sentences). In *numerical tables,* the focus is on presenting data, such as the means and standard deviations or the calculated values from a single complex analysis or a large number of simpler analyses. Round the data to *two decimals* in most cases. Numerical tables are desirable to use if providing the data in sentences would make the text dense with numbers and confusing to read. Figure A.12 presents a table from the sample manuscript. You can see the table number on the first line, followed by a title that describes the types of data the table contains. Any notes that are needed are listed below the table.

Verbal tables focus on presenting words or sentences. A verbal table might be used to present several terms in one column and the corresponding definitions of the terms in another column. Another use for a verbal table would be to present a survey or a list of stimuli that is not so long that it would require an appendix.

Figures and Figure Captions

Figures in research reports are usually graphs, diagrams, illustrations, or photographs, and each one has a caption, or title. A *figure caption* is not given on the same page with the figure because different departments of publishers produce them. So, all figure captions for a report are listed together, beginning on a new page, and *each figure has its own separate page* massed at the very end of the manuscript. The *pages with figures have no header or pagination,* and the figure number and partial caption are written on the back. Because figures use a lot of space and are expensive to produce, they are used sparingly in journal articles. Figure A.13 shows a page (at top) with a figure caption and a page (at bottom) with the corresponding figure from the sample manuscript.

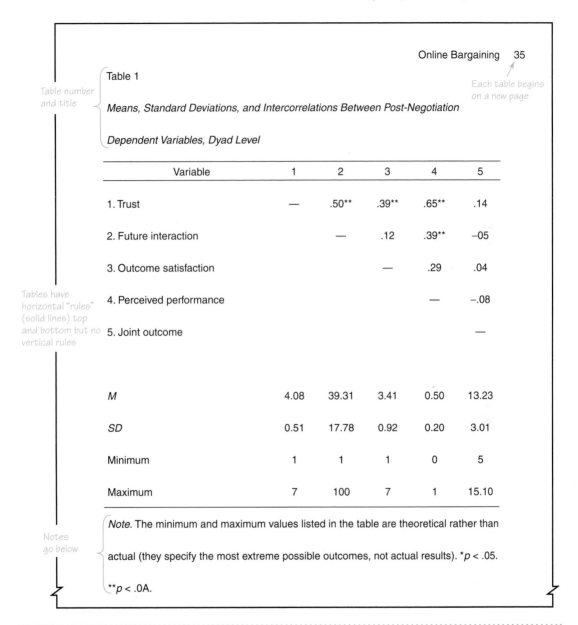

Table number and title

Table 1

Each table begins on a new page

Means, Standard Deviations, and Intercorrelations Between Post-Negotiation

Dependent Variables, Dyad Level

Variable	1	2	3	4	5
1. Trust	—	.50**	.39**	.65**	.14
2. Future interaction		—	.12	.39**	−05
3. Outcome satisfaction			—	.29	.04
4. Perceived performance				—	−.08
5. Joint outcome					—
M	4.08	39.31	3.41	0.50	13.23
SD	0.51	17.78	0.92	0.20	3.01
Minimum	1	1	1	0	5
Maximum	7	100	7	1	15.10

Tables have horizontal "rules" (solid lines) top and bottom but no vertical rules

Notes go below

Note. The minimum and maximum values listed in the table are theoretical rather than

actual (they specify the most extreme possible outcomes, not actual results). *$p < .05$.

**$p < .0A$.

FIGURE A.12

A numerical table (page 35 of the sample manuscript). Notice that it contains a great deal of data that would be confusing and difficult to read if included in sentences.

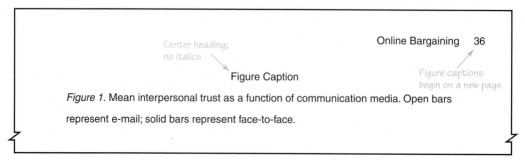

Center heading;
no italics

Online Bargaining   36

Figure captions
begin on a new page

Figure Caption

Figure 1. Mean interpersonal trust as a function of communication media. Open bars

represent e-mail; solid bars represent face-to-face.

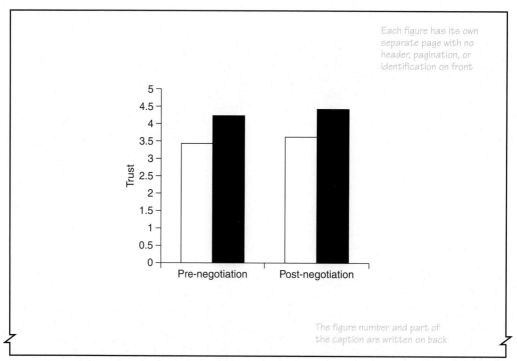

Each figure has its own
separate page with no
header, pagination, or
identification on front

The figure number and part of
the caption are written on back

FIGURE A.13

Two full pages of the sample manuscript (top is page 36, bottom is the last page but has no header or pagination) depicting a figure caption and corresponding graph.

APPENDIX B
STATISTICAL PROCEDURES

Formulas for Manual Calculations

Preparing Tables and Graphs
Tables
Graphs

Standard Statistical Tables
List of Tables

OVERVIEW

Like Appendix A on report writing, Appendix B takes a "how-to" approach—in this case with regard to performing statistical procedures. It will tell you *how to*

- Prepare the data for analysis, including methods for organizing the data, finding errors or other problems in the data, and methods for dealing with missing data.

- Calculate the statistics you've chosen to perform, using computer and manual approaches. Although there are several major computer statistical programs—such as SPSS, SAS, Systat, and Minitab—we'll use SPSS in our examples because it appears to be the most popular statistics software in psychology, and a student version of it is available with this book. Instructions for other programs are given in the Companion Website for this book. The student version of SPSS includes all the statistics we will discuss, except for repeated measures ANOVA, which requires an advanced version of SPSS.

- Construct tables and figures.

At the end of this appendix are standard statistical tables, including a *table of random numbers* that can be used to randomize the order of items or conditions for presentation in the study and the selection or assignment of participants. Most of the other statistical tables give critical values for deciding whether a finding is significant when calculating analyses manually.

PREPARING THE DATA FOR ANALYSIS

The raw data we collect are not generally ready for statistical analysis. We must perform a number of initial activities and make some decisions in the process of preparing the data for analysis.

INITIAL ACTIVITIES AND DECISIONS

We begin the process of analyzing data by making sure they are in the correct form for our needs. For example, if we collect data in a survey, we may need to total the scores for the whole questionnaire, calculate scores for certain subscales, or convert the scores to percentages. Our hypotheses will determine the form of the scores we'll need. Let's look at a couple of examples.

Suppose we collected survey data for a study on coping with stress, but there are several ways of coping that are very different from one another, such as planful problem solving, seeking social support, and escape–avoidance (Folkman & Lazarus, 1988). Our hypothesis might be that the type of coping people use depends on whether a stressful experience appears to be modifiable. For instance, if people think they can do something to reduce the source of stress, they may use planful problem solving; if they think they can't change the source, they may use escape–avoidance. Questionnaires to measure coping can yield an overall score and separate subscale scores for each type of coping. Clearly, we'd need subscale scores to test our hypothesis.

As another example, suppose we did a study in which hungry rats learned to run down the "stem" (long section) in a T-shaped runway to a choice point: turning one way led to a chamber containing food; turning the other way led to a chamber with no food. The walls had these three paint patterns: the stem was a solid medium gray, the chamber with food had vertical black and white stripes, and the chamber without food had horizontal black and white stripes. The rats were then tested while hungry in an identical runway, except that the walls of the middle 2-foot section of the stem was painted with one of the three patterns—solid gray, vertical stripes, or horizontal stripes. We are testing two theories that predict different outcomes. One theory states that having the middle section painted like the food chamber should elevate the subjects' motivation, getting them to run faster in that section and reach the actual food chamber sooner than the rats in the other conditions. The second theory states that having the middle section painted like the food chamber should confuse the subjects, so that they'd run slower in that section and reach the food chamber later than the rats in the other conditions. Testing these hypotheses requires time (or speed) scores for the middle section of the stem and for the entire runway, from start to finish.

Scoring, Coding, and Organizing the Data

Researchers usually record their data on sheets of paper. For instance, if the researchers assess overt behavior, such as running speed, they put the scores on *data sheets,* usually one sheet per subject. The data sheets for the study with rat subjects we just considered might contain running times for each foot of the runway, an indication of whether the animal turned in the correct (food) direction, and comments on extraneous behaviors that may have occurred. If researchers collect data with a survey, the questionnaire is the data sheet.

As we've already seen, scoring a questionnaire may require calculating subscale scores, and the items for each subscale may be scattered throughout the survey. If so, we must keep track of what each item measures. In addition, if some items are stated in one direction, such as "I often feel nervous," but others are in the opposite direction, such as "I am usually calm," we'll probably have to use *reverse scoring* for some of the items. Reverse scoring yields an overall score for a set of items that is in one direction. If we are using a previously developed questionnaire, scoring procedures are probably given in a manual for the test or in a published report. As we saw earlier, the scoring we do can involve combining the data from separate variables to create a *composite variable,* such as an overall total, sum of subscale scores, or product of two or more scores. If we are performing analyses manually, we would calculate the values of composite variables and write them on the data sheets, but if we are using a computer statistical program, we can have the program create the composite variables from the component scores, as we'll see later.

Each entry in a data sheet is a score for a variable, including performance on the dependent variable(s), designation of the research condition or group, and demographic information, such as gender, age, and ethnicity. Some of these data are in numerical form because they were assessed with an *interval* or *ratio* measurement scale, such as rating scores or age. *Ordinal* data are ranks across all subjects in an analysis. Other data are in words and were collected with a nominal scale, such as gender and ethnicity. *Nominal* data can be converted, or coded, as numerical in an arbitrary manner, such as 1 = female and 2 = male, but these numbers do not make the data interval or ratio for statistical analyses—they're still nominal: We're just "naming" them with a number. When we code data in an arbitrary way, we should keep track of the coded meanings; if we don't and forget, we'll need to do some work later to figure out what they mean.

Next, we need to organize the data, typically in a *summary table* arranged in columns and rows. *Each column represents a variable, and each row represents one subject.* Thus, the first row will be for the first subject and will contain the data for each variable in each column horizontally. A column can contain data representing the condition the subject was tested in (that is, the level of an independent variable), a dependent variable, or any other variable we may want to keep track of in our analyses, such as demographic characteristics. The data we enter into the table will come from the data sheets, and all the data for a particular variable will appear in a single column. If we are performing our statistical analyses on a computer, the *data file* is the summary table; it has rows for subjects (often called "cases") and columns for variables. If we are doing the analyses manually, we'll need to construct a table on paper with rows for subjects and columns for variables. In either case, each column should be given a name—and if it must be abbreviated, the name should be meaningful or easy to decipher. For example, the dependent variable "reaction time" might be abbreviated as "reactime."

As we set up the table of data, it's a very good idea to create a *variables key* that specifies what each column represents and the data values it can contain. For instance, in a study on people's anxiety and reaction time, we could write in the key:

> Column 1: gender (1 = male, 2 = female)
>
> Column 2: age (17–31 years)
>
> Column 3: ethnic = ethnicity (1 = Caucasian, 2 = African American, 3 = Hispanic, 4 = Asian)
>
> Column 4: reactime = reaction time (0.000–999.999)
>
> Column 5: anxiety (0–125)

The data in parentheses are the possible values each variable can have. Notice that we can also use the variables key to keep track of any abbreviations for variables and the coded values for variables measured on a nominal scale—in this case, gender and ethnicity. If we do our analyses on a computer, the program will probably have a way to enter the information for the variables key. In SPSS, we'd click on the *Variable View* tab at the bottom of the data file and use the *Label* and *Values* columns to record the full name or meaning of an abbreviation and the possible values, respectively.

Eliminating Subjects from the Analysis

Although rare, sometimes we must consider eliminating from the analysis the data of some subjects. This can occur if we find that the equipment did not function properly during testing, large or critical sections of the data sheets have no data, or the data are "weird," such as if all scores are extremely high or low, no matter what the variable measures. Why would the latter two problems happen? The lack of data may occur if an observer or participant made a mistake, such as by skipping a page in a survey, or if a participant did not want to answer those questions. Although the absence of a small amount of data usually does not justify dropping a subject, sometimes lacking data on just one variable can exclude a subject from the analysis, particularly if it is the only way to identify the level of an independent variable—for example, age or gender. For the weird data, having extremely high or low scores for all assessments regardless of what the variables measure suggests that the subject was ill, disordered, or not taking the task seriously. Deciding to eliminate subjects from analyses should be reserved *only for cases in which the data are clearly not usable,* and never because they do not confirm a research hypothesis. If subjects are eliminated, we must indicate in the report (usually in the Method section) their number and the reasons.

Checking for Erroneous and Outlying Data

Once we have entered the data into the summary table, we can examine them for two types of problems a data grouping can have: erroneous data and outliers. *Erroneous data* result from mistakes, usually in recording scores on a data sheet or entering the data into the summary table. There are two ways to tell that erroneous data exist. First, we can check the summary table data against the data sheets. Second, we can check whether summary table data fall outside the range of possible scores. For instance, in the variables key given earlier, the range of values for gender spans from 1 to 2. If we find in the summary table a value of 11 for gender, we can see that there is an error, and we'd need to check the data sheet to be certain of the correct value.

There are two ways to check whether any data fall outside the possible range for the variable. First, if our summary table is a data file in a computer statistics program, we can perform a frequency analysis for each variable. In SPSS, we would click in the menu bar on *Analyze → Descriptive Statistics → Frequencies*; then we would enter the names of the variables we want to check and click on *OK*. This will yield an output that gives the number of subjects (cases) with each score, and if it shows scores outside the possible range, we know that errors exist. As part of a frequency analysis in SPSS, we can also have the output presented graphically as a histogram or bar chart (click on *Charts* before *OK*), which enables us to see more clearly how the scores are distributed for a variable. Second, if we are doing the analysis manually and our summary table is on paper, we would scan each column, looking for scores that are outside the possible range.

In the problem of *outliers,* the data include one or more extreme scores that are within the range of possible values but are improbable or "don't fit" because they deviate so much from the main body of scores in the data grouping. How do we identify outliers, and what should we do about them? A good way to identify outliers is to define them statistically, such as scores that fall three or more standard deviations from the mean. We can find outliers in three ways:

- Calculate the *M* and *SD* for each variable, add and subtract 3 *SDs* from the *M,* and use the frequency analysis to find scores that exceed these limits.
- Perform a *stem-and-leaf plot* in SPSS by clicking on *Analyze → Descriptive Statistics → Explore* in the menu bar and then the "Plots" button. The stem-and-leaf plot lists in numerical order the "stems," which are the first digit(s) of each score, and to the right of each stem, each "leaf," the last digit for scores that share the same stem. The plot looks like a numerical form of histogram, enabling us to see the distribution of the data and identify outliers.
- For correlational analyses, perform a scatterplot manually or in SPSS by clicking in the menu bar on *Graphs → Interactive → Scatterplot.*

What to do about outliers is a controversial issue, and there are at least four reasonable approaches. One possibility is to do nothing—that is, leave outliers in the data we analyze and point out their presence in the Results or Discussion. Second, we can do the analyses with and without them, noting the similarities and differences in outcomes. Third, we can convert data, such as by substituting for an outlier a score that is slightly larger (or smaller) than the next most extreme value in the data set. Fourth, we can simply exclude outliers from our analyses. None of these approaches provides a perfect solution, but whatever action we take should be explained in the research report.

DEALING WITH MISSING DATA

Sometimes a datum is missing for a subject, either because an observer neglected to enter one or a participant failed to respond, such as by skipping a question in a survey. Missing a few data when other comparable data are available for the subject is often not a serious problem, but how to deal with the missing data is controversial, and several reasonable approaches have been used (Schafer & Graham, 2002). One approach is to delete the case, or subject—an extreme method that has serious shortcomings. We'll describe a couple of other approaches that replace the missing values with estimated scores.

A traditional method for replacing missing data is to *average the available data* from that subject on that variable. For instance, if we measured a person's stress with a 10-item scale but one item was skipped, we could replace the missing value with the mean of the nine completed items. In SPSS, we would click in the menu bar on *Transform → Replace Missing Values* and then apply the *series mean* method, which is the most commonly used approach for replacing values. If we are doing our analyses manually, we can calculate the mean and write it in the correct place in the summary table. Regardless of whether we perform the replacements by computer or by hand, it's a good idea to keep track of them. For instance, when writing a replacement datum in the summary table, we could circle it.

A newer and very complex method for replacing missing data is called *multiple imputation* (Schafer & Graham, 2002). For this procedure, a computer program examines the range of possible values for a missing datum and then uses regression (correlational) statistics to predict many simulated values for it. Analyses are performed with each of the simulated values, and the outcomes are then averaged. Multiple imputation and other new approaches appear to produce more accurate replacement values for missing data than traditional methods do, and widely used statistical programs such as SPSS and SAS are beginning to incorporate some of them.

To summarize the discussion of problems in the data we collect, eliminating the data for some subjects and dealing with missing data and outliers involve careful decision making in choosing among reasonable procedures. When writing a research report for a research methods course, check with your instructor for guidance in the approaches to use with these problems and specify in the report exactly how you dealt with each problem.

CALCULATING STATISTICS

Given that most students do their statistical analyses on computers these days, this section will focus mainly on how to input the data and run analyses with a statistics program. As stated earlier, many statistics programs are available, and we'll use SPSS (version 11.0) in describing statistical procedures. Each program has its own appearance and procedures for inputting data and running each analysis. If you need to use another program, the instructions given here may not apply. If a newer version of SPSS is published during the run of this edition, updates for changes to the procedures of will be given in the Companion Website for this book.

Because research methods students often have forgotten how to perform specific statistical analyses, this section provides step-by-step directions for each inferential test specified in Table 4.1 (see inside front cover). *Use that table as we have in the past to decide which analyses to compute.* The tests we'll cover will be separated into two types, *parametric* and *nonparametric*.

A FEW SPSS DATA MANAGEMENT FUNCTIONS

Before we consider how to do specific statistical analyses with SPSS, let's describe a few useful functions we can use in managing the data file. Three of these functions are *copy, cut,* and *paste,* which we can access by clicking on *Edit* in the menu bar. Highlight the material to be copied, cut, or pasted before using the functions.

SPSS has a nifty function for creating new variables, such as composite variables. We would click in the menu bar on *Transform* → *Compute*, which takes us to a box that we'll describe in terms of its left and right sides. On the left is a blank space (labeled "Target Variable") for naming the new variable we want to create and a list of all existing variables in the data file. On the right is a blank box ("Numeric Expression") in which we will compose the formula for creating the target variable. To compose a formula, we transfer variable names from the list, inserting as appropriate the arithmetic functions and numbers listed on the right, below the numeric expression box (we won't cover here the long list of "functions" on the far right). After naming the target variable and composing the formula, we click on OK, and the program adds a column for the new variable at the right end of the data file.

The last SPSS data management function we'll discuss allows us to split the data file into separate groups of cases, based on the data for one or more of the variables. For example, suppose we had data for several variables, including gender (coded as 1 = male, 2 = female), and wanted to do an analysis for only one of the sexes—say, females. We would click in the menu bar on *Data* → *Select Cases*, which brings up a box that has all variables in the data file listed on the left and several "select" options on the right. We'd click on the second option, "If condition is satisfied" and on the "If" button, which brings up a box with a space to fill in a formula that specifies *which cases we want to include*. In our example, because we coded females as "2," we would specify the formula: "gender = 2." If we also had data for the variable of age and wanted to select females older than 18 years, we'd use the formula: "gender = 2 & age > 18." Once you select the cases, look at the data file and see that the cases not selected—for instance, males—are crossed off. This means that they will not be included in any analyses conducted while this "select cases" function is in force. To eliminate the function and use the whole data file again, simply go to the select cases box and click on the "Reset" button.

SPSS STEP BY STEP: PARAMETRIC ANALYSES

As we examine instructions for calculating *parametric tests* on SPSS, we'll consider how to do statistics for *assessing relationships* before statistics for *assessing differences*. Inputting data in parametric analyses is most efficient if we assign each column in the data file according to the order in which the needed data appear in the data sheets. Thus, suppose we did a study that assessed participants' demographic variables, self-esteem, and social attitudes regarding attractive and unattractive women, and those variables appear in that order in the data sheets. We'd label the columns in the data file in that order so we can input the data for each participant (case) in the same order they have in the data sheet. The inputting process will go more smoothly and with fewer errors.

The directions for each parametric analysis will tell you how to *enter the data, run the analysis,* and *read the output.* Because parametric outputs are often very wide, it's usually best to print them in *landscape* mode: click in toolbar on *File* → *Print* → *Properties* → *Basic* → *Landscape.* Each analysis has variations and options that we won't discuss—our directions will focus on the basics and commonly used options, usually applying default settings in the program. We'll start with statistics to assess relationships.

Pearson Product-Moment Correlation (r)

Pearson's *r* is used to assess the degree of relationship between two variables when we have data measured on an interval or ratio scale. *Review and keep handy the material in Chapter 6* on Pearson's *r* for information not covered here.

To enter the data in the SPSS data file,
1. Assign and name columns according to the order in which the data for the corresponding variables appear in the data sheets. Set up a variables key by using the *Label* and *Values* columns in the *Variable View* screen.
2. Enter data for each variable in its own column, one subject (case) at a time.
3. Create new or composite variables, if needed, and add them to the variables key.

To run a Pearson's *r*, make sure the data file is open and:
1. Use the *select cases* function if you want to analyze data for only some of the subjects.
2. Click in the menu bar on *Analyze → Correlate → Bivariate*, which produces a box called "Bivariate Correlations." The default correlation coefficient is Pearson.
3. Move the variables you want to analyze from the list on the left to the box labeled "Variables." If you want to do more than one Pearson's *r*, you can put more than two variables in the box. Be sure *not* to use variables measured on nominal scales, such as gender or ethnicity.
4. Click on the "Options" button, then "Means and standard deviations," and then the "Continue" button.
5. Click on the "OK" button, and the analysis runs.

To read the output, you'll see the *M*s and *SD*s for the variables in a "Descriptive Statistics" table at the top of the printout and a matrix called "Correlations" with each variable listed vertically and horizontally. Each cell of the matrix contains three values for the two variables involved: the *r* ("Pearson Correlation"), *p* value ("Sig. [2-tailed]"), and number of subjects ("*N*"). If the *p* is less than .05, the correlation for that pair of variables is significant. The output doesn't give the *df*, which is easy to calculate: the number of cases minus 2.

Multiple Regression

Multiple regression analysis is a correlational procedure that is used to predict the level of a criterion variable on the basis of a combination of two or more predictor variables. Although special forms of multiple regression can be used with nominal or ordinal data, we'll consider the more usual case of having data measured on an interval or ratio scale. *Review and keep handy the material in Chapter 6* on multiple regression for information not covered here.

To enter the data in the SPSS data file,
1. Assign and name columns according to the order in which the data for the corresponding variables appear in the data sheets. Set up a variables key by using the *Label* and *Values* columns in the *Variable View* screen.

2. Enter data for each variable in its own column, one subject (case) at a time.

3. Create new or composite variables, if needed, and add them to the variables key.

To run a multiple regression, make sure the data file is open and:

1. Use the *select cases* function if you want to analyze data for only some of the subjects.

2. Click in the menu bar on *Analyze* → *Regression* → *Linear,* which produces a box called "Linear Regression."

3. Move the variables you want to analyze from the list on the left to the boxes labeled "Dependent," which is the criterion variable, and "Independent(s)," which are the predictor variables.

4. The default setting for "Method" is *Enter,* which we won't change here, but other methods are very commonly used. This setting determines the process by which each predictor variable is entered into the analysis. Considering how to choose the most appropriate method is beyond the scope of this book.

5. Click on the "Statistics" button, then "Descriptives" (which will give you the *M*s and *SD*s), and then the "Continue" button.

6. Click on the "OK" button, and the analysis runs.

To read the output, you'll see the *M*s and *SD*s for the variables in a "Descriptive Statistics" table at the top of the printout followed by a complex series of tables, each with a name. The main elements of the outcome will be found in two tables. In the "Model Summary" table, you'll find out which combination of predictor variables accounted for a significant amount of variance in the criterion variable and the overall amount of variance they accounted for (the "R square" value). For example, an R square of .42 means that the combined predictor variables accounted for 42% of the variance in the criterion variable. In the "Coefficients" table, you'll see the amount of variance (in the "Beta" column) in the criterion variable accounted for by each predictor variable. And the column labeled "Sig." provides the p values—a p less than .05, confirms that the variable is a significant predictor.

The remaining parametric statistics we'll consider are designed to assess differences between data groupings for two or more conditions or groups in a study.

Independent-Samples t Test (t)

The independent-samples t test is applied to examine differences between two data groupings when the independent variable has two levels, each subject receives only one level of the variable, and the data were measured on an interval or ratio scale. *Review and keep handy the material in Chapter 7* on the independent-samples t test for information not covered here.

To enter the data in the SPSS data file,

1. Assign and name columns according to the order in which the data for the corresponding variables appear in the data sheets. One column must designate levels of the independent variable (coded, for example,

1 = experimental group, 2 = control group). Set up a variables key by using the *Label* and *Values* columns in the *Variable View* screen.

2. Enter data for each variable in its own column, one subject (case) at a time. Each column will have data pertaining to both of the groups (the codes in the column for the independent variable will tell the program which group a datum belongs to).

3. Create new or composite variables, if needed, and add them to the variables key.

To run an independent-samples *t*, make sure the data file is open and:

1. Use the *select cases* function if you want to analyze data for only some of the subjects.

2. Click in the menu bar on *Analyze → Compare Means → Independent-Samples T Test*, which produces a box called "Independent-Samples T Test."

3. Identify the dependent variables you want to analyze from the list on the left and move them to the box labeled "Test Variable(s)." If you want to do more than one *t* test for the same independent variable, you can put additional dependent variables in the box.

4. Move the independent variable from the list on the left to the box called "Grouping Variable" and click on the "Define Groups" button, which produces a box called "Define Groups."

5. Insert the group codes (for example, "1" for the experimental, "2" for the control) in the spaces under "Use specified values" and click on the "Continue" button.

6. Click on the "OK" button, and the analysis runs. (Note: You'll need to calculate effect sizes manually, using one of the formulas in Table 7.3, see inside back cover.)

To read the output, you'll see two tables. The table called "Group Statistics" gives the *M*s and *SD*s for the variables without your having to request them. The table called "Independent Samples Test" is more complicated than it looks. On the left are two columns pertaining to a Levene's test, which checks an assumption of the *t* test: that the variances of the two groups are similar. If this test is significant (if the value in the "Sig." column is less than .05), the variances are not similar, and the *t* test will need to use an adjustment for unequal variances. Notice that all the remaining columns in the table have two rows, one for equal variances and one for unequal variances. If the variances are similar (the Levene's test is not significant), use the values in the upper row (equal variances) of each column, but if the variances are not equal, use the values in the lower row. The main columns to consider now give the *t* (in the "*t*" column), *p* ("Sig. [2-tailed]"), and *df*. If the *p* is less than .05, the difference is significant.

Paired-Samples t Test (t)

The paired-samples *t* test is used to assess whether two sets of interval or ratio data differ when collected in a dependent-groups design—that is, the subjects in the two conditions were the same individuals or matched. If the same subjects were tested in each of the conditions, a repeated-measures or within-subjects design was used. *Review and keep handy the material in Chapter 8* on the paired-samples *t* test for information not covered here.

To enter the data in the SPSS data file,

1. Assign and name columns according to the order in which the data for the corresponding variables appear in the data sheets. Set up a variables key by using the *Label* and *Values* columns in the *Variable View* screen.

2. Enter data for each variable in its own column, one subject (case) at a time. Each level of the independent variable is considered a separate variable and *has its own column* and name, such as "pretest" and "posttest."

3. Create new or composite variables, if needed, and add them to the variables key.

To run a paired-samples *t*, make sure the data file is open and:

1. Use the *select cases* function if you want to analyze data for only some of the subjects.

2. Click in the menu bar on *Analyze → Compare Means → Paired-Samples T Test*, which produces a box called "Paired-Samples T Test."

3. Identify the two variables you want to analyze from the list on the left and move them to the box labeled "Paired Variables." The two must be moved as a pair. If you want to do more than one paired-samples *t*, you can put additional pairs of variables in the box, one pair at a time.

4. Click on the "OK" button, and the analysis runs. (Note: You'll need to calculate effect sizes manually, using one of the formulas in Table 7.3, see inside back cover.).

To read the output, you'll see two tables. The one called "Paired-Samples Statistics" gives the *M*s and *SD*s for the variables without your having to request them (disregard the other columns in most cases). The table called "Paired-Samples Test" gives the *t* (in the "*t*" column), *p* ("Sig. [2-tailed]"), and *df*. If the *p* is less than .05, the difference is significant.

One-Way ANOVA (F) for Independent Groups

The one-way ANOVA for independent groups is applied to examine differences among more than two data groupings when there is one independent variable, each subject received only one of the three or more levels of that variable, and the data are on an interval or ratio scale. *Review and keep handy the material in Chapter 7* on the one-way ANOVA for information not covered here.

To enter the data in the SPSS data file,

1. Assign and name columns according to the order in which the data for the corresponding variables appear in the data sheets. One column must designate levels of the independent variable (coded, for example, 1 = experimental group, 2 = control group, 3 = placebo). Set up a variables key by using the *Label* and *Values* columns in the *Variable View* screen.

2. Enter data for each variable in its own column, one subject (case) at a time. Each column will have a variable's data pertaining to all the groups (the codes in the column for the independent variable will tell the program which group a datum belongs to).

3. Create new or composite variables, if needed, and add them to the variables key.

To run a one-way ANOVA for independent groups, make sure the data file is open and:

1. Use the *select cases* function if you want to analyze data for only some of the subjects.

2. Click in the menu bar on *Analyze → Compare Means → One-Way ANOVA*, which produces a box called "One-Way ANOVA."

3. Identify the dependent variables you want to analyze from the list on the left and move them to the box labeled "Dependent List." If you want to do more than one ANOVA for the same independent variable, you can put additional dependent variables in the box.

4. Move the independent variable from the list on the left to the box called "Factor."

5. Click on the "Options" button, which brings up a box called "One-Way ANOVA Options." Click on "Descriptive" (to get the *M*s and *SD*s) and "Homogeneity of variance test" (Levene's test), which checks an assumption of the ANOVA: that the variances in the groups are similar. Then click on the "Continue" button.

6. If you will use post hoc comparisons, click on the "Post Hoc" button, which gives a box that allows you to choose the one(s) you want. If the Levene's test (see step #5) of homogeneity of variance found that the variances are significantly different, we would choose one of the post hoc tests under "Equal Variances Not Assumed." It is OK to use more than one post hoc test at the same time. After selecting the post hoc analysis, click on the "Continue" button.

7. If you will use contrasts (planned comparisons), you can simply compute *t* tests for two data groupings at a time. You can also click on the "Contrasts" button, which gives a box called "One-Way ANOVA: Contrasts," but the next steps are more complicated than they should be.

8. Click on the "OK" button, and the analysis runs. (Note: You'll need to calculate the effect size manually, using one of the methods described in Chapter 7, such as the formula for eta squared $[\eta^2]$.)

To read the output, you'll see at least two tables. The table called "Descriptives" gives the *M*s and *SD*s for the variables. The table called "ANOVA" has the sums of squares, *df*s, mean squares, *F* value, and *p* value. The main columns to use are the *F*, *p* ("Sig."), and *df*. If the *p* is less than .05, the difference among the groups is significant in this omnibus test, and more analyses may be needed. If the Levene's test found that the variances are not equal, we'd state that fact in the report and probably still use the outcome shown in the ANOVA table (see **Box B.1**). If we did post hoc comparisons, there would be another table called "Multiple Comparisons," and we'd use the comparisons that correspond with the outcome of the homogeneity of variance (Levene's) test—that is, either the ones for "Equal Variances Assumed" or the ones for "Equal Variances Not Assumed."

One-Way ANOVA (F) with Repeated Measures (requires SPSS Advanced version)

The repeated-measures one-way ANOVA is used to test for differences among data groupings when there is one independent variable with more than two levels, each subject is tested at all of the levels, and the data were measured on an

---

BOX B.1 UNEQUAL VARIANCES IN AN ANOVA

One assumption of the ANOVA is that the variances should be similar for data across groups. What effect does having unequal variances have, and how should researchers deal with them? The main practical effect of unequal variances is to reduce the power of the test, but the extent of this effect is not as great as was once thought (Winer, 1962). If a test of the homogeneity of variance, such as the Levene's test, finds that the variances are significantly different across groups, researchers can consider three options:

■ Transform the data. Converting each datum with the same arithmetic function, such as taking the square root, can alter the form of the data's distribution and bring it into compliance with ANOVA assumptions. Deciding whether to transform data and which of many available methods to use is a complex process that is beyond the scope of this book, but it is an acceptable option that can be done easily in SPSS with the *Transform → Compute* process described earlier.

■ Use a nonparametric test. Because nonparametric methods are not based on the idea of equal variances, they can be applied when the data do not meet the assumptions underlying parametric tests. But there are two problems with this approach. First, nonparametric tests typically have less power than their parametric counterparts. If the concern about using an ANOVA with unequal variances is that the power is reduced, switching to a nonparametric statistic may not help. Second, nonparametric tests can provide acceptable alternatives for one-way designs, but they do not provide a complete analysis for factorial designs, as we saw in Chapter 9.

■ Use the ANOVA anyway. Given that the main practical concern regarding unequal variances is the reduced power of the ANOVA, researchers often use ANOVAs when the variances are not equal and state in the report that they did so. If an analysis found significant effects with reduced power, it's a conservative test. If an ANOVA did not find an expected difference with reduced power, this difficulty can be addressed in the report.

interval or ratio scale. *Review and keep handy the material in Chapter 8* on the re-peated-measures ANOVA for information not covered here.

To enter the data in the SPSS data file,

1. Assign and name columns according to the order in which the data for the corresponding variables appear in the data sheets. Set up a variables key by using the *Label* and *Values* columns in the *Variable View* screen.

2. Enter data for each variable in its own column, one subject (case) at a time. Each level of the independent variable is considered a separate variable and *has its own column* and name, such as "pretest," and "postest1," and "postest2."

3. Create new or composite variables, if needed, and add them to the variables key.

To run a repeated-measures one-way ANOVA, make sure the data file is open and:

1. Use the *select cases* function if you want to analyze data for only some of the subjects.

2. Click in the menu bar on *Analyze* → *General Linear Model* → *Repeated Measures,* which produces a box called "Repeated Measures Define Factors" where you must type in the number of levels the within-subjects variable has (you can also give it a name to replace "factor1") and click on the "Add" button. Then click on the "Define" button, which produces a box called "Repeated Measures."

3. Identify the three or more conditions (variables, each of which has a column, such as "pretest," in the data file) you want to analyze and move them to the box called "Within-Subjects Variables."

4. Click on the "Options" button, and then "Descriptive Statistics" and "Estimates of Effect Size" (which computes eta squared η^2). Then click on the "Continue" button.

5. If you want to do planned comparisons, you can compute separate paired-samples t tests later or use the "Contrasts" button. Post hoc comparisons are not available in the repeated measures one-way ANOVA.

6. Click on the "OK" button, and the analysis runs.

To read the output, you'll see several tables. The one called "Descriptive Statistics" gives the *M*s and *SD*s for the variables. A table called "Mauchly's Test of Sphericity" reports a test of an ANOVA assumption about the data: if it is significant (p ["Sig."] less than .05), an adjustment to the ANOVA is needed, which appears in the next table called "Tests of Within-Subjects Effects." This table gives the *F, p,* and *df* values: if the test of sphericity was not significant, use the top row of values; the other rows give adjusted values calculated with two different methods (Greenhouse-Geisser and Huynh-Feldt). This table also has the effect size estimate, eta squared (η^2) in the column called "Partial Eta Squared." If the p is less than .05, a significant difference exists among the groups in this omnibus test, and additional analyses may be needed.

Two-Way ANOVA: All Independent Groups

The two-way ANOVA for independent groups is applied to examine differences among more than two data groupings when there are two independent variables (factors), each subject received a condition consisting of one level of each variable, and the data are on an interval or ratio scale. *Review and keep handy the material in Chapter 9* on the two-way ANOVA for information not covered here.

To enter the data in the SPSS data file,

1. Assign and name columns according to the order in which the data for the corresponding variables appear in the data sheets. Create separate columns to designate levels of each factor: one column will be for one independent variable (coded, for example, 1 = experimental group, 2 = control group, 3 = placebo), and another column will be for the other independent variable. Set up a variables key by using the *Label* and *Values* columns in the *Variable View* screen.

2. Enter data for each variable in its own column, one subject (case) at a time. Each column will have a variable's data pertaining to all the groups (the codes in the two columns for levels of the independent variables will tell the program which group a datum belongs to).

3. Create new or composite variables, if needed, and add them to the variables key.

To run a two-way ANOVA for independent groups, make sure the data file is open and:

1. Use the *select cases* function if you want to analyze data for only some of the subjects.

2. Click in the menu bar on *Analyze → General Linear Model → Univariate,* which produces a box called "Univariate."

3. Identify the dependent variables you want to analyze from the list on the left and move them to the space labeled "Dependent Variable." You can only run one dependent variable at a time.

4. Move the two independent variables from the list on the left to the box called "Fixed Factor(s)." You're not likely to need the remaining boxes.

5. Click on the "Options" button, which brings a box called "Univariate: Options." Click on "Descriptive statistics" (to get the *Ms* and *SDs*), "Estimates of effect size" (which computes eta squared [η^2] for each factor and the interaction), and "Homogeneity tests" (Levene's test, which checks an assumption of the ANOVA: that the variances in the groups are similar). Then click on the "Continue" button.

6. If you will use post hoc comparisons or contrasts, follow steps # 6 and # 7 in the instructions given earlier for the one-way ANOVA for independent groups. After selecting these analyses, click on the "Continue" button.

7. Click on the "OK" button, and the analysis runs.

To read the output, you'll see at least two tables. The table called "Descriptive Statistics" gives the *Ms* and *SDs* for each cell (condition or group) in the factorial. The table called "Tests of Between-Subjects Effects" has the sums of squares, *df*s, mean squares, *F* values, *p* values ("Sig."), and effect sizes (the column is called "Partial Eta Squared"). Refer to Table 9.1, which shows the rows of interest. The main columns to use are ones giving the *F*s, *p*s, *df*s, and effect size (η^2) estimates. Recall that each of these outcomes will be calculated for each factor and the interaction. If the *p* for any *F* is less than .05, the difference is significant in this omnibus test, and additional analyses may be needed. If the Levene's test found that the variances are not equal, we'd state that fact in the report and probably still use the outcome shown in the ANOVA table (see Box B.1). If we did post hoc comparisons or contrasts, there would be additional tables.

Two-Way ANOVA: All Dependent Groups (requires SPSS Advanced version)

A two-way ANOVA for all dependent groups is applied to examine differences among more than two data groupings when there are two independent variables (factors), each subject received all levels of each independent variable, and the data are on an interval or ratio scale. *Review and keep handy the material in Chapter 9* on the two-way ANOVA for information not covered here.

To enter the data in the SPSS data file,

1. Assign and name columns according to the order in which the data for the corresponding variables appear in the data sheets. Set up a variables key by using the *Label* and *Values* columns in the *Variable View* screen.

2. Enter data for each variable in its own column, one subject (case) at a time. Each level of the independent variable is considered a separate variable and has its own column and name, such as "pretest," and "postest1," and "postest2."

3. Create new or composite variables, if needed, and add them to the variables key.

To run a two-way ANOVA with all dependent groups, make sure the data file is open and:

1. Use the *select cases* function if you want to analyze data for only some of the subjects.

2. Click in the menu bar on *Analyze → General Linear Model → Repeated Measures*, which produces a box called "Repeated Measures Define Factors." You must type in, one at a time, the number of levels each within-subjects variable has (you can also give it a name to replace "factor1") and click on the "Add" button. Then click on the "Define" button, which produces a box called "Repeated Measures."

3. Identify the four or more conditions (variables, each of which has a column, such as "pretest," in the data file) you want to analyze and move them to the box called "Within-Subjects Variables."

4. Click on the "Options" button, and then "Descriptive Statistics" (to get the *M*s and *SD*s) and "Estimates of Effect Size" (which computes eta squared [η^2] for each factor and the interaction). Then click on the "Continue" button.

5. If you want to do planned comparisons, you can compute separate paired-samples *t* tests later or use the "Contrasts" button. Post hoc comparisons are not available in SPSS for ANOVAs with all dependent groups.

6. Click on the "OK" button, and the analysis runs.

To read the output, you'll see several tables. The one called "Descriptive Statistics" gives the *M*s and *SD*s for each cell (condition or group) in the factorial. A table called "Mauchly's Test of Sphericity" reports a test of an ANOVA assumption about the data: if it is significant (*p* ["Sig."] less than .05), an adjustment to the ANOVA is needed, which appears in the next table called "Tests of Within-Subjects Effects." This table gives the *F*, *p*, and *df* values: if the test of sphericity was not significant, use the top row of values; the other rows give adjusted values calculated with two different methods (Greenhouse-Geisser and Huynh-Feldt). This table also has the effect size estimate, eta squared (η^2) for each *F* in the column called "Partial Eta Squared." If the *p* is less than .05, a significant difference exists among the groups in this omnibus test, and additional analyses may be needed.

Two-Way ANOVA: Mixed Factorial Designs (requires SPSS Advanced version)

A two-way ANOVA for mixed factorial designs is applied to examine differences among more than two data groupings when there are two independent variables (factors), one tested as independent groups and the other tested as dependent groups (within-subjects or matched), and the data are on an interval or ratio scale. *Review and keep handy the material in Chapter 9* on the two-way ANOVA for information not covered here.

To enter the data in the SPSS data file,

1. Assign and name columns according to the order in which the data for the corresponding variables appear in the data sheets. One column must specify levels of the between-subjects factor—coded, for example, 1 = experimental group, 2 = control group, 3 = placebo. Set up a variables key by using the *Label* and *Values* columns in the *Variable View* screen.

2. Enter data for each variable in its own column, one subject (case) at a time. Each level of the within-subjects (repeated measures) factor is considered a separate variable and has its own column and name, such as "pretest," and "postest1," and "postest2."

3. Create new or composite variables, if needed, and add them to the variables key.

To run a two-way ANOVA for a mixed factorial design, make sure the data file is open and:

1. Use the *select cases* function if you want to analyze data for only some of the subjects.

2. Click in the menu bar on *Analyze → General Linear Model → Repeated Measures*, which produces a box called "Repeated Measures Define Factors," where you must type in the number of levels the within-subjects has (you can also give it a name to replace "factor1") and click on the "Add"

button. Then click on the "Define" button, which produces a box called "Repeated Measures."

3. Identify from the list on the left the two or more repeated measures conditions (variables, each of which has a column, such as "pretest," in the data file) you want to analyze and move them to the box called "Within-Subjects Variables." Then move the variable that specifies the levels of the between-subjects factor to the box called "Between-Subjects Factor(s)."

4. Click on the "Options" button, and then "Descriptive Statistics" (to get the *M*s and *SD*s) and "Estimates of Effect Size" (which computes eta squared [η^2] for each factor and the interaction). Then click on the "Continue" button.

5. If you want to do planned comparisons, you can compute separate paired-samples *t* tests later or use the "Contrasts" button. Post hoc comparisons are not available in SPSS for the repeated measures two-way ANOVA.

6. Click on the "OK" button, and the analysis runs.

To read the output, you'll see several tables. The one called "Descriptive Statistics" gives the *M*s and *SD*s for each cell (condition or group) in the factorial. The table called "Mauchly's Test of Sphericity" reports a test of an ANOVA assumption about the data: if it is significant (*p* ["Sig."] less than .05), an adjustment to the ANOVA is needed, which appears in the next table called "Tests of Within-Subjects Effects." This table gives the *F, p,* and *df* values for variables that include repeated measures testing: if the test of sphericity was not significant, use the top row of values; the other rows give adjusted values calculated with two different methods (Greenhouse-Geisser and Huynh-Feldt). The table called "Tests of Between-Subjects Effects" gives the *F, p,* and *df* values for variables that do not include repeated measures testing. If the *p* for an *F* value in these tables is less than .05, a significant difference exists among the groups in this omnibus test, and additional analyses may be needed. These tables also have effect size estimates, eta squared (η^2) for each *F* in columns called "Partial Eta Squared."

Three-Way ANOVA

Three-way ANOVAs are used with designs that involve three independent variables, are basically done as an extension of the two-way procedures, and, of course, require interval or ratio data. Use the preceding two-way directions for the corresponding type of design (all independent groups, all dependent groups, and mixed), using the following adjustments:

- *All independent groups* (Access the same way via *Analyze → General Linear Model → Univariate*). Add a third factor to the "Fixed Factors" box in step # 4.
- *All dependent groups* (Access the same way via *Analyze → General Linear Model → Repeated Measures,*). Include all conditions (variables, each of which has a column in the data file) you want to analyze, moving them to the box called "Within-Subjects Variables" in step # 3.
- *Mixed factorial* (Access the same way via *Analyze → General Linear Model → Repeated Measures,*). If the third factor involves repeated measures: in

step # 2, type in the number of levels for that factor (and label, if desired); in step # 3, add the corresponding conditions to the box called "Within-Subjects Variables." If the third factor involves independent groups: in step # 3, move the variable that specifies the levels of that factor to the box called "Between-Subjects Factor(s)."

The outputs will be similar (but more extensive) for the corresponding type of two-way design. *Review and keep handy the material in Chapter 9* on the three-way ANOVA for information not covered here.

SPSS STEP BY STEP: NONPARAMETRIC ANALYSES

As we examine instructions for calculating *nonparametric tests* on SPSS, we'll consider how to do a statistic for *assessing relationships* before we discuss statistics for *assessing differences*. Keep in mind that for nonparametric statistics, *M*s and *SD*s are usually not needed. In contrast to parametric statistics, which use interval or ratio data that enable us to calculate meaningful *M*s and *SD*s, nonparametric statistics use nominal or ordinal data that are not normally distributed in the population from which the subjects are drawn or do not yield meaningful *M*s and *SD*s.

The directions for each nonparametric analysis will tell you how to *enter the data, run the analysis,* and *read the output.* Nonparametric outputs are usually not very wide, so it's OK to print them in the *portrait* mode (default). Each analysis has variations and options that we won't discuss—our directions will focus on the basics and commonly used options, usually applying default settings in the program. Let's begin with a nonparametric statistic to assess relationships.

Spearman (rho) Rank Correlation (r_s)

The Spearman rank correlation, sometimes called *rho,* is used to assess the degree of relationship between two variables when the data for one are on an ordinal scale and the other are on an ordinal, interval, or ratio scale. *Review and keep handy the material in Chapter 6* on the correlational analyses for information not covered here.

To enter the data in the SPSS data file,
1. Assign and name columns according to the order in which the data for the corresponding variables appear in the data sheets. Set up a variables key by using the *Label* and *Values* columns in the *Variable View* screen.
2. Enter data for each variable in its own column, one subject (case) at a time.
3. Create new or composite variables, if needed, and add them to the variables key.

To run a Spearman rank correlation, make sure the data file is open and:
1. Use the *select cases* function if you want to analyze data for only some of the subjects.
2. Click in the menu bar on *Analyze* → *Correlate* → *Bivariate,* which produces a box called "Bivariate Correlations." Although the default procedure in the area labeled "Correlation Coefficients" is Pearson's *r,* we can change it to Spearman.

3. Move the variables you want to analyze from the list on the left to the box labeled "Variables." If you want to calculate more than one Spearman analysis, you can put more than two variables in the box. Be sure *not* to use variables measured on nominal scales, such as gender or ethnicity.

4. Click on the "OK" button, and the analysis runs.

To read the output, you'll see a matrix called "Correlations" with each variable listed vertically and horizontally. Each cell of the matrix contains three values for the two variables involved: the Spearman r_s ("Correlation Coefficient"), p value ("Sig. [2-tailed]"), and number of subjects ("N," this statistic does not involve df). If the p is less than .05, the correlation for that pair of variables is significant.

Chi-Square (χ^2)

The chi-square statistic is used to assess whether nominal data—the number of times certain events or subjects fall into clearly defined categories—are distributed evenly. The category names provide nominal data. Chi-square can be applied when there are at least two categories that are independent—that is, the same individual or event cannot be in more than one category. Each category can be defined by one or more factors. The categories of male and female are defined by one factor (gender); the categories of male–White, male–Black, male–Asian, female–White, female–Black, and female–Asian are defined by two factors (gender and ethnicity). As an example, we might do a study of the frequency distribution of individuals with a specific mental disorder across categories. We could have reason to suspect, for instance, that frequency of the disorder is much higher for one category than the others. *Review and keep handy the material in Chapters 7 and 9* on the chi-square test for information not covered here.

To enter the data in the SPSS data file,
1. Create a code for the levels of each factor—for example: male = 1 and female = 2; White = 1, Black = 2, and Asian = 3.

2. Assign and name columns, such as gender and ethnicity, according to the order in which the data for the corresponding variables appear in the data sheets. Set up a variables key by using the *Label* and *Values* columns in the *Variable View* screen.

3. Enter the codes for each variable in the corresponding column, one subject (case) at a time. A Black male participant would have a 1 in the gender column and 2 in the ethnicity column. With nominal data, there are no "scores"—the program will just count the frequencies of individuals in each category, such as male–Black.

4. Create new or composite variables, if needed, and add them to the variables key.

To run a chi-square test, make sure the data file is open and:
1. Use the *select cases* function if you want to analyze data for only some of the subjects.

2. Click in the menu bar on *Analyze → Descriptive Statistics → Crosstabs,* which produces a box called "Crosstabs."

Nonparametric
tests on SPSS

3. Move one of the variables (say, gender) from the list on the left to the box labeled "Row(s)." If the category is defined by two variables, move the other (ethnicity) to the box labeled "Columns." The lowest box ("Layer 1 of 1") is used if there are three or more variables to define categories.

4. Click on the "Cells" button, then "Total" in the "Percentages" area, leaving the default request for "Observed" and "Expected" in the "Counts" area. These requests will produce for each cell its percent of the total cases, the expected number of cases if the null hypothesis is correct, and the actual number of cases. Then click on the "Continue" button.

5. Click on the "OK" button, and the analysis runs. (Note: You'll need to calculate effect sizes manually, using the formula in Table 7.3, see inside back cover.)

To read the output, you'll see two tables. The upper table gives the observed count, the expected count, and the percentages for each cell. The lower table gives the chi-square outcome, using more than one method for calculating it (they're usually very similar); the most commonly used method is the Pearson chi-square. This table also has the *df* ("D of Freedom") and *p* value ("Significance"). If the *p* is less than .05, the observed and expected counts are significantly different. This is an omnibus test if there are more than two data sets, and additional analyses may be needed.

Mann-Whitney (U)

The Mann-Whitney *U* is used for ordinal (ranked) data to test whether the data groupings for two independent groups or conditions are significantly different. The data must have been measured in an ordinal scale or will be analyzed as such because they do not meet the assumptions for parametric analysis. *Review and keep handy the material in Chapter 7* on the Mann-Whitney test for information not covered here.

To enter the data in the SPSS data file,

1. Assign and name columns according to the order in which the data for the corresponding variables appear in the data sheets. One column must designate levels of the independent variable (coded, for example, 1 = experimental group, 2 = control group). Set up a variables key by using the *Label* and *Values* columns in the *Variable View* screen.

2. Enter the data (ranks) for each variable in the corresponding column, one subject (case) at a time. If the data are on an interval or ratio scale, SPSS will convert them to ranks automatically in the analysis. Each column will have data pertaining to both of the groups (the codes in the column for the independent variable will tell the program which group a datum belongs to).

3. Create new or composite variables, if needed, and add them to the variables key.

To run a Mann-Whitney *U*, make sure the data file is open and:

1. Use the *select cases* function if you want to analyze data for only some of the subjects.

Nonparametric tests on SPSS

2. Click in the menu bar on *Analyze → Nonparametric Tests → 2 Independent Samples,* which produces a box called "Two-Independent-Samples Tests."

3. Identify the dependent variables you want to analyze from the list on the left and move them to the box labeled "Test Variable List." If you want to do more than one test for the same independent variable you can put additional dependent variables in the box.

4. Move the independent variable from the list on the left to the box called "Grouping Variable" and click on the "Define Groups" button, which produces a box called "Define Groups."

5. Insert the group codes (for example, "1" for the experimental, "2" for the control) in the spaces under "Use specified values" and click on the "Continue" button.

6. Click on the "OK" button, and the analysis runs. (Note: You'll need to calculate effect sizes manually, using the formula in Table 7.3, see inside back cover.)

To read the output, you'll find a table called "Test Statistics." The main values of interest in the table are the *z* score (in the "Z" column) and *p* value ("Asymp. Sig. [2-tailed]"). If the *p* is less than .05, the two groupings of ranked data are significantly different.

McNemar Test

The McNemar test is used with nominal data in dependent-groups (repeated measures or matched) designs to determine whether the distributions of dichotomous scores (yes/no) assessed at two different times are significantly different. It operates like a chi-square test and yields a χ^2 value. *Review and keep handy the material in Chapter 8* on the McNemar test for information not covered here.

To enter the data in the SPSS data file,

1. Create a yes/no code—for example: no = 0, yes = 1—for each variable (time of assessment). *Note:* SPSS will not calculate a χ^2 value if there are fewer than 35 cases.

2. Assign and name columns, such as "pretest" and "posttest," according to the order in which the data for the corresponding variables appear in the data sheets. Set up a variables key by using the *Label* and *Values* columns in the *Variable View* screen.

3. Enter the codes for each variable in the corresponding column, one subject (case) at a time.

4. Create new or composite variables, if needed, and add them to the variables key.

To run a McNemar test, make sure the data file is open and:

1. Use the *select cases* function if you want to analyze data for only some of the subjects.

2. Click in the menu bar on *Analyze → Nonparametric Tests → 2 Related Samples,* which produces a box called "Two-Related-Samples Tests." Click on McNemar in the "Test Type" area.

3. Identify the two variables you want to analyze from the list on the left and move them to the box labeled "Test Pair(s) List." The two must be moved as a pair. If you want to do more than one McNemar test, you can put additional pairs of variables in the box, one pair at a time.

4. Click on the "OK" button, and the analysis runs. (Note: You'll need to calculate effect sizes manually, using the formula for chi-square analysis in Table 7.3, see inside back cover.)

To read the output, you'll find two tables, one gives data for each cell. The other table ("Test Statistics") gives the N, χ^2 value, and p ("Asymp. Sig."). If the p is less than .05, the observed and expected counts are significantly different.

Wilcoxon Matched-Pairs Signed-Ranks Test

The Wilcoxon matched-pairs signed-ranks test uses ordinal (ranked) data to determine whether the data groupings for two dependent (repeated measures or matched) groups are significantly different. The data must be on an ordinal scale or will be analyzed as such because they do not meet the assumptions for parametric analysis. *Review and keep handy the material in Chapter 8 on the* Wilcoxon test for information not covered here.

To enter the data in the SPSS data file,

1. Assign and name columns according to the order in which the data for the corresponding variables appear in the data sheets. Set up a variables key by using the *Label* and *Values* columns in the *Variable View* screen.

2. Enter the data (ranks) for each variable in the corresponding column, one subject (case) at a time. If the data are on an interval or ratio scale, SPSS will convert them to ranks automatically in the analysis.

3. Create new or composite variables, if needed, and add them to the variables key.

To run a Wilcoxon matched-pairs signed-ranks test, make sure the data file is open and:

1. Use the *select cases* function if you want to analyze data for only some of the subjects.

2. Click in the menu bar on *Analyze → Nonparametric Tests → 2 Related Samples,* which produces a box called "Two-Related-Samples Tests" (the default "Test Type" is the Wilcoxon test).

3. Identify the two variables you want to analyze from the list on the left and move them to the box labeled "Test Pair(s) List." The two must be moved as a pair. If you want to do more than one Wilcoxon test, you can put additional pairs of variables in the box, one pair at a time.

4. Click on the "OK" button, and the analysis runs. (Note: You'll need to calculate effect sizes manually, using the formula for analyses that yield z scores in Table 7.3, see inside back cover.)

To read the output, you'll find two tables. The main values of interest are in the "Test Statistics" table—the z score (in the "Z" row) and p ("Asymp. Sig. [2-tailed]"). If the p is less than .05, the two sets of ranked data are significantly different.

Kruskal-Wallis (H)

The Kruskal-Wallis H statistic is a nonparametric one-way analysis of variance used for ordinal (ranked) data to test whether the data groupings for more than two independent groups or conditions are significantly different. The data must be on an ordinal scale or will be analyzed as such because they do not meet the assumptions for parametric analysis. The H statistic operates like a chi-square test and yields a χ^2 value. *Review and keep handy the material in Chapter 7* on the Kruskal-Wallis test for information not covered here.

To enter the data in the SPSS data file,

1. Assign and name columns according to the order in which the data for the corresponding variables appear in the data sheets. One column must designate levels of the independent variable (coded, for example, 1 = experimental group, 2 = control group, 3 = placebo). Set up a variables key by using the *Label* and *Values* columns in the *Variable View* screen.

2. Enter the data (ranks) for each variable in the corresponding column, one subject (case) at a time. If the data are on an interval or ratio scale, SPSS will convert them to ranks automatically in the analysis. Each column will have data pertaining to all the groups (the codes in the column for the independent variable will tell the program which group a datum belongs to).

3. Create new or composite variables, if needed, and add them to the variables key.

To run a Kruskal-Wallis *H*, make sure the data file is open and:

1. Use the *select cases* function if you want to analyze data for only some of the subjects.

2. Click in the menu bar on *Analyze* → *Nonparametric Tests* → *K Independent Samples*, which produces a box called "Tests for Several Independent Samples."

3. Identify the dependent variable you want to analyze from the list on the left and move them to the box labeled "Test Variable List." If you want to do more than one test for the same independent variable you can put additional dependent variables in the box.

4. Move the independent variable from the list on the left to the box called "Grouping Variable" and click on the "Define Range" button, which produces a box called "Several Independent Samples: Define Range." Put in the spaces the minimum and maximum values of the independent variable codes (for example, "1" for the experimental, "3" for the placebo) and click on the "Continue" button.

5. Click on the "OK" button, and the analysis runs. (Note: You'll need to calculate effect sizes manually, using the formula for chi-square analysis in Table 7.3, see inside back cover.)

To read the output, you'll find two tables. One gives the values for the chi-square (in the "Chi-Square" row), *df,* and *p* ("Asymp. Sig."). If the *p* is less than .05, a significant difference exists among the groups in this omnibus test, and additional analyses may be needed.

k-Sample Median Test

Like the Kruskal-Wallis *H* statistic, the *k*-sample median test uses ordinal (ranked) data to test whether the data sets for more than two independent groups or conditions are significantly different and yields a χ^2 value. The *procedure in SPSS is the same as for the Kruskal-Wallis,* except that you would click on "Median" in the "Test Type" area of the box called "Tests for Several Independent Samples." Although the *k*-sample median test is less powerful than the Kruskal-Wallis test, it is often applied if the underlying variable for the ranks is not likely to have a continuous distribution, which the Kruskal-Wallis assumes. *Review and keep handy the material in Chapter 7 on the k-sample median test for in-*formation not covered here.

Cochran (Q)

The Cochran *Q* test is a nonparametric one-way analysis of variance for nominal data with three or more dependent groups. It is used to determine whether the distributions of dichotomous scores (yes/no) for a variable are significantly different. The *Q* statistic operates like a chi-square test and yields essentially a χ^2 value. *Review and keep handy the material in Chapter 7 on the Cochran Q test for in-*formation not covered here.

To enter the data in the SPSS data file,
1. Create a yes/no code—for example: no = 0, yes = 1—for each variable (time of assessment, such as pretest, first posttest, and second posttest).
2. Assign and name columns, such as "pretest," "postest1," and "postest2," according to the order in which the data for the corresponding variables appear in the data sheets. Set up a variables key by using the *Label* and *Values* columns in the *Variable View* screen.
3. Enter the codes for each variable in the corresponding column, one subject (case) at a time.
4. Create new or composite variables, if needed, and add them to the variables key.

To run a Cochran *Q* test, make sure the data file is open and:
1. Use the *select cases* function if you want to analyze data for only some of the subjects.
2. Click in the menu bar on *Analyze → Nonparametric Tests → K Related Samples,* which produces a box called "Tests for Several Related Samples." Click on Cochran's *Q* in the "Test Type" area.
3. Move the variables you want to analyze from the list on the left and to the box labeled "Test Variables."

4. Click on the "OK" button, and the analysis runs. (Note: You'll need to calculate effect sizes manually, using the formula for chi-square analysis in Table 7.3, see inside back cover.)

To read the output, you'll find two tables. One table gives the data for each cell. The other table gives the Cochran's Q and p values ("Asymp. Sig."). If the p is less than .05, a significant difference exists among the groups in this omnibus test; additional analyses may be needed.

Friedman χ^2

The Friedman χ^2 test is a nonparametric one-way analysis of variance used for ordinal (ranked) data to determine whether the rankings for more than two dependent groups or conditions are significantly different. The data must be on an ordinal scale or will be analyzed as such because they do not meet the assumptions for parametric analysis. *Review and keep handy the material in Chapter 8* on the Friedman test for information not covered here.

To enter the data in the SPSS data file,
1. Assign and name columns according to the order in which the data for the corresponding variables appear in the data sheets. One column must designate levels of the independent variable (coded, for example, 1 = experimental group, 2 = control group, 3 = placebo). Set up a variables key by using the *Label* and *Values* columns in the *Variable View* screen.
2. Enter the data (ranks) for each variable in the corresponding column, one subject (case) at a time. If the data are on an interval or ratio scale, SPSS will convert them to ranks automatically in the analysis. Each column will have data pertaining to all the groups (the codes in the column for the independent variable will tell the program which group a datum belongs to).
3. Create new or composite variables, if needed, and add them to the variables key.

To run a Friedman χ^2 test, make sure the data file is open and:
1. Use the *select cases* function if you want to analyze data for only some of the subjects.
2. Click in the menu bar on *Analyze → Nonparametric Tests → K Related Samples,* which produces a box called "Tests for Several Related Samples" (the default "Test Type" is the Friedman test).
3. Move the variables you want to analyze from the list on the left and to the box labeled "Test Variables."
4. Click on the "OK" button, and the analysis runs. (Note: You'll need to calculate effect sizes manually, using the formula for chi-square analysis in Table 7.3, see inside back cover.)

To read the output, you'll find two tables. The upper table gives data for each cell. The lower table gives the χ^2 and p values ("Asymp. Sig."). If the p is less than .05, a significant difference exists among the groups in this omnibus test, and additional analyses may be needed.

Nonparametric tests on SPSS

FORMULAS FOR MANUAL CALCULATIONS

This section presents and explains the arithmetic actions for calculating several of the more likely statistical tests students may need to perform manually. The tests we'll cover are the simpler parametric ones and the chi-square, each of which is discussed in the chapters of this book and in the preceding section on SPSS analysis. The formulas we'll use are designed to make calculations as easy as possible. Other formulas for the same statistics that you see elsewhere may look different, but they are arithmetically equivalent and yield the same outcomes when applied to the same data. If you do analyses manually, remember that you need to check your work for errors. Here's a rule of thumb: *repeat each analysis at least twice.* If it comes out the same two times, assume that the identical outcomes are correct.

As we examine the procedures for manual calculations, we'll use hypothetical data for a study done with second-graders on their ability to recall and spell words that are read to them. Assume in the examples that the words were three to five letters in length and that the children had learned previously and spelled each word correctly in classroom tests about 6 months earlier. No words used in the study had a homophone, that is another word pronounced the same but with a different spelling, as in *reed* and *read*. Also assume that the method for each condition of the study has an individual child listen through earphones to a tape-recorded reading of 10 words, one at a time, and spell each one 5 seconds after hearing it. The precisely measured volume of the voice through the earphones is moderate and the same for each word.

At this time, we won't describe all features of the research design, such as the number of groups, because the relevant aspects of the design will be introduced for each of the appropriate statistics. For now, let's look at the data for one condition in the study in which sound from the earphones is pure—that is, with no background noise—as each child is tested. Each of the 10 scores represents the number of correctly spelled words (out of 10) for one of the 10 participants:

9   10   8   9   9   8   10   7   9   8

Arithmetic Operations

In the formulas we'll examine, you'll need to carry out some arithmetic functions that you may not remember how to do, so we'll illustrate how they're done here using the spelling scores you just read. The Xs and Ys in the illustrations represent individual scores. Three arithmetic functions are especially critical. They are: (1) *summation X,* which involves simply totaling the individual scores; (2) *summation X, the quantity squared,* or squaring the total of the scores; and (3) *summation X squared,* squaring each score before adding them together. Here are the symbols for each of these functions and how to calculate them with the above data:

1. $\sum X = 9 + 10 + 8 + 9 + 9 + 8 + 10 + 7 + 9 + 8 =$ **87**
2. $\left(\sum X\right)^2 = (9 + 10 + 8 + 9 + 9 + 8 + 10 + 7 + 9 + 8)^2 = 87^2 =$ **7569**

3. $\sum X^2 = 9^2 + 10^2 + 8^2 + 9^2 + 9^2 + 8^2 + 10^2 + 7^2 + 9^2 + 8^2$, which equals $81 + 100 + 64 + 81 + 81 + 64 + 100 + 49 + 81 + 64 = $ **765**

Refer to these examples if you use the following formulas and forget how to perform these functions.

Standard Deviation (SD)

The *SD* is equal to the square root of the variance in a data grouping. We've already calculated the values for some of the elements with our example data, and we'll plug them into the formula.

$$ SD = \sqrt{\frac{\sum X^2 - \frac{\left(\sum X\right)^2}{N}}{N-1}} = \sqrt{\frac{765 - \frac{7569}{10}}{9}} = \sqrt{\frac{8.1}{9}} = \textbf{0.94} $$

In normal distributions of data, the *SD* is approximately one sixth the range. By this rule, if our data were exactly normally distributed, the *SD* would have been about 0.50 (that is, $3 \div 6$). Try to visualize the distribution: Most of the scores are 9s and 10s, with a few 8s and one 7. The distribution departs to some degree from the "bell shape" of a perfect normal distribution.

Pearson Product-Moment Correlation (r)

Suppose in the example study in which we assessed children's ability to spell words that were read to them that our purpose was to see if their spelling scores correlated with their scores on an IQ test. Here are the IQs (100 is average), presented for the children in the same order as earlier:

120   140   118   121   127   116   138   106   133   123

We'll call these scores *Y* in our formula for calculating Pearson's *r*:

$$ r = \frac{N\left(\sum XY\right) - \left(\sum X\right)\left(\sum Y\right)}{\sqrt{\left[N\left(\sum X^2\right) - \left(\sum X\right)^2\right]\left[N\left(\sum Y^2\right) - \left(\sum Y\right)^2\right]}} $$

To calculate $\sum XY$ in the numerator, we'll need to multiply the *X* and *Y* scores for each child and then add those products. To illustrate for just the first two children, 1080 for the first child (that is, 9×120) would be added to the 1400 (10×140) for the second. The remaining arithmetic functions were covered earlier. Plugging into the formula the values for the functions in parentheses, with $N = 10$ in this analysis, we have:

$$ \frac{N(10887) - (87)(1242)}{\sqrt{[N(765) - (7569)][N(155248) - (1542564)]}} = \frac{816}{\sqrt{[81][9916]}} = .91 $$

For Pearson's *r*, the $df = N - 2$; thus, it is 8 for this analysis. The *df* would enable us to determine whether the correlation is significant by checking the table of critical values of *r* at the end of this appendix. Because we were not sure in advance that the scores would have a positive correlation, we would use a two-tailed test. Checking the table, we find that the critical value of *r*(8) is .632 for the .05 level of confidence and .765 for the .01 level. Thus, the outcome is significant, and we'd express it in a report as: *r*(8) = .91, *p* < .01. If you calculate *r* manually, *review and keep handy the material in Chapter 6* on the Pearson's *r* for information not covered here.

Independent-Samples t Test (t)

Suppose in our example study, the purpose was to assess the effects of background noise through the earphones on the children's performance, using two groups of 10 children. We want to see whether the two groups will differ, using an independent-samples *t* test for our analysis. Although the statistical analysis would be the same if we used either an experimental or a quasi-experimental strategy, we randomly assigned the children to the conditions so we could conduct the study as an experiment. The research condition we've already discussed (no background noise) constitutes the control group; the experimental group (we'll label "noise 25") hears the same 10 words at exactly the same volume, but with a background hissing sound that is 25% as loud as the voice reading the words. Here are the individual data for number of words spelled correctly:

Noise 25	7	9	6	8	7	9	8	6	7	6
Control	9	10	8	9	9	8	10	7	9	8

We'll use two subscripts, "*n25*" and "*c*" to distinguish between data for the two groups in our calculations. Thus, for example, X_{n25} and X_c refer, respectively, to scores from the experimental and control groups, and n_{n25} and n_c refer to the number of participants in each group. The formula for the independent-samples *t* test is

$$t = \frac{M_{n25} - M_c}{\sqrt{\left[\dfrac{\sum X_{n25}^2 - \dfrac{\left(\sum X_{n25}\right)^2}{n_{25}} + \sum X_c^2 - \dfrac{\left(\sum X_c\right)^2}{n_c}}{n_{n25} + n_c - 2}\right]\left[\dfrac{1}{n_{n25}} + \dfrac{1}{n_c}\right]}}$$

Plugging into the formula the values for the functions in parentheses, with each $n = 10$ in this analysis, we have

$$\frac{7.30 - 8.70}{\sqrt{\left[\dfrac{545 - \left(\dfrac{5329}{10}\right) + 765 - \left(\dfrac{7569}{10}\right)}{10 + 10 - 2}\right]\left[\dfrac{1}{10} + \dfrac{1}{10}\right]}} =$$

$$\frac{-1.40}{\sqrt{\left[\dfrac{12.1 + 8.1}{18}\right][.20]}} = \frac{-1.4}{.474} = -2.95$$

Notice that the *t* has a negative value; this is simply because the numerator subtracted the larger mean from the smaller. If the two means had been positioned oppositely, the result would have been a +2.95. The sign has no importance in a *t* value. For an independent-samples *t*, the $df = N - 2$ (that is, $n_{n25} + n_c - 2$); thus, it is 18 for this analysis. Using the *df*, we can determine whether the difference in means is significant by checking the table of critical values of *t* at the end of this appendix. Because we knew in advance that the noise would interfere with performance, we can use a one-tailed test. Checking the table, a footnote says to halve the two-tailed *p* value for a one-tailed test. Thus, the critical value of $t(18)$ is 1.734 for the .05 level of confidence and 2.878 for the .005 level. The outcome is significant, and we'd express it in a report as: $t(18) = -2.95$, $p < .005$ (one-tailed). We'd also calculate and report the effect size, using the formula in Table 7.3 (see inside back cover). If you calculate the *t* manually, *review and keep handy the material in Chapter 7* on the independent-samples *t* test for information not covered here.

Paired-Samples t Test (t)

Suppose in our example study, the purpose was to assess the effects of background noise through the earphones on the children's performance, testing one group of 10 children in two conditions. Although the experimental and control conditions are essentially the same as those we saw with the independent-samples *t* test analysis, we are now using repeated measures, and the analysis will be with a paired-samples *t* test. Assume that the method includes needed counterbalancing and that the data are the same as we saw in the section on the independent-samples *t* test.

Most formulas for calculating a paired-samples *t* use *difference scores (Ds)* that we get by subtracting for each participant the score for one condition from the other (note that some difference scores may be negative). The scores and the *Ds* (subtracting the experimental from the control scores) are:

Noise 25	7	9	6	8	7	9	8	6	7	6
Control	9	10	8	9	9	8	10	7	9	8
D	+2	+1	+2	+1	+2	−1	+2	+1	+2	+2

The difference score formula for calculating a paired-samples *t* test, along with the calculations for this analysis, are:

$$t = \sqrt{\frac{n - 1}{[n(\Sigma D^2)/(\Sigma D)^2] - 1}} = \sqrt{\frac{9}{[10(28)/1(196)] - 1}} = \sqrt{\frac{9}{.429}} = \textbf{4.58}$$

For a paired-samples *t*, the $df = n - 1$; thus, it is 9 for this analysis. Using the *df*, we can determine whether the difference in means is significant by checking the table of critical values of *t* at the end of this appendix. Because we knew in advance that the noise would interfere with performance, we can use a one-tailed test. Checking the table, a footnote says to halve the two-tailed *p* value for a one-tailed test. Thus, the critical value of $t(9)$ is 1.833 for the .05 level of confidence and 3.250 for the .005 level. The outcome is significant, and we'd express it in a report as: $t(9) = 4.58$, $p < .001$ (one-tailed). We'd also calculate and report the effect size, using the formula in Table 7.3 (see inside back cover). If you calculate the t manually, *review and keep handy the material in Chapter 8* on the paired-samples t test for information not covered here.

One-Way ANOVA (F) for Independent Groups

Suppose in our example study, the purpose was to assess the effects of background noise through the earphones on the children's performance, using three groups of 10 children. We want to see whether the groups will differ, using a one-way ANOVA for our analysis. Although the statistical analysis would be the same if we used either an experimental or a quasi-experimental strategy, we randomly assigned the children to the conditions so we could conduct the study as an experiment. The research condition with no background noise constitutes the control group, and two experimental groups hear the same 10 words at exactly the same volume, but with a background hissing sound that is either 25% or 50% as loud as the voice reading the words. We'll label the former group "noise 25" and the latter group "noise 50." Here are the individual data for number of words spelled correctly:

Noise 50	3	4	2	6	4	7	6	3	3	4
Noise 25	7	9	6	8	7	9	8	6	7	6
Control	9	10	8	9	9	8	10	7	9	8

We'll use three subscripts—"$n50$," "$n25$," and "c"—to distinguish between data for the three groups in our calculations. Thus, for example, X_{n50}, X_{n25}, and X_c refer, respectively, to scores from the two experimental groups and the control group, and n_{n50}, n_{n25}, and n_c refer to the number of participants in each group. The one-way ANOVA for independent groups requires a series of formulas that use symbols we'll need to define: k refers to the number of groups in the study and the subscript "$1-k$" means each group, one at a time. The formulas we'll use are a little different from those we saw in Chapter 7, which were given to help you see what the computations were doing conceptually. Our interest now is in making the calculations as easy as possible, which requires different formulas. We'll cover the calculations as a series of steps with separate formulas.

Step 1: Calculate the total sum of squares (SS_{tot}) with the following formula.

$$SS_{tot} = \sum X_{1-k}^2 - \frac{\left(\sum X_{1-k}\right)^2}{N}$$

For our example study with $N = 30$, this formula translates to

$$SS_{tot} = \sum X_{n50}^2 + \sum X_{n25}^2 + \sum X_c^2 - \frac{\left(\sum X_{n50} + \sum X_{n25} + \sum X_c\right)^2}{N}$$

$$200 + 545 + 765 - \frac{(42 + 73 + 87)^2}{30} = 1510 - 1360.13 = \mathbf{149.87}$$

Step 2: Calculate the sum of squares between groups (SS_{bg}) with this formula, having already calculated the last part of it (as 1360.13) in the previous step.

$$SS_{bg} = \frac{\left(\sum X_{n50}\right)^2}{n_{n50}} + \frac{\left(\sum X_{n25}\right)^2}{n_{n25}} + \frac{\left(\sum X_c\right)^2}{n_c} - \frac{\left(\sum X_{n50} + \sum X_{n25} + \sum X_c\right)^2}{N}$$

$$\frac{42^2}{10} + \frac{73^2}{10} + \frac{87^2}{10} - 1360.13 = 1466.2 - 1360.13 = \mathbf{106.07}$$

Step 3: Calculate the sum of squares within groups (SS_{wg}, or error sum of squares) by simply subtracting the SS_{bg} from the SS_{tot}.

$$SS_{wg} = SS_{tot} - SS_{bg} = 149.87 - 106.07 = \mathbf{43.80}$$

Step 4: Calculate the degrees of freedom associated with the SS_{bg} and SS_{wg}.

$$df_{bg} = k - 1;\ \text{in the example study, it would be } 3 - 1 = \mathbf{2}$$

$$df_{wg} = N - k;\ \text{in our example, it would be } 30 - 3 = \mathbf{27}$$

Step 5: Calculate the mean squares between groups (MS_{bg}) and within groups (MS_{wg}) by dividing each SS by its associated df.

$$MS_{bg} = SS_{bg} \div df_{bg};\ \text{in our example, } 106.07 \div 2 = \mathbf{53.03}$$

$$MS_{wg} = SS_{wg} \div df_{wg};\ \text{in our example, } 43.80 \div 27 = \mathbf{1.62}$$

Step 6: Calculate the *F* value.

$$F = MS_{bg} \div MS_{wg} = 53.03 \div 1.62 = \mathbf{32.73}$$

Using the *df*s, we can determine whether the omnibus difference in means is significant by checking the table of critical values of *F* at the end of this appendix. The *df* associated with the numerator in the *F* test is the df_{bg} (in our example, 2), and the *df* associated with the denominator in the *F* test is the df_{wg} (27). Checking the table, we see that the critical value of $F(2, 27)$ is 3.35 for the .05 level of confidence and 9.02 for the .001 level. The outcome is significant, and we'd express it in a report as: $F(2, 27) = 32.73$, $p < .001$. We would also calculate and report the effect size, using the formula in Chapter 7, and post hoc comparisons or contrasts.

If you calculate the *F* manually, *review and keep handy the material in Chapter 7* on the one-way ANOVA for information not covered here. We will not cover manual computations for ANOVAs for factorial designs because they are even more complex, and they're almost never performed today without a computer statistics program.

Chi-Square (χ^2)

To illustrate computations for the chi-square, a nonparametric statistic, we need to use a different example study because the data from the study on children's spelling words that were read to that them were not measured on a nominal scale. Suppose we did marketing research on 300 randomly selected adults' favorite ice cream flavors—chocolate, vanilla, or strawberry. We simply asked which of the three was their favorite, and the frequencies looked like this:

Chocolate	Vanilla	Strawberry
143	47	110

We would do a chi-square test to determine whether these frequencies differ significantly from the null hypotheses of an equal distribution—100 in each cell. In the formula, k is the number of conditions (in our example, 3), O is the observed frequency, and E is the expected frequency if the null hypothesis were true; the subscripts "c," "v," and "s" refer to the flavors. The formula is

$$\chi^2 = \sum [\frac{(O - E)^2_{1-k}}{E_{1-k}}] \text{ which, translates in the example study to}$$

$$[\frac{(O - E)^2_c}{E_c}] + [\frac{(O - E)^2_v}{E_v}] + [\frac{(O - E)^2_s}{E_s}]$$

Plugging in the numbers, the calculations and outcome are

$$[\frac{(143 - 100)^2}{100}] + [\frac{(47 - 100)^2}{100}] + [\frac{110 - 100^2}{100}]$$

$$= 18.49 + 28.09 + 1.0 = \mathbf{47.58}$$

For a one-way χ^2, $df = k - 1$; thus, it is 2 for our example study because there are three groups. (If we had designed a study that needed a two-way χ^2 analysis, the formula to calculate the χ^2 would be the same, but the formula for the df would change.) We can find whether the difference in frequencies is significant by checking the table of critical values of χ^2 at the end of this appendix. The table shows that the critical value of $\chi^2(2)$ is 5.99 for the .05 level of confidence and 13.82 for the .001 level. The difference is significant, and we'd express it in a report as: $\chi^2(2) = 47.58$, $p < .001$. We'd also calculate and report the effect size, using the formula in Table 7.3 (see inside back cover). If you calculate the χ^2 manually, *review and keep handy the material in Chapters 7 and 9* on the chi-square statistic for information not covered here.

PREPARING TABLES AND GRAPHS

Appendix A described that tables and figures can provide efficient ways to display data in research reports and discussed how to present them in a manuscript. The material we will give here supplements the discussion in Appendix A, and you will need to *coordinate the two discussions* if you are considering including tables or figures in a paper. You may recall that tables can provide verbal and numerical information, and figures can present diagrams, photographs, illustrations, or graphs. We will focus here on *statistical* displays, describing *how to prepare* tables that display *numerical data* and figures that present *graphs*. Although numerical tables and graphs can occur in any text section of a research report, they are most commonly used in the Results section. Be sure to refer to the table or figure in the text of the report, such as by stating, "Table 1 presents. . . ."

TABLES

A numerical table provides data organized in columns and rows that are labeled with titles that can be interpreted without consulting the text. Abbreviated labels must be spelled out somewhere in the body of the table or in a note that appears just below the table. Most often, the data are rounded to *two decimals*. The task of making a table can be done with a typewriter, but it is much easier with a computer word processor. We'll describe the procedure in *Microsoft Word,* using figures to display the tables as illustrations. Make sure the standard toolbar and formatting toolbar are available at the top of the screen (if they are not, use the *View* menu to add them).

In Appendix A, we examined Figure A.12, which presents a table from a sample manuscript. As you can see in that figure, the table starts at the top of a new page with the table number on the first line. The title (italic font) begins on the second line. Now look at Figure B.1, which presents two tables as they might appear in a journal article. *Word* has a nice feature for composing tables: you'll find in the standard toolbar an icon that looks like a matrix of cells with a dark band across the top. If you steady the cursor on the icon, the label "Insert Table" appears. Click on the icon, and a matrix appears. If you drag the cursor across the cells while pressing the left mouse button, you highlight cells, and the size of the matrix is reported at the bottom to tell you the number of rows and columns the table will have if you release the mouse. I created Table 1 and Table 2 in Figure B.1 by releasing the mouse at "9 × 10 Table" for each (using an extra column to enable horizontal spacing plans I had that are not absolutely necessary).

The table that appears on releasing the mouse has dark horizontal and vertical solid lines, which we don't want. Dark solid lines will print. We can determine where lines will and won't be by using a feature that has an icon (a square that surrounds a vertical cross in dotted lines) on the formatting toolbar. If you steady the cursor on the icon, the label "Outside Border" appears. Click on the arrow to the right of that icon, and an array of possible line placements appears. All you need to do is highlight the section of the table you want to change, click on the arrow, and click on the line pattern you want. I generally start by highlighting the entire matrix and clicking on the last listed pattern,

TABLE 1

Descriptive Statistics and Bivariate Correlation Coefficients for Directional and Accuracy Reasoning Scores with Validation Variables (N = 103)

Variables	ACC	IHBS	MON	BLUN	CON	OPEN	AGR	M (SD)
DIR: Directional reasoning	−.14	.50**	.01	.20*	−.23*	−.21*	−.19*	120.80 (16.69)
ACC: Accuracy reasoning	—	−.11	.23*	.00	.13	.26**	.00	79.74 (10.38)
IHBS: Irrational Health Belief Scale		—	.03	.07	−23*	−.30**	−.30**	40.02 (11.50)
MON: Monitoring			—	−.37**	−.20*	.13	.13	10.78 (3.26)
BLUN: Blunting				—	−.13	−.04	−.11	4.14 (2.68)
CON: Conscientiousness					—	.19*	.29**	37.15 (20.97)
OPEN: Openness to experience						—	.24*	29.27 (21.22)
AGR: Agreeableness							—	37.29 (13.47)

*p < .06, two-tailed (only the DIR-AGR p was > .05);** p < .01, two tailed

TABLE 2

Descriptive Statistics for and Comparisons Between High Foreclosure (High Directional and Low Accuracy) Participants and Low Foreclosure (High Accuracy and Low Directional) Participants on Several Personality Variables

Variables	High Foreclosure			Low Foreclosure			t	p
	N	M	SD	N	M	SD		
Agreeableness	26	34.27	15.36	26	38.12	12.37	.99	ns
Conscientiousness	26	27.88	19.20	26	42.62	18.37	2.83	.007
Openness to experience	26	23.20	21.92	26	44.56	13.07	4.27	.000
Irrational health beliefs	26	48.38	13.02	26	34.67	6.72	4.77	.000
Monitoring	26	9.88	2.90	26	11.58	2.98	2.07	.043
Blunting	26	5.19	2.42	26	4.15	2.75	1.45	ns
Monitoring-blunting difference[1]	26	13.69	4.36	26	16.42	4.37	2.25	.029

[1]Calculated as monitoring score minus blunting score plus 9 (to eliminate negative values).

FIGURE B.1

Examples of APA-style tables. Table 1 gives Pearson's *r* coefficients among several variables, along with means and standard deviations. Table 2 presents the means and standard deviations for several variables and *t* test comparisons of those variables for individuals whose cognitive style reflects either high foreclosure (the tendency to make judgments impulsively and with biased logic) or low foreclosure.

which removes all the lines in the table (light lines remain on the screen but don't print) so I can add lines where I want them. Other useful icons in the formatting bar for use in the table are the ones for italic font and alignment, especially "Center." If your computer has *Word,* try playing with these features. If you have a different word processor, see if it has similar features.

GRAPHS

Although there are many types of graphs, two are by far the most common in psychology research reports and are constructed with a horizontal axis (often called the "abscissa" or "*x*-axis") and a vertical axis (the "ordinate" or "*y*-axis"). *Line graphs* use straight lines to connect successive data points, usually representing the group means, placed at intersects for the scaled values along the horizontal and vertical axes. The lines between points are straight because our best guess or assumption is that the relationship is linear in between. *Bar graphs* generally use vertically arranged rectangles to represent data points scaled along the vertical axis. The horizontal axis almost always represents the independent variable, and the vertical axis scales the dependent variable.

Choosing the Type of Graph

Which type of graph should you use? The choice depends on whether the variables are continuous or discrete. A *continuous variable* contains values representing a numerical progression of number, amount, or degree, as occurs in interval or ratio scales. Examples of continuous variables include age, amount of medication or therapy received, number of words recalled, income, running speed, and chronological time. A *discrete variable* has values representing separate categories—as in nominal scales—rather than a progression of numerical values. Examples of discrete variables include gender, college major, religion, political party affiliation, and the type (not amount) of therapy people received. When both variables are discrete, we wouldn't use a graph at all. In choosing the type of graph to use, the *general rule of thumb* is

- Use a line graph if the variables scaled on the horizontal and vertical axes are both continuous.
- Use a bar graph if the variable on the horizontal axis is discrete and the variable on the vertical axis is continuous.

There is a main *exception* to this rule: A line graph is acceptable when one variable is discrete if we need to display an interaction between the variables. Interactions are usually clearer when shown in line graphs than in bar graphs.

Making a Graph

Graphs can be prepared by hand or with a computer graphics program. Regardless of the approach you use, start by making a freehand sketch of what the graph will look like, including all labels it will have and a tentative caption describing its contents. Make sure the graph's proportions will enable you to present what you want it to say—for example, if you want to show a significant difference between conditions with a large effect size, make the distance between those means large. A well-planned and well-prepared graph:

- Is easy to read and understand.
- Contains only essential information and leaves out visually distracting detail.
- Creates a clear and fair picture of what the data indicate.
- Uses distinct black-and-white patterns to distinguish different sets of data. In a line graph, for example, use solid and dashed lines and different geometric forms, such as circles and squares, for data points. In a bar graph, use shading or crosshatching. If the patterns are different, the data sets should be different; patterns that are the same indicate that there is a similarity or connection between data sets. Don't use colors in a graph for a research report because journals virtually never print in color.

Use graphs contained in this book as models. For line graphs, look at Figures 6.1, 7.3, and 9.5, for example. For a bar graph, look at Figure A.13.

When preparing a graph manually, print labels clearly and use graph paper and a ruler to make all lines neat and straight. Many computer programs are available to make graphs, and you may already own one if you have *Microsoft Excel* or *Works,* for instance. If you perform your statistical analyses on a computer, all major statistics programs have graphing features—and your data would already be in the data file. In SPSS, you can access graphing functions in more than one way, such as by clicking on *Graphs* in the menu bar or right-clicking on a set of values in the SPSS output and selecting "Create Graph." Each of these approaches gives options to make line or bar graphs. More details on using SPSS graphing functions are available in the Companion Website for this book. Don't forget that you can use the *select cases* function described earlier in this appendix to limit the data used in a graph.

STANDARD STATISTICAL TABLES

LIST OF TABLES

Random Numbers

Table B.1: Table of Random Numbers

Critical Values: Parametric Statistics

Table B.2: Table of Critical Values of F

Table B.3: Table of Critical Values of Pearson's r

Table B.4: Table of Critical Values of t

Critical Values: Nonparametric Statistics

Table B.5: Table of Critical Values of χ^2

Table B.6: Table of Critical Values of r_s (Spearman rho)

Table B.7: Table of Critical Values of z

Table of Random Numbers

03 47 43 73 86	36 96 47 36 61	46 98 63 71 62	33 26 16 80 45	60 11 14 10 95
97 74 24 67 62	42 81 14 57 20	42 53 32 37 32	27 07 36 07 51	24 51 79 89 73
16 76 62 27 66	56 50 26 71 07	32 90 79 78 53	13 55 38 58 59	88 97 54 14 10
12 56 85 99 26	96 96 68 27 31	05 03 72 93 15	57 12 10 14 21	88 26 49 81 76
55 59 56 35 64	38 54 82 46 22	31 62 43 09 90	06 18 44 32 53	23 83 01 30 30
16 22 77 94 39	49 54 43 54 82	17 37 93 23 78	87 35 20 96 43	84 26 34 91 64
84 42 17 53 31	57 24 55 06 88	77 04 74 47 67	21 76 33 50 25	83 92 12 06 76
63 01 63 78 59	16 95 55 67 19	98 10 50 71 75	12 86 73 58 07	44 39 52 38 79
33 21 12 34 29	78 64 56 07 82	52 42 07 44 38	15 51 00 13 42	99 66 02 79 54
57 60 86 32 44	09 47 27 96 54	49 17 46 09 62	90 52 84 77 27	08 02 73 43 28
18 18 07 92 46	44 17 16 58 09	79 83 86 19 62	06 76 50 03 10	55 23 64 05 05
26 62 38 97 75	84 16 07 44 99	83 11 46 32 24	20 14 85 88 45	10 93 72 88 71
23 42 40 64 74	82 97 77 77 81	07 45 32 14 08	32 98 94 07 72	93 85 79 10 75
52 36 28 19 95	50 92 26 11 97	00 56 76 31 38	80 22 02 53 53	86 60 42 04 53
37 85 94 35 12	83 39 50 08 30	42 34 07 96 88	54 42 06 87 98	35 85 29 48 39
70 29 17 12 13	40 33 20 38 26	13 89 51 03 74	17 76 37 13 04	07 74 21 19 30
56 62 18 37 35	96 83 50 87 75	97 12 25 93 47	70 33 24 03 54	97 77 46 44 80
99 49 57 22 77	88 42 95 45 72	16 64 36 16 00	04 43 18 66 79	94 77 24 21 90
16 08 15 04 72	33 27 14 34 09	45 59 34 68 49	12 72 07 34 45	99 27 72 95 14
31 16 93 32 43	50 27 89 87 19	20 15 37 00 49	52 85 66 60 44	38 68 88 11 80
68 34 30 13 70	55 74 30 77 40	44 22 78 84 26	04 33 46 09 52	68 07 97 06 57
74 57 25 65 76	59 29 97 68 60	71 91 38 67 54	13 58 18 24 76	15 54 55 95 52
27 42 37 86 53	48 55 90 65 72	96 57 69 36 10	96 46 92 42 45	97 60 49 04 91
00 39 68 29 61	66 37 32 20 30	77 84 57 03 29	10 45 65 04 26	11 04 96 67 24
29 94 98 94 24	68 49 69 10 82	53 75 91 93 30	34 25 20 57 27	40 48 73 51 92
16 90 82 66 59	83 62 64 11 12	67 19 00 71 74	60 47 21 29 68	02 02 37 03 31
11 27 94 75 06	06 09 19 74 66	02 94 37 34 02	76 70 90 30 86	38 45 94 30 38
35 24 10 16 20	33 32 51 26 38	79 78 45 04 91	16 92 53 56 16	02 75 50 95 98
38 23 16 86 38	42 38 97 01 50	87 75 66 81 41	40 01 74 91 62	48 51 84 08 32
31 96 25 91 47	96 44 33 49 13	34 86 82 53 91	00 52 43 48 85	27 55 26 89 62
56 67 40 67 14	64 05 71 95 86	11 05 65 09 68	76 83 20 37 90	57 16 00 11 66
14 90 84 45 11	75 73 88 05 90	52 27 41 14 86	22 98 12 22 08	07 52 74 95 80
68 05 51 18 00	33 96 02 75 19	07 60 62 93 55	59 33 82 43 90	49 37 38 44 59
20 46 78 73 90	97 51 40 14 02	04 02 33 31 08	39 54 16 49 36	47 95 93 13 30
64 19 58 97 79	15 06 15 93 20	01 90 10 75 06	40 78 78 89 62	02 67 74 17 33
05 26 93 70 60	22 35 85 15 13	92 03 51 59 77	59 56 78 06 83	52 91 05 70 74
07 97 10 88 23	09 98 42 99 64	61 71 62 99 15	06 51 29 16 93	58 05 77 09 51
68 71 86 85 85	54 87 66 47 54	73 32 08 11 12	44 95 92 63 16	29 56 24 29 48
26 99 61 65 53	58 37 78 80 70	42 10 50 67 42	32 17 55 85 74	94 44 67 16 94
14 65 52 68 75	87 59 36 22 41	26 78 63 06 55	13 08 27 01 50	15 29 39 39 43
17 53 77 58 71	71 41 61 50 72	12 41 94 96 26	44 95 27 36 99	02 96 74 30 83
90 26 59 21 19	23 52 23 33 12	96 93 02 18 39	07 02 18 36 07	25 99 32 70 23
41 23 52 55 99	31 04 49 69 96	10 47 48 45 88	13 41 43 89 20	97 17 14 49 17
60 20 50 81 69	31 99 73 68 68	35 81 33 03 76	24 30 12 48 60	18 99 10 72 34
91 25 38 05 90	94 58 28 41 36	45 37 59 03 09	90 35 57 29 12	82 62 54 65 60
34 50 57 74 37	98 80 33 00 91	09 77 93 19 82	74 94 80 04 04	45 07 31 66 49
85 22 04 39 43	73 81 53 94 79	33 62 46 86 28	08 31 54 46 31	53 94 13 38 47
09 79 13 77 48	73 82 97 22 21	05 03 27 24 83	72 89 44 05 60	35 80 39 94 88
88 75 80 18 14	22 95 75 42 49	39 32 82 22 49	02 48 07 70 37	16 04 61 67 87
90 96 23 70 00	39 00 03 06 90	55 85 78 38 36	94 37 30 69 32	90 89 00 76 33

53 74 23 99 67	61 32 28 69 84	94 62 67 86 24	98 33 41 19 95	47 53 53 38 09
63 38 06 86 54	99 00 65 26 94	02 82 90 23 07	79 62 67 80 60	75 91 12 81 19
35 30 58 21 46	06 72 17 10 94	25 21 31 75 96	49 28 24 00 49	55 65 79 78 07
63 43 36 82 69	65 51 18 37 88	61 38 44 12 45	32 92 85 88 65	54 34 81 85 35
98 25 37 55 26	01 91 82 81 46	74 71 12 94 97	24 02 71 37 07	03 92 18 66 75
02 63 21 17 69	71 50 80 89 56	38 15 70 11 48	43 40 45 86 98	00 83 26 91 03
64 55 22 21 82	48 22 28 06 00	61 54 13 43 91	82 78 12 23 29	06 66 24 12 27
85 07 26 13 89	01 10 07 82 04	59 63 69 36 03	69 11 15 83 80	13 29 54 19 28
58 54 16 24 15	51 54 44 82 00	62 61 65 04 69	38 18 65 18 97	85 72 13 49 21
34 85 27 84 87	61 48 64 56 26	90 18 48 13 26	37 70 15 42 57	65 65 80 39 07
03 92 18 27 46	57 99 16 96 56	30 33 72 85 22	84 64 38 56 98	99 01 30 98 64
62 95 30 27 59	37 75 41 66 48	86 97 80 61 45	23 53 04 01 63	45 76 08 64 27
08 45 93 15 22	60 21 75 46 91	98 77 27 85 42	28 88 61 08 84	69 62 03 42 73
07 08 55 18 40	45 44 75 13 90	24 94 96 61 02	57 55 66 83 15	73 42 37 11 61
01 85 89 95 66	51 10 19 34 88	15 84 97 19 75	12 76 39 43 78	64 63 91 08 25
72 84 71 14 35	19 11 58 49 26	50 11 17 17 76	86 31 57 20 18	95 60 78 46 75
88 78 28 16 84	13 52 53 94 53	75 45 69 30 96	73 89 65 70 31	99 17 43 48 76
45 17 75 65 57	28 40 19 72 12	25 12 74 75 67	60 40 60 81 19	24 62 01 61 16
96 76 28 12 54	22 01 11 94 25	71 96 16 16 88	68 64 36 74 45	19 59 50 88 92
43 31 67 72 30	24 02 94 08 63	38 32 36 66 02	69 36 38 25 39	48 03 45 15 22
50 44 66 44 21	66 06 58 05 62	68 15 54 35 02	42 35 48 96 32	14 52 41 52 48
22 66 22 15 86	26 63 75 41 99	58 42 36 72 24	58 37 52 18 51	03 37 18 39 11
96 24 40 14 51	23 22 30 88 57	95 67 47 29 83	94 69 40 06 07	18 16 36 78 86
31 73 91 61 19	60 20 72 93 48	98 57 07 23 69	65 95 39 69 58	56 80 30 19 44
78 60 73 99 84	43 89 94 36 45	56 69 47 07 41	90 22 91 07 12	78 35 34 08 72
84 37 90 61 56	70 10 23 98 05	85 11 34 76 60	76 48 45 34 60	01 64 18 39 96
36 67 10 08 23	98 93 35 08 86	99 29 76 29 81	33 34 91 58 93	63 14 52 32 52
07 28 59 07 48	89 64 58 89 75	83 85 62 27 89	30 14 78 56 27	86 63 59 80 02
10 15 83 87 60	79 24 31 66 56	21 48 24 06 93	91 98 94 05 49	01 47 59 38 00
55 19 68 97 65	03 73 52 16 56	00 53 55 90 27	33 42 29 38 87	22 13 88 83 34
53 81 29 13 39	35 01 20 71 34	62 33 74 82 14	53 73 19 09 03	56 54 29 56 93
51 86 32 68 92	33 98 74 66 99	40 14 71 94 58	45 94 19 38 81	14 44 99 81 07
35 91 70 29 13	80 03 54 07 27	96 94 78 32 66	50 95 52 74 33	13 80 55 62 54
37 71 67 95 13	20 02 44 95 94	64 85 04 05 72	01 32 90 76 14	53 89 74 60 41
93 66 13 83 27	92 79 64 64 72	28 54 96 53 84	48 14 52 98 94	56 07 93 89 30
02 96 08 45 65	13 05 00 41 84	93 07 54 72 59	21 45 57 09 77	19 48 56 27 44
49 83 43 48 35	82 88 33 69 96	72 36 04 19 76	47 45 15 18 60	82 11 08 95 97
84 60 71 62 46	40 80 81 30 37	34 39 23 05 38	25 15 35 71 30	88 12 57 21 77
18 17 30 88 71	44 91 14 88 47	89 23 30 63 15	56 34 20 47 89	99 82 93 24 98
79 69 10 61 78	71 32 76 95 62	87 00 22 58 40	92 54 01 75 25	43 11 71 99 31
75 93 36 57 83	56 20 14 82 11	74 21 97 90 65	96 42 68 63 86	74 54 13 26 94
38 30 92 29 03	06 28 81 39 38	62 25 06 84 63	61 29 08 93 67	04 32 92 08 00
51 29 50 10 34	31 57 75 95 80	51 97 02 74 77	76 15 48 49 44	18 55 63 77 09
21 31 38 86 24	37 79 81 53 74	73 24 16 10 33	52 83 90 94 76	70 47 14 54 36
29 01 23 87 88	58 02 39 37 67	42 10 14 20 92	16 55 23 42 45	54 96 09 11 06
95 33 95 22 00	18 74 72 00 18	38 79 58 69 32	81 76 80 26 92	82 80 84 25 39
90 84 60 79 80	24 36 59 87 38	82 07 53 89 35	96 35 23 79 18	05 98 90 07 35
46 40 62 98 82	54 97 20 56 95	15 74 80 08 32	16 46 70 50 80	67 72 16 42 79
20 31 89 03 43	38 46 82 68 72	32 14 82 99 70	80 60 47 18 97	63 49 30 21 30
71 59 73 05 50	08 22 23 71 77	91 01 93 20 49	82 96 59 26 94	66 39 67 98 60

Source: Abridged from Fisher, R. A., & Yates, C. B. E. (1963). *Statistical tables for biological, agricultural, and medical research* (6th ed.). Table XXXIII. Darien, CT: Hafner Publishing Co.

TABLE B.2

Table of Critical Values[a] of F

df (denominator)[b]	p (or α)	df (numerator)[b] 1	2	3	4	5	6	8	12	24	∞
1	.05	161.40	199.50	215.70	224.60	230.20	234.00	238.90	243.90	249.00	254.30
	.01	4052	4999	5403	5625	5764	5859	5982	6106	6234	6366
	.001	405284	500000	540379	562500	576405	585937	598144	610667	623497	636619
2	.05	18.51	19.00	19.16	19.25	19.30	19.33	19.37	19.41	19.45	19.50
	.01	98.50	99.00	99.17	99.25	99.30	99.33	99.37	99.42	99.46	99.50
	.001	998.50	999.00	999.20	999.20	999.30	999.30	999.40	999.40	999.50	999.50
3	.05	10.13	9.55	9.28	9.12	9.01	8.94	8.84	8.74	8.64	8.53
	.01	34.12	30.82	29.46	28.71	28.24	27.91	27.49	27.05	26.60	26.12
	.001	167.00	148.50	141.10	137.10	134.60	132.80	130.60	128.30	125.90	123.50
4	.05	7.71	6.94	6.59	6.39	6.26	6.16	6.04	5.91	5.77	5.63
	.01	21.20	18.00	16.69	15.98	15.52	15.21	14.80	14.37	13.93	13.46
	.001	74.14	61.25	56.18	53.44	51.71	50.53	49.00	47.41	45.77	44.05
5	.05	6.61	5.79	5.41	5.19	5.05	4.95	4.82	4.68	4.53	4.36
	.01	16.26	13.27	12.06	11.39	10.97	10.67	10.29	9.89	9.47	9.02
	.001	47.18	37.12	33.20	31.09	29.75	28.84	27.64	26.42	25.14	23.78
6	.05	5.99	5.14	4.76	4.53	4.39	4.28	4.15	4.00	3.84	3.67
	.01	13.74	10.92	9.78	9.15	8.75	8.47	8.10	7.72	7.31	6.88
	.001	35.51	27.00	23.70	21.92	20.81	20.03	19.03	17.99	16.89	15.75
7	.05	5.59	4.74	4.35	4.12	3.97	3.87	3.73	3.57	3.41	3.23
	.01	12.25	9.55	8.45	7.85	7.46	7.19	6.84	6.47	6.07	5.65
	.001	29.25	21.69	18.77	17.19	16.21	15.52	14.63	13.71	12.73	11.69
8	.05	5.32	4.46	4.07	3.84	3.69	3.58	3.44	3.28	3.12	2.93
	.01	11.26	8.65	7.59	7.01	6.63	6.37	6.03	5.67	5.28	4.86
	.001	25.42	18.49	15.83	14.39	13.49	12.86	12.04	11.19	10.30	9.34
9	.05	5.12	4.26	3.86	3.63	3.48	3.37	3.23	3.07	2.90	2.71
	.01	10.56	8.02	6.99	6.42	6.06	5.80	5.47	5.11	4.73	4.31
	.001	22.86	16.39	13.90	12.56	11.71	11.13	10.37	9.57	8.72	7.81
10	.05	4.96	4.10	3.71	3.48	3.33	3.22	3.07	2.91	2.74	2.54
	.01	10.04	7.56	6.55	5.99	5.64	5.39	5.06	4.71	4.33	3.91
	.001	21.04	14.91	12.55	11.28	10.48	9.92	9.20	8.45	7.64	6.76
11	.05	4.84	3.98	3.59	3.36	3.20	3.09	2.95	2.79	2.61	2.40
	.01	9.65	7.20	6.22	5.67	5.32	5.07	4.74	4.40	4.02	3.60
	.001	19.69	13.81	11.56	10.35	9.58	9.05	8.35	7.63	6.85	6.00
12	.05	4.75	3.88	3.49	3.26	3.11	3.00	2.85	2.69	2.50	2.30
	.01	9.33	6.93	5.95	5.41	5.06	4.82	4.50	4.16	3.78	3.36
	.001	18.64	12.97	10.80	9.63	8.89	8.38	7.71	7.00	6.25	5.42
13	.05	4.67	3.80	3.41	3.18	3.02	2.92	2.77	2.60	2.42	2.21
	.01	9.07	6.70	5.74	5.20	4.86	4.62	4.30	3.96	3.59	3.16
	.001	17.81	12.31	10.21	9.07	8.35	7.86	7.21	6.52	5.78	4.97
14	.05	4.60	3.74	3.34	3.11	2.96	2.85	2.70	2.53	2.35	2.13
	.01	8.86	6.51	5.56	5.03	4.69	4.46	4.14	3.80	3.43	3.00
	.001	17.14	11.78	9.73	8.62	7.92	7.43	6.80	6.13	5.41	4.60

TABLE B.2 (CONTINUED)

df (denominator)[b]	p (or α)	df (numerator)[b]									
		1	2	3	4	5	6	8	12	24	∞
15	**.05**	4.54	3.68	3.29	3.06	2.90	2.79	2.64	2.48	2.29	2.07
	.01	8.68	6.36	5.42	4.89	4.56	4.32	4.00	3.67	3.29	2.87
	.001	16.59	11.34	9.34	8.25	7.57	7.09	6.47	5.81	5.10	4.31
16	**.05**	4.49	3.63	3.24	3.01	2.85	2.74	2.59	2.42	2.24	2.01
	.01	8.53	6.23	5.29	4.77	4.44	4.20	3.89	3.55	3.18	2.75
	.001	16.12	10.97	9.00	7.94	7.27	6.81	6.19	5.55	4.85	4.06
17	**.05**	4.45	3.59	3.20	2.96	2.81	2.70	2.55	2.38	2.19	1.96
	.01	8.40	6.11	5.18	4.67	4.34	4.10	3.79	3.45	3.08	2.65
	.001	15.72	10.66	8.73	7.68	7.02	6.56	5.96	5.32	4.63	3.85
18	**.05**	4.41	3.55	3.16	2.93	2.77	2.66	2.51	2.34	2.15	1.92
	.01	8.28	6.01	5.09	4.58	4.25	4.01	3.71	3.37	3.00	2.57
	.001	15.38	10.39	8.49	7.46	6.81	6.35	5.76	5.13	4.45	3.67
19	**.05**	4.38	3.52	3.13	2.90	2.74	2.63	2.48	2.31	2.11	1.88
	.01	8.18	5.93	5.01	4.50	4.17	3.94	3.63	3.30	2.92	2.49
	.001	15.08	10.16	8.28	7.26	6.62	6.18	5.59	4.97	4.29	3.52
20	**.05**	4.35	3.49	3.10	2.87	2.71	2.60	2.45	2.28	2.08	1.84
	.01	8.10	5.85	4.94	4.43	4.10	3.87	3.56	3.23	2.86	2.42
	.001	14.82	9.95	8.10	7.10	6.46	6.02	5.44	4.82	4.15	3.38
21	**.05**	4.32	3.47	3.07	2.84	2.68	2.57	2.42	2.25	2.05	1.81
	.01	8.02	5.78	4.87	4.37	4.04	3.81	3.51	3.17	2.80	2.36
	.001	14.59	9.77	7.94	6.95	6.32	5.88	5.31	4.70	4.03	3.26
22	**.05**	4.30	3.44	3.05	2.82	2.66	2.55	2.40	2.23	2.03	1.78
	.01	7.94	5.72	4.82	4.31	3.99	3.76	3.45	3.12	2.75	2.31
	.001	14.38	9.61	7.80	6.81	6.19	5.76	5.19	4.58	3.92	3.15
23	**.05**	4.28	3.42	3.03	2.80	2.64	2.53	2.38	2.20	2.00	1.76
	.01	7.88	5.66	4.76	4.26	3.94	3.71	3.41	3.07	2.70	2.26
	.001	14.19	9.47	7.67	6.69	6.08	5.65	5.09	4.48	3.82	3.05
24	**.05**	4.26	3.40	3.01	2.78	2.62	2.51	2.36	2.18	1.98	1.73
	.01	7.82	5.61	4.72	4.22	3.90	3.67	3.36	3.03	2.66	2.21
	.001	14.03	9.34	7.55	6.59	5.98	5.55	4.99	4.39	3.74	2.97
25	**.05**	4.24	3.38	2.99	2.76	2.60	2.49	2.34	2.16	1.96	1.71
	.01	7.77	5.57	4.68	4.18	3.86	3.63	3.32	2.99	2.62	2.17
	.001	13.88	9.22	7.45	6.49	5.88	5.46	4.91	4.31	3.66	2.89
26	**.05**	4.22	3.37	2.98	2.74	2.59	2.47	2.32	2.15	1.95	1.69
	.01	7.72	5.53	4.64	4.14	3.82	3.59	3.29	2.96	2.58	2.13
	.001	13.74	9.12	7.36	6.41	5.80	5.38	4.83	4.24	3.59	2.82
27	**.05**	4.21	3.35	2.96	2.73	2.57	2.46	2.30	2.13	1.93	1.67
	.01	7.68	5.49	4.60	4.11	3.78	3.56	3.26	2.93	2.55	2.10
	.001	13.61	9.02	7.27	6.33	5.73	5.31	4.76	4.17	3.52	2.75
28	**.05**	4.20	3.34	2.95	2.71	2.56	2.44	2.29	2.12	1.91	1.65
	.01	7.64	5.45	4.57	4.07	3.75	3.53	3.23	2.90	2.52	2.06
	.001	13.50	8.93	7.19	6.25	5.66	5.24	4.69	4.11	3.46	2.70

TABLE B.2 (CONTINUED)

df (denominator)[b]	p (or α)	df (numerator)[b] 1	2	3	4	5	6	8	12	24	∞
29	**.05**	4.18	3.33	2.93	2.70	2.54	2.43	2.28	2.10	1.90	1.64
	.01	7.60	5.42	4.54	4.04	3.73	3.50	3.20	2.87	2.49	2.03
	.001	13.39	8.85	7.12	6.19	5.59	5.18	4.64	4.05	3.41	2.64
30	**.05**	4.17	3.32	2.92	2.69	2.53	2.42	2.27	2.09	1.89	1.62
	.01	7.56	5.39	4.51	4.02	3.70	3.47	3.17	2.84	2.47	2.01
	.001	13.29	8.77	7.05	6.12	5.53	5.12	4.58	4.00	3.36	2.59
40	**.05**	4.08	3.23	2.84	2.61	2.45	2.34	2.18	2.00	1.79	1.51
	.01	7.31	5.18	4.31	3.83	3.51	3.29	2.99	2.66	2.29	1.80
	.001	12.61	8.25	6.60	5.70	5.13	4.73	4.21	3.64	3.01	2.23
60	**.05**	4.00	3.15	2.76	2.52	2.37	2.25	2.10	1.92	1.70	1.39
	.01	7.08	4.98	4.13	3.65	3.34	3.12	2.82	2.50	2.12	1.60
	.001	11.97	7.76	6.17	5.31	4.76	4.37	3.87	3.31	2.69	1.90
120	**.05**	3.92	3.07	2.68	2.45	2.29	2.17	2.02	1.83	1.61	1.25
	.01	6.85	4.79	3.95	3.48	3.17	2.96	2.66	2.34	1.95	1.38
	.001	11.38	7.32	5.79	4.95	4.42	4.04	3.55	3.02	2.40	1.54
∞	**.05**	3.84	2.99	2.60	2.37	2.21	2.10	1.94	1.75	1.52	1.00
	.01	6.64	4.60	3.78	3.32	3.02	2.80	2.51	2.18	1.79	1.00
	.001	10.83	6.91	5.42	4.62	4.10	3.74	3.27	2.74	2.13	1.00

[a]Critical values with one decimal place in the original tables were rounded to two decimals by adding a zero; values with no decimals were not altered.

[b]The *df*s are used in calculating the numerator and denominator mean squares that yield an *F* value in the ANOVA. The formulas for computing *df*s vary with the type of research design. See book Chapters 7 and 8 for one-way designs and Chapter 9 for factorials.

Source: Abridged from Fisher, R. A., & Yates, C. B. E. (1963). *Statistical tables for biological, agricultural, and medical research* (6th ed.). Table V: Variance Ratio. Darien, CT: Hafner Publishing Co.

TABLE B.3

Table of Critical Values of Pearson's r

df[b]	Two-tailed level of significance (p or α)[a]			
	.10	.05	.01	.001
1	.98769	.99692	.999877	.9999988
2	.90000	.95000	.990000	.99900
3	.8054	.8783	.95873	.99116
4	.7293	.8114	.91720	.97406
5	.6694	.7545	.8745	.95074
6	.6215	.7067	.8343	.92493
7	.5822	.6664	.7977	.8982
8	.5494	.6319	.7646	.8721
9	.5214	.6021	.7348	.8471
10	.4973	.5760	.7079	.8233
11	.4762	.5529	.6835	.8010
12	.4575	.5324	.6614	.7800
13	.4409	.5139	.6411	.7603
14	.4259	.4973	.6226	.7420
15	.4124	.4821	.6055	.7246
16	.4000	.4683	.5897	.7084
17	.3887	.4555	.5751	.6932
18	.3783	.4438	.5614	.6787
19	.3687	.4329	.5487	.6652
20	.3598	.4227	.5368	.6524
25	.3233	.3809	.4869	.5974
30	.2960	.3494	.4487	.5541
35	.2746	.3246	.4182	.5189
40	.2573	.3044	.3932	.4896
45	.2428	.2875	.3721	.4648
50	.2306	.2732	.3541	.4433
60	.2108	.2500	.3248	.4078
70	.1954	.2319	.3017	.3799
80	.1829	.2172	.2830	.3568
90	.1726	.2050	.2673	.3375
100	.1638	.1946	.2540	.3211

[a] The p value is halved for a one-tailed test by doubling the two-tailed α; thus, one-tailed .05 uses the .10 column.

[b] df = number of pairs − 2.

Source: Abridged from Fisher, R. A., & Yates, C. B. E. (1963). *Statistical tables for biological, agricultural, and medical research* (6th ed.). Table VII. Darien, CT: Hafner Publishing Co.

TABLE B.4

Table of Critical Values of t

df[b]	Two-tailed level of significance (p or α)[a]			
	.10	.05	.01	.001
1	6.314	12.706	63.657	636.619
2	2.920	4.303	9.925	31.598
3	2.353	3.182	5.841	12.924
4	2.132	2.776	4.604	8.610
5	2.015	2.571	4.032	6.869
6	1.943	2.447	3.707	5.959
7	1.895	2.365	3.499	5.408
8	1.860	2.306	3.355	5.041
9	1.833	2.262	3.250	4.781
10	1.812	2.228	3.169	4.587
11	1.796	2.201	3.106	4.437
12	1.782	2.179	3.055	4.318
13	1.771	2.160	3.012	4.221
14	1.761	2.145	2.977	4.140
15	1.753	2.131	2.947	4.073
16	1.746	2.120	2.921	4.015
17	1.740	2.110	2.898	3.965
18	1.734	2.101	2.878	3.922
19	1.729	2.093	2.861	3.883
20	1.725	2.086	2.845	3.850
21	1.721	2.080	2.831	3.819
22	1.717	2.074	2.819	3.792
23	1.714	2.069	2.807	3.767
24	1.711	2.064	2.797	3.745
25	1.708	2.060	2.787	3.725
26	1.706	2.056	2.779	3.707
27	1.703	2.052	2.771	3.690
28	1.701	2.048	2.763	3.674
29	1.699	2.045	2.756	3.659
30	1.697	2.042	2.750	3.646
40	1.684	2.021	2.704	3.551
60	1.671	2.000	2.660	3.460
120	1.658	1.980	2.617	3.373
∞	1.645	1.960	2.576	3.291

[a] The p value is halved for a one-tailed test by doubling the two-tailed α; thus one-tailed .05 uses the .10 column.

[b] df (for independent samples) = total number of subjects − 2; df (for paired samples) = number of pairs − 1.

Source: Abridged from Fisher, R. A., & Yates, C. B. E. (1963). *Statistical tables for biological, agricultural, and medical research* (6th ed.). Table III. Darien, CT: Hafner Publishing Co.

TABLE B.5

Table of Critical Values of χ^2

df^a	Level of significance (p or α) .05	.01	.001	df^a	Level of significance (p or α) .05	.01	.001
1	3.841	6.635	10.827	16	26.296	32.000	39.252
2	5.991	9.210	13.815	17	27.587	33.409	40.790
3	7.815	11.345	16.266	18	28.869	34.805	42.312
4	9.488	13.277	18.467	19	30.144	36.191	43.820
5	11.070	15.086	20.515	20	31.410	37.566	45.315
6	12.592	16.812	22.457	21	32.671	38.932	46.797
7	14.067	18.475	24.322	22	33.924	40.289	48.268
8	15.507	20.090	26.125	23	35.172	41.638	49.728
9	16.919	21.666	27.877	24	36.415	42.980	51.179
10	18.307	23.209	29.588	25	37.652	44.314	52.620
11	19.675	24.725	31.264	26	38.885	45.642	54.052
12	21.026	26.217	32.909	27	40.113	46.963	55.476
13	22.362	27.688	34.528	28	41.337	48.278	56.893
14	23.685	29.141	36.123	29	42.557	49.588	58.302
15	24.996	30.578	37.697	30	43.773	50.892	59.703

[a]df = number of conditions (categories) -1.

Source: Abridged from Fisher, R. A., & Yates, C. B. E. (1963). *Statistical tables for biological, agricultural, and medical research* (6th ed.). Table IV. Darien, CT: Hafner Publishing Co.

TABLE B.6

Table of Critical Values of r_s (Spearman rho)

N (number of pairs)	Two-tailed test p (or α) level .05	.01	N (number of pairs)	One-tailed test p (or α) level .05	.01
11	.620	.815	11	.520	.735
12	.591	.766	12	.485	.691
13	.566	.744	13	.475	.671
14	.544	.715	14	.456	.645
15	.524	.688	15	.440	.622
16	.506	.665	16	.425	.601
17	.490	.644	17	.411	.582
18	.475	.625	18	.399	.564
19	.462	.607	19	.388	.548
20	.450	.591	20	.377	.534
21	.438	.576	21	.368	.520
22	.428	.562	22	.359	.508
23	.418	.549	23	.351	.496
24	.409	.537	24	.343	.485
25	.400	.526	25	.336	.475
26	.392	.515	26	.329	.465
27	.384	.505	27	.323	.456
28	.377	.496	28	.317	.478
29	.370	.487	29	.311	.415
30	.364	.478	30	.305	.432

[a]Critical values were calculated from $\sum d^2$ and n data in Olds (1938, Table V) and Olds (1949, Table V [extended]) using the formula:

$$r_s = 1 - \frac{6 \sum d^2}{n^3 - n}$$

TABLE B.7

Table of Critical Values of z

Instructions:
- Find the *z* values in the table by using the left-most column, which has the values to one decimal, and the top row, which has the added data to obtain the second decimal place. For example, if you calculated a *z* of 2.13, you would find that value in the table by scanning down the left column to "2.1" and following that row to the right to the column labeled ".03": $2.1 + .03 = 2.13$.
- The body of the table gives the *one-tailed p* (or α) levels of significance for each *z* value listed. Double the *p* value for a two-tailed test.
- Values of *z* that are less than 1.64 for a one-tailed test or 1.96 for a two-tailed test (see shaded cells) are not significant ($p > .05$); all values of *z* that are greater than 3.30 are significant at the .001 level of confidence for one-tailed and two-tailed tests.
- No *df*s are used with tests based on *z* values.

z	.00	.01	.02	.03	.04	.05	.06	.07	.08	.09
1.6	.0548	.0537	.0526	.0516	.0505	.0495	.0485	.0475	.0465	.0455
1.7	.0446	.0436	.0427	.0418	.0409	.0401	.0392	.0384	.0375	.0367
1.8	.0359	.0351	.0344	.0336	.0329	.0322	.0314	.0307	.0301	.0294
1.9	.0287	.0281	.0274	.0268	.0262	.0256	.0250	.0244	.0239	.0233
2.0	.0228	.0222	.0217	.0212	.0207	.0202	.0197	.0192	.0188	.0183
2.1	.0179	.0174	.0170	.0166	.0162	.0158	.0154	.0150	.0146	.0143
2.2	.0139	.0136	.0132	.0129	.0125	.0122	.0119	.0116	.0113	.0110
2.3	.0107	.0104	.0102	.0099	.0096	.0094	.0091	.0089	.0087	.0084
2.4	.0082	.0080	.0078	.0075	.0073	.0071	.0069	.0068	.0066	.0064
2.5	.0062	.0060	.0059	.0057	.0055	.0054	.0052	.0051	.0049	.0048
2.6	.0047	.0045	.0044	.0043	.0041	.0040	.0039	.0038	.0037	.0036
2.7	.0035	.0034	.0033	.0032	.0031	.0030	.0029	.0028	.0027	.0026
2.8	.0026	.0025	.0024	.0023	.0023	.0022	.0021	.0021	.0020	.0019
2.9	.0019	.0018	.0018	.0017	.0016	.0016	.0015	.0015	.0014	.0014
3.0	.0013	.0013	.0013	.0012	.0012	.0011	.0011	.0011	.0010	.0010
3.1	.0010	.0009	.0009	.0009	.0008	.0008	.0008	.0008	.0007	.0007
3.2	.0007									
3.3	.0005									

Source: Siegel, S. (1956). *Nonparametric statistics for the behavioral sciences.* Table A. New York: McGraw-Hill.

GLOSSARY

AB design Intrasubject research design involving one baseline phase (A) and one intervention phase (B).

ABA design A reversal design in intrasubject research consisting of three phases: baseline (A), intervention (B), and reversal baseline (A).

ABAB design A reversal design in intrasubject research consisting of four phases: baseline (A), intervention (B), baseline (A), and intervention (B).

absolute threshold The lowest intensity of a stimulus that a participant can sense, assessed as an average across many trials.

all possible orders A control procedure for order effects that involves identifying every possible sequence of conditions and having each subject receive one of them; also called *complete counterbalancing*.

alternating-treatment designs A type of intrasubject research design in which two or more treatments are conducted during the same intervention phase to compare their effectiveness. Also called *simultaneous-treatment* or *multielement designs*.

analysis of variance (ANOVA) A parametric inferential statistical test for determining whether the means for data groupings are significantly different; typically applied when comparing more than two groups or conditions.

Animal Care and Use Committee A group of professionals and nonprofessionals who evaluate the care and treatment of animals used in research.

anonymity The state of being unknown or having one's identity masked.

applied behavior analysis A field of applied research that studies ways to apply conditioning principles to solve socially relevant problems.

applied research Research conducted mainly to address a current real-life problem.

archival data Representations of variables stored as hard copy or electronically.

asymmetric transfer A counterbalancing problem in repeated measures designs in which the carryover effects are greater for one sequence of conditions than for another sequence.

authority A method Peirce proposed by which people acquire and solidify knowledge or beliefs by accepting information as valid because it comes from a source that they respect or perceive to be an expert.

balancing Equating conditions for methodological details by making sure each group has the same degree of variation in a potential extraneous variable.

baseline A period of time before an intervention is introduced *or* the data collected during a baseline phase for comparison with intervention data.

basic research Research conducted mainly to gain knowledge about fundamental principles of behavior.

between-subjects design Research design that compares two or more separate groups of subjects that have different levels of an independent variable; also called *independent-groups design*.

between-subjects factorial ANOVA An analysis of variance procedure used with interval or ratio data for factorial designs with all independent groups.

blind A method of control in which the observer is unaware of the condition of the study for which a subject is being assessed.

block randomization A control procedure for order effects that involves giving each subject many trials in each condition presented as a series of sets (blocks), each of which contains one testing in each condition in a random order.

Bonferroni adjustment A statistical approach for dealing with the inflated risk of Type I error when multiple tests are performed; divide the desired alpha by the number of tests to get a more stringent alpha level for each test.

case study A type of research that involves preparing a detailed biography or assessment to describe a person's characteristics, such as to illustrate an unusual disorder or a case that contradicts common ideas about people or psychological processes.

causal inference Concluding that one event or condition causes another. Making a causal inference requires that the study meet three criteria: covariation of variables, causal time sequence, and elimination of other plausible causes (confounding).

ceiling effect The circumstance of performance reaching its maximum level and can't go higher, usually because the measurement scale does not extend high enough.

changing-criterion design A type of intrasubject research design in which the effect of an intervention is examined by altering the standards of correct performance periodically and seeing if the behavior matches the new standards.

chi-square (χ^2) A nonparametric inferential statistic used with nominal data to evaluate whether the observed frequencies differ from the expected frequencies.

clinical significance An evaluation of an intervention's success in terms of the degree to which the change in behavior is meaningful to the participant's everyday life.

closed-ended items Survey items that restrict the responses by requiring respondents to select from a set of answers.

cluster sampling A type of probability sampling in which researchers identify units ("clusters") of subjects who share a common feature, select clusters randomly, and try to recruit all members in each cluster as subjects.

Cochran Q A nonparametric inferential statistical procedure for nominal data in a dependent-groups design to determine whether a difference exists among more than two conditions of the study.

coefficient of determination For two correlated variables, the proportion of the variance of one that can be accounted for by the other; the square of r (the correlation coefficient).

coercion In research, the act or process of pressuring or strongly influencing a person's decision to participate.

cohort In testing age differences, individuals born in the same time period.

complete counterbalancing A control procedure for order effects that involves identifying every possible sequence of conditions and having each subject receive one of them; also called *all possible orders*.

concurrent validity A method for establishing a measure's criterion validity; the degree to which scores on the measure correlate with scores on an already validated measure of the *same* concept.

confidentiality In research, the principle that information about participants obtained in a study should not be disclosed to others unless the participant or a legal procedure authorizes otherwise.

confounding The circumstance when an uncontrolled factor (extraneous variable) may be responsible for variations of a dependent variable, rendering the effect of the independent variable unclear. Occurs when an extraneous variable covaries with the independent variable.

construct validity The extent to which scores on a measure are consistent with the way the construct it is intended to assess should operate (see *convergent validity* and *discriminant validity*).

constructs Hypothetical, not directly observable entities or processes, such as learning or motivation, that are inferred from behavior and assumed to follow from particular circumstances, such as experience.

content analysis A procedure by which narrative data can be categorized or rated to produce numerical data.

continuity assumption The view that psychological processes are similar across subjects, settings, and time periods unless there are reasons to think otherwise.

contrast A type of follow-up analysis to an ANOVA to compare only two conditions for which the researchers had identified an explicit prior hypothesis (also called a *planned comparison* or an *a priori test*).

control Procedures used in research to manage or isolate conditions or events that could influence the dependent variable.

control group A comparison group that does not receive the experimental treatment.

controlled within-subjects design A research design in which subjects are tested with repeated measures in a true experiment.

convenience sampling A nonprobability sampling method in which researchers ask for volunteers from individuals who are readily available, without trying to mirror the characteristics of the population.

convergent validity A method for establishing a measure's construct validity; the degree to which its scores correlate with scores on a validated measure of a *similar* concept.

correlation coefficient A statistic that can range from -1.00 to $+1.00$ and expresses the direction and magnitude of association between variables.

correlational strategy A research approach designed to assess the magnitude and direction of association between variables in a single group of subjects.

cost–benefit ratio An assessment of the extent to which the cost of an intervention is exceeded by the amount of money it saves in the long run.

counterbalancing An approach for controlling order effects in repeated measures that involves changing the sequence in which subjects experience levels of the independent variable; can be accomplished with methods of individual counterbalancing and overall counterbalancing.

criterion validity The extent to which scores on a measure match an existing standard or forecast a future variable (see *concurrent validity* and *predictive validity*)

criterion variable In regression analysis, the variable to be predicted by the predictor variable (for example, the criterion variable of school grades can be predicted to some degree from scores on an earlier IQ test).

Cronbach's alpha A statistic that serves as an index of a measure's reliability by demonstrating its internal consistency.

cross-lagged panel correlations A statistical procedure that gives all possible correlation coefficients for two variables assessed at two points in time; used in addressing the directionality problem in correlational research.

cross-sectional design In developmental research, observing different individuals at about the same time who differ in age.

curvilinear relationship A pattern of data that is not linear in a distribution of scores; the trend of the data does not follow a straight line.

data Factual information, usually expressed in numbers.

debriefing A procedure in which participants are told the nature and details of the study after participation.

deception In research, the process of misleading participants or withholding information to hide the nature of the study or manipulate a variable.

dehoaxing Describing to participants any deceptions that were used and the reasons for them.

demand characteristics Features of a study that participants may use in an effort to determine its purpose.

dependent-groups design Research design that compares two or more related sets of subjects that have different levels of an independent variable; includes *within-subjects* and *matched-subjects designs* (compare with *independent-groups* and *between-subjects designs*).

dependent variable A measurable aspect of subjects, objects, or events that is assessed to determine if its value varies with levels of the independent variable.

descriptive statistics Measures, such as the mean or standard deviation, that summarize the distribution of the data for variables in a study.

descriptive strategy A research approach that involves observing events or phenomena with the goal of detailing or categorizing them or charting their course.

desensitizing A counseling process used in debriefing to reduce any negative emotional states the research may have produced in participants.

difference threshold The smallest discrepancy between stimuli that a participant can sense, assessed as an average across many trials.

differential attrition The circumstance of subjects failing to complete a study at a higher rate when under one condition than another.

directionality A problem in correlational interpretation: any causal relationship underlying a correlation between two variables could operate in either direction.

discriminant validity A method for establishing a measure's construct validity—the measure should *not* correlate with scores for dissimilar or unrelated constructs; also called *divergent validity*.

double-blind A control procedure in which neither the participant nor the observer is allowed to know which condition the participant is receiving, thereby reducing the chances of bias.

duration As a type of quantitative data for measuring behavior, the time it lasts from beginning to end.

E × N design A factorial design that includes at least one independent variable tested with an experimental strategy and one tested with a nonexperimental strategy.

effect size A correlational measure of the degree of association between the independent and dependent variables.

empirical questions Queries or problems that can be resolved through systematic, objective observation.

empiricism A method Peirce proposed by which people acquire and solidify knowledge or beliefs by observation of events or phenomena.

error variance Nonsystematic variation in the scores in a data grouping, much of which reflects individual differences among subjects.

ethics A set of principles or values describing behaviors that are morally correct or incorrect.

event sampling In assessing naturally occurring behavior, restricting observations to a period of time following a predetermined situation.

experimental analysis of behavior A field of basic research that examines the role of conditioning in behavior.

experimental group A group of subjects that receives a treatment condition to compare with the control group.

experimental realism The degree to which the research situation has an impact on the subjects, getting them involved in the study and taking it seriously.

experimental strategy A research approach that examines differences in the effects of specific conditions by manipulating an independent variable, observing a dependent variable, and applying a high level of control to isolate or eliminate the role of extraneous factors.

external validity The degree to which the research findings generalize to individuals, settings, and time periods other than those examined in the study.

extraneous variable An uncontrolled factor that is not being examined in a study but could affect the results.

extreme-groups method The procedure of separating individuals into groups who score at the upper and lower levels of a distribution of data for a variable so that they can be compared for differences on another variable.

face validity In evaluating the validity of a measure, considering the degree to which a measure looks like it assesses what it is intended to measure,

factor analysis A complex correlational procedure to identify clusters of variables that correlate with each other, suggesting that those variables share an underlying theme, or "factor." (Note that the word *factor* here does not mean "independent variable," as it does in other terms.)

factorial design A research design with two or more independent variables (factors), organized so that all possible combinations of levels of each factor is tested.

falsifiability A characteristic of good theories in which they make clear statements that allow researchers to propose and disprove hypotheses.

falsifying data The act of fabricating or changing research data.

field research Research that takes place in a real-life setting, rather than in a laboratory.

floor effect The circumstance of performance reaching its minimum level and can't go lower, usually because the measurement scale does not extend low enough.

frequency As a type of quantitative data for measuring behavior, the number of times the act occurs.

Friedman χ^2 A nonparametric inferential statistical procedure for ordinal data in a dependent-groups design to determine whether a difference exists among more than two conditions of the study.

graph A diagram that generally shows how one variable changes as a function of another variable.

graphic analysis A procedure for examining graphs of data from intrasubject research to evaluate whether an intervention succeeded in changing a behavior substantially.

graphic rating scales A measurement approach in which participants express judgments by marking a point along a line of standard length with descriptors at each end.

history A potential extraneous variable in research with a pretest and posttest whereby an uncontrolled factor that is present between the tests is responsible for changes in the dependent variable.

holding conditions constant Equating conditions for methodological details by making all experiences in the study identical for all subjects in all conditions except for variations in the independent variable.

hypothesis A type of theory that gives a very tentative view or applies to a small range of phenomena; *also,* a prediction for a research outcome.

independent-groups design Research design that compares two or more separate and unrelated groups of subjects that have different levels of an independent variable; also called *between-subjects design* (compare with *dependent-groups, within-subjects,* and *matched-subjects designs*).

independent variable A factor of interest in conducting a study that is tested for its influence on a dependent variable.

inferential statistics Mathematical procedures for assessing the likelihood that the relationships or differences in groups of data collected from subjects in a sample actually exist in the population.

informed consent The procedure of telling participants in advance all features that might affect their willingness to take part in the study and obtaining their voluntary agreement to participate.

Institutional Review Board A group of professionals and nonprofessionals who review the ethical features of research at a particular institution, such as a university, to protect the rights and safety of participants.

interaction In factorial designs, the combined influence of two or more independent variables (factors) such that the effect of one factor depends on the level of the other factor(s).

inter-item reliability An approach for assessing the reliability of a measure that uses only a single testing, separates the items into halves, and conducts a correlational analysis of the scores for the two sets of items (see *split-half method* and *internal-consistency method*).

internal-consistency method An inter-item reliability procedure that repeatedly divides a measure's items into halves and computes a correlation; it then averages the coefficients for an index of internal consistency (see *Cronbach's alpha*).

internal validity The degree to which variations in the dependent variable can be attributed unambiguously to the independent variable; a study with high internal validity has little or no confounding.

interobserver reliability An indicator of measurement reliability that assesses the degree of consistency in the data obtained by different observers of the same behaviors or events. Also called *interrater reliability* or *interobserver agreement*.

interrupted time-series design A quasi-experimental design that compares a series of assessments before and after an event or treatment to evaluate changes that the event or treatment may have produced.

interval scale A measure characterized by distances between numerical values that are known or reasonably assumed to be equal in size.

intervention A program or treatment designed and implemented to change behavior.

intrasubject design A research approach that examines changes in behavior for one individual at a time, usually to compare performance while an intervention or condition is either in effect or absent. Also called a *single-subject, single-case,* or *small-N design.*

introspection A self-observation method in which people pay close attention to and describe their own sensations and perceptions.

intuition A method Peirce proposed by which people acquire and solidify knowledge or beliefs by accepting information as valid because it appears self-evident.

Kruskal-Wallis *H* A nonparametric inferential statistical procedure used with ordinal data to test for differences between more than two independent data groupings.

***k*-sample median test** A nonparametric inferential statistical procedure used with ordinal data to test for differences between more than two independent data groupings.

laboratory research Research that takes place in a setting that allows the researcher substantial control over who is present, how data are collected, and what the subjects will experience at any given time.

Latin square A control procedure for order effects that involves arranging sequences of conditions into a matrix so that each condition occurs equally often in each serial position and appears before and after each other condition once.

lawful The scientific assumption that the occurrence of events is basically orderly and predictable, following rules of cause and effect.

Likert scales Closed-ended measurement approaches in which survey respondents rate items along a continuum with labels at the ends (such as "strongly agree" and "strongly disagree") and at intervals (preferably equal) in between.

line graph A diagram that uses straight lines connecting data points to show changes in one variable in relation to another variable.

longitudinal design In developmental research, observing the same individuals across time at different ages to assess age-related changes in variables.

magnitude As a type of quantitative data for measuring behavior, assessing the intensity, degree, or size of the action or its effect.

main effect In a factorial design, the separate influence of one independent variable, ignoring the effects of the other factor(s) tested.

manipulation check An assessment of whether variations in the independent variable had their intended effects on the subjects.

Mann-Whitney *U* A nonparametric inferential statistical procedure used with ordinal data to test for differences between two independent data groupings.

matched-subjects design A research design in which subjects in different groups are equated by using the technique of matching.

matching A procedure for equating subjects in a matched-groups design; the researcher assesses the subjects on a matching variable (it should correlate highly with the dependent variable) and then randomly assigns to groups the subjects who score very similarly on the matching variable.

maturation A potential extraneous variable in research with a pretest and a posttest whereby physical or psychological growth that occurs between the tests is responsible for changes in the dependent variable.

McNemar test A nonparametric inferential statistical procedure for nominal data in a dependent-groups design to determine whether a difference exists between two conditions of the study.

mean A measure of central tendency: the mathematical average of a set of scores.

mean squares between-groups (MS_{bg}) An index of the variance associated with the independent variable; calculated by dividing the sum of squares between groups by the associated degrees of freedom.

mean squares within-groups (MS_{wg}) An index of the error variance; calculated by dividing the sum of squares within groups by the associated degrees of freedom.

median A measure of central tendency: the middlemost score of a rank-ordered distribution.

median-split method The procedure of separating individuals into groups who score above and below the median in a distribution of data for a variable so that they can be compared for differences on another variable.

meta-analysis Statistical procedures for analyzing and integrating the results of prior research on a topic to assess the relationship between variables across studies.

minimal risk A category of potential risk for participants in a study; the likelihood and magnitude of harm or discomfort is comparable to what they encounter in daily life activities.

mixed factorial design A factorial design that tests at least one factor with independent groups and one with dependent groups (either repeated measures or matched).

mode A measure of central tendency: the most frequently occurring score in a set of scores.

model A description of processes in a phenomenon *or* an analogous entity or process.

multiple-baseline, across-behaviors A type of multiple baseline design in which each AB design examines the effects of an intervention on a *different behavior* for a single individual in a particular situation.

multiple-baseline, across-situations A type of multiple baseline design in which each AB design examines the effects of an intervention on a particular behavior in a *different situation* for a single individual.

multiple-baseline, across-subjects A type of multiple baseline design in which each AB design examines the effects of an intervention on a particular behavior for a *different individual* in a specific setting.

multiple-baseline designs Intrasubject research designs in which two or more AB designs are conducted, with all baseline phases starting simultaneously but continuing for different lengths of time.

multiple regression A statistical regression analysis for predicting a criterion variable from data on two or more predictor variables.

multivariate analysis Inferential statistical procedures that involve more than one dependent variable in an analysis.

multivariate analysis of variance A procedure for examining the difference between two or more means, using more than one dependent variable at the same time.

mundane realism The degree of resemblance between the research situation and the subjects' real-life experiences.

natural-groups design A quasi-experimental independent-groups design in which groups are formed on the basis of a naturally occurring factor, a subject variable.

naturalistic observation A method for observing behavior in its natural setting without trying to affect it; used in descriptive research.

nominal scale A measure characterized by simply categorizing individuals based on their behavior or other variable, such as gender, and using the number in each category as the data.

nonequivalent control group design A quasi-experimental design with an experimental group that receives a treatment and a control group, but the groups are not equated, such as with random assignment or matching techniques.

nonparametric statistics Inferential statistical procedures used mainly with nominal or ordinal data, and sometimes with interval or ratio data that seriously violate the parametric assumptions that data groupings have reasonably normal distributions and equal variances.

nonprobability sampling Methods that recruit subjects without trying to obtain a sample that is representative of the population, usually because the researchers cannot identify all members of the population or estimate the chances of selecting any specific individual (see *convenience sampling*).

numerical rating scales Closed-ended measurement approaches in which survey respondents rate items along a continuum with numbers spanning the range of the scale and labels at the ends, such as "never" and "always."

objective A characteristic of science in which researchers strive to be impartial, such as in taking steps to reduce or eliminate subjectivity in their observations.

observer bias Making systematic errors in observations favoring one condition over another in a study, usually due to the observer's expectations.

omnibus test A statistical analysis that compares more than two data groupings simultaneously.

open-ended items Survey items that do not restrict respondents' responses, allowing them to answer in any way they wish.

operational definition The meaning of a concept or variable expressed in terms of the procedures used to produce or measure different levels of it.

order effects The influence on a dependent variable of the specific sequence in which levels of the independent variable were tested in a within-subjects design; also called *sequence effects*.

ordinal scale A measure in which scores represent rank orders or relative amounts.

outliers Scores that fall well outside the main distribution in a data grouping.

paired-samples *t* test A parametric inferential statistical procedure for determining whether the means for two groups or conditions in a dependent-groups design are significantly different.

parametric statistics Inferential statistical procedures used with interval or ratio data, particularly if the data groupings have reasonably normal distributions and equal variances.

parsimonious A characteristic of good theories that involves providing simple and straightforward explanations of events or phenomena, relying as little as possible on assumptions or constructs.

partial correlation A statistical technique that calculates a correlation coefficient after removing the variance associated with a third variable; used in evaluating the role of the third variable.

participants The preferred term for referring to people examined in research. (Other acceptable terms are more specific—for instance, *respondents* can be used to refer to people who complete surveys.)

physical traces Remnant measures that consist of material fragments or products of past behavior.

pilot study A trial run of the research method during the design of a study.

placebo control group A set of participants that receives a condition that looks like an experimental condition but is not; the purpose is to create a false belief that the treatment may be active.

placebo effect A physiological or psychological change in response to the participant's expectation that the change will occur.

plagiarism Presenting another individual's ideas or words without giving credit to the source or using the proper format, thereby implying that the material is one's own creation.

population The full set of individuals of interest for a study from which a sample is drawn.

post hoc comparisons Follow-up analyses to an ANOVA with a significant *F* value to compare all possible pairs of conditions without having made prior hypotheses (also called *unplanned comparisons, multiple comparisons,* or *a posteriori tests*).

power The degree to which a test is able to detect a relationship or difference between data groupings; affected by the sample size, statistical procedure used, alpha, and effect size.

predictive validity A method for establishing a measure's criterion validity; the degree to which scores on the measure correlate with a future event or variable.

predictor variable In regression analysis, the variable being used to predict a criterion variable (for example, scores on an earlier IQ test might be a predictor variable for the criterion variable of school grades).

pretest sensitization A potential extraneous variable in research with a pretest and a posttest whereby the pretest itself changes the subject and is responsible for changes in the dependent variable at posttest.

primary source The original, firsthand statement or description of information.

privacy In research, participants' freedom from unauthorized observation or recording of their behavior, feelings, and thoughts in situations that people reasonably expect are free of observation.

probability sampling Approaches for recruiting subjects that attempt to obtain a sample that is representative of the population; the researchers can specify the likelihood of selecting any member of the population (methods include *cluster sampling, simple random sampling,* and *stratified random sampling*).

program evaluation Applied research procedures for assessing the need for and success of programs (interventions or policies) implemented on a large scale, such as throughout a city.

prospective approach A quasi-experimental method whereby characteristics of subjects are assessed and at a later time examined for relationships to future behaviors or events.

pseudoscience A system of knowledge that people may erroneously assume is valid, but which relies mainly on casual observation, such as anecdotes, as evidence and evades disproof.

psychophysics A field of study that focuses on relations between characteristics of stimuli and subjects' perception of and reactions to them.

PsycINFO An electronic database of abstracts of psychology related reports and books.

quasi-experimental strategy A research approach that tests for differences between conditions but does not create equivalent groups, manipulate the independent variable, or fully control other extraneous factors.

random A process or event that happens purely by chance and without bias; it does not mean "haphazard."

random assignment A procedure for creating equivalent groups by making sure that each subject has an equal chance of being chosen to serve in each group in the study.

range A measure of variability in a set of data: the span from the highest to the lowest scores.

ratio scale A measure with equal distances between numerical values and a true zero point, reflecting an absence of the variable; these characteristics mean that a ratio of one score to another can be formed.

rationalism A method Peirce proposed by which people acquire and solidify knowledge or beliefs through logical thinking, particularly deductive and inductive reasoning.

reactivity The influence of being observed on a participant's behavior.

regression analysis A statistical procedure that develops an equation to predict scores on a criterion variable from scores on a predictor variable.

regression line A straight line that best represents the data in a scatterplot by following a path that minimizes the summed squared deviations of the scores.

regression to the mean A potential extraneous variable in research with a pretest and a posttest whereby subjects who score uncommonly high or low on the pretest tend to score more toward the middle of the distribution at posttest.

reliability The degree to which a measurement procedure produces scores consistently and dependably, such as when applied repeatedly or by another observer.

remnant measures Assessments of past events or states based on remains, outcomes, or other evidence of behavior.

repeated-measures ANOVA A parametric inferential statistical procedure for use in dependent-groups designs to determine whether the means for the groups or conditions are significantly different; typically used with more than two data groupings.

repeated-measures factorial ANOVA A parametric inferential statistical procedure for use in factorial designs with at least one dependent-groups factor; used to test whether the means for the groups or conditions are significantly different.

replication Performing a retest of a study's conditions to see if the same results occur.

research design The plan for implementing a study's research strategy; identifies, for instance, the variables to be examined and whether the research will test for differences or for associations between data groupings or individual subjects.

research strategy The scientific approach (experimental, quasi-experimental, correlational, or descriptive) used in a study to accomplish its goal.

residual variance A portion of the overall error variance that excludes variation resulting from individual differences and is used in a one-way repeated-measures ANOVA to compute the F value.

response set bias Invalid self-reporting in which a respondent consistently gives answers that are not related to the content of the items, such as agreeing with pro and con statements on an issue.

restricted range The circumstance of a limited dispersion or span of scores for one or both of the variables in a scatterplot; lowers the calculated correlation coefficient.

retrospective approach A quasi-experimental method whereby past behaviors or events are examined for relationships—for example, using them as independent and dependent variables.

reversal designs Intrasubject research formats with a series of phases that involve alternations in the presence and absence of an intervention.

reverse counterbalancing A control procedure for order effects in within-subjects designs that involves having the subjects experience levels of the independent variable in two sequences, with the second order being the opposite of the first.

risk In research, a category of likelihood and magnitude of harm or discomfort for participants that is greater than that encountered in daily life activities.

risk–benefit analysis An assessment comparing the potential benefits of conducting a study against the risks it may present for participants.

sample The subjects selected to participate as a subset of the population of interest for a study.

sampling The process by which subjects are recruited or selected to participate in a study.

scatterplot In correlational procedures, a graphical representation of subjects' scores on two variables, with the pattern of data points depicting their relationship.

scholarly source High level literature intended for professionals and students.

science A system of knowledge and procedures characterized by the use of careful and unbiased observation.

segmented rating scales Closed-ended measurement approaches in which respondents rate items in a survey by marking one of the segments that divide a continuum with labels at the ends, such as "never" and "always."

self-correcting A characteristic of science in which its knowledge is revised on the basis of new evidence when errors are found.

self-report A method for observing covert behavior by having participants provide information about themselves, such as their feelings or past experiences.

significant In inferential statistics, an outcome that is very unlikely to have occurred just by chance if the null hypothesis is actually true.

simple-effects analysis A follow-up statistical procedure for an ANOVA with a factorial design; examines the effect of one factor at a particular level of another factor.

simple random sampling A type of probability sampling in which each member of the population has an equal and unbiased likelihood of being recruited to participate in a study.

single-case experiments Intrasubject research that use experimental strategies, thereby meeting the three criteria for making cause-effect conclusions.

social desirability bias Invalid self-reporting in which a respondent behaves in ways he or she believes are socially preferred or permissible.

social validity An evaluation by a client and individuals in his or her life of the social utility and adaptiveness of the change in behavior produced by an intervention.

Solomon four-group design A two-way factorial design in which the presence or absence of a pretest and an intervening treatment are the independent variables; used in controlling for confounding from history or maturation and the pretest.

speciesism A form of discrimination in which humans disregard the welfare of animals in research with the view that the potential benefits of research outcomes for humans outweigh the rights of animals.

split-half method An inter-item reliability procedure that divides items in a measure into halves and computes a correlation as an index of the measure's reliability.

standard deviation A measure of variability; the average deviation of scores from the mean of the data grouping (which is also the square root of the variance).

stratified random sampling A type of probability sampling that selects individuals in a random manner, but the population is separated into particular subgroups so that they will be represented in the sample proportionally.

structural modeling A statistical research approach in which an expected pattern of correlations among specific variables is identified and tested.

subjects The term for referring to individuals tested in research when they are animals or could be either animals or humans.

subject variable A characteristic of the subjects, such as gender, that is used in a quasi experiment to separate them into groups for comparisons (see *natural-groups design*).

sum of squares (*SS*) The sum of squared deviations between individual scores and the mean of the data grouping.

sum of squares between-groups (*SS*$_{bg}$) An index of the variance associated with the independent variable, calculated as the sum of squared deviations between the mean for each condition and the grand mean.

sum of squares within-groups (*SS*$_{wg}$) An index of error variance, calculated as the sum of variances of the scores for each condition in the analysis.

survey A self-report method in which participants answer a set of questions on one or more topics.

***t* test** A parametric inferential statistical procedure for determining whether the means for two groups or conditions are significantly different.

tenacity A method Peirce proposed by which people acquire and solidify knowledge or beliefs by accepting information as valid because it has been encountered so often and for a long time.

testing changes A potential extraneous variable in research with a pretest and a posttest if the assessment process is in some way different in the two tests.

test-retest reliability An approach for evaluating the consistency of scores on a measure by testing the subjects with the same measure at two different times and then calculating the correlation between the two sets of scores.

theory A logically organized set of statements that attempts to explain why and under what circumstances specific phenomena occur, thereby providing a source for hypotheses to test with empirical methods.

third variable In correlational analyses, an uncontrolled factor that may be responsible for the correlation between two other variables.

time sampling In assessing naturally occurring behavior, restricting observations to predetermined time intervals within larger periods of time.

twin studies A quasi-experimental approach in which researchers compare the members of identical and fraternal twin-ships for their degree of similarity; finding greater similarity for identical twins supports a genetic basis for the variable assessed.

validity In measurement, the degree to which a procedure assesses what it is intended to measure.

variance The degree to which the scores in a data grouping differ from one another, expressed as a numerical index; the average squared deviation of the scores from the mean of the distribution.

waiting list control group A research condition in which subjects who will receive the experimental treatment eventually do not receive it initially so that they can be compared with those who are already receiving it; often used when the presence or absence of therapy is the independent variable.

Wilcoxon matched-pairs signed-ranks test A nonparametric inferential statistical procedure for ordinal data in a dependent-groups design to determine whether a difference exists between two conditions of the study.

within-subjects design A type of dependent-groups design in which each subject is tested on the dependent variable more than once—that is, in more than one condition of the study; also called a *repeated measures design*.

yoked control group A research condition in which each subject's experience in the study is tied to and exactly the same as that of an experimental subject except for the operation of the independent variable.

REFERENCES

Allport, G. W., & Postman, L. J. (1947). *The psychology of rumor.* New York: Holt.

Altman, L. K. (1997, December 23). More orgasms, more years of life? *New York Times,* p. F7.

American Psychiatric Association. (1994). *Diagnostic and statistical manual of mental disorders* (DSM-IV, 4th ed.). Washington, DC: Author.

Anderson, C. A., Lepper, M. R., & Ross, L. (1980). Perseverance of social beliefs: The role of explanation in the persistence of discredited information. *Journal of Personality and Social Psychology, 39,* 1037–1049.

Anderson, C. A., Lindsay, J. J., & Bushman, B. J. (1999). Research in the psychology laboratory: Truth or triviality. *Current Directions in Psychological Science, 8,* 3–9.

Anderson, K. J. (1990). Arousal and the inverted-U hypothesis: A critique of Neiss's "reconceptualizing arousal." *Psychological Bulletin, 107,* 96–100.

Anderson, N. H. (2002). Methodology and statistics in single-subject experiments. In H. Pashler & J. Wixted (Eds.), *Stevens' handbook of experimental psychology* (3rd ed., pp. 301–337). New York: Wiley.

APA (American Psychological Association). (1953). *Ethical standards of psychologists.* Washington, DC: Author.

APA (American Psychological Association). (1982). *Ethical principles in the conduct of research with human participants.* Washington, DC: Author.

APA (American Psychological Association). (2002). *Ethical principles of psychologists and code of conduct.* Washington, DC: Author.

APA (American Psychological Association). (2001). *Publication manual of the American Psychological Association* (5th ed.). Washington, DC: Author.

Aronson, E., Brewer, M., & Carlsmith, J. M. (1985). Experimentation in social psychology. In G. Lindzey & E. Aronson (Eds.), *Handbook of social psychology* (3rd ed., Vol. 1, pp. 441–486). New York: Random House.

Atkinson, R. C., & Shiffrin, R. M. (1971, August). The control of short-term memory. *Scientific American,* pp. 82–90.

Bailey, J. M., Kim, P. Y., Hills, A., & Linsenmeier, J. A. W. (1997). Butch, femme, or straight acting? Partner preferences of gay men and lesbians. *Journal of Personality and Social Psychology, 73,* 960–973.

Bailey, J. S., Timbers, G. D., Phillips, E. L., & Wolf, M. M. (1971). Modification of articulation errors of pre-delinquents by their peers. *Journal of Applied Behavior Analysis, 4,* 265–281.

Bandura, A., Ross, D., & Ross, S. A. (1963). Imitation of film-mediated aggressive models. *Journal of Abnormal and Social Psychology, 66,* 3–11.

Barlow, D. H., & Hayes, S. C. (1979). Alternating treatments design: One strategy for comparing the effects of two treatments in a single subject. *Journal of Applied Behavior Analysis, 12,* 199–210.

Barlow, D. H., Sakheim, D. K., & Beck, J. G. (1983). Anxiety increases sexual arousal. *Journal of Abnormal Psychology, 92,* 49–54.

Bartlett, F. C. (1932). *Remembering: A study in experimental and social psychology.* New York: Macmillan.

Baumrind, D. (1964), Some thoughts on ethics of research: After reading Milgram's "Behavioral Study of Obedience." *American Psychologist, 19,* 421–423.

Baumrind, D. (1985). Research using intentional deception: Ethical issues revisited. *American Psychologist, 40,* 165–174.

Becker, L. J., Rabinowitz, V. C., & Seligman, C. (1980). Evaluating the impact of utility company billing plans on residential energy consumption. *Evaluation and Program Planning, 3,* 159–164.

Becker, M. H., & Rosenstock, I. M. (1984). Compliance with medical advice. In A. Steptoe & A. Mathews (Eds.), *Health care and human behaviour* (pp. 175–208). London: Academic Press.

Bell, S. E. (2000). Events in the Tuskegee Syphilis Study: A timeline. In S. M. Reverby (Ed.), *Tuskegee's truths: Rethinking the Tuskegee Syphilis Study* (pp. 34–37). Chapel Hill: University of North Carolina Press.

Beloff, H. (1962). The structure and origin of the anal character. *Genetic Psychology Monographs, 55,* 275–278.

Berkowitz, L., & Macaulay, J. (1971). The contagion of criminal violence. *Sociometry, 34,* 238–360.

Bio-Chart. (2002, February 9). *What are biorhythms?* Retrieved from http://bio-chart.com.

Birnbaum, M. H. (2001). *Introduction to behavioral research on the Internet.* Upper Saddle River, NJ: Prentice Hall.

Blagrove, M. (1996). Effects of length of sleep deprivation on interrogative suggestibility. *Journal of Experimental Psychology: Applied, 2,* 48–59.

Blakemore, C., & Cooper, G. F. (1970). Development of the brain depends on the visual environment. *Nature, 228,* 477–478.

Bostow, D. E., & Bailey, J. B. (1969). Modification of severe disruptive and aggressive behavior using brief timeout and reinforcement procedures. *Journal of Applied Behavior Analysis, 2,* 31–37.

Bourne, L. E., Dominowski, R. L., Loftus, E. F., & Healy, A. F. (1986). *Cognitive processes* (2nd ed.). Englewood Cliffs, NJ: Prentice Hall.

Brady, J. V. (1958). Ulcers in "executive" monkeys. *Scientific American, 199*(4), 95–100.

Brady, J. V., Porter, R. W., Conrad, D. G., & Mason, J. W. (1958). Avoidance behavior and the development of gastroduodenal ulcers. *Journal of the Experimental Analysis of Behavior, 1,* 69–72.

Bragg, R. (2002, February 10). In skating, perfection is in the judge's eye. *New York Times,* pp. 1, 30.

Bramel, D., & Friend, R. (1981). Hawthorne, the myth of the docile worker, and class bias in psychology. *American Psychologist, 36,* 867–878.

Brandt, A. M. (2000). Racism and research: The case of the Tuskegee Syphilis Experiment. In S. M. Reverby (Ed.), *Tuskegee's truths: Rethinking the Tuskegee Syphilis Study* (pp. 15–33). Chapel Hill: University of North Carolina Press.

Bransford, J. D., & Johnson, M. K. (1972). Contextual prerequisites for understanding: Some investigations of comprehension and recall. *Journal of Verbal Learning and Verbal Behavior, 11,* 717–726.

Bremner, J. D., & Narayan, M. (1998). The effects of stress on memory and the hippocampus throughout the life cycle: Implications for childhood development and aging. *Development and Psychopathology, 10,* 871–885.

Brennen, T., Baguley, T., Bright, J., & Bruce, V. (1990). Resolving semantically induced tip-of-the-tongue states. *Memory & Cognition, 18,* 339–347.

Brown, R., Cazden, C., & Bellugi-Klima, U. (1969). The child's grammar from I to III. In J. P. Hill (Ed.), *Minnesota symposia on child psychology* (Vol. 2, pp. 28–73). Minneapolis: University of Minnesota Press.

Buckner, R. L., & Logan, J. M. (2001). Functional neuroimaging methods: PET and fMRI. In R. Cabeza & A. Kingstone (Eds.), *Handbook of functional neuroimaging of cognition* (pp. 27–48).Cambridge, MA: MIT Press.

Buela Casal, G., Caballo, V. E., & Cueto, E. G.(1990). Differences between morning and evening types in performance. *Personality and Individual Differences, 11,* 447–450.

Buss, A. R. (1973). An extension of developmental models that separate ontogenetic changes and cohort differences. *Psychological Bulletin, 80,* 466–479.

Cahill, L., Prins, B., Weber, M., & McGaugh, J. L. (1994). β−adrenergic activation and memory for emotional events. *Nature, 371,* 702–704.

Calhoun, K. S., & Lima, P. P. (1977). Effects of varying schedules of timeout on high- and low-rate behaviors. *Behavior Therapy and Experimental Psychiatry, 8,* 189–194.

Campbell, D. T. (1969). Reforms as experiments. *American Psychologist, 24,* 409–429.

Campbell, D. T., & Stanley, J. C. (1963). *Experimental and quasi-experimental designs for research.* Boston: Houghton Mifflin.

Campbell, P. E., Batsche, C. J., & Batsche, G. M. (1972). Spaced-trials reward magnitude effects in the rat: Single versus multiple food pellets. *Journal of Comparative and Physiological Psychology, 81,* 360–364.

Chapman, C. R., Casey, K. L., Dubner, R., Foley, K. M., Gracely, R. H., & Reading, A. F. (1985). Pain measurement: An overview. *Pain, 22,* 1–33.

Childress, A. R. (1996, March). *Cue reactivity and drug craving.* Paper presented at the Society of Behavioral Medicine, Washington, DC.

Chira, S. (1991, November 20). Where children learn how to learn: Inner-city pupils in Catholic schools. *New York Times,* p. B8.

Christensen, L. (1988). Deception in psychological research: When is its use justified? *Personality and Social Psychology Bulletin, 14,* 664–675.

Clark-Carter, D. (1997). *Doing quantitative research: From design to report.* East Essex, UK: Psychology Press.

Cohen, J. (1988). *Statistical power analysis for the behavioral sciences* (2nd ed.). Hillsdale, NJ: Erlbaum.

Cook, T. D., & Campbell, D. T. (1979). *Quasi-experimentation: Design & analysis issues for field settings.* Chicago: Rand McNally.

Creer, T. L., Chai, H., & Hoffman, A. (1977). A single application of an aversive stimulus to eliminate chronic cough. *Journal of Behavior Therapy and Experimental Psychiatry, 8,* 107–109.

Cronan, T. A., Groessl, E., & Kaplan, R. M. (1997). The effects of social support and education interventions on health care costs. *Arthritis Care and Research, 10,* 99–110.

Cunningham, A. J., Edmonds, C. V. I., Jenkins, G. P., Pollack, H., Lockwood, G. A., & Warr, D. (1998). A randomized controlled trial of the effects of group psychological therapy on survival in women with metastatic breast cancer. *Psycho-Oncology, 7,* 508–517.

Curtiss, S. (1977). *Genie: A psycholinguistic study of a modern-day "wild child."* New York: Academic Press.

D.A.R.E. (Drug Abuse Resistance Education). (2000). *D.A.R.E. overview.* Retrieved May 6, 2000 from http://www.dare.com.

Darley, J. M., & Latané, B. (1968). Bystander intervention in emergencies: Diffusion of responsibility. *Journal of Personality and Social Psychology, 8,* 377–383.

Dasen, P. R., & Heron, A. (1981). Cross-cultural tests of Piaget's theory. In H. C. Triandis & A. Heron (Eds.), *Handbook of cross-cultural psychology: Developmental psychology* (Vol. 4, pp. 295–341). Boston: Allyn & Bacon.

DeLongis, A., Coyne, J. C., Dakof. G., Folkman, S., & Lazarus, R. S. (1982). Relationship of daily hassles, uplifts, and life events to health status. *Health Psychology, 1,* 119–136.

De Luca, R. V., & Holborn, S. W. (1992). Effects of a variable-ratio reinforcement schedule with changing criteria on exercise in obese and nonobese boys. *Journal of Applied Behavior Analysis, 25,* 671–679.

DeVries, J. E., Burnette, M., & Redmon, W. K. (1991). AIDS prevention: Improving nurses' compliance with glove wearing through performance feedback. *Journal of Applied Behavior Analysis, 24,* 705–711.

Dewing, K., & Hetherington, P. (1974). Anagram solving as a function of word imagery. *Journal of Experimental Psychology, 102,* 764–767.

Diamond, M., & Sigmundson, H. K. (1997). Sex reassignment at birth: Long-term review and clinical implications. *Archives of Pediatric and Adolescent Medicine, 151,* 298–304.

Dishman, R. K. (1986). Mental health. In V. Seefeldt (Ed.), *Physical activity and well-being* (pp. 304–341). Reston, VA: American Alliance for Health, Physical Education, Recreation, and Dance.

Dittmar, M. L., Berch, D. B., & Warm, J. S. (1982). Sustained visual attention in deaf and hearing adults. *Bulletin of the Psychonomic Society, 19,* 339–342.

Dush, D. M., Hirt, M. L., & Schroeder, H. (1983). Self-statement modification with adults: A meta-analysis. *Psychological Bulletin, 94,* 408–422.

Ebbinghaus, H. (1964). *Memory: A contribution to experimental psychology* (H. A. Ruger & C. A. Bussenius, Trans.). New York: Dover. (Original work published 1885).

Edelman, S., Lemon, J., Bell, D. R., & Kidman, A. D. (1999). Effects of group CBT on the survival time of patients with metastatic breast cancer. *Psycho-Oncology, 8,* 474–481.

Eibl-Eibesfeldt, I. (1970). *Ethology: The biology of behavior.* New York: Holt, Rinehart & Winston.

Eibl-Eibesfeldt, I. (1972). Similarities and differences between cultures in expressive movements. In R. A. Hinde (Ed.), *Non-verbal communication* (pp. 297–312). Cambridge, England: Cambridge University Press.

Ekman, P. (1993). Facial expression and emotion. *American Psychologist, 48,* 384–392.

Elkind, D. (1974). *Children and adolescents: Interpretive essays on Jean Piaget.* New York: Oxford University Press.

Erhardt, D., & Baker, B. L. (1990). The effects of behavioral parent training on families with young hyperactive children. *Journal of Behavior Therapy and Experimental Psychiatry, 21,* 121–132.

Eron, L. D., Huesmann, L. R., Lefkowitz, M. M., & Walder, L. O. (1972). Does television violence cause aggression? *American Psychologist, 27,* 253–263.

Evans, R., & Donnerstein, E. (1974). Some implications for psychological research of early versus late term participation by college subjects. *Journal of Research in Personality, 8,* 102–109.

Fancher, R. E. (1979). *Pioneers of psychology.* New York: W. W. Norton.

Fawzy, F. I., Fawzy, N. W., Hyun, C. S., Elashoff, R., Guthrie, D., Fahey, J. L., & Morton, D. L. (1993). Malignant melanoma: Effects of an early structured intervention, coping, and affective state on recurrence and survival 6 years later. *Archives of General Psychiatry, 50,* 681–689.

Ferster, C. B., & Skinner, B. F. (1957). *Schedules of reinforcement.* New York: Appleton-Century-Crofts.

Feshbach, S. (1964). The function of aggression and the regulation of aggressive drive. *Psychological Review, 71,* 257–272.

Festinger, L., Riecken, H. W., & Schachter, S. (1956). *When prophecy fails.* Minneapolis: University of Minnesota Press.

Field, D. (1981). Can preschool children really learn to conserve? *Child Development, 52,* 326–334.

Finney, J. W., Rapoff, M. A., Hall, C. L., & Christopherson, E. R. (1983). Replication and social validation of habit reversal treatment for tics. *Behavior Therapy, 14,* 116–126.

Fisher, R. A. (1935). *The design of experiments.* Edinburgh and London: Oliver & Boyd.

Fisher, R. A., & Yates, C. B. E. (1963). *Statistical tables for biological, agricultural, and medical research* (6th ed.). Darien, CT: Hafner Publishing Co.

Fisher, R. P., Geiselman, R. E., & Amador, M. (1989). Field test of the cognitive interview: Enhancing the recollection of actual victims and witnesses of crime. *Journal of Applied Psychology, 74,* 722–727.

Fisher, R. P., McCauley, M. R., & Geiselman, R. E. (1994). Improving eyewitness testimony with the cognitive interview. In D. F. Ross, J. D. Read, & M.P. Toglia (Eds.), *Adult eyewitness testimony: Current trends and developments* (pp. 245–269). New York: Cambridge University Press.

Folkman, S., & Lazarus, R. S. (1988). Coping as a mediator of emotion. *Journal of Personality and Social Psychology, 54,* 466–475.

Foster, S. L., & Mash, E. J. (1999). Assessing social validity in clinical treatment research: Issues and procedures. *Journal of Consulting and Clinical Psychology, 67,* 309–319.

Fox, D. K., Hopkins, B. L., & Anger, W. K. (1987). The long-term effects of a token economy on safety performance in open-pit mining. *Journal of Applied Behavior Analysis, 20,* 215–224.

Fredrikson, M., & Matthews, K. A. (1990). Cardiovascular responses to behavioral stress and hypertension: A meta-analytic review. *Annals of Behavioral Medicine, 12,* 30–39.

Friedman, H. S., Tucker, J. S., Schwartz, J. E., Tomlinson-Keasy, C., Martin, L. R., Wingard, D. L., et al. (1995). Psychosocial and behavioral predictors of longevity: The aging and death of the "Termites." *American Psychologist, 50,* 69–78.

Gagnon, M., & Ladouceur, R. (1992). Behavioral treatment of child stutterers: Replication and extension. *Behavior Therapy, 23,* 113–129.

Gallup, G. G., & Suarez, S. D. (1985). Alternatives to the use of animals in psychological research. *American Psychologist, 40,* 1104–1111.

Gannon, L., Luchetta, T., Rhodes, K., Pardie, L., & Segrist, D. (1992). Sex bias in psychological research. *American Psychologist, 47,* 389–396.

Garcia, J., Hankins, W. G., & Rusiniak, K. W. (1974). Behavioral regulation of the milieu interne in man and rat. *Science, 185,* 824–831.

Garcia, J., & Koelling, R. A. (1966). Relation of cue to consequence in avoidance learning. *Psychonomic Science, 4,* 123–124.

Gibson, E. J., & Walk, R. D. (1960). The "visual cliff." *Scientific American, 202*(4), 64–71.

Gillespie, R. (1988). The Hawthorne experiments and the politics of experimentation. In J. C. Morawski (Ed.), *The rise of experimentation in American psychology* (pp. 114–137). New Haven, CT: Yale University Press.

Ginsburg, H. J., Pollman, V. A., & Wauson, M. S. (1977). An ethological analysis of nonverbal inhibitors of aggressive behavior in male elementary school children. *Developmental Psychology, 4,* 417–418.

Glass, D. C., Krakoff, L. R., Contrada, R. J., Hilton, W. F., Kehoe, K., Mannucci, E. G., Collins, C., Snow, B., & Elting, E. (1980). Effects of harassment and competition on cardiovascular and plasma catecholamine responses in Type A and B individuals. *Psychophysiology, 17,* 453–463.

Glass, G. V. (1976). Primary, secondary, and meta-analysis of research. *Educational Researcher, 5,* 3–8.

Goodman, S. H., Lahey, B. B., Fielding, B., Dulcan, M., Narrow, W., & Regier, D. (1997). Representativeness of clinical samples of youths with mental disorders: A preliminary population-based study. *Journal of Abnormal Psychology, 106,* 3–14.

Gruen, W. (1975). Effects of brief psychotherapy during the hospitalization period on the recovery process in heart attacks. *Journal of Consulting and Clinical Psychology, 43,* 223–232.

Haber, L. R., & Haber, R. N. (1982). Does silent reading involve articulation? Evidence from tongue twisters. *American Journal of Psychology, 95,* 409–419.

Hadaway, C. K., Marler, P. L., & Chaves, M. (1993). What polls don't show: A closer look at U.S. church attendance. *American Sociological Review, 58,* 741–752.

Hagenaars, J. A., & Cobben, N. P. (1978). Age, cohort and period: A general model of the analysis of social change. *Netherlands Journal of Sociology, 14,* 58–91.

Hains, A. H., & Baer, D. M. (1989). Interaction effects in multielement designs: Inevitable, desirable, and ignorable. *Journal of Applied Behavior Analysis, 22,* 57–69.

Hall, J. A., & Veccia, E. M. (1990). More "touching" observations: New insights on men, women, and interpersonal touch. *Journal of Personality and Social Psychology, 59,* 1155–1162.

Hall, J. F. (1966). *The psychology of learning.* Philadelphia: J. B. Lippincott.

Hartup, W. W. (1974). Aggression in childhood: Development perspectives. *American Psychologist, 29,* 336–341.

Haynie, N. A. (2001). Wundt, Wilhelm (1832–1920). In W. E. Craighead & C. B. Nemeroff (Eds.), *The Corsini encyclopedia of psychology and behavioral science* (3rd ed., p. 1775). New York: Wiley.

Helmstadter, G. C. (1970). *Research concepts in human behavior: Education, psychology, sociology.* New York: Appleton-Century-Crofts.

Hetherington, E. M., & Brackbill, Y. (1963). Etiology and covariation of obstinacy, orderliness, and parsimony in young children. *Child Development, 34,* 919–943.

Hilliard, R. B. (1993). Single-case methodology in psychotherapy process and outcome research. *Journal of Consulting and Clinical Psychology, 61,* 373–380.

Holloway, S. M., & Hornstein, H. A. (1976, December). How good news makes us good. *Psychology Today,* pp. 76–78, 106–108.

Holmes, D. S. (1976a). Debriefing after psychological experiments. I. Effectiveness of postdeception dehoaxing. *American Psychologist, 31,* 858–867.

Holmes, D. S. (1976b). Debriefing after psychological experiments. II. Effectiveness of postexperimental desensitizing. *American Psychologist, 31,* 868–875.

Holroyd, K. A., & Penzien, D. B. (1986). Client variables and the behavioral treatment of recurrent tension headache: A meta-analytic review. *Journal of Behavioral Medicine, 9,* 515–536.

Hsu, L. M. (1989). Random sampling, randomization, and equivalence of contrasted groups in psychotherapy outcome research. *Journal of Consulting and Clinical Psychology, 57,* 131–137.

Hulse, S. H., Deese, J., & Egeth, H. (1975). *The psychology of learning* (4th ed.). New York: McGraw-Hill.

IIHS (Insurance Institute for Highway Safety). (2002, August 31). *Passenger vehicles fatality facts tables.* Retrieved from http://www.hwysafety.org.

Izard, C. E. (1979). Emotions as motivations: An evolutionary developmental perspective. In H. E. Howe & R. A. Dienstbier (Eds.), *Nebraska Symposium on Motivation, 1978: Vol. 26* (pp. 163–200). Lincoln: University of Nebraska Press.

Jacobson, N. S., Roberts, L. J., Berns, S. B., & McGlinchey, J. B. (1999). Methods for defining and determining the clinical significance of treatment effects: Description, application, and alternatives. *Journal of Consulting and Clinical Psychology, 67,* 300–307.

James, J. (1981). Behavioral self-control of stuttering using time-out from speaking. *Journal of Applied Behavior Analysis, 14,* 25–37

Jarrard, L. E. (1963). Effects of d-lysergic acid diethylamide on operant behavior in the rat. *Psychopharmacologia, 5,* 39–46.

Jemmott, J. B., Ditto, P. H., & Croyle, R. T. (1986). Judging health status: Effects of perceived prevalence and personal relevance. *Journal of Personality and Social Psychology, 50,* 899–905.

Jemmott, J. B., & Locke, S. E. (1984). Psychosocial factors, immunologic mediation, and human susceptibility to infectious diseases: How much do we know? *Psychological Bulletin, 95,* 78–108.

Jennings, G., Nelson, L., Nestel, P., Esler, M., Korner, P., Burton, D., et al. (1986). The effects of changes in physical activity on major cardiovascular risk factors, hemodynamics, sympathetic function, and glucose utilization in man: A controlled study of four levels of activity. *Circulation, 73,* 30–40.

Johnston, L. D., O'Malley, P. M., & Bachman, J. G. (2000). *Monitoring the Future: National survey results on drug use from the Monitoring the Future Study, 1975–1999. Volume I: Secondary school students.* (NIH Publication No. 00–4802). Bethesda, MD: National Institute on Drug Abuse.

Jospe, M., Shueman, S. A., & Troy, W. G. (1991). Quality assurance and the clinical health psychologist: A programmatic approach. In J. J. Sweet, R. H. Rozensky, & S. M. Tovian (Eds.), *Handbook of clinical psychology in medical settings* (pp. 95–112). New York: Plenum.

Kaplan, R. M. (1989). Health outcome models for policy analysis. *Health Psychology, 8,* 723–735.

Kazdin, A. E. (2003). *Research design in clinical psychology* (4th ed.). Boston: Allyn & Bacon.

Kendall, P. C., Marrs-Garcia, A., Nath, S. R., & Sheldrick, R. C. (1999). Normative comparisons for the evaluation of clinical significance. *Journal of Consulting and Clinical Psychology, 67,* 285–299.

Keppel, G. (1991). *Design and analysis: A researcher's handbook* (3rd ed.). Englewood Cliffs, NJ: Prentice Hall.

Kiecolt-Glaser, J. K., Dura, J. R., Speicher, C. E., Trask, O. J., & Glaser, R. (1991). Spousal caregivers of dementia victims: Longitudinal changes in immunity and health. *Psychosomatic Medicine, 53,* 345–362.

Kimmel, A. J. (1996). *Ethical issues in behavioral research: A survey.* Cambridge, MA: Blackwell.

Kirnan, J., Bragge, J. D., Brecher, E., & Johnson, E. (2001). What race am I? The need for standardization in race question wording. *Public Personnel Management, 30,* 211–220.

Kohler, F. W., & Greenwood, C. R. (1990). Effects of collateral peer supportive behaviors within the classwide peer tutoring program. *Journal of Applied Behavior Analysis, 23,* 307–322.

Kritch, K. M., & Bostow, D. E. (1998). Degree of constricted-response interaction in computer-based programmed instruction. *Journal of Applied Behavior Analysis, 31,* 387–398.

Landrum, R. E., & Chastain, G. (1999). Subject pool policies in undergraduate-only departments: Results from a nationwide survey. In G. Chastain & R. E. Landrum (Eds.), *Protecting human subjects: Department subject pools and institutional review boards* (pp. 25–42). Washington, DC: American Psychological Association.

Langer, E. J., & Rodin, J. (1976). The effects of choice and enhanced personal responsibility for the aged: A field experiment in an institutional setting. *Journal of Personality and Social Psychology, 34,* 191–198.

Latané, B., Williams, K., & Harkins, S. (1979). Many hands make light the work: The causes and consequences of social loafing. *Journal of Personality and Social Psychology, 37,* 822–832.

Lee, D. N., & Aronson, E. (1974). Visual proprioceptive control of standing in human infants. *Perception & Psychophysics, 15,* 529–532.

Levine, J. D., Gordon, N. C., & Fields, H. L. (1978, September 23). The mechanism of placebo analgesia. *Lancet,* 654–657.

Levitt, L., & Leventhal, G. (1986). Litter reduction: How effective is the New York State bill? *Environment and Behavior, 18,* 467–479.

Leynes, P. A., & Bink, M. L. (2002). Did I do that? An ERP study of memory for performed and planned actions. *International Journal of Psychophysiology, 45,* 197–210.

Likert, R. (1932). A technique for the measurement of attitudes. *Archives of Psychology, 140,* 5–55.

Loftus, E. F. (1975). Leading questions and the eyewitness report. *Cognitive Psychology, 7,* 560–572.

Loftus, E. F., & Burns, T. E. (1982). Mental shock can produce retrograde amnesia. *Memory & Cognition, 10,* 318–323.

Loftus, E. F., & Ketcham, K. (1991). *Witness for the defense.* New York: St. Martin's Press.

Lowe, C. F., & Chadwick, P. D. J. (1990). Verbal control of delusions. *Behavior Therapy, 21,* 461–479.

Lubin, B., Zuckerman, M., Breytspraak, L. M., Bull, N. C., Gumbhir, A. K., & Rinck, C. M. (1988). Affects, demographic variables, and health. *Journal of Clinical Psychology, 44,* 131–141.

Ludwig, T. E., Jeeves, M. A., Norman, W. D., & DeWitt, R. (1993). The bilateral field advantage on a letter-matching task. *Cortex, 29,* 691–713.

Luparello, T. J., Lyons, H. A., Bleecker, E. R., & McFadden, E. R. (1968). Influences of suggestion on airway reactivity in asthmatic subjects. *Psychosomatic Medicine, 30,* 819–825.

Lynam, D. R., Milich, R., Zimmerman, R., Novak, S. P., Logan, T. K., Martin, C., et al. (1999). Project DARE: No effects at 10-year follow-up. *Journal of Consulting and Clinical Psychology, 67,* 590–593.

Mangione, T. W. (1998). Mail surveys. In L. Bickman & D. J. Rog (Eds.), *Handbook of applied social research methods* (pp. 399–427). Thousand Oaks, CA: Sage.

Martinetti, M. P., Andrzejewski, M. E., Hineline, P. N., & Lewis, M. J. (2000). Ethanol consumption and the matching law: A choice analysis using a limited-access paradigm. *Experimental and Clinical Psychopharmacology, 8,* 395–403.

Marx, M. H., & Hillix, W. A. (1963). *Systems and theories in psychology.* New York: McGraw-Hill.

Matarazzo, J. D. (1972). *Wechsler's measurement and appraisal of adult intelligence* (5th ed.). Baltimore: Williams & Wilkins.

May, C. P., Hasher, L., & Stoltzfus, E. R. (1993). Optimal time of day and magnitude of age differences in memory. *Psychological Science, 4,* 326–330.

Meehl, P. E. (1993). Philosophy of science: Help or hindrance? *Psychological Reports, 72,* 707–733.

Mehl, M. R., & Pennebaker, J. W. (2003). The sounds of social life: A psychometric analysis of students' daily social environments and natural conversations. *Journal of Personality and Social Psychology, 84,* 857–870.

Melamed, B. G., & Bush, J. P. (1985). Family factors in children with acute illness. In D. C. Turk & R. D. Kerns (Eds.), *Health, illness, and families: A life-span approach* (pp. 183–219). New York: Wiley.

Melamed, B. G., & Siegel, L. J. (1975). Reduction of anxiety in children facing hospitalization and surgery by use of filmed modeling. *Journal of Consulting and Clinical Psychology, 43,* 511–521.

Merikle, P. M., & Skanes, H. E. (1992). Subliminal self-help audiotapes: A search for placebo effects. *Journal of Applied Psychology, 77,* 772–776.

Milgram, S. (1963). Behavioral study of obedience. *Journal of Abnormal and Social Psychology, 67*, 371–378.

Miller, N. E. (1984). Value and ethics of research on animals. *Laboratory Primate Newsletter, 23*(3), 1–10.

Miller, S. M., & Green, M. L. (1984). Coping with stress and frustration: Origins, nature, and development. In M. Lewis & C. Saarni (Eds.), *The socialization of emotions* (pp. 263–314). New York: Plenum.

Miller, W. R., & DiPilato, M. (1983). Treatment of nightmares via relaxation and desensitization: A controlled evaluation. *Journal of Consulting and Clinical Psychology, 51*, 870–877.

Mondics, C. (2002, July 14). Animal-test alternatives are lacking, many agree. *Philadelphia Inquirer*, p. A15.

Mook, D. G. (1983). In defense of external invalidity. *American Psychologist, 38*, 379–387.

Morier, D., & Keeports, D. (1994). Normal science and the paranormal: The effect of a scientific method course on students' beliefs. *Research in Higher Education, 35*, 443–453.

Moscovitch, M., Winocur, G., & Behrmann, M. (1997). What is special about face recognition? Nineteen experiments on a person with visual object agnosia and dyslexia but normal face recognition. *Journal of Cognitive Neuroscience, 9*, 555–604.

Naquin, C. E., & Paulson, G. D. (2003). Online bargaining and interpersonal trust. *Journal of Applied Psychology, 88*, 113–120.

Narrow, W. E., Rae, D. S., Robins, L. N., & Regier, D. A. (2002). Revised prevalence estimates of mental disorders in the United States: Using a clinical significance criterion to reconcile 2 surveys' estimates. *Archives of General Psychiatry, 59*, 129–130.

Needham, J. (1975). *A history of embryology* (3rd ed.). New York: Arno Press (New York Times).

Newhagen, J. E., & Ancell, M. (1995). The expression of emotion and social status in the language of bumper stickers. *Journal of Language and Social Psychology, 14*, 312–323.

Nickerson, R. S. (1999). Basic versus applied research. In R. J. Sternberg (Ed.), *The nature of cognition* (pp. 409–444), Cambridge, MA: MIT Press.

Nodine, C. F., & Simmons, F. G. (1974). Processing distinctive features in the differentiation of letterlike symbols. *Journal of Experimental Psychology, 103*, 21–28.

Novaco, R. W. (1977). Stress inoculation: A cognitive therapy for anger and its application to a case of depression. *Journal of Consulting and Clinical Psychology, 45*, 600–608.

O'Brien, A., Fries, E., & Bowen, D. (2000). The effects of accuracy of perceptions of dietary-fat intake on perceived risk and intentions to change. *Journal of Behavioral Medicine, 23*, 465–473.

Olds, E. G. (1938). Distribution of sums of squares of rank differences for small numbers of individuals. *Annals of Mathematical Statistics, 9*, 133–148.

Olds, E. G. (1949). The 5% significance levels for sums of squares of rank differences and a correction. *Annals of Mathematical Statistics, 20*, 117–188.

Orne, M. T. (1962). On the social psychology of the psychology experiment: With particular reference to demand characteristics and their implications. *American Psychologist, 17*, 776–783.

Orne, M. T., & Evans, T. J. (1965). Social control in the psychological experiment: Antisocial behavior and hypnosis. *Journal of Personality and Social Psychology, 1*, 189–200.

Parrott, A. C. (1999). Does cigarette smoking *cause* stress? *American Psychologist, 54*, 817–820.

Parry, H. J., & Crossley, H. M. (1950). Validity of responses to survey questions. *Public Opinion Quarterly, 14*, 61–80.

Parsons, H. M. (1974). What happened at Hawthorne? *Science, 183*, 922–932.

Passell, P. (1993, March 9). Like a new drug, social programs are put to the test. *New York Times*, pp. C1,10.

Peirce, C. S. (1957). *Essays in the philosophy of science*. New York: Liberal Arts Press. (Originally published as a series of essays, beginning in 1877.)

Pennebaker, J. W., Mayne T. J., & Francis, M. E. (1997). Linguistic predictors of adaptive bereavement. *Journal of Personality and Social Psychology, 72,* 863–871.

Perin, C. T. (1942). Behavior potentiality as a joint function of the amount of training and the degree of hunger at the time of extinction. *Journal of Experimental Psychology, 30,* 93–113.

Peterson, L., Ridley-Johnson, R., & Carter, C. (1984). The supersuit: An example of structured naturalistic observation of children's altruism. *Journal of General Psychology, 110,* 235–241.

Petraitis, J., Flay, B. R., Miller, T. Q., Torpy, E. J., & Greiner, B. (1998). Illicit substance use among adolescents: A matrix of prospective predictors. *Substance Use and Misuse, 33,* 2561–2604.

Pfungst, O. (1911). *Clever Hans (the horse of Mr. Von Osten): A contribution to experimental animal and human psychology* (C. L. Rahn, Trans.). New York: Holt, Rinehart & Winston.

Piaget, J. (1929). *The child's conception of the world.* London: Routledge & Kegan Paul.

Piaget, J. (1952). *The origins of intelligence in children* (M. Cook, Trans.). New York: International Universities Press. (Originally published in 1936.)

Piaget, J. (1977). Judgment and reasoning in the child. In H. E. Gruber & J. J. Voneche (Eds.), *The essential Piaget* (pp. 89–117). New York: Basic Books.

Pihl, R. D., Zacchia, C., & Zeichner, A. (1981). Follow-up analysis of the use of deception and aversive contingencies in psychological experiments. *Psychological Reports, 48,* 927–930.

Pingitore, R., Dugoni, B. L., Tindale, R. S., & Spring, B. (1994). Bias against overweight job applicants in a simulated employment interview. *Journal of Applied Psychology, 79,* 909–917.

Pinto, R. P., & Hollandsworth, J. G. (1989). Using videotape modeling to prepare children psychologically for surgery: Influence of parents and costs versus benefits of providing preparation services. *Health Psychology, 8,* 79–95.

Plous, S. (1991). An attitude survey of animal rights activists. *Psychological Science, 2,* 194–196.

Posavac, E. J., & Carey, R. G. (1997). *Program evaluation: Methods and case studies* (5th ed.). Upper Saddle River, NJ: Prentice Hall.

Poulton, E. C. (1982). Influential companions. Effects of one strategy on another in the within-subjects designs of cognitive psychology. *Psychological Bulletin, 91,* 673–690.

Powers, R. (1999, April 18). Eyes wide open. *New York Times Magazine,* pp. 80–83.

Randi, J. (1982). *Flim flam! Psychics, ESP, unicorns, and other delusions.* Buffalo, NY: Prometheus Books.

Renne, C. M., & Creer, T. L. (1976). Training children with asthma to use inhalation therapy equipment. *Journal of Applied Behavior Analysis, 9,* 1–11.

Riskind, J. H., & Maddux, J. E. (1993). Loomingness, helplessness, and fearfulness: An integration of harm-looming and self-efficacy models of fear. *Journal of Social and Clinical Psychology, 12,* 73–89.

Roberts, A. H. (1995). The powerful placebo revisited: Magnitude of nonspecific effects. *Mind/Body Medicine, 1,* 35–43.

Rodin, J., & Langer, E. J. (1977). Long-term effects of a control-relevant intervention with the institutional aged. *Journal of Personality and Social Psychology, 35,* 897–902.

Ronen, T. (1991). Intervention package for treating sleep disorders in a four-year-old girl. *Journal of Behavior Therapy and Experimental Psychiatry, 2,* 141–148.

Rosenhan, D. L. (1973). On being sane in insane places. *Science, 179,* 250–258.

Rosenhan, D. L., & Seligman, M. E. P. (1984). *Abnormal psychology.* New York: Norton.

Rosenman, R. H., Swan, G. E., & Carmelli, D. (1988). Definition, assessment, and evolution of the Type A behavior pattern. In B. K. Houston & C. R. Snyder (Eds.), *Type A behavior pattern: Research, theory, and intervention* (pp. 8–31). New York: Wiley.

Rosenthal, R. (1984). *Meta-analytic procedures for social research.* Beverly Hills, CA: Sage.

Rosenthal, R. (1990). How are we doing in soft psychology? *American Psychologist, 45,* 775–776.

Rosenthal, R., & DiMatteo, M. R. (2002). Meta-analysis. In H. Pashler & J. Wixted (Eds.), *Stevens' handbook of experimental psychology* (3rd ed., pp. 391–428). New York: Wiley.

Rosenthal, R., & Rosnow, R. L. (1975). *The volunteer subject.* New York: Wiley.

Rosenthal, R., & Rosnow, R. L. (1984). *Essentials of behavioral research: Methods and data analysis.* New York: McGraw-Hill.

Ross, A. S., & White, S. (1987). Shoplifting, impaired driving, and refusing the breathalyzer: On seeing one's name in public places. *Evaluation Review, 11,* 254–260.

Rozlog, J. Z., Kiecolt-Glaser, J. K., Marucha, P. T., Sheridan, J. F., & Glaser, R. (1999). Stress and immunity: Implications for viral disease and wound healing. *Journal of Periodontology, 70,* 786–792.

Ruddy, M. G., & Bornstein, M. H. (1979). Cognitive correlates of infant attention and maternal stimulation over the first year of life. *Child Development, 53,* 183–188.

Rutter, M. (1979). Maternal deprivation. *Child Development, 50,* 283–305.

Saari, L. M., & Latham, G. P. (1982). Employee reactions to continuous and variable ratio reinforcement schedules involving a monetary incentive. *Journal of Applied Psychology, 67,* 506–508.

Salapatek, P. (1968). Visual scanning of geometric patterns by the human newborn. *Journal of Comparative and Physiological Psychology, 66,* 247–258.

Sarafino, E. P. (1979). An estimate of nationwide incidence of sexual offenses against children. *Social Welfare, 58,* 127–134.

Sarafino, E. P. (1985). Peer–peer interaction among infants and toddlers with extensive daycare experience. *Journal of Applied Developmental Psychology, 6,* 17–29.

Sarafino, E. P. (2001). *Behavior modification: Principles of behavior change* (2nd ed.). Mountain View, CA: Mayfield.

Sarafino, E. P. (2002). *Health psychology: Biopsychosocial interactions* (4th ed.). New York: Wiley.

Sarafino, E. P., & Armstrong, J. W. (1986). *Child and adolescent development* (2nd ed.). St. Paul, MN: West.

Sarafino, E. P., & Ewing, M. (1999). The Hassles Assessment Scale for Students in College: Measuring the frequency and unpleasantness of and dwelling on stressful events. *Journal of American College Health, 48,* 75–83.

Sarafino, E. P., Gates, M., & DePaulo, D. (2001). The role of age at asthma diagnosis in the development of triggers of asthma episodes. *Journal of Psychosomatic Research, 51,* 623–628.

Scarr, S., & Kidd, K. K. (1983). Developmental behavior genetics. In P. H. Mussen (Ed.), *Handbook of child psychology* (Vol. II, pp. 345–433). New York: Wiley.

Schachter, S., & Gross, L. P. (1968). Manipulated time and eating behavior. *Journal of Personality and Social Psychology, 10,* 98–106.

Schafer, J. L., & Graham, J. W. (2002). Missing data: Our view of the state of the art. *Psychological Methods, 7,* 147–177.

Schaie, E. W. (1965). A general model for the study of developmental problems. *Psychological Bulletin, 64,* 92–107.

Schau, C. G. (1987). Sex differences: Developmental. In R. J. Corsini (Ed.), *Concise encyclopedia of psychology.* New York: Wiley.

Scheier, M. F., & Carver, C. S. (1985). Optimism, coping, and health: Assessment and implications of generalized outcome expectancies. *Health Psychology, 4,* 219–247.

Schuman, H., & Presser, S. (1996). *Questions and answers in attitude surveys: Experiments on question form, wording, and content.* Thousand Oaks, CA: Sage.

Schwartz, M. D., Lerman, C., Miller, S. M., Daly, M., & Masny, A. (1995). Coping disposition, perceived risk, and psychological distress among women at increased risk for ovarian cancer. *Health Psychology, 14,* 232–235.

Schwarz, N. (1999). Self-reports: How the questions shape the answers. *American Psychologist, 54,* 93–105.

Scoville, W. B., & Milner, B. (1957). Loss of recent memory after bilateral hippocampal lesions. *Journal of Neurology, Neurosurgery, and Psychiatry, 20,* 11–21.

Scruggs, T. E., & Mastropieri, M. A. (1998). Summarizing single-subject research: Issues and applications. *Behavior Modification, 22,* 221–242.

Sears, R. R., Whiting, J. W. M., Nowlis, V., & Sears, P. S. (1953). Some child rearing antecedents of dependency and aggression in young children. *Genetic Psychology Monographs, 47,* 135–234.

Seligman, M. E. P., Castellon, C., Cacciola, J., Schulman, P., Luborsky, L., Ollove, M., et al. (1988). Explanatory style change during cognitive therapy for unipolar depression. *Journal of Abnormal Psychology, 97,* 13–18.

Shepard, R. N., & Metzler, J. (1971). Mental rotation of three-dimensional objects. *Science, 171,* 701–703.

Shiffman, S., & Stone, A. A. (1998). Introduction to the special section: Ecological momentary assessment in health psychology. *Health Psychology, 17,* 3–5.

Sidman, M. (1960). *Tactics of scientific research.* New York: Basic Books.

Siegel, S. (1956). *Nonparametric statistics for the behavioral sciences.* New York: McGraw-Hill.

Siegel, S., Hinson, R. E., Krank, M. D., & McCully, J. (1982). Heroin "overdose" death: Contribution of drug-associated environmental cues. *Science, 216,* 436–437.

Sigall, H., & Ostrove, N. (1975). Beautiful but dangerous: Effects of offender attractiveness and nature of the crime on juridic judgment. *Journal of Personality and Social Psychology, 31,* 410–414.

Silverman, G. (2002, July 15). It's a bird, it's a plane, its plagiarism buster! *Newsweek,* p. 12.

Slater, L. (2002, February 3). The trouble with self-esteem. *New York Times Magazine,* pp. 44–47.

Skinner, B. F. (1938). *The behavior of organisms.* New York: Appleton-Century-Crofts.

Skinner, B. F. (1953). *Science and human behavior.* New York: Macmillan.

Sledzik, P. S., & Bellantoni, N. (1994). Brief communication: Bioarcheological and biocultural evidence for the New England vampire folk belief. *American Journal of Physical Anthropology, 94,* 269–294.

Smith, C. P. (2000). Content analysis and narrative analysis. In H. T. Reis & C. M. Judd (Eds.), *Handbook of research methods in social and personality psychology* (pp. 313–335). Cambridge: Cambridge University Press.

Smith, C. S., Reilly, C., & Midkiff, K. (1989). Evaluation of three circadian rhythm questionnaires with suggestions for an improved measure of morningness. *Journal of Applied Psychology, 74,* 728–738.

Solomon, R. L. (1949). An extension of control group design. *Psychological Bulletin, 46,* 137–150.

Spearman, C. (1904). "General intelligence" objectively determined and measured. *American Journal of Psychology, 15,* 210–293.

Spiegel, D., Bloom, J. R., Kraemer, H. C., & Gottheil, E. (1989). Effect of psychosocial treatment on survival of patients with metastatic breast cancer. *Lancet, 334,* 888–891.

Sroufe, L. A. (1979). Socioemotional development. In J. D. Osofsky (Ed.), *Handbook of infant development* (pp. 462–516). New York: Wiley.

Stein, J. A., Newcomb, M. D., & Bentler, P. M. (1987). An 8-year study of multiple influences on drug use and drug use consequences. *Journal of Personality and Social Psychology, 53,* 1094–1105.

Stern, S. E., & Faber, J. E. (1997). The lost e-mail method: Milgram's lost-letter technique in the age of the Internet. *Behavior Research Methods, Instruments, & Computers, 29,* 260–263.

Stevens, S. S. (1951). Mathematics, measurement, and psychophysics. In S. S. Stevens (Ed.), *Handbook of experimental psychology* (pp. 1–49). New York: Wiley.

Stone, G. C. (1979). Health and the health system: A historical overview and conceptual framework. In G. C. Stone, F. Cohen, & N. E. Adler (Eds.), *Health psychology: A handbook* (pp. 1–17). San Francisco: Jossey-Bass.

Streiner, D. L. (2003). Starting at the beginning: An introduction to coefficient alpha and internal consistency. *Journal of Personality Assessment, 80,* 99–103.

Stroop, J. R. (1992). Studies of interference in serial verbal reactions. *Journal of Experimental Psychology: General, 121,* 15–23. (Reprinted from 1935 article in *Journal of Experimental Psychology, 18,* 643–662)

Suls, J., & Swain, A. (1993). Use of meta-analysis in health psychology. In S. Maes, H. Leventhal, & M. Johnston (Eds.), *International review of health psychology* (Vol. 2, pp. 3–28). Chichester, England: Wiley.

Sulzer, B., & Mayer, G. R. (1972). *Behavior modification procedures for school personnel.* Hinsdale, IL: Dryden.

Sutton, W. S. (1987). Determinism/indeterminism. In R. J. Corsini (Ed.), *Concise encyclopedia of psychology.* New York: Wiley.

Swain, J. C., & McLaughlin, T. F. (1998). The effects of bonus contingencies in a class-wide token program on math accuracy with middle-school students with behavioral disorder. *Behavioral Interventions, 13,* 11–19.

Swann, W. B., Wenzlaff, R. M., Krull, D. S., & Pelham, B. W. (1992). Allure of negative feedback: Self-verification strivings among depressed persons. *Journal of Abnormal Psychology, 101,* 293–306.

Swazey, J. P., Anderson, M. S., & Lewis, K. S. (1993). Ethical problems in academic research. *American Scientist, 81,* 542–553.

Tabachnick, B. G., & Fidell, L. S. (2001). *Computer-assisted research design and analysis.* Boston: Allyn & Bacon.

Talbot, M. (2002, September 22). Sexed ed. *New York Times Magazine,* pp. 17–18.

Taylor, S. E. (1983). Adjustment to threatening events: A theory of cognitive adaptation. *American Psychologist, 38,* 1161–1173.

Terman, L. M., & Oden, M. H. (1947). *Genetic studies of genius: The gifted child grows up* (Vol. 4). Stanford, CA: Stanford University Press.

Thomas, G. V., & Blackman, D. (1992). The future of animal studies in psychology. *American Psychologist, 47,* 1679.

Thorndike, E. L. (1898). Animal intelligence: An experimental study of the associative processes in animals. *Psychological Monographs, 2*(4), 1–109.

Thumin, F. J. (1962). Identification of cola beverages. *Journal of Applied Psychology, 46,* 358–360.

Trull, T. J., Nietzel, M. T., & Main, A. (1988). The use of meta-analysis to assess the clinical significance of behavior therapy for agoraphobia. *Behavior Therapy, 19,* 527–538.

Tucker, J. S., Friedman, H. S., Wingard, D. L., & Schwartz, J. E. (1996). Marital history at midlife as a predictor of longevity: Alternative explanations to the protective effect of marriage. *Health Psychology, 15,* 94–101.

Turner, C. F., Ku, L., Rogers, S. M., Lindberg, L. D., & Pleck, J. H. (1998). Adolescent sexual behavior, drug use, and violence: Increased reporting with computer survey technology. *Science, 280,* 867–873.

Turner, S. M., Beidel, D. C., & Jacob, R. G. (1994). Social phobia: A comparison of behavior therapy and atenolol. *Journal of Consulting and Clinical Psychology, 62,* 350–358.

Ulrich, R. S. (1984). View through a window may influence recovery from surgery. *Science, 224,* 420–421.

Underwood, B. J., & Shaughnessy, J. J. (1975). *Experimentation in psychology.* New York: Wiley.

USDHHS (United States Department of Health and Human Services). (1982). *Protection of human subjects.* Washington, DC: U.S. Government Printing Office.

USDHHS (United States Department of Health and Human Services). (2003). *Medical privacy—national standards to protect the privacy of personal health information.* Retrieved September 24, 2003, from http://www.hhs.gov/ocr/hipaa

Van Kammen, W. B., & Stouthamer-Loeber, M. (1998). Practical aspects of interview data collection and data management. In L. Bickman & D. J. Rog (Eds.), *Handbook of applied social research methods* (pp. 375–397). Thousand Oaks, CA: Sage.

Vaughn, B. E., Kopp, C. B., & Krakow, J. B. (1984). The emergence and consolidation of self-control from eighteen to thirty months of age: Normative trends and individual differences. *Child Development, 55,* 990–1004.

Walters, R. H., & Brown, M. (1963). Studies of reinforcement of aggression: III. Transfer of responses to an interpersonal situation. *Child Development, 34,* 563–571.

Watson, J. B., & Rayner, R. (2000). Conditioned emotional reactions. *American Psychologist, 55,* 313–317. (Reprinted from 1920 article in *Journal of Experimental Psychology, 3,* 1–14)

Watson, R., Glick, D., Hosenball, M., McCormick, J., Murr, A., Begley, S., et al. (1993, December 27). America's nuclear secrets. *Newsweek,* pp. 14–18.

Webb, E. J., Campbell, D. T., Schwartz, R. D., & Sechrest, L. (2000). *Unobtrusive measures* (2nd ed.). Thousand Oaks, CA: Sage.

Weigel, R. H., Loomis, J. W., & Soja, M. J. (1980). Race relations on prime time television. *Journal of Personality and Social Psychology, 39,* 884–893.

Weiss, J. M. (1968). Effects of coping response on stress. *Journal of Comparative and Physiological Psychology, 65,* 251–260.

Weiss, J. M. (1977). Psychological and behavioral influences on gastrointestinal lesions in animal models. In J. D. Maser & M. E. P. Seligman (Eds.), *Psychopathology: Experimental models* (pp. 232–269). San Francisco: W. H. Freeman.

Weitzman, M., Gortmaker, S., & Sobol, A. (1992). Maternal smoking and behavior problems of children. *Pediatrics, 90,* 342–349.

Westmaas, J. L., Wild, T. C., & Ferrence, R. (2002). Effects of gender in social control of smoking cessation. *Health Psychology, 21,* 368–376.

Whitman, T. L., Mercurio, J. R., & Caponigri, V. (1970). Development of social responses in two severely retarded children. *Journal of Applied Behavior Analysis, 3,* 133–138.

Wiederman, M. W. (1999). Sexuality research, institutional review boards, and subject pools. In G. Chastain & R. E. Landrum (Eds.), *Protecting human subjects: Department subject pools and institutional review boards* (pp. 201–219). Washington, DC: American Psychological Association.

Winer, B. J. (1962). *Statistical principles in experimental design.* New York: McGraw-Hill.

Wolf, M. M. (1978). Social validity: The case for subjective measurement *or* how applied behavior analysis is finding its heart. *Journal of Applied Behavior Analysis, 11,* 203–214.

Wood, J. M., Bootzin, R. R., Rosenhan, D., Nolen-Hoeksema, S., & Jourden, F. (1992). Effects of the 1989 San Francisco earthquake and content of nightmares. *Journal of Abnormal Psychology, 101,* 219–224.

Wood, S. J., Murdock, J. Y., Cronin, M. E., Dawson, N. M., & Kirby, P. C. (1998). Effects of self-monitoring on on-task behaviors of at-risk middle school students. *Journal of Behavioral Education, 8,* 263–279.

Woodworth, R. S., & Schlosberg, H. (1965). *Experimental psychology* (rev. ed.). New York: Holt, Rinehart & Winston.

CREDITS

Box 1.3
(a) B.F. Skinner Foundation; (b) John Garcia; (c) Mary D. Salter Ainsworth, Pearson Education/PH College; (d) Richard S. Lazarus; (e) Larry Squire, PhD; (f) Ellen Berscheid, PhD.

Figure 2.1
This PsycINFO record is reprinted with permission of the American Psychological Association, publisher of the PsycINFO Database, 2004, all rights reserved.

Chapter 3 quotes
"Ethical Principles of Psychologists and Code of Conduct" from *American Psychologist*, 2002, 57, pp. 1060–1073. Copyright © 2002 by the American Psychological Association. Reprinted with permission.

Figure 4.1
Professor Joseph Campos, University of California, Berkeley.

Figure 4.2
Reprinted with permission from *Science*, 171: 701–703, 1971. Copyright © 1971 AAAS.

Figure 4.3
From Ekman & Friesen, 1975. ©Paul Ekman 1975.

Figure 6.2
From "The Long-Term Effects of a Token Economy on Safety Performance in Open-Pit Mining" by D.K. Fox, B.L. Hopkins, & W.K. Anger. *Journal of Applied Behavior Analysis*, 20, pp. 215–224, 1987. Reprinted with permission.

Figure 6.3
Ross, A. S., & White, S. *Evaluation Review*, 11, pp. 254–260, copyright © 1987 by Sage Publications. Reprinted by permission of Sage Publications, Inc.

Figure 6.4
Adapted from Haganaars, J. A. & Cobben, N. P., *Netherlands Journal of Psychology*, 1978.

Figure 6.5
From *Pioneers of Psychology*, Francer, R. F. (1979). Copyright © W.W. Norton & Company.

Figure 6.7
Eron, L. D., Huesmann, L. R., Lefkowitz, M. M., & Walder, L. O., "Does Television Violence Cause Aggression?," *American Psychologist, 27,* 1972. Copyright © 1972 by the American Psychological Association. Adapted with permission.

Table 6.2
Eron, L. D., Huesmann, L. R., Lefkowitz, M.M., & Walder, L. O. Does Television Violence Cause Aggression?, *American Psychologist, 27,* 1972, pp. 253–263. Copyright © American Psychological Association.

Table 6.3
Schier, M. F., & Carver, C. S. Optimism, Coping, and Health: Assessment and Implications of Generalized Outcome Expectancies. *Health Psychology,* 4, 1985, pp. 219–247. Copyright © American Psychological Association.

Figure 7.2
Blakemore, C., & Cooper, G. F. Development of the Brain Depends on the Visual Environments, *Nature,* 228, pp. 477–478, 1970.

Figure 7.3
Perin, C. T., "Behavior Potentially as a Joint Function of the Amount of Training and the Degree of Hunger at the Time of Extinction," *Journal of Experimental Psychology,* 1942. American Psychological Association.

Figure 7.4
Bransford, J. D. & Johnson, M. K., "Contextual Prerequisites for Understanding: Some Investigations of Comprehension and Recall," *Journal of Verbal Learning and Verbal Behavior,* 1972.

Figure 8.1
From Lee, D. N., & Arronson, E. Visual proprioceptive control of standing in human infants. *Perception & Psychophysics, 15,* 529–532, 1974. The Psychonomic Society.

Figure 9.4
"Loomingness, Helplessness, and Fearfulness: An Integration of Harm-Looming and Self-efficacy Models of Fear"

Author Index

Subject Index

Questions and answers			Designs and strategies	
Ss in conditions of IV are independent?	IV manipulated?	Equated Ss in groups?	Research design (where covered)*	Research strategy
YES (independent groups)	YES	YES	Randomized groups (Ch. 5)	Experimental
	YES	NO	Nonequivalent control group (6)	Quasi-experimental
	NO (events occur on own)	NO	Nonequivalent control group (6)	Quasi-experimental
	NO (IV is a S variable)	NO	Natural groups (6)	Quasi-experimental
NO (dependent groups)	YES	YES (same Ss)	Controlled within-Ss (5)	Experimental
	YES	YES (matched)	Matched-Ss (5)	Experimental
	NO (IV is a S variable)	YES (same Ss)	Longitudinal (6)	Quasi-experimental
	NO (events occur on own)	YES (same Ss)	Time-series (6)	Quasi-experimental

*Chapter numbers where the research designs are covered are given in parentheses. For additional information about each design, use the index to find the exact pages and check the glossary (at back of book) to find definitions.

FIGURE 7.1

Diagram with questions and answers about a study's independent variable (IV) and subjects (Ss) to determine the type of research design and research strategy (follow arrows) it uses.